Implementing IP Services at the Network Edge

David Ginsburg
Marie Hattar

♠Addison-Wesley

Boston • San Francisco • New York • Toronto • Montreal
London • Munich • Paris • Madrid
Capetown • Sydney • Tokyo • Singapore • Mexico City

Many of the designations used by manufacturers and sellers to distinguish their products are claimed as trademarks. Where those designations appear in this book, and Addison-Wesley was aware of a trademark claim, the designations have been printed with initial capital letters or in all capitals.

The authors and publisher have taken care in the preparation of this book, but make no expressed or implied warranty of any kind and assume no responsibility for errors or omissions. No liability is assumed for incidental or consequential damages in connection with or arising out of the use of the information or programs contained herein.

The publisher offers discounts on this book when ordered in quantity for special sales. For more information, please contact:

Pearson Education Corporate Sales Division
201 W. 103rd Street
Indianapolis, IN 46290
(800) 428-5331
corpsales@pearsoned.com

Visit AW on the Web: www.aw.com/cseng/

Library of Congress Cataloging-in-Publication Data
Ginsburg, David
    Implementing IP services at the network edge / David Ginsburg and Marie Hattar.
       p.   cm.
    Includes bibliographical references and index.
    ISBN 0-201-71079-X (alk. paper)
    1. Computer networks. 2. Telecommunication. 3. TCP/IP (Computer network protocol) 4. Internet service providers.   I. Hattar, Marie. II. Title.

TK5105.5 .G55 2002
004.6'2–dc21

2001053364

Copyright © 2002 Pearson Education, Inc.

All rights reserved. No part of this publication may be reproduced, stored in a retrieval system, or transmitted, in any form, or by any means, electronic, mechanical, photocopying, recording, or otherwise, without the prior consent of the publisher. Printed in the United States of America. Published simultaneously in Canada.

For information on obtaining permission for use of material from this work, please submit a written request to:

Pearson Education, Inc.
Rights and Contracts Department
75 Arlington Street, Suite 300
Boston, MA 02116
Fax: (617) 848-7047

ISBN: 0-201-71079-X

Text printed on recycled paper

1 2 3 4 5 6 7 8 9 10—CRS—0504030201

First printing, December 2001

*To our fathers, N. Ginsburg and H. Hattar,
who would have embraced the Internet.*

Contents

Preface xi

Chapter 1 The New IP Services Network: The Importance of the Network Edge 1
The Origins of Data Services 2
   Optimizing Data Network Efficiency: Packet Switching 3
   Network Convergence 5
The Evolution of Carriers: Divestiture and Its Consequences 6
   Carriers' Technological Problems 7
   The Evolution of Regulation 8
The Evolution of ISPs and Internet Architecture 13
   High-Level Internet Architecture 13
   Transit Providers 14
   Exchange Points 15
   ASPs and CSPs 16
   Access Providers 17
Subscriber Evolution and the Provider Quandary 18
   Requirements for Large Enterprises 19
   Requirements for SMEs 20
   Requirements for and Economics of SOHO Users 21
   Requirements for and Economics of Residential Users 22
The Role of IP Services at the Network Edge 25

The Future of Edge Services   28
Conclusion   30

Chapter 2   Broadband Access Technologies: Physical Connectivity   31
The Last Meter: Business, SOHO, and Residential LANs   31
Access Devices at the Subscriber Site   33
The Access Network   34
   DSL Access Technologies   35
   Cable Access Technologies   41
   Fixed Wireless Access Technologies   47
   Mobile Wireless Access Technologies   49
   Metropolitan Ethernet Access Technologies   55
   Traditional Dedicated Access Technologies   58
   Dial-Up Remote Access Servers   59
Conclusion   60

Chapter 3   Security and Tunneling Technologies: The Services Enablers   61
Security   62
   Firewalls   63
   Preventing Attacks   70
   Network Address Translation   74
   Content Filtering   77
   Authentication, Authorization, and Accounting   79
   Encryption   79
   Key Management   80
   Certificates and Digital Signatures   82
Tunneling Technologies   83
   L2TP   84
   PPTP   87
   IPSec   87
   GRE, IP in IP, and UTI   89
   MPLS   90
Subscriber Segregation   93
   Virtual Routers   93
   Multiple Routers   95
Conclusion   95

Chapter 4   Higher-Layer Technologies   97
Content Management   98
   Content Caching   100
   Content Switching   103
   Content Routing   107
   Content Distribution and Management   108

Contents   vii

                Video Distribution   117
                Voice Distribution   119
                   Voice Protocols   119
                   ATM-Based Voice Services   120
                   IP-Based Voice Services   123
                   Other Voice Services Possibilities   126
                Virtual Hosting Services   127
                Conclusion   129

Chapter 5   The IPSS and Its Role in Service Provisioning   131
                The IPSS   131
                   IPSS Architecture   134
                   Packet Flow through an IPSS   136
                   IPSS Deployment   137
                   Network Engineering with IPSSs   140
                   Edge Routers versus IPSSs   142
                   IPSS Vendor Revenue Opportunity   143
                IPSS Provisioning   146
                   The Need for Effective Provisioning   147
                   Element Provisioning   149
                   Services Provisioning   152
                   External Management Systems   159
                   Client Software   162
                   Customer Network Management   164
                   Service Level Agreements   165
                Conclusion   167

Chapter 6   Deploying Basic Services   169
                Service Basics   170
                   Basic Services   172
                   Location for Services   172
                Subscriber Aggregation and Basic Internet Access   173
                   DSL Access and Market Opportunity   173
                   Cable Access and Market Opportunity   180
                   Wireless Access and Market Opportunity   182
                   Satellite Access   184
                   Comparison of DSL, Cable, and Fixed Wireless   185
                   MDU/MTU Market Segment   185
                   Dial Access Aggregation   186
                   Mobile Wireless Access   187
                Traffic Management   190
                   The Role of the IPSS   190
                   Bandwidth   191
                   Oversubscription   192
                   Additional QoS Guarantees   193

　　　　　　　　　　　Traffic Management Concepts　　194
　　　　　　　　　　　MPLS　　201
　　　　　　　　　　　Deploying QoS　　202
　　　　　　　　　　　Dynamic QoS　　206
　　　　　　　　Wholesaling　　207
　　　　　　　　　　　Active Wholesaling　　208
　　　　　　　　　　　Transit Wholesaling　　212
　　　　　　　　　　　Wholesaling Financial Comparisons　　212
　　　　　　　　　　　Subscriber Experience in the Wholesale Environment　　215
　　　　　　　　Loyalty and Lockin　　216
　　　　　　　　　　　Minimizing Customer Churn　　217
　　　　　　　　　　　Customer Support　　218
　　　　　　　　Conclusion　　218

Chapter 7　　Deploying Higher-Layer Services　　219
　　　　　　　　Firewalls and IP-VPNs　　219
　　　　　　　　　　　Firewalls　　220
　　　　　　　　　　　IP-VPNs　　224
　　　　　　　　Content Services Deployment　　248
　　　　　　　　　　　Business Relationships　　248
　　　　　　　　　　　Topologies for Content-Enabled Networks　　250
　　　　　　　　　　　The Result　　253
　　　　　　　　　　　The Content Distribution Market Opportunity　　255
　　　　　　　　Voice Services Deployment　　256
　　　　　　　　Service Bundling　　258
　　　　　　　　　　　Residential　　259
　　　　　　　　　　　Telecommuters　　259
　　　　　　　　　　　Small Business　　259
　　　　　　　　　　　Multiservice Bundling　　260
　　　　　　　　Conclusion　　261

Chapter 8　　Deployment Examples　　263
　　　　　　　　Residential PPPoE DSL Service　　263
　　　　　　　　　　　Background　　264
　　　　　　　　　　　Services Description　　265
　　　　　　　　　　　Advantages　　268
　　　　　　　　　　　The Financial Model　　268
　　　　　　　　DSL Wholesaling and Portals　　274
　　　　　　　　　　　Background　　274
　　　　　　　　　　　Services Description　　274
　　　　　　　　　　　Advantages　　278
　　　　　　　　　　　The Financial Model　　279
　　　　　　　　Cable Open Access　　283
　　　　　　　　　　　Background　　283
　　　　　　　　　　　Services Description　　284

Advantages 286
The Financial Model 287
Fixed Wireless Wholesaling 291
Background 291
Services Description 292
Advantages 294
3G Mobile Wireless Services 295
Background 295
Services Description 296
The Financial Model 297
Advantages 301
IP-VPNs and Firewalls 303
Background 303
Services Description 304
Advantages 310
Broadcast Video Distribution 310
Background 311
Services Description 312
Advantages 317
Internet Data Center 317
Background 317
Services Description 318
Advantages 320
Conclusion 321

Appendix **Resources** 323
Standards and Recommendations 323
Well-Known Applications 328
Representative List of Service Providers 328
Representative List of Vendors 332
Industry Forums and Associations 334

Glossary 335

Bibliography 341

Index 347

Preface

This book is about the network edge and about how to effectively deploy a new class of internetworking device, the Internet protocol services switch (IPSS). The edge is the point in the network joining the various access technologies such as digital subscriber line (DSL), cable, and wireless with the high-speed routed and optical core. The IPSS is a new type of internetworking platform that has fundamentally changed the way service providers deploy and offer services.

Why is the network edge the subject of such intense interest among the service providers, the equipment vendors, and the analyst community? It is the strategic point in the network where the provider has subscriber identity and may therefore apply value-added services before handing the traffic off to the core. The edge has gained prominence with broadband deployments, as service providers are called upon to provide a host of services beyond basic connectivity. IP-VPNs, content management and distribution, storage networking, and voice are just a few of the more obvious of these services. Support for these services requires a new class of internetworking platform, a platform that did not even exist before mass-market broadband deployments. This is the IP services switch.

The IPSS is a platform that builds on the basic capabilities of the traditional router but provides much more in terms of provider-based services support and subscriber policy provisioning. Depending on the type of IPSS, it may

- Provide basic residential broadband subscriber management
- Adapt Frame Relay-based businesses into an IP backbone
- Offer more sophisticated firewalling, IPSec-based IP-VPNs, and content management

- Play a critical role in cable open access, permitting subscribers to have access to the ISP of their choice
- Act as the point of IP services aggregation and adaptation for next-generation wireless systems

The IPSS's provisioning capabilities permit the provider to quickly adapt the service parameters across any of these access technologies, sometimes even under subscriber control. The net result is that the IPSS enables a new set of network-based services, services that result in additional revenue and subscriber lock-in opportunities for the service provider be it ILEC, CLEC, IXC, or ISP.

One important point is that the IPSS is increasingly being thought of as a function within the network as opposed to something that must exist as a standalone platform. As an example, edge routers and even ATM switches are increasingly being equipped with the additional hardware and software to perform IPSS functions that previously may have required a dedicated system.

This book will help the reader understand the role of the IPSS in the network (be it a discrete device or a part of another platform); its effect on both the service provider and the subscriber; where it should be deployed; and what alternative solutions exist. The book accomplishes this by paralleling the reader's decision process in evaluating the IPSS—first looking at the industry as a whole and then delving into the various technologies that play a role in the broadband services edge. Then the IPSS and services provisioning are introduced, and the various end-to-end services enabled by the IPSS are detailed.

Implementing IP Services at the Network Edge closes with a number of deployment examples. In focusing on these examples, it is a practical guide to IP services deployment. In fact, this is the first book covering all IP services, in contrast to other books in the broadband space that focus on individual access technologies or protocols.

The chapters are organized as follows:

- Chapter 1 provides an overview of the service provider landscape and then introduces network-based services and the market opportunity.
- Chapter 2 details the broadband access network, introducing technologies such as DSL, cable, and fixed and mobile wireless.
- Chapter 3 offers an introduction to the different tunneling technologies, including L2TP, IPSec, and MPLS. It details how subscriber traffic arriving via any of the access technologies described in chapter 2 may be extended across an arbitrary backbone.
- Chapter 4 outlines the technologies at the core of the more sophisticated services offerings. These technologies include content networking, voice, and video.

- Chapter 5 is the culmination of the first half of the book, introducing the IPSS and provisioning.
- Chapter 6 looks at implementing access services on the IPSS and also covers traffic management and wholesale deployments in detail.
- Chapter 7 details the more sophisticated service possibilities made possible by the IPSS, including network-based security and IP-VPNs, as well as content networks.
- Chapter 8 ties together everything that is discussed in chapters 1 through 7 by detailing a number of actual implementations and their financial models.

The material in this book is applicable to a wide audience, including network engineering and service development teams within carriers and ISPs, industry analysts and consultants, and anyone else wishing to understand the evolution of the network edge.

Acknowledgments

We would like to thank Steve McGeown, Reinaldo Penno, and Shubh Agarwal, all from Nortel Networks. We'd also like to thank Alan White, formerly of BellSouth, Robert McCormick from Savvis Communications, Joe Mosher from Aliant Telecom, Regis Oliveira and Mauro Garcia, both from Canbras, and Bruce van Nice from Redback. We're especially thankful to Howard Berkowitz from Nortel and his assistance as another author in helping with the flow of the book and to Dave Callisch for the cover artwork. Finally, we'd like to thank our current and past employers for support and flexibility.

Chapter 1

The New IP Services Network

The Importance of the Network Edge

Today we are facing a new kind of IP services network, one that has major opportunities for financial risk and reward. This market is evolving because the needs and technologies of several market segments—including customers, Internet service providers (ISPs), traditional telephony carriers, and other new types of customer-facing service providers—are converging. Where these market segments are coming together is the network *edge*—the area between the customer and the service provider. The edge is no longer a simple demarcation point between customer and provider; rather, it needs to contain a great deal of intelligence to meet the requirements of both new technologies and the regulatory and business environment. If customers are to receive reliable and affordable service, and if providers are to be able to do business in a way that generates profit, new tools are needed to efficiently manage edge services.

To understand the edge, you have to understand the different perspectives involved: those of the user, the ISP, and the carrier. You have to know how all these perspectives are changing and how a common and mutually beneficial business model can result from these changes.

Traditional carriers evolved from telephone companies. Telephone companies (or their governmental monopoly equivalents in many countries) originally provided circuit-switched services, which, in a more modern context, can be viewed as providing raw bandwidth. The fundamental assumption of circuit switching is that bandwidth in the carrier's infrastructure is allocated exclusively to the circuit user, as long as the circuit exists. Circuits can be dedicated, or they can be set up on demand, for example, by using conventional dial-up and user signaling protocols in integrated services digital network (ISDN) or asynchronous transfer mode (ATM) networks.

Unlike carriers, ISPs began by offering packet-based, not circuit-switched, services. The fundamental assumption of packet switching is that the underlying bandwidth can be shared among multiple users, because the nature of packet-based communications is that it occurs in bursts. While one user's communication is bursting, another can be assumed to be idle, so the various users' communications can be interleaved. The differences between circuit and packet switching, and between the carriers and the ISPs, have influenced how networks are deployed and what kinds of technologies and services are offered.

New access technologies are enabling both ISPs and traditional carriers to offer *broadband* services, at data rates far beyond the practical 53 Kbps limit of analog dial-up or of the 64 Kbps channels of ISDN. Even before these improvements in bandwidth at the subscriber side of the edge, optical technologies led to massive improvements in backbone bandwidth.

The evolution to a new edge model includes a proliferation of service provider types and ancestries. Much of this evolution has been the result of three trends—the explosive growth of the Internet and its ability to support multiple types of services (e.g., data, voice, video), the availability of broadband technology, and deregulation. The net result is a service delivery chain developed in such a way that different types of providers bring different value propositions to the table. We no longer live in a world dominated by the baby Bells, known as the incumbent local exchange carriers (ILECs), in the United States, or by the governmental post, telephone, and telegraph (PTT) monopolies in much of the rest of the world. Throughout the world, deregulation has permitted new providers offering specialized services to enter the market.

The remainder of this chapter provides an introduction to the industry—where it has been, the current environment, and where it is going. It looks at the origins of data services, the advent of packet switching, and a much-debated term, *convergence*. It then goes on to look at the evolution of the incumbent carriers, competitive carriers, and the ISPs in light of the regulatory environment. Finally, it looks at subscriber expectations and the concept of IP services. This provides a lead-in to the technology discussions of the next few chapters.

The Origins of Data Services

Initially, data service providers offered basic point-to-point connectivity via leased lines over the existing public switched telephone network (PSTN), which was designed for voice services. Voice services are inherently analog, and the original PSTN backbones were analog. Even with the earliest telephone systems, carriers had a strong cultural tradition of providing extremely reliable service. Clichés of switchboard operators staying at their posts in burning buildings and of cable splicers struggling through torrential storms have a strong base in reality.

Voice communications are quite sensitive to latency, and the telephone network met this requirement by dedicating circuit-switched bandwidth for the duration of a call. There are, however, significant idle periods in voice communications, and dedicating bandwidth for a call is wasteful.

In the early 1960s, digital technologies began to enter the PSTN backbone, but the PSTN remained analog at the edges. Digital technologies were introduced not to enhance data services, but to make analog services more scalable.

Widespread use of digital networking occurred in the 1970s, when carriers began providing digital interfaces to the digital backbone (e.g., T1); at this point, the backbone still used copper pairs, coaxial cable, and microwave transmission systems. This period also saw rapid growth in mainframe-based data networks, which, while meeting important corporate goals, shared the inflexibility and the commitment to reliability of telephony networks. There was a clear demarcation between providing bandwidth and providing application services.

The mid-1970s saw major changes in business models. Despite the breakup of former carrier monopolies, it was still the enterprise's job to implement applications, which often meant dealing with multiple carriers. More and more equipment that had previously been controlled by the carrier (e.g., modems) came under the control of the enterprise. Enterprises that attempted networking during this period needed to have strong in-house engineering capabilities, which generally only large business, government, and academic institutions could afford.

The 1980s saw the introduction of optical transmission systems with far higher reliability and capacity than earlier alternatives. Telephone-oriented providers could deliver high reliability and tightly controlled quality of service (QoS), although in a much more resource-intensive manner than the separately evolving packet-switched data networks.

Optimizing Data Network Efficiency: Packet Switching

Traditional carriers began to recognize the inefficiencies of using dedicated or circuit-switched resources for all applications, especially data applications that were even burstier than voice. Carriers began to create packet-switching technologies that fit into their administrative models, which still made a sharp distinction between subscriber and provider. The original carrier-oriented packet technology was X.25, optimized for operating over the analog backbones characteristic of 1970s technology. Frame Relay, ISDN, and ATM, generically called *fast packet services*, were optimized for the digital backbones of the 1980s. These new services offered the enterprise additional flexibility in backbone architectures because links between sites became more cost-effective.

IP Networking

Also in the early 1970s, in competition with X.25 services, research networks were exploring a different model of packet switching, realized with the Internet Protocol (IP) suite in the ARPANET and its successors. IP networks have fundamentally different assumptions from those of X.25 networks. In an IP network, the end hosts have much of the intelligence and are responsible for ensuring reliable delivery when applications require it. In X.25 networks, the provider is responsible for reliable delivery. The internal switching elements of X.25 networks, given these responsibilities, are slower and more complex than IP routers

The history of the Internet can be seen as one of intelligence moving to the edge, away from the core. We started with dumb terminals in the 1970s, and as personal computers were introduced and became more powerful, all error correction, retransmission, caching, and other functions were delegated to them.

IP networks historically have been far more flexible and resource-efficient than telephony-oriented services, but they have also lacked the demonstrated reliability and QoS controls of circuit-switched and telephony-oriented packet services.

The global, public Internet is a collaborative system that involves the voluntary cooperation of many ISPs. Since no single organization is in control, it is unrealistic to expect high reliability or QoS control from the public network. There is a classic engineering proverb: "Good, cheap, fast. Pick two." The public network is fast to implement and cheap with respect to the efficiency of resource use, but it has unpredictable quality.

Although it is impossible to guarantee the quality of the Internet as a whole, ISPs can go quite far toward providing good service quality in their own network segments. A single ISP can use the same protocol families that are used in the public Internet to build virtual private networks (VPNs), and thus offer QoS across its own backbone.

Mass-Market IP Services

The first IP-based services required dedicated hardware at the customer's location (that is, *customer premises equipment* [CPE]) or hardware operated on behalf of the subscriber by the provider at the point of presence (PoP). Because of the cost of hardware and ongoing provisioning, the option of using CPE was suitable only for large enterprises. True mass-market IP services (that is, those services designed to appeal to a very large customer base) offered by the provider require a different class of network-based IP service nodes that support hundreds or even thousands of subscribers. Figure 1.1 outlines this evolution from leased lines to managed CPE to network-based services.

Mass-market IP services have to deal with the "skills gap," or the lack of IP engineering expertise of most small and medium enterprises (SMEs), telecommuters, and residential users. The mass-market offerings require that the provider

The Origins of Data Services

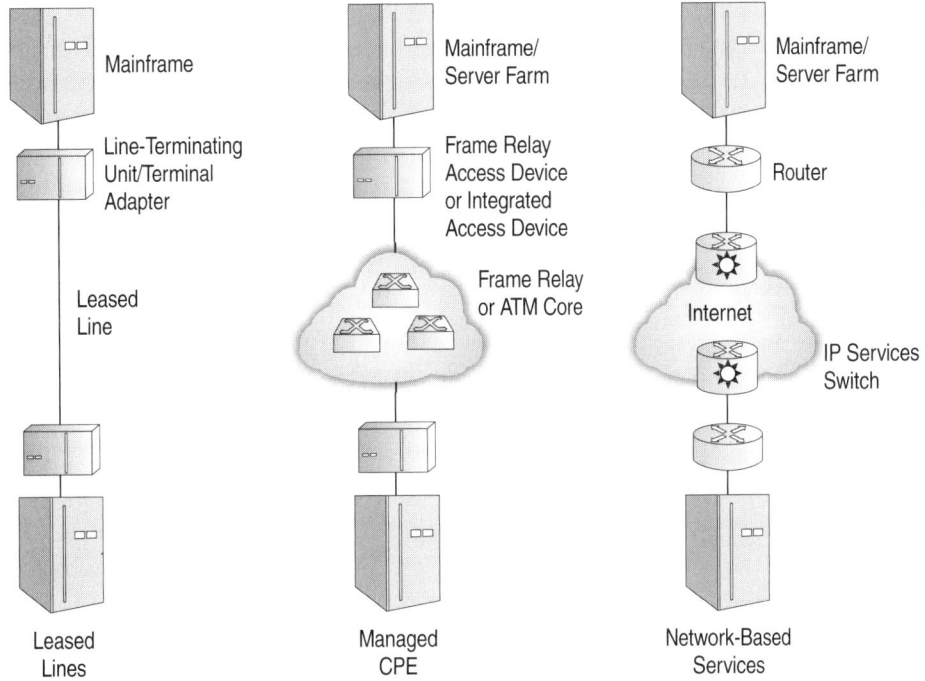

FIGURE 1.1 Transition from Leased Lines to Managed CPE to Network-Based Services

take on a much greater role in network operations than had been the case with the more traditional services.

Another aspect of the mass market is the need to unify seemingly directly opposed goals. On the one hand, the potential subscriber is frustrated by dealing with a plethora of service providers for voice, corporate data, video, and public Internet services. On the other hand, regulators push for even more differentiation and competition.

Network Convergence

An unfortunately overused term, *convergence*, refers to an environment in which the union of data, voice, and video is recognized. In principle, the subscriber has a wide range of competitive providers that can meet a range of application requirements. In reality, of course, no single provider can be proficient at all technologies. Nor is any single provider even permitted to compete against all possible competitors. Real-world converged networks may involve a single primary point of user contact, but the provider that deals with the subscriber also must deal with an assortment of other service providers. Many of these other providers, especially those that provide high-speed access services, are wholesalers and do not directly sell to end users.

An ideal converged network must offer the flexibility and cost model of the Internet with the QoS and reliability of the PSTN. This cost model is compelling: Deploying an IP-centric network on average costs about 70 percent less than installing and operating traditional phone switches. Furthermore, routing, transmission, and operational systems double in performance per price approximately every 18 months. In addition, by virtue of its flexibility in offering revenue-generating services with reduced time to market, investment is more readily available for IP deployments.

We are witnessing the initial deployment of these next-generation converged network infrastructures. They combine support for voice, video, and data; include an awareness of application QoS support in their design; and are rich in value-added services made possible by more intelligent edge platforms and distributed application and content servers. Subscribers enter the network via a mix of broadband and narrowband technologies, key aspects of which are detailed in chapter 2.

Associated with these new transmission and access technologies is a variety of higher-layer services such as secure networking, application service providers (ASPs), content service providers (CSPs), and content distribution providers (CDPs).

The Evolution of Carriers: Divestiture and Its Consequences

The telephone industry has gone through cycles of competition, consolidation, and divestiture resulting in new competitive models. At the outset, the market was completely competitive and cursed by interoperability problems. It was often necessary to have several telephones on one's desk—one for each telephone company.

Many of the initial telephone companies merged into, or were replaced by, AT&T, known as the Bell System. In 1907, Theodore Vail, CEO of AT&T, introduced the model of *universal service*. Universal service meant that every telephone should be able to connect to every other telephone. Vail did not assume, however, that every individual would have a telephone.

Small, independent operators always coexisted with the Bell System. The modern versions of these firms are known as independent operating companies (IOCs). Initially, the Bell System refused to interconnect with IOCs, but this situation was resolved by the 1913 Kingsbury Commitment. This regulatory agreement established the roles of local exchange carriers (LECs) and inter-exchange carriers (IXCs), with IOCs in the role of LECs and Bell in the IXC function. Within the limitations of analog copper transmission systems, it was reasonable to consider the LEC function as a natural and technical monopoly, subject to regulation. The incumbent local exchange carrier is the first LEC in a given area, and it owns the copper wire plant.

The next major evolution occurred in 1975, when AT&T was broken into several categories of new companies. The first category included the Regional Bell Operating Companies (RBOCs), which were ILECs created from the breakup of AT&T. The original RBOCs included Bell South, SBC, Nynex, and so on, but several of these have since merged to become large carriers such as Verizon.

More recently, a new class of provider has emerged—the competitive local exchange carrier (CLEC). These providers offer data, and sometimes voice services, by leasing copper from the ILEC or by using alternate local loops.

Carriers' Technological Problems

Before delving into the current regulatory environment and its effect on the ILECs and the CLECs, it is worth spending a little more time on the technological problems that carriers face. An understanding of these problems will clarify why the ILECs and CLECs push for regulations that permit them to offer different types of services.

The Last-Mile Problem

A continuing aspect of technical monopoly on the part of the traditional telephone companies has been the "last mile," or the copper wire pairs connecting subscriber sites to the entry point to the telephone network. This entry point is usually called the *end office*, the *serving central office*, or the *Class 5 office*. Depending on the service, the "last mile" may actually extend up to 18,000 feet from the end office.

To avoid huge proliferation of telephone poles or underground conduits, it has been attractive for a single company to maintain the copper local loops. New technologies offer alternatives to copper pairs, such as coaxial cable for television, fixed wireless services, and various optical fiber systems. Even some of these newer alternatives face obsolescence; for example, coaxial cable is inadequate to meet the bandwidth requirements of a large number of high-definition television (HDTV) stations.

Industry practice has been to have the ILEC operate the local loops, but to lease pairs to alternative access providers. Such providers place equipment in collocation space at the central office and convert the signals associated with their particular technology to high-speed digital streams. Depending on the technology and business model, these streams may reenter the ILEC network or go by facilities owned by the access provider to aggregation points higher in the access provider's communication chain.

Access providers either directly or indirectly feed the digital streams into higher-level service providers. At present, the most common kind of higher-level provider is the ISP. Other provider types include independent voice service providers and providers of content such as video on demand.

The Second-Mile Problem

The introduction of broadband services has created what is sometimes called the *second-mile problem*, where subscribers now have high-speed connectivity across the local loop via cable, DSL, or wireless, only to have their bandwidth and response times degraded within their ISP's backbone or between their ISP and other ISPs. This happens for the following reasons.

Subscribers' expectations about available bandwidth depend on the monthly rate they are paying. For example, a $40-per-month DSL subscriber may expect DSL bandwidth to Web sites on the other side of the world. This conflicts with the realities of Internet finances, where it is usually impractical for the local ISP to provide this bandwidth into the Internet backbone because of costs to connect with upstream providers.

A second major issue is that many ISPs base their business plans on continued subscriber growth. By 2004, subscriber growth is expected to have slowed from the exponential growth of today to a more stable rate of 13 percent (Ovum, 2000c). The goal, therefore, is to be capable of generating additional profits from an existing subscriber base.

The Evolution of Regulation

The deployment of broadband access in the United States is a function of both the technology and the regulatory environment. To some, it would seem that the latter plays center role in deployment decisions. Modern telecommunications history began in the United States with the Telecommunication Act of 1996, the starting point of many years of litigation. One area of focus has been on who may deploy DSL services and in what capacity. Any regulation impacts the IOCs and IXCs as well as the ILECs.

The ILECs and the CLECs

The 1996 act set the parameters by which the ILECs (that is, the RBOCs, Verizon, and Sprint) could enter the long-distance market. They could enter this lucrative market only by opening their local loops to competition. The act resulted in the creation of a new type of carrier, the CLEC. Currently, Covad is probably the best remaining example of a pure data CLEC. The act also required the ILECs to provide access to the bare copper wires, but then left it to the states to determine the types of equipment permitted by the ILECs as part of collocation agreements. Finally, it also left to the states the question of sub-loop unbundling, where different providers have access to different segments of the frequency spectrum. The competition order resulted in a number of legal challenges. One of the most interesting points is the intelligence permitted as part of collocation, which left it to the individual states to determine whether the new CLECs could deploy more intelligent devices such as DSL access multiplexers (DSLAMs) in the central offices.

The next significant ruling by the Federal Communications Commission (FCC)—the United States telecommunications regulatory body—was the Advanced Services Order of 1998. This reinstated one of the contested provisions of the original loop competition order, requiring ILECs to provide CLECs with DSL-capable loops as well as information about availability. This act also stated that packet services offered by the ILECs could be regulated, but at the same time it permitted the ILECs to create deregulated entities as long as they were managed separately. This led to the creation of ISPs and advanced data services affiliates within the ILECs. It was unclear whether the DSLAMs deployed by the ILECs would be subject to regulation, or whether they could be operated by the deregulated affiliate. The ILECs also wondered whether they would have to unbundle some of the data equipment (the DSLAMs) and offer advanced capabilities to the CLECs.

In 1999, the next major regulatory change affected not only local loops, but also the ability of CLECs to place equipment in ILECs' physical offices; CLECs had to meet ILECs' standards for equipment that would go into ILEC facilities. The same year, the U.S. Supreme Court struck down most of the decisions in the earlier challenge, giving the FCC authority over unbundled network element (UNE) pricing once again. However, the act also required that the FCC prove that a given UNE was required by the CLEC before requiring that an ILEC offer it. A subsequent ruling, also in 1999, clarified the types of equipment permitted as part of collocation. It permitted hardware-supporting enhanced services, and it lowered the cost of collocation by mandating cageless or shared-cage deployments.

Despite all the regulations that benefit the CLECs, they still sometimes encounter problems in the form of timely loop qualification, information about the availability of floor space in the central offices, actual access to this floor space, hardware standards that are sometimes more strict than those required by the ILECs for their own deployments, and other miscellaneous problems resulting from being critically dependent on the competitor.

The regulatory environment established by these decisions has been most relevant to broadband provisioned with various forms of DSL, although its principles apply to other broadband services such as cable. Like ILECs, cable operators historically have local area monopolies, with varying amounts of regulation. They are therefore impacted by what is happening in the regulatory space to the ILECs and CLECs.

As cable technology extended to include IP-based services beyond the original analog video, the cable providers naturally wanted to optimize their profit by requiring their subscribers to come to them for IP services. Competitive IP and voice service providers, however, have insisted that a business with a technical monopoly should grant *open access* to any willing provider. There have been court rulings in both directions. Similar open access debates go on with other technologies (for example, third-generation IP-enabled cellular radio services).

By 2001, the regulatory debate had evolved to encompass the incumbents, the CLECs, and the multiservice operators—the cable operators. The incumbents were in favor of the Internet Freedom and Broadband Deployment Act (HR 1542), which would lift requirements on them to open their local phone service to competition before they could offer long-distance services. In addition, they would not be required to lease at wholesale prices elements of their data network to competitive providers. The CLECs, as would be expected, were not in favor of this regulation, but the ILECs contended that the MSOs were already enjoying the same regulatory relief. The ILECs also contended that it would give them an incentive to increase their investments in broadband access since they would have a more assured revenue model. By the end of 2001, the outcome of this debate was still to be determined, although the ILECs seemed to have the upper hand.

The ILECs and the DSL Providers

The ILECs, in an enviable position because they own the physical copper infrastructure to the subscriber, must permit other service providers to offer services over this infrastructure per the regulations described in the previous section. CLECs offer a variety of services, but many of them focus on broadband access. Such an access network has several components:

- An access device at the subscriber premises, which may be provider-owned or customer-owned.
- An access network between the subscriber location and the ILEC end office. This network may be no more than the copper pairs in most DSL systems, but it may involve various bandwidth-aggregating or distance-extending devices in the field, such as equipment in multitenant buildings or freestanding copper-to-fiber pedestals.
- Wire distribution equipment, operated by the ILEC in the central office. Usually called the *main distribution frame* (MDF), this cross-connects signals from subscriber pairs into cables leading to the CLEC's area inside the ILEC end office.
- CLEC-owned equipment to convert signals on the subscriber pair to pure data streams, which are multiplexed into high-speed aggregates that the CLECs will distribute to ISPs and other customers. In DSL, this equipment is called the DSLAM.
- The DSLAM may be integrated with or connect to an IPSS that manages distribution of individual subscriber streams to the appropriate provider and may offer value-added services.

Complicating the model even further is the ability of data and voice providers to share copper pairs. Access to the copper loop is also evolving, with bandwidth unbundling now becoming a reality (see Figure 1.2). Bandwidth unbundling permits the ILEC and CLEC to share a single copper pair, with the ILEC offering basic telephony services and the CLEC offering DSL.

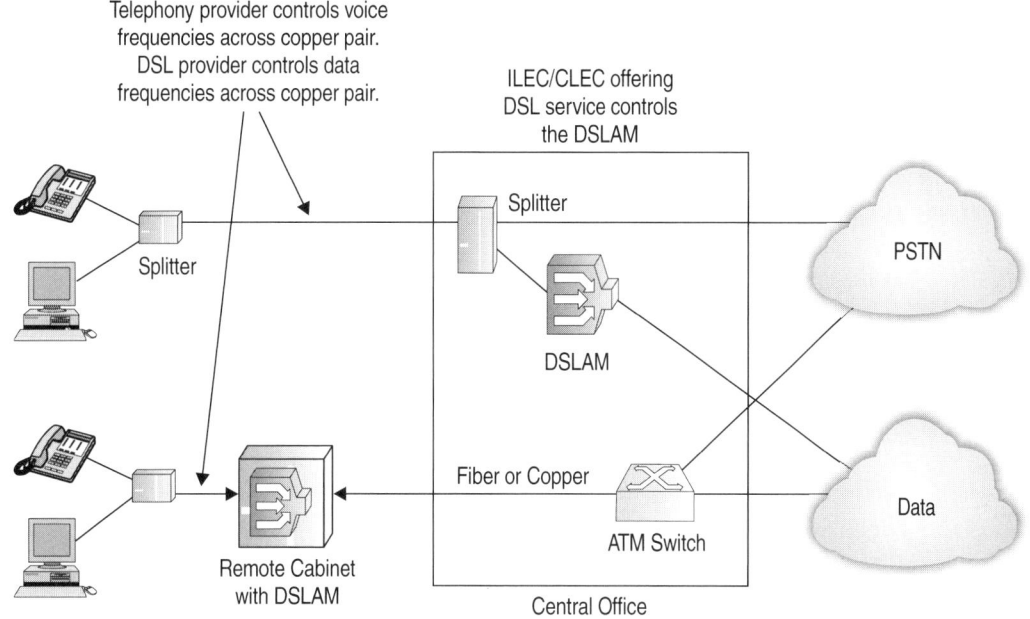

FIGURE 1.2 Loop Unbundling

Although much industry interest has been on the new data CLECs, the more traditional voice CLECs are also evolving; many of them offer services in communities that were initially bypassed by the early DSL buildouts. For example, although Covad's buildout was expected to hit 165 metropolitan statistical areas (MSAs) (major metropolitan areas) by the end of 2000, its initial deployment addressed only 5 (Oakland, San Diego, San Francisco, San Jose, and Los Angeles) of the 25 MSAs within California.

Some CLECs have developed business models targeting specialized markets, such as wireless, high-speed access to large businesses via optical networks, and services targeted at the multidwelling unit/multitenant unit (MDU/MTU) and hospitality (that is, apartment buildings, condominiums, and hotels). In these areas, the providers have highly evolved business plans specifically targeting the services required by subscribers in these different environments. Sometimes they operate as ISPs, and other times they focus on basic access.

The IOCs and IXCs

Along with CLECs and ILECs, traditional voice-focused independent operating companies have also joined the broadband fray. These IOCs have provided basic services to communities not served by the ILECs, and in fact they serve a very large geographical area (primarily low-density regions), if not a very large proportion of the U.S. population.

The IXCs are also undergoing change, no longer providing only long-distance telephony service. In fact, the IXCs, most notably AT&T and Worldcom, have evolved to become the largest data operators and ISPs, and they are actively entering the broadband arena. IXCs are also players in providing U.S. and international Internet connectivity.

Newer carriers, most notably Qwest, Level 3 Communications, and Williams Communications, have taken an active role in data wholesaling, buildout of data centers, and in some cases deployment of broadband access. They of course play a vital role in providing data and voice transit services for the ILECs and CLECs. The competitive environment in this space is also changing, as the ILECs are permitted to offer long-distance services and as the IXCs re-enter the local telephony market.

The MSOs and Metropolitan Carriers

Cable system operators are more formally known as *multiservice operators* (MSOs). They are the only true vertically integrated providers of any scale in today's marketplace in that many offer voice and data services as well as video. Their ability to offer a full range of services enrages the regulated ILECs, who feel that this is unfair competition.

The fact that they may offer multiple services, along with the fact that the majority of their Internet subscribers are bound to their own ISP, has created a great deal of debate within the industry. Some MSOs are now providing what is known as "open access" or "equal access," where their subscribers have access to multiple ISPs (along similar lines to the DSL model), though this is still an issue in the courts. This evolution is described in greater detail within the deployment examples in chapter 8.

At this point we don't know just how far the MSO model will evolve. Will the MSOs be required to open their local loops in the same way as the ILECs, permitting third parties to offer video and voice services? Although the MSOs contend that they have funded their cable buildouts, this was done in the context of local franchises. You can draw parallels between the MSO situation and the copper buildouts that occurred many years earlier; both AT&T and the MSOs are independent companies but were placed in an advantageous position because of regulation and barrier to entry. It is still too early to judge the outcome of this debate.

Economic Viability of CLECs

Funding problems that many of the CLECs began to experience during the second half of 2000 were indicative of the need to differentiate their service offerings and enter the market with a well-thought-out business plan. These CLECs, created out of the Telecommunications Act of 1996, specialize in data or voice services. How-

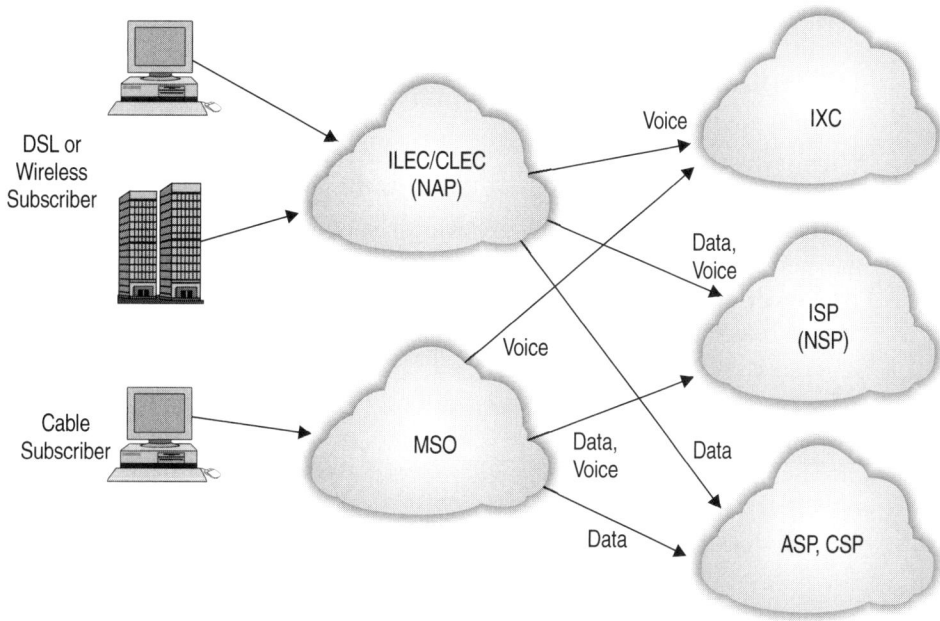

FIGURE 1.3 Service Providers

ever, while there are only so many subscribers, there are a very large number of providers. Providers that are best able to articulate their strategies and services while minimizing the cost of service deployment are most likely to survive.

Figure 1.3 details the different types of providers and how they connect with each other within a network. Recently, some CLECs have begun to act as ISPs by connecting at the IP layer (also known as peering) directly with content providers and ASPs. The CLEC may be a wholesaler, contracting with ISPs rather than end users, or it may offer direct consumer services.

The Evolution of ISPs and Internet Architecture

ISP business models have also been evolving. These models evolve very quickly because ISPs are in large part unregulated. To understand how this evolution is taking place, let's first review the architecture of the Internet and the types of providers involved.

High-Level Internet Architecture

The global Internet is composed of a large number of organizations that exchange IP routing information among each other and that operate autonomously. This is how data from a computer in San Jose, for example, that is connected to one service provider knows how to reach a computer served by a second provider in London. Each organization is normally associated with an autonomous system (AS).

An AS is a set of routers having a single routing policy, running under a single technical administration. Each AS, be it an ISP or enterprise, has a identifying number, which is assigned to it by an Internet registry or a provider. The Border Gateway Protocol, version 4 (BGP-4) is the routing protocol of choice to exchange reachability information between ASs. There are two kinds of economic relationship between providers:

- Peering, where two providers connect as equals; and
- Transit, where one provider is paid by another provider or enterprise to provide connectivity to the rest of the Internet.

The basic technical relationship between a subscriber such as an enterprise and a service provider is one of default forwarding behavior. When the enterprise network does not know where to send a packet with a particular address, it sends it to a default route that delivers it to the transit provider. The transit provider is expected to have more information and know where to deliver the packet.

Enterprises may have more sophisticated relationships with multiple service providers, and they can receive varying amounts of information on the addresses that each provider reaches. The enterprise, in a multi-homing strategy, picks the "best" upstream provider to reach a given destination. Even in multi-homed designs, however, there often is a single primary provider to which traffic defaults.

Transit Providers

Some of the largest providers with national and international reach form the "backbone" of the Internet. These are the *transit* providers, who provide connectivity to other providers and learn all their routing information through bilateral agreements with other large providers. The economic relationship among these providers, called *peering*, is one of equals. In a basic bilateral peering arrangement, the two parties advertise their customers' routes to one another and share the costs of the physical links between them. There is therefore no financial exchange. A provider connected to a sufficiently large number of peers, even though it does not receive full routes from any of them, will be able to build a full Internet routing table and belong to the default-free zone (DFZ).

These large providers may also be called *Tier-1* providers, a term that has no rigorous technical definition and is sometimes abused by marketing to enhance the stature of a given provider. The general definition of a Tier-1 provider, however, is as follows:

- It owns or controls a national or continental backbone of appreciable speed (commonly OC-48 or better).

- It does not pay any other providers for routes, but it learns all its routing information through bilateral peering arrangements.
- It has network operations and engineering staff accessible to other carriers on a 24-hour basis.

Examples of Tier-1 providers are Worldcom (UUnet), AT&T, and Cable and Wireless. Although new lower-level providers, especially at the local level, constantly enter the business, national providers have largely acquired the original regional, or Tier-2, providers.

Exchange Points

At a regional level, there are special cases of bilateral peering among local ISPs as well as among content providers and ISPs. Such peering takes place at neutral exchange points, which have many names, including Metropolitan Area Ethernet (MAE). Exchange points have a long history in the Internet, and their original functions differ from their use today. Urban legend says that most interprovider traffic exchange takes place at exchange points. However, the largest providers exchange traffic through private links, the existence of which is often considered sensitive proprietary information. These providers may have secondary presence at exchange points for their less critical traffic.

It is increasingly common, however, for metropolitan areas to include cooperative exchanges to avoid the need to forward local traffic across a continent or ocean. As an example, for many years, it was cheaper for Asian countries to backhaul traffic across the Pacific to points on the U.S. West Coast where major carriers interconnected. Therefore, it is very attractive to put local exchanges in Singapore, Sydney, and so forth, so traffic originating there and destined for a local server on a different local provider network need not cross an ocean.

Metropolitan exchange points are also becoming increasingly popular in North American cities that are not meeting points of the largest carriers. St. Louis and Toronto, for example, have active local exchanges that avoid the need for national backhaul.

Even more complex relationships involve centers that provide hosting service under various business models but have enough user traffic to justify their peering to large providers on behalf of their subscribers. Some of these hosting centers include Equinix, Exodus Communications, and Verio. In some cases, as with Verio, the organization may offer both hosting and Tier-1 connectivity.

Increasingly, these provider exchanges also provide full hosting facilities—sort of a one-stop shop for Internet infrastructure and peering. Other providers more focused on hosting, such as Exodus, connect to the major exchange points within a metropolitan area. The close linkage between hosting and network peering is especially valuable for broadband content delivery (Exchange Point, 2000; Cook, 2001).

The majority of local and regional players focus on basic connectivity, and the transit providers derive revenue from payments and from connecting the smaller ISPs into their backbones. The smaller players are at risk, and they might evolve their business models in one of two ways: they may consolidate, building economies of scale, or they may focus on customer retention through more personalized customer support.

Given that an ISP's greatest asset is its subscriber base, another alternative is to outsource its physical infrastructure to a larger provider. The ISP then operates only its application servers; the Web, e-mail, file transfer, and domain name servers provide the actual subscriber services. In fact, these ISPs begin to look very much like ASPs and are sometimes referred to as "virtual ISPs."

The Development of Modem Wholesaling

As ISPs grew beyond a local calling area, it quickly became apparent that it was expensive and inefficient for them to establish their own physical modem pools in multiple physical areas to ensure that their subscribers could make toll-free calls.

Modem or ISDN access device pools feed into remote access servers (RASs) or network access servers (NASs). RASs validate the user, set up connectivity with the Point-to-Point Protocol (PPP), and then negotiate an IP address with the dial-up subscriber. Each RAS appears as an IP subnet inside the access provider network.

In the past, the individual ISP controlled these RASs, and a subscriber, if traveling, required a list of local access numbers (or a more expensive toll-free number). This meant that the ISP had to deploy a RAS in any city with local access. This ISP was therefore forced to maintain a rather extensive physical access infrastructure, and that could detract from the ISP's primary business of subscriber management. Over the past few years, a different model has gained popularity: The ISP hands off access to a wholesaler.

Even when the ISP outsources the access infrastructure, it still needs to participate in *roaming* software structures. The access provider rarely has access to the ISP's customer and password lists, so this provider must act as an authentication proxy for the ISP. The access provider interacts with the dialing-in host, but it forwards the access request to the ISP for validation. After validation, the access provider still may need to track the call length in order to be able to send call accounting data back to the ISP, which will bill the user for connection time.

ASPs and CSPs

Several kinds of provider generate content. ASPs are the descendants of the traditional time-sharing service bureaus. They provide resources and operational services for enterprises that do not want to operate their own servers. ASPs may or may not make content available on the public Internet, and they also may or may not peer with both ISPs and wholesalers.

CSPs generate content for advertising revenue (e.g., CNN), for sales (e.g., Amazon), or to carry out independently funded missions (e.g., government information sites). For an assortment of performance and economic reasons, CSPs may not focus on delivering content to the ultimate user, but may outsource content delivery to specialized CDPs. This peering relationship is of increasing importance because it provides the CSP with better (in terms of QoS and reach) access to a wider mix of subscribers—the CSP is no longer limited to peering with individual ISPs. CDPs optimize service delivery to ISP customers. A CDP might operate its own physical network or contract with many ISPs to provide a virtual content backbone.

When looking at service delivery models, you therefore first need to understand the types of service providers and the role they play within the network's physical and logical infrastructure. This infrastructure extends beyond what is commonly considered the Internet, since many providers may offer services and connectivity that are totally unrelated to public Internet services.

Access Providers

As mentioned earlier, modem pool operators pioneered the outsourcing of ISP customer access. Broadband connectivity methods, such as DSL and cable, also lend themselves to outsourcing of the access function. Such DSL access providers, cable MSOs, or wireless access providers are sometimes referred to as *access wholesalers* because, in most cases, these providers are capable of reselling their access infrastructure to multiple upstream providers.

ISPs are the subscriber's primary entry point into the Internet and, in most cases, provide the IP address to hostname lookup via the Domain Naming System (DNS), e-mail, and subscriber Web services. They also own and operate the physical router (but usually not the transmission) infrastructure upstream from the access provider. The "virtual" or "vanity" ISPs own no infrastructure, and they rely on the wholesaler for address management and physical connectivity. This class of ISP is interested only in subscriber management and content.

Traditionally, an Internet subscriber will connect to an ISP that controls a local, regional, or sometimes national backbone, as well as the access to this backbone in the form of dial or ISDN RASs.

With access wholesaling, a larger subscriber base now shares the RAS infrastructure, and the ISP may quickly add local (or international) markets. Typical access wholesalers include ILECs, CLECs, and some of the larger transit ISPs. The DSL (and soon MSO) deployment model lends itself to this wholesaling in that the ISP rarely operates the DSLAM. Rather, the DSL access provider operates the DSLAM on behalf of many ISPs within a given metropolitan area. If a given ISP contracts with an ILEC or a CLEC with national reach, then it may offer DSL service to subscribers nationwide (as is now the case with many formerly local ISPs).

Subscriber Evolution and the Provider Quandary

In the same way that both the network infrastructure and the providers have evolved over time, so have the subscribers. This has placed service providers in a quandary. They are under pressure to offer sophisticated services while at the same time being pressured by the financial community to show profitability. These pressures oppose one another, since the cost of infrastructure buildout and service deployment results in a longer time to profitability. However, because of bandwidth commoditization (that is, the constant price reductions due to increased competition) and the cost of subscriber acquisition and retention, an offer of basic connectivity no longer is sufficient. Data service providers must therefore evolve their offerings, in the same way that voice providers have added increasing value to their service offerings. Network-based voicemail and caller ID are probably the most well-known examples of these more advanced services. Facilities-based carriers are looking to garner additional revenue from their infrastructure. Conversely, ISPs are looking for ways to focus on their subscribers and value-added services rather than on the physical infrastructure buildout. In the end, there are three major, conflicting forces:

- Subscribers have growing expectations of their providers, and they expect a premium service. They require speed, security, reliability, service-level guarantees, ubiquitous access, and rich media, all at a reasonable price.
- Subscribers do not have the expertise to deploy these capabilities on their own, and this situation cuts across different market segments, including those of the residential Internet user, the telecommuter, and the business user.
- Some subscribers are more sensitive to price than to quality. The entire network cannot change instantly to a model that gives all subscribers premium service without either excluding the price-sensitive user or operating at a financial loss.

To effectively meet these conflicting forces, providers and the services they offer must be responsive to the requirements of various market segments, including the following:

- Large enterprises (such as Fortune 500, government, and academia with in-house networking capability)
- Small and medium businesses
- Small and home offices
- Residential users

The analysis in this section focuses on the residential market more than any other, for a good reason: the sheer scale of the solution required. Predictions are that up to 80 million U.S. households could have some form of broadband connectivity in the coming years (CIMI, 2001). At a yearly fee of $500 per household, this represents a $40 billion opportunity. In contrast, there are 6 million single-site businesses, representing a total opportunity of $12 billion; the multisite market, consisting of 150,000 principal sites and 1.35 million branches, represents an $18.5 billion opportunity. Any solution offering services and subscriber policy must therefore scale for the residential sector 10 times as much as it would for the business market.

Requirements for Large Enterprises

Large businesses are always interested in lowering their costs. Assuming that they continue to use dedicated access facilities, broadband service alternatives that provide equivalent services at lower cost are always attractive.

One of the important differences between large enterprises and other subscriber types is the extent to which it is cost-effective to put intelligent hardware on the customer premises (such as a branch bank). Large enterprises can afford to purchase and operate complex equipment such as routers. The model for smaller customers requires that a commodity device be installed on the customer premises, with the intelligence at the edge. In other words, the only option here is CLE.

◆ Special Geographic Issues

The FCC report on broadband access (FCC, 2000) found the lack of widespread broadband connectivity still to be acute in rural areas. Whereas 57 percent of zip codes (equating to 72 percent of the population) in small towns had at least one high-speed provider (DSL or cable), this dropped to 19 percent in the outlying areas. Although a new class of CLECs (at least the ones that have survived) targeting the smaller communities and continued ILEC buildout are helping to address this deficit, there is a more fundamental problem in connectivity from the small town to the Internet at large. In many cases, the total Internet bandwidth for a given town cannot support the content services demanded by DSL and cable modem subscribers. The report also focused on the availability of high-speed access to schools. As is obvious, rural schools are at more of a disadvantage, though they are sometimes served by state-funded Frame Relay and ATM networks and are therefore buffered from the lack of residential high-speed service. In comparison, upwards of 95 percent of the population in metro areas (greater than 268 persons per square mile) have access to DSL or cable modem service (Figure 1.4).

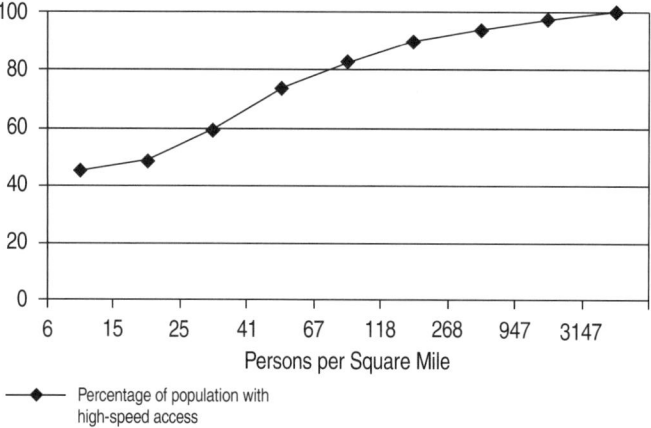

FIGURE 1.4 Broadband Availability   *Source:* FCC, 2000.

Large users can choose between customer located equipment (CLE) and CPE, based on the extent to which they want to outsource their network operations.

Large users must closely examine some of the new broadband- and Internet-based services. Traditional dedicated services, such as T1/E1 and Frame Relay, have been priced not simply based on the cost of the equipment, but to include the cost of business-grade operational support. Problem response times of 1 to 4 hours are typical for traditional services, whereas consumer-grade broadband may have 24-hour or longer waits for repair.

While some may believe that an expensive Frame Relay service somehow can be replaced by a $30-per-month, Internet-based virtual private network, these perceptions can doom a business. One case in point is the problems businesses in California experienced during the first quarter of 2001, when Northpoint declared bankruptcy. Small enterprises were at danger of having their broadband access disconnected without warning.

Requirements for SMEs

If we look at the last 20 years of internetworking, the top thousand or so large firms have been quite successful in deploying their own network and services infrastructures. They began by using leased lines interconnecting mainframes and then migrated to Frame Relay and ATM, while at the same time deploying any necessary QoS, security, and content management to meet the needs of their enterprises. They had both the in-house skills and the funding for these deployments, and, where in-house skills did not exist, they were able to bring in outside assistance.

Unfortunately, this "roll your own" approach is not applicable to a whole new class of always-on business customers—the SMEs, sometimes referred to as the Fortune 5,000,000. They have neither the in-house skills to deploy advanced ser-

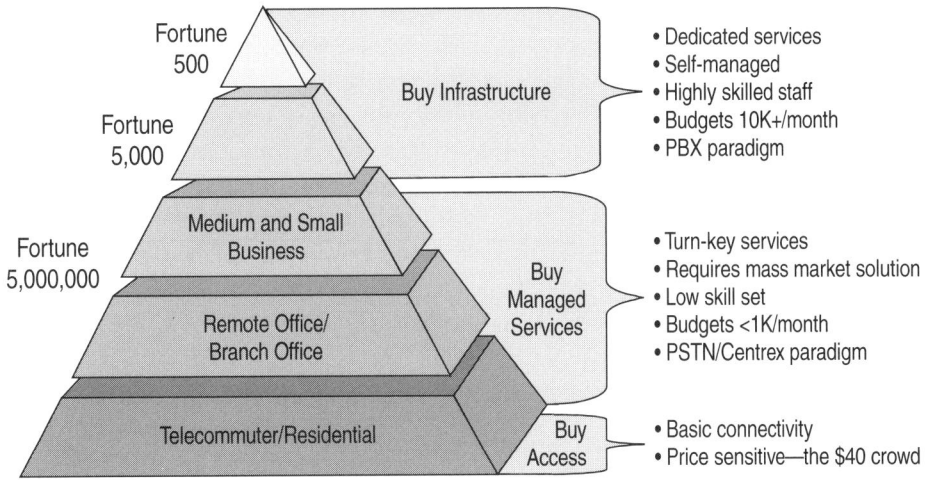

FIGURE 1.5 Market Segmentation

vices on their own nor the finances to handle managed services offerings more suited for large corporations. Figure 1.5 depicts these different customer segments along with their requirements. According to a 1998 CIMI report (CIMI, 1998), in 1982, 86 percent of network administrators were capable of planning and supporting their network infrastructure, but this had dropped to 14 percent by 1996 because of the exponential growth of the types of customers connected to the Internet. The report states that this will drop again to 1 percent in the coming years. This gap, resulting in a demand for services outsourcing, presents a major opportunity for service providers. Drawing an analogy to voice, the SME market is like the Centrex market—in which the telephone company is responsible for all technical operations—as opposed to the PBX market, where each enterprise operates its own internal network.

There remains a significant difference between business- and residential-grade services. Business-grade services, even in the SME market, are mission-critical. Businesses expect, for example, the same availability from voice over IP (VoIP) service as they do from traditional telephony. However, the difference between consumer and business grade often blurs with home workers in the small office/home office (SOHO) environment.

Requirements for and Economics of SOHO Users

The SOHO market is intimately entwined with large enterprise markets, as large enterprises make increasing use of telecommuting. There are two distinct classes of users within business-focused Internet households—those who must fund their total online experience and those partially (or totally) funded by an employer.

The first group of SOHO subscribers is very aware of the cost of connectivity, but considers high-speed access to be one of the costs of doing business. In most cases, Internet access is a business write-off. In contrast, cost sensitivities are less important to the telecommuter because of corporate sponsorship. (This is not to imply that the corporation itself is not cognizant of connectivity costs. In fact, during economic downturns, sponsored DSL or cable modem access is often one of the first benefits to fall by the wayside.)

Some of the most well-defined business applications include the following:

- Training and information broadcasts
- E-mail services
- Access to corporate-hosted applications, databases, and file systems
- Home office monitoring
- Office phone extension

Table 1.1 outlines total revenue opportunities from personal Internet households, business households, and late adopters (individuals who are slow to adopt new technologies such as the Internet). The telephony access device (TAD)—a hybrid telephone and Internet terminal—is an interesting development and is indicative of major changes in Internet access. Whereas in the past, households connected to the Internet via PCs, now there are other options, such as that offered by WebTV. In the future, this trend will accelerate, with many of the 64.3 million offline households connecting via combined settop boxes and Web browsers or via hybrid phone and Web terminals (TADs). This latter class of device is already available for purchase in the sub-$250 range and will serve as an additional point of Internet access in many PC-based households.

Requirements for and Economics of Residential Users

The guiding factor in residential access is the cost of connectivity. In fact, many DSL and cable subscribers paying only $40 or $50 a month still believe that they are being overcharged. This is probably driven by a perception that the additional bandwidth has little content value beyond basic dial-up connectivity; this perception is especially disturbing given that many of the same subscribers will not question a $100-per-month cell phone bill. One conclusion is that subscribers would be more comfortable with a lower monthly entry price, where they would then be given the option of purchasing additional value-added services. These services could run anywhere from $5 to $10 per month before subscribers would resist. With the deployment of the IPSS, services for less than $5 a month are a reality. One problem is that subscribers will quickly shift to providers who offer these lower rates. This results in additional churn. At the same time, customers expect a

TABLE 1.1 Household Revenue Opportunities

	Personal Internet	*Business Internet*	*Late Adopter*
Characteristics	High-speed access for audio, video, and data TAD used but not a given Advertising subsidized by basic but not paid services Home network	High-speed access for audio, video, and data TAD not a given Multiple phone lines Security Hosted services	Internet at low cost TAD and advertising subsidize services May not have PC
Basic access—telephony, messaging, music, Web information and services, meter reading	$0–60	$0–80	$0–40
TAD—combines voice and Internet capabilities	$0–20—TAD often combined with home gateway and home network	$0–20—gateway to home office LAN	$0–10
Pay services—long distance, CD streaming, conferencing, video streaming, pay per game, software download, monitoring	$0–130	$0–178	$0–110
Ads—targeted and sponsored	$50–112	$0–112	$50–112

price advantage when bundling two or more services. This price advantage is a reality because providers can offer discounts of $5 per month and up, depending on usage, for multiple-service bundles.

These price sensitivities provide a partial view into the revenue opportunity with residential users. Providers must grow beyond viewing broadband access as a continuation of business as usual; they must look at the ways the technology can change how family members interact with the outside world while at home as opposed to considering it as just higher-speed Internet dial-up access. They must look at typical household entertainment (and even nonentertainment) expenses and determine the role the Internet might play. This involves understanding the demographics and targeting the appropriate market segments.

Of the 103 million households in the United States, 45.4 million were online at the end of 1999. Total online penetration is expected to grow to more than 80 million by 2005. The offline 57.6 million (55 percent) present a massive opportunity given proper targeting. These offline households fall into three categories based on income:

- The upper 12 million offline households have a household income of greater than $50,000 per year, which makes them prime targets for new services.
- The middle 6 million offline households earn between $35,000 and $50,000 per year, which makes them possible targets for basic services and puts them in the late adopter category with the lower 40 million households.
- The lower 40 million offline households earn less than $35,000 per year, which makes them late adopters unless the government takes a role in providing basic Internet connectivity (GAO, 2001; IDC, 1999b; Jupiter, 2000) (see Figure 1.6).

Within the total residential segment of the market, the same IDC report states that 34.8 percent are basic consumers, 22.8 percent are telecommuters, and 27.2 percent are evening telecommuters. SOHO users account for the remaining 15 percent.

Beyond basic connectivity and security (PC-, CPE-, or network-based), requested residential services include Internet accelerators, streaming media, personal caching, and content filtering. An Internet accelerator permits a subscriber to speed up his or her connection for a specific download or streaming event. This of course requires some mechanism within the network to signal and then account for the request. The portals and active agents described in chapter 5 provide this capability. Personal caching is intriguing in that it permits a subscriber to

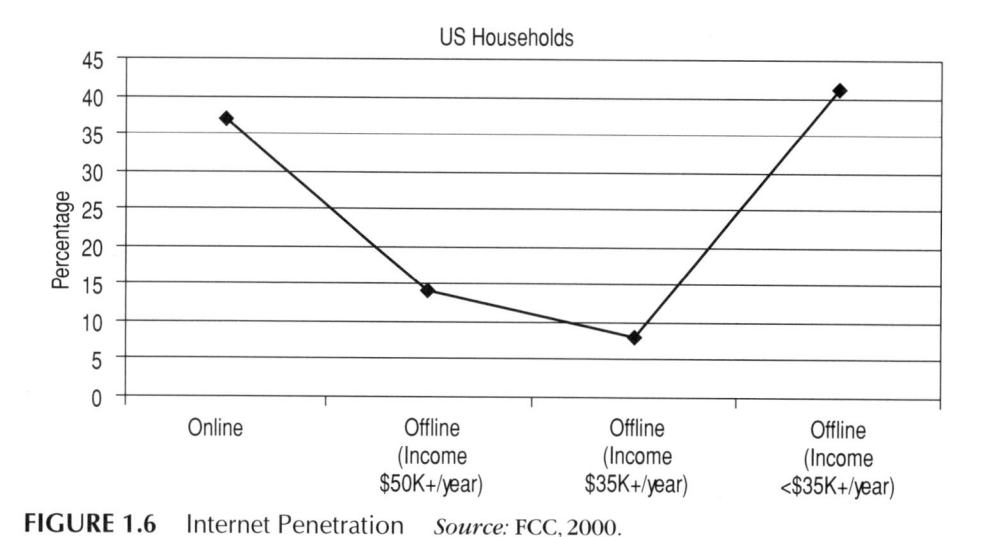

FIGURE 1.6 Internet Penetration *Source:* FCC, 2000.

store often-accessed data within the network, accessible from anywhere. Given the proliferation of wireless PDAs and standalone Internet terminals, this could be a powerful capability. An extension of the terminal concept is the capability to download data from this cache, alter the data, and then upload the information back into the network.

The typical connected household spends upwards of $150 per month on information services, including the following:

- *Messaging*—for example, phone, long distance, cell phone, Internet
- *Monitoring*—for example, utilities, security, health
- *Information*—for example, newspapers, magazines, reference books, financial information
- *Video*—for example, cable or satellite TV, video rentals, video purchases
- *Music*—for example, tapes, CDs, satellite radio
- *Software and games*—rental and purchase of single and multiplayer games and software downloads

Table 1.2 itemizes current and possible future expenditures within this budget.

The Role of IP Services at the Network Edge

Customer requirements for advanced services call for the deployment of a new class of internetworking platform that needs to do the following:

- It must sit at the edge of the network, between the broadband (i.e., DSL or cable) collector network and the ISP, video, or voice service provider. It must manage the complex interactions between subscribers, providers, and services.
- It needs to provide services independent of the hardware topology of the ILEC, cable operator, or other facility provider.

The platform that can do this is the IPSS. The cost-effective operation of broadband service providers requires wholesaler-oriented platforms that operate between the subscriber and the ISP, offering, at a minimum, the ability to collect the traffic of many subscribers and deliver it as a high-speed stream to the ISP. These devices manage network-based services for up to tens of thousands of residences and small businesses.

While this book uses the term IPSS, various vendors use other terms for the same device, including broadband service nodes (BSNs), universal access concentrators (UACs), and subscriber management systems (SMSs). Such platforms often

TABLE 1.2 Household Online Expenses Affordable within $150/Month Budget

Service Category	Brick and Mortar (traditional approaches)	Click and Mortar (revenues to the service provider) (Internet-based)
Messaging	Local telephony, long distance, cellular, paging, voice mail	Internet access ($0–40/month) Multiple virtual phone lines ($10/month) Other enhanced voice services ($10/month)
Video	Cable TV, satellite TV, video rentals and purchase, movie theaters, pay TV	Movies on demand (advertising driven) Broadcast TV (per-event, say, $4) Pay per view ($10/month) Videoconferencing
Music	Tapes, CDs, satellite music	Music on demand ($.05/song) Broadcast radio (advertising driven) Pay-per-listen live events ($5) Music purchase (MP3) ($.99/song; $1/album)
Gaming	Online games, rental or purchase of games, arcades, game console purchase and rental, lotteries	Pay per play ($10/month) Software purchases (varies) Online gambling (losses) Online lotteries (up to $25) Free online games (advertising driven)
Software Applications	Software rental and purchase	Outsourced applications ($4.95/month) Pay-per-use applications (advertising driven) Network applications
Monitoring	Home security, health monitoring	Home monitoring ($10/month) Health monitoring ($20/month when required) Day care monitoring
Information	Newspapers, magazines, reference books, financial information	Real-time stock quotes (advertising driven) E-zines ($24/year) Shopping, banking, community (part of basic Internet access)
IP-Network-Based Services		Firewalls ($5/month) Personal information caches ($10/month) Online backups ($20+/year)
Education	University, college, seminars	Online courses ($400+)

also provide value-added services beyond simple bandwidth collection and aggregation, including the following:

- High-density subscriber aggregation
- QoS support
- Security services, such as traffic filtering, firewalling, and IP virtual private networks (IP-VPNs)
- Portal services where subscribers may select content or destinations

Platforms may be differentiated by number of subscribers, speed and number of broadband uplinks, access technologies, and value-added services.

The network edge is the location of the IPSS. It may be attractive to locate certain content sources, or more likely content caches, at the same physical location as the IPSS. Placing content devices at this point minimizes the subscriber's delay in accessing content and also can reduce upstream bandwidth requirements from the edge to the content home location.

Although carriers and customer-facing providers such as ISPs may differ in the details of their services deployments, their basic goals and philosophies are the same. They need to be proactive to customer demands, and then they need to effectively translate those demands into new, differentiated service offerings within the required market window. This requires network platforms and provisioning infrastructures on which they may quickly deploy and adapt services across each of the market segments described in the previous section. Fortune 500 requirements could be met by deploying hardware on their premises (that is, customer located equipment/customer premises equipment), but the SME and residential markets—two segments offering great revenue potential—require a new class of internetworking device if their requirements are to be met.

This evolution of the network edge enables a paradigm shift in the way both subscribers and service providers view the network. No longer are service offerings static because of provisioning inefficiencies or inflexible hardware and software platforms. The network is dynamic, and depending on the sophistication of the offering, subscribers may even have control of their services on the fly via provisioning portals. Service providers now have more direct control over their subscribers, since, via these platforms, they "know" these subscribers for the first time.

The deployment of this new class of platform at the network edge is a critical piece of the puzzle in enabling the feature-rich broadband Internet. We've witnessed the buildout of DSL, cable, and more recently wireless; the deployment of optical backbones and terabit routing; and the consolidation of the essence of the Internet—the servers—into large hosting facilities connected to content switches

TABLE 1.3 Subscriber and Service Provider Requirements

Requirement	Solution	Where Applied	Challenges
High-speed access	DSL, cable modems, fixed wireless, other	Network edge	Bandwidth into ISP backbone, QoS, universal access
Quality of service	DiffServ, ATM, Frame Relay, and 802.1p QoS, MPLS	Network edge, CPE, core	Mapping between layers, peering between providers, payments, security
Security	Firewalls, antispoofing, scanning, intrusion detection, IP-VPNs, encryption hardware, denial-of-service back-tracing	Network edge, CPE	Provisioning, application support, security policies, scalability
Content	IP multicast, content distribution networks, caches, content switching	Network edge, hosting sites	QoS, provisioning, payments, security
Provisioning	RADIUS, LDAP, COPS, SNMP	Network edge, CPE, core	Internetworking with existing OSSs, end to end across multiple vendors

(the content edge) capable of Web site load balancing and communication with Web caches and content distribution networks. The rest of the equation is therefore in place. What the edge adds to the equation is the completion of the business model, permitting service providers to efficiently and profitably deploy end-to-end broadband services.

The edge also permits the intelligent placement of content services. With the growth of broadband access, subscribers increasingly demand rich content. The question, then, is where to place this content for maximum efficiency. Since the network edge is the one point where the provider has true subscriber identity, this is the most logical point. In fact, with the growth of content-networking providers, this is now a reality. Table 1.3 outlines many subscriber and service provider requirements and demonstrates that the network edge plays an important role in meeting these requirements.

The Future of Edge Services

The demand for advanced services highlights the provider's quandary—how to derive additional revenue from the substantial broadband investment. This investment is substantial, running into the billions of dollars, and providers are experiencing increasing pressure from their shareholders to show profitability. Unfortunately, in many cases, time to profitability is far out in the future. Level 3 Communications has predicted breakeven on its infrastructure investment only in 2003, and both Covad and Rhythms had predicted 2004 (Redpoint, 2000). Unfortunately for Rhythms, time has run out. Furthermore, basic connectivity, though an effective tactical market entry strategy, provides profitability to only a very small number of carriers and ISPs over time. For the carrier, this is due to the continued growth in metro and global optical connectivity, resulting in a supply of bandwidth exceeding demand and competition pushing bandwidth pricing to commodity levels.

Different types of service providers will approach this market with different goals. While the ILECs and ISPs will deploy new infrastructures with a hope of preserving profitability and investment, the CLECs and IXCs are looking for competitive advantage over these existing players. The former have an evolutionary paradigm; the latter have a disruptive paradigm. However, for the incumbents, the problem is especially acute, with defection of customers to long-distance bypass services (including VoIP) and mobile operators a major concern. The incumbents' major difficulty is the maintenance of the legacy systems.

ISPs are in a bind, facing increasing pricing pressures for basic access (with failed attempts at "free ISP" services an unfortunate occurrence). They must upgrade their infrastructures and support systems to permit deployment of these advanced services. To their advantage is credibility in the IP space, credibility that they may leverage in offering IP-VPN and portal services. Their challenges include implementing provisioning systems and ensuring availability that is at least as high as the incumbents'.

Finally, the CLECs have both an opportunity and a risk. They are in an enviable position in that they are often building infrastructure from scratch, but a rack of routers and DSLAMs does not a service make. Strong finances, an awareness of the business model for a given service offering, customer support, and focus are critical. Those that lose sight of these points are destined to fail, as we have witnessed all too often. The failure of Northpoint and Rhythms are probably the best examples of this. Those that are successful in differentiating their services while building on established business models will succeed. As an example, CLECs that have built a customer base via voice services have a supporting revenue stream for the entry into broadband.

Looking forward, how do we expect the network to further evolve in the coming years? The network will transition into a services-rich edge and a high bandwidth optical core. Subscriber traffic will enter the network within a metropolitan area via one of a number of broadband access technologies and will then be directed to a service and content PoP. Most traffic is expected to terminate within the metropolitan area, at Web caches, content servers, and ASPs associated with these PoPs. Traffic that is destined for the WAN will be mapped into all-optical, traffic-engineered paths. These optical paths will terminate at the distant metropolitan areas. For example, if traffic originating in San Francisco is destined for London, it will enter the optical domain at its source, and even though it may pass through switching nodes in Chicago and New York, it will not leave the optical domain until it reaches London. In some but not all cases, the providers will use Multiprotocol Label Switching (MPLS)—a protocol described in the following chapters—to map data onto these optical paths at the edge of the network.

Content networking will also evolve, with providers deploying the necessary content switches, caches, and peering to provide a rich set of services to their subscribers. Much of this content will flow through separate distribution networks from the origination site to the metro area. Ultimately, providers will be able to take a service-centric approach, working with their subscribers to identify the required service profile and then drawing on a rich hardware, software, and provisioning infrastructure to deploy the service at an acceptable cost and within the required market window. A smaller set of providers than exists today will deploy the necessary physical infrastructure, offering everything from dense wavelength division multiplexing (DWDM) transport to virtualized routing, leaving the customer-facing providers to focus on their real strengths—subscribers and services.

As networks evolve, so too will the regulatory environment. Legislation will evolve from simply dealing with copper pairs and equal access to encompassing some of the basic issues surrounding network evolution. Common regulations will address both the PSTN and the Internet and will not focus on any single technology or geography—it will take a broader, services-focused approach and will mandate only where necessary.

Conclusion

Service providers and their business models are undergoing a transformation, and this chapter documents these changes as they relate to competition, the types of services demanded by subscribers, revenue opportunities for these services, and, by association, revenue opportunities for the equipment vendors providing hardware for these services.

A new class of internetworking equipment meets the needs of both service providers and subscribers. These devices enable the carriers and ISPs to deploy enhanced services in a cost-effective way, while solving many of the service delivery problems facing the subscriber community. The remainder of this book covers this new service environment in detail, describing the financials, topologies, protocols, and actual service offerings found at the network edge. We are still in the early days of this enhanced network, with the first generation of edge devices for broadband service access just now seeing wide deployment, while second-generation platforms are undergoing testing.

Chapter 2
Broadband Access Technologies
Physical Connectivity

It is important to be able to establish high-speed data streams between the subscriber's edge device and the intelligent edge at the point of presence (PoP), and from the PoP to content and service providers. This chapter details the principles and components by which information enters the network at the subscriber premises and flows to the PoP or other edge-demarcation point. This part of the information exchange process involves physical and data link layers issues, including the "last meter" in the home, access devices at the subscriber site, and the various access network technologies.

We look at the various methods of accessing the network, including the elements commonly found at the residence or business and the devices used to connect the customer with the provider's network, and the last-mile technologies. This last section warrants the longest discussion, and it is here that we detail DSL, cable, wireless, metropolitan Ethernet, and other technologies found in the provider's access network.

The Last Meter: Business, SOHO, and Residential LANs

Offices have long had local area networks (LANs). As broadband-enabled services proliferate, there is an increasing need for small LANs in the small office/home office (SOHO) and residential settings. This is the *last meter*, the connection between the subscriber's desktop and the service provider network. The subscriber's choice of technology will influence the types of services the subscriber may ultimately take advantage of.

A telecommuter may have more than one computer. However, even when there is only one computer, LAN connectivity to printers and other peripherals is more attractive than proliferating the number of peripheral ports. The problem of "footprint" for peripheral ports is especially acute with laptops.

As shown in Figure 2.1, SOHO LAN options include traditional Ethernet installations based on Category 5 unshielded twisted pair (UTP, the standard Ethernet cable one sees in office buildings), reuse of the existing phone wiring based on the Home Phone Networking Alliance (PNA) standard (HomePNA, 2000), or one of a number of wireless solutions based on 802.11b (IEEE, 1999), a wireless Ethernet standard often referred to as the Wi-Fi solution. While not strictly a LAN technology, universal serial bus (USB) is quite useful for interconnecting peripherals, and it can interface to Ethernet.

The PCs, laptops, printers, and media servers installed within the home commonly connect to what is termed a *home gateway,* a device that provides the data and telephony interface to the service provider and possibly also includes storage. Many household devices may leverage some of the residential-focused, network-based, value-added services described in chapter 1. Devices connecting to these services include home security, gaming consoles, media servers, and traditional PCs. Subscriber DSL and cable modems now integrate home gateway functionality. For example, a DSL modem may support the Home PNA or the 802.11b standard—or even both.

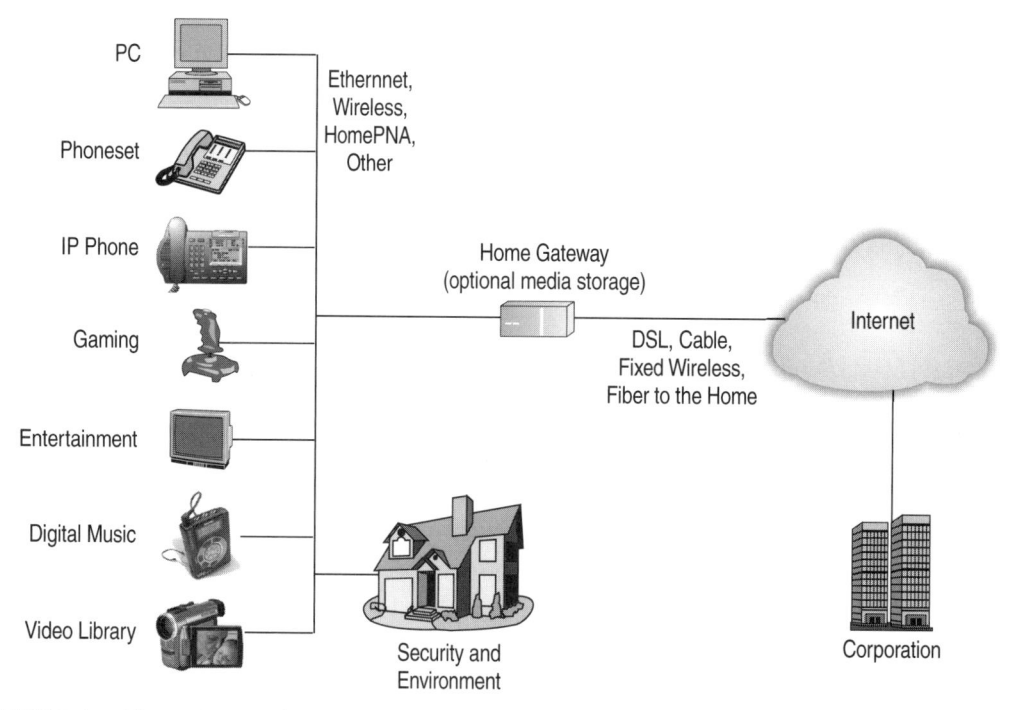

FIGURE 2.1 Home Networking

Large businesses have more traditional LAN installations, primarily based on Ethernet switching and, more recently, on 802.11b wireless. Compared to the residential and SOHO markets, large businesses usually require more sophisticated gateways into the access network, as described in the next section.

Access Devices at the Subscriber Site

The various forms of residential, SOHO, and business LANs connect to the broadband access network via access devices (see Figure 2.2). What are the requirements of these devices across the different market segments, how do they differ, when is routing or bridging a requirement, and what are the trade-offs?

The characteristics of the devices differ greatly, depending on the type of customer. For DSL, a basic residential subscriber (i.e., approximately $40/month) with a single PC connects via Ethernet, USB, or wireless to a simple DSL modem. This modem operates as a bridge, forwarding the subscriber's traffic at the link layer into the provider's network.

Cable or fixed wireless connectivity takes place in much the same way as DSL connectivity, with one or more PCs connected to an access device that functions as a bridge connecting to the provider's access network. Differences here involve

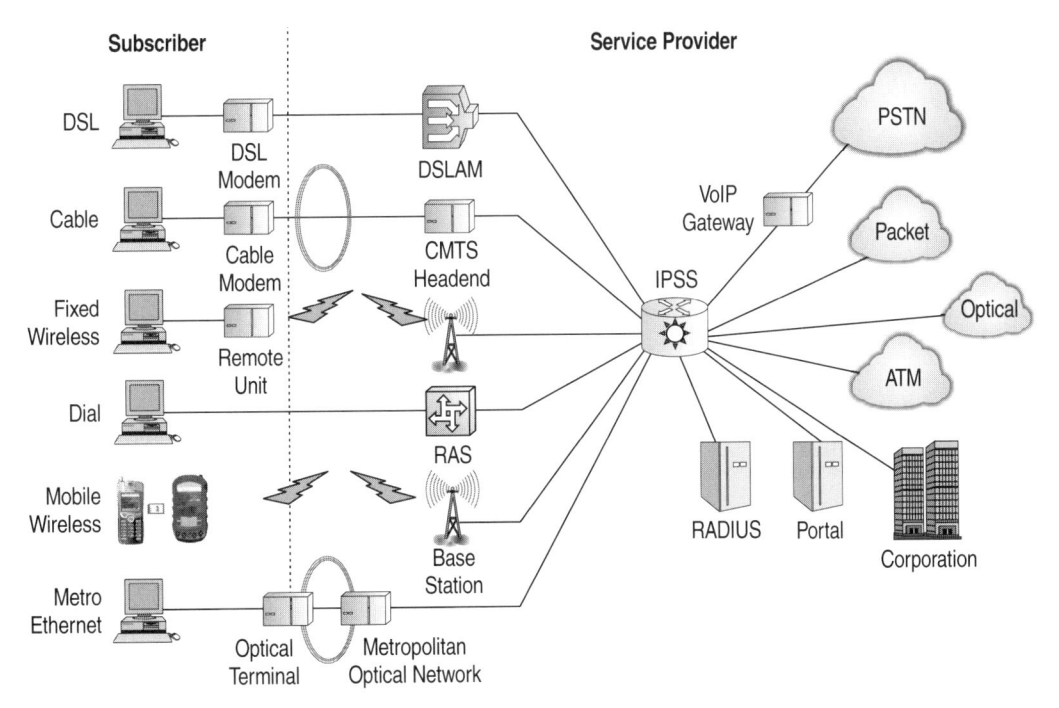

FIGURE 2.2 Access Technologies

the choice of uplinks. In the case of cable modems, uplinks integrate the required radio frequency (RF) technology to connect to the cable plant, whereas wireless modems connect to an external antenna mounted on the side of the building, which then connects to the provider's wireless base station.

SOHO users may have more sophisticated requirements since they almost always have a LAN and multiple devices. Although bridged access is a possibility, the provider must provide the SOHO user with a public IP address for each connected device. This is a workable, though expensive, solution; a DSL ISP provider is likely to charge $5 per month for each IP address. A more scalable and cost-effective solution for the SOHO user is to deploy a router. In this case, the user may have an arbitrary number of devices on his or her own subnet, routed into the provider's network. Depending on the deployment, the customer's subnet could employ public routable IP addresses, or the router could implement network address translation/protocol address translation (NAT/PAT) (described in chapter 3) to map nonroutable local IP addresses into the Internet.

Separate from the discussion of whether the device supports bridging or routing is what additional services it integrates. Firewalling, sophisticated traffic prioritization, and IP-VPN support are just a few of the possibilities.

Mobile wireless access is a bit different, since a single device will in almost all cases replace what are discrete devices for wireline access. These 2.5G or 3G devices may take the form of PDAs, cellphones, or laptops with integrated wireless modems.

Other, more mature technologies are relevant as well. A customer-located bridge or router connecting to a Frame Relay service is sometimes known as a Frame Relay access device (FRAD), and it connects to a port on a Frame Relay edge switch. The same customer device deployed as part of an asynchronous transfer mode (ATM) service is known as an integrated access device (IAD), and it connects directly to an ATM switch. (Note that the term *IAD* is also coming into favor in the DSL space as part of DSL-based voice services.)

As an aside, one of the goals of providers is to transition these end-to-end Frame Relay or ATM subscribers to an IP backbone. This transition is described in chapter 3 and is one of the uses of an IP service switch.

The Access Network

The different on-premises networking technologies connect to the provider's central office or PoP and then into the IPSS via a number of different access technologies. Factors influencing the choice of technology include the provider's background (i.e., incumbent local exchange carrier [ILEC] or multiservice operator [MSO]), the bandwidth required, whether the provider is targeting static or mobile customers (or both), and whether the provider is focusing on the residential or business market (or both). Access technologies include DSL, cable, fixed and mobile wireless, metropoli-

> ◆ **CPE versus CLE**
>
> If a device is owned and operated by the provider, it is commonly called *customer located equipment* (*CLE*) or *customer premise equipment* (*CPE*). In contrast, a device owned and operated by the subscriber is always referred to as CPE. Service providers often provide a *managed service*. This term has come to mean that the service provider installs CLE at the customer or subscriber site, but the service provider actually operates and manages the device. Chapter 3 discusses split-horizon management, an evolution of traditional CLE in which the subscriber and the provider manage different parameters within the CLE. As services become more sophisticated, this capability is becoming increasingly popular.

tan Ethernet, legacy technologies (including T1 and greater time-division multiplexing (TDM), Frame Relay, and ATM services) and remote access servers.

DSL Access Technologies

Digital subscriber line (DSL) is probably the most well known broadband access technology, at least in the business space, and in the coming years it will account for up to half of residential, telecommuter, and small business deployments. Both the ILECs and CLECs are ambitiously focusing on DSL buildout, and the type of DSL can greatly affect the types of services available to the subscriber.

In a typical DSL deployment, the subscriber's PC connects directly to the DSL modem via Ethernet or USB. Where there are multiple devices connected to the DSL modem, they attach via a hub or LAN switch (see Figure 2.3). An alternative available since 2000 is to equip the PC with an integrated DSL modem. In all cases, the DSL modem then connects to the copper pair. In the case of asymmetric digital subscriber line (ADSL), the modem may also be equipped with a plain old telephone service (POTS) splitter, though external splitters are more common. POTS splitters split the copper pair between the data and the analog or ISDN voice traffic. A variation on the traditional residential DSL modem is the DSL IAD. These IADs support both data and voice over DSL and permit small businesses or even telecommuters to connect multiple analog or digital voice lines across the copper loop. The voice traffic is carried in separate ATM permanent virtual circuits (PVCs) from the traditional data traffic. The DSL access provider then switches this PVC to a special voice gateway, which connects to the PSTN.

On entering the central office (CO), the copper pairs traverse the main distribution frame (MDF) and terminate at the digital subscriber line access multiplexer (DSLAM), which is the CO-side complement to the subscriber-side DSL modem. The one variation is with ADSL, where the pairs first pass through a splitter bank, permitting the access provider to split the voice traffic from the data. Then, the

FIGURE 2.3 DSL Topology

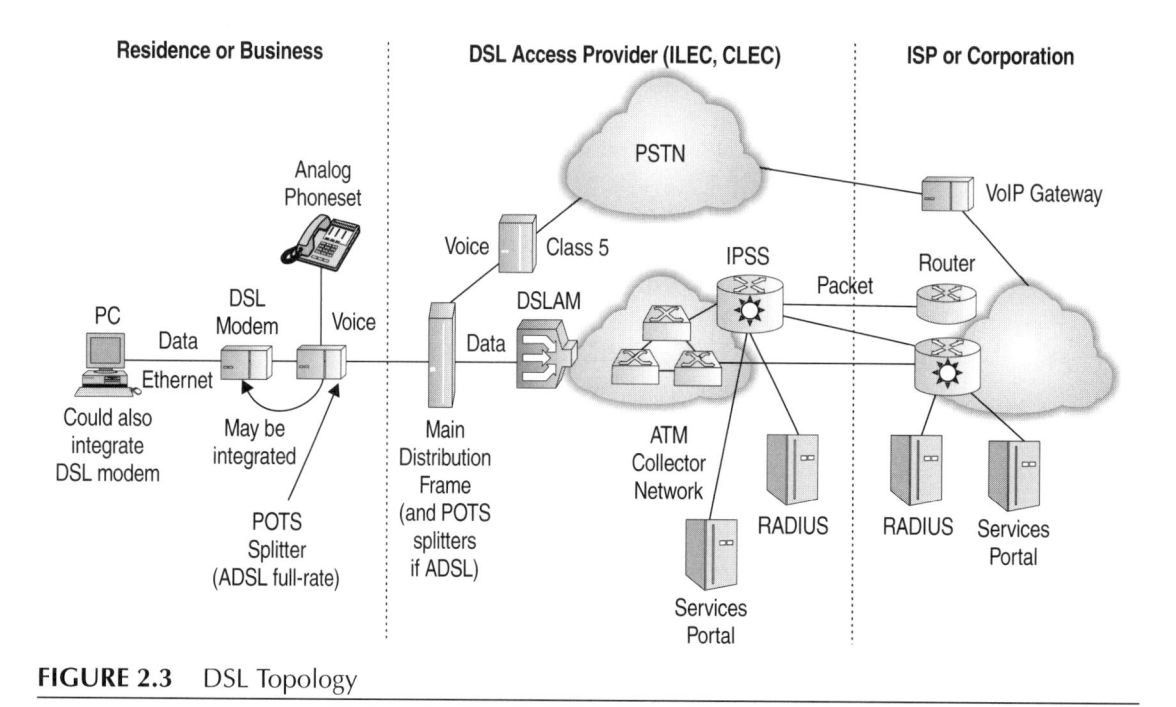

access provider forwards the voice traffic to the existing voice switches. The DSLAM is a chassis-based device, capable of terminating up to hundreds of subscribers, and it usually includes the capability to terminate multiple flavors of DSL (for example, ADSL, SDSL, IDSL, HDSL). A typical DSLAM contains different types of modem cards, control modules, trunks, and power supplies. In many cases, the DSLAM is capable of supporting redundant control and trunk modules. Per-card modem densities available in 2001 commonly range from 32 per blade (interface card) for SDSL or G.lite to 16 per blade for full-rate discrete multitone (DMT) ADSL. Traffic entering the DSLAM passes through the DSL modems and then onto the backplane or into the DSLAM's switching fabric.

The next few sections detail the different types of DSL technologies in use, as well as DSLAM architectures.

DSL Technologies

DSL refers to a set of copper-loop-based technologies, including the following:

- Asymmetric DSL (ADSL), including variations once referred to as rate-adaptive DSL (RADSL) and G.lite/DSL-lite
- Symmetric DSL (SDSL)
- High-speed DSL (HDSL), including HDSL2
- ISDN DSL (IDSL)

- Very-high-speed DSL (VDSL)
- Symmetric HDSL (SHDSL)

Figure 2.4 shows the different DSL technologies in terms of bandwidth, distance, copper pairs required, and encoding scheme.

ADSL and G.Lite/DSL-Lite ADSL is by far the most popular of the DSL technologies, but it is considered primarily a residential technology because it offers greater downstream (toward the subscriber) than upstream (from the subscriber) bandwidth and it uses a single copper pair.

Typical ADSL deployments range from 128 Kbps for low-end residential service to 8 Mbps for premium business and entertainment services. In all cases, ADSL's upstream bandwidth is capped at about 1 Mbps. As with all the other DSL technologies, the distance from the access provider's central office (CO) to the subscriber determines the maximum bandwidth available.

	IDSL	HDSL: SDSL	HDSL2	SHDSL	ADSL	DSL-Lite (G.lite)	VDSL
Maximum Reach	26 Kft	20 Kft	24 Kft (with repeater)	25 Kft	13 Kft typical	24 Kft	3–5 Kft typical
Typical Reach	20 Kft	10 Kft (T1)	9 Kft (T1)	14 Kft (T1)	6 Kft (T1)		1 Kft
Maximum Bandwidth (downstream/upstream)	144 Kbps / 144 Kbps	2 Mbps / 2 Mbps	2 Mbps / 2 Mbps	2.3 Mbps / 2.3 Mbps	7 Mbps / 1 Mbps	1 Mbps+ / 256 Kbps+	52 Mbps / 6.4 Mbps
Typical Bandwidth (downstream/upstream)	144 Kbps / 144 Kbps	144 Kbps / 144 Kbps	1.5 Mbps / 1.5 Mbps	1.5 Mbps / 1.5 Mbps	1 Mbps / 764 Kbps	256 Kbps / 128 Kbps	26 Mbps / 3.2 Mbps
Copper Pairs	1	1	1	1	1	1	1
Encoding	2B1Q (ISDN)	2B1Q (and others)	OPTIS/TC-PAM	TC-PAM	DMT	DMT	CAP/QAM or DMT variant
Standard	ISDN		G.991.1	G.991.2	G.992.1	G.992.2	

FIGURE 2.4 DSL Taxonomy

Some analysts predict that by 2003, more than 20 million ADSL lines will be deployed globally, with over 10 million in the United States alone (FCC, 2000; IDC, 2000b). Initially, the ILECs deployed ADSL, but CLECs (which at one time focused on SDSL and IDSL-only deployments) are now deploying ADSL as well. ADSL is the one DSL flavor that supports the transport of the existing analog or digital voice traffic in a frequency spectrum below that of the ADSL data. In a typical deployment, a POTS splitter is deployed at the customer site, separating the baseband voice traffic from the data, avoiding the need for a second copper loop, and therefore permitting the use of ADSL where copper pairs are extremely limited (and without the additional cost of any of the DSL-focused voice technologies based on ATM or VoIP). The splitter includes the necessary filters to avoid interference of either the voice or the data traffic.

A variation of ADSL, known as DSL-lite or G.lite (ITU, 1999b), is also aimed at the residential market. G.lite is limited to bandwidths lower than full-rate ADSL, but it permits greater density at the DSLAM and may simplify POTS splitter deployment. Some PCs equipped with ADSL support G.lite. Although G.Lite wasn't available as early as expected, most DSLAMs now support it.

One problem with ADSL is that there are still some incompatibilities in the chipsets deployed. For this reason, there is no guarantee that a DSL modem from one vendor will operate with a DSLAM from another. Two bright notes are that many of the major incompatibility problems are now in the past and that only a few vendors provide the DSLAMs used by the majority of subscribers. In fact, DSL modems are finally available in retail outlets.

SDSL and HDSL SDSL, a single-pair symmetric service, is focused more on business subscribers than is ADSL, and is primarily offered by the CLECs. The symmetry involved in SDSL is important in business applications, which often require bilateral file sharing (as opposed to residential applications, in which users are often Web browsing and do not upload many files, one reason for ADSL's popularity in the residential space). Another reason for SDSL's popularity in business settings is that it does not support voice via POTS splitters, as ADSL does. Businesses generally do not need the POTS splitter functionality because they usually have multiple voice

◆ **Early ADSL Interoperability Problems: CAP versus DMT**

Early ADSL interoperability problems based on differences in the fundamental coding technology have all but disappeared. These problems had to do with two competing technologies: carrier amplitude and phase (CAP) and discrete multitone (DMT). ANSI and the ITU selected DMT for standardization, and it is therefore now the single global standard for ADSL.

lines that are separate from the data connection. With the deployment of the voice over DSL (VoDSL) solutions described in the section "Circuit-Oriented DSLAMs" later in this chapter, this lack of traditional voice support is even less of an issue for businesses. Access providers offer SDSL at speeds up to 1.5 Mbps, and as with ADSL, the bandwidth is a function of the distance from the CO.

HDSL is also focused on business subscribers, and it is available at symmetric speeds of up to 1.5 or 2 Mbps, depending on location. Although HDSL in the past relied on two pairs of wire, the more recent HDSL2 requires only a single pair. One advantage of HDSL is its data encoding, which permits longer reach than the other DSL technologies. HDSL has a long history of deployment in T1/E1 services, replacing earlier repeater-based technologies.

IDSL and VDSL IDSL is considered a telecommuter service because of its bandwidth limitation of 144 Kbps. Like SDSL and HDSL, IDSL does not support analog voice. Although IDSL saw some early growth within the CLECs, momentum has shifted to ADSL and SDSL because they have greater bandwidth capabilities. One advantage of IDSL, however, is its reach. IDSL can extend up to 24,000 ft, far beyond the range of most other technologies (except digital-loop-carrier-based (DLC-based) deployments and some vendor proprietary encoding). One reason for its distance capabilities is that IDSL uses ISDN encoding and can be deployed in the presence of most ISDN-compatible transmission equipment such as repeaters, amplifiers, and loop extenders.

VDSL is a higher-speed technology, promising data rates of up to 52 Mbps. However, VDSL has seen minimal deployment to date because of the requirement for fiber buildout and cost. VDSL is limited to distances of about 3,000 ft, and bandwidth drops quickly with distance. To achieve top bandwidths, the provider must deploy fiber within the access network to a pedestal located near the subscriber. Today, Ethernet extension is being deployed in volume, while VDSL is still a niche technology. Given the effect of volume manufacturing on component pricing, Ethernet's advantage may be insurmountable.

SHDSL A fairly recent development is SHDSL (ITU, 2000), which offers up to 2 Mbps of symmetric service. SHDSL is designed to overcome many of the vendor and encoding incompatibilities between HDSL, IDSL, and SDSL. The new SHDSL standard was completed in 2000; the most interesting component of the standard is SHDSL's capability to negotiate the service type during the start-up phase. Using a variation of the G.hs handshake protocol (ITU, 1999a), SHDSL modems select the use of T1, E1, ISDN, ATM, or even IP framing across the link. This optimizes performance because it avoids unnecessary overhead and reduces latency. The ability to support IP also reduces complexity in IP-centric deployments, while TDM support is best for voice across low-speed links.

DSLAMs

DSLAMs fall into two categories—those based on ATM or Frame Relay and configured through virtual circuits, and those integrating IP functionality and configured much like a router. Although circuit-mode DSLAMs comprise the majority of the installations and are preferred by the ILECs, with the growth of the CLECs toward the end of the 1990s, many thought that IP DSLAMs would be the future. However, this has not quite been the case, and circuit-mode DSLAMs still comprise the majority of new installations. Some DSLAMs are also being adapted for DLC deployment, an advance that will greatly extend the reach of DSL deployments.

Circuit-Oriented DSLAMs Traditionally, at least in the ADSL space, the DSL CPE and the DSLAMs all operate in ATM mode, with subscriber PVCs extended across the DSLAM's trunk via an ATM backbone to the provider's Layer 3 PoP. ATM is essentially a connection-oriented cell-based technology that allows the service provider to create either permanent virtual circuits (PVCs) or switched virtual circuits (SVCs). These PVCs or SVCs are created to connect two points and will support a certain amount of bandwidth defined by the ATM switch. ATM technology has traditionally been used to provide effective bandwidth management and quality of service (QoS) in service provider networks. Since these providers were responsible for initial DSL deployment, and favored ATM, the DSLAM vendors complied by implementing ATM-centric platforms. Because of this, the DSLAMs traditionally have no visibility into the IP-layer subscriber traffic. The exception has been with IDSL and SDSL on the subscriber side, where a number of DSLAMs operate as frame mode bridges. In addition, although a DSLAM may operate in ATM mode on the subscriber side for ADSL, nothing precludes bridging into Frame Relay or even Fast Ethernet on the trunk side. The next logical step is to provide the DSLAM with full IP functionality, described in the next section.

Depending on how sophisticated the DSLAM is, it may support prioritization of the subscriber PVCs (or even SVCs) at the ATM layer. This capability is in fact critical for support of the IAD-based VoDSL service described previously. After crossing the fabric, the DSLAM forwards the traffic over one or more trunks to the metropolitan or regional ATM network and then onto the IPSS. Alternatively, the provider may deploy *subtending*, where DSLAMs in more remote locations or within a PoP aggregate through a second DSLAM. This architecture minimizes the number of upstream trunk connections.

IP-DSLAMs A more recent offering, the IP-DSLAM, incorporates full routing within the DSLAM and provides a choice of upstream trunk interfaces, including Fast Ethernet and PPP over SONET/SDH. This DSLAM architecture has advantages and disadvantages. IP-DSLAMs have an advantage when it comes to IP multicast because they permit effective video distribution (as described in chapter 7). In a broadcast environment, multiple subscribers on the DSLAM might want to view a single channel. Because of the bandwidths involved, it is inefficient to send an individual stream for each and every subscriber from the IPSS. Thus, IP-layer replication must take place at the DSLAM. Disadvantages include additional cost of deployment and operation, as well as an inability to offer some forms of wholesaling since IP addressing DSLAM is dedicated to a single IP provider. This architecture is therefore more suitable for those providers specifically targeting video distribution.

In any case, the IP-DSLAM will still probably connect to an IPSS for additional IP services processing. If this is not the case, the DSLAM will forward traffic directly across the IP backbone to ISPs and corporate customers. Although the IP-DSLAM is a good concept in theory, it has in fact seen limited acceptance by the ILECs, which favor the more traditional DSLAMs offered by Alcatel and others. In addition, those most supportive of the IP-DSLAM concept, the business-focused CLECs, have experienced financial difficulties and have therefore backed off on their DSL deployments or have gone out of business.

Extensions to DLCs In addition to traditional CO-based DSLAM deployment, placement within the digital loop carrier (DLC) environment is now taking place. DLCs are street cabinets placed close to business or residential subscribers that help the service provider optimize the installed copper plant while permitting more advanced services. DSLAMs installed within these DLC cabinets must conform to certain size and environmental profiles (such as temperature and humidity). In meeting these requirements, they usually have lower modem density than their CO counterparts. There are also additional challenges when deploying in this environment, including the total upstream bandwidth from the DLC (sometimes limited to multiples of T1 [1.544 Mbps]) and the variations in DLCs that require vendors to support multiple platforms.

Cable Access Technologies

When it comes to residential high-speed Internet access, cable modems are even more popular than DSL at present. In fact, by 2003 the two technologies are expected to be about evenly deployed, with 20 million cable modems installed globally—10 million in the United States alone (IDC, 2000b). However, unlike with DSL, the focus for cable modem service has been on residential service. In some areas, especially overseas, this is changing as providers deploy cable modem service to multitenant units (MTUs) for small business applications. The technology reuses the existing cable TV infrastructure by reserving one or more channels for data. Each of these channels offers up to 38.8 Mbps of downstream bandwidth (depending on the encoding used), which is shared by up to 500 subscribers. A cable modem deployment consists of the subscriber modems, the required fiber and coaxial infrastructure, and the cable modem termination system (CMTS).

Cable Modems

As in the DSL scenario, the user's PC connects via Ethernet to a cable modem that contains the hardware it needs to connect to the cable infrastructure. As more CMTS headends and subscriber cable modems from multiple vendors came into the market, CableLabs (*www.cablemodem.com*) created the Data over Cable Systems Interface Specification (DOCSIS) standard to ensure interoperability (CableLabs, 1999). This standard is also intended as a framework for an end-to-end IP solution. The cable service providers can mix and match vendor equipment as long as it is DOCSIS compliant, allowing service providers to have alternative hardware and vendor choices. Additionally, DOCSIS-compliant equipment is easier to configure and provision than prestandard modems.

Although early cable modem deployments relied on proprietary techniques, all new deployments are based on DOCSIS, and earlier deployments will be replaced over time. The first DOCSIS specification, 1.0, covered basic interoperability and system management. The more recent, Version 1.1, includes provisions for QoS in support of Internet telephony. Version 2.0, finalized in September 2001, added new physical layer encoding. Through the use of Synchronous COMA, the upstream bandwidth was raised to 30 Mbps, introducing better symmetry between upstream and downstream bandwidth. DOCSIS 2.0-compliant systems are expected to see initial deployment during 2002.

Internationally, a Euro-DOCSIS standard supports the 8 MHz channel separation for European broadcast systems (in contrast to the 6 MHz channels used in North America). It is identical to the North American standard in most other regards. An alternative standard for data over cable, the Digital Video Broadcasting (DVB) standard (*www.dvb.org*), has also seen deployment, and some vendors support this technology.

The Headend

At the MSO's PoP, a cable modem headend (also referred to as a CMTS) aggregates traffic from the subscriber modems. The cable headend then connects into the provider's backbone, similar to DSL (see Figure 2.5). The cable plant may also connect to a voice gateway in parallel with the CMTS. (Broadband voice technologies are discussed in greater detail in chapter 4.)

The type of connection into the provider's backbone differs, depending on the size of the deployment, the service model of the cable operator, and the type of equipment deployed. For smaller deployments where the subscribers connect into a single ISP (normally a partner with the cable operator), an IPSS may not be needed, and the CMTS headends may connect directly to the provider's core routing infrastructure, as shown in Figure 2.6, Option 1. This connection is via Fast Ethernet (FE), Gigabit Ethernet (GE), or PPP over synchronous optical network/synchronous digital hierarchy (SONET/SDH).

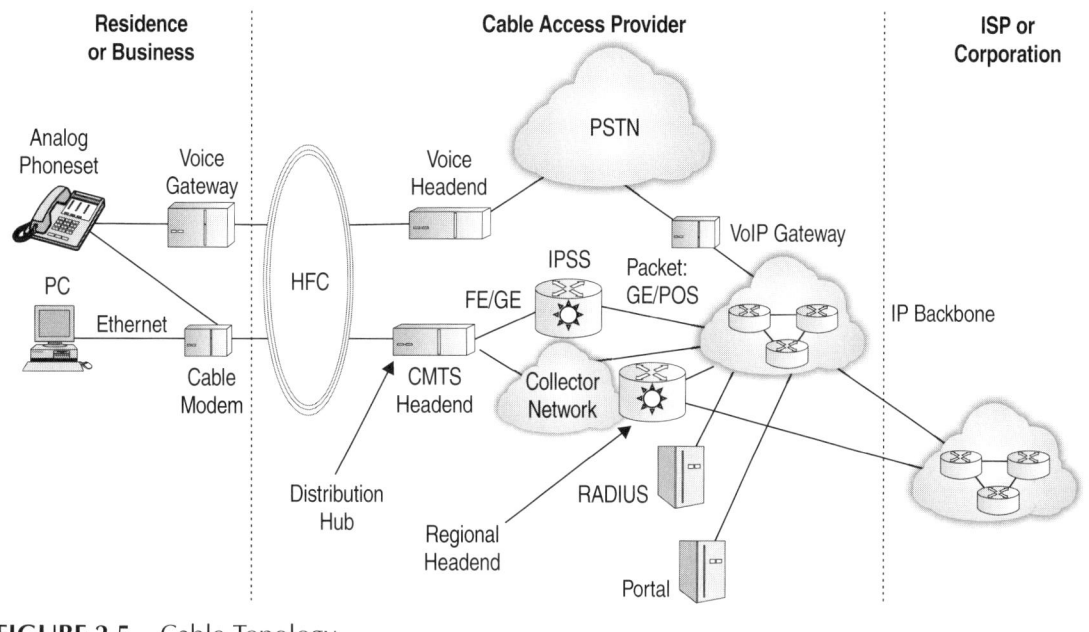

FIGURE 2.5 Cable Topology

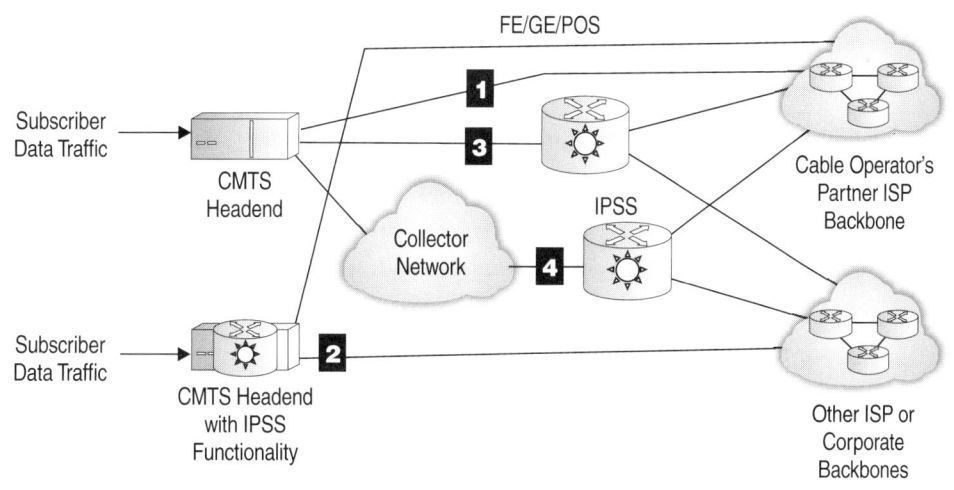

FIGURE 2.6 Beyond the Cable Headend

Where connectivity to multiple ISPs or corporate networks is required (known as *open access*), either the CMTS headend will integrate IPSS functionality if it operates as a router (Option 2 in Figure 2.6) or the operator will deploy a standalone IPSS for additional scalability and network-based services (for example, a CMTS headend might integrate provider selection via tunneling, but not firewalling or more complex IP-VPNs). If the headend operates as a bridge, it will usually connect to an IPSS. This IPSS may be collocated with a bank of headends connected via a LAN switch (Option 3 in Figure 2.6), or it may be collocated at an aggregation PoP reached via a Layer 2 or 3 access network (Option 4 in Figure 2.6).

The Evolving Role of Fiber in Cable Systems

Within neighborhoods, the coaxial system transitions from coax to fiber. Thus the term *hybrid fiber-coax* (HFC) is used to refer to these newer buildouts, a requirement for two-way cable data services. This HFC deployment results in an infrastructure that is capable of bringing higher-bandwidth symmetric services to the customers. Rather than the cable company then providing data services to business customers, it could partner with a third party to provide these services.

Figure 2.7 shows a typical HFC plant. Off-air and satellite channels all arrive at the provider's headend facility and are modulated onto different frequencies for transmission across the fiber/coax infrastructure. At this point, the Internet traffic is also mapped into one or more frequencies. This data channel connects to the Internet via the CMTS. In the direction of the subscriber, the combined video and

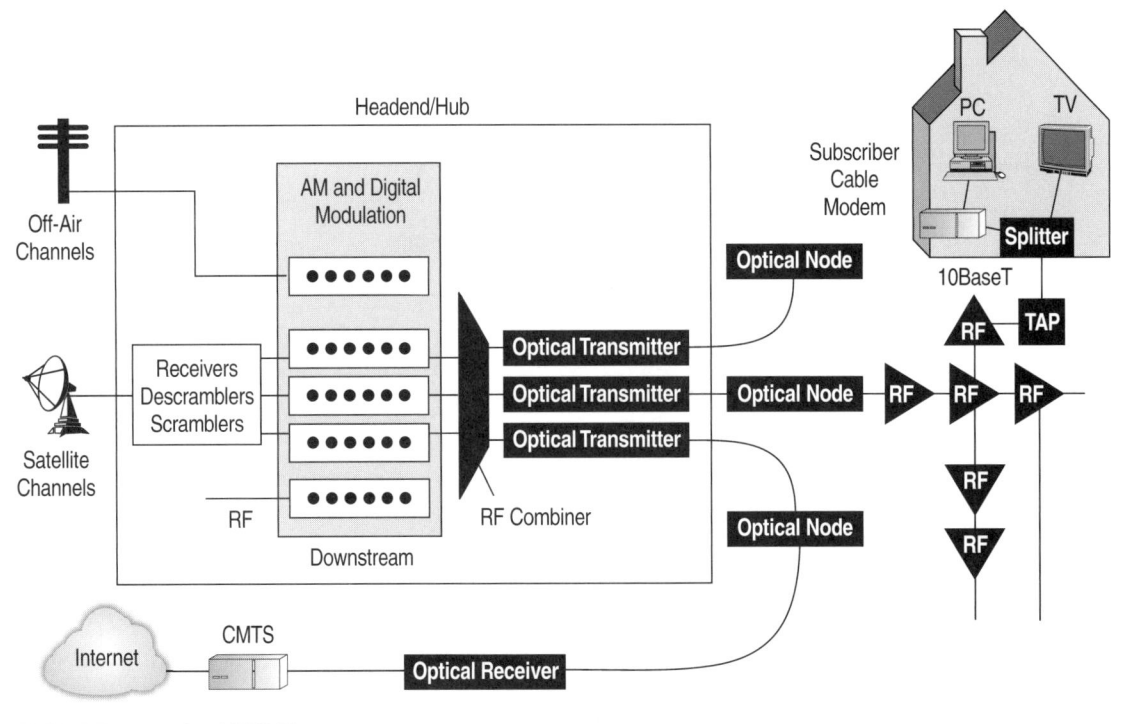

FIGURE 2.7   An HFC Plant

data signal follows a fiber infrastructure until it reaches an optical node close to the subscriber's neighborhood. At this point, the signal is mapped onto coaxial cable for the final leg to the subscriber. As part of a tree topology, branching off within the neighborhood, the signal passes through multiple RF splitters before arriving at the tap servicing the household (or apartment). Here the signal is split, with the data diverted to a cable modem. The subscriber's PC (or hub servicing multiple PCs) connects to this modem via Ethernet or USB.

An HFC plant is configured as a single headend topology (shown in Figure 2.8) or as a central headend with secondary hub topology (shown in Figure 2.9). The central headend with secondary hub topology is the more common architecture in new HFC plants because it allows the cable providers to reuse the same transmission channel across the various secondary hubs since each channel is effectively terminated at these hubs. In the central headend architecture, a different channel is used for each optical node, resulting in less efficient use of the frequency spectrum provided to the cable provider since no reuse is possible.

Figure 2.10 depicts a data deployment using cable modems. In a cable modem environment, data is transmitted over shared media. Additionally, a differentiation is made between upstream and downstream data. *Downstream data* is data going

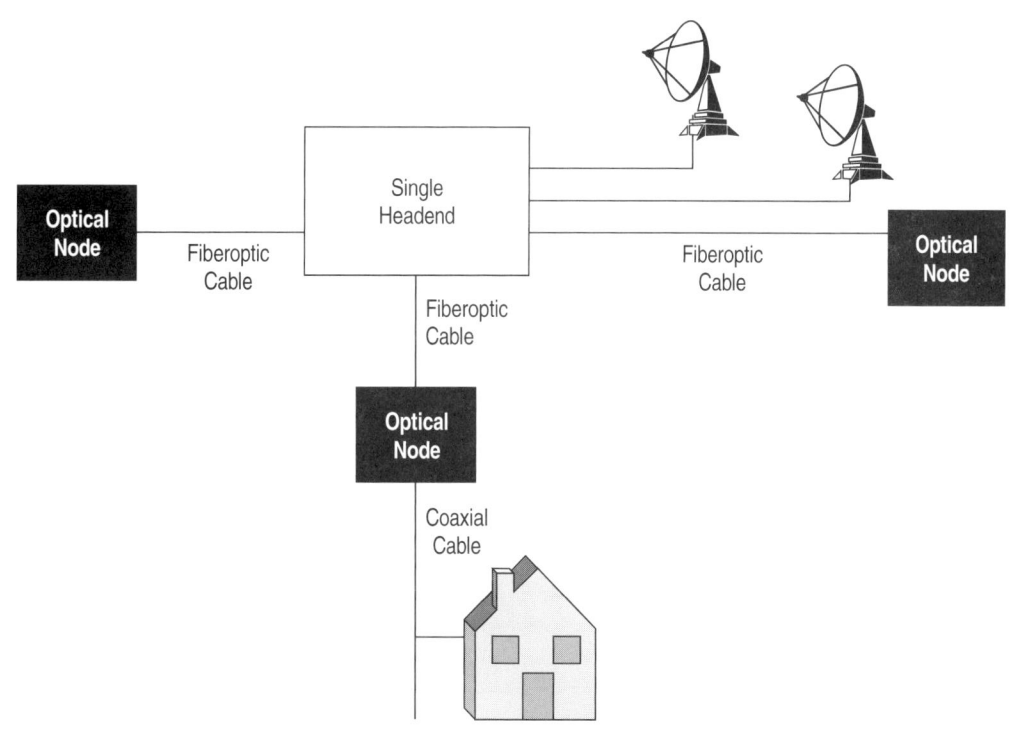

FIGURE 2.8 Single Headend Architecture

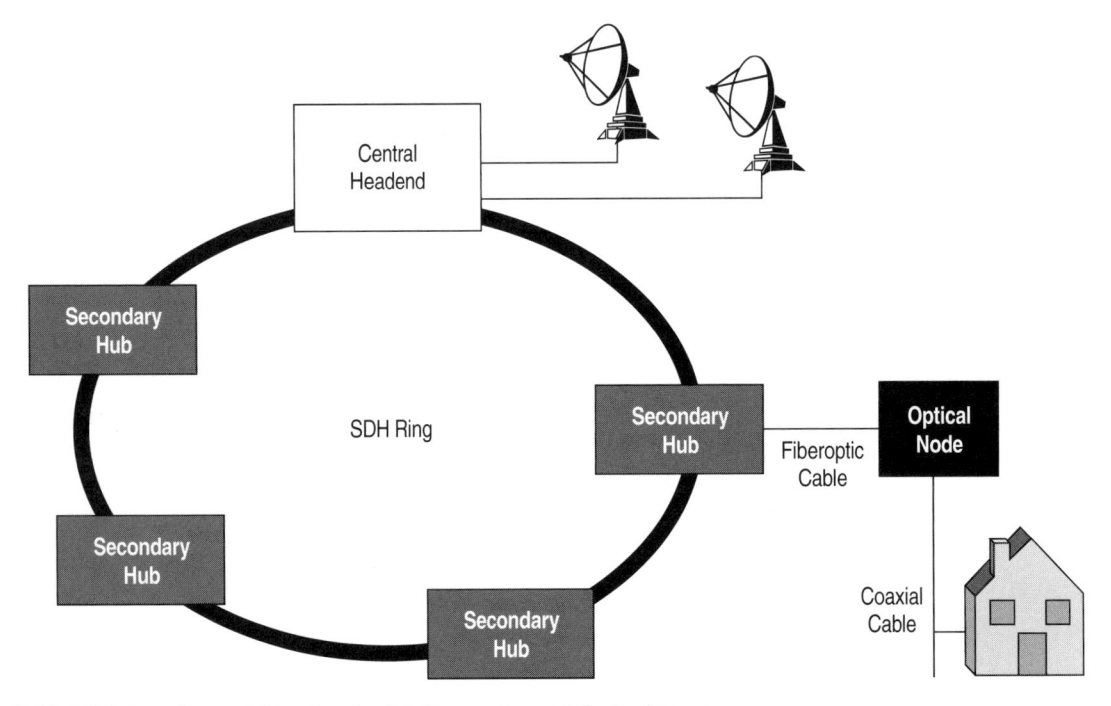

46   **Chapter 2** *Broadband Access Technologies: Physical Connectivity*

FIGURE 2.9   Central Headend with Secondary Hub Architecture

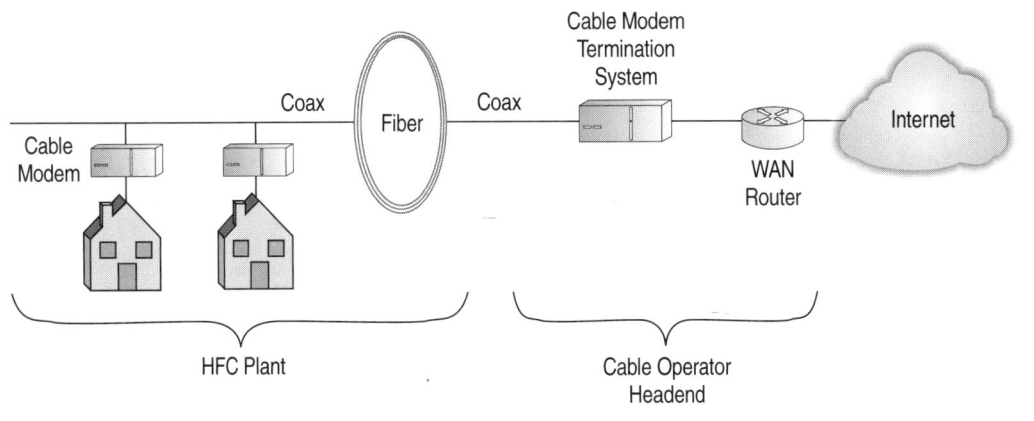

FIGURE 2.10   Cable Modem Deployment

from the Internet to the CMTS down to the cable modem. *Upstream data* is subscriber data being transmitted from a PC up to the cable modem then to the CMTS and onward to the Internet. Downstream data is transmitted over a 6 MHz analog channel (a TV broadcast channel, rendering the data traffic transparent to the existing cable plant), with all data transmitted using the full bandwidth. This results in a maximum throughput per channel of 38.8 Mbps when using quadrature amplitude modulation (QAM) 256 or 26.9 Mbps when using QAM64 modulation. The downstream channels can be sent over a frequency spectrum ranging from 88 to 860 MHz.

The upstream, or return, channels run on a different frequency from the downstream channels. They can run only on frequencies ranging from 5 to 42 MHz. Unfortunately, this bandwidth is not all usable because of noise, which results in a limited number of return paths. Under ideal conditions, up to 11 return paths can be set up. The upstream channel width is up to 3.2 MHz and is user-definable; in contrast, the downstream bandwidth is set. With a 3.2 MHz channel, the maximum throughput is 10.24 Mbps using QAM16 or 5 Mbps using quadrature phase shift keying (QPSK). The asymmetrical bandwidth was initially geared toward residential users. However, as cable modem usage spread into the business environment, the upstream bandwidth was not sufficient for bandwidth-intensive applications such as videoconferencing. As a result, many CMTS headends are capable of multiple upstream channels. The number of upstream and downstream connections depends on the service model of the MSO, and determines the bandwidth available to a subscriber in the return direction. For example, a DOCSIS card may include one upstream channel using QPSK or 16QAM modulation, for a total bandwidth of 5 or 10 Mbps.

At the distribution hub operated by the cable provider, the fiber transitions once again to coax, which then terminates at a bridge or router acting as a CMTS.

Fixed Wireless Access Technologies

It is still too early to judge the success of fixed wireless buildouts, since real deployments began only in late 2000. However, based on announced plans by both AT&T and Sprint, more than 50 percent of the U.S. population is expected to be in range of this type of service by the end of 2003. This will result in up to 4 million new residential and 450,000 new business subscribers in this short amount of time. Note that these wireless technologies also include the shorter-range (3 to 5 miles) local multipoint distribution system (LMDS, 28 and 39 GHz) systems as well as the longer-range (25 to 35 miles) multichannel multipoint distribution system (MMDS, 2 GHz) networks.

Fixed wireless technology is a relative newcomer to broadband residential connectivity, though business customers have utilized various forms of wireless access over the last few years. For residential broadband deployment, incumbent cellular operators are able to reuse their infrastructure by placing new antennas

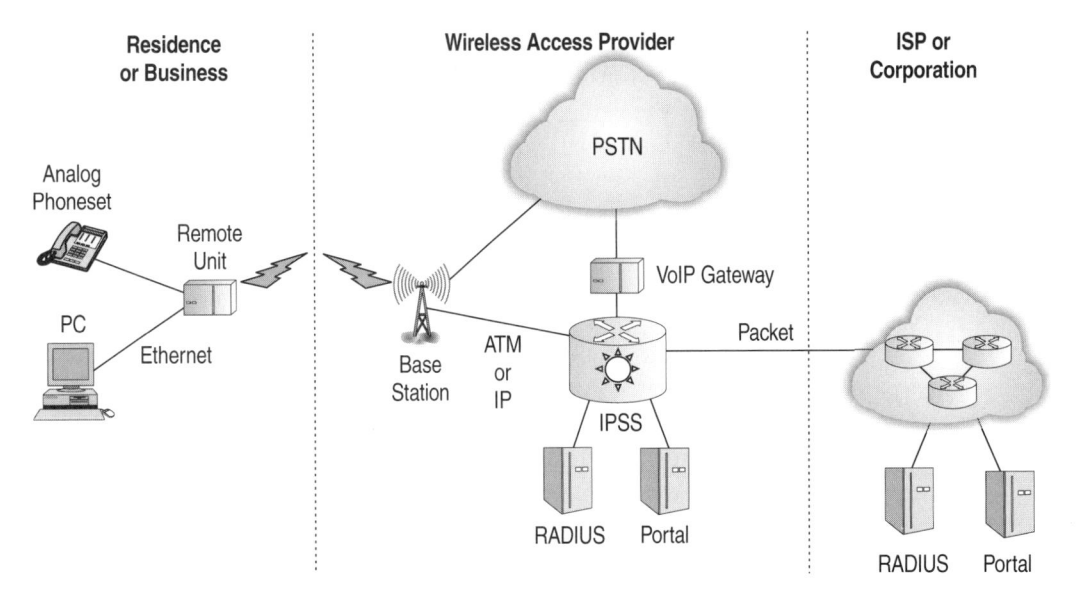

FIGURE 2.11 Fixed Wireless Deployment

on their existing cellular masts and new radios collocated with their existing cellular systems (see Figure 2.11). The technology for these radios varies from vendor to vendor, as there is not yet a standard. Multiple radios within a metropolitan area connect via Frame Relay or ATM to one or more IPSSs located within the provider's Layer 3 PoP. Within the PoP, the access provider forwards the subscriber traffic to the various ISPs and content providers. At the residence, multiple PCs attached to a home LAN (for example, HomePNA) connect to the wireless remote unit located on the outside of the house. The technology as initially deployed offers bandwidths up to 256 Kbps, at a monthly cost not much greater than that of Internet dial-up. As an added advantage, fixed broadband wireless also supports traditional telephony service. It therefore permits the broadband wireless operator to address the local phone market in locations where it may not be the incumbent carrier. It also permits the operator to offer data services in locations where it may not have a cable franchise or access to the local loop for DSL.

In businesses, LMDS and MMDS are the primary fixed wireless contenders. LMDS offers up to 155 Mbps at a range of 5 miles and is used for high data rates in concentrated areas. MMDS spans an entire metropolitan area of about 50 miles in diameter but at bandwidths to only 27 Mbps. Both technologies multiplex multiple customers into this bandwidth, much as Ethernet hubs do. Typically, a router within the business will connect to the remote unit for either of these technologies. The LMDS or MMDS base stations connect to the provider's ATM or packet backbone, with some traffic terminating on the IPSS for additional IP services processing.

Mobile Wireless Access Technologies

Mobile wireless services are expected to be the greatest area of growth over the next decade, and as with wired services, wireless subscribers have the need for sophisticated services. The focus here is on next-generation, IP-centric mobile systems, which first appeared during 2001. Initial deployments are variations of the existing second-generation digital wireless technologies, including global system for mobile communication (GSM), time division multiple access (TDMA), and code division multiple access (CDMA) systems. In the case of GSM and TDMA, the next-generation technology is known as the general packet radio service (GPRS) and offers up to 128 Kbps per subscriber. CDMA systems will evolve to CDMA 1xRTT, also offering 128 Kbps. The real breakthrough is expected to occur after 2002, with third-generation universal mobile telecom systems (UMTSs) offering bandwidth of up to 2 Mbps per subscriber and allowing for near-broadband content.

In a typical mobile wireless deployment, the subscriber's GPRS, 1xRTT, or UMTS handset connects to the wireless operator's base station (see Figure 2.12). The telephony traffic is then separated from the data traffic and forwarded into the

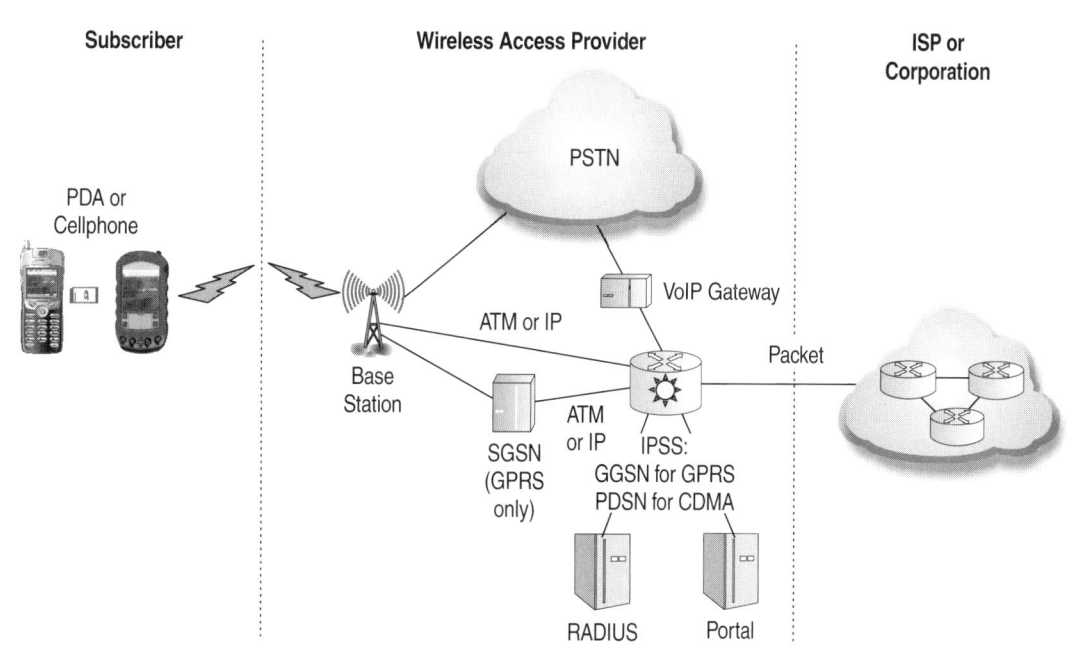

Note: GSM and TDMA evolve to GPRS and then UMTS. CDMA evolves to CDMA 1xRTT and then UMTS.

FIGURE 2.12 Wireless System Architecture

existing voice infrastructure. The difference between third-generation and previous technologies is that with third-generation technologies, the data traffic is forwarded to a dedicated IP services node unique to these next-generation deployments. For GPRS, this is known as the gateway GPRS support node (GGSN), and the CDMA 1xRTT equivalent is the packet data serving node (PDSN). The GGSN or PDSN, both of which may be functions of IPSSs, is responsible for tunnel termination, security, management of the subscriber's IP traffic, and routing traffic into the provider's backbone or server farm. Any content servers, including wireless access protocol (WAP), are placed upstream from the GGSN/PDSN. Chapter 8 includes a detailed GPRS and third-generation services example.

There are three major methods of wireless access—FDMA, TDM, and CDMA—which have different ways of dividing the radio spectrum into channels and allocating the channels to system users. Frequency division multiple access (FDMA) divides the spectrum into fixed channels, and each channel is allocated to a call. Most analog techniques are based on FDMA.

TDMA starts out with a slice of the spectrum referred to as one carrier. Each carrier is then divided into timeslots that are referred to as channels. Only one subscriber is assigned to a timeslot at any given time, and no other conversation can access the channel until the user is finished or until the system hands off the original call to a different channel. GSM is a TDMA/FDMA hybrid, dividing the available spectrum by frequency, then dividing by time within the frequency.

CDMA technology allows multiple conversations to share the same frequency. CDMA systems are equipped with intelligent codes that enable them to separate one conversation from another. They use unique digital codes rather than separate time channels to differentiate subscribers. The mobile terminals and the base station share these codes with all users sharing the same range of radio spectrum. The impact to the end consumer because of these different technologies is that terminals based on one standard cannot be used in another network based on a different standard.

Mobile networks consist of four major components:

- The *terminal*, sometimes called mobile terminal or mobile station (or phone), is the device that subscribers use to access mobile services.
- The *radio network,* or radio access network (RAN), consists of radio base stations and equipment to monitor and manage these base stations. The base stations receive and transmit radio communications to and from the mobile terminals.
- The *core network* focuses on switching and routing voice and data traffic from radio base stations. Traditionally, it has been based on circuit-switched technology, but with a UMTS rollout, it is being adapted to better support data services.

- The *service creation platforms* enable the service implementation in the various components via application programming interfaces (APIs).

Components of a Mobile Wireless Deployment

In an actual deployment, a wireless network consists of a base station system (BSS), a network subsystem, and an operation and support system (OSS). The network subsystem contains elements of the core network and service creation platform described earlier, and the base station system equates to the radio network. Figure 2.13 shows a typical example of a GSM architecture, and the following sections describe the components.

The BSS The BSS consists of two main components: the base station controller (BSC) and the base transceiver station (BTS). Together this hardware and software combination makes up 70 percent of capital expenditure for wireless providers.

The BSC is responsible for radio resource management and handoff between base stations as a user changes from one cell to another. It handles the connections between the mobile terminal and the mobile switching center (MSC).

The BTS controls the radio interface by transmitting and receiving signals from the subscriber's terminal. It also houses the radio transceivers that define a cell and handles the radio link protocols with the mobile terminals. It provides such functions as access control, traffic concentration, and signal processing and protocol conversion.

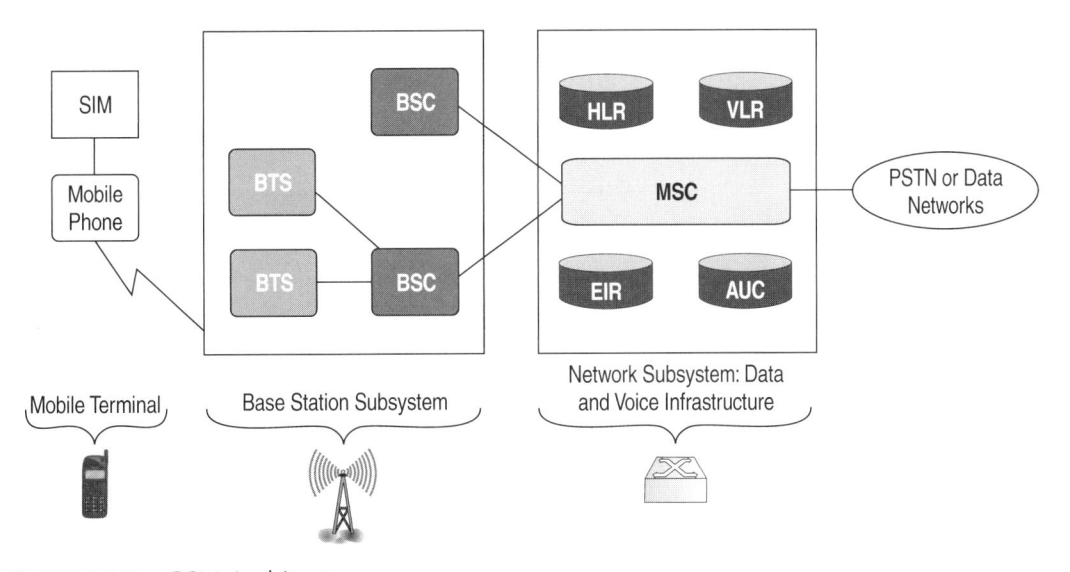

FIGURE 2.13 GSM Architecture

The Network Subsystem The network subsystem performs the routing, switching, call control, charging, and accounting functions. It can also interact with intelligent network (IN) platforms for additional services such as call forwarding. In mobile environments, IN is often used to provide the service creation and control environments. In GSM networks, CAMEL (customized applications for mobile enhanced logic) enables mobile roaming between different networks, voice-mail services, and customized value-added services. Elements of this subsystem include the following:

- A *mobile switching center* (MSC) is responsible for call setup and connection of the various elements of the switching system to the base station system. It is also the interface to other networks such as the public switched telephone network (PSTN).
- A *home location register* (HLR) is a centralized database that stores subscriber services and current location information on subscribers and assigns a subscriber profile. The HLR may be used in conjunction with the provisioning of more advanced services described in the rest of this list.
- A *visitor location register* (VLR) is another database that keeps records of all mobile subscribers currently in a specific MSC. It is used for roaming services.
- An *authentication center* (AUC), yet another database, contains the authentication register of all subscribers and is used to minimize fraud by allowing only authorized users on the mobile network.
- The *equipment identity register* (EIR) is a database that maintains information about the mobile terminals. An MSC can check with the EIR to ensure that a stolen terminal cannot be used on the network.

The OSS The OSS manages the whole network and all network elements from a central point. It supports cell network planning and traffic statistics. The OSS can be located within the switching center and/or at the base station system.

Cellular Evolution

The cellular world is divided into three different generations, based on the technology deployed:

- *First-generation (1G) deployments* are the traditional analog cellular systems that use FDMA technology. In 1G deployments, the voice-switching segment is based on digital circuit switches.
- *Second-generation (2G) deployments* were the first to use digital cellular systems based on TDMA and CDMA. The voice-switching segment is still based

on digital circuit switches. There have been evolutions to existing 2G systems to obtain increased data rates, such as the high-speed circuit-switched data (HSCSD) protocol that enables rates of 115 Kbps, although the terminals realistically support 57.8 Kbps and the technology is an inefficient use of spectrum because of the circuit switching.

- *Third-generation (3G) systems* are based on wideband CDMA (WCDMA). In 3G systems, both voice- and data-switching segments are based on packet switches. Existing CDMA operators will evolve to CDMA 1xRTT, later evolving to 3xRTT and TDMA, and GSM operators will evolve to GPRS and then UMTS.

An important interim option fits between 2G and 3G networks; the industry typically refers to it as 2.5G. The name 2.5G does not refer to a specific technology but to a migration phase between circuit-switched voice wireless networks (2G) and the packet-based voice and data wireless networks (3G). Some 2.5G solutions, including GPRS and the enhanced data rates for GSM evolution (EDGE), are based on the introduction of a packet overlay network on top of the existing 2G circuit-switch-based networks. To support packet data, a small modification is made to the RAN. Other existing technologies such as CDMA 1xRTT and TDMA require additional changes to the radio infrastructure. Voice is still carried over the existing circuit switches and TDM-based network. Figure 2.14 shows the mobile

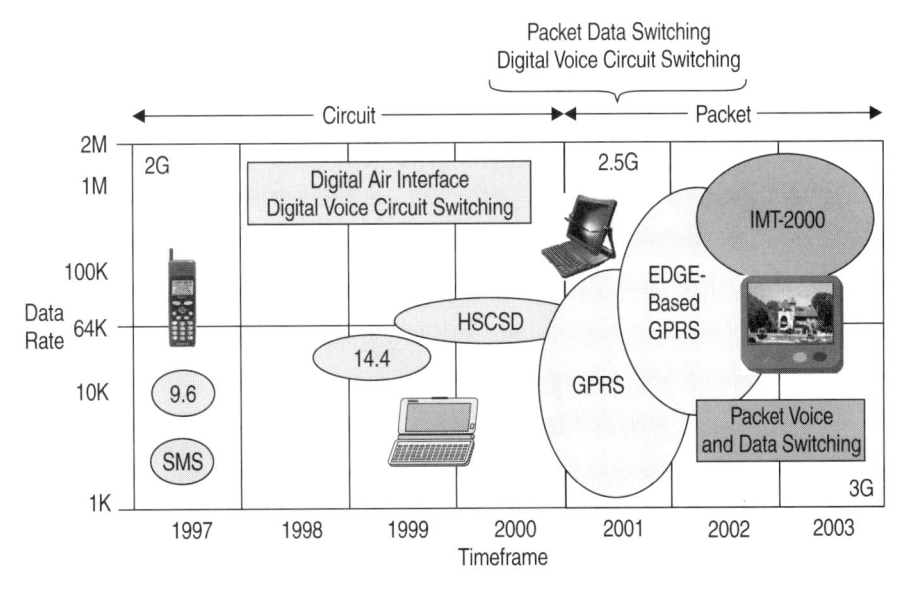

FIGURE 2.14 Wireless Technology Evolution *Source:* Nortel Networks

wireless technology evolution and its rollout timeframe. The sections below describe GPRS, EDGE, and UMTS/3G in detail.

GPRS   GPRS is the first standard for carrying data traffic over an existing 2G wireless network. It involves an overlay of a packet-based (air) interface on top of the existing circuit-switched GSM network. This gives the user an option to use a packet-based data service. GPRS can be embedded in an existing GSM network by adding three new network elements:

- The *packet control unit support node* (PCUSN) manages the channel and radio link control and is sometimes an integrated function in the base station controllers. The connection between a PCUSN to the SGSN is usually Frame Relay.
- The *serving GPRS support node* (SGSN) performs mobility management, implements authentication procedures, and routes packet data.
- The *gateway GPRS support node* (GGSN) provides the interconnection with fixed packet data networks for GPRS. It stores routing information for attached GPRS users. This information is used to tunnel the subscriber's protocol data units (PDU) to the current point of attachment of the mobile station such as the SGSN. The tunneling protocol between the SGSN and the GGSN is IP based.

EDGE   EDGE is a radio-based, high-speed mobile data standard that allows data transmission speeds up to 384 Kbps and is an evolution of GPRS. It was initially developed as a technology for providers that failed to obtain a UMTS license, since it enables the incumbent providers to participate in offering data services at speeds that are close to those offered via UMTS. EDGE technology rollout began in 2001, although it is not clear how widely this technology will be deployed given that UMTS deployment is expected by the end of 2002. One advantage of EDGE is that it permits the operator to use the same frame structure, channels, and 200 kHz carrier bandwidth as used within GSM.

3G Wireless Access and UMTS   Third-generation wireless access is the latest major access technology, and it will have a major impact on the types of network services delivered to mobile subscribers. An evolution from today's cellular networks, which offer 14.4 Kbps at best, 3G mobile technologies will offer anywhere from 128 Kbps to 2 Mbps beginning around late 2002. This bandwidth will open up a new class of applications and access to content that were heretofore available only to fixed subscribers. It also introduces a set of mobility and content adaptation requirements, described in chapter 4. Over the next decade, 3G deployments—which may attract hundreds of millions of subscribers—could dwarf all other forms of broadband access. In fact, when analysts speak of the billion-subscriber Internet, more than 750 million of these subscribers are expected to be wireless. If current wireless revenues are any guide, 3G will eventually generate hundreds of billions of dollars annually, and in fact, depending on cost points, many users may use wireless as their primary means of Internet connectivity in the same way that many people now use cellphones from their homes. This revenue estimate assumes that the wireless operators, with their massive investments in 3G licenses, are actually capable of offering higher-revenue services to subscribers beyond basic voice. 3G is a precursor to even more advanced technologies, known as 4G, which offer 20 Mbps and higher.

UMTS is a 3G mobile phone system with expected early commercial availability in 2002. It is a natural evolution for existing GSM operators. By utilizing a 5 Mhz carrier within the wireless spectrum (as opposed to GSM's 200 kHz), UMTS will enable data speeds between 384 Kbps and up to 2 Mbps. The radio interface technology for UMTS relies on WCDMA. Note that UMTS is one of a number of IMT-2000 (International Mobile Telecommunications) technologies. Others include multicarrier CDMA, known as CDMA 2000. This permits existing CDMA operators to evolve their networks. Yet a third technology is time division duplex (TDD) CDMA.

Metropolitan Ethernet Access Technologies

The access technology that is receiving the greatest amount of interest at present is metropolitan fiber extension. Although some of the previously mentioned technologies such as DSL and cable will use fiber as part of the backhaul into the PoP, the focus here is on the extension of fiber all the way to the enterprise or multidwelling units (MDUs) such as condominiums and multitenant units (MTUs) such as office buildings. Most of these buildings or enterprises are prewired with Ethernet and are using this as the mode of connectivity. The individual Ethernet segments within the building aggregate at a LAN switch within the wiring closet and are then mapped onto the metropolitan fiber backbone via technology offered by a number of vendors. Some of these techniques permit many customers to share the same fiber backbone. The traffic traverses the fiber, eventually reaching the provider's PoP. The provider forwards some traffic directly into the IP backbone, and other traffic is diverted to the IPSS for additional IP services processing. Which direction the traffic goes is based on the customer's requirement for additional network-based services. As mentioned earlier, the provider may deploy the IPSS at the subscriber's site if justified by the traffic volume or services required.

The reason for the growth in metropolitan fiber extensions is that hardware now exists to allow the mapping of subscriber traffic into fiber at much reduced costs compared to earlier SONET/SDH-based systems. There are two key capabilities here. The first is the mapping of subscriber Ethernet traffic across the fiber backbone in such a way as to separate traffic from multiple subscribers and, at the same time, permit statistical sharing of the bandwidth for QoS guarantees. This is one reason that these types of deployments are often referred to as *Ethernet extension*. Though the subscriber-side interface is FE or GE, Ethernet as a physical medium is not extended across the metropolitan area in most cases.

The second major development is the availability of reasonably priced wavelength division multiplexing (WDM) hardware that permits the provider to reuse the fiber strands across multiple subscribers, with each subscriber or fiber potentially at a different frequency (or "color"). In metro deployments, coarse WDM has traditionally been the most cost-effective hardware, offering anywhere from 4 to 16 lambdas (as opposed to the dense WDM deployed in the core, which offers from 40 to 320 lambdas, but at additional cost). Recently, vendors have begun to introduce cost-effective metro dense wavelength division multiplexing (DWDM) systems. In WDM, fiber extension permits true broadband connectivity, potentially orders of magnitude beyond DSL and cable. Early deployments provide 10 or at most 100 Mbps per subscriber, but future installations will scale this into the gigabit range. We may consider the extension of Ethernet services to residences within a DLC infrastructure to be a variant of this solution.

In a typical deployment, the provider's fiber network extends to most office, apartment, and mixed-use buildings within a metropolitan area (see Figure 2.15). As a prelude to offering the service, the provider installs small fiber terminating devices in each of the buildings, which are capable of mapping TDM and LAN traffic onto the backbone. Depending on the volume of traffic expected, these terminals may include DWDM capabilities, permitting even greater capacity across the

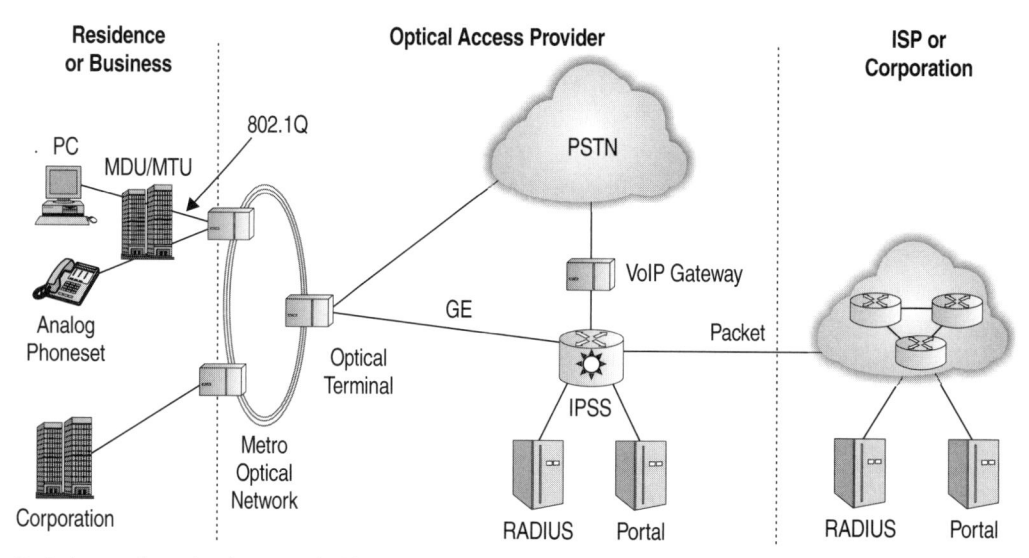

Note: Optical network may break out to in-building DSL.

FIGURE 2.15 Metropolitan Fiber Extension

fiber backbone since multiple subscribers may now map into different colors across the fiber. Businesses and residential subscribers usually connect to the terminal via Ethernet, with 802.1Q tagging (IEEE, 1998) providing for separation. This virtualization is preserved when mapping the subscriber traffic across the backbone based on techniques described in the next section.

Because copper is copper, an alternative to Ethernet is a single-building DSL, terminated at a small DSLAM in the wiring closet that then connects to the fiber terminal. This solution eliminates the need for recabling the building, since the DSL reuses the existing copper pairs. In both the Ethernet and DSL cases, subscriber traffic leaving the building traverses the fiber backbone, terminating at an aggregation PoP for Layer 3 processing. Note that for enterprise customers, we expect the provider initially to forward most traffic directly into the backbone, bypassing the IPSS.

Residential Ethernet extension, though not as caught up in the fiber reuse and DWDM buzz, is still a major area of interest. Ethernet minimizes the number of protocol conversions and encapsulations between the subscriber's PC and the backbone, and Ethernet hardware is readily available at low cost. The focus here is on neighborhoods equipped with next-generation DLCs capable of supporting both data and voice, and usually backhauled to the CO via DS3 or above. DSL, especially VDSL, is one option here, given the availability of DSLAMs fitting the required form factor. However, more interesting are solutions based on Ethernet, which provide bandwidths of 10 Mbps and above. With these Ethernet-based solutions, the provider deploys technology between the pedestal and the residence that is capable of mapping Ethernet across the existing copper pair. In some locations, the provider is installing new cabling that is capable of supporting the full Fast Ethernet bandwidth of 100 Mbps or, in some cases, deploying fiber.

The technology used to map the subscriber Ethernet traffic into the fiber is worth a closer look. The provider must enable sharing of the fiber bandwidth while protecting security. One approach is to use techniques (such as Cisco's Dynamic Packet Transport or Nortel's OPTera Packet Edge) that create a media access control (MAC) layer across the fiber. Each edge device connecting subscribers is provided an address, and it encapsulates the traffic in such a way as to identify its source, destination, and owner. These edge devices attached to the fiber contend for the bandwidth, but no bandwidth is preallocated. This results in significant efficiency compared to TDM-based approaches. In fact, one could consider it to be a next-generation architecture, similar to a fiber distributed data interface (FDDI), that is extended across the metropolitan area network (MAN). The two vendor proposals from Nortel and Cisco form the basis for work within IEEE 802.17. Another approach across the metropolitan fiber network is to map subscriber traffic via 802.1Q virtual local area networks (VLANs), while preserving QoS via 802.1p. Here, the switches would connect via point-to-point trunks as opposed to a ring.

The other major trend is the deployment of WDM within the metro area. Consider the Ethernet mapping described in the previous paragraph. If only one "color" or lambda was in use, the total throughput across a single fiber pair would be limited to about 2xGE (given that the per-fiber bandwidth limitation of most metropolitan systems is 2.5 Gbps). Although this may seem like a lot, in a major metro area, this bandwidth could be quickly exhausted, especially when connecting multiple sites of a major enterprise. WDM acts as a bandwidth multiplier, increasing the available bandwidth across the fiber by 4 or more times by mapping into different lambdas. Existing systems have this capacity and are sometimes used for the transparent transport of other protocols in addition to Ethernet. As noted above, this is the exception where Ethernet as a protocol is actually extended across the fiber infrastructure. Some of these protocols, in addition to Ethernet, include ESCON and Fiber Channel, both used primarily for mainframe communication and backup. The technology may also of course be used to map the technologies described in the previous paragraph into one or more wavelengths. In those instances where dark fiber (fiber that is not yet lit with transmission equipment) is used as opposed to WDM hardware, a LAN switch could trunk across multiple fiber strands, creating a single logical trunk via 802.3ad bonding.

Traditional Dedicated Access Technologies

Although considered by some as passé, traditional access via leased lines (such as T1/E1), Frame Relay, and ATM still provides the primary source of data revenue for the major providers. As described in chapter 3, many service providers intend to offer IPSS-delivered services to this installed base. These services continue to drop in price as DSL increases in market share, and at some point, we should reach equilibrium for a given bandwidth and service level agreement (SLA) across the different technologies. As of the end of 2000, typical monthly T1 charges ranged from $450 to $2,000 in metro areas. Added to this is a $750 to $5,500 installation fee (sometimes waived) plus the cost of CPE. In contrast, a T1 Frame Relay service requires a monthly fee of $575, with an up-front installation of $990 and CPE (Copper Mountain, 2000). The palette of services described in this chapter and chapter 3 also applies to customers connected via leased lines, Frame Relay, and ATM, and in fact, supporting this market has been a major goal of the IPSS vendors. As an example of market stability, Infonetics (Infonetics, 2000) predicts that edge router sales will enjoy substantial growth over the next four years, with the majority of these purchases by T1 and above customers.

One technology left out of the discussion is ISDN. Although ISDN as a data service has seen success overseas, it did not really reach critical mass in the United States, where fractional T1 and Frame Relay services became the access methods of choice. Looking forward, those customers with ISDN data services are expected to migrate to DSL in the coming years because of lower fees, higher bandwidths, and lower-cost CPE. For example, my employer provided an ISDN line for me, and then I disconnected it when ADSL became available.

Dial-Up Remote Access Servers

Because of its relevance to understanding the wholesale and tunneling architectures described in chapter 3, we briefly talk here about dial-up Internet access. Dial access is the oldest and most widespread form of Internet access. The key element of this architecture is the remote access server (RAS) or network access server (NAS). Subscribers use a PC modem or an external modem to connect across the existing telephone network to the RAS, which then aggregates traffic into a trunk that connects to the provider's backbone (see Figure 2.16). A typical RAS supports anywhere from 1 to more than 1,000 subscriber modems in a modular chassis. This chassis contains the modem cards, commonly connected to the provider's access network via T1/E1 or even DS3. In a few cases, discrete modem connections are still found. The RAS also includes the necessary control modules, as well as one or more upstream trunks. These trunks are packet, ATM, or even Fast or Gigabit Ethernet if connecting to a collocated core router. The different line, trunk, and control cards within a RAS are connected via a bus, though in some cases switch fabrics are used.

The RAS interfaces to the provider's authentication and accounting systems, such as remote authentication dial in user service (RADIUS) (Rigney, 1997b) and plays a key role in the tunneling architectures used within dial wholesaling. RADIUS is an Internet Engineering Task Force (IETF) protocol, the most common protocol used by ISPs for dial access authentication and accounting. Originally, ISPs owned and operated RASs on behalf of their subscribers. More recently, the trend has been for wholesale access operators such as facilities-based carriers to

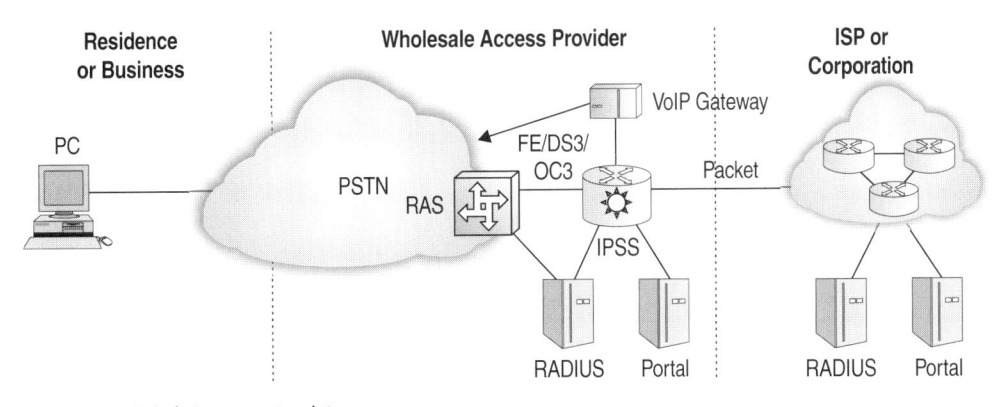

FIGURE 2.16 Dial Access Architecture

provide RAS services on behalf of multiple ISPs. This provides the facilities-based carrier with a new, high-margin service, while permitting the ISP to focus on customers and service as opposed to physical infrastructure buildout.

With the growth of this dial wholesaling, and with the deployment of dial infrastructures supporting on the order of hundreds of thousands of subscribers, providers have recognized the need for the IPSS to support optimized tunneling and wholesale architectures, as well as additional services on behalf of the subscribers.

Conclusion

This chapter details the physical architecture of the access network, from the subscriber to the provider's PoP. Its focus is on the various last-mile technologies for broadband access, including DSL, cable, fixed and mobile wireless, and metropolitan Ethernet. Although these technologies warrant individual books on their own, they are just a prelude to our primary focus—the higher-layer technologies and services at the network edge. The next chapter begins to introduce these technologies.

Chapter 3
Security and Tunneling Technologies
The Services Enablers

The next step beyond providing basic and premium access is to secure the service. Increasingly, providers are bundling CLE, network, and even desktop-based security services with their basic service offerings because customers are demanding it. Of all the internetworking topics, security receives the greatest amount of coverage in the press, because of the effect (on both financials and mind-set) of security on the Internet community in general. Users focus on different aspects of security for a number of reasons:

- Corporations want to protect their intranets from intrusion.
- Always-on DSL and cable subscribers are at increasing risk since they now have a permanent connection into the Internet.
- Parents, schools, and corporations want to enforce proper use of the Internet.

Security is a broad topic, which includes methods of preventing attack against subscribers and service providers, mechanisms for authenticating subscribers, and content management when invoking content filtering and blocking. A complete security service provides a firm foundation for many of the applications in use across the Internet. It also helps prevent embarrassing incidents, such as Web site hacks, which detract from the overall user experience and introduce questions about the security of the Internet in general. In this chapter, we cover the key concepts of security, including *firewalls* and *encryption*—methods of ensuring that unwanted hackers do not enter the network as well as ways that data is encrypted so that only the recipient can understand it. Other security concepts covered include hiding subscriber addresses from the Internet at large through network address translation (NAT) and user authentication.

From security, we move to the techniques used to tunnel subscribers across the network backbone. We then cover subscriber segregation. Although many consider this to be one and the same with tunneling, the two functions are in fact very different. Tunneling helps transport the subscribers across the backbone once segregated, but on its own is insufficient to effectively secure the user's data. The security and tunneling technologies described here form the technology basis for the firewalling and IP-VPNs services introduced in chapter 7.

Security

Although the focus of most security discussions is on firewall capabilities or how well a given platform prevents denial-of-service (DoS) attacks, in reality a complete security service integrates a number of data and management path functions. This is an important distinction, in that there are many dedicated firewalling products available, but these products don't suit everyone's needs. For example, a small business might be looking for a managed solution that provides the following capabilities: a firewall to protect against intrusion and denial of service; assurance that its addresses are not spoofed; application filtering and network address translation to hide internal IP addresses, IP-VPNs; service level agreements (SLAs) that describe the security guarantee and any penalties; and the capability to log attacks and communicate security advisories.

The following sections address how a managed service may offer these services. In particular, the topics addressed are the following:

- Firewalls
- Preventing attacks (antispoofing, denial-of-service attacks)
- Network address translation
- Content filtering

> ### ◆ Security through Obscurity?
>
> Often, one hears the phrase *security by obscurity* when referring to dial-up users. The contention here is that a dial-up user is connected for only a short period of time and always via a dynamic IP address generated during the establishment of the PPP session. Although this may have been true a few years back, the average dial-up hold time has increased significantly, as has the sophistication of hacker tools. It is also not too difficult for a hacker to obtain listings of the IP address spaces assigned by different ISPs in a retail or dial-up wholesale environment. For this reason, the firewalls that are commonly associated with always-on subscribers are also applicable to dial-up users.

- Authentication, authorization, and accounting (AAA)
- Encryption
- Key management
- Certificates and digital signatures

Firewalls

A firewall is probably the most visible security feature. It involves setting rules on which traffic to accept and which traffic to discard and possibly log. Figure 3.1 shows a typical business policy permitting access to a Web server, a mail server, DNS, and denying all else. Users internal to the business have full access to the Internet.

There is much confusion regarding firewalls because the word *firewall* is used to describe many different devices with many different capabilities. In the following sections we cover the different types of firewalls used in the industry and then compare and contrast their capabilities.

Types of Firewalls

You commonly hear of three types of firewalls: packet-filtering firewalls, stateful firewalls, and application proxy firewalls. Each is effective in certain circumstances and provides some measure of protection for the end user. In order to ascertain which type is the most useful for your organization, an understanding of the underlying technology is necessary so that they can be compared and contrasted.

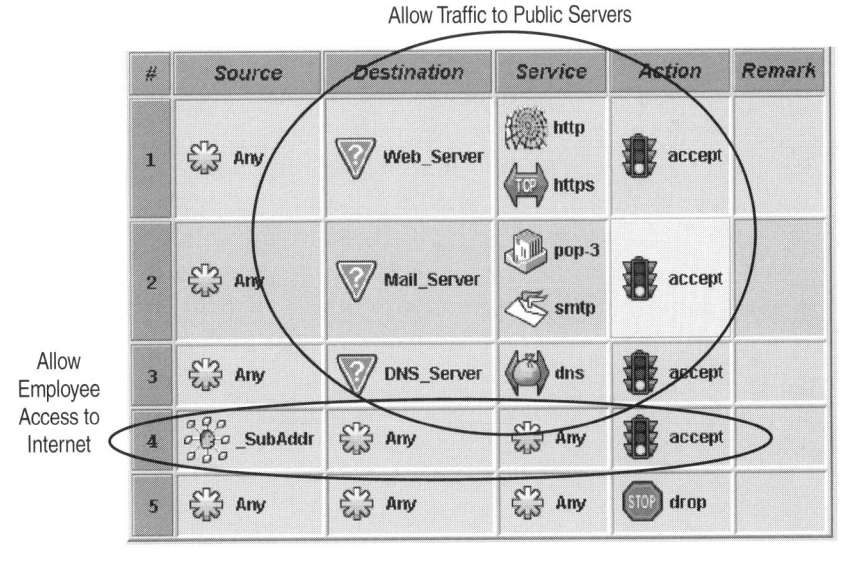

FIGURE 3.1 An Example of a Firewall Policy

Packet-Filtering Firewalls   The most basic firewall is a packet-filtering router. Packet filters look at incoming and outgoing packets and apply a fixed set of rules to determine whether the packets will be allowed to pass. The packet-filtering firewall is typically very fast (compared with other firewall techniques) because it does not examine any of the data in the packet. It looks at the type of packet along with the source and destination IP address, as well as port combinations, and then it applies filtering rules. The list of rules is called an *access control list* (ACL). ACLs allow data belonging to certain ports of known applications to enter and exit the network. Packets are dropped if they arrive at unauthorized ports.

To understand packet filtering, think of a parking lot with assigned parking spots. A port can be thought of as an assigned parking spot in the lot. A car arriving at the monitored garage has to tell the guard (the firewall) which spot it is going to park in (the port). If the guard was given permission to allow a visiting car (network packet) to use that spot, then the car is allowed into the lot. A packet-filtering router works in a similar manner. A packet-filtering router is stateless and does not take into consideration any conversations or data flows. Although the router may make determinations based on the contents of the IP or TCP/UDP header, it has no way to associate packets with bidirectional flows. It is also incapable of following the initial control flows to determine what additional data ports have been allocated. For this reason, packet filtering is not useful for complex protocols, such as H.323, unless the network administrator allows incoming UDP packets to all high ports, which would be a bad security practice.

Stateful Firewalls   Stateful inspection goes beyond simple packet filtering by following the actual application flow, opening ports as required for the control and data connections. Stateful inspection is sometimes called a *circuit-level firewall*. In stateful inspection firewalls, all connections are monitored, and only those connections that are found to be valid are allowed to pass through the firewall. This generally means that a client behind the firewall can initiate any type of session, but clients outside the firewall cannot see or connect to a machine protected by the firewall. This of course requires that the firewall is able to understand all applications in use across the network. Some firewalls do not implement application-based stateful inspection but instead understand that a specific application uses UDP in a "query" or "session" manner that is fairly symmetrical and can be generalized into a few heuristics. For example, a rule may allow responses for outgoing packets. With the addition of a NAT function, this firewall may effectively hide internal addressing or may permit more efficient address allocation. However, the firewall must then include the necessary functionality to make the required changes to addressing within the control flows, an added level of sophistication.

Application Proxy Firewalls   With an application proxy firewall, all client applications use the firewall as the gateway. The firewall then authorizes each packet for each protocol differently. Some of the disadvantages of application proxy firewalls are that every client program needs to be set up to use a proxy, and the firewall must have a proxy in it for each type of protocol that can be used. If a protocol is not supported by the application proxy firewall, protocol implementation has to be delayed. The biggest disadvantage of application proxy firewalls is that they can be quite slow. The greatest advantage is that they are very secure. After initial setup, application proxy firewalls can be so transparent that clients do not even realize they are going through a firewall.

Say that a session proxy is transparent to the user's application, but because this type of proxy does not understand the application, it might limit functionality in some instances. A good example of this is with H.323 (a videoconferencing protocol), where the proxy might preclude incoming calls because of lack of support for address translation. Although they are complex, application proxies are widely deployed, especially at corporate gateways for Web access.

A Comparison of Firewalls

As mentioned earlier, the type of firewall used depends on what is being protected and what the performance requirements are. Without an understanding of the requirements, a comparison of firewall types is not very useful. However, once the requirements and the type of protection are defined, then the correct type of firewall can be selected to accommodate the requirements and optimize performance. Stateful firewalls are typically faster than application proxy firewalls but do not provide the same level of network security. Application proxy firewalls, on the other hand, are very CPU-intensive and are not as fast or as scalable as stateful inspection firewalls. When an application proxy firewall is in use, the external user does not have a direct connection to the internal network but only to the proxy server. Trade-offs need to be considered between stateful inspection and application proxy firewalls depending on how scalable and fast the firewall needs to be.

At the subscriber edge, a truly stateful firewall is the most useful type of firewall because it provides the necessary security while precluding the need for complex configuration and administration of an application proxy. The firewall follows each and every subscriber data session, making a determination about which applications (for example, FTP, HTTP) to permit and which to deny. This capability also has the effect of preventing most common attacks since attacks rely on well-known ports, and contrasts with approaches based on "static" extended ACLs, which do not permit following dynamic applications. Table 3.1 contrasts stateful firewalls with simple packet filters and with proxy firewalls.

Firewalls and Protocols

Firewalls recognize applications by following TCP (for example, FTP), UDP (for example, BOOTP or SNMP), ICMP (for example, ICMP-PROTO), and IP (for example, OSPF) "ports"—identifiers used by applications at the transport layer that permit

TABLE 3.1 Firewall Comparison

Stateful Inspection Firewall	Packet-Filtering Firewall	Application Proxy Firewall
• Follows every subscriber data session • Results in effective blocking of complex applications (e.g., VoIP) • Eliminates security holes from packet filtering	• Uses ACLs, employing "all-or-nothing" approach • Introduces insecurities such as "allow all TCP high ports" • Involves specification of complex rules	• Is a dedicated firewall • Terminates incoming sessions and establishes new sessions • Requires different proxy for each application, delaying use of firewall for new applications • Poses difficulty for VPN clients • Results in limited throughput

the destination computer to associate an incoming data stream with an application. Since some applications use a combination of well-known ports plus some dynamic ports that are negotiated during the session, following a protocol can be rather complex.

For example, a simple protocol such as HTTP (based on TCP) starts a session with a packet sent from the subscriber that does not belong to any previous conversation. The firewall must therefore initiate a new conversation, maintaining state for this new conversation. If the policy allows this protocol (HTTP), the packet is allowed, and packets in the reverse direction to the originating port number at the same IP address are considered part of this conversation and are therefore allowed as well. However, if the subscriber did not initiate the conversation, the incoming packets are dropped. This is therefore a relatively simple protocol to follow.

FTP is a bit more complex, in that it relies on both a control and a data connection. As in the HTTP example, a PC initiates the initial TCP connection. However, FTP uses this connection to negotiate a new TCP connection for any data transfer. This connection in most cases uses a random port number. A state-following firewall recognizes the original connection requests in the control channel and then parses the subsequent data connections. It derives the new TCP connection information from this parsing, associating the new ports with the original FTP conversation.

Even more complex than FTP and HTTP is H.323, a family of protocols for Internet telephony (and videoconferencing) that includes gateways to ISDN and the PSTN, as well as additional control functions to manage address resolution, call acceptance, multipoint conferencing, QoS, and connectivity from the enterprise to the outside world via proxies. H.323 is complex because it creates a number of data flows for both the control and data connections, all of which the firewall must understand (see Figure 3.2). An H.323 call is first established by exchanging Q.931 signaling packets via a TCP connection on a well-known port (port 1720). This is the easy part. As part of this exchange, the two parties select an ephemeral

FIGURE 3.2 H.323 Firewalling

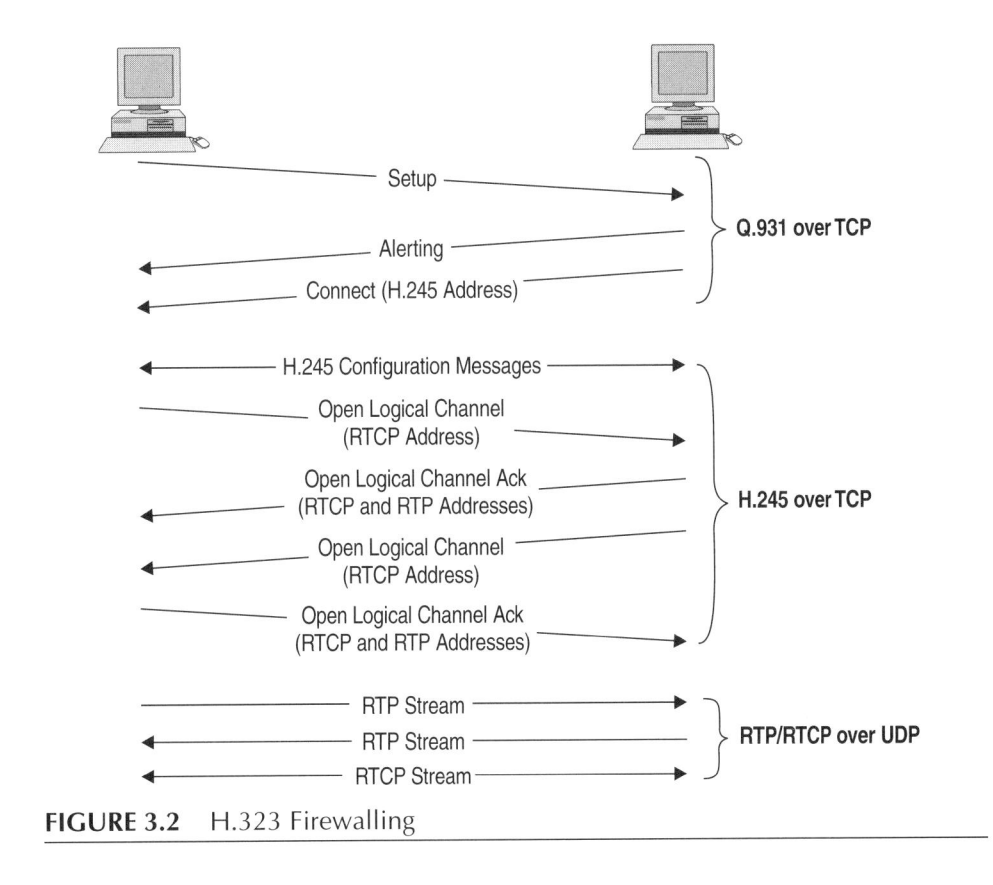

(that is, dynamic and greater than 1024) port for the H.245 TCP control connection. If the firewall has not properly interpreted the Q.931 exchange, it has no way of determining this dynamic port. One complexity here is the use of ASN.1 encoding within the Q.931 messages, creating a challenge for firewall developers because of its complexity. However, let us assume that the firewall has properly decoded the Q.931 exchange.

Now the parties must ensure that all H.245 exchanges are unsecured because if they were secured, the firewall would have no way to interpret the data. This precludes the use of the procedures outlined in H.235 to secure the control connection. As part of the H.245 exchange, the parties agree to use the RTP and RTCP ports, which are UDP ports, so the firewall then enables them. Although the H.245 flow must be in the clear (unsecured), the parties may secure the RTP data flow without an adverse effect on the firewall. H.323 is just one example of the increasingly large number of sophisticated applications that a firewall must be capable of accepting or blocking. As you can imagine, creating firewall software to understand and follow this conversation is difficult. With the number of applications in use—and the rate of development of new applications—this is a daunting task for firewall developers.

In an actual implementation, the firewall device will contain a database that describes the port numbers used by many of the most popular applications. This database will contain descriptions for both well-known (registered through the Internet Assigned Numbers Authority [IANA]) applications, such as Lotus Notes, and also vendor-specific assignments (some HTTP-based and others relying on RPCs) for various enterprise-reporting, customer management, e-commerce, and industry-specific applications. Note that these application descriptions also form a basis for the various traffic management and IP-VPN policies described later.

Firewall Policy Definition

When deploying the firewall policy, an administrator may define the action as applying to an individual host, a router, a network of hosts, a selected IP address range, or any combination of these. Defining scope is more complex when attempting to define a bulk policy that will apply to multiple businesses, each with its own IP address space. To ease deployment of these policies, the provisioning system may define *abstract objects* (see Figure 3.3), which are variables left undefined within a specific subscriber policy until final provisioning. In the figure, the abstract objects

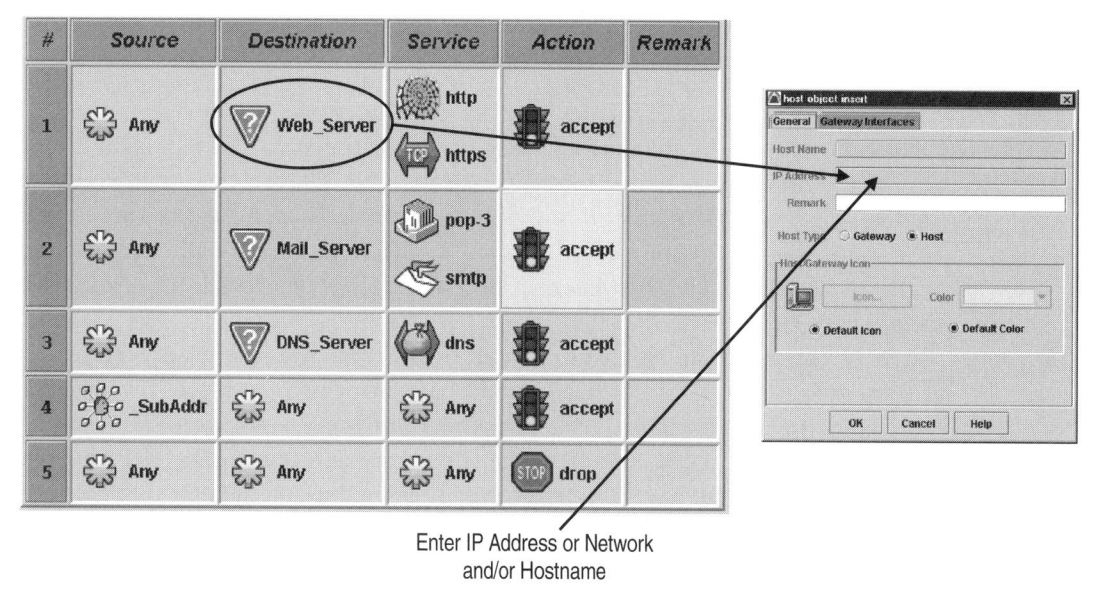

FIGURE 3.3 An Example of an Abstract Object

◆ The Internet Assigned Numbers Authority (IANA)

The IANA is responsible for assignment of most well-known Internet numbers, including those dealing with vendors, protocols, and IP addressing. Within an IP environment, TCP and UDP applications are identified via ports opened at the transport layer between hosts. The IANA has divided the range of possible TCP/UDP ports (a 2-byte field) into the following three ranges.

Port Numbers	Application Description
0–1023	Well-known applications
1024–49151	Registered to specific vendors/entities (updated at www.isi.edu/in-notes/iana/assignments/port-numbers)
49152–65535	Dynamic and/or private

An example of a well-known application is the File Transfer Protocol (FTP), which includes both TCP and UDP versions. Although both TCP and UDP ports have been reserved for some applications, it is not necessarily the case that the UDP or TCP version of the application actually exists.

Port Numbers	Protocol	Application Description
20	TCP	FTP—default data
20	UDP	FTP—default data
21	TCP	FTP—Control
21	UDP	FTP—Control

An example of a registered application is Microsoft-SQL, which also consists of multiple sets of ports.

Port Numbers	Protocol	Application Description
1433	TCP	Microsoft-SQL-Server
1433	UDP	Microsoft-SQL-Server
1434	TCP	Microsoft-SQL-Monitor
1434	UDP	Microsoft-SQL-Monitor

One of the challenges in developing any port-aware traffic prioritization or firewalling mechanism is tracking new applications, such as videoconferencing and gaming.

Port Numbers	Protocol	Application Description
1673	TCP	Intel Proshare Multicast
1673	UDP	Intel Proshare Multicast
1674	TCP	Intel Proshare Multicast
1674	UDP	Intel Proshare Multicast
26000	TCP	Quake
26000	UDP	Quake

Finally, some vendors have mapped applications to ports in the registered space without actually requesting assignments. This, of course, complicates platform development.

Port Numbers	Application Description
3300 + 3301	SAP R/2—unregistered

are those shown as triangles with a question mark in the middle indicating that they are not completely defined. At a later stage, when the actual server address is known, this information can be filled in, and hence the abstract object can be substituted with a known object.

For example, service definition personnel within a provider may define a policy called *BusinessFirewall* that consists of a set of incoming and outgoing rules to follow if the business applications are well understood. However, since this is a business, it probably operates both a Web server and an e-mail server. Since IP addressing is different for each business, the portion of the policy relating to these servers must be left unresolved in regard to the IP addresses of these servers, until a time when a specific business is provisioned. Only then will the order entry personnel know the actual addresses for these servers. The policy is then completely defined (see Figure 3.4). This is an evolving capability in the industry and one that service providers seek from equipment vendors. However, many customers develop their own applications, and these are usually unsupported by generic firewalls. Network operator expertise is needed to troubleshoot the firewall in conjunction with these applications and to modify the rules.

Preventing Attacks

Many types of attacks can be directed at a user from the network. Unfortunately, new types of attacks are constantly being created, ensuring that firewall software engineers will be employed for some time to come. One of the most common types of attack is for a hacker to assume a user's identity or spoof him or her.

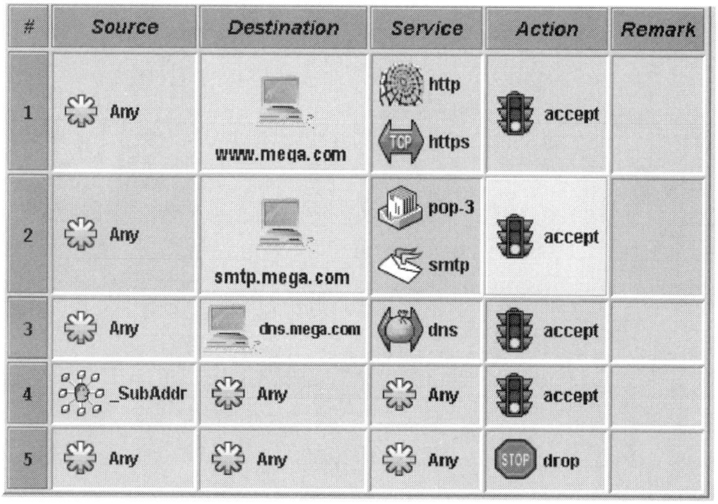

FIGURE 3.4 A Complete Policy

Other attacks include denial of service, where a server has so many simultaneous hits that it cannot serve the requests and is inaccessible. Even more creative is distributed denial of service (DDoS), where the DoS attack arrives from multiple machines. The most common ones are covered here along with the technologies that identify, stop, or at least slow down these attacks.

Antispoofing

Antispoofing, also known as *ingress filtering,* prevents IP address masquerade attacks. In an IP address masquerade attack, a packet tries to assume the IP address of a different source. Spoofing an IP address is done for several malicious reasons, but the most common ones are to hijack a specific address and to use the address as a source to hide behind in a "SMURF" attack. Spoofed packets have a false source address and should not gain access to the network. For example, an ISP assigns (either statically or as a result of Dynamic Host Configuration Protocol [DHCP] after a login) the residential subscriber *marie* the IP address 199.242.50.1. It knows that *marie* is now associated with this address, and it may create a rule to discard any traffic from *marie* with an IP source address that is different from 199.242.50.1. This is ingress antispoofing, and it prevents a user from launching attacks with fake source addresses. In the opposite direction, egress antispoofing (that is, egress filtering) prevents any traffic from the Internet with *marie*'s IP from entering her network because the firewall recognizes that *marie*'s IP address needs to come from the subscriber side and not the network side. This prevents a third party from seeming to be native to *marie*'s network and accessing internal resources (see Figure 3.5).

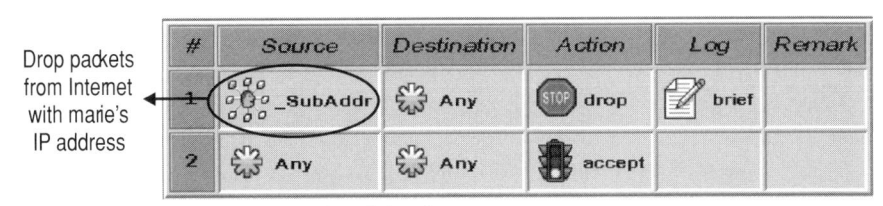

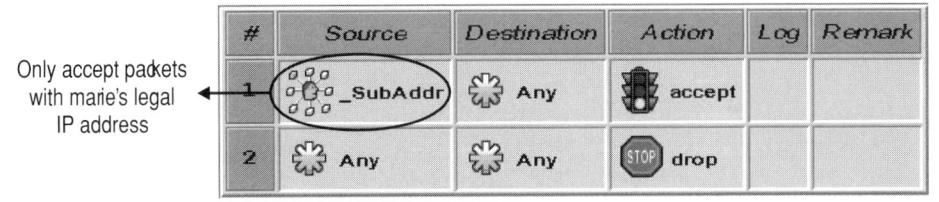

FIGURE 3.5 An Example of Antispoofing

SMURF Attacks

A special case of antispoofing is SMURF attacks. SMURF attacks are named after a program used to perform the attack (as opposed to cute blue dwarves). A hacker sends traffic to a site that can result in a virtual explosion of traffic at the intended site. SMURF attacks typically work this way:

1. The attacker issues ICMP echo request packets with a spoofed source IP address of the target being attacked.
2. The echo request packets are sent to addresses of remote LANs using directed broadcast address. The connected router then broadcasts these packets out on the LAN.
3. All active hosts on the LAN respond with an ICMP echo reply back to the source IP address (the address being spoofed). This results in a huge flood of traffic at the real source IP address.

One common defense against SMURF attacks is to turn off IP-directed broadcast in routers everywhere, as this prevents the broadcast from being forwarded to the subnet. Another is to turn on egress filtering at the network boundaries—that is, don't forward packets with a source address that is not on your network.

DoS and DDoS

One type of attack that antispoofing prevents is denial of service and, in some situations, as described later in this section, distributed DoS attacks. A DoS attack is characterized as an attack in which the primary goal is to deny the victim(s) access to a particular attacked site. The following are some examples:

- "Flooding" of the network, which prevents legitimate network traffic
- Disrupting connections between two machines and hence disabling access to a service
- Preventing a particular individual from accessing a service
- Disrupting a service to a specific person or system
- Illegitimate use of resources such that an intruder may use disk space anonymously

Some DoS attacks can be executed with limited resources against a large sophisticated site. This is called an *asymmetric attack*. DoS attacks are most frequently executed against network connectivity. The goal is to prevent hosts or networks from communicating. A typical example of this type of attack is the SYN flood attack. In this type of attack, the attacker begins the process of establishing a connection to the victim machine but does it in a way to prevent the ultimate completion of the connection. The victim machine reserves one of a limited number of data structures required to complete the connection. The result is that legitimate connections are denied, while the victim machine waits to complete bogus "half-open" connections initiated by the attacker.

Another DoS attack is where the intruder uses the victim's resources against the victim. For example, an intruder forges UDP packets to connect the *echo* service on one machine to the *chargen* service on another machine. These two services then consume all available network bandwidth between them.

Yet another example is an intruder consuming all available bandwidth on the network by generating a large number of packets directed to the victim's network. These packets are usually ICMP echo packets, but they could be anything. Additionally, the intruder does not need to operate from a single machine but may be able to coordinate or co-opt several machines on different networks to achieve the same effect (hence the DDoS attack).

Typically, a DDoS attack implants a rogue program within an unsuspecting host. This program launches the attack and uses the legitimate IP address of a host machine. This, however, makes it easy to trace the host machine, understand how it has been breached, and remove the rogue program. If the IP address is legitimate (within the subnet), antispoofing does protect against DDoS attacks. Many DDoS programs set a random-source IP address to avoid detection. The reason for this is as follows. Many Web sites implement antiflood protection, but this type of protection is based on a certain level of traffic from a single-source IP address. Obviously, this will not protect against packets sourced from a large number of random IP addresses. This is why antispoofing is necessary, because it results in the discard and logging of all packets generated by the rogue DDoS program.

DDoS attacks are designed to effectively shut down a given Web site by saturating it with certain types of traffic from a large number of sources. Motivation may be political, economic (an electronic picket fence), or just maliciousness. Because of the number of sources, traditional DoS prevention techniques are ineffective, since they are designed to combat attacks from a single known source or sources.

A "master" computer carries out the DDoS attack by planting a DDoS agent on thousands of "slaves" (see Figure 3.6). It implants these slaves via various vulnerabilities within the machine's OS or by accessing public machines and compromising password files. Under the control of the master, these slaves launch the attack against the intended Web site.

Recently, cable- and DSL-attached PCs have been used as sources for DDoS attacks. This is possibly more of a threat than older, more confined attacks based on academia, in that many of the security holes that enabled the first round of attacks have been addressed at the OS level or by service providers. In the case of the residential PC, the subscriber will have no knowledge that his or her PC is even being used as a source for the attack, since the attack does not exhibit the behavior of a virus and interfere with normal operation.

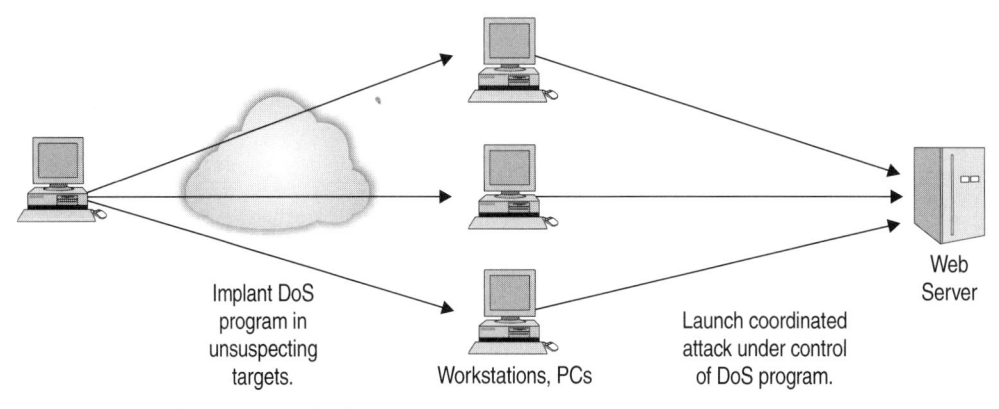

FIGURE 3.6 Distributed Denial-of-Service

Image description: Diagram showing an attacker implanting DoS programs in unsuspecting workstations/PCs through a cloud network, which then launch a coordinated attack against a Web Server.

The firewalling and antispoofing techniques described in this chapter help prevent DDoS attacks in two ways. When launching the DDoS attack, the master must establish a session with the slave computer. Proper firewalling prevents the establishment of unsolicited sessions from untrusted sites. In addition, ingress antispoofing prevents traffic sourced from a subscriber with an IP address other than that assigned by the service provider.

DDoS attacks result in loss of time and money for many organizations. The following are some of the precautions that enterprise IS staff should perform in conjunction with a firewall:

- Use TCP SYN flood protection.
- Disable any unused or unneeded network services.
- Observe system performance and establish activity baselines for normal usage.
- Implement a tool (for example, Tripwire) to detect changes in configuration information or other files.

Table 3.2 summarizes these various forms of attacks against hosts and networks.

Network Address Translation

Network address translation permits a provider to hide a subscriber's or a corporation's internal IP addressing from the outside world, with the effect of conserving IP address space and enhancing security. Because of this, many providers consider NAT to be an element of their IP-VPN strategy.

NAT operates in the following way (see Figure 3.7). A corporation may assign its hosts any range of IP addresses, limiting the scope to the extent of the corporate

Security

TABLE 3.2 Network and Host Attacks

Activity	Type of Attack Tool	Method of Access
Access violation	Password cracking/guessing; IP spoofing; Trojan horse; Java applet	Telnet; remote control program
User/host discovery	Ping sniffer	ICMP tools on corrupted system
Exposure of vulnerabilities	Scanner	Tools on corrupted system
Corruption of information	Virus; worm	E-mail/file transfer corrupted on system
Theft of information	Password cracking/guessing; IP spoofing	Corrupted system
Denial of service	Ping of death; SYN flooding; e-mail virus	ICMP; TCP; e-mail

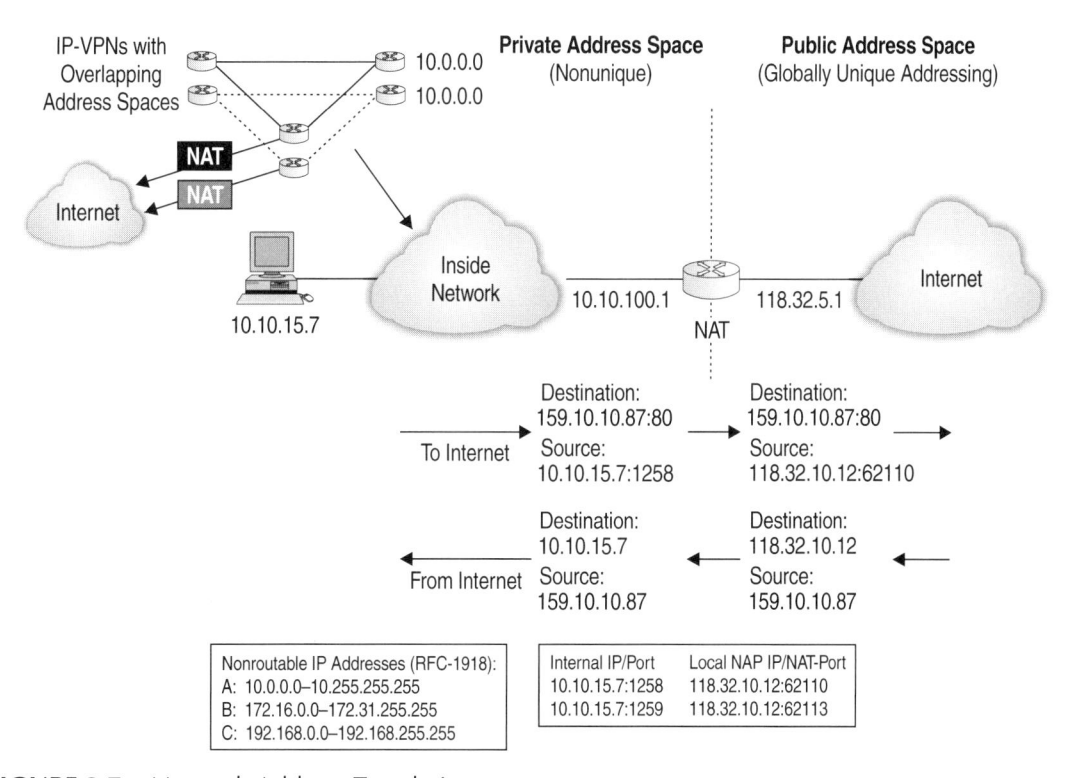

FIGURE 3.7 Network Address Translation

intranet. In most cases, this assignment will conform to the guidelines outlined in RFC 1918, which lists a set of address ranges that are not routed across the global Internet (sometimes referred to as "10 networks"). The question then is how hosts within the corporation communicate to the world at large.

Traditionally, a corporation implements NAT at its border router with the Internet, dynamically mapping host addresses within its private space to public IP addresses. Often NAT is implemented as 1:1 or N:1 or N:M. What this means is that in 1:1 NAT, a public IP address is reserved for each private IP address. When the private IP address arrives at the NAT gateway, the NAT gateway maps it to a public IP address. The N:1 or N:M cases are extensions of 1:1 in that a number of private addresses are mapped to one or more public IP addresses. The N:1 and N:M, where M is less than N, use an extension of NAT called port address translation (PAT).

PAT maps multiple hosts into a single external IP address. With any TCP/IP connection, a particular user comes in on a specific port socket as part of either TCP or UDP. The port number in addition to the private IP address is used to uniquely identify a user. In either case, public addressing is conserved since only a percentage of the total hosts within the corporation are connected to the Internet at any point in time. Thus, a corporation's internal addressing may use large blocks of private addresses but needs only a handful of publicly routable IP addresses.

If instead of being implemented at the enterprise edge, as just described, NAT was implemented at the service provider, it would be at a central point (or a few points) within the customer's IP-VPN, with the service provider mapping the customer's internal addressing to its (the provider's) public address space. In this scenario, the corporation has no need or requirement for any public addressing, as the IP-VPN provider handles this task. This architecture supports multiple IP-VPNs with overlapping address ranges.

Although NAT has some advantages in terms of address space conservation, it does present problems with a number of common applications. If these limitations are taken into account when designing a service, then NAT is an option. It is also unfair to generalize and state that NAT breaks IP Security Protocol (IPSec). (IPSec is covered later in this chapter, in the section "IPSec.") You need to understand what breaks and if there are any workarounds.

The encapsulating security payload (ESP) for IPSec provides encryption across an IPSec tunnel. (ESP is described later in this chapter, in the section "IPSec.") If a NAT gateway is operating in one-to-one mode (i.e., single interior IP addresses mapped to single exterior IP addresses), then operation is unaffected. However, this mode of operation may not result in the address efficiencies desired. In most cases, a NAT gateway operates in many-to-one mode, or PAT. Here, the IPSec ESP will not work since the gateway performs port remapping. This would require remapping of the ESP security parameter index field, something that cannot take place since it would look as if the IPSec tunnel had been compromised. IPSec, of course, avoids this, and any modification of the field will cause the receiving end of the IPSec tunnel to discard the packets. A workaround whereby IPSec was altered to allow such remapping would defeat the purpose of IPSec, since the source and destination would have no way of knowing where in the network the tampering took place. Note that if the IPSec tunnels all originate and terminate within the private domain, then there is no problem. Therefore, NAT could be deployed between the IP-VPN and the Internet. NAT also interferes with a number of the more complex applications (e.g., multimedia) that involve dynamic port selection and multiple control and data flows, but vendors and providers are making progress in identifying these applications and adding support within their NAT gateways. The only real solution here is to evaluate the planned applications and verify support on the proposed NAT platform.

Content Filtering

With increasingly powerful hardware and software at the network edge, the service provider has the opportunity to deploy even more sophisticated forms of security. Operations such as URL filtering and content filtering require parsing deep within the IP packet header or even the payload (see Figure 3.8). In the past, these capabilities required dedicated hardware, usually at the subscriber's site. Using a network-based device (detailed in chapter 5) and offload servers, the provider may now offer these services to many subscribers from a central location. For example, a service provider may offer an e-mail or URL filtering and rating service, precluding access to certain Web sites or e-mail content (see Figure 3.9). A URL-filtering service involves parsing a given subscriber's Web traffic against a rating database (i.e., "G" or "R") or a customized dictionary.

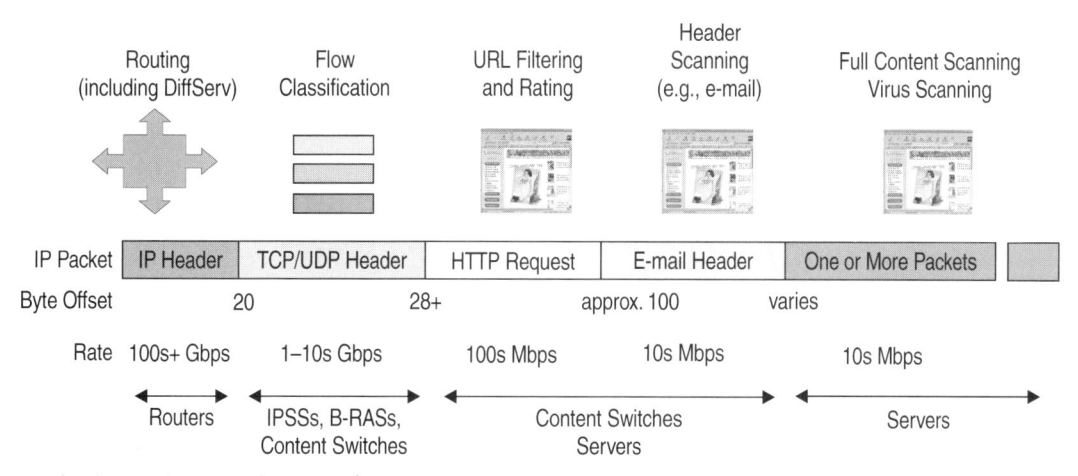

Note: IP header is 20 bytes; TCP header is 24+ bytes; UDP header is 8+ bytes.

FIGURE 3.8 Filtering Requirements

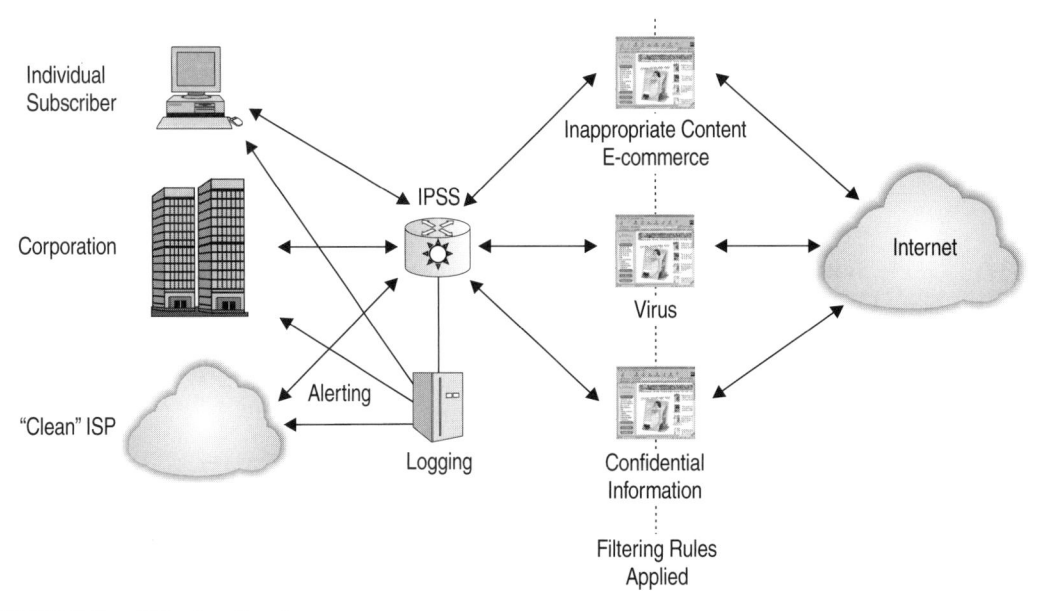

FIGURE 3.9 Filtering Services

More sophisticated services include smart content parsing where content is not automatically blocked. Instead, it is examined as part of the context to determine whether it should be blocked or not. As part of this service, an ISP may invoke an alerting system, notifying parents, for example, if a child attempts to access a blocked site, or at the extreme, shutting down the account. URL filtering applies to enterprise subscribers as well, reducing lost time due to Internet surfing, as many employees have gotten into the habit of doing their shopping on the job whether for clothes or groceries or through online auctions. Depending on the level of control desired, an enterprise may block access to certain sites or may just log such access for future action.

Virus scanning is another area of intense interest (for obvious reasons). Here, the ISP will deploy a filtering server, with virus definitions updated automatically from a server operated by the virus-scanning software provider. Some filtering software also has the capability of identifying unknown virus types based on characteristics and behaviors of known viruses.

In addition to filtering, a complete security service also includes a set of service guarantees. For example, the subscriber should have access to any logging and the ability to dynamically change the logged parameters, such as the source and destination addresses and ports, traffic types and volumes, and any action performed. The provider should be capable of offering a service-level guarantee as to the type of prevention offered and any penalties for attacks that are not prevented. There are firewall certification standards bodies, the most common one being International Computer Security Association (ICSA), which run a given firewall through a standard set of tests. Only after passing these tests is the firewall deemed certified. It is recommended that providers implement industry-certified firewalls and that they have the necessary talent on staff to properly formulate the required policies. Finally, the provider should maintain communication with the subscriber as to security updates and warnings.

Note that network-based security services are only one element of an end-to-end security architecture available to a typical corporation or end user. This architecture exists on many layers and includes authentication and encryption on the application layers as well as desktop security. As an example, most transactions between Web browsers and commerce servers rely on the secure sockets layer (SSL). The configuration of browser security parameters is as close as most users get to the details of network security.

Authentication, Authorization, and Accounting

Closely related to the basic security services are Authentication, Authorization, and Accounting (AAA) services. These perform the following:

- Authentication: verifying username and password
- Authorization: allowing the user to access information upon authentication
- Accounting: recording when the user has started and stopped accessing the network for billing or other recording purposes

A subscriber who is accessing network services is required to authenticate with a username and password. Authentication relies on a number of mechanisms, including Password Authentication Protocol (PAP), Challenge Handshake Authentication Protocol (CHAP), and tokens (that is, cards or other devices associated with a given user). Within the Internet access environment, RADIUS (Remote Authentication Dial-in User Service) is the mechanism that has the widest acceptance.

The login process, of course, also identifies whether a given subscriber is to be associated with other security services. Less visible but just as important (though sometimes neglected) is security within the network—securing the network devices from malicious internal attack and logging all access. Solutions here include securing console or remote access via SSL/SSH, as well as securing SNMP and any routing protocols.

Encryption

Encryption is the art of hiding sensitive data from individuals other than the intended recipient(s). It is one of the most interesting and frustrating areas of internetworking. It is interesting because it has required the development of ever more powerful ciphers to counter increasingly powerful decryption systems, and it is frustrating because artificial barriers to export and import of technology are imposed by some countries. (Who can forget having to remove the 128-bit encryption browser from their PCs when traveling to Europe and having to use the 56-bit encryption browser instead?) Within the Internet, a number of encryption algorithms are relevant, including the following:

- The Data Encryption Standard (DES), a block cipher based on 56-bit keys and, until recently, universally used for commercial encryption.
- Triple DES (3DES), which extends DES by encrypting a block of data three times with three different keys. Essentially a 168-bit key is used to generate three subkeys that are used to encrypt and decrypt the data. The "effective" key length of 3DES is 112 bits (i.e., 2^{112} of brute force is required to crack the three keys). 3DES has all but replaced DES for most encryption purposes because of the ease with which users with powerful computers can decrypt DES56.
- The Rivest-Shamir-Adelman (RSA) public-key algorithm, supporting a variable key length, though 512 bits is most common. RSA is commonly used to create the keys used to verify sender/receiver identities, but is much slower for bulk encryption than DES/3DES.
- The Advanced Encryption Standard (AES) algorithm, a new standard that is even stronger in encryption than 3DES and is based on a Rijndael encryption formula. It will be the new Federal Information Processing Standard (FIPS) that will specify the cryptographic algorithm for the U.S. government. It is expected to also spread to the private sector.

One barrier to international security deployment (at least from the perspective of U.S.-based equipment suppliers) was the restriction on 3DES encryption export. Until the beginning of 2000, export of network-based encryption in support of multiple end subscribers required a time-intensive licensing process for every overseas service provider. Although export of CLE-based encryption was simpler, this restriction slowed deployment of network-based IP-VPN services based on IPSec. Luckily, with changes in the U.S. export regulations as of January 2000, a simple report is all that is now required. Note that this does not imply that 3DES may actually be exported to anywhere overseas; some nations still impose their own import restrictions.

Key Management

Encryption of user data is just a small part of a complete security architecture. There must be some way to distribute the keys used by the sender and receiver to encrypt and then decrypt the data. Although secured distribution of keys in support of manual keying is a possibility—and in fact is still used by many governments and is supported within IPSec—it is not scalable for widespread deployment within a corporation or between users who have no a priori knowledge of one another. Thus, we need a more scalable solution. This is the role of public-key encryption (such as RSA), which introduces the concept of public and private keys. For example, Bob publishes his public key. Ann then uses this key to send a secure message to Bob, and Bob decrypts the message using his private key. Ann must know that Bob's public key is really from Bob. Implementing a key distribution architecture requires *authentication*, the process of identifying users and proving that they are who they claim to be, as discussed earlier. Authentication is a basic part of most users' everyday experience with ISPs or with the corporate intranet. Passwords, smart cards, and biometric systems are all forms of authentication.

Many service providers must make decisions about deploying pre-shared keys versus implementing a public key infrastructure (PKI). Pre-shared keys are configured ahead of time on any internetworking devices participating in IPSec and are simpler to implement and roll out than PKI. However, they do not enable large scaling of the solution, especially among multiple service providers. When using pre-shared keys, the service provider agrees with the customer on the key used for the setup of the security association. This key may be used across multiple sites or only between two sites. Thus pre-shared keys provide similar security to PKI but could result in an "n^2" situation (the number of keys increase n^2 as the number of endpoints grows) as multiple tunnel endpoints are used. PKI, on the other hand, solves the scalability problem and eliminates a potential man-in-the-middle security concern.

PKI prevents man-in-the-middle attacks by having partners or enterprises register with the Certificate Authority (CA). When an enterprise wants to communicate with another unknown enterprise, it exchanges the keys through the CA, which certifies that Enterprise A is who it says it is and Enterprise B is also who it claims

♦ Man-in-the-Middle Attacks

A man-in-the-middle attack may occur when a pre-shared key is set up without the party or partner at the other side being known. An unknown party could claim to be this partner and exchange the pre-shared key with the initiator. The man-in-the-middle attacker then repeats this process with the intended party and sits in the middle, receiving the traffic. This is much like a blind date where you've made arrangements to see someone whom you've never met and someone else shows up. Of course, in a blind date scenario, this may work to your advantage, depending on the date. However, in business arrangements, you want to ensure that you are communicating with the correct party and not a party crasher.

to be. PKI addresses the scalability of keys by forming a hub that distributes the key to whoever needs it. The enterprise needs only to register the key with the CA, and the CA then distributes the key. This reduces the scalability algorithm to "$2n$" range versus "n^2". In practicality, although PKI addresses scalability concerns and possible person-in-the-middle attacks, most service providers do not choose to roll it out because of its complexity and instead prefer to use pre-shared keys.

Certificates and Digital Signatures

Keys are contained in a certificate, which identifies both the individual and the validity of the certificate itself. This is the basis of a PKI, which permits individuals to post their public keys, while at the same time providing assurance that a given public key belongs to a given individual (see Figure 3.10). The certificate, conforming to the X.509 standard (and usually accessed via Lightweight Directory Access Protocol [LDAP] mechanisms), includes information regarding the individual, his or her public key, the timeframe for validity of the certificate, and the issuing authority. This last entity, the CA, is critical, in that it validates the certificate itself. This requires validation of a hierarchy of CAs, eventually reaching a trusted entity such as a government, large corporation, or nonprofit entity. The major CAs include VeriSign, Entrust, GTE, Baltimore, Thawte, and some vendor-operated sites,

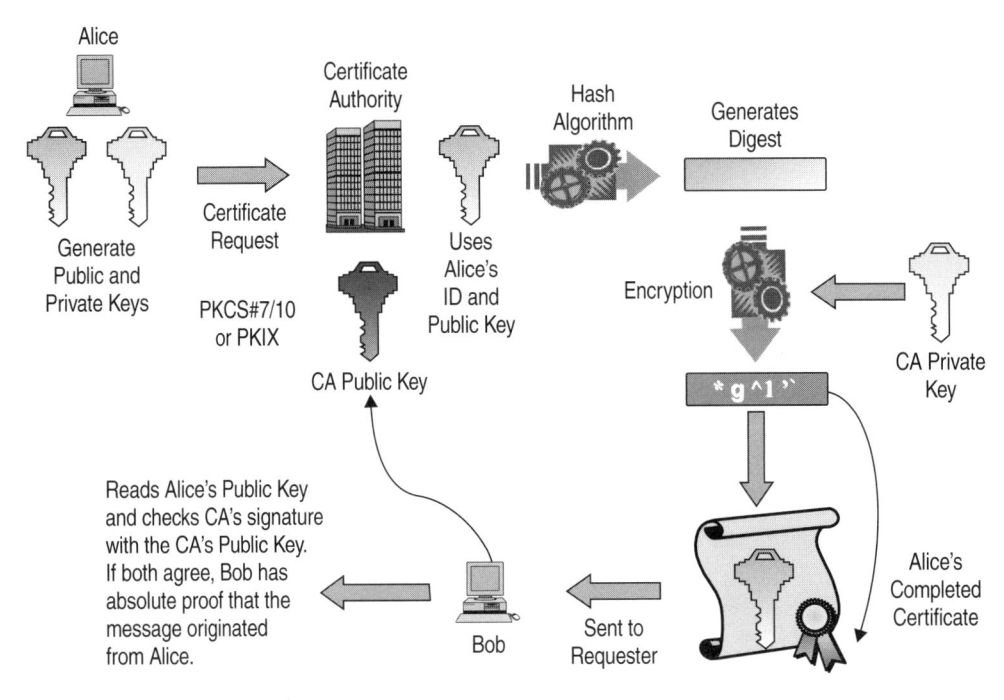

FIGURE 3.10 Public Key Infrastructure

such as that offered by Microsoft. For example, a PKI in the public domain may require a CA rooted at the local government, while one confined to a single corporation could use a CA maintained internally.

In an actual encryption deployment, the public-private key exchange is normally used only to generate a session key for data encryption. This is due to the fact that public-key encryption systems such as RSA are too computationally intensive for bulk data encryption. Therefore, once session keys are created and exchanged, DES or 3DES is used for the actual data encryption.

With an understanding of security, we can now look at how it is maintained by tunneling subscribers across the backbone and segregating them at the network edge.

Tunneling Technologies

Tunneling technologies and associated tunneling services evolved as a result of using the IP infrastructure to transport private data between two entities. In much the same way that an underground car tunnel provides a path between two points that is segregated from the rest of the external environment, tunneling isolates communications in networking. Once data is placed in the tunnel, it is effectively segregated from other IP traffic. If there is concern that someone can somehow break into the tunnel to access the data (this question is always asked by the security purists), then a simple solution is to encrypt it. Typically, service providers use nonencrypted tunnels if the data is being transported over their own infrastructure but may encrypt it if it is traversing the public Internet.

Tunneling by its nature is a point-to-point technology. The tunnel starts at an initial node, possibly a user's PC, and ends at another node, such as a content server. Along the way, the tunnel may be merged with other tunnels, and a bigger tunnel may be created. Alternatively, there may be many tunnels starting from different networks that are intended to go to the same site. Instead of creating multiple tunnels that are duplicated, many service providers are entering into the tunnel grooming service. Minimizing the number of tunnels by aggregating tunnels to the same destination is a new service offering. Not only does this optimize network resource utilization, but it allows access service providers to introduce additional revenue-generating services on top of tunnel grooming, such as QoS for certain tunnel sets. Customers can subscribe and pay more for a service that ensures that their tunneled data receives the best possible service across the network.

In this section, we cover the popular Layer 2 and 3 tunneling protocols and examine how tunnels serve as the basic building block for additional services such as IP-VPNs. The various tunneling protocols covered include the following:

- L2TP
- PPTP

- IPSec
- GRE, IP in IP, and UTI
- MPLS

The underlying protocols that offer IP-VPNs are covered in this chapter, but IP-VPN implementations are covered in chapter 7. These technologies serve as the infrastructure on which IP-VPNs can be offered. Since IP-VPNs leverage many of the new services, such as security, tunneling, and traffic management, they are discussed in chapter 7 after the other concepts are explained.

L2TP

L2TP (Townsley, 1999) evolved as a result of standardizing PPTP (Point-to-Point Tunneling Protocol) and L2F (Layer 2 Forwarding, a Cisco proprietary protocol). L2TP is now commonly used as the tunneling protocol for Internet dial architectures. The protocol encapsulates PPP frames within most link-layer technologies or within IP. L2TP defines two types of messages, control and data. The control message is used for tunnel maintenance, and the data message is for user traffic. Both message types are carried over UDP, even though the original encapsulated user data may be UDP or TCP. L2TP supports encryption and compression of data. More recently, with the growth of telecommuters and concern about security of tunneling over public IP infrastructures, dual-mode PC clients now support both L2TP and IPSec, combining the remote-access capabilities of L2TP with the security capabilities of IPSec. These clients insert the IPSec header between the IP and the UDP headers. The protocol also supports many authentication mechanisms, the most common being CHAP, MS-CHAP(v2), and the Extensible Authentication Protocol (EAP), which permits use of token cards.

Within L2TP, two modes of tunneling are possible:

Compulsory tunneling—A RAS or an IPSS establishes the L2TP tunnel to a corporate or ISP gateway. Traffic then flows from one or more subscribers within the created tunnel. In fact, the end users have no idea that they are being tunneled. To the subscriber, it appears as if the modem is just doing the modem communication across to a modem bank. This type of tunneling forms the basis for Internet wholesale dial services where a single RAS is shared among multiple corporations or ISPs. The traffic of different ISPs or corporations is partitioned via the creation of separate tunnels across an arbitrary IP backbone.

Voluntary tunneling—The PC originates the L2TP (or L2TP/IPSec) tunnel. The tunnel then terminates at either a service provider's tunnel gateway or a corporation. Windows 2000 is an example of an operating system with this functionality.

Figure 3.11 shows these two modes of operation.

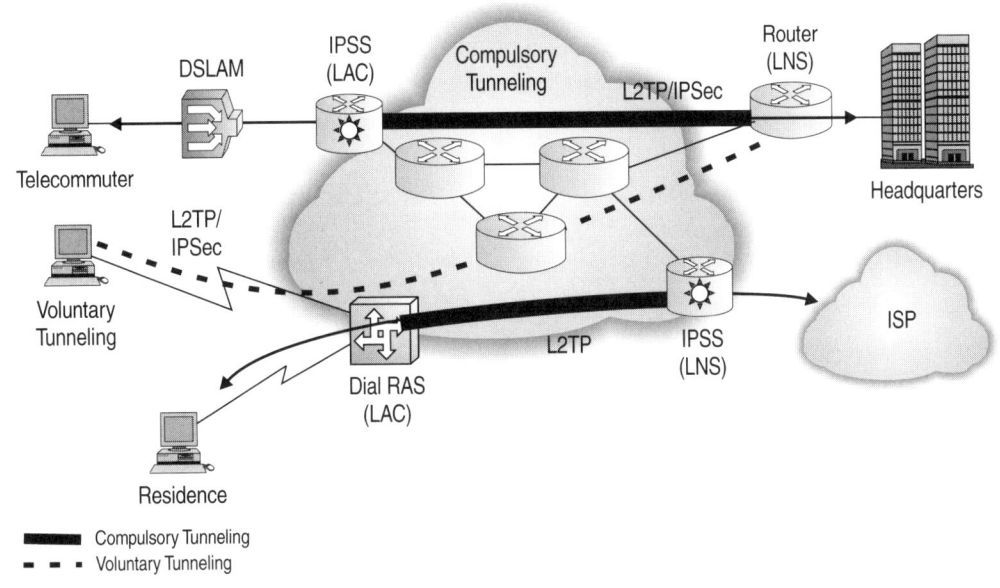

FIGURE 3.11 Compulsory and Voluntary Tunneling

The L2TP protocol defines a sequence of events that take place between the subscriber, the tunnel origination point (known as an L2TP Access Concentrator [LAC]), and the tunnel termination point, the L2TP Network Server (LNS). When a user first initiates a PPP session to a given destination based on a fully qualified username (e.g., cats@thirasystems.com), the LAC determines whether an L2TP tunnel to the LNS handling the thirasystems.com domain is in place. If a tunnel does not exist, the LAC establishes this control connection. This control connection supports messages for the establishment, maintenance, and clearing of tunnels and calls. The user's call now initiates a session within this tunnel for the PPP traffic.

L2TP enables a number of different applications across the network. The most common is Internet dial wholesaling, where a wholesale provider virtualizes a RAS among multiple ISPs. Each ISP contracts for a number of modem ports on the platform and is provided with a tunneled connection back to its own backbone. Think of this as having a permanent gym locker versus using any open locker and putting on a lock for the duration of use. When a company has a permanent locker (or the RAS), it is responsible for its maintenance, but the locker's functionality is to provide storage space. If the company instead uses any available open locker (modem wholesale), it receives the same service but now is no longer responsible for the maintenance. The financial difference is that instead of a capital cost, the company now has a monthly expense.

The other benefit to the ISP is that now it can provide service beyond the geographic reach of its own RAS deployment. Another method of geographic extension

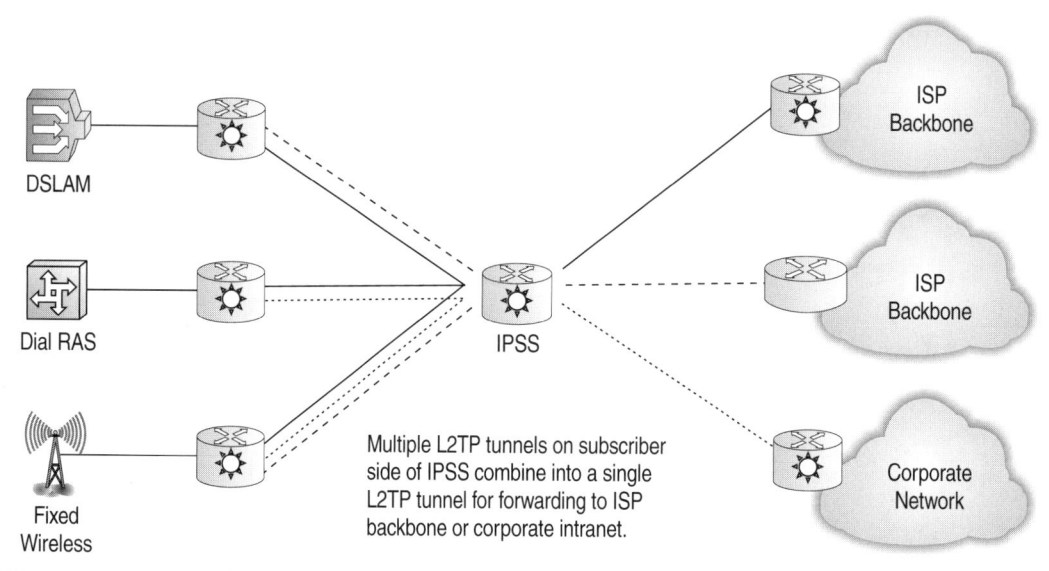

FIGURE 3.12 Tunnel Optimization

is L2TP support on a DSL aggregation platform that permits the operator to securely backhaul subscriber traffic to multiple ISPs. In some deployments, the L2TP tunnels from the RAS terminate at this broadband aggregation platform and are then remapped into a second set of tunnels terminating at the ISP (see Figure 3.12). Thus, both dial and DSL subscriber traffic share the same backbone L2TP tunnels.

A second type of L2TP deployment is client-based. Although this architecture fell out of favor during 1999, by 2000 it was once again accepted as a way of securely tunneling subscribers across an arbitrary access technology. Part of this renewed acceptance may be due to the inclusion of L2TP within Windows 2000 and Windows ME. It is much simpler for users to leverage a technology if it is already included than if they have to install a new client. This L2TP client architecture also supports IP addressing at the PC separate from that of the actual access network. For example, a wireless access provider could assign private addresses native to the service. Subscribers would then tunnel to ISPs that would assign the actual globally routable addresses. Another advantage of L2TP is its compatibility with both Layer 2 and Layer 3 access technologies. In contrast, an access encapsulation such as PPPoE (described in chapter 6 in detail) operates only across a Layer 2 access infrastructure (or across a Layer 3 infrastructure if routing is disabled).

One interesting application that some service providers and enterprises are implementing is to use L2TP to tunnel all dial clients to a single location where one firewall is used for all the dial traffic. This minimizes the need to deploy a large firewall at each PoP. This centralization of services is similar to the airport hub concept where airplanes end up at certain hubs, which have all the expensive maintenance equipment (in this case, the firewall). From the hub, the planes then continue to their destination. Closely related to L2TP are PPTP and L2F. These protocols also provide for secure tunneling from the client or across the backbone. PPTP is described next. L2F is a proprietary protocol that is being phased out in favor of L2TP.

Advantages of L2TP to the provider include the ability to either extend the geographic range of its coverage if a retail ISP or reuse its access infrastructure if a wholesaler. The subscriber of course has access to a selected ISP or corporation across a larger set of access providers. As open access to select the desired ISP is implemented by cable providers, L2TP will play a key role in tunneling the user traffic to the selected ISP in this environment as well.

PPTP

Like L2TP, PPTP (Hamzeh, 1999) also enjoys some popularity as part of Internet dial architectures. PPTP was designed to include both the authentication and encryption capabilities between a client and the network and therefore does not require a separate encryption standard. It also supports use of NAT. It relies on a TCP connection for the tunnel maintenance and GRE for encapsulating the user PPP frames. As with L2TP, a PC client initiates a tunneled connection to a corporate gateway. PPTP is used extensively for voluntary tunneling because it is readily available with Microsoft Windows software (that laziness factor rears its head again). However, PPTP is not as widely deployed in support of compulsory tunneling, the domain of L2TP.

IPSec

IP Security Protocol (IPSec) defines a complete architecture for securing data, authenticating users, and managing security. IPSec specifies the creation of a secure tunnel between two endpoints and therefore is considered a tunneling service. The following are the main techniques that IPSec uses:

- The Diffie-Hellman key exchange for delivery of secret keys
- Public key cryptography for verification of the Diffie-Hellman key exchange
- DES, 3DES, and other lesser-known encryption algorithms for securing the data
- Keyed hash algorithms, such as HMAC+MD5 or HMAC+SHA-1, for packet authentication
- Digital certificates for public key validation

IPSec (Kent, 1998c) first defines a security association (SA) between two entities that want to establish a secure connection. This SA defines the encryption and authentication algorithm to be used and the method of key exchange, and then provides for the key exchange itself. Every secure connection between a sender and a receiver requires at least one SA, and sometimes two if encrypting and authenticating. A concept closely aligned with the SA is the domain of interpretation (DOI), which defines which protocols are expected within the SA.

Two important components in an IPSec implementation are the two types of packet encapsulation. These include the encapsulating security payload (ESP; IP Protocol 50) (Kent, 1998b) for encryption and authentication, and the authentication header (AH; IP Protocol 51) (Kent, 1998a) for authentication only.

The AH contains a checksum of the packet's data and is inserted between the IP and TCP headers. The most important part of the AH is the authentication data, generated by applying the authentication algorithm (HMAC+MD5, HMAC+SHA-1) to the packet's contents. During operation, the sender generates a checksum based on the data and the authentication algorithm. This is placed in the AH. After receipt of the data, the receiver calculates a checksum based on that data and compares it to the original. Note that the AH itself is secure via public keying (i.e., someone could not intercept the data, alter it, and then add a new checksum corresponding to the new data).

In contrast to the AH, the ESP is used for data encryption as well as authentication. ESP protocols include DES and 3DES. If the ESP is used for authentication as well, which is optional, a checksum is generated from the data in the same way as with the AH. Both the AH and ESP are deployable in two modes—tunnel and transport. Tunnel mode is designed for operation between two security gateways (e.g., routers with IPSec capabilities) and involves encapsulating the original encrypted packet in a new IP header, totally hiding the original source and destination. In contrast, transport mode maintains the original IP header and therefore does not protect the original IP source and destination addresses from eavesdropping.

IPSec relies on the Internet Security Association and Key Management Protocol (ISAKMP) (Maughan, 1998) for its key management and authentication framework and the Internet Key Exchange (IKE) protocol (Harkins, 1998) for the actual key exchange technique. Where IPSec operates between hosts or internetworking devices, a simple password (known as a pre-shared authentication key) may be sufficient. The use of certificates and a CA is more scalable and permits IPSec deployments across multiple management domains. Finally, in a Windows environment spanning a single domain or multiple trusted domains, Kerberos is an option. In all cases, IPSec will use DES or 3DES for actual encryption. The IKE is responsible for creating a way for individuals to agree on the encryption and authentication algorithms for confirming user identity and for key management. Within IKE, there are multiple modes of establishing the SA depending on the level of security required. IKE involves two phases of negotiation. Phase 1 has two possible methods of negotiation, Main Mode and Aggressive Mode. Phase 2 is based only on Quick Mode. Main Mode is the most secure method, but is more complex than Aggressive Mode. The tradeoffs are speed and protecting the identities of the two parties. Quick Mode is used for IPSec parameter negotiation and key exchange updates.

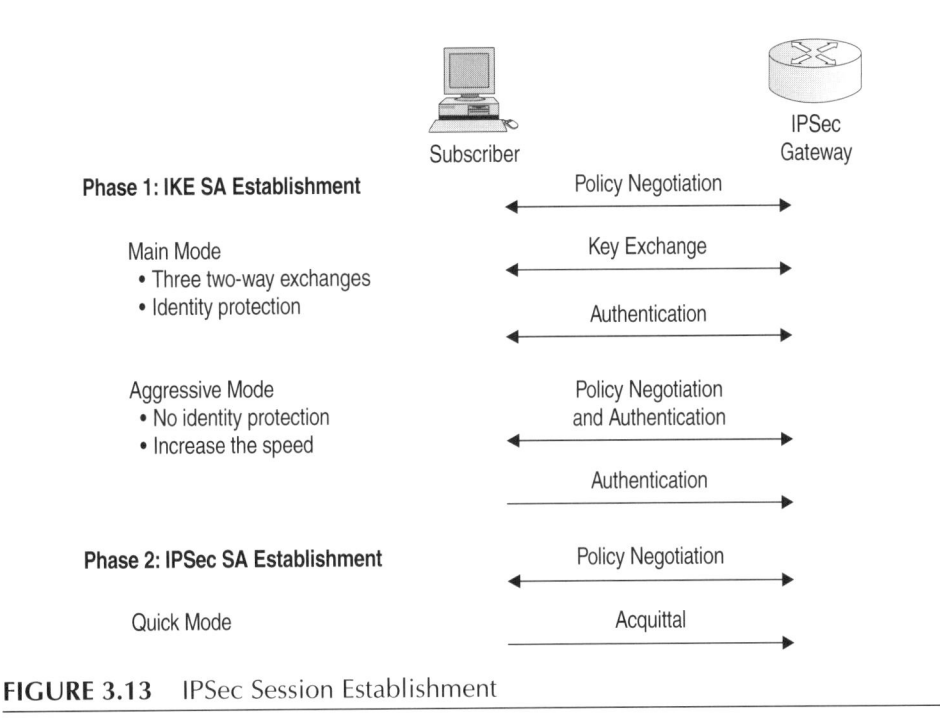

Tunneling Technologies

```
Phase 1: IKE SA Establishment                    Subscriber                           IPSec Gateway

                                                 ←── Policy Negotiation ──→

  Main Mode                                      ←──── Key Exchange ────→
    • Three two-way exchanges
    • Identity protection                        ←──── Authentication ───→


  Aggressive Mode                                ←── Policy Negotiation ──→
    • No identity protection                         and Authentication
    • Increase the speed
                                                 ───── Authentication ───→


Phase 2: IPSec SA Establishment                  ←── Policy Negotiation ──→

  Quick Mode                                     ──────── Acquittal ─────→
```

FIGURE 3.13 IPSec Session Establishment

In deployment, IPSec operates as follows (see Figure 3.13): Two entities that want to establish a secure connection first establish an IKE SA via the Main or the Aggressive mode. As mentioned, Main provides identity protection, while Aggressive is quicker. The two parties now establish the full IPSec SA using Quick Mode. Within the policy negotiation phase, parameters exchanged include which ciphering algorithm, hash algorithm, and method for authentication will be used.

One major shortcoming with the existing IPSec specifications is in support for remote VPN access. Both the tunnel and transport modes are effective for security within a network backbone, or between a service provider's edge and the backbone, but neither includes the user authentication and IP address assignment (DHCP) mechanisms required for telecommuter access. Although some vendors have added proprietary extensions to solve this shortcoming, none are standardized. The preferred method is to place L2TP within IPSec operating in Transport mode.

GRE, IP in IP, and UTI

Other tunneling mechanisms of note, which are, in fact, fairly common, are GRE and IP in IP. Both permit the extension of a single subscriber's or corporation's traffic across an arbitrary IP backbone without the use of encryption and with very little overhead. This lack of encryption is a potential problem, requiring that the customer trust the backbone provider.

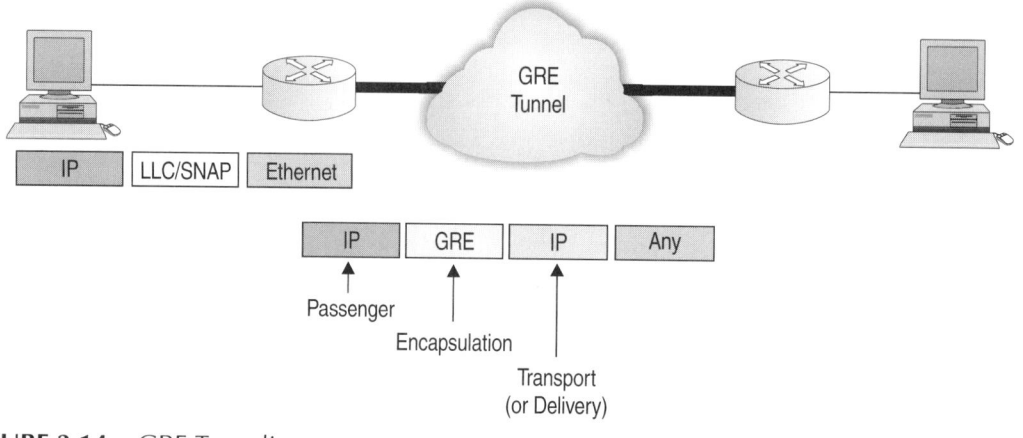

FIGURE 3.14 GRE Tunneling

GRE, as defined in RFCs 1701 and 1702, encloses the original data and protocol, known as the "passenger," in an encapsulation, in this case GRE (Figure 3.14). It then wraps this in a "transport" protocol, IP. The advantage of GRE is that it is capable of handling both multiprotocol and IP multicast traffic between two points that have only IP unicast connectivity. In a service provider network, this capability is probably the more relevant. Since GRE also hides the underlying addressing, it eliminates the need for NAT since the tunnels may extend between two sites using private addressing.

The IP in IP encapsulation protocol, as defined in RFC 1853, encapsulates the original data and protocol within another IP header. This differs from other protocols that typically insert a special data header between IP headers. Instead, with IP in IP, the original unadorned IP header is maintained and simply wrapped in another standard IP header. Unlike GRE, IP in IP is limited to IP traffic and does not handle multiprotocol traffic. A newer alternative to both GRE and IP in IP is the Universal Tunnel Interface (UTI). It offers lower overhead than the other techniques, important on high-speed backbones.

MPLS

Multiprotocol label switching (MPLS) (Callon, 2000) was originally envisioned as a way to optimize the transport of IP traffic over an ATM backbone. It accomplishes this by labeling ATM cells with Layer 3 (IP) forwarding information. The MPLS label is placed in the VPI/VCI cell header. The ATM switches that are MPLS-enabled then switch based on this information instead of based on the standard VPI/VCI contained in the cell header.

Although MPLS was originally conceived as a method to provide effective traffic engineering for IP networks and to empower ATM switches to participate in IP networks, the MPLS concepts are being extended in various IETF working groups to be utilized across other Layer 1/Layer 2 technologies. There is now work underway at the IETF to support other protocols such as Frame Relay, ATM, and Ethernet via MPLS (Martini, 2001a; Martini, 2001b). An alternative proposal by Juniper is known as the Circuit Cross Connect (CCC) and is actually implemented in their JUNOS™ software. If these efforts become a standard (and even if they don't), MPLS may well be utilized to offer Layer 2 VPNs. Even more interesting are evolving techniques for the support of TDM traffic across MPLS, referred to as circuit emulation service over MPLS (Malis, 2001). If this is perfected, MPLS could be deployed as a universal convergence layer. Also worth mentioning are the efforts to extend MPLS for the signaling of LSPs across native synchronous optical network (SONET) transmission, DWDM, and optical cross-connect architectures. Within the IETF, this is known as generalized MPLS (Ashwood-Smith 2000; Ashwood-Smith, 2001).

Since its original creation, MPLS has found acceptance as a traffic-engineering technique for congested packet backbones by virtue of its capability to label QoS paths and direct traffic along these paths. With its traffic-engineering capabilities, MPLS is also suitable for IP-VPNs across the backbone, combining virtualization of the backbone and application QoS support. RFC 2547 (updated by Rosen, 2000) defines the use of BGP4 extensions to carry per-VPN reachability information across a provider's backbone. With BGP4 extensions, the provider offers a full IP-VPN service, as opposed to basic Internet connectivity. Customers to this IP-VPN service may include single enterprises, multiple enterprises connected into an extranet, ISPs, ASPs, and even other providers offering an IP-VPN service of their own, possibly targeted to specific market segments.

Providers create MPLS IP-VPNs as shown in Figure 3.15. Customers (sites) connect to the provider's backbone via hosts, switches, or, in most cases, routers, all acting as customer edge (CE) devices. For the remainder of this description, we'll use *router* as a generic term for these devices. A CE router connects to a provider edge (PE) router via a variety of access technologies. The IP-VPN provider operates this PE router. PEs connect to the provider's core routers, referred to as provider (P) routers. These P routers do not connect to customers. The CE router is a routing peer to the PE router and only to the PE router, while the PE router maintains multiple IP forwarding tables, one for each IP-VPN instance for which it has customers attached via CE routers. Between the CE and the PE router, static routing, RIPv2, OSPF, and BGP4 are all possibilities.

In a large network where there are many PE routers, only those routers servicing a given IP-VPN will have routes for it. The PE identifies individual IP-VPNs via ATM PVCs, VLANs, or tunnels on the subscriber side. This permits multiple IP-VPNs over a single physical interface. It also permits a single customer site to participate in multiple IP-VPNs. Although this technique supports multiple overlapping IP address spaces (i.e., two or more IP-VPNs each using 10.0.0.0), if two customers using this private addressing wish to interconnect, either they need to adjust their addressing or they must implement NAT (Rosen, 2000).

FIGURE 3.15 MPLS IP-VPNs

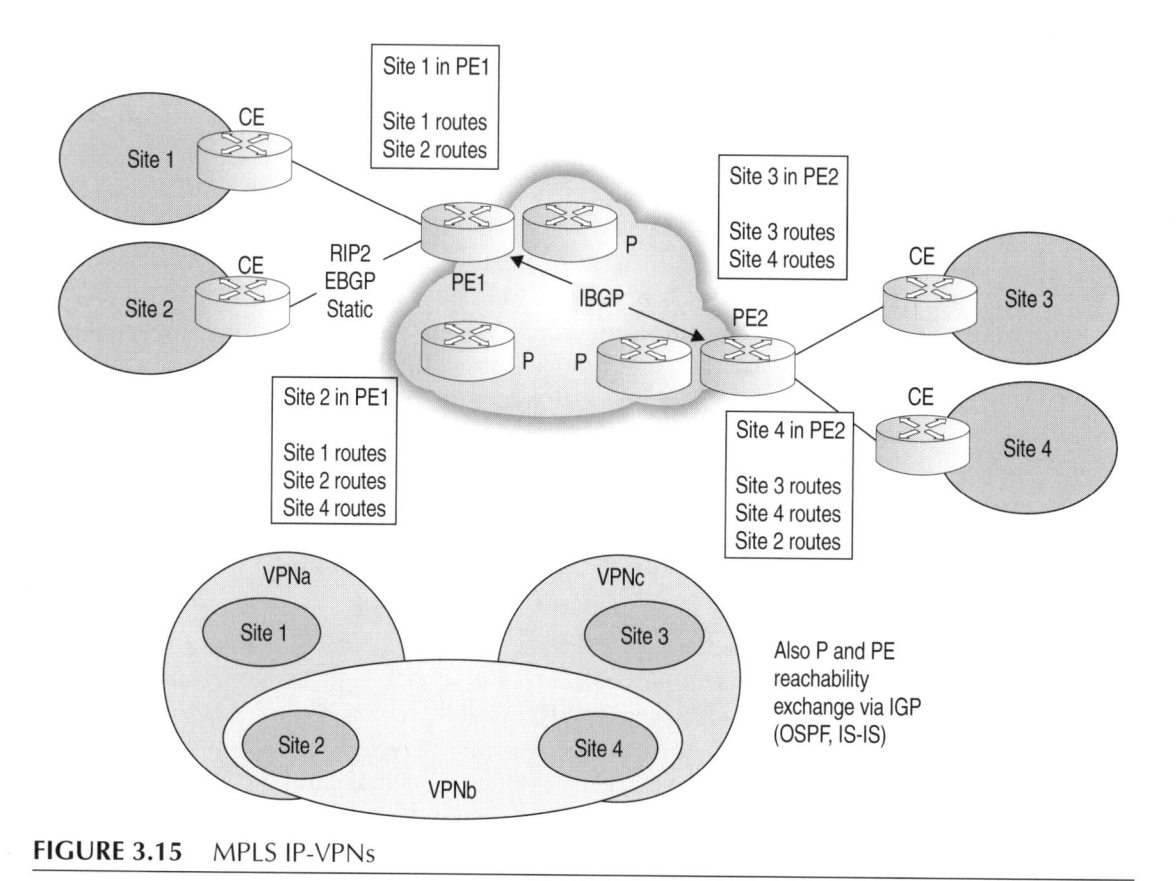

Under actual operation, the PE learns from the CE the routes at the CE's site that belong to a given IP-VPN. It then distributes this reachability information to other PEs servicing the same IP-VPN. The distant PE then forwards this information to any connected CEs in the given IP-VPN. They use this information to forward data across the backbone. The use of a new address family (VPN-IPv4) as a route distinguisher permits the identification of per-VPN routes within BGP4. Note that the P routers do not maintain any per-VPN forwarding information—this is the role of the PE routers. They need to know only how to route between the PE routers themselves.

The use of MPLS IP-VPNs has created great controversy at many IETF meetings, with probably the greatest concern being the use of BGP to exchange this reachability information. Opponents of the technique focus on the complexity of BGP configuration, and the requirement to implement BGP on every device. Proponents focus on scalability and the fact that the vast majority of providers already have BGP expertise. In any case, this technique is beginning to see acceptance. In fact, a full IP-VPN offering may include IPSec or L2TP at the edge and MPLS within the core. Although MPLS does not natively support encryption, in the majority of cases the customer will be satisfied that the provider will maintain security between IP-VPNs. This is no different than a provider properly configuring an FR or ATM backbone. However, if required, encryption is a possibility.

Subscriber Segregation

The tunneling techniques just described are only some of the ways service providers deal with traffic from multiple customers across a backbone. Consider multiple enterprises connecting to an IP edge device at the provider's PoP. If the provider wishes to maintain the individual identities of these enterprises across the backbone, including their routing and QoS, it must have some way of segregating these enterprises within the edge device. This segregation applies mainly to enterprises, since individual subscribers are most likely to rely on the tunneling techniques just described. Subscribers entering the network with RADIUS authentication who are then mapped into L2TP or PPTP tunnels are naturally segregated or require no segregation as they are mapped into a common IP backbone. In addition, if the L2TP or IPSec (or even GRE) tunnel originates at the CPE, the customer is already segregated on arrival at the network edge.

The real question, then, is how to effectively segregate enterprise customers at the edge before forwarding their traffic across the backbone using techniques such as GRE, IP in IP, MPLS, and even IPSec. Virtual routing, where a single edge device is partitioned into multiple routers, is a well-understood concept and is implemented by a number of vendors. This technique has some limitations, addressed by more recent multi-router implementations. In any case, the goal is to extend the customer's network, including its routing domain, across the provider's network, while maintaining the required level of security and QoS.

Virtual Routers

The term *virtual router* (VR) is often used to describe IP routing support on a Frame Relay or ATM switch, as well as on many recent edge routers. In the case of Frame Relay and ATM, this capability provides an excellent migration path for multiservice operators seeking to leverage their installed base of switching equipment in support of IP services. Adding this capability usually requires a hardware upgrade, with the platform capable of supporting anywhere from hundreds to thousands of individual routing entities depending on the strength of the routing engine. Newer edge routers also support upward of hundreds of VRs. This is accomplished by maintaining multiple copies of the routing table, one for each customer, in the device's memory. In a full VR implementation, the routing table belonging to a specific customer receives routing updates across the backbone from

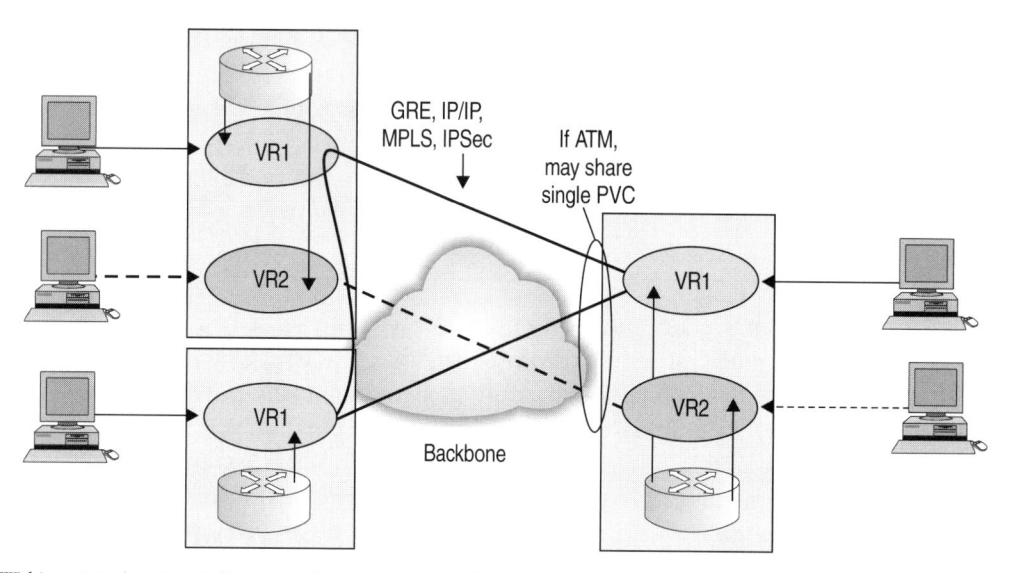

Note: Within a virtual router platform, a single route processor distributes route table updates to the individual VRs. These VRs maintain their own routing tables based on this information.

FIGURE 3.16 Virtual Routers

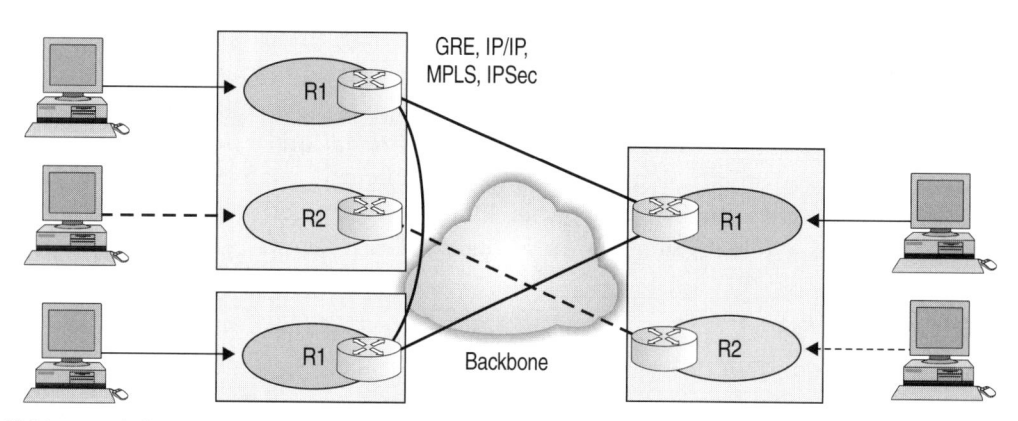

Note: Multi-router platforms equip each forwarding table (R) with a separate route processor.

FIGURE 3.17 Multi-routers

other VR-enabled edge devices. From the perspective of the customer, the VR operates just as an ordinary router (but not quite; see the next section).

Customers arriving on "always-on" DSL connections or Frame Relay PVCs map into the VRs, and then the provider maintains customer identity across the backbone via a number of different mechanisms depending upon the technology. In the case of ATM, the VRs map into individual PVCs or SVCs or, in some cases, into an aggregate PVC using a tagging mechanism (see Figure 3.16). In the case of a router, the VRs will map into GRE or IP in IP, MPLS-VPNs, or IPSec tunnels. This is at the discretion of the provider based on throughput, interoperability, and security requirements.

Multi-Routers

At a high level, the concept of the multi-router (Figure 3.17) is much like that of the virtual router. However, the architecture of the multi-router is very different, presenting some advantages. One deficit of a virtual router architecture is that a single route processor calculates the routing tables for all customers served on the platform. This has obvious performance implications for large enterprises. In addition, the provider cannot provide a view into the individual customer's configuration.

The alternative is to provide dedicated routing resources (processing and memory) for each and every customer. This is the concept of the *multi-router*, with the customer traffic then forwarded across the provider's backbone as just described, using GRE, IP in IP, MPLS, or dedicated channels or wavelengths. Within a multi-routing architecture, no single customer may adversely affect the forwarding performance, routing connectivity, or services available to any others.

Conclusion

This chapter looks at the various security, segregation, and tunneling services available to the broadband subscriber. Security services play a vital role in protecting both the subscriber and the network operator; tunneling permits the provider to extend the subscriber's backbone across a public infrastructure, a feature unavailable with conventional routing protocols; and segregation helps the provider identify subscribers and enterprises. These technologies form the underlying building blocks for additional services that the service provider can bundle and offer. These services (covered in greater detail in chapters 5 through 7) are the key to providing additional value to the end user and a continuous revenue stream for the service provider. The next chapter covers additional technologies, including content management, video, and voice, critical in enabling rich services at the network edge.

Chapter 4
Higher-Layer Technologies

Beyond connectivity and tunneling, there is a complete gamut of technologies available for service providers to offer to end customers and generate additional revenues. These services extend beyond Layers 1 through 3, which are traditionally the connectivity layers in networking. Instead, these services base their technology on leveraging and utilizing Layers 4 through 7. The most important of these technologies focus on broadband content management and distribution. They are important because users connect to the network to reach specific services and content sites. In fact, there is a fear that Internet adoption has slowed down because of a lack of compelling content—broadband subscribers just have nowhere to go. And, although we are witnessing the beginning of true convergence between the Internet and the media industry, as evidenced by the merger of AOL and Time-Warner, this is only the beginning.

This chapter covers content services and discusses the technologies associated with these higher-layer services—services that operate at Layers 4 through 7. Content services tie together technologies and protocols such as caching, service selection portals, content switching and server load balancers, and content distribution networks. In the residential space, content services will prove to be a major source of revenue to service providers. Chapter 7 discusses the actual deployment of these services.

After covering content management, the chapter discusses in more depth coverage of technologies that rely on content management. Broadcast video distribution, though considered a form of content management, is really a service separate from services such as content caching and content distribution networks since some providers are building networks (and receiving funding) solely to disseminate broadcast video. This video distribution application introduces a new set of complexities into the network buildout and is discussed separately in this chapter.

In addition, edge-based voice services add a separate set of concerns and introduce an entirely new set of protocols and server functions. In fact, voice integration is probably the most difficult offering because of the management and quality requirements. Finally, we cover virtual hosting services, which migrate functions and services traditionally served at the enterprise to a network or data service.

Content Management

Content providers, spanning the continuum from AOL Time-Warner or Virgin to the smallest Web developer, generate or broker content. Typically, the role of the network infrastructure is to carry this content to the subscribers. Subscribers require a means to identify what content is available, at what cost, and at what quality. Depending on the access technology in question, such as dial-up, DSL/cable, or wireless, these parameters may be quite different. The service provider must have a way to recover expenses for carrying this content, either from the subscriber or from the content provider. A content distribution architecture therefore must incorporate a number of elements:

- Methods for peering between access providers/wholesalers, retail ISPs, and content providers, to include revenue recognition
- Methods for ensuring delivery of the content at the requested QoS
- Methods for caching this content where appropriate
- Methods for subscribers to identify what content is available and to access this content

The most basic requirement for content delivery is an infrastructure capable of delivering the content where it is required, when it is required, and at the requested QoS. This is, of course, a challenge in today's Internet, where access providers massively oversubscribe residential subscribers, even if they connect via DSL or cable. The content servers require Internet connectivity bandwidth commensurate with the QoS of the material and the number of subscribers served. For example, a small Web site catering to a small number of subscribers may require only a T1, while a major sporting events site may require many OC3s. The servers themselves may be located either at a hosting site (more common) or on the premises of the content provider. Note that hosting presents advantages in proximity to Internet peering by providing the proper facilities and the ability to utilize on-demand sites active for only a single event (e.g., the Olympics, the World Cup, or a presidential election). The content providers have done a good job of delivering content into the network and, over the past few years, have evolved increasingly sophisticated content delivery architectures.

However, this is only the beginning. In May 2001, *Wired* (*Wired,* 2001) pointed out that the success of the transition to broadband will depend on multiple forces coming together—the re-engineering of the network infrastructure to support higher bandwidths for millions of subscribers, the implementation of new billing systems, the compression and copy protection of content for efficiency and security, and the buy-in from the major content producers to open their archives to the Internet (which is dependent on the other three forces being in place).

Content management as a service is a bit different from the technologies described in the previous chapters in that it has only recently taken center stage as part of next-generation service offerings. You are constantly hearing about content partnerships between network and content providers, startups focusing on content delivery and mediation, content portals, and the growth of video and voice across the Internet. *Content* is any type of information with intrinsic or derived value and may be paid for by the subscriber, a service, or the content provider. It may include text, audio, or video, but in most cases it refers to stored or streamed multimedia. The term *content management* is also difficult to define since it encompasses peering relationships between ISPs or wholesalers and content providers; the various caching architectures; traffic management; and some recent work in optimized content delivery (a next-generation cache architecture, if you will).

Within a network, the various content management, distribution, and mediation functions come together within a content delivery or content distribution network (CDN). Figure 4.1 shows an example of a CDN, a content PoP with redundancy. One part of a CDN is the *content edge,* the location where content is delivered to the transport mechanism that will take it to the subscriber. Devices at the content edge, including the IPSS, interface with the various content servers, LAN switches, Web caches, and CDNs, and participate in content distribution intelligence. Contrast this to the *subscriber edge,* which currently focuses on providing individual subscribers with high-touch IP services—the realm of the IPSS. A third edge is the *border edge,* which consists of traditional edge routers offering ISP and leased-line connectivity and focuses on basic IP connectivity and forwarding. As time progresses, we are beginning to see the integration of some subscriber edge functions into the CDN and vice versa. One thing to note is that the content edge is also creeping closer, pushed by the service providers.

Functions within a CDN include the following:

- Content caching
- Content switching
- Content routing
- Content distribution and management

A CDN also requires the various QoS, security, multicast, and IP-VPN capabilities described elsewhere in this book. Although these technologies are important to other services, they are especially critical in the content space.

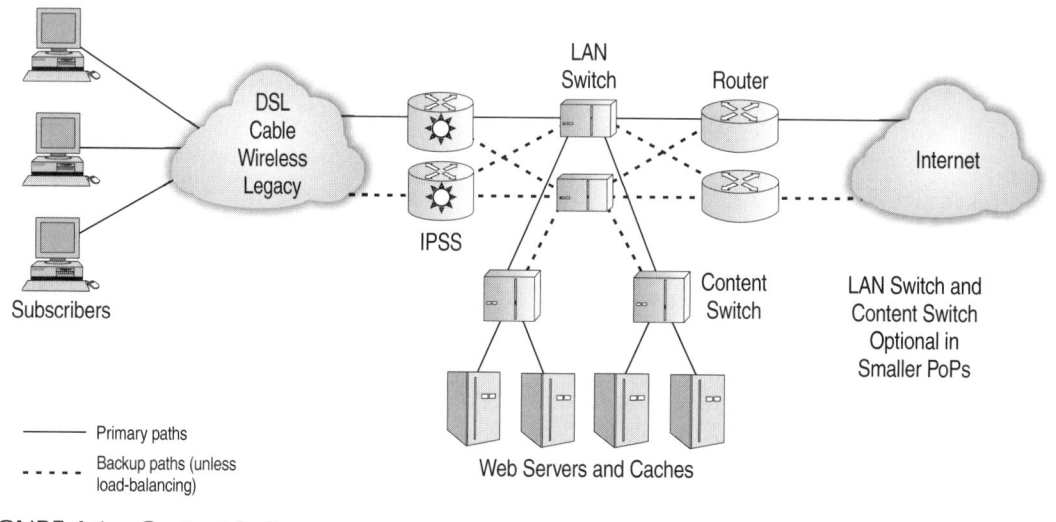

FIGURE 4.1 Content PoP

Content Caching

Caching servers evolved as a method to store commonly accessed content on a separate device—the cache. If the cache had the content (that is, if it got a hit), it would serve the content back to the user. If the cache did not have the content (that is, if there was a cache miss), it would forward the request to the origin server and receive the content, which would then be served to the user. Over time and because of the importance of caching, special names have resulted based on the location of the cache and its deployment. The common names associated with caching are proxy caching and reverse proxy caching. Depending on where the cache is placed, the characteristics and value it provides differ.

Proxy Caches

Initially, simple Web caches were collocated with the subscriber's edge router, and subscribers would point their browsers directly to this cache. This is called *proxy caching* and requires the user to reconfigure his or her browser to point to the cache. It has the disadvantage of no redundancy in that a single browser must point to a single cache. If the cache fails, the user cannot be served any content even though the origin server may be fine. This is still a common practice at many corporations, which implement proxies at their corporate boundaries to the Internet, often leading to less than acceptable performance.

The most common type of cache, and the most successful, is edge caching, sometimes referred to as *network-side caching* or *forward caching*. Edge caching helps accelerate network performance by freeing bandwidth across the backbone between the origin servers and the network edge. Having the content closer to the subscriber also results in a better customer experience. The Akamai network, described in the section "The Evolution of Content Distribution," later in this chapter, is an example of intelligent edge caching. The provider deploys these edge caches in conjunction with suitably equipped routers that intercept the user's traffic and redirect the traffic to the cache. These devices cache content from many Web sites and are usually capable of about a 35 percent hit rate.

Reverse Proxy Caches

Reverse proxy caching involves collocating the cache with origin servers in the data center. Other names for this technique include *Web acceleration server* and *server-side* caching. Using this type of cache results in a 95 percent hit rate on average, but such caches are suitable for only static content. Benefits of reverse caching are improved server performance and protection of the origin servers from flash crowds, though content switches provide many of the same advantages. To avoid sending all subscriber data through the server-side cache, providers now deploy these devices in conjunction with content switches, forwarding only relevant requests to the cache (i.e., a request will go to the cache only if the requested data is actually stored).

Cache Characteristics

A Web cache does not provide the redundancy of most other internetworking devices and is therefore not the most suitable platform to impose in the data plane for all traffic, as was done in the early days of proxy caching and transparent proxy caching. Although some early caches were deployed in this configuration, it is not recommended. Unlike traditional file systems, a Web cache will use the URL namespace for indexing and storage. Depending on the scalability required, a cache will contain anywhere from 4 GB to more than 300 GB of disk storage, supported by anywhere from 128 MB to more than 4 GB of RAM (figures from the year 2001). Note that this capacity is usually sufficient, as the cache must store only a small fraction of the total Internet content available. Larger systems will support sustained rates to 155 Mbps or above, and they will support redundancy and DC power. The actual characteristics of the hardware to be used differ depending on where the cache is utilized in the network.

Ideally, a cache should have a high hit rate, it should respond quickly to subscriber requests, it should not unnecessarily duplicate the cached traffic, it should have no impact on non-Web traffic, it should offer 100 percent uptime and redundancy, and it should require no administration of clients and intermediate systems. Realistically, if it achieves 50 percent of these capabilities, significant savings are realized.

For example, a single Web acceleration server will eliminate the need for three origin servers and therefore portions of any Layer 4 switches and firewalls installed that are load balancing and protecting the origin servers. This results in a savings of about $80,000 over a three-year period in a typical configuration. Savings due to a reduction in rack charges raise this to a total savings of about $85,000. After taking into account the initial deployment cost of the Web acceleration server in Year 1, the savings achieved through deployment of the single Web accelerator are therefore $23,250 in Years 2 and 3. The provider may also choose to deploy an IPSS in conjunction with the Web acceleration server to provide firewalling capabilities. Given an IPSS supporting on the order of 1 Gbps worth of firewall capacity, it could easily serve most of the customers within a typical data center. The provider could charge $200 per month per Mbps for this service and achieve a good return on its investment, given an initial deployment cost of $300,000 for the IPSS.

The financial advantages of deploying a caching architecture are compelling for the typical service provider. Consider a network-side cache with the following assumptions:

Cost per Mbps/month to the provider	$700
Cost of T3/year to the provider	$380,000
Cachable traffic	40 percent of the T3 = 18 Mbps
Hit rate	40 percent of the cached traffic = 7.2 Mbps

Based on these assumptions, the savings per year on the T3 are $60,480. Given that a carrier-class network cache is on the order of $70,000, the payback period for the deployment is 14 months. The cache also results in surge protection across the T3 and performance enhancements from the perspective of the subscriber.

Caches face some ongoing problems regarding subscriber tracking. Traditional cache architectures presented problems if the creator of the content was expecting statistics on impressions for advertising. This resulted in the content providers tagging more and more Web content as noncachable, many times defeating the intent of caching. Offline statistics processing is a possibility, though it is somewhat complex to implement. Caching does have identified advantages, however. In a study by CacheFlow, Web page response times for DSL subscribers were reduced from about 10 seconds to 2 seconds. If the results for DSL were this good, you can imagine the results for dial. Major cache vendors include Cisco, Inktomi, Cacheflow, and Volera.

More recently, a new type of dynamic server-side (origin) caching known as *content condensation,* first introduced by FineGround, has been made available. For example, say that at the beginning of the day, a user first accesses a Web site. With no Web cache in place, all HTML and graphics information is delivered because no information is cached locally. A second visit to the site finds that most of the user interface graphics are cached locally and only the updated HTML and ad information is transmitted. On a typical Web page, this reduces the amount of information by about 50 percent, resulting in less bandwidth required and a quicker download time. If the content provider implements edge caching, further optimizations are possible. This cache fulfills the ad and content graphics needs because other users have probably requested the same information. Only about a third of the original page is therefore transmitted. The final step is the implementation of the condensation technology at the origin servers, reducing the amount of changed HTML transmitted to the order of a few kilobytes. The net result is a savings in both bandwidth and download time.

In a large cache deployment, a host or service provider may have numerous caches deployed. To ensure that caches communicate effectively with routers or Web switches, protocols were developed for intercache communication. The Cisco Web Cache Coordination Protocol (WCCP) (Cieslak, 2000) is a good example of this type of protocol. WCCP provides for the following:

- Discovery of the caches of each other
- Load distribution of the caching across a number of physical cache devices
- Connection of a cache to multiple routers
- Security between the router and cache
- Procedure for the cache to decline a cache request

Although many companies are developing additional protocols beyond WCCP for cache discovery and mappings, WCCP currently is the most common.

Content Switching

Content switches, Layer 4 through 7 switches, and Web switches are common names for *server load balancers,* a class of device that provides server acceleration. There are two main classes of server load balancers. The first are *local load balancers,* collocated with the origin servers, distributing incoming Web traffic across multiple servers and bypassing any that are unavailable. The content provider does not really have an incentive to deploy server-side (reverse proxy) Web caching, since most static content is cached at the edge of the network. Server-side caching would just add additional complexity. *Global load balancers* operate by providing the authoritative DNS reply for a given URL domain name. Traffic to a given domain can therefore be distributed to multiple data centers, avoiding sites that may be temporarily unavailable.

Content switching includes the switching functions required to direct the user accessing content to the right content server at the origin site. The benefit of content switching is the ability to load-balance caches and origin servers and, by doing so, help manage flash crowds by directing users to less utilized or crowded content servers. Thanks to content switches, the annual Victoria's Secret catalog launch can be viewed easily by people worldwide.

Content Switch Features

Content switches consist of combination hardware and software or pure software applications that can run on a multipurpose computing machine. The content switch is used in front of a series of Web servers and caches. Some of the common features of a content switch are as follows:

- High-performance cache redirection
- Local and global server load balancing
- Firewall load balancing
- The ability to handle a high rate of HTTP requests
- A large choice of interfaces
- Bandwidth management
- QoS support
- Routing (though not on the level of core routers)
- Network address translation (NAT)
- Redundancy

Content switches interact more effectively with Web caches and servers than do traditional routers, since they operate up to the application layer in some cases. They are capable of identifying Web traffic requests and directing the subscriber to the proper reverse proxy cache or local content server. For example, a content switch may route a given URL requesting a specific content object to a server that is optimized for commerce or for streaming media. It accomplishes this by relying on cookies inserted into the subscriber's browser for HTTP or SSL session identifiers embedded in HTTPS.

A *cookie* identifies the subscriber and permits a content switch to track a given session to a commerce server, to name one example. It may go beyond this by offering enhanced session QoS if the commerce site identifies frequent customers via the cookies. Since a visit will consist of multiple TCP sessions, this is the only way to track an individual subscriber. The content switch operates by terminating the subscriber's initial TCP connection and then reissuing the request to the best server available. This is sometimes known as *TCP splicing* (see Figure 4.2).

Cookies do have their downside, as described in the sidebar "Maintaining State." In fact, even the source IP address is not guaranteed to be static because of the use of proxy servers and NAT.

Content Management

```
Subscriber                    Content Switch                     Web Servers
    |─────────── 1 ───────────>|─────────── 2 ───────────>|
```

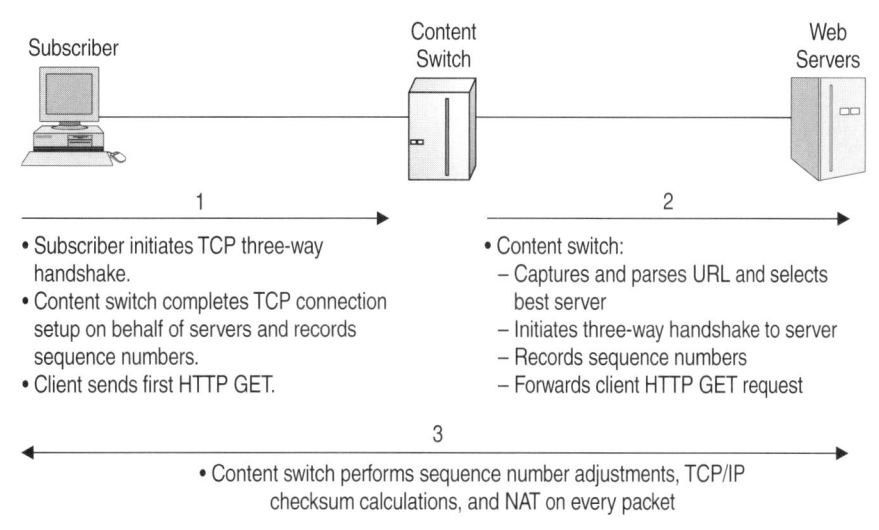

- Subscriber initiates TCP three-way handshake.
- Content switch completes TCP connection setup on behalf of servers and records sequence numbers.
- Client sends first HTTP GET.

- Content switch:
  – Captures and parses URL and selects best server
  – Initiates three-way handshake to server
  – Records sequence numbers
  – Forwards client HTTP GET request

```
        <─────────────── 3 ───────────────>
```
- Content switch performs sequence number adjustments, TCP/IP checksum calculations, and NAT on every packet

FIGURE 4.2 TCP Splicing

Content switches are a fairly new class of internetworking device, operating on URLs, applications, and even actual data such as an e-mail header or the contents of a graphics file. Content switches are one of many equipment pieces coexisting with the various Layer 2 and Layer 3 switches, routers, IPSSs, and physical aggregation devices found within a provider's PoP or data center. Although content switches do not fall directly into the IPSS category, they many times operate in conjunction with these devices within the data center. In the future, with advances in technology, many IPSSs may incorporate most, if not all, current content-switching capabilities. One may envision content-switching capability implemented on a card and added on demand if the provider requires it. Better-known content switching vendors include Nortel Networks' Alteon Web Systems, Foundry's BigIron, Cisco's ArrowPoint, and F5 Networks' Big-IP.

The total capacity of a given platform is an important parameter; it determines whether the platform can be placed in the data path for all subscriber traffic or for a subset of the traffic, or whether it should operate as more of a server, adjunct to the data path. For example, Layer 2 switches (the traditional LAN switches), and, more recently, Layer 3/4 switches, scale to 100 Gbps or more (see Figure 4.3). They form the core of many PoPs and connect the subscriber-side devices (for example, RASs, DSLAMs, CMTS headends, IPSSs) to the core routers and to the server farms. Since the beginning of 2001, Web redirectors, content caches, and IP-VPN devices have offered anywhere from 100 Mbps to 10 Gbps maximum throughput. It is therefore essential that the provider forward to these devices

◆ Maintaining State

Early video distribution models required that the subscriber start watching movies and other content at a fixed time. Customers are far happier, however, with the model offered by the video recorder, where they can stop and start viewing content at their discretion. In the retail segment, customers are happiest if they are recognized when they go into a store, and the salesperson knows their preferences.

To offer a service as flexible as a VCR or a retail store, Internet servers and clients operated by a given content or commerce provider must retain state on the status of active transactions, and possibly on the history of the user's activity. The retention of state presents both technical and privacy issues, though most individuals now consider this retention as part of the price of effectively doing business over the Internet.

The two basic strategies for maintaining state are to store state information on the server (or set of servers) and to store state information on the subscriber client. The first method tends to require a means of identifying the client, such as a login. The second method is commonly associated with cookies stored on the client.

Although cookies help to streamline e-commerce and access to content, they do have their downside in that a given Web site is capable of identifying a subscriber, along with the content viewed. If the subscriber has conducted commerce at the site, a great deal of information may be known. This is not a problem if the Web site does not redistribute this data. Unfortunately, many sites offer this information to third parties, usually to advertisers. These agencies may correlate cookies from multiple Web sites to build a complete profile of a given subscriber. This correlation is not too difficult, given identification information such as the subscriber's IP address. At the extreme, Web site viewing habits may be used against a given user by slowing his or her response times.

Consider the following cookies from a Netscape browser:

```
some-browser.com   TRUE/FALSE   1293839397   UIDC
    199.242.50.141:0952131438:448515
www.some-airline.com   FALSE/FALSE   1293753600
    XX_ID199.242.50.141-787351648.29329187
```

Two different Web sites have gathered the subscriber's identity via an Internet provider address. Cookies also include usernames, with correlation a possibility because the majority of users enter the same name when queried at a new Web site. Other cookies are more difficult to decrypt, but may still contain the subscriber's encoded IP address or username, as in the following case:

```
some-news.com   TRUE/FALSE   1281665642   xxxid   Gcf1947fb-11339-952736464-1
```

FIGURE 4.3 Switch Throughput

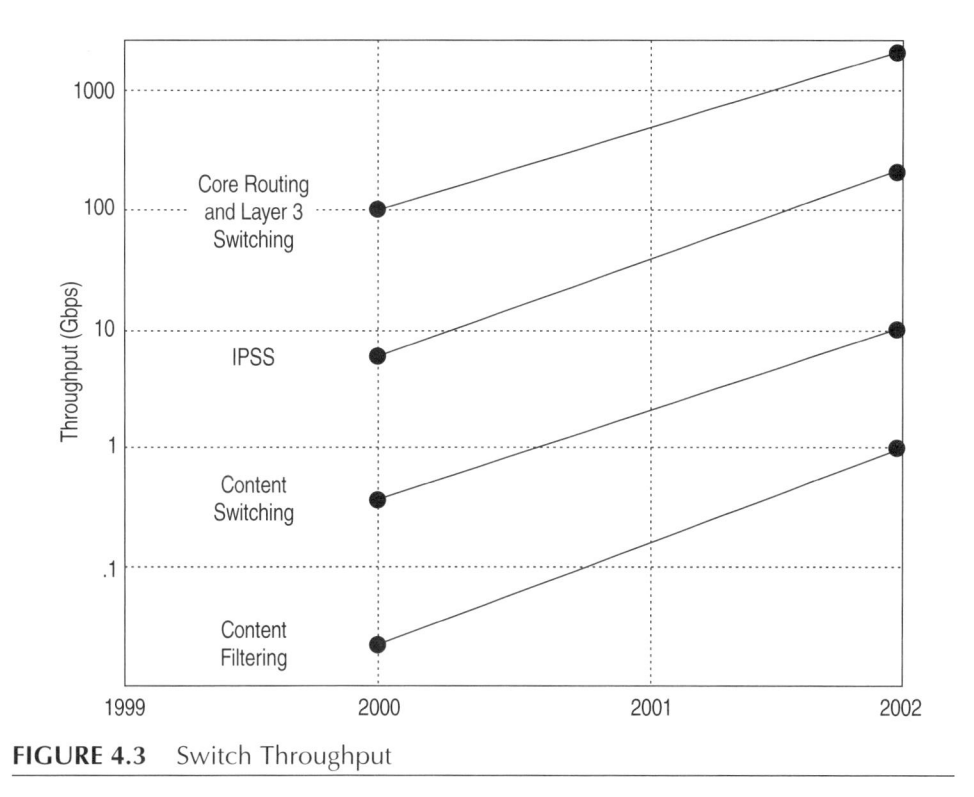

only traffic that is relevant to a given service. Finally, full-content filters are limited to about 10 Mbps, though this is expected to increase in the future. For this scalability reason, full-content filtering is a limited service within the service provider at present (although it enjoys wide use within the enterprise).

Although early content switches were derived from off-the-shelf hardware, the current generation of hardware relies on custom ASICs for Layer 2 through 7 switching and on very sophisticated software. Depending on the capacity of the system, it will rely on a bus or a switching fabric. Data enters the system through a variety of interface types and is held in queues for processing.

Content Routing

Determination of the best content delivery site is the responsibility of content routing, a function of traditional routers. A new device, called the *request-to-content router*, is being introduced in content networking. In much the same way that a traditional Layer 3 router would send a packet on the best path to its destination, the content router looks at the content request (the URL) and sends the user to the best content site. Content routing also adapts to network failures and congestion.

In typical deployments, a user requests content via a URL. The URL maps to a domain that the content originator (for example, *www.allegronetworks.com*) has placed under the control of a content distribution architecture. The subscriber's request is routed to the closest content cache, determined by a number of techniques. If the content is available at the cache, it is served locally; if not, the cache requests the content from the origin server.

Traditional content routing is DNS-based in that a user would request content via an HTTP request to *www.thirasystems.com*, for example. The request would be sent to the DNS server to resolve *www.thirasystems.com* to an IP address. If the local DNS server could not resolve the address, it would forward it to the authoritative DNS server. This server, if it were content-routing-enabled, would resolve the request to the IP address closest to the local DNS server. The concern with this type of resolution is that the selected content site is closest to the DNS server and not necessarily the user (although often the local DNS server is close to the user machine). The other disadvantage is that the DNS does not support Layer 7 attributes, nor does it look into the actual HTTP request to understand the specific content being sought. New content routers are being offered that can inspect the packet and determine the optimum content location closest to the user. The request is then redirected to this optimal site. This is accomplished by a variety of techniques, one of which is a race between various content sites to see who gets to the user first. The winner becomes the site to route content to until the next race, in which a new winner may be found.

Using a more sophisticated content router allows content providers to better segment their servers and achieve better reliability. Imagine a typical scenario where a content provider may have an HTTP server along with a Wireless Access Protocol (WAP) server. Suppose that the WAP server fails. In a typical DNS-based content-routing scenario, the defective site is removed from the list of active content sites. Unfortunately, this means also taking out the HTTP server even though it is functioning correctly. An L7-based content router would understand whether the request was an HTTP browser or a WAP browser and accommodate the request accordingly. The content request then arrives at the content edge, which is responsible for the delivery of content to the subscriber and includes caching and streaming media services (both video and audio).

Content Distribution and Management

Content distribution and management include provisioning of the content delivery, monitoring, and ensuring that any content delivered to the subscriber is current. In order to provide the best content experience, there are several challenges to overcome in content distribution (see Table 4.1).

The need to properly address content distribution issues is accentuated by the fact that 50 percent of Internet users are outside of the United States, whereas 80 percent of the content is in the United States (Gilder, 2000). Fetching one Web

Content Management

TABLE 4.1 Content Distribution Challenges

Challenge	Possible Solution
Bandwidth constraint	Add additional bandwidth to the network. This is already occurring, as observed in the optical core buildout and its extensions to the optical metro, though the routed network edge is still a bottleneck.
Server overload	Add additional servers and load balancers to ensure good content distribution and server response.
Speed-of-light delay	New experiments claim to beat the speed of light. However, the easiest course of action is to locate the content servers closer to the subscriber and optimize paths.
State retention	To have the provider offer a service as flexible as a VCR and as personalized as a retail store, the content store must maintain state for each individual user.

object takes as many as seven round trips, resulting in an average Web delay per object of 300 to 600 msec or more. As a result, since most global users have to traverse large distances to get to the United States for the content source, this introduces significant delay. Solving the content distribution and delivery problem will go a long way in bringing the broadband service experience to subscribers.

The basic method of improving content distribution is to have content as close as possible to the content user. The conceptual content distribution model can be seen as a tree, with content creation at its root and many content distribution points near users. These content distribution points store static or dynamic content, but, in either case, they buffer between content provider and content subscriber, reducing the amount of bandwidth and server processing the content provider must provide directly to users. Moving content distribution closer to the user also minimizes speed-of-light delay. Holding state information is a problem to be solved by retaining state in smaller servers only for the group of subscribers connected to that server.

To better understand content distribution and management, let's look at the evolution of content distribution. We will also examine the impact of streaming content, as well as the role of digital rights management and hosted applications in content distribution networks.

The Evolution of Content Distribution

Initially, corporations manually replicated their Web content by copying files between servers, both for intranet users and for those accessing content from the Internet (see Figure 4.4, Scenario 1). This solution was called *mirroring,* or using *mirrored sites*. One advantage of this solution is the elimination of delays in data retrieval caused by distance. As an example, establishing a connection between a Web browser in the United States and a server in Asia may take on the order of

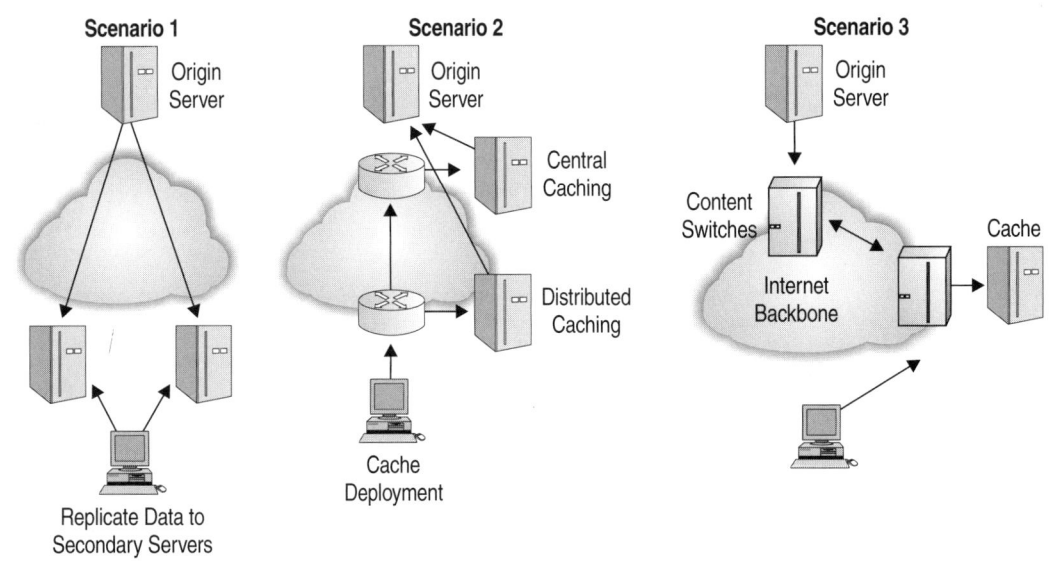

FIGURE 4.4 Content Distribution Evolution

seconds. The immediate effect of replication is therefore a reduction in the latency for Web page downloads. This, in turn, has a direct effect on revenue for commerce sites in high-latency environments, borne out by the following statistic: For a typical 70 Kb Web page, over 50 percent of people attempting to download this content abandon the operation before it is completed (Zona, 1999a). This results in a loss of billions of dollars each year in terms of advertising revenue for portals, sales revenue for commerce sites, and event revenue for streaming media sites. However, mirroring does not provide intelligent routing of the content and provides no guarantee that the content will in fact be served from the server closest to the subscriber (unless the content is generated and hosted locally).

With the deployment of the various caching, content-switching, and data-replication architectures, the network has evolved to include content-distribution intelligence (see Scenarios 2 and 3 in Figure 4.4). This includes provisions for traffic monitoring and analysis within the network, permitting providers to identify which content should be replicated or cached. In addition, it permits scheduled content delivery if this is part of the provider's business model. Part of this infrastructure will include interfaces to existing billing and operational systems. A good example of this is the Akamai network, which permits content providers to preposition select content more closely to the subscribers on a global basis through caching and network intelligence.

Figure 4.5 illustrates the Akamai architecture. It consists of a large number of geographically dispersed servers connected across the Internet and used to preposition content belonging to customers of the Akamai service. These customers

Content Management 111

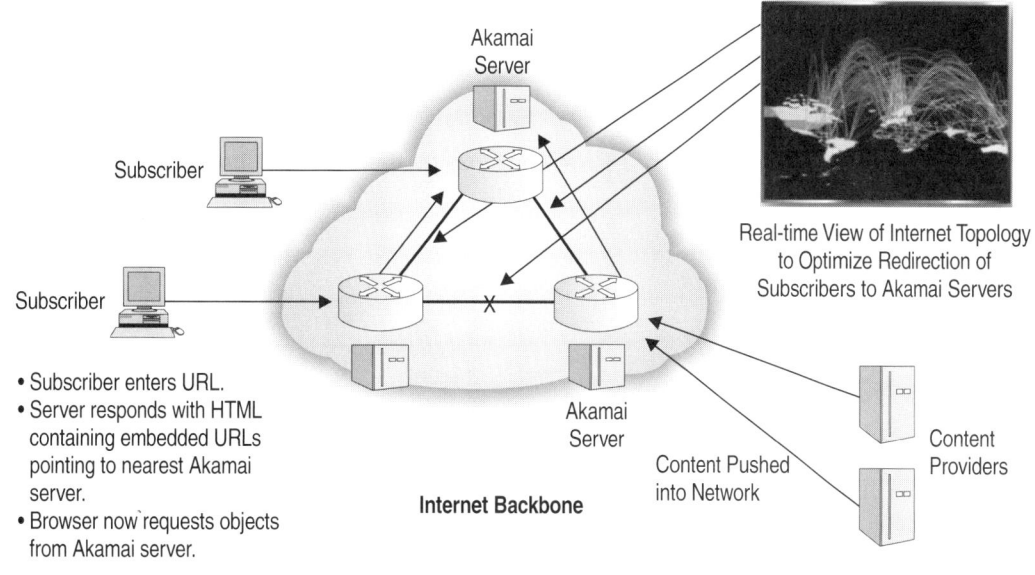

FIGURE 4.5 Akamai Architecture

tag certain Web content, which is then distributed to these servers. A subscriber accessing the customer's Web site is first served the original home page, permitting visitor counting and placement of cookies. However, if the subscriber now requests content that has been distributed to an Akamai server, the returned URL points to this server. In fact, up to 90 percent of typical Web content may be distributed in this way. The choice of server, and therefore the actual Akamai URL, depends on the real-time state of the network in terms of network and server loading, performance, and, most important, reachability. Digital Island offers a content-distribution service much like that offered by Akamai.

One type of content distribution is the ability to automatically distribute browser content. An evolution from the early push technologies of a few years back, or the polling technologies currently in use that require a client to periodically query a server, newer architectures create a persistent connection between the server and the user's browser. As information is updated (for example, financial data), it is distributed to the user as objects across an overlay network (see Figure 4.6). The technology developed by Bang Networks is one example of this. A Web server is equipped with a "data pump," which delivers updates into an overlay consisting of content routers. These routers are distributed across the Internet backbone and maintain user session state for up to millions of endpoints. Content that is to take this path is tagged with HTML extensions. In addition to simply displaying the distributed content in a browser window, it may also be fed into a client-side application via an API. This permits further processing.

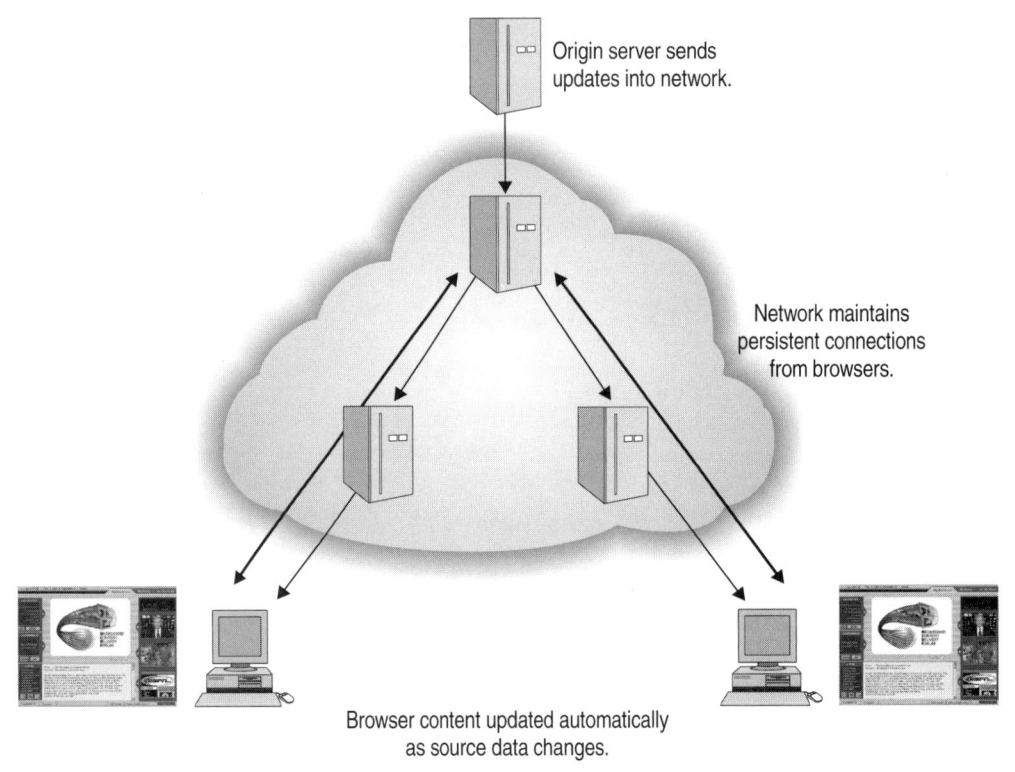

FIGURE 4.6 Dynamic Updates

Other types of intelligence include the ability to target content based on the subscriber's location. One system, Quova's GeoPoint, relies on a user's IP address to determine the location via a database lookup. As these databases become more sophisticated, they will be better able to handle subscribers whose IP addresses do not necessarily correlate with their actual location (for example, through the use of tunneling architectures or toll-free numbers). The system permits geographic-specific content, advertising, or even the locking out of certain content based on the user's location (for example, a movie not available in a certain country).

Streaming Content

The next level in sophistication for content networking is the support of real-time streaming media. This has always presented a challenge to network engineers because of the need to efficiently replicate thousands of streams across a wide area. When folks speak of scaling the Internet to the size of a broadcast network, they are usually talking about streaming media. And, if you judge scalability by a typical performance experienced during some of the more popular online concerts or fashion shows, the Internet has a long way to go, as it is barely able to support a large number of narrowband streams, much less streams at broadband rates. The media distribution architectures now in place are designed to address this problem by incorporating intelligent replication of the data within the core of the network. Proprietary techniques that include provisions for retransmission are used to distribute the content to the network edge. At this point, the edge caches generate the individual subscriber streams. Note that initial deployments, such as that put in place by Akamai, do not rely on native support within the network for IP multicast (IPmc) because multicast support across multiple providers (or even within a single ISP) is not a given.

A different approach is that offered by Cisco (via its Sightpath acquisition) and Volera (a Novell spin-off). The Sightpath and Volera solutions include centralized content control, distribution of the content to servers closer to the subscribers, and redirection of subscriber Web requests to these edge servers (see Figure 4.7). A difference in this architecture and network caching is the ability to push the content to the distributed caches ahead of any subscriber requests. This approach consists of intelligent content-routing functions that work to redirect a content request to the nearest server from the perspective of the subscriber. The network administrator selects which content to replicate, either entire Web sites or single files, and establishes via the DNS (or a request-to-content router) a rule to reroute all requests for this content. The relevant content is then replicated to servers at the edge (Step 1 in Figure 4.7). Now, when subscribers request this content via a

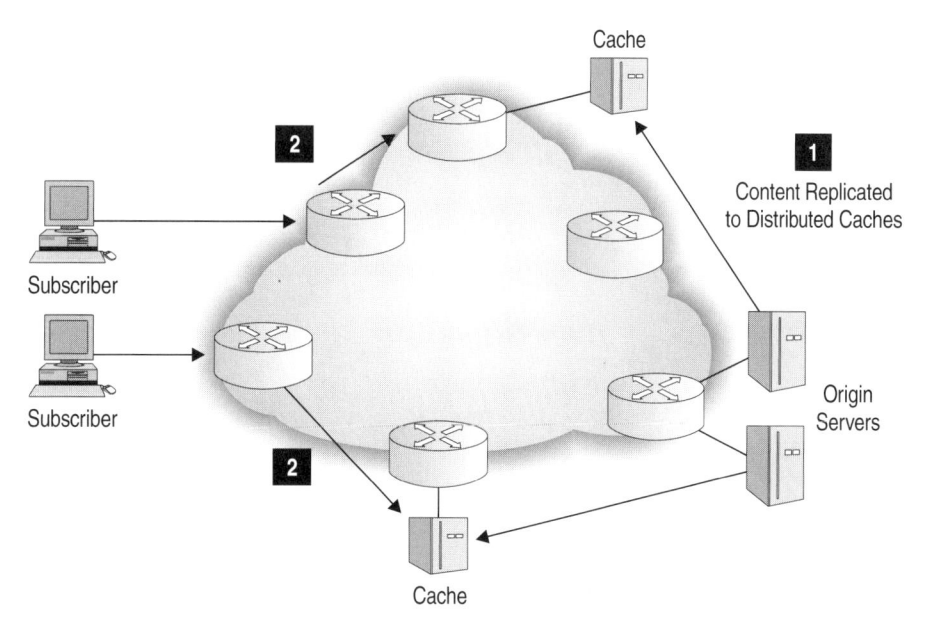

FIGURE 4.7   Content Distribution

URL, they are redirected to the nearest server based on proximity, presence of the content, server loading and availability, and network loading (Step 2 in Figure 4.7).

Yet another approach, offered by iBlast, is designed to eliminate the "last-mile" bottleneck of best-effort residential broadband. Instead of relying on conventional technologies such as DSL or cable modems for delivery, iBlast streams content via digital broadcast signals. A backbone network connects content suppliers and the broadcasters, and the iBlast signal occupies a 7 Mbps slice of a single digital channel. This still leaves room for an HDTV broadcast signal. The 7 Mbps feed is capable of delivering 150 GB of content to a market over the course of a day, content that may include videos, music, localized news, magazines, computer programs, and games. The system relies on the availability of cheap storage at the household, with the subscriber selecting the desired content ahead of time. This content, protected via digital rights management (DRM) techniques if applicable, is then available locally. Even more sophisticated means of identifying and delivering content have been proposed.

The Content Tunnel (CT) protocol, which is under development, involves creating a QoS-assured path between a given subscriber and requested content (see Figure 4.8). Devices along the data path recognize these CT requests and direct

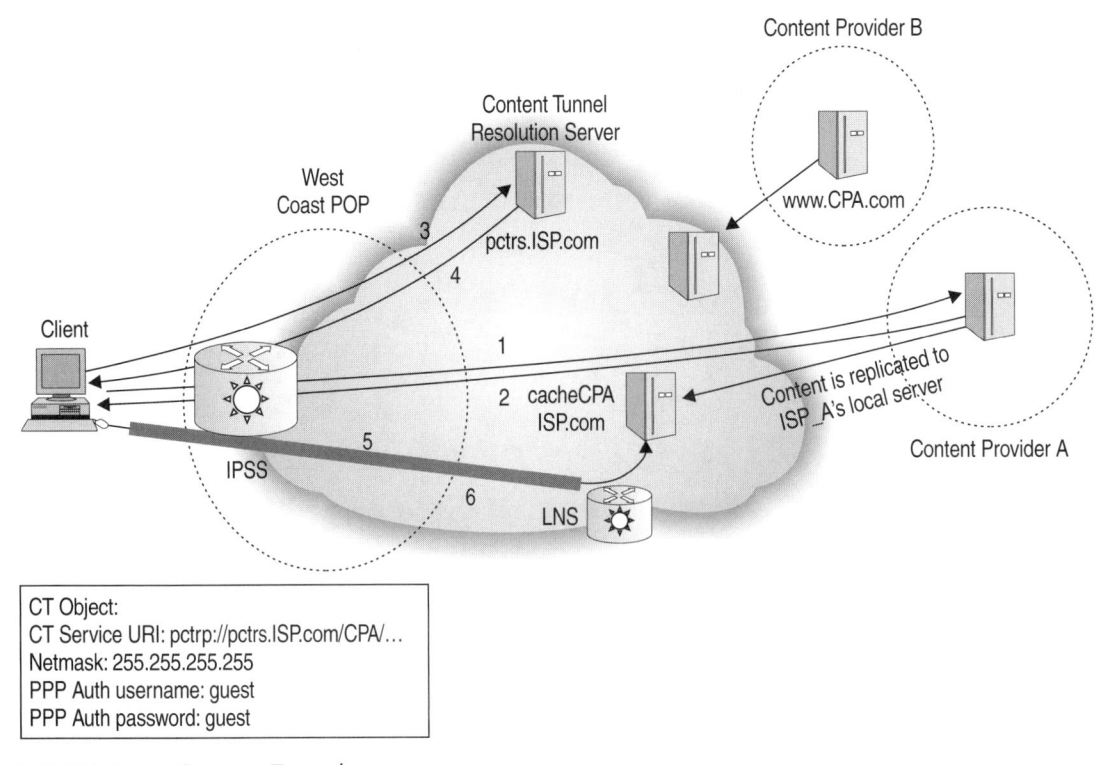

FIGURE 4.8 Content Tunnels

them to the nearest server capable of servicing the request. Content could be locally cached or made available at a central site depending on the size and geographic distribution of the subscribers interested in the content. The CT permits the service or content provider to offer on-demand content and to bill accordingly.

A CT implies some way of identifying a given content object. This object may be as simple as a JPEG image or as complex as a broadcast news feed. Although the various forms of content may seem chaotic, they are in fact well defined in terms of a number of basic parameters, including source, restrictions (in terms of audience and network capabilities), QoS, and cost. To accomplish this identification, we may define a universal content locator (UCL)—a tag identifying the content in terms of these parameters. For example, a news photo may have a certain encoding, may be unrestricted in terms of audience, may be free to an end subscriber but not to an ISP, and may have no QoS requirements (other than differences in download speed over different access media). Other images, intended for more specific audiences (of the naughty variety) may include restrictions and will probably require payment from both service providers and subscribers. A motion picture will include QoS components as well as restrictions and costs. Finally, a real-time video feed will definitely impose end-to-end QoS requirements on the network. Note that a content object may also reference a program or service offered by an ASP. Possible parameters for the UCL include the following:

- *Source*
- *Size:* KBytes, MBytes, GBytes
- *QoS:* Minimum streaming rate at a given encoding—in other words, MPEG1, MPEG2, MP3, proprietary, and so forth
- *Restrictions:* Associated with encoding—in other words, do not permit transmission at less than MPEG2; may also relate to the subscriber—in other words, rating, geography, IP-VPN member
- *Cost:* The content object at a given QoS; may include costs for partial or full delivery; may also include parameters for payment—in other words, subscriber, service provider, content provider pays, and so forth

The CT could be deployed to dynamically adapt content to the subscriber's access technology. For example, the subscriber may have selected a set of content sites via a portal. At home, via DSL or cable, a certain QoS is possible. However, when mobile, the QoS capabilities of a 3G wireless system are quite different. Improving the QoS of mobile systems is the goal of content-mediation servers, now being deployed, which are capable of adapting content for a particular technology.

Under actual operation, CTs could function as follows (see Figure 4.8). The subscriber, via his or her browser, issues a request for the URI (Step 1) *http://www.CPA.com/trailers.clip.avi*. This arrives at the content server, and instead of returning the actual content, it returns a CT object (Step 2). Note that this is no different from the techniques used for other types of content delivery networks. The CT object (Step 3), of the form *pctrp://pctrs.ISP.com/CPA/trailers/clip.avi,* is now resolved by the CT resolution server. This server returns the best location for the requested content (Step 4 in Figure 4.8), in this case *http://cacheCPA.ISP.com/trailers/clip.avi.* The subscriber now opens a connection to this cache, in this case an L2TP tunnel (Step 5), and the requested content is viewed (Step 6).

In this example, the cache is located within the access provider's backbone, with the assumption that all access PoPs have adequate bandwidth across the backbone to the content cache. An alternative places the cache at each access PoP, closer to the subscriber but requiring additional replication. Yet another possibility is to direct the subscriber via tunnels directly back to the content provider. This assumes adequate bandwidth between the access provider and the content provider, but provides the content provider with additional control. In any case, the content provider must have some means of effectively delivering the content into the access provider's network. Ultimate control of this delivery may be achieved through a routed overlay, separate from the access provider's network and guaranteeing both QoS and security.

Digital Rights Management

Closely related to any content distribution architecture is the ability to track and secure the content itself. This field is known as digital rights management, and has been in the forefront of most debates concerning how and when to distribute content across the Internet. In fact, probably the most visible Internet policy issue of the past few years—that surrounding *Napster.com*—focused on DRM issues.

When a content provider sends content that has value into the network, it must have an assurance that only those subscribers who have paid for the content will be able to make use of it. The most common technique at present is a client program that interacts with requested content that is downloaded in a nonviewable form onto the subscriber's hard disk. The reason for this download, as opposed to viewing online via some streaming technology, is that most Internet connections (even DSL and cable) cannot support real-time, high-quality video. As an example, the subscriber wishes to download a certain video and then have access to it for 24 hours. Via the client program, the subscriber accesses the provider's Web site, makes a payment, and receives a decryption key permitting viewing for the day.

One problem is that, as of yet, there is no single DRM standard. The result is a proliferation of PC clients for each distributor or provider, much like the proliferation of browser plug-ins for different media types. More important, the studios have been slow to open their archives, fearing piracy and loss of control. It is hoped the current generation of DRM schemes will address this. In fact, in comparison to the widespread piracy of DVDs across the Internet due to the cracking of the DVD security scheme (though not the "mass" piracy of MP3 because of the file size of the typical "ripped" DVD), the existing DRM mechanisms seem pretty secure.

Hosted Applications

One use of a content distribution architecture is in support of applications hosted by service providers. Here, an application service provider (ASP) works with application developers to offer hosted applications to telecommuters, the SOHO market, and small and medium enterprises. Types of applications include sales tracking, payroll, and database, to name a few. When using hosted applications, the subscriber is no longer relying on the service provider for basic connectivity—it is now relying on the provider for its very livelihood. Therefore, the techniques that have been described in this section, along with the various security, traffic management, and IP-VPN architecture described in the previous sections, are critical.

Video Distribution

Although closely related to the content distribution described in the previous section, high-quality video distribution is a very different service because of the demands placed on the network as well as the financial model driving this service. In a repeat of early DSL pilots that focused on video, service providers are now looking to the various broadband access media (most notably DSL and metro Ethernet) as a basis for entertainment-quality video distribution. Driving this is the need to compete against cable operators offering high-speed Internet connectivity, telephony (traditional or VoIP), and, of course, video distribution. The move toward video distribution over the Internet is a major shift in strategy for both the broadcast industry and networking in general and is the first time bandwidth and quality demands have been placed on an IP infrastructure for such a wide audience. Unlike in the early trials, the networking hardware, servers, and clients now exist to make this application financially viable with incremental up-front investments.

In its simplest form, the access provider, acting as an ISP, peers with the various broadcasters, delivering video at multiple levels depending on the application. "Entertainment quality" is usually MPEG2 at about 3.5 Mbps, while special interest programs and secondary feeds for primary programs are at MPEG1 rates (1.5 Mbps). A typical offering will also support lower rate streaming at about 300 to 800 Kbps. Over time, as technology advances, these rates are expected to increase, with a goal of delivering HDTV-quality video to the subscriber. The integration of the broadcast feed with IP lends itself to the concept of "interactive TV," providing a two-way path between the content provider and the subscriber. For example, a sports program may display statistics and replays, while a game show may include online quizzes (possibly for money, where permitted). The client is either a PC or, more commonly, an IP-enabled settop box. Chapter 1 dealt with these types of Internet-enabled appliances for a much more diverse audience than that currently served by PCs.

Broadcast video distribution introduces some challenges for DSL providers because of bandwidth requirements. Consider a provider wishing to compete with the cable providers, offering upward of 50 feeds to the subscribers. If these feeds were delivered individually to each and every subscriber, the required bandwidth would quickly exceed that available within most DSL access networks and would also destroy the cost model. In the majority of cases, multiple subscribers attached to the DSLAMs within a given CO will wish to receive the same video feed. This is very much the case for the three to five major networks within a given service area. Since this video distribution is at the IP layer, we must have a way of effectively replicating the data. This is the role of IP multicasting, with IP-equipped DSLAMs or DSLAMs operating in conjunction with collocated multicast engines responsible for data replication (see Figure 4.9). Under this solution, only one copy of a given broadcast feed must traverse the access network. In addition, the IPSS forwards to the DSLAMs only those feeds actually requested. Even if 1,000 subscribers are served from a given CO, it is unlikely they will request more than 50 channels at any given time. Therefore, a single OC3/STM1 will suffice in most cases. In a metro Ethernet environment, bandwidth is less of an issue, though the CLE located in MDUs/MTUs must still support IP multicast. Subscriber selection of a given channel is via the PC, a settop box, or a network-based portal.

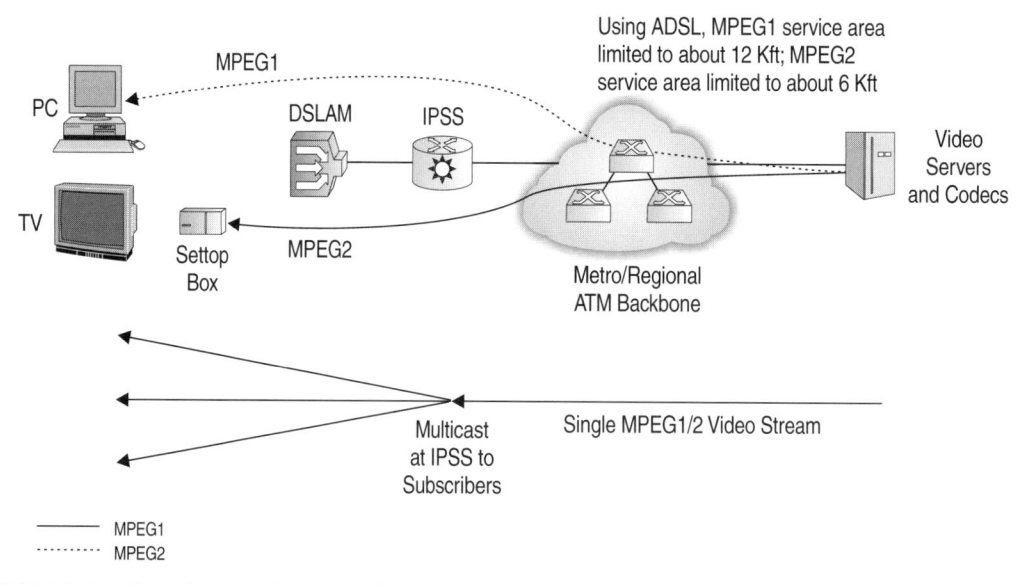

FIGURE 4.9 Broadcast Video Distribution Architecture

Voice Distribution

Voice support at the subscriber edge is a complex topic but a source of great potential revenue for the service provider. It is a natural extension of broadband access deployment, in that the provider may now optimize use of the copper pair. In the past, a copper pair supported a single analog phone line or, at most, 64 Kbps of data. Although some enterprises deployed technology capable of supporting multiple voice channels, this technology did not apply to the telecommuter or small office. This is because most of these technologies relied on a T1 or fractional T1, with a breakeven at six to nine voice channels. The coupling of the voice technologies described in this section with Internet access will help drive the overall business case, as described in chapter 1. Depending on the physical access technology—be it DSL, cable, wireless, or leased line—this voice support will take a number of forms. Whether the provider forwards the traffic into the PSTN or offers an end-to-end Internet telephony service will also influence the architecture and the types of services offered. One thing is in common: Most of the technologies support the full range of traditional voice services, permitting use as a primary line replacement for small businesses and telecommuters. ILECs, CLECs, and MSOs may all benefit from these architectures. However, the CLECs and MSOs may have the most to gain, in that they may offer an integrated voice and data service for the first time.

To implement a voice distribution network, an understanding of the underlying voice protocols is required. Beyond that, voice services can be implemented over a variety of networks. Here, we look at ATM-based and IP-based voice service implementations in addition to some other technologies supporting voice-based services.

Voice Protocols

Next-generation voice services rely on the necessary server and gateway architecture, as well as on a set of protocols handling voice encoding, signaling, and management. H.323 is one such protocol that may be familiar to many. It was originally developed within the ITU for videoconferencing but now has been adapted for VoIP. The protocol includes end terminals, voice gateways, gatekeepers, and multipoint control units (MCUs) for multipoint conferencing (see Figure 4.10). The end terminals, usually PCs at present, support signaling and contain the voice-coding capability (codecs). Gateways interface the packet to the voice network, while gatekeepers, optional to the architecture, support functions such as admission and bandwidth control. Although many in the industry consider H.323 as dated or less flexible than more modern standards, it does have a large installed base. The Session Initiation Protocol (SIP), in contrast, has its roots in the Internet community and is considered by many to be more scalable and easier to implement because of

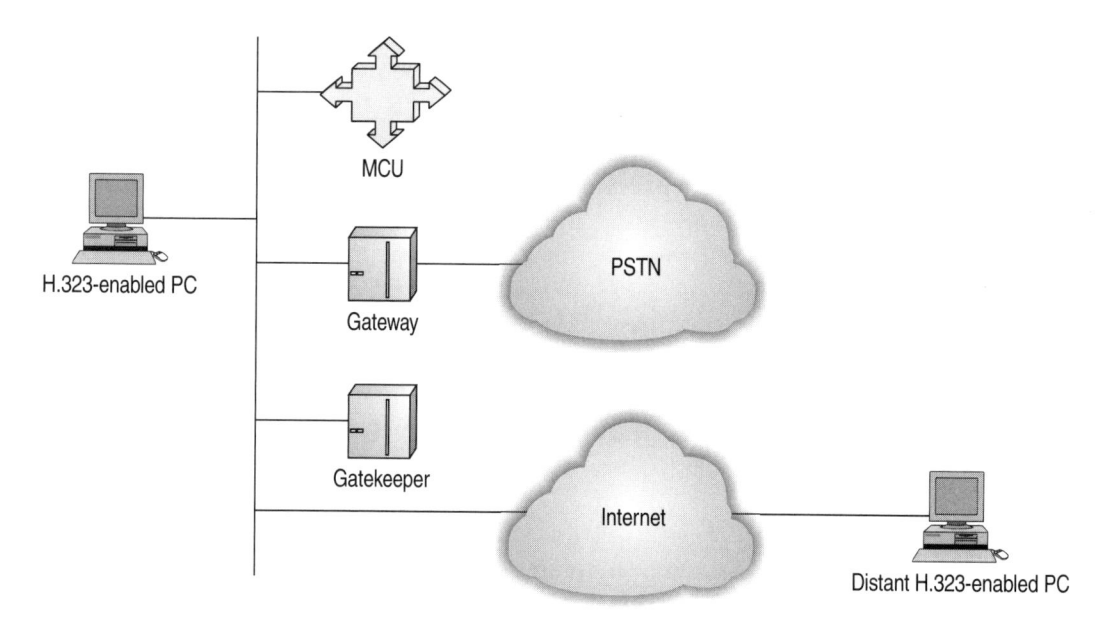

FIGURE 4.10 H.323 Voice Architecture

a simpler message structure. It also offers greater interoperability with other Internet protocols, such as IPSec.

Unlike H.323 and SIP, the Media Gateway Control Protocol (MGCP) runs internal to a network and is used by call agents (also called *soft switches*) to control media gateways connecting the packet network to the PSTN as well as signaling gateways for Signaling System 7 (SS7)—the PSTN signaling and control system—conversion. Figure 4.11 contrasts the encapsulations for the different voice protocols.

H.323, SIP, and MGCP protocols form the core of a next-generation IP telephony network. Within an MGCP deployment, SIP or H.323 could be used between the client and the media gateway. However, MGCP also supports lightweight (dumb) clients. These could be connected to a settop box under the control of MGCP. Megaco is an evolution of MGCP (plus MDCP) and is undergoing standardization within the ITU as H.248.

ATM-Based Voice Services

The ATM-based voice services rely on an integrated access device (IAD) at the subscriber site and a PSTN gateway within the provider's network (see Figure 4.12). This architecture encapsulates the subscriber voice traffic in an ATM AAL2 for carriage over the provider's metropolitan ATM network to the gateway.

In the case of VoDSL, the IAD establishes one or more additional AAL5 PVCs for the data traffic. In this environment, the DSLAM must be equipped with adequate

Voice Distribution

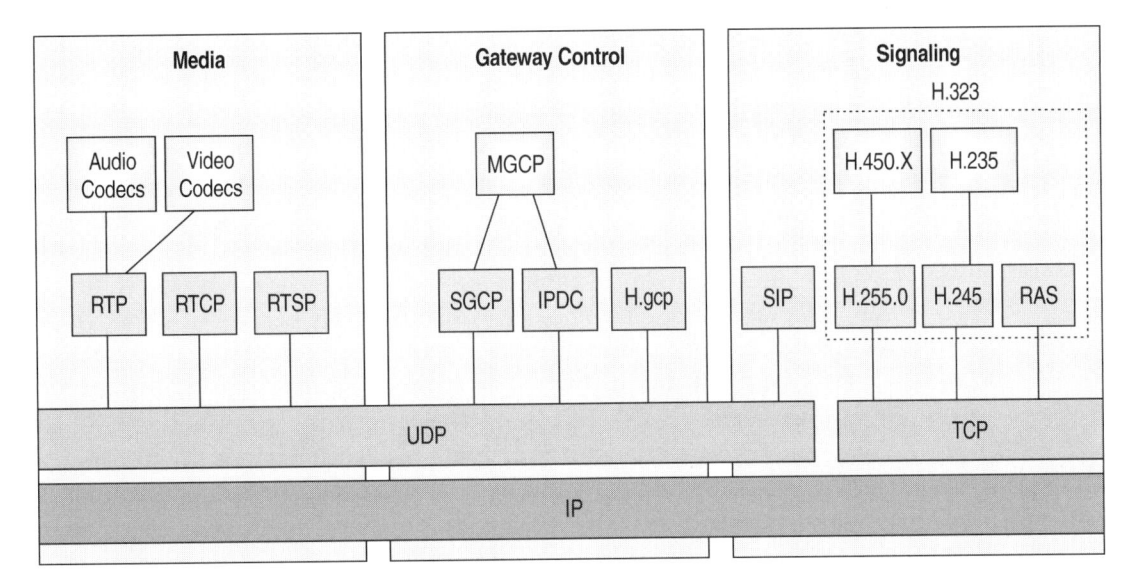

FIGURE 4.11 Voice Protocol Comparison

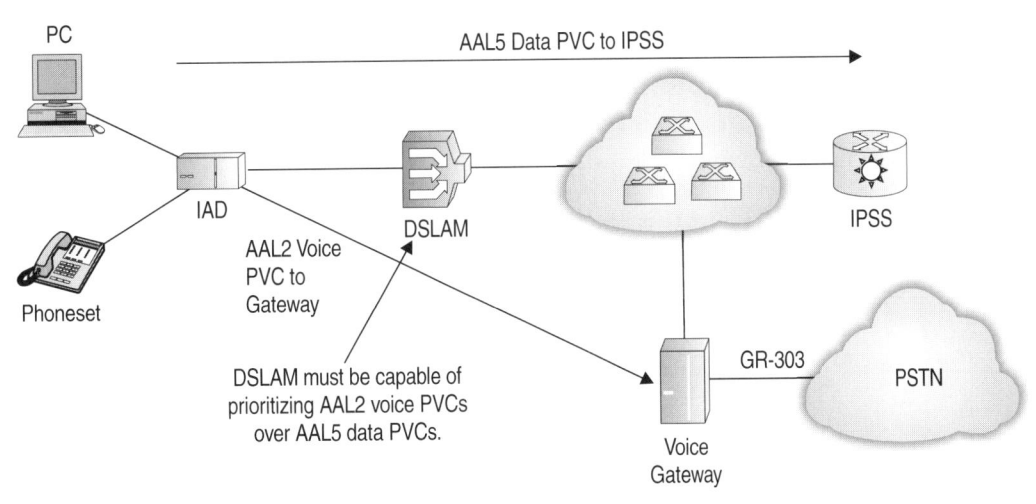

FIGURE 4.12 ATM Voice IAD and PSTN Gateway

QoS support to prioritize the AAL2 versus the AAL5 PVCs. A typical IAD supports anywhere from 4 to 24 voice interfaces and will include an SDSL (most common), ADSL (for telecommuter voice extension), or T1 uplink. The voice gateway connects to the ATM aggregation network via DS3 or OC3 and then connects to the PSTN via a GR-303 interface running discrete DS1s, STS1s, or OC3s (see sidebar below). Encoding across this interface includes G.711 pulse code modulation (mu-law and A-law) at 64 Kbps for uncompressed voice as well as G.726 adaptive PCM (ADPCM) at 32 Kbps and low-distortion-code excited linear prediction (LD-CELP) at 16 Kbps for compressed voice. Echo cancellation based on G.168 is also expected by the subscriber. In some cases, the gateway may include Frame capabilities as well. In the DSL space, this architecture is referred to as the *broadband loop emulation service* (BLES).

An advantage of an ATM-based architecture is that it extends the full range of advanced voice (CLASS and AIN) services across to the subscriber. Some of the well-known services include caller ID, call waiting, three-way calling, call forwarding, and Centrex for business. Signaling between the IAD and the gateway is carried via Q.921/931. A typical gateway will support on the order of 2,000 simultaneous subscribers, equating to a user population of 8,000, assuming 4:1 business oversubscription, or 18,000 at a 9:1 residential oversubscription. The gateway, as part of the voice infrastructure, is also expected to support full redundancy,

♦ A Brief Tutorial on GR-303

GR-303, defined by Telcordia, is the voice and management interface between a Class 5 voice switch—such as the Nortel DMS-100 or 500, the Lucent 5ESS, or the Siemens EWSD—and a voice gateway or DLC. The physical interface between the two devices is via multiple T1s, which may also be carried via STS1 or OC3. GR-303 defines interface groups (IGs) that may contain up to 28 DS1s, although 2 DS1s, a primary and a secondary, are always required. The primary and secondary contain two special DS0 channels, leaving 22 channels for voice, while the other DS1s within the IG have all 24 channels available for voice. Of the two special channels, the control plane is the timeslot management channel (TMC) and is used by the voice gateway to inform the Class 5 switch when it is originating a call and is used by the Class 5 switch to inform the gateway of an incoming call as well as the selected DS0 within a given DS1 for the call. The devices use the second channel, the embedded operations channel (EOC), for path-protection switching (shifting control from the primary to the secondary), fault management, and performance management. Note that, although GR-303 and TR-008 are the North American standards of choice, the V5.2 interface is used internationally.

Voice Distribution 123

including 1+1 protection on common modules, hot swap and hot software upgrade, and protection switching via GR-303.

This architecture operates in the following way. When a subscriber lifts the phone handset, the IAD signals the voice gateway that a call is in progress. This gateway then relays the message to the Class 5 switch, which actually generates the dial tone. Each digit dialed is relayed to the PSTN switch, which then completes the call. Since this architecture involves connections from IAD to gateway to Class 5 switch, even two subscribers on the same IAD must communicate via the switch. This is one of the limitations of this architecture. Currently, major vendors in VoDSL include Jetstream and CopperCom.

IP-Based Voice Services

The second voice option relies on IP, but is not VoIP in the sense that most people consider (see Figure 4.13). In fact, it is much like the IAD and a PSTN gateway solution described in the previous section. The methodology used is the following:

1. Instead of encapsulating the voice traffic and signaling directly into ATM or Frame, the IAD encapsulates it in IP.

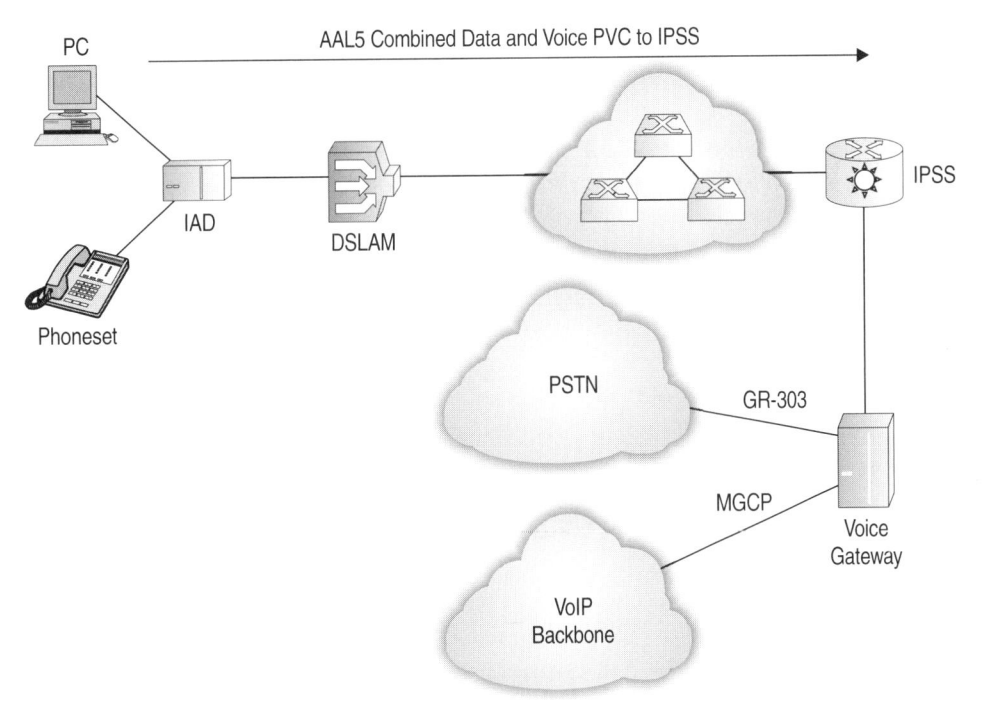

FIGURE 4.13 VoIP IAD and PSTN Gateway—Traditional Class 5 and MGCP

2. The IAD forwards this voice traffic across the same AAL5 PVC as the data (in the case of DSL), prioritizing the voice over the data at the IP layer. As with other solutions, the DSLAMs must have some mechanism to prioritize these combined voice and data PVCs over the best-effort, data-only PVCs.

3. Upon reaching the gateway, the voice traffic enters the PSTN via a GR-303 or V5.2 interface to the Class 5 switch or into a VoIP backbone via MGCP. This additional option, MGCP, is not available within the native ATM solution. This architecture is also a type of BLES.

Although voice traffic passes through the IPSS (since there is no routing functionality in the network between the IAD and the IPSS, and all traffic flows over the single PVC between the subscriber and the IPSS), the real interaction is between the IAD and the gateway. In this architecture, the only role the IPSS may play is in prioritizing or firewalling the voice traffic; it performs no signaling or protocol conversion. The signaling in an IP-based voice service is similar to the ATM-centric architecture in that it takes place between the IAD, the gateway, and the Class 5 switch. Although it is effective, opponents of this technology highlight the inefficiency of two subscribers on the same IAD having to pass through the gateway to communicate, resulting in nonoptimal voice traffic flows.

The architecture is quite different when the gateway connects to an IP Class 5 switch, known as a *soft switch*. The IAD then acts as an MGCP client, communicating via the gateway to an MGCP server emulating most Class 5 switch functions. This switch includes SS7/C7 trunk gateways via TDM whereby the soft switch generates all signaling. Note that this signaling function need not be collocated with the trunk termination function. The MGCP server instructs the IAD to generate the dial tone or voice prompts and to accept dialed digits. If the call terminates locally, or on another IAD connected to the same IPSS, the voice traffic no longer has to hairpin back to the gateway. This is a real advantage of this IP-centric architecture. If the IAD connects over the loop to a soft switch, this architecture is known as *voice over multiservice broadband networks* (VoMBN) when it relates to DSL.

In addition to DSL, T1, and wireless, IP-based voice technologies also support cable since they rely only on the IP layer. The cable modem acts as an IAD, connecting traditional phonesets as well as PCs to the cable infrastructure. However, in conjunction with cable, voice deployment will need to rely on the QoS capabilities found within the DOCSIS 1.1 specification for proper QoS support. TollBridge and General Bandwidth are representative of vendors offering products in this segment.

The next option is true VoIP, generated at a VoIP-capable end device or router (see Figure 4.14). Here, in the case of DSL, the voice traffic shares the same AAL5 PVC with the data traffic. However, the IPSS now plays a more central role as opposed to being just a forwarding device. The IPSS may simply forward the VoIP traffic to a PSTN media gateway, or it may act on the traffic, routing it directly into

Voice Distribution

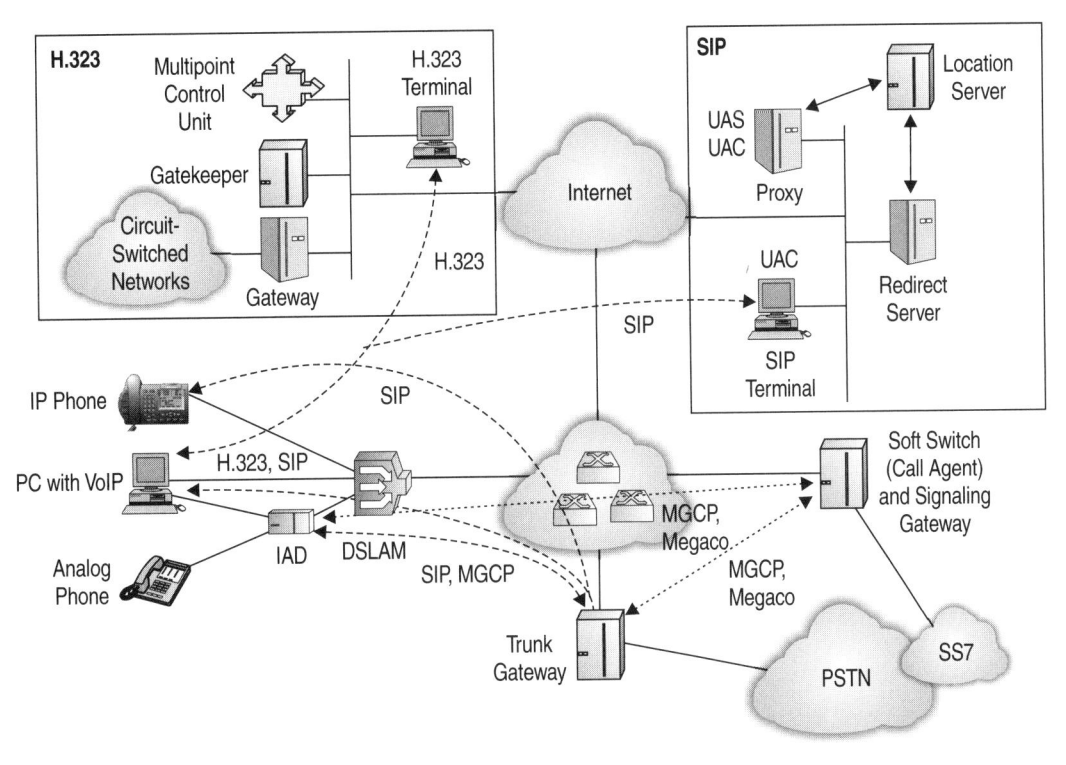

FIGURE 4.14 Internet Telephony

the provider's core or performing more intelligent functions, such as firewalling. To effectively provide this feature, the IPSS must be capable of following the H.323, SIP, or Megaco protocols generated at the subscriber site (and described in an earlier section in this chapter).

The PSTN gateway performs the actual VoIP-to-PSTN encoding and will generate the signaling into the PSTN over a GR-303 interface. This signaling may include T1 RBS (CAS), T1/E1 ISDN PRI, and E1 R1/R2 (Europe). Actual subscriber services supported by this gateway may include POTS, Centrex, ISDN signaling, emergency and operator services, Local Number Portability, and the Communications Assistance for Law Enforcement Act (CALEA) for monitoring of suspect traffic by government agencies. In the future, the IPSS may incorporate this gateway functionality, initially for smaller installations but later for wide-scale conversion of existing voice networks to IP. However, it is unlikely that the IPSS will ever incorporate full soft switch capabilities, as these are usually resident on an external server platform.

Recently, some vendors have begun to deliver voice over DSL via TDM techniques. They carve away frequency across the copper pair and dedicate the available

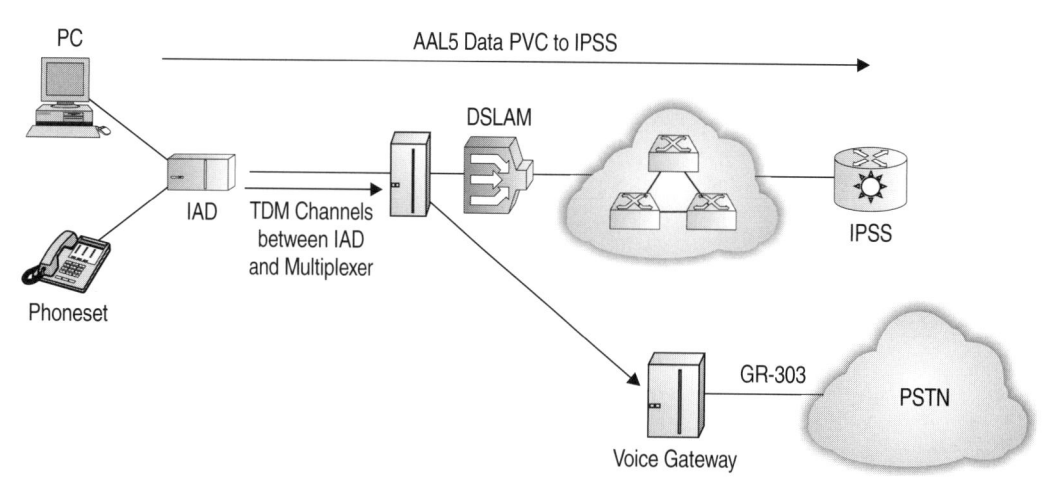

FIGURE 4.15 A TDM-based IAD and PSTN Gateway

bandwidth to four or more channels of voice traffic (see Figure 4.15). In the PoP, a device forwards the voice traffic to the PSTN. Using this architecture, the frequencies devoted to DSL carry only the data traffic.

Other Voice Services Possibilities

Like DSL, cable also supports voice traffic via separate channels from the data. As an example, a cable data offering may dedicate one or more 6 Mhz channels within the cable infrastructure for the data. In addition, the MSO now reserves one or more channels for voice. Note that this architecture does not preclude the installation of CPE capable of supporting both voice and data, though a coax splitter and two devices may be more common (see Figure 4.16). Some cable providers solve the voice problem in an entirely different way, by laying twisted pair alongside the coaxial cable. This architecture, whereby the provider offers a traditional PSTN service, is more common in Europe.

Fixed wireless also introduces some new possibilities regarding voice distribution. In the majority of residential fixed wireless deployments, the technology supports transport of the subscriber's voice traffic via TDM techniques. That is, the access bandwidth is divided into both voice and data channels. The provider diverts the voice traffic to a PSTN gateway before it even arrives at the IPSS. VoIP across fixed wireless is a bit more complex, since QoS guarantees are not as strong as those under cable or DSL. For this reason, the provider may not be able to offer a business-grade VoIP service unless the wireless technology provides some prioritization for the voice traffic. An option is to implement different degrees of contention for different classes of subscribers, ensuring premium access for businesses.

FIGURE 4.16 Voice over Cable and Wireless

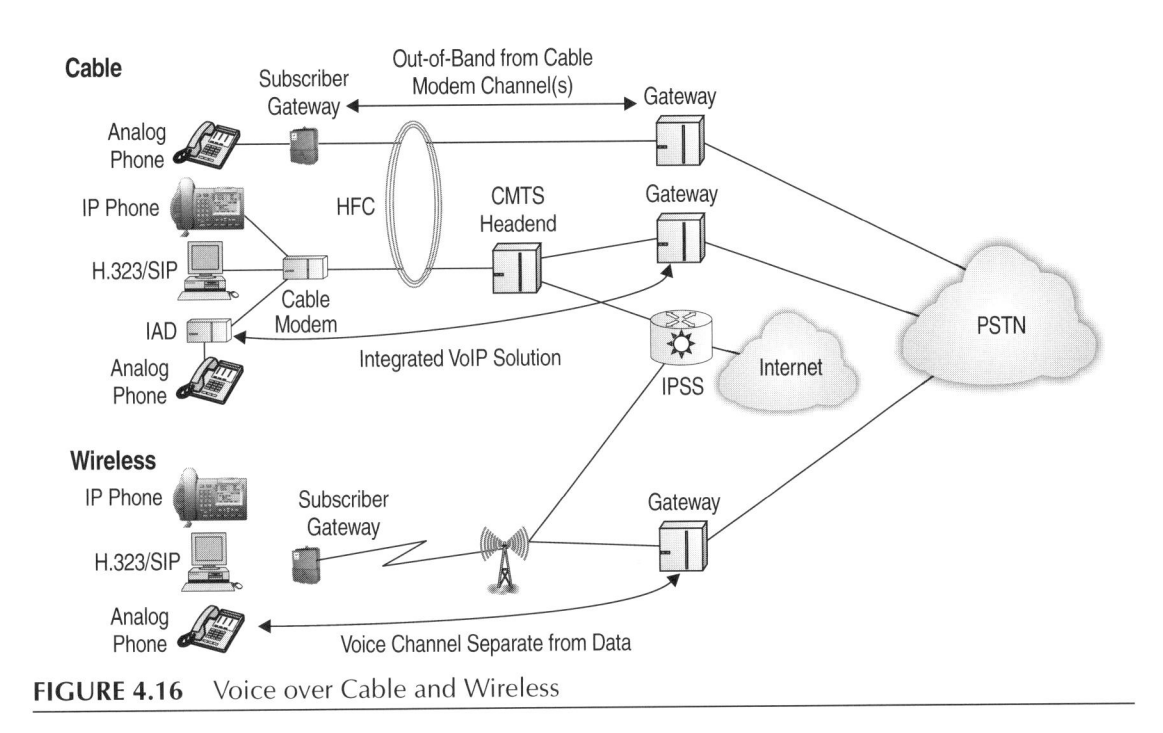

Mobile wireless, of course, goes hand in hand with voice. Architecturally, mobile wireless initially looks much the same as fixed wireless, with the voice and data traffic split at the base station or controller. Only the data or VoIP traffic arrives at the IPSS, with all other voice traffic forwarded into the provider's existing voice network. As 3G mobile wireless networks evolve, VoIP will play an increasingly important role until the traditional voice traffic all but disappears and all voice traffic passes through the IPSS acting as a packet data serving node (PDSN) or gateway GPRS support node (GGSN).

Virtual Hosting Services

Another type of end-user service is closely related to hosting but extends beyond content hosting to offering a virtual hosting service. A virtual hosting service is separate from content distribution, in that it relies on server components within the provider's infrastructure. *Virtual hosting services* include online backup, hosted applications, personal information caches, and hosted Web servers (see Figure 4.17). As described in chapter 1, these types of services should see acceptance by both residential and business broadband subscribers. Online backup permits a subscriber to dispense with onsite storage, by providing a centralized

FIGURE 4.17 New Services

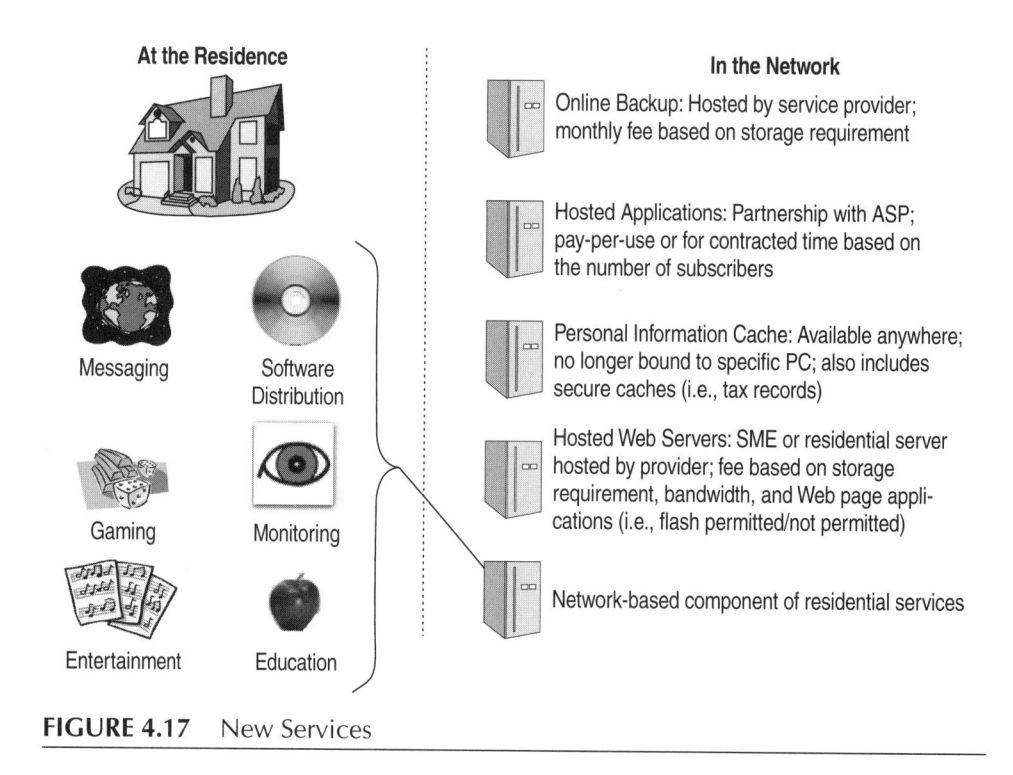

secure backup site. Advantages of this service include disaster recovery and access to the information from anywhere on the Internet in a secure way. A provider will usually tariff this service by the megabyte or gigabyte, and in most cases it will be bundled with an access and/or Web-hosting service.

Hosted applications fall into the domain of the ASP, and they permit the subscriber to access required applications on demand without the requirement of a large up-front investment. These types of hosted applications figure heavily in the enterprise resource planning (ERP) and sales space. An added advantage is that a remote user need only install a client, accessing the application on a centralized server. In fact, nothing precludes a client from accessing an application server locally. This server then uses a centralized database.

Personal information caches are a fairly new concept, permitting subscribers to store commonly accessed information at a central location. This information may include identity information, files of interest, or documents that the subscriber may wish to access while traveling (for example, at an airport kiosk). Web hosting is probably the most well-known service, whereby the provider operates the server on behalf of the subscriber. Advantages of Web hosting include better security, access to backbone connectivity, and economies of scale (e.g., server virtualization, support, and upgrades). The IPSS brings to the table advantages for all of these hosted applications, including additional security, IP-VPNs, QoS management, and personalization via portal services.

Blurring the line between true services and applications are many of the additional "up-sells" expected within a broadband deployment. Given firewalling, application QoS support, network-based caching, and, for the telecommuter, IP-VPN access to the corporate intranet, what additional services might we expect? For the consumer, telephony and video distribution will play a major role. As described in chapter 1, a typical household currently subscribes to a full range of messaging, monitoring, entertainment, information, and education services. A broadband provider will look at how these services are delivered currently and develop analogies in the broadband space.

The following new services are evolving from the common services described in chapter 1: Messaging may evolve to the ability to offer multiple virtual phone lines via the Internet, videoconferencing, and, of course, basic Internet e-mail access. Monitoring is a major area for differentiation and includes health, security, and utilities. The ability to monitor an empty house or cabin or the daycare center via a video feed is desired and embraced by a large portion of the population. Those requiring constant medical attention are already connected to remote monitoring centers, and many utilities companies now read meters via phone lines and will soon read them via the Internet. Entertainment includes music on demand, Internet radio, gaming, video on demand, and online gambling. Finally, information services include access to software (possibly pay-per-use), reference libraries, and financial information.

Conclusion

This chapter covers the various technologies that exist at the core of many provider advanced-service offerings. With an understanding of the last mile from chapter 2, security and tunneling from chapter 3, and content and media from this chapter, we are now in a position to examine the role of the IP services switch in the network and how it ties these technologies together to enable network-based services. The next chapter introduces the IPSS and the provisioning of value-added services.

Chapter 5
The IPSS and Its Role in Service Provisioning

So far this book has introduced the different technologies encountered at the network edge, first looking at the physical infrastructure and then at the various tunneling, security, content, and media protocols relevant to residential and business subscribers. This chapter focuses on the hardware and provisioning platform that brings all these technologies together—the IP services switch (IPSS). The IPSS sits at the edge of the provider's network between the access infrastructure and the core, providing a wide range of basic connectivity and value-added services. The IPSS may exist as a standalone platform or as a blade on a more conventional edge router or ATM switch. Or these router or ATM platforms, without any additional hardware assistance, may perform a subset of IPSS functionality. This chapter introduces the architecture of the IPSS and then details provisioning.

Although the IPSS may provide the brawn behind many of the value-added services, the required brain is the services-provisioning system—otherwise, the service provider will not be able to effectively roll out a profitable service. An understanding of the unique characteristics of the IPSS and how services are provisioned is essential for grasping the more detailed service descriptions in the remaining chapters of this book.

The IPSS

The IPSS is the hardware platform that provides logical (and sometimes physical) aggregation of subscriber traffic across the access technologies described in chapter 2, including DSL, cable, wireless, or other more traditional means of connectivity. The IPSS provides basic subscriber aggregation over these technologies, and it also extends this functionality by providing additional high-touch services—that is, services that require the device to maintain subscriber or application state, and thus additional processing, such as firewalling, content mediation, and IP-VPNs. This state awareness and the ability to provision complex subscriber policies are major differences between an IPSS and a more traditional subscriber management system (or broadband remote access servers [B-RASs]). In this section, although we cover B-RAS from a historical perspective, the focus is on the IPSS.

The easiest way to visualize an IPSS is to compare it to a router located at the customer (see Figure 5.1). Traditionally, this router provides connectivity, as well as more sophisticated functions such as firewalling, traffic management, and IP-VPNs if required. Within an IPSS, these functions are integrated into a provider-owned platform. In effect, each customer is provided with a logical CPE router with the same functions as the standalone router. However, the platform supports literally thousands of these routers, which contributes to the great cost and management efficiencies of an IPSS. These logical CPE routers, one for each subscriber, connect inside the platform to a logical router for the backbone operator, usually an ISP. In addition, if the subscriber requires IP-VPN functionality, the subscriber's logical CPE router may connect into a logical VPN router and then into the backbone.

The first platform optimized for subscriber management was the Redback SMS 1000, introduced in early 1998. It quickly received acceptance by a number of providers. One of the reasons for the development of the Redback 1000 was to address protocol and scalability limitations of traditional routers when deployed for broadband subscriber aggregation. The Cisco 6400 followed the Redback 1000 in the fall of that same year. In turn, Shasta Networks (now Nortel), SpringTide

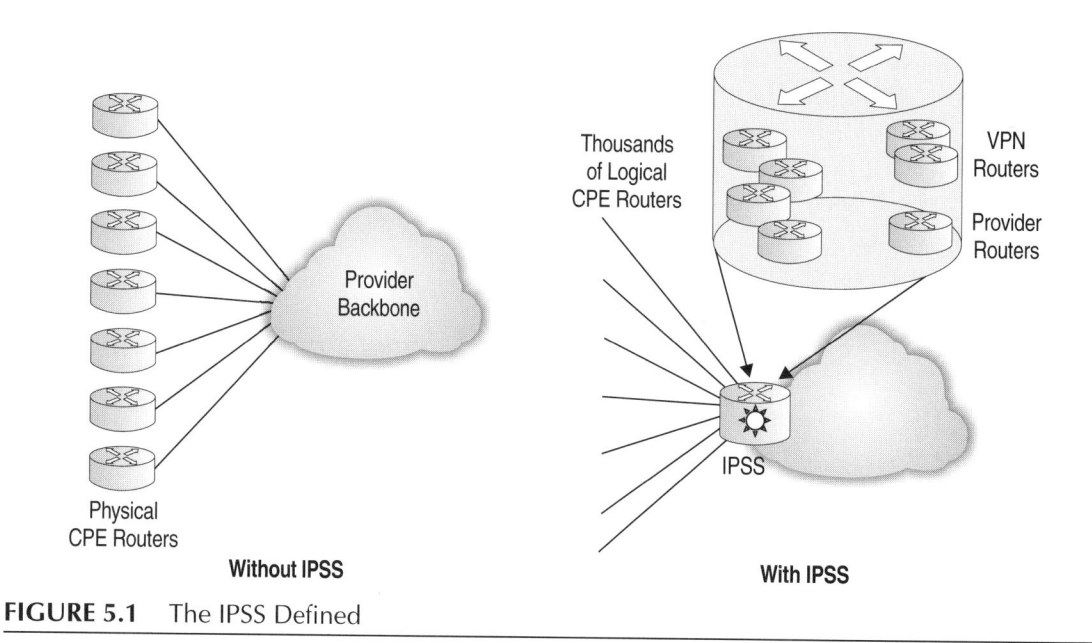

FIGURE 5.1 The IPSS Defined

(now Lucent), Redstone (now Unisphere), Assured Access (now Alcatel), and CoSine all introduced platforms in 1999. The Shasta, SpringTide, and CoSine solutions all included security and IP-VPN functionality based on IPSec and encryption in addition to subscriber management. In 2000, an additional set of startups announced their intention to deliver products in this space. These included Quarry, Ellacoya, Celox, Crescent Networks, and several other multiservice edge platforms such as Amber Networks (now Nokia) and Gotham Networks. In addition, a few vendors have introduced platforms optimized for specific access technologies (rather than the more general approach of the systems just listed). RiverDelta (now Motorola), which offers a cable platform, is probably the best example of this. We also expect platforms optimized for subscriber management within third-generation (3G) wireless deployments, focusing on tunneling, interaction with voice gateways, interoperability with cellular provisioning systems, and content.

These IPSS platforms provide basic subscriber management and advanced services for residential subscribers, telecommuters, and small businesses. Although larger in absolute numbers than the total number of small business subscribers, the residential market segment offers less revenue per capita. For the residential subscriber, the platform not only addresses the problem of connecting broadband subscribers to the network in a cost-effective way, but also helps provide the basis for more profitable security and localized content services. This last point is important, and it is the basis of most of the current interest at the subscriber edge. As part of the case studies in chapter 8, we look at the various business cases for these different sectors in much greater detail, taking into account the many considerations that go into deploying a service offering.

The IPSS differs from traditional edge and core routers in a number of crucial ways: Its operational paradigm is different from that of an average router, in that routers, optimized for basic packet forwarding, maintain identity based on ISPs and subinterfaces. As an example, routers are effective in routing traffic from a business customer consisting of a large number of PCs, but they are not designed to recognize the subscribers at these PCs or apply individualized policies. In addition, the IPSS's design focuses on the application of subscriber- and application-aware packet processing to individual traffic flows, as opposed to aggregates, while its provisioning is based on a paradigm of identified subscribers, as opposed to the maintenance of IP address tables. This provisioning is optimized for the efficient deployment of individualized or bulk service policies, areas in which traditional router provisioning architectures present major barriers to effective service deployment.

The next sections look at the IPSS in detail, covering architecture, packet flow, where it is deployed in the network, how to properly engineer these deployments, coexistence of the IPSS with traditional edge routers, and, finally, the vendor revenue opportunity for IPSSs, edge routers, and B-RASs.

IPSS Architecture

Architecturally, the IPSS is very different from a typical core or edge router. Routers implement the necessary processing to quickly forward IP (or multi-protocol) packets based on their IP header information and maintain little persistent subscriber state (i.e., the subscriber's transaction or flow). For this reason, router architectures based on generalized processing in conjunction with hard-wired application specific integrated circuits (ASICs), programmable ASICs, or even FPGAs will suffice. The router generates the IP routing table on a central processor and distributes it to forwarding engines associated with the I/O modules. In most current designs, a nonblocking data fabric interconnects these I/O modules. One vendor offers a variation on this design, placing a large number of route processors on a single platform and distributing the routing information over a separate control fabric to the I/O modules.

On a traditional router, the amount of processing available for a given speed of packet processing is optimized for general packet forwarding. One rule of thumb is that this amount of processing takes about 1 MIPS per Mbps of forwarded data. Thus, a router with 1 Gbps capacity will include 1,000 MIPS of processing (Ginsburg, 2000). In fact, this is very much the case with most edge (T1/E1 aggregation) and core routers. Therefore, you would not deploy an IPSS where pure routing is all that is necessary, and you would not deploy a router where more complex services were required.

The IPSS is very different from traditional routers, having to parse IP packets beyond the header and maintain per-subscriber state. (By *state*, we mean, in addition to keeping a record in memory of which subscribers have connected to the network through the system, also keeping a record of and implementing any policies applying to these subscribers.) Because of these requirements, the IPSS is designed to maximize the amount of processing applied to each packet, as opposed to routers that minimize this processing while focusing on throughput.

Because of the many types of potential services supported, it is difficult to estimate the amount of per-subscriber processing required. However, a good estimate is that 10 times the processing capability of a typical router will result in desired performance (see Figure 5.2). There is also no way to anticipate the types of new services required over time. In the same way that an IPSS differs from a router, it also differs from a B-RAS. Since a B-RAS is required to perform only simple broadband aggregation and routing, it need not incorporate the same processor performance as the IPSS. This architectural limitation precludes the majority of B-RASs from evolving to IPSSs. An additional characteristic of the IPSS is expandability; a provider can deploy the necessary processing and memory incrementally as the subscriber base grows. This permits a lower cost of service entry and enables the service provider to expand as its customer base grows, without the requirement for a forklift upgrade. The service provider is able to add additional cards with additional processing in order to offer more services to more subscribers.

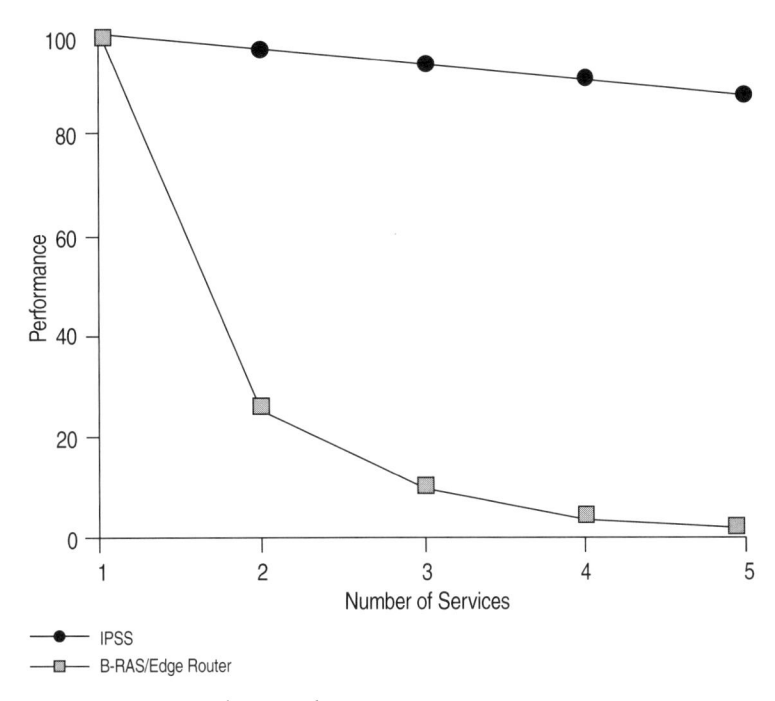

FIGURE 5.2 IPSS Forwarding Performance

A typical IPSS is modular and contains a switch fabric, a control module, multiple I/O modules, and high-touch packet-processing modules. Of the three IPSSs commercially available in 2001, two relied on an ATM fabric and one on an internal ring architecture. Within the IPSS, the control module is responsible for management, assignment of subscribers to the packet-processing modules, and centralized route table calculation. The packet-processing modules perform the service processing and also include the encryption coprocessors used for IPSec. Typical IPSS I/O modules available in 2001 include the following:

- OC3/STM1 ATM, OC12/STM4 ATM, and DS3/E3 ATM
- Channelized DS3 and OC3/STM1 Frame Relay
- T1/E1 Frame Relay
- Fast Ethernet and Gigabit Ethernet
- OC3/STM1 POS and OC12/STM4 POS

During late 2001 and into 2002, vendors introduced OC48/STM16 POS, OC192/STM64 POS, ChOC12 Frame, 10GE, and 802.17 (or vendor-proprietary versions of 802.17, such as Cisco's DPT). Some of the higher-speed interfaces may initially be deployed as trunks into the provider's core routers or transmission systems. Note that deployment of these higher-speed interfaces on IPSSs normally trails that of deployment on traditional edge or core routers because of the additional processing required for a given throughput. On average, technology that has evolved to the point of being able to deliver OC192 on a core router or traditional edge router, for example, will enable OC48 on an IPSS.

An IPSS also typically includes the following:

- Common element redundancy (i.e., the chassis includes spares for the control and fabric modules, known as 1:1 redundancy)
- Services processing redundancy (with one space-processing module shared among all the active modules, also know as 1:N redundancy)
- Automatic protection switching (APS) on the optical access links (or a vendor-proprietary protocol offering the same functionality on the linecards for physical link failure)
- The Virtual Router Redundancy Protocol (VRRP) between systems for additional redundancy in case a system totally fails

Packet Flow through an IPSS

Let's look at an example of the packet flow through one IPSS example, the Nortel Shasta 5000 BSN. Subscriber side packets enter via the input/output (I/O) modules and are forwarded across the backplane to the switch fabric (see illustration on the

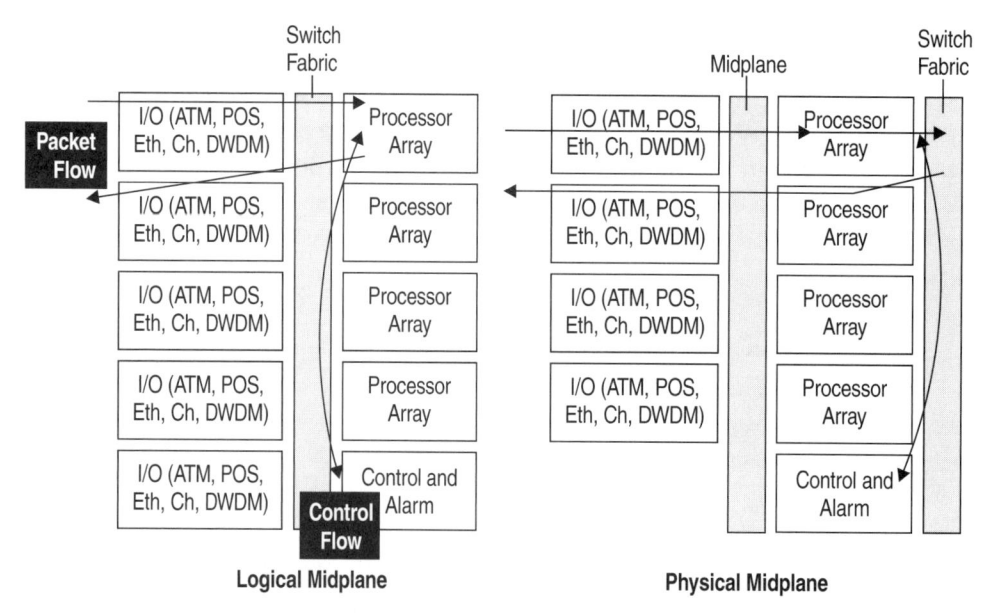

FIGURE 5.3 IPSS Architecture—Logical and Physical Midplane Designs

left in Figure 5.3). In the case of a Frame interface (channelized DS3, FE/GE), packets first pass through a segmentation and reassembly (SAR) function before entering the backplane. From the switch fabric, the system then forwards an individual subscriber's packets to a specific packet-processing blade based on the assignment of the control module (i.e, the control module distributes different subscribers' traffic across the various processor modules). Once processing is complete, packets are once again forwarded to the switch fabric and then to the proper I/O module.

An alternative design, shown on the right in Figure 5.3, relies on a physical midplane interconnecting the I/O modules with the service-processing modules. The Lucent/Springtide IPSS 7000 and the Redback 10,000 are examples of systems that rely on this design. Although most IPSSs are based on traditional "closed" operating systems that integrate the different IP services capabilities, at least one vendor, CoSine Communications, has taken a different approach. The CoSine IPSX 9000 is built on an open platform that integrates software modules from third parties. For example, CoSine bases its security capabilities on the Gauntlet software from Network Associates and on Check Point.

IPSS Deployment

Within the PoP, the different access technologies connect to the IPSS via ATM, Frame Relay, or FE/GE. For example, DSLAMs usually connect via an ATM aggregation network, presenting the IPSS with one or more E3/DS3, OC3/STM1, or OC12/STM4 trunks (Figure 5.4, Option 1), though in some deployments the DSLAMs may connect directly to the IPSS. In contrast, an IPSS providing services to Frame Relay or leased-line subscribers may receive traffic via a channelized DS3 interface (Figure 5.4, Option 2). Finally, a cable or LAN extension may appear as multiple FEs, a GE aggregate, or PPP over SONET/SDH from either a collocated CMTS or a separate LAN switch if the CMTS is remote from the IPSS (Figure 5.4, Option 3). An IPSS deployed within a metro optical network may leverage FE, GE, or PPP over SONET/SDH for subscriber connectivity, connecting to an optical edge device (Figure 5.4, Option 4).

On the trunk side, the IPSS connects with the core routers or ATM switches, though in some smaller networks, the IPSS itself may function as a core router, directly peering with other ISPs. For ATM backbones, and if QoS is an issue, the provider may assign these PVCs or SVCs to variable bit rate-real time (VBR-rt), GFR, and the like. VBR-rt and GFR are ATM classifications that commit to certain levels of service.

Core router connectivity is usually via PPP over SONET/SDH or FE/GE, and in many cases, it takes place via an intermediate LAN switch serving the PoP. As optical switching and routing become more common, the IPSS will connect to these technologies as well and, in fact, will begin to integrate many optical components. Servers, either belonging to the provider or hosted by the provider, also connect to the IPSS via LAN switches. In most cases, these servers attach via the content switch, as described in chapter 4.

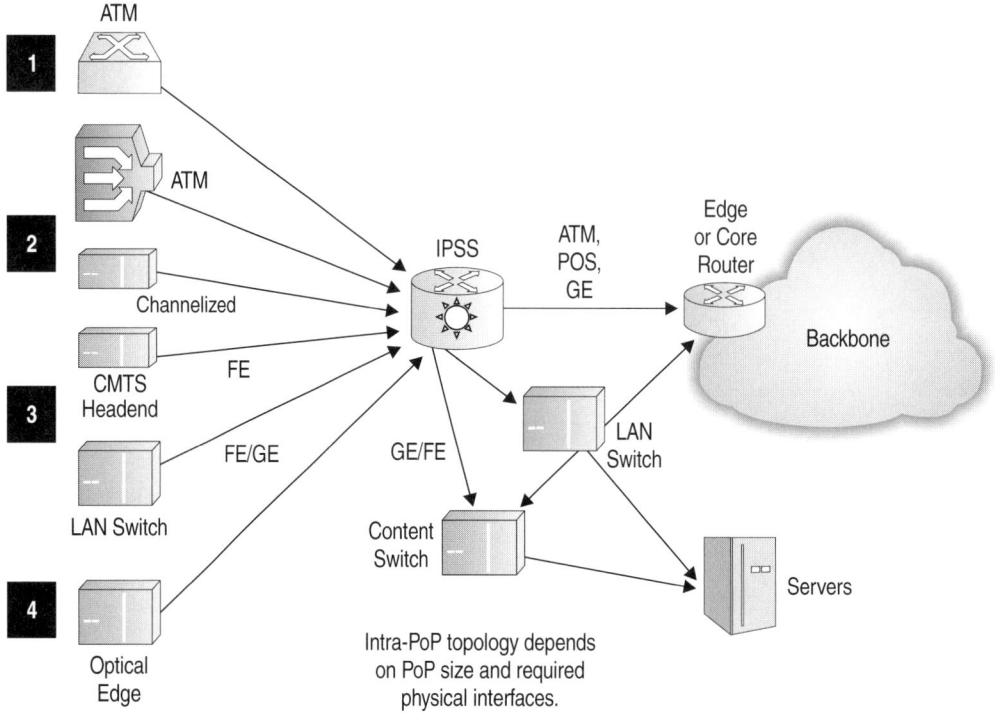

FIGURE 5.4 IPSS Connectivity within a PoP

The location for IPSS deployment depends on whether the provider is acting as an access wholesaler or as ISP, ASP, or CSP. In an early DSL deployment, the access provider would not even deploy an IPSS and would run ATM PVCs from the DSLAMs directly to the ISPs (Figure 5.5, Option 1). This evolved to the provider collocating the IPSS with the physical aggregation platforms, such as the DSLAMs or cable modem headends (Figure 5.5, Option 2). In the case of DSL, this type of deployment would conserve PVCs across the ATM aggregation network. Once the access provider embraces the IPSS, there are two deployment options, with the provider in most cases no longer collocating the IPSSs with the DSLAMs because of the extent of the deployment. The first option originates the L2TP tunnels within the provider's backbone, but then terminates them on an IPSS operated by the ISP (Figure 5.5, Option 3). If the ISP does not have an IPSS, the access provider could terminate the tunnels within its network and route traffic to the ISP (Figure 5.5, Option 4). Depending on the access technology, these networks may be based on ATM or on the mapping of FE/GE directly into optical transport.

If an ISP (or a corporation) operates the IPSS, it will be placed at the edge of the provider's router or ATM backbone (except in the case of a virtual ISP, in

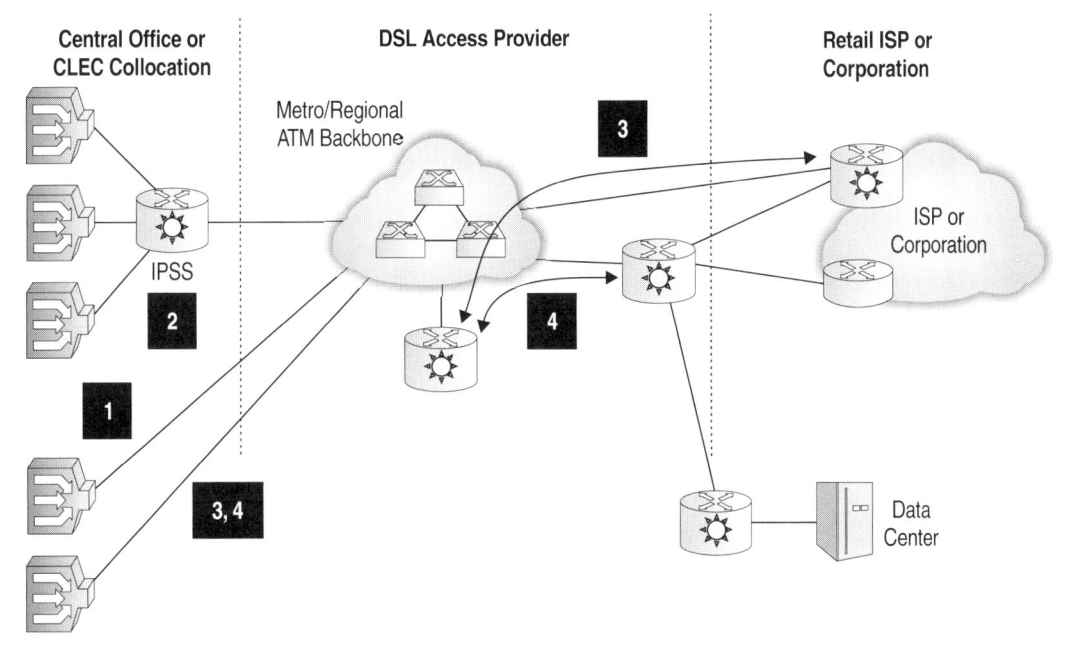

FIGURE 5.5 Options for IPSS Deployment: Access Wholesaler

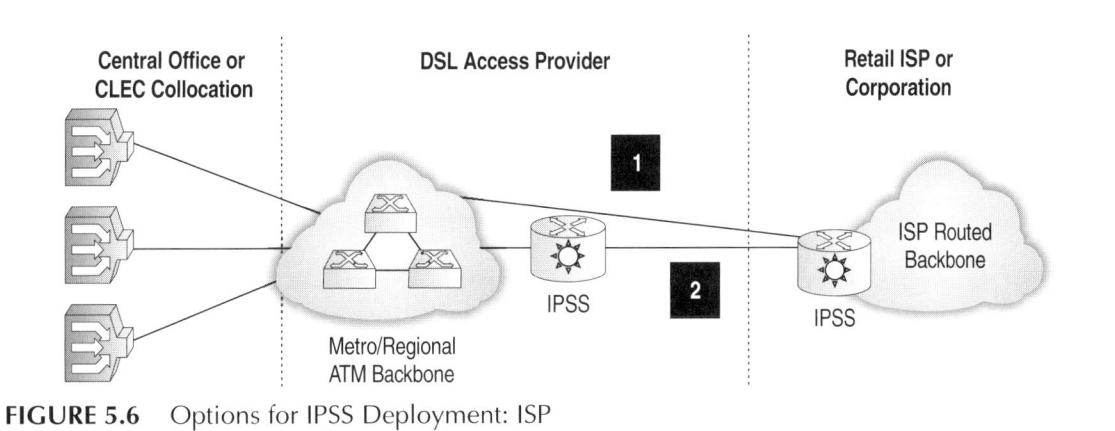

FIGURE 5.6 Options for IPSS Deployment: ISP

which the IPSS connects with the provider's e-mail, Web, and provisioning servers). As noted earlier, depending on the service model of the access provider and the capabilities of the ISP, the ISP either may terminate tunnels from the access provider (Figure 5.6, Option 1) or may connect via a routed connection without tunneling (Figure 5.6, Option 2).

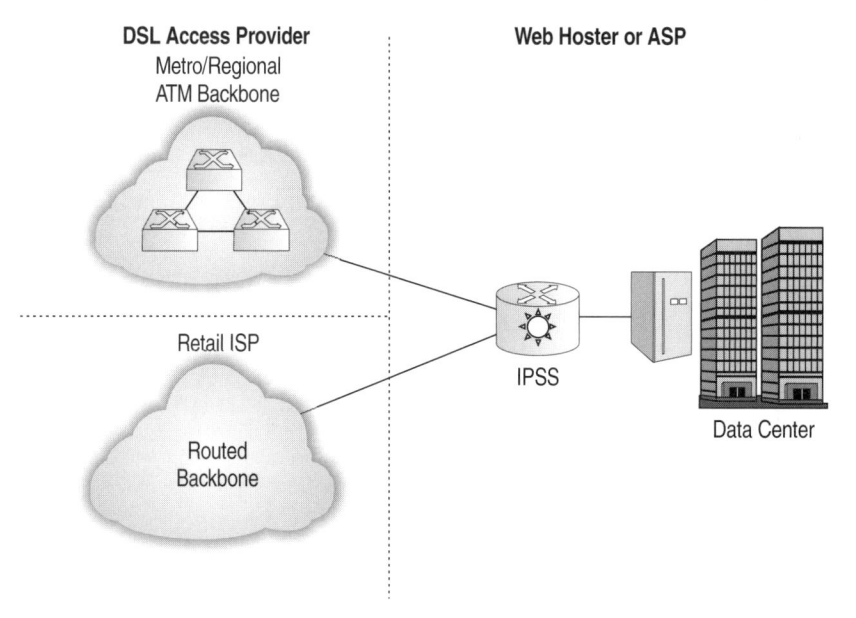

FIGURE 5.7 Options for IPSS Deployment: ASP

Although the most common use for the IPSS is as a subscriber aggregation and services platform, there is a second use within an Internet data center. Consider a Web-hosting operation or an ASP (see Figure 5.7). In either of these two cases, the hosting operator deploys the IPSS at its data center in support of the hosted Web sites—the subscribers. The operator can then offer a set of services to these subscribers, including traffic management, security, address management, and mapping into IP-VPNs.

As an example, bigbrokerage.com might want to provide some of its clients with preferential service, and it will surely want some type of firewalling and prevention of denial-of-service attacks. The IPSS offers these capabilities. Another customer segment is the virtual ISP, with the hosting operator providing facilities for the ISP's servers. Here, the ISP requires address space management, QoS, peering with other ISPs, and security. The ASP connects to both access providers (ILECs and CLECs) as well as to ISPs.

Network Engineering with IPSSs

Deploying an IPSS, as described in the previous section, is very different from deploying a traditional router. Whereas router deployments focus on peering sessions, raw Layer 3 throughput, and the effectiveness of route redistribution, the IPSS metrics are in general harder to define. This also applies to the types of IPSS scalability testing that a provider may carry out—the metrics are different from those of any router testing.

The easiest engineering approach, given the differences in IPSS implementations and lack of industry institutional knowledge, is to model the service definition, such as basic subscriber aggregation or firewalling, and then test it for a set number of subscribers. Components of this test may include processor and memory load, latency through the system, and the time to provision new subscribers. The number of subscribers may be increased until a predictable model results. This model will also help prove or disprove whether the box actually scales based on the number of subscribers. The next step is to determine the IPSS scalability required for the network in question. There are two approaches:

- The provider can over-engineer the deployment (an approach quite familiar to those who have worked with IP), realizing that it is sometimes more expensive to constantly revisit the network plan (i.e., engineering resources are more scarce than capital or bandwidth).

- In a more capital-constrained environment, over-engineering may not be possible. The engineering loop is therefore compressed, and the provider must be capable of adding capacity in terms of platforms and bandwidth at short notice. This requires better automated feedback. In the current environment, providers are probably gaining familiarity with this approach, whether they want to or not.

The requirement to engineer the network based on the services needed also precludes the bottom-up engineering common in Frame Relay and ATM deployments. These networks are deterministic, with the network planners designing an end-to-end approach based on known traffic requirements in a connection-oriented environment. IP networks operate on a per-hop basis, precluding any end-to-end determinism; the services deployed determine the resource requirements, even more so with an IPSS than with a router. Given knowledge of IPSS scalability, these considerations are at least a starting point for network engineering.

When developing IPSS test plans, the provider or lab must understand how the IPSS architecture differs from those of traditional routers and ATM or Frame Relay switches. Routers have one major function—to quickly decide where to forward a packet and then send it to an outgoing interface. The measurement of this performance is simple for a range of deployment scenarios, and it has been the subject of in-depth testing for at least a decade. The same applies to ATM switches, which provide ATM transport and switching for predefined service classes. In fact, some of the most rigorous network engineering and testing have been in support of Frame Relay and ATM switches.

In contrast, IPSS is not intended to be a generic transport device; its reason for existence is not basic packet or frame forwarding. One of its major characteristics, because of its intended audience and location in the network, is optimization in terms of provisioning, interface management, and buffering (i.e., queue depth) for very large numbers of lower-bandwidth subscribers (1 Mbps and below) as opposed to a smaller number of high-bandwidth customers. This is almost the exact opposite of most router designs. The ability to handle tens of thousands of these subscribers is basic to its design and must be reflected in any test scenarios. One valid metric is the number of subscribers supported for a given number of subscriber policies. The best way to measure this is via the latency and packet throughput (percentage of line rate) across the system.

Edge Routers versus IPSSs

It is sometimes difficult to determine when to deploy an IPSS (see Figure 5.8, Option 1) and when to use a traditional edge router or a subscriber management system. For example, subscribers connected to DSL and other subscriber-based access technologies such as cable will, in most cases, require subscriber management (e.g., a Redback 10000), but may not require the additional services offered by an IPSS. In some cases, subscribers requiring firewalling and IP-VPNs may de-

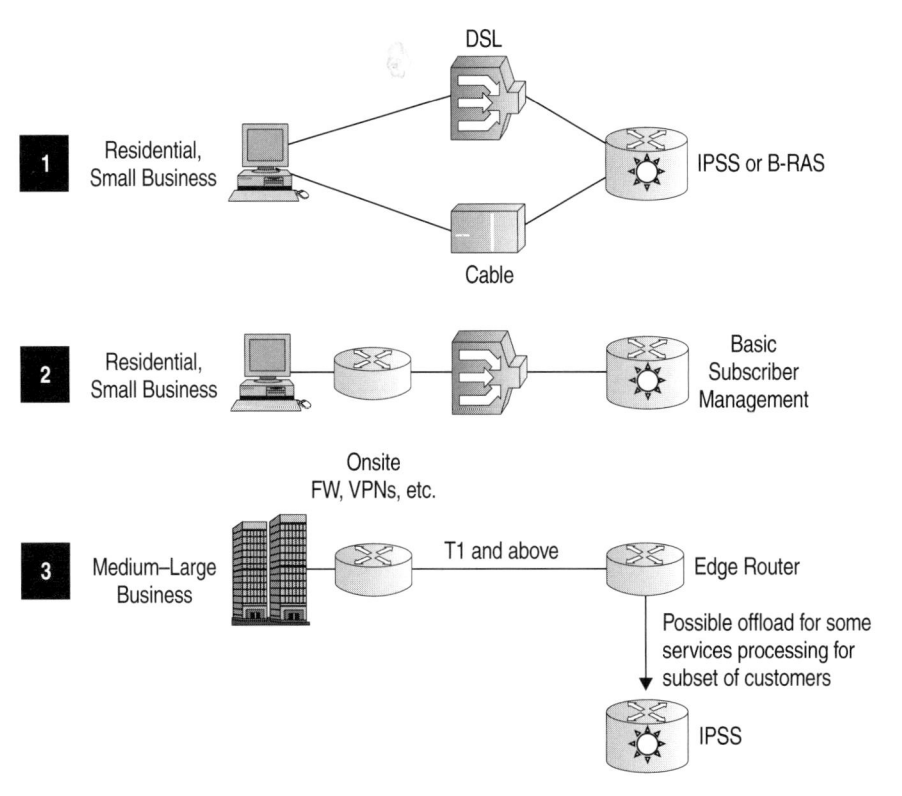

FIGURE 5.8 IPSS and Edge Router Coexistence

ploy some of the more advanced services on hardware at their premises so they will not require an IPSS (see Figure 5.8, Option 2).

Because of these complex onsite deployments, edge routers may sometimes take the place of subscriber management platforms and provide the necessary protocol support if the customer has implemented the functionality onsite. (The Cisco 7500 actually provided the first subscriber management before the development of the Redback 1000.) In addition, as DSL access speeds evolve and "always-on" connectivity becomes the expectation, today's session-based access protocols such as PPP over Ethernet (PPPoE) will evolve to more traditional bridged or routed encapsulations that don't require authentication or maintenance of subscriber state. An observer looking back in a few years may consider subscriber management platforms to be just a tactical market entry during the early days of DSL.

Some customers, especially those requiring T1 and above access, don't require any subscriber management and are not willing to pay for the more sophisticated IPSS-based services (see Figure 5.8, Option 3). This traffic should therefore follow the path of least resistance into the Internet backbone, flowing through a more traditional edge router. As mentioned earlier in the chapter, technology supporting OC48 linecards on IPSSs will support OC192 linecards on traditional routers. The cost differential is roughly at the same ratio, so from the financial standpoint, a provider should deploy the platform that is most suitable for the given traffic profile.

The most interesting trend is the incorporation of IPSS-like functionality into other platforms. For example, edge routers such as the Cisco 10000 Edge Services Router now support IP-VPN blades. This same type of functionality is expected on ATM switches as well. It is therefore increasingly difficult to pin down just what an IPSS is and is not. For this reason, both providers and analysts may reconsider how they look at this marketplace in future.

In any case, the task of the service provider is therefore to intelligently deploy a network that offers both IPSS and non-IPSS paths, depending on the subscriber's requirements. The reason for this is that it is not financially viable for the provider to send all subscriber traffic through the more expensive IPSS path, especially those subscribers who do not require and are not willing to pay for its capabilities. Therefore, we expect a continued strong market for the more traditional edge router in addition to the IPSS. A next-generation provider PoP will often contain both platforms, each performing the functions for which it is optimized. Given that the PoP connects to either an ADM or a metro GE switch, shunting customer traffic to one device or the other is not difficult.

IPSS Vendor Revenue Opportunity

Given the role of the IPSS in network deployments, what is the revenue opportunity from the perspective of the equipment vendor? When looking at the subscriber edge, analysts characterize three types of devices. Providers usually deploy edge aggregation routers to connect ISPs and large customers into a backbone. These platforms offer high-density channelized interfaces or, more recently, Gigabit Ethernet interfaces, routing, traffic prioritization, and packet filtering. Table 5.1 shows revenue, number of units, and growth rate for this market segment.

The next category listed in the table is subscriber management routers, or B-RASs, which bring in subscribers from a variety of access technologies and route them into the provider's core. Although B-RASs were first deployed within DSL, they are now seeing use within cable in support of open access, within wireless, as part of large-scale dial wholesaling, and as gateways between Frame access and IP backbones. In many cases, an edge router may be repurposed into the subscriber management space to address additional customer segments. Over time, some of these B-RASs may evolve into the next class of edge device, IPSSs. The third category listed in the table is the IPSS, with market growth expected to be highest of the three categories over the next few years.

As of the end of 2001, edge aggregation routers include but are not limited to the Cisco 7300/7600/10000/GSR, Ericsson AXI 540, and Unisphere ERX-700 and

TABLE 5.1 Vendor Revenue Opportunities

	2000	2001	2002	2003	2004
Edge Aggregation Routers and Multiservice Edge Devices					
Revenue	1.17B	1.53B	2.41B	3.55B	4.84B
Growth Rate	84%	31%	58%	48%	36%
Units	11,329	16,132	23,542	32,668	42,921
Growth Rate	39%	42%	46%	39%	31%
Subscriber Management Routers (Broadband Remote Access Servers)					
Revenue	610M	731M	896M	962M	886M
Growth Rate	496%	20%	23%	7%	−8%
Units	12,630	14,306	18,279	20,148	19,091
Growth Rate	677%	13%	28%	10%	−5%
IP Services Routers (IPSSs)					
Revenue	180M	251M	696M	1.48B	2.64B
Growth Rate	na	40%	178%	113%	79%
Units	801	893	2,376	4,811	8,574
Growth Rate	na	13%	166%	102%	78%

Source: Infonetics, 2001 ("Service Provider Core and Edge Hardware—Quarterly Worldwide Market Share and Forecasts for 1Q01"). Used with permission.

Note for comparison: Synergy Research reported $118M in subscriber management revenues for 1999 based on 1792 units, growing to $614M in 2000 based on 13,272 units. IP services switches were first reported in 2000, generating $198M in revenues on 945 units. Extrapolations into future years were not provided.

1440, as well as newer systems by Nokia, Amber, Gotham, and Allegro Networks' Multi-Router. As noted in the previous section, some of these devices are beginning to integrate B-RASs IPSS functionality.

Subscriber management routers include the Cisco 6400, 7200, 7400, the Redback SMS-500/1800/10000, the Alcatel Onestream Broadband Access Server, the Lucent DSL Terminator 100, and the Unisphere system. One difficulty in judging this market is that some platforms considered to be subscriber management in fact integrate IPSS-like functionality.

IP services routers (the IPSS market) include the Cisco VPN 5000 Concentrator, CoSine Communications IPSX 9500/3500, the Lucent/SpringTide IPSS 7000, the Nortel/Shasta 5000 BSN, and new entrants into this space such as Quarry and Celox.

Note that it is still too early to determine the amount of growth in the 3G/4G wireless space, but it is expected to be immense (possibly double or triple these wireline projections). The conclusion here is that the IP services platform market will enjoy greater growth opportunity in the coming years than almost any other segment of the internetworking market. In fact, 2001 was the inflection point—a shift from tactical broadband market entry via subscriber management to a more strategic IP-services-based solution resulting in a more sustainable business model.

Besides the IPSS, there are many other systems within the broadband PoP or central office. These include the Web and provisioning servers, the Layer 2 and Layer 3 switches, the content switches, and core routing devices. Beginning in 2000, some DSLAMs and CMTS headends began to integrate subscriber management and IP services functionality. How this will impact the sales of the standalone platforms listed in Table 5.1 is still unknown. For an appreciation of these two market segments, look at sales of DSLAMs in 2000, which reached $3.8 billion (Infonetics, 2001), while CMTS headends generated $834 million in revenue to vendors. In addition, some vendors are beginning to look at adding subscriber management to their content switches. This segment alone was a $652 million market in 2000, expected to grow to $4 billion by 2004 (IRG, 2000).

One less positive statistic is the ratio of lines in service versus the installed capacity. By the end of 2000, the data CLECs deployed more than 7 million ports with DSL access capacity, but they had filled only 930,000. Although the overall ratio is better across all types of providers—2.5 million out of 10 million—it is still a troubling number. There was also evidence of a slowdown in overall Internet penetration, as most of the available mass market was already connected. In fact, these types of statistics were common by 2001 across a number of different technology areas and contributed to the massive dropoff in new service provider contracts that the industry experienced during that year.

This overbuild has led to a new degree of realism across all segments of the internetworking industry, with providers scrutinizing their deployment plans much more closely and balancing spending with actual subscriber revenue. From a higher level, one could say that the industry as it relates to both IPSSs and the

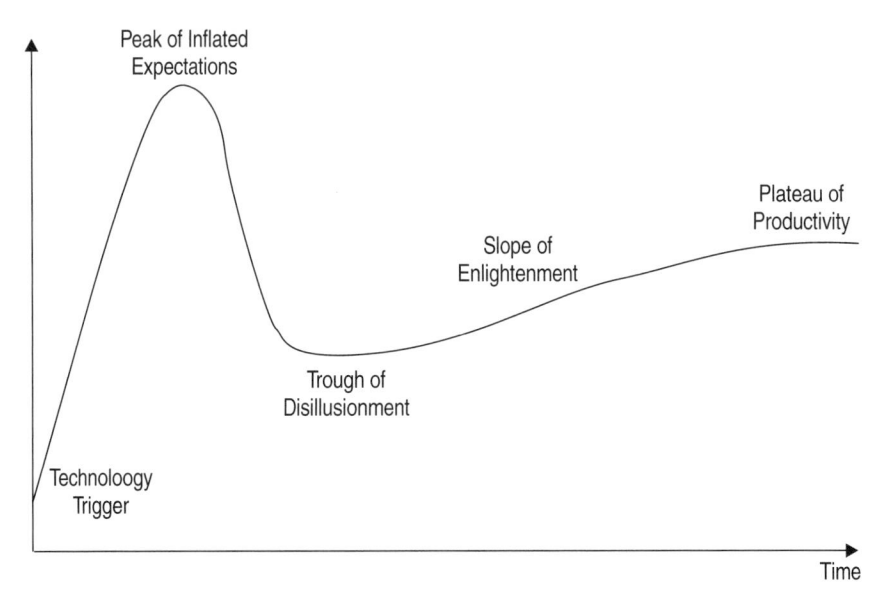

FIGURE 5.9 The Hype Cycle of Emerging Technologies

concept of network-based services, is in the "Trough of Disillusionment" as characterized by the Gartner Group (see Figure 5.9). The IPSS is not the cure-all that some have made it out to be, but there is still validity in the concept of network-based services, and thus the reality is somewhere between the two extremes. The goal is to deliver compelling services and content across the network, as described in chapter 7.

IPSS Provisioning

The IPSS's service-provisioning capabilities are just as critical as the data-forwarding path, and they permit the service provider to offer customized services on behalf of large numbers of subscribers. More than in any other internetworking platform, IPSS discussions revolve around the provisioning and billing of subscriber services. This provisioning is critical if the provider is to target the evolving DSL, cable, and wireless marketplace. We introduce provisioning by first looking at the need in the IP services space, setting a basis for a discussion of element and services provisioning. It is here that we introduce concepts such as the common open policy service (COPS) and the Lightweight Directory Access Protocol (LDAP). Any provisioning system must allow for open interfaces to external systems. Finally, the end subscriber is most interested in the support of client software, customer network management, and service level agreements.

The Need for Effective Provisioning

To understand how critical provisioning of IPSSs is and how providers actually go about implementing this capability, a brief review of network management in general is helpful. The ITU's Telecommunications Management Network (TMN) framework has four levels of management:

- *Business management:* offering services to customers, doing necessary customization, and implementing acceptable day-to-day relationships between consumer and provider.
- *Service management:* the provider side of business management, in which the provider defines a service it will offer and then organizes all the technical, operational, documentation, billing, provisioning, and other resources needed to implement the service.
- *Network management:* designing and operating the end-to-end flow through the provider system that will deliver the service. This can include collecting information, but actual billing is not at this level.
- *Element management:* configuring and troubleshooting the components, including customer site equipment, collection network components, IP service switches, backbone routers, and so forth, that are the hops along the end-to-end path.

Once a service is defined and offered, and a customer contracts for it, the provisioning process begins. This process invokes the hardware and software configuration steps, the dispatch of technicians to customer sites (i.e., "truck rolls") and collocation facilities, and all the other operations that must take place before the subscriber can receive service. The skill with which the provider addresses these requirements will make or break any service offering.

Consider horror stories surrounding DSL deployments requiring multiple truck rolls, or small businesses relying on hosted e-mail services that are either unavailable or proven to be unsecure. In the case of DSL deployment, just one additional truck roll, costing anywhere from $150 to $300, can destroy the revenue potential of a low- to mid-range subscriber. In fact, the cost of service deployment in the DSL space has caused more than one CLEC to fail. For example, a recent article on broadband deployment (*EETimes,* 2001) estimates that the average DSL installation takes 51.5 hours, requiring $1,950 in labor. The average service activation time is 62.4 days, sometimes taking as long as 120 days. Clearly this is unacceptable. In the same way, problems with hosted services can cause the subscriber to question the capabilities of the service provider and will impact SLAs, and thus the bottom line.

These are extreme examples, but they prove the point that an appreciation for the complexity of service provisioning must span from the customer to the network core and from service inception to its retirement.

More common impacts to the provider's business model are the help desk requests. For broadband services, the frequency of these requests and the support costs run over three times those of traditional dial access connectivity. One reason for this is that because of the complexity of the broadband deployment, the provider is faced with having to field many questions unrelated to the actual service. These many times focus on the user's PC or third-party software as well as any specialized hardware required.

Although the focus here is on provisioning of subscriber services at the network's edge, an end-to-end service touches every network component across the data path. Remember from chapter 2 that data path provisioning for a DSL service will include a client (PC or otherwise) connected to the DSL modem. This in turn connects across the copper loop to the DSLAM, which trunks the subscriber data into an ATM aggregation network in all but the smallest of deployments. The data now enters IPSS and is either terminated locally or passes into a core ATM or router network. Depending on the deployment, more than one operator may manage these components (see Figure 5.10).

At a minimum, the ILEC offers combined DSL access and ISP service. Although this is common in the residential space, for business customers the situation is a bit different. The business customer may contract with the ILEC and a separate ISP. In a more complex configuration, the customer's ISP partners with a CLEC for the service. This CLEC in turn must partner with the local ILEC. There therefore may be three parties involved in offering the service, an unenviable situation if

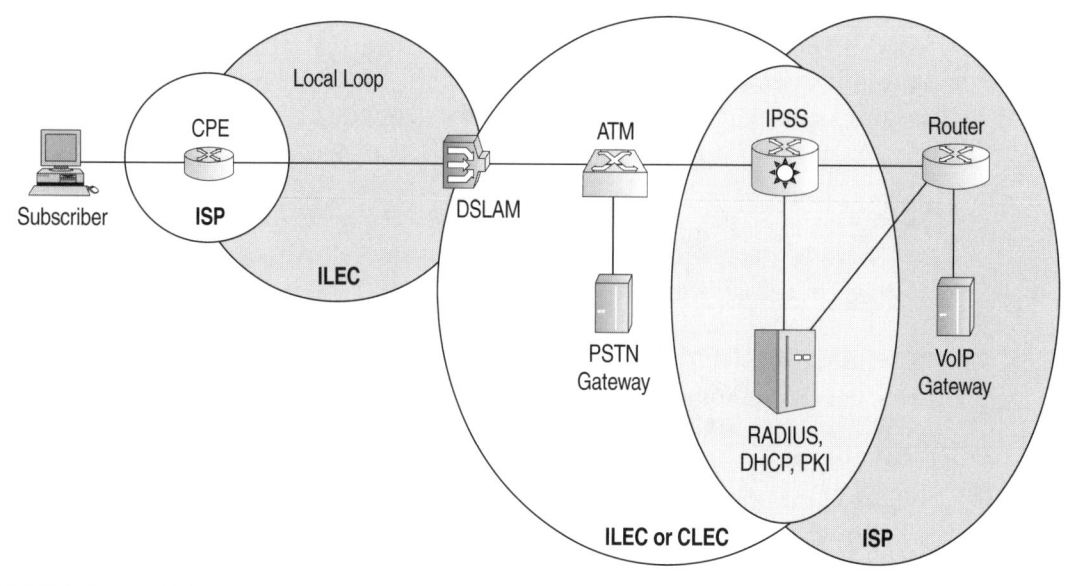

FIGURE 5.10 DSL Management Domains

something goes wrong (*NYT*, 2000). Each of these providers controls a subset of the equipment required for the complete service, be it the CPE, the local loop, the DSLAM, the ATM switch, or the IPSS and routers.

Possibly more complex than the data path is dynamic subscriber layer provisioning, which at its most basic will include RADIUS and DHCP. More complex services will rely on policy management systems and, in the case of IPSec, a complete security management infrastructure. In most cases, the provider will have an existing back-office system responsible for some provisioning functions, along with billing and customer care. The provisioning components for any new service, which are often based on new hardware, will need to interface with these existing systems. This last requirement is sometimes the most complex (and costly to implement). The challenge then is to deploy an effective management infrastructure capable of both element (device) management and end-to-end provisioning. This infrastructure not only must permit the provider to deploy the service cost-effectively, but must also include the ability to properly maintain, upgrade, and bill for the service. Probably the best way to look at provisioning is to analyze a few typical services, examining the various provisioning technologies at the element, network, service, and business layers.

Element Provisioning

According to the TMN model, element and network provisioning is responsible for device configuration and the establishment of the path through the provider's network. Techniques for element provisioning include SNMP, Common Object Request Broker Architecture (CORBA), XML, and Web-based interfaces. Management may be via a vendor's proprietary system or a third-party open platform.

Consider a residential DSL service made available through the cooperation of a DSL access provider and an ISP. In this environment, DSL access providers usually provision DSL modems en masse before shipping them to the subscriber. The intent is for the end user to play no part in modem configuration, and in most cases the operator does not provide the user with the configuration password. Once in service, the DSL provider may conduct basic monitoring and troubleshooting of the device from a centralized management station via one of the DSL line MIBs using SNMP. Although the copper pair may not seem manageable, over the last few years, vendors have introduced devices that permit the provider to actively troubleshoot the loop between the DSLAM and the subscriber. One very specialized type of device, used for initial loop qualification (which determines whether an individual is eligible for DSL service and at what bandwidth), is an essential component of mass-market DSL deployment.

The DSLAM is manageable either via SNMP or via a vendor's proprietary management system. In both cases, the DSL access provider deploys a centralized management platform capable of managing the DSLAMs within a given metropolitan area. (DSLAM vendors are just now introducing management platforms capable of extending beyond a limited number of platforms.) Management of the ATM aggregation network also occurs via SNMP or a vendor's legacy system. Although IPSS management is also possible via SNMP, its role in the network is very different from that of the DSLAM or ATM switch. Whereas provisioning of the DSLAM and ATM switch is static—done once for the service duration—provisioning of the IPSS is dynamic, taking place mostly at the IP layer and above. Subscriber traffic, if not terminated within the IPSS's PoP, is handed off to the network core. Centralized SNMP or proprietary provisioning also applies to these core ATM switches and routers. Note that most of the devices described here also support a command line interface (CLI), though in most cases it is used only as a local troubleshooting interface and, in the case of most DSL CPE, is disabled. The one exception is with the routers, which some providers centrally provision by creating CLI scripts and pushing them down to the routers across the network. Also note that a provider may purchase two or more components of the solution from a single vendor. In this case, one would hope that they are managed via a common platform. An example of this would be the DSLAM and ATM switching, or the DSLAM and IPSS.

The DSL access provider provisions the subscriber's PVC from the DSL CPE and across the DSLAM and ATM switch (see Figure 5.11). It then terminates within the DSLAM (if it is IP-equipped), or at an IPSS, or continues to an ISP. Effective provisioning, of course, requires coordination between the back-office systems, especially if different vendors supply different platforms. A major help is bulk provisioning, where the access provider preconfigures a range of PVCs within the DSLAM, across the ATM network, and into the IPSS. When a new subscriber requests service, the provider need only provision the local loop and the necessary IP layer information for the subscriber within the IPSS. The access provider

ILEC, DLEC
1. Configure and verify ATM PVC between subscriber CPE, DSLAM, ATM switch, and ISP router.
2. If IPSS is deployed, PVC terminates at IPSS and maps into routed context or L2TP tunnel.
3. Configure optional PVC for voice gateway and configure GR-303 interface to PSTN.

ISP
1. Configure subscriber at router or IPSS.
2. Configure subscriber router if part of service.
3. Configure VoIP gateway if part of service.

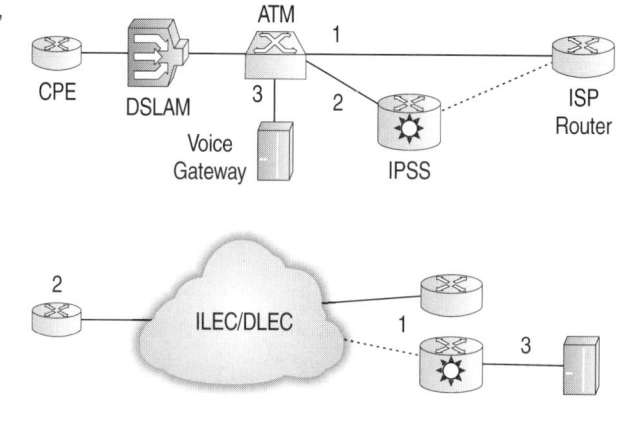

FIGURE 5.11 DSL Provisioning Tasks

also controls the copper loop qualification system and may in fact prequalify most of the loops within a CO, saving on subscriber provisioning time. Ultimately, the objective on the part of the access provider is to automate and streamline as many elements of the process as possible.

The ISP has a similar set of requirements, terminating the PVC or routed connection from the access provider at the IPSS or router and entering the necessary subscriber information. Most of this provisioning takes place at the services layer, described later in this chapter. The ISP also maintains its routed backbone, though this requires no per-subscriber provisioning. In some deployments, the ISP will also configure the subscriber router and may deploy a VoIP gateway.

One of the complexities of DSL provisioning is the interface between the access provider and the ISP. If the subscriber contracts with the access provider, how is the ISP informed? This requires automated (or many times manual) interfaces between the two groups. In some cases, the subscriber acts as the single point of interface and receives bills from both the ILEC/CLEC and the ISP.

The types of devices found within a dial, cable, wireless, or Frame Relay deployment are not so different from those found within DSL, though they go by different names. Traditional dial access consists of a remote access server (RAS) trunked into the ISP's backbone. The ISP or dial wholesaler manages the RAS via SNMP, usually with the addition of a vendor-proprietary platform permitting management of the more complex features such as modem pools for ISPs. Since dial is session-oriented, relying on PPP, the RAS also connects to either RADIUS or TACACS+ (terminal access controller access control server) for authentication and accounting. The next section describes these AAA servers in detail.

In cable modem deployments, the DSLAM equivalent is the cable modem headend (that is, CMTS). ATM is rare within cable modem deployments, while IPSS-type devices are still in the early phase of deployment. Although there is no loop qualification per se within cable, the MSOs must still ensure that they have the required hybrid fiber-coax (HFC) buildout to be able to offer cable modem service. Within cable, a central data over cable system interface specification (DOCSIS) provisioning system both controls the headend and configures the individual modems—the end user plays no part in this phase of provisioning (see Figure 5.12). In an open access environment, the headends connect locally or across a metropolitan router network to an IPSS, also controlled by the cable operator. Subscriber traffic is then forwarded to an ISP, which may also operate an IPSS, paralleling the DSL deployment. In fact, a provider offering both DSL and cable access may deploy a single IPSS for both services.

Wireless operators are faced with the same provisioning challenges. Within a fixed wireless deployment, the subscriber device is known as a remote unit (RU). A central provisioning system located at the operator's PoP provisions the RUs as well as the base stations (see Figure 5.12). These base stations connect to an IPSS, with the remainder of the architecture paralleling that of DSL.

Cable
1. Configure subscriber modems and CMTS headends via DOCSIS provisioning system.
2. Configure MSO's router, or:
3. If IPSS deployed, configure policies and routing at IPSS, and tunnels to ISP's router.
4. ISP configures tunnel termination.

Wireless
1. Configure subscriber gateways and base station via wireless provisioning system.
2. Configure policies and routing at IPSS, and tunnels to ISP's router.
3. ISP configures tunnel termination.

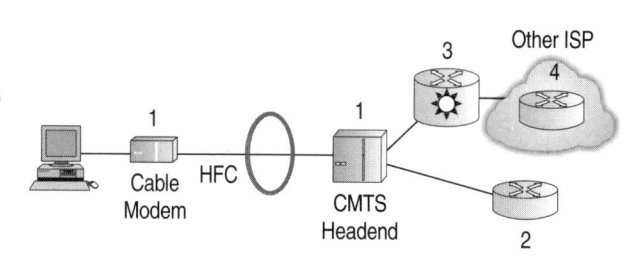

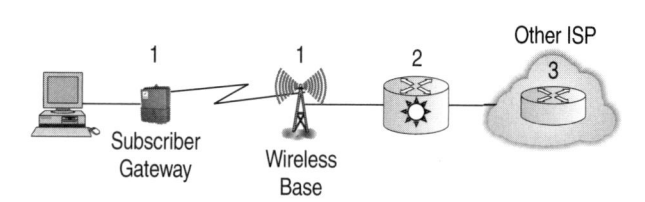

FIGURE 5.12 Cable and Wireless Provisioning

Mobile wireless (cellular, PCS, GSM, and so forth) relies on a completely different architecture and includes subscriber-provisioning systems more complex than those deployed as part of traditional Internet access. However, once the subscriber traffic reaches the IPSS (known as a GGSN or PDSN in this environment), provisioning looks much like that in DSL.

Services Provisioning

Element and network management providing device-level configuration is only a starting point for enabling the various services supported by the IPSS. If all we were interested in was a basic transport service, traditional element management would be all that is required. However, the intent here is for the service provider to add additional value to its service offering.

As an example, the provider may wish to create individualized subscriber policies that permit customization of security, traffic management, and VPN services. Or a small business or enterprise branch may have specialized security or traffic management requirements, requiring customization. Service provisioning also introduces the concept of bulk policies that allow a provider to create a template policy for a large number of subscribers, greatly reducing the provisioning expense. For example, the provider may create a service profile that offers preset firewalling and QoS policies optimized for a given class of residential subscriber. In the consumer broadband space, bulk policy capability is critical, as one cannot expect a low-end residential DSL service operator to individually provision hundreds of thousands of subscribers.

When looking at subscriber provisioning, the focus is on the IPSS and the various external servers and databases. Depending on the service and architecture, the CPE and the subscriber's desktop also play a role. What providers are ultimately looking for are solutions that provide centralized management with the following goals:

- Ensure QoS for mission-critical applications.
- Provide differentiated CoS for other traffic.
- Simplify configuration of security services such as access control, IPSec configuration, and VPN usage.
- Focus on ease of use for installation, configuration, authoring, and deployment.
- Support a heterogeneous network environment.
- Provide fault tolerance and a secure environment.
- Integrate with fault monitoring, performance analysis, and accounting.

To accommodate these requirements, an extensible architecture, the common open policy service (COPS), provides the support for policy-manageable elements or policy enforcement points (PEPs) and new action across these PEPs obtained from a policy decision point (PDP). Additionally, the architecture provides secure communication between management components and supports both legacy and policy-aware environments. Another protocol of importance, currently implemented by many vendors and deployed throughout networks, is the Lightweight Directory Access Protocol, or LDAP. Finally, subscriber self-provisioning also plays a role in bringing dynamic service capabilities to the end user.

COPS

COPS is an IETF protocol initially designed for managing Resource Reservation Protocol (RSVP) admission policy but expanded to include policy-based configuration under the extension COPS-PR (policy provisioning) (Herzog, 2000). The protocol is based on two models: an outsourcing model used to address the requirement for an instantaneous policy decision (authorization) and a configuration model (or provisioning model) that does not assume a 1:1 correlation between a PEP-request PDP decision. Instead the configuration model of COPS can be triggered by external events, PEP events, or a combination of the two.

COPS defines a query and response protocol that can be used to exchange policy information between a policy server (PDP) and its clients (PEPs). The PEP enforces predetermined policies. The PEP also includes classification, traffic policing, and admission control. There is at least one PDP in each controlled administrative domain. Building on the strengths and weaknesses of SNMP (SNMP is pervasive for network monitoring but not for configuration), COPS is a connection-oriented, stateful protocol that is TCP-based. It uses a client/server

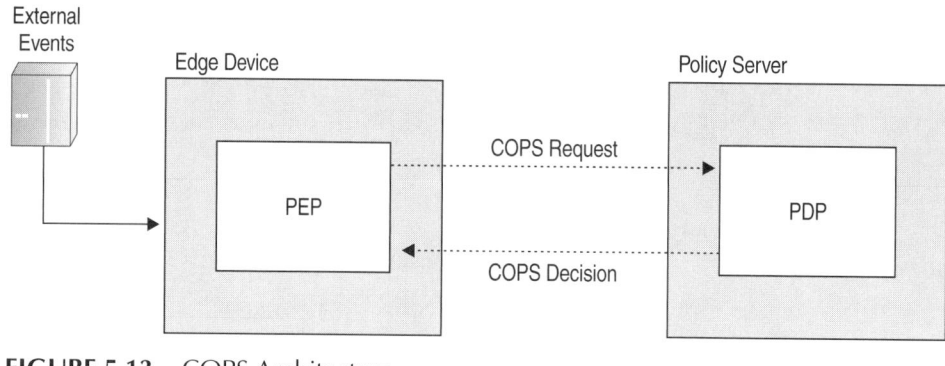

FIGURE 5.13 COPS Architecture

architecture along with efficient message passing. Figure 5.13 depicts the basic COPS architecture.

COPS is extensible by design in that it has both an outsourcing mode for managing signaled QoS and a configuration mode for managing provisioned QoS. As part of the protocol, it establishes secure communications between the client (PEP) and the server (PDP) to ensure appropriate authentication and integrity. COPS-PR is based on extending the configuration mode to enable the provisioning of various policies, although the initial focus was on QoS. Compared to SNMP-based systems for policy provisioning, COPS is thought to be technically superior. However, SNMP remains a more economical alternative because of its well-established user base. One obvious question is whether the IPSS is a PEP or both a PEP and PDP. In fact, it may play both roles given stored subscriber policies.

Although COPS and a centralized policy-based management system are a good end goal, a number of other protocols are more familiar to those working with IP services switches. An IPSS includes subscriber-level awareness and therefore will interface to the provider's existing authentication, authorization, and accounting (AAA) and directory servers. It therefore requires more sophisticated subscriber policy provisioning than that available through SNMP. For this reason, most IPSS vendors have developed proprietary systems for this policy creation. The types of policies implemented at the IPSS, including access, security, and QoS, will play a major role in any service definition.

Currently deployed AAA servers include RADIUS and TACACS+, although the latter has all but disappeared from most deployments and is not covered here.

RADIUS RADIUS, as defined in RFCs 2138 (authentication and authorization) and 2139 (accounting), forms the bulk of the authentication architecture for Internet dial and, now, DSL. An internetworking device such as an IPSS or RAS acts as a client to a RADIUS server, exchanging data as to subscriber identity and accounting through Access Request, Access Response, Accounting Start, and Accounting Stop commands (see Figure 5.14). Note that RADIUS also handles L2TP tunneling parameters as part of logins based on fully-qualified domain names (FQDNs). The server responds with the proper L2TP tunnel for the subscriber.

In the example shown in Figure 5.14, the ISP offering the service requires a provisioning infrastructure capable of supporting dynamic subscriber logins. The IPSS interfaces to both the vendor's proprietary system as well as to RADIUS. Via the IPSS's provisioning system, the ISP bulk provisions the access PVCs and creates a set of bulk policies that determine how subscribers are treated when first logging into the network. The policy states that the subscriber's authentication request is handed off to the ISP's RADIUS server, which validates the username, password, and, optionally, the domain (if the ISP uses more than one or operates as a host for multiple vanity ISPs). If authentication is successful, the subscriber receives an IP address via DHCP and is free to surf the Web. Either the IPSS provisioning system or RADIUS may contain additional parameters relating to QoS or security. At subscriber login, the RADIUS server may also generate an accounting record, though these are uncommon within flat-rate DSL services (unlike with hourly Internet dial-in, where accounting is essential). In the future, with the

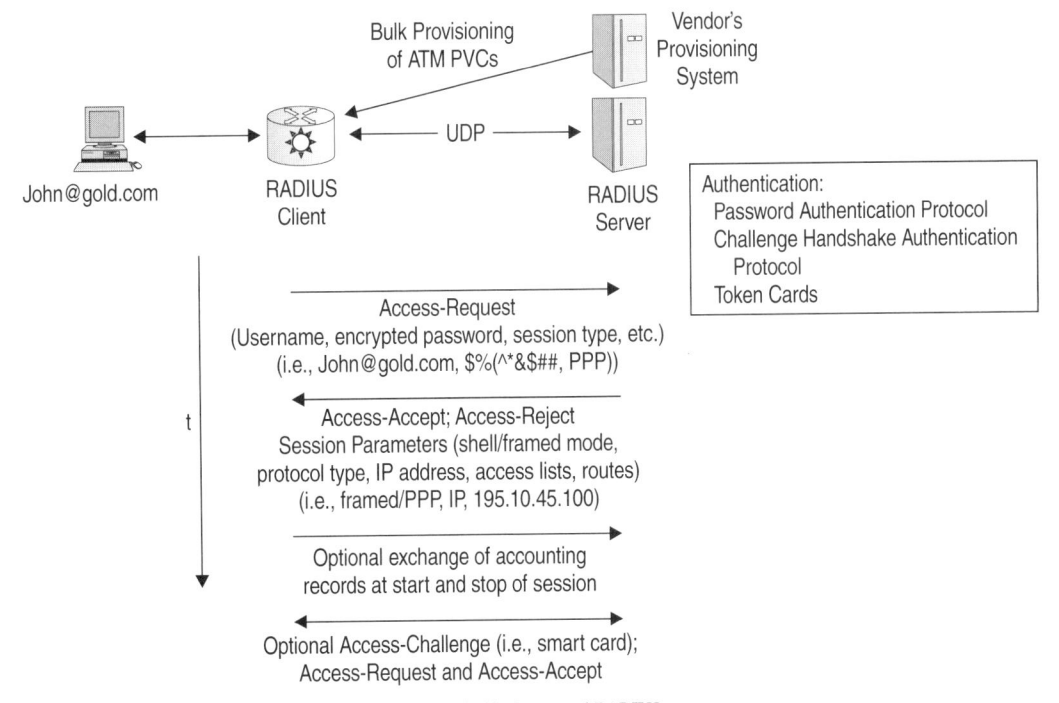

Note: Option is proxy RADIUS where NAS/LAC acts on behalf of external RADIUS server.

FIGURE 5.14 IPSS Interaction with RADIUS

growth of DSL for telecommuting (mainly at hotels), DSL wholesalers (or the hotels themselves) may apply hourly access fees.

Dial Wholesaling and RADIUS One of the most complex uses of RADIUS is in support of dial wholesaling. Consider a subscriber connected to a dial RAS, which then connects via an IPSS to the ISP's router. Figure 5.15 shows an L2TP tunneling deployment, with the RAS acting as the L2TP access concentrator (LAC) and the IPSS as an L2TP network server (LNS). The dial wholesaler and the ISP both operate RADIUS servers. The subscriber first issues an access request. If accepted, the wholesaler's RADIUS server returns the tunnel parameters. If no tunnel exists between the RAS and the IPSS, a tunnel gets established. The RAS now forwards the subscriber's PPP traffic via this tunnel to the IPSS. A second tunnel between the IPSS and the ISP router is then requested. This router (the LNS) now issues an access request to the ISP's RADIUS server, which then (it is hoped) responds with an access response containing the necessary PPP parameters. The LNS now establishes an end-to-end PPP session with the subscriber.

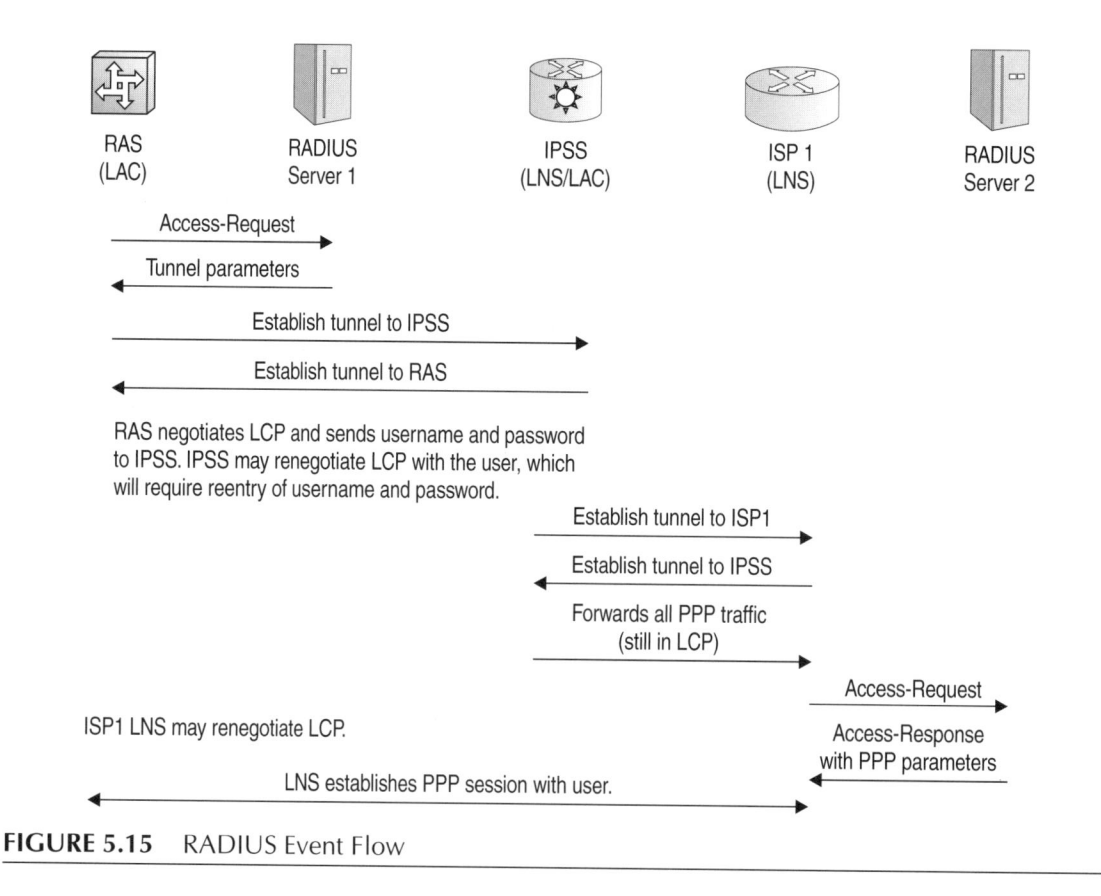

FIGURE 5.15 RADIUS Event Flow

RADIUS defines a set of standard attributes, along with vendor-specific attributes (VSAs) that pertain to a given hardware platform or services capability. Examples of standard RADIUS attributes include the username of the form username@isp, the user PAP password, the protocol type such as PPP, and, in the case of PPP, session and idle timeouts An interesting attribute for PPPoE subscribers in the DSL space is the calling station ID that contains the hostname, B-RAS/IPSS slot, port, and ATM virtual path identifier (VPI) and virtual circuit identifier (VCI). RADIUS accounting parameters are also identified via these attributes. Parameters include the number of input packets and the total session time. VSAs are identified via unique vendor codes and attribute numbers. An example within Vendor ID 3199 (Nortel IP Services) is the telnet user privilege. Values for this VSA include 0 for a standard user, 1 for a superuser, and 2 for a super-superuser. Some attributes have their origin as VSAs and then migrate to standard attributes because of wide use. Many of the accounting parameters, as well as those relating to multilink PPP and L2TP, fall into this category. Other VSAs may include firewall and IP-VPN parameters.

LDAP

The Lightweight Directory Access Protocol (Wahl et al., 1997) is a client/server protocol for directory access. Although originally deployed in conjunction with X.500, LDAPv3 is now decoupled and may be deployed standalone or in conjunction with other directory servers. It is very much suited for the needs of the Internet and many enterprises.

Within the enterprise, an individual's first contact with LDAP is in the context of an e-mail address lookup. However, its use extends beyond simple enterprise directories because of its extensibility. An LDAP directory contains information about objects. When used within an Internet access environment, the object usually refers to an individual, and the directory will store various attributes, which may include a name, password, location, service description, and even photos and sounds relating to that individual. The service provider maintains the central directory, accessible by any internetworking device. These devices, including the IPSSs, RASs, routers, and ATM switches, act as clients to the LDAP servers (see Figure 5.16). One feature of LDAP is its resilience through directory replication. This prevents single points of failure because of server or reachability problems. Although LDAP is a powerful mechanism for storing subscriber parameters, it does not replace existing management systems based on SNMP or CORBA. This is due to the fact that the directory system does not offer the real-time performance required for online device management.

Interaction between the IPSS and the RADIUS server is changing as providers implement LDAP. The provider now enters the subscriber's profile into a central database, which then pushes the data down to the RADIUS server and to the IPSS's provisioning system. In fact, LDAP will distribute this information to any internetworking device, and service providers are heading in this direction. As an example, the directory could contain ATM-layer or CLE-provisioning data.

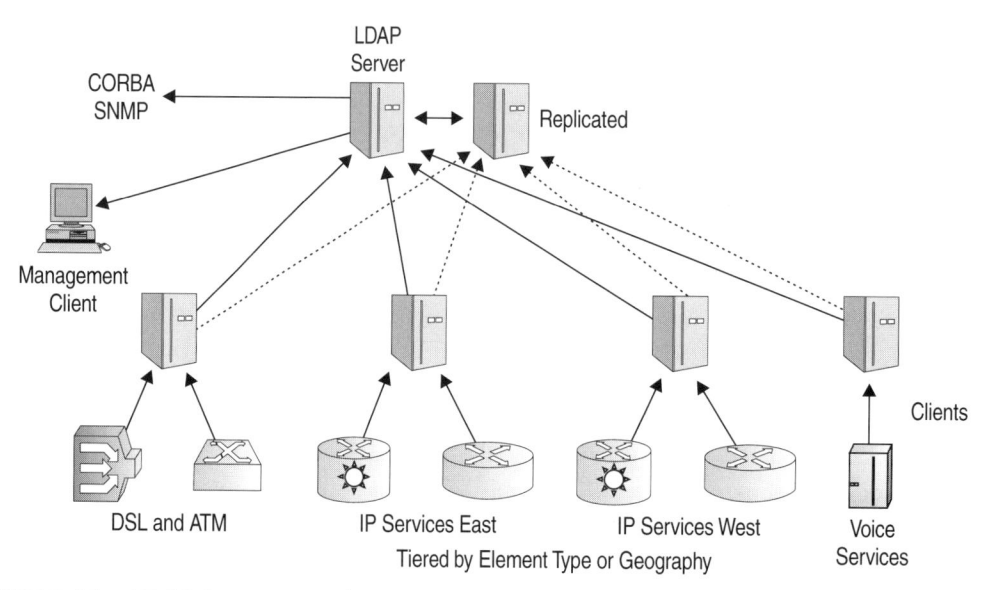

FIGURE 5.16 LDAP Structure and Hierarchy

Subscriber Self-Provisioning

In an extension of the traditional provisioning environment, the provider presents the subscriber with a Web- or client-based portal for service activation, authentication, and possibly service enhancement. In the case of the portal, the IPSS redirects the subscriber's browser to a specific Web page. Note that this redirection is very different from preloading a browser with a specific home page, a technique easily defeated. If the provider is so inclined, it may also provide the subscriber with client software. Advantages of using a portal include more of a presence on the desktop, and disadvantages include the requirement to ship and support a client. These issues are addressed toward the end of this chapter.

There are a variety of portals, all with different roles. Service activation portals are nothing new; they have been used as part of Internet dial provisioning for a while. In this environment, the ISP provides the (potential) subscriber with a toll-free number that forces a connection to a Web page through which the new subscriber may enter contact and billing information. What is new is the extension of this paradigm to the DSL, cable, or wireless markets. In those contexts, the IPSS forces a connection to a provisioning URL. Only after subscribers enter the required information are their accounts activated (see Figure 5.17). The concept of a provisioning portal is critical for the evolving free access services described earlier, in that it is the single point of ongoing contact between the provider and the subscriber.

Building on the basic provisioning portal, the provider may choose to mandate authentication via a Web interface. An advantage of this is that the provider is

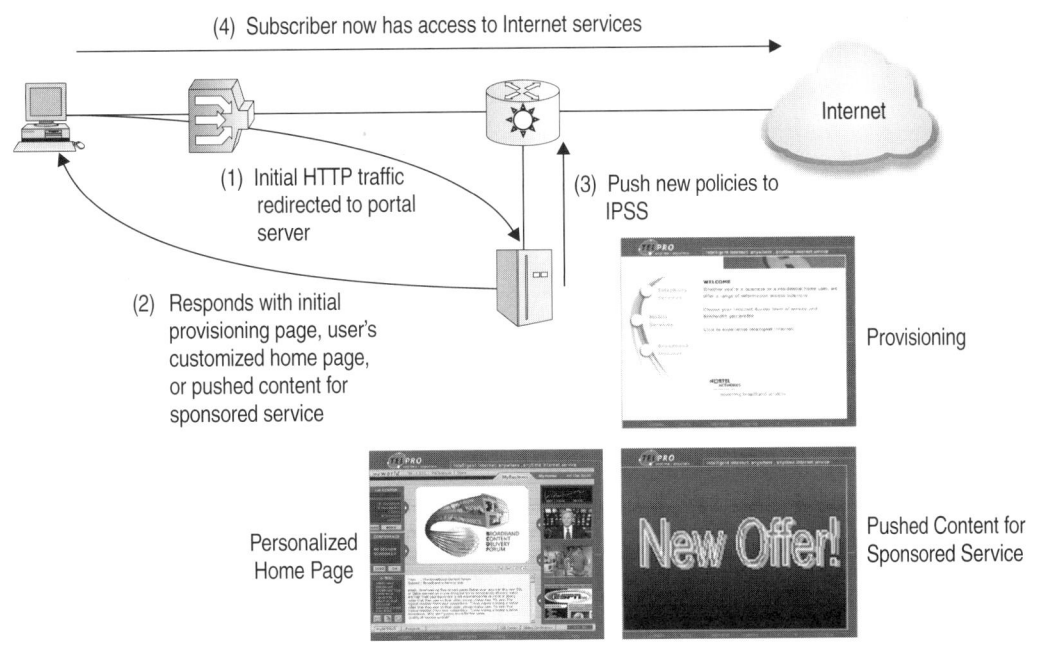

FIGURE 5.17 Subscriber Self-Provisioning

able to customize the subscriber's login experience with targeted content. This is a capability not available through traditional PC dialer programs or PPPoE clients. The next level in sophistication is offering the capability to the subscriber of enhancing his or her basic service. For example, the subscriber may request a higher bandwidth or additional security features. Rather than bringing order entry personnel into the loop or forcing the subscriber to endure a hierarchy of voice prompts, all provisioning could take place via the Web.

External Management Systems

Although the focus thus far has been on the various element and policy management systems associated with the hardware in delivering a service, these systems are only one part of the provisioning puzzle within a typical service provider. Consider an ILEC delivering voice and various types of data services. The ILEC introduces DSL, deploying some new hardware (the DSL CPE, DSLAMs, and IPSS) but reusing components from other data services. Alternatively, an ISP provides DSL services and must seamlessly interface the IPSS with its existing billing and customer care systems. The challenge in both cases is to integrate the management systems associated with the new hardware with existing operational support system (OSS). Table 5.2 outlines some of the most common billing, customer care,

TABLE 5.2 Management Systems and Vendors

Management System	Vendors
Element Management and Provisioning (only systems specific to IPSS/subscriber aggregation listed here)	Alcatel's 1135 Service Management Center Cisco's CiscoWorks 2000/Service Connection Manager CoSine's InVision SMS/InGage CNM Ennovate's EnSight Service Automation System Lucent's (SpringTide's) LightShip Nortel's (Shasta's) Service Creation System Redback's Director and Abatis Unisphere's NMC-RX
Performance Reporting	Concord Net Health, Remedy
SLA Service Assurance	Micromuse Netcool, Agilent Firehunter
Fault Management	Micromuse Netcool, Seagate NerveCenter, HP OpenView, RiverSoft Network Management Operating System
Customer Care	Clarify
Billing	Portal, XACCT, Belle Systems, Bridgewater, CSG Systems
Flow-Through Provisioning	Syndesis, CPlane Service Control Platform
Other	Redundancy—Veritas Interprocess Messaging—TIBCO, Vitria Automated ordering and provisioning—NightFire Software

and provisioning systems. It also lists many of the vendor-proprietary systems in the subscriber aggregation and services market.

Some of the most important capabilities of these systems in terms of service deployment include the following:

- *Service monitoring:* Provides view into the subscriber's services (DSL, IP-VPN, and so forth) across different technology platforms. Includes QoS monitoring.
- *Performance monitoring:* Monitors performance of the network in support of the subscriber services. Used to generate SLA reports.
- *Performance reporting:* Provides network statistics including trending. Used for resource optimization and planning.
- *SLA planning:* Identifies conformance problems and offenders. Defines SLA contracts and evaluates targets based on network capabilities.
- *SLA negotiation:* Maps customer contracts to SLAs created in the planning phase.
- *SLA assessment:* Tracks compliance and generates reports. Will identify customers impacted by a network outage.
- *Service activation:* Provides configuration management, including audit and rollback.

- *Service assurance*
  - Alarm surveillance and fault diagnosis, including auto-discovery and problem advisor
  - Performance monitoring, including packet loss, congestion, jitter, latency, and so forth
  - Trend analysis and reporting
  - Traffic flow and routing analysis
- *Customer care and billing*
  - IP services accounting, including aggregation of performance monitoring and SLA data
  - Trouble ticketing, including collection, mediation, and distribution
  - Gathering via push or pull, normalizing, and storing of data
  - Validating and distributing storage of data
  - Correlating events
  - Distributing resulting data via standard accounting and billing records
  - Bulk or real-time; push or pull

In many cases, an IPSS vendor will partner with a vendor in one of these areas based on requirements that are specific to a given deployment. For example, an ISP may use Portal Software for accounting and might want to offer QoS selection as part of its DSL offering. The interface used for QoS selection must therefore interface not only into the IPSS but also into portal software. Another example is order entry within an ILEC. Here, the provider requires a common interface for ATM PVC provisioning across the DSLAM, the ATM switches, and into the IPSS. Syndesis is often used as this common platform and requires device-specific interfaces for the actual provisioning.

An evolving and very powerful architecture is the use of a messaging bus to connect the various management systems both within and between service providers. In the DSL space, Vitria BusinessWare connects the customers, ISPs, data local exchange carrier (DLEC), and ILECs for flow-through provisioning. Partner interaction models (PIMs) based on XML define the necessary interactions between these different entities. Figure 5.18 depicts one possible flow-through provisioning model. Also relevant in the provisioning space is Telcordia, formerly Bellcore, which delivers a variety of service, network, and element management solutions to many of the major service providers. For this reason, vendors introducing new hardware into these environments, many times, must provide either direct management interfaces or APIs into existing Telcordia-developed systems.

Admittedly, providers are still in the early phases of this end-to-end integration, because of both the unavailability of the necessary interfaces and the time-to-market requirements. Tactical systems deployed in support of these requirements could of course backfire, in that near-term shortcuts may result in longer-term pain.

FIGURE 5.18 Flow-Through Provisioning

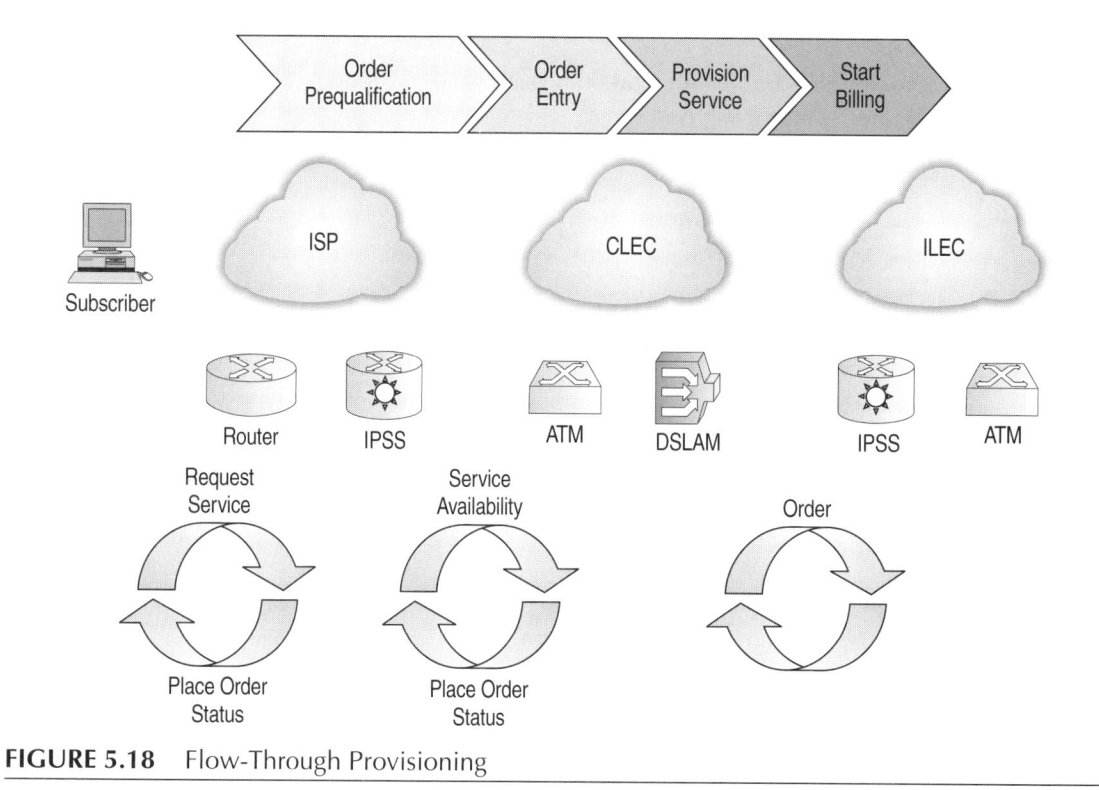

Figure 5.19 depicts the various components of a complete OSS deployment. Although the number of components may seem excessive at first, they are all essential parts of a system providing for provisioning, billing, monitoring, customer support, and facilities management.

Client Software

One difficulty in delivering some of the advanced services desired by the residential or business customer is the requirement for a PC client. This is due to lack of support within the operating system for some of the encapsulations required (e.g., PPPoE or IPSec) or the requirement for a permanent presence on the subscriber's desktop under some business models (e.g., free DSL). Traditionally, the broadband access provider or ISP would provide the subscriber with the client. For DSL, where PPPoE is a major factor, client vendors include Wind River (carrying the former RouterWare product), NTS (now Siemans/Efficient), and BroadJump. In all cases except that of BroadJump, the service provider has no real control over this client, in that it is delivered to the subscriber via CD, is installed, and quickly grows obsolete (unless there is a provision for automatic updates). In addition, support costs for these clients are a known problem within the industry. Although native

IPSS Provisioning

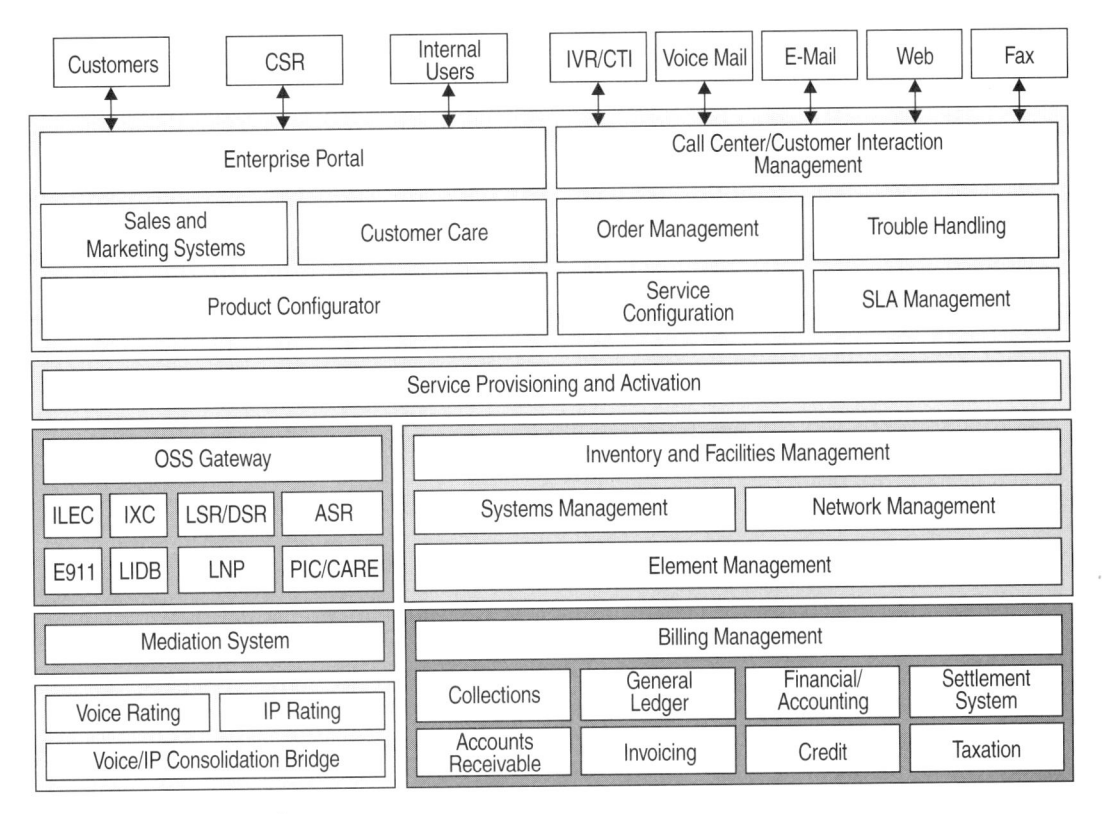

FIGURE 5.19 OSS Architecture

support within the operating system is sometimes used as the answer, one cannot expect that Windows, the Mac operating system, or even Linux will keep up with every change in the provisioning model.

A novel approach is to couple a PC client, or "agent," with a provider-based management platform. This platform takes an active role in client updates and provisioning, but goes beyond this basic functionality by permitting the provider to configure the subscriber's system, monitor it in real time (with the agreement of the subscriber, of course) to identify the source of network or access problems, and push network information to the subscriber (see Figure 5.20). Additional functions include client registration, used to identify new subscribers within the network, and integration with back-office systems. One vendor, BroadJump, has coined the term *virtual truck* to refer to the capabilities of this active agent architecture. Stated advantages to the service provider include acceleration of market penetration through ease of installation, reduction of support costs resulting in increased margins, increased customer loyalty, and the ability to market, upgrade, and customize services. Likewise, subscriber benefits include ease of self-installation and

FIGURE 5.20 Active Agent Architecture

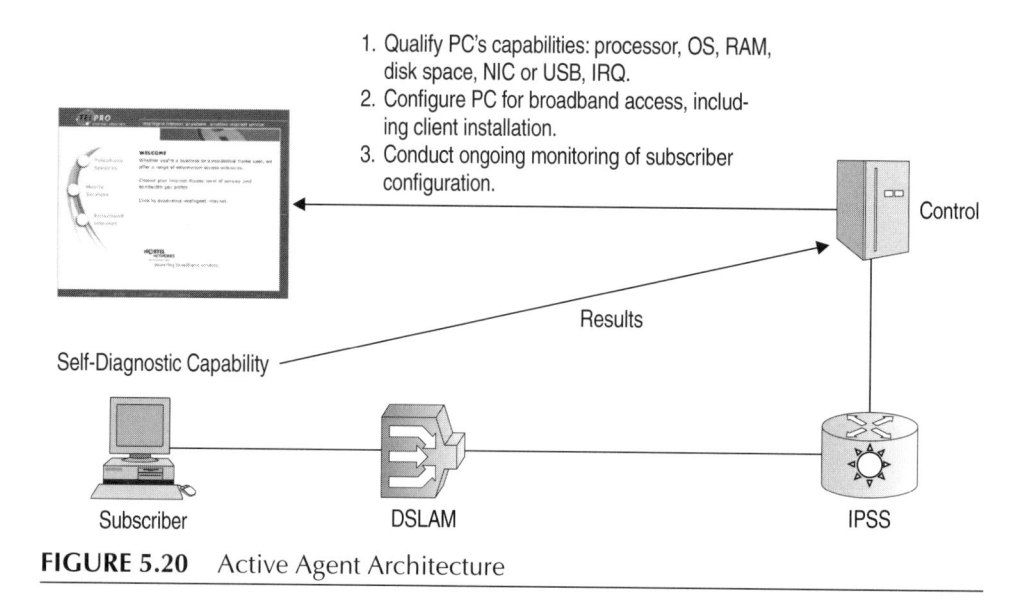

configuration, streamlined support, access to real-time status data, and ease of service upgrades.

Customer Network Management

The final challenge in delivering many edge-based services is the requirement for customer visibility into network configuration and service monitoring. This customer network management (CNM) capability is a given in services such as firewalling and IP-VPNs. For example, as part of a managed firewall service, the customer will wish to configure firewall rules or monitor and log policy violations. In essence, the subscriber to a managed service requires the same management capabilities as would be available if the device was on the subscriber's premises. IP-VPN services are another good example of CNM requirements, where a subscriber may wish to change group membership or QoS on demand and to monitor performance and utilization. Only in the last few years have providers begun to take an active role in the development of these CNM capabilities, capabilities extending beyond the support some vendors provide for their Fortune 500 customers.

Extending the concept of CNM, some providers now permit customers to monitor and even alter the configuration of their CLE devices. The provider accomplishes this by implementing what is known as *split-horizon* capabilities, with both the subscriber and the service provider permitted to alter certain device-level characteristics (see Figure 5.21). For example, the provider may have access to loop monitoring and configuration, while the subscriber may be able to alter Layer 3 traffic-shaping parameters, as well as monitor throughput. The one

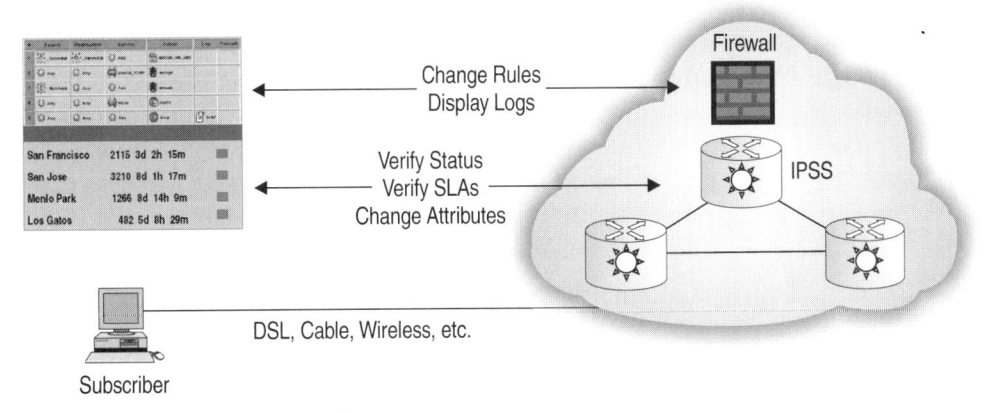

FIGURE 5.21 Customer Network Management

challenge here is to ensure that the subscriber has access to only those parameters made visible by the service provider. Not all CLE devices are capable of this.

Service Level Agreements

Ultimately, the subscriber is interested in a reliable service offering. A provider characterizes this by what is known as a service level agreement (SLA), which outlines any security, QoS, and uptime guarantees, and many times is monitored by the subscriber via CNM (described in the preceding section). The SLA will have a major influence on service pricing and will determine whether the customer may rely on a primary provider for all services or must contract a second provider for backup. Once SLAs are in place, the provider is liable financially for violations. For example, if the provider offers 99.9 percent uptime over the course of a month, it must refund the subscriber a percentage of the monthly fee if availability slips below that number.

This financial penalty to a service provider is perhaps the best way to ensure the reliability of the service offering. In other words, if during the course of the month, the subscriber experiences more than 44 minutes downtime (calculated by 60 minutes × 24 hours × 31 days/1,000 parts), the provider is in violation. Like all interactions that involve lawyers (i.e., contract agreements), there are complexities. One such complexity is the time window of the SLA. In the course of a month, a single outage in this case may last 44 minutes if it is not time-bounded. This may be unacceptable to the customer. A solution is to define SLAs over the course of a day or even an hour, each with acceptable limits. From the perspective of the service provider, these SLAs balance against what the provider must have in place to actually deliver a given SLA. In fact, the provider may deploy a network statistically capable of offering an SLA of 99.5 percent, for example, but may offer

SLAs at 99.9 percent. In this case, the provider is betting that the network will not fail and will discount the projected subscriber revenue to deal with unforeseen outages. There is therefore a bit of due diligence that the customer of the service must undertake when evaluating SLAs. In addition, any SLA guarantees will not reflect the financial stability of a provider, which in itself may have a major impact on network uptime (especially if the customer wakes up and discovers that the provider has declared bankruptcy during the dark of the night).

Although most interest in SLAs seems to revolve around service uptime, parameters of the service are just as critical. For example, an SLA will usually define the average bandwidth available to the customer, the latency, and the packet loss, possibly mapped to different QoSs. Security SLAs, briefly described earlier, will include logging, notification, and the probability that a provider will successfully block a given attack. It goes without saying that effective SLAs across provider boundaries are still in their infancy.

A challenge is in calculating the expected network downtime. This is often difficult, given the number of internetworking devices and physical links across

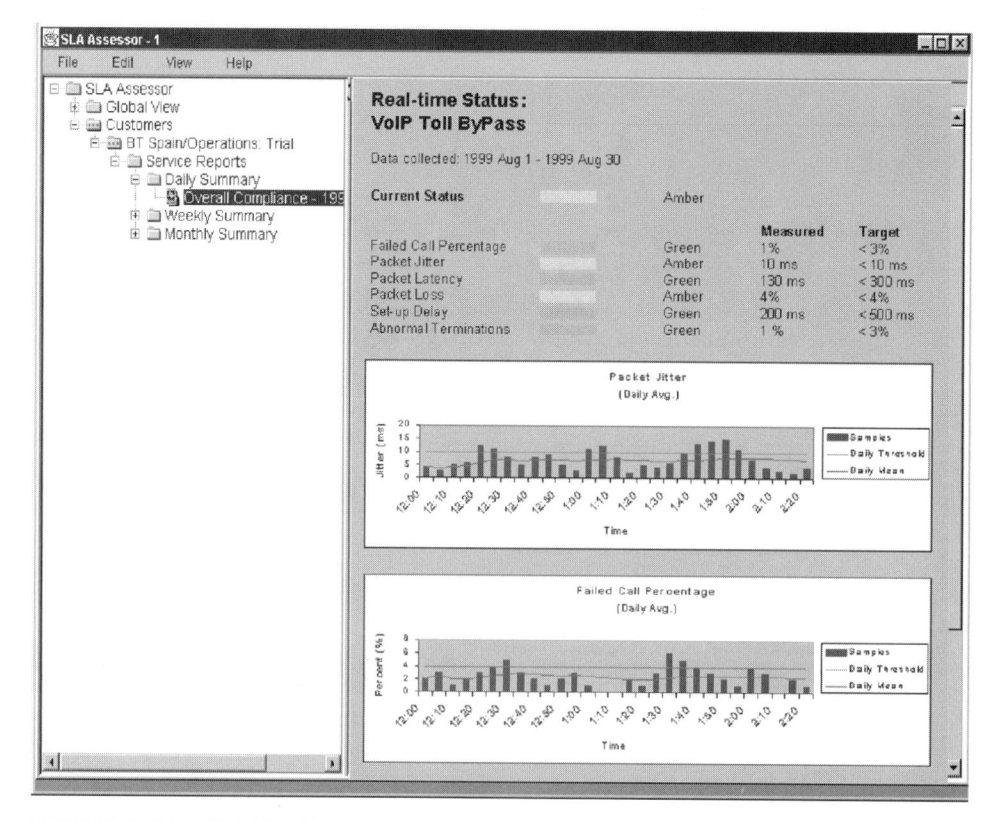

FIGURE 5.22   SLA Tracking

the path between the subscriber and a hosting site or between two subscribers connected via an IP-VPN. Here, the provider must be very careful to calculate expected outages for each component, the mean time between failures (MTBFs), as well as the expected restoration times. A given internetworking device may in fact be capable of providing different restoration levels for different subscriber classes (premium, best effort, and so forth). This capability will of course influence the calculation. Figure 5.22 depicts a typical value-added service, along with failure rates and network performance.

Conclusion

This chapter is really the core of the book. The technologies introduced in earlier chapters lay the groundwork for understanding the IPSS, its role in the network, and its provisioning. With this understanding, we may now look at how the IPSS plays an essential role in end-to-end service deployment. Chapter 6 looks at the basic connectivity services, while chapter 7 builds on this by introducing IP-VPNs and content management.

Chapter 6
Deploying Basic Services

Subscribers buy services, not the specific technologies with which services are deployed. IP services break down into two categories: basic and enhanced. In today's IP services network, basic services include physical access to the service, bandwidth, and general availability. Certain network implementations, such as an open access environment, use L2TP and related tunneling technologies to pass the user connection to the service provider as part of basic services. Tunneling for open access may be invisible to the subscriber, just as the DSL or cable is invisible if the primary contact point of the subscriber is an ISP.

This chapter focuses on the deployment of these basic services: what the user sees. As with any business, financial success rests on offering services that people want to buy (and not just try) and then implementing these services with pricing and support that are acceptable to the user, while covering costs and enabling profitability. After a description of the basic services concept, subscriber aggregation and basic Internet access are discussed, including the various access technologies. Once connectivity is achieved, additional services covered include traffic management and wholesaling.

Application QoS support is key in permitting business subscribers to fully utilize the network in support of mission-critical applications. For example, a business may utilize the network for site-to-site connectivity, or it may have an accounting or a manufacturing application that requires a certain QoS across the backbone to operate effectively. The business may also offer e-commerce services, with its customers expecting a certain experience.

The chapter concludes with a look at what it takes to maintain customer loyalty and ensure lockin to minimize expensive subscriber churn.

Service Basics

Service is a confusing term because it means different things to different audiences, depending on their backgrounds. Carriers refer to ATM and Frame Relay as services, and ISPs make use of the domain name service (DNS). In this book, we use *service* to refer to the various network-edge-based connectivity, tunneling, security, and content services that ILECs, CLECs, and ISPs are currently rolling out. These services come in a variety of formats and either are being offered today or are planned for the near future. Many service providers have traditionally offered managed customer located equipment (CLE) services, and now they are looking to move some of these CLE products into the network for easier management and lower-cost deployment. Scaling a network device to offer the same set of services as a CLE device requires a new type of platform, previously unavailable in the marketplace. This new services device has to support a myriad of services but also has to scale to multiple customers since it is now located in the PoP, where real estate is at a premium. Service providers are also bundling services in a variety of ways to make gaining entry into new market segments attractive. In much the same way that customers shifted to a Centrex voice service, they are now shifting to network-based services. This chapter demystifies these new services and service models.

The service definitions presented here have been collected from service providers and equipment vendors. Chapter 8 builds on these service definitions as well as on the technology and provisioning descriptions from chapters 2 through 5, by describing actual end-to-end service implementations.

Defining just what a service is can be a challenge. Different standards bodies define services differently. For example, the IETF Policy Framework Working Group defines a service by focusing on a set of policies (Westerinen et al., 2000). Other standards bodies use a different definition. The service definition used in this book is that a service is an offer that provides value to the subscriber as well as the service provider and enables the service provider to generate revenue. A service is not dependent solely on a pure technology play but is technology-independent. It can be offered through different technologies. Also, a service is not an application (but an application can sit on top of a service). For example, are DSL and cable service offerings or technologies? In reality, they should be considered technologies. Be warned, however, that in the industry there are misconceptions about what is considered a technology and what is considered a service.

DSL, cable, analog dial, and Frame Relay technologies are based on different access hardware or protocols. Some of these technologies, such as Frame Relay, have evolved into service offerings that go way beyond the physical technology definition. However, true services are very different from access technologies and include offerings such as basic subscriber aggregation in support of basic Internet access, security, traffic management for premium access, IP-VPNs, and content management. These services are all independent of the underlying physical technology.

TABLE 6.1 Technologies, Services, and Applications

Technology	Service	Application
ATM	Subscriber aggregation	Residential voice
Frame Relay	Managed firewalls/security	Video distribution
DSL	IP-VPNs	Gaming
Cable	Traffic management	Business-to-business exchanges
Wireless	Wholesaling	Web
Optical		
IP		

Another misconception in the industry concerns the difference between a service and an application. For example, while videoconferencing, gaming, and even telephony are commonly considered services, in reality they are applications, visible at the subscriber's desktop (or at a server) and using a set of technologies and services (Table 6.1). Two services described later, video distribution and voice, fall into both the services and applications categories. They are covered within the service descriptions because of their impact on network design, as well as a provider's ability to offer them as part of a service bundle. However, they are also applications because the subscriber can "touch and feel" them.

As part of creating the service definition of what is offered to customers, the provider must decide on the approach—whether the offering is network-based, relies on a given CPE/CLE device, or leverages more powerful PC platforms. The service offer will depend on the intended audience, time-to-market requirements, price sensitivities, and service penetration, as well as any partnerships the provider may have. A provider may eventually determine that the best service will combine all three elements, as exemplified by the IP-VPN offering described in chapter 7. Trade-offs between CPE-based versus network-based services include the cost of deploying and supporting customer-based hardware and software versus the speed of service deployment. Although some PC-based approaches to services, such as firewalling, may seem attractive at first glance, whether or not subscribers or even corporate IT departments are willing to support these is another story. Finally, a provider must make a conscious decision as to where the service will be offered within the service value chain. If all is on the desktop, what is the opportunity for additional revenue, and where is the subscriber lock-in? This service differentiation is therefore very important when looking into how providers market and price their service and application offerings. In addition, certain classes of services may be suited to only subsets of the total subscriber population. Thus, the service (or "product") development arm of a provider must be careful about service definition as well as service bundling. The following sections describe basic services and service bundling in detail.

Basic Services

Basic services are those offerings that permit market entry and also serve as a basis over which the provider may offer more sophisticated services based on customer demand or the evolution of the provider's provisioning capabilities. As an example, broadband subscriber aggregation is required to connect the subscriber to the network. Without an effective aggregation platform and provisioning system, the other services are moot. Subscriber aggregation is where discussions of PPP, PPPoE, and bridging come into play in the DSL market segment, and concerns such as oversubscription and its resulting impact on network performance play a role in cable and wireless service definitions. Premium Internet access that provides application QoS support builds on this basic aggregation functionality. Techniques such as differentiated services (DiffServ) marking, policing and shaping, and MPLS traffic engineering come into play. Very rarely do you see a traffic management service on its own—it is usually subsumed within a set of access, content management, and IP-VPN services. In fact, traffic management is a requirement for the effective delivery of broadband services.

Security, which relies on stateful firewalling, antispoofing capabilities, and prevention of denial-of-service (DoS) attacks, builds on both basic and premium access. Although in the past many have considered security a premium service, it too is now a requirement and forms the basis of a number of the more complex services described later in this chapter. A service provider may include both traffic management and security in support of a basic service bundle.

Location for Services

One important question is, where is the best point in the network for service application? Is it in the PoP at the IP service switch (IPSS), at the customer site, or possibly at both locations? The proper answer depends on the service offering, the business model of the provider, the skill set of the subscriber, and network reach. Although the focus here is on the provider-controlled network edge, by no means does this imply that this is the only proper point in the network for services application. In fact, a provider may service a single customer that has some connectivity to the provider's backbone (known as "on-net"), but also has offices at which the first provider does not provide service. Here, a second provider would provide connectivity for these locations, and the customer is "off-net" from the first provider. However, if the first provider wanted to offer a common set of services to the customer, it could provide CLE-based devices for the customer's sites connected to the second provider.

There is therefore no single correct answer for the best point of services deployment, and providers have come to the conclusion that a fully developed security, traffic management, or IP-VPN service will consist of a number of network- and CPE-based components optimized for different market segments. As an example, an IP-VPN offering may consist of IPSec-based PC clients serving mobile workers via dial, DSL, and cable; larger CLE boxes serving major sites; and a network-edge-based IPSS serving branch offices. Traffic management services also require end-to-end support from the CLE to the network core if they are to provide true end-to-end capabilities. One of the major criteria in hardware and software selection is whether the provider is actually managing a service or whether the subscribers implement different functionality ad hoc. For example, a PC-based firewall may be adequate as a personal security solution, but it may not have the necessary centralized management and logging to be usable as part of a managed offering.

Comparisons between the more sophisticated CLE devices and network-based solutions are difficult because many times the subscriber does not know the level of sophistication required going into the service selection process. The choice of what services to deploy may come down to a matter of pricing; if the provider can offer the network-based solution at a lower monthly cost and is capable of addressing any security and CNM concerns, then the subscriber is more likely to accept this offering. Another qualifier is terminology. In many cases, there is confusion when describing a set of capabilities or services. For example, firewalling means different things to different people, and when defining a service, the provider must be very careful to be detailed in describing its exact characteristics.

Subscriber Aggregation and Basic Internet Access

Subscriber aggregation, often referred to as *subscriber management,* is the process of connecting broadband—that is, DSL, cable, wireless, and others to a wholesaler's or ISP's backbone in support of basic Internet access. The following sections describe the access and market opportunities for broadband services.

DSL Access and Market Opportunity

For DSL, an access wholesaler provides the basic DSL access and, in most cases, operates the DSLAMs, while the ISP terminates only the subscriber traffic that originates on the wholesaler's DSLAMs. A later section, "Wholesaling," describes this access wholesaling in greater detail.

Subscriber aggregation is the most basic and most widespread of network edge services. As part of the subscriber aggregation function, the IPSS performs protocol conversion, terminates ATM or other access link-layer technologies, terminates or forwards into the backbone any access side tunnels (L2TP, PPTP, IPSec, and so forth), and supports multiple ISP contexts (or virtual routers) if deployed as part of a wholesale access deployment. Devices capable of basic subscriber aggregation have been available since 1999 and are sometimes referred to as IPSSs, subscriber management systems (SMSs), or broadband RASs (B-RASs). In most cases, SMSs and B-RASs perform aggregation, while IPSSs are capable of performing more sophisticated state-aware packet processing. Major vendors in the subscriber management market segment include Alcatel (via the Assured Access acquisition), Cisco, Unisphere, and Redback. CoSine, Nortel Networks (via the Shasta Networks acquisition), Lucent (via the SpringTide acquisition), and a few new entrants such as Quarry and Celox fall under the IPSS category but are also capable of providing simple subscriber aggregation.

On the periphery of subscriber aggregation are platforms from Abatis (since acquired by Redback) and Ellacoya that are mainly focused on policy provisioning via their portal capabilities, as opposed to focusing on raw IP services throughput. The subscriber aggregation function common to all these platforms is critical in broadband access, and it is a capability that was not really a strong point of traditional edge router designs (as described in the section in chapter 5, "Edge Router versus IPSSs") because of the scalability required in subscriber session processing. As an example, before Redback announced its first SMS platform, which supported more than 1,000 subscribers, the typical core router was capable of supporting only on the order of 255 subscribers in the DSL space.

Across the access connection, subscribers arrive at the IPSS via different interfaces and encapsulations depending on the underlying technology. In the case of DSL, subscribers usually appear on ATM PVCs as PPP, PPPoE, or RFC 2684 bridged or routed traffic (see Figure 6.1). In a telecommuting environment, the subscriber's PC or DSL modem may originate an L2TP, PPTP, or IPSec tunnel above one of these basic encapsulations. The IPSS terminates the subscriber PVCs and forwards the traffic into the access wholesaler's or ISP's backbone. In addition, some newer DSLAMs with IP capability combine the DSL modems with this subscriber aggregation function, directly forwarding the routed IP traffic into the provider's backbone. Although a provider may not require a standalone IPSS in this application, it still would be used to enable the more sophisticated IP services described in the following sections since the basic IP-DSLAM would be capable of subscriber management only.

The choice of access encapsulation will depend on the wholesaler's and ISP's service delivery model as well as their confidence (or lack thereof) in a PC client. RFC-2684 bridging is simple to implement, but does not allow the provider to effectively identify multiple subscribers within a household unless a subscriber management platform that identifies subscribers via their IP addresses is in place. This, however, is not a problem if the provider implements flat-rate, per-household pricing. Of the flat-rate, per-household pricing models, many consider the bridged model to be the most effective because of its ease of use and true "always-on" con-

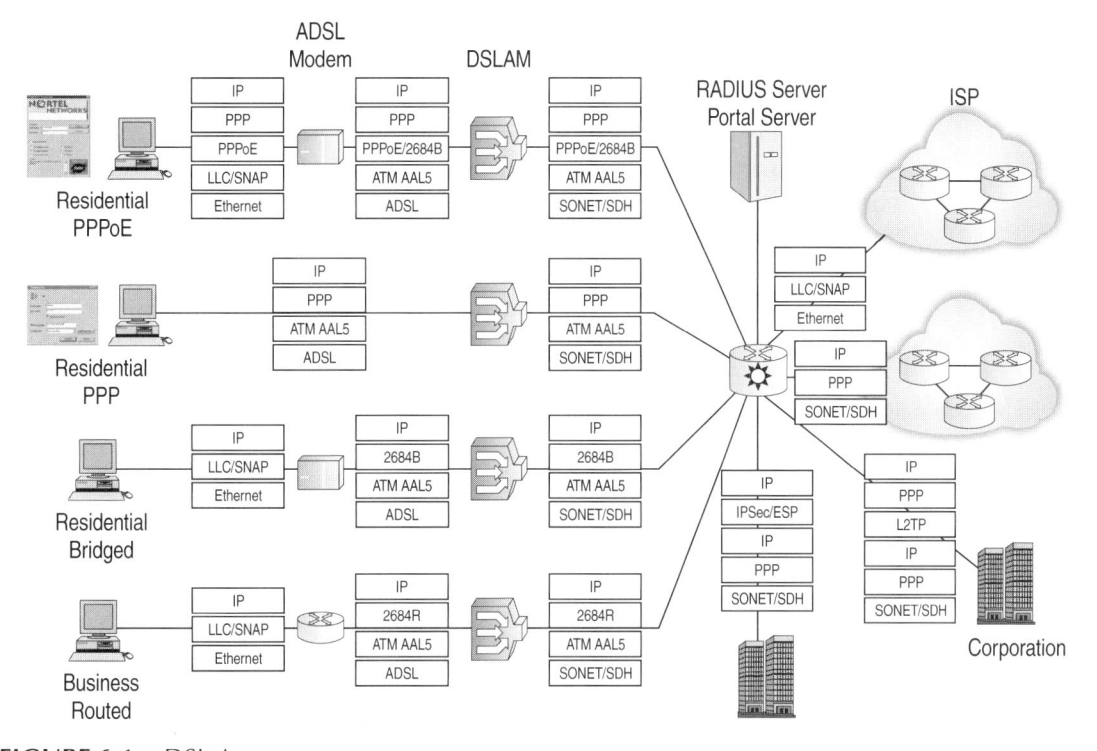

FIGURE 6.1 DSL Access

nectivity. In addition, bridging does not create an issue with reachability between PCs within the household since all PCs are assigned IP addresses belonging to a single subnet. If one user within the household wishes to reach a corporate network, the IP-VPN client (for example, Check Point SecuRemote) will normally allow the user simultaneous access to both the household LAN and the corporate network, only encrypting traffic with IP addresses destined for the corporate intranet. Both PPPoE and L2TP, in contrast, assign IP addresses to the PC that belong to the provider's network. This creates in-home reachability problems unless the PC is set up as a default gateway. One concern with typical bridged configurations is scalability limitations caused by broadcast traffic and the potential for broadcast storms because of misbehaving applications. In the DSL market segment, all subscriber management platforms implement the necessary filters and enhancements to basic bridging, such as half-bridging, to eliminate these threats.

In PPPoE's favor is its ability to identify individual users within a household through unique logins. In addition, the provider has the ability to reuse the RADIUS infrastructure deployed as part of Internet dial offerings, as well as the capability to implement timeouts (as with dial) to permit additional oversubscription of the service. The majority of low-end residential DSL services now implement PPPoE, with the provider now charging extra for the "luxury" of permanent IP addressing via a bridged service. PPP over ATM, supported on some ADSL modems and on some PCs, also permits session authentication, but is more suitable for single-user deployments unless the DSL modem supports multiple subscribers. For business subscribers, both RFC-2684 bridging and routing enjoy use, in that they permit the business to view the DSL connection no differently than a leased line or Frame Relay circuit.

The speed with which providers deploy DSL and the resulting pricing are related to the overall market opportunity. According to PointTopic (2000), in the United States the ILECs (such as Verizon [Bell Atlantic/GTE], BellSouth, SBC, and Qwest [with US West]) reported that the number of DSL-qualified lines grew from 20 million in 1999 to anywhere from 38 to 50 million in 2000 depending on the survey. The CLECs report on coverage on both loops served and on a PoP basis. By the end of 2000, Covad reported more than 30 million loops served, while AT&T and WorldCom reported coverage in more than 1,000 PoPs. Note that much of this CLEC coverage overlaps the population base serviced by the ILECs.

This growth is paralleled elsewhere in the world, and by the end of 2000, 44 percent of the lines in Germany, 48 percent of those in France, 2.5 million lines in Korea, 1 million in Hong Kong, and 1.5 million in Taiwan were DSL-capable. By mid-2001, more than 50 percent of U.K. lines were DSL-capable. These figures, which document loops served, are roughly equivalent to wireless operators stating the number of PoPs or the percentage of their subscriber base served by a wireless infrastructure. They are important in informing the marketplace as to the status of their broadband buildout and therefore the potential subscriber base.

However, the more telling number is the number of active DSL subscribers. Between the ILECs and CLECs, more than 2 million customers were connected in the United States by the end of 2000, a number expected to grow to somewhere around 13 million by the end of 2004. This figure would be a 27 percent penetration and is based on the assumption of 80 percent of the households falling within a DSL service area. Given new initiatives to push the technology into the digital loop carrier (DLC) space, this is likely. Worldwide, this figure is expected to top 25 million, though it could be significantly greater by 2004 based on aggressive buildout plans in Europe and in Asia (FCC, 2000). We must of course balance these buildout plans with the reality of the capital markets, and in some cases the buildout plans are predicated on partnerships that may not occur.

In the authors' opinions, the best estimate yet is a Yankee report (Yankee, 2000), which places the market for high-speed access at 41 percent of the Internet population by the middle of the decade. This figure is based on a survey evaluating the willingness to pay among all PC-equipped households. What is just as interesting is the overall interest level, at 63 percent within the PC-equipped household category and 82 percent among telecommuters (comprising more than 25 percent of all U.S. households). The conclusion here is that the market could be even greater if service providers addressed some of the service pricing concerns. In any case, given 100 million Internet-connected households, a conservative estimate calls for 40 million or more households with DSL, cable, or wireless connectivity by the middle of the decade. Worldwide, the total could be between 100 and 150 million, though even this number may be low based on the growth of digital TV and other broadband devices in the home that lay a path for true convergence (see Figure 6.2). An earlier survey (Ovum, 2000a) projected 54 million DSL and 20 million cable households globally by 2005.

One way to build subscriber base is to offer incentives for signing up for the DSL access service, the DSL ISP, or a combination of the two. An example of these incentives is discounts for long-term commitments, where the installation fee or CPE charge is waived for a one- or two-year term. More sophisticated bundles include a PC. The subscriber is of course subject to early termination fees. The provider may also offer a discount as part of a service bundle, offering advantages for long-distance, local-service, or wireless subscribers. Note that this bundling is

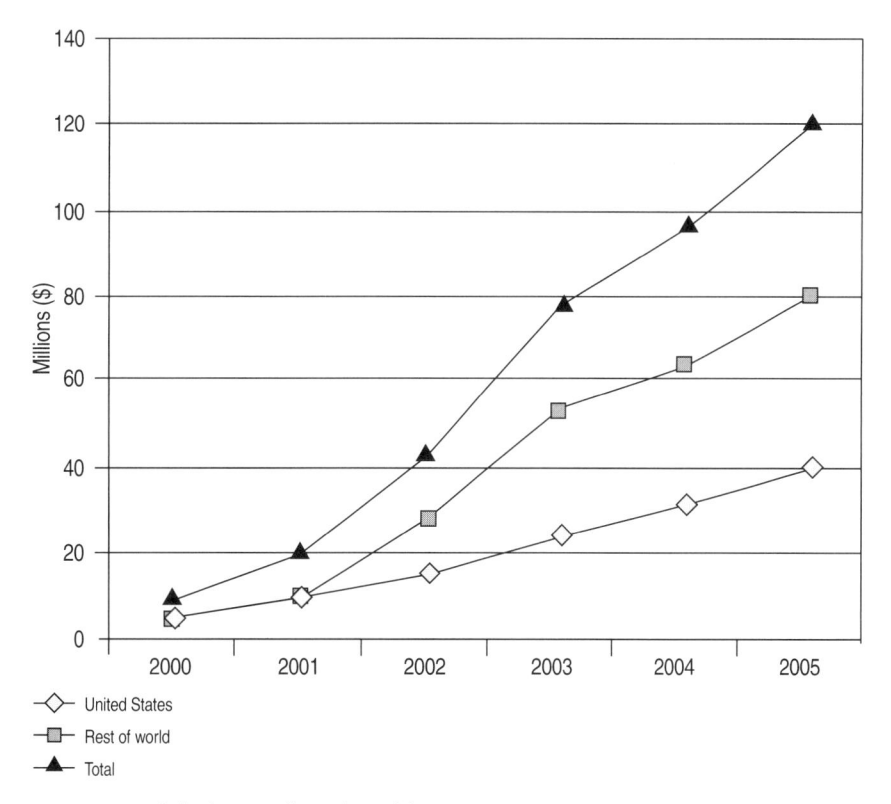

FIGURE 6.2 Global Broadband Buildout

the norm within cable modem services. In many cases, the service is now bundled with the ISP, offering additional price breaks. This prevents the subscriber from having to deal with two sets of providers and monthly statements. Self-installation also minimizes up-front costs to the provider resulting in savings passed on to the subscriber.

So, what are realistic charges for the various services? Of the different broadband services, DSL is all over the map because of the different target markets. At the low end, residential PPPoE services, such as those offered by PacBell, are now offered at $39.95 or lower for ADSL access and ISP. The prospectuses for these services sometimes state that because of oversubscription, average downstream bandwidth may vary from 1.5 Mbps to 384 Kbps, while upstream bandwidth may be only on the order of 128 Kbps. These low-end services also offer very little in terms of qualified support or SLAs. Still, in comparison to Internet dial, the average user is quite satisfied, and the access provider has accomplished its mission of offloading the PSTN (probably the real reason for residential bargain-basement pricing). Covad's closest service offering in this space in 2001, TeleSurfer, approximated these rates, with 608 Kbps downstream and 128 Kbps upstream available at $49 to $69 per month, depending on choice of ISP. A 1.5 Mbps/384 Kbps service was offered at $69 to $89 per month.

A concern with these low-end services is the type of services possible when the subscriber is limited to 128 Kbps in the upstream direction. A recent FCC report (FCC, 2000) defines *advanced services* as those offering greater than 200 Kbps in the upstream direction. These bandwidths permit rich content, such as video and Web sourced from the subscriber, and also enable more effective telecommuting. Based on this definition, it is anticipated that most high-speed users (that is, those with 128 Kbps and below upstream) will transition to higher bandwidths as technology becomes more readily available.

Telecommuters and home workers require greater available bandwidth in both the downstream and upstream directions and often wish to work with ISPs that offer more stringent service guarantees. In addition, since the user's employer is almost always paying for the service, there is less sensitivity to pricing. Typical telecommuters pay on the order of $100 to $150 per month for service, depending on the choice of technology (ADSL, SDSL, IDSL) and bandwidth. As an example, a combined ADSL and ISP service offered by PacBell in mid-2000 for $59.95 per month offered the same bandwidths as the $39.95 PacBell residential PPPoE service described earlier but permitted static addressing (5 IP addresses maximum) and therefore multiple PCs. Increasing the bandwidth to between 1.5 and 6 Mbps downstream and 384 Kbps upstream resulted in a monthly fee of $179.95, a significant increase, though still within the bounds of high-end telecommuters. Covad's offerings in this space, known as TeleSpeed, included symmetric rates of 144, 192, 384 Kbps and 1.1 Mbps. Monthly rates for these bandwidths ranged from $89 to $150 at the low end to $249 to $400 for the 1.1 Mbps service, and all of Covad's services supported multiple users and routing.

The technology also plays an important role in the pricing model, since a subscriber beyond the reach of ADSL may have access only to IDSL. Providers consider IDSL to be a business offering in most cases, and they charge more for it than for ADSL, even though the customer's bandwidth may be below that of ADSL. This is a bit of a disconnect working against the CLECs' offering this technology.

Another way providers differentiate themselves is through the access protocol. The $39.95 service from PacBell described earlier is based on PPPoE, a session protocol requiring a login. A PPPoE service precludes deployment of a Web server at the residence because of dynamic IP addressing and also incorporates timeouts based on inactivity. Those subscribers wishing to deploy servers will need to subscribe to a bridged or routed service at a higher rate. In many cases, the same ADSL access provider will offer all three services (PPPoE, bridged, and routed).

Business subscribers will look much like telecommuters but will be more demanding in bandwidth and will require SLAs. In most cases, these SLAs are available only as part of SDSL, HDSL, or SHDSL services. As businesses rely on DSL as a fractional T1 (less than 1.544 Mbps) or Frame Relay replacement, their SLA demands will approach those of the incumbents' SLA service offerings for fractional T1 and Frame Relay. For this reason, pricing for high-end business services will be very different from that for residences or telecommuters. Services in this market segment will be $250 per month or more depending on bandwidth requirements and service guarantees. Looking at PacBell once again (and based on published 2000 fees), available bandwidths are the same as those for the telecommuter service, but the monthly rates rise to $238 per month and $328 per month, because of a larger IP address space of 32 available addresses, the ability to deploy routed CPE, and more proactive monitoring. An interesting point is that shifting to a third-party ISP (that is, PacBell as the ADSL provider and a separate ISP) would result in the $328 fee growing to the $400 per month range. This is for equivalent services, though with different installation and termination agreements. Probably the closest approximation to a T1 service in this space is Covad's partnership with third-party ISPs. The SLA is 1.5 Mbps downstream and 1.5 Mbps upstream with a committed information rate (CIR) of 1.2 Mbps and 29 IP addresses allocated to the site. Here, the monthly rate is $499.

Across all these markets, the price for installation, the cost of equipment purchase or rental, and the requirement for a long-term service agreement vary greatly. In many cases, it is not difficult to obtain a promotion whereby the initial installation and hardware are free of charge, as long as the subscriber is willing to commit to the service for more than 6 months or a year. In addition, more residential services now offer self-installation, eliminating the $100 or higher technician installation fee. Promotions are obviously most readily available in areas where the DSL provider faces competition from cable or fixed wireless.

> ◆ **Yet Another Provider Type?**
>
> It is still too early to judge a third type of DSL service, one optimized for the distribution of broadcast video. Although the technology supports this type of service, it has not yet been widely deployed because of costs. Still, some of the more forward-looking providers have taken the leap when threatened by the cable operators.
>
> Chapter 8 describes one such service based on this video distribution. As the DSL access providers enable higher DSL bandwidths via remote placement of DSLAMs, this video service should become more viable. Ultimately, it may become the second conduit of entertainment video for many households.
>
> Interestingly, when the numbers are compared, the total cable subscriber base over the next few years may exceed that of DSL, but the total bandwidth served by DSL and the total revenue generated will exceed that of cable. This is because of the business emphasis, as well as planned wide deployment into the 6 Mbps range based on DLC systems. Other access technologies, including fixed wireless and satellite, also play a role in the broadband services space but are not as widely deployed at the moment.

In the United States alone, residential DSL revenues are expected to grow from $290 million in 2000 to more than $2.3 billion in 2003. The growth in the business sector is even greater, from $299 million to more than $5.6 billion (IDC, 1999b). The European market is much the same, with combined residential and business revenues growing from $333 million to $5.7 billion in the same timeframe (IDC, 2000a). Central and Latin America (CALA) and Asia–Pacific Rim deployment could equal Europe by 2004.

Cable Access and Market Opportunity

Analyzing cable access is a bit different from analyzing DSL access. Whereas you can identify the number of DSL subscribers fairly easily (based on individual ATM virtual circuits), it's difficult to guess how many cable TV subscribers are using cable Internet access. There are two types of headends within cable: those that support IP routing and those that operate as bridges. In the former case, the cable headend presents the IPSS with a routed trunk connection. If the headend is configured to forward all subscriber traffic to the IPSS across this link, you can implement firewalling, tunneling, and ISP selection on the IPSS. The connection between the headend and the IPSS will depend on whether the two devices are collocated or separated via a metropolitan area network (MAN). If collocated, FE and GE are common, while most intra-MAN connectivity is via PPP over SONET or more sophisticated and optimized methods of mapping the IP traffic onto the optical backbone. Where the cable headend operates as a bridge, it should also forward all subscriber traffic to the IPSS for processing. Access encapsulations across cable include Ethernet bridging, PPPoE, L2TP, and IPSec. One challenge is in identifying individual subscribers (for both routed and bridged headends) since there is no link-layer separation as is the case with DSL ATM PVCs. Where the cable operator has deployed a session protocol such as PPPoE or L2TP, this does not present a problem since subscribers arrive on individual tunnels. However, in a nontunneled environment, the IPSS must be capable of identifying the subscribers based on their IP source addresses (see Figure 6.3).

As is the case with DSL, the choice of access encapsulation within a cable deployment depends on the MSO wholesaler as well as the ISP(s). The majority of current deployments rely on Ethernet bridging, although some providers now equip the subscriber with PPPoE or L2TP clients. These tunneling protocols are the only way of identifying individual subscribers in environments where the provider does not have an IPSS with the subscriber identification capability just described.

Low-end cable offerings roughly parallel those in the ADSL space, though some MSOs have been even more aggressive in their monthly fees. Where DSL competition exists (and remember that this competition is a two-way street), the MSOs sometimes offer an introductory rate of $19.95 or even $9.95 a month, with installation waived. After the trial period, the rate usually increases to $29.95 if the customer owns the modem or $39.95 with a provider modem. These rates are on par with DSL. The MSOs do have an advantage, however, in that they have taken

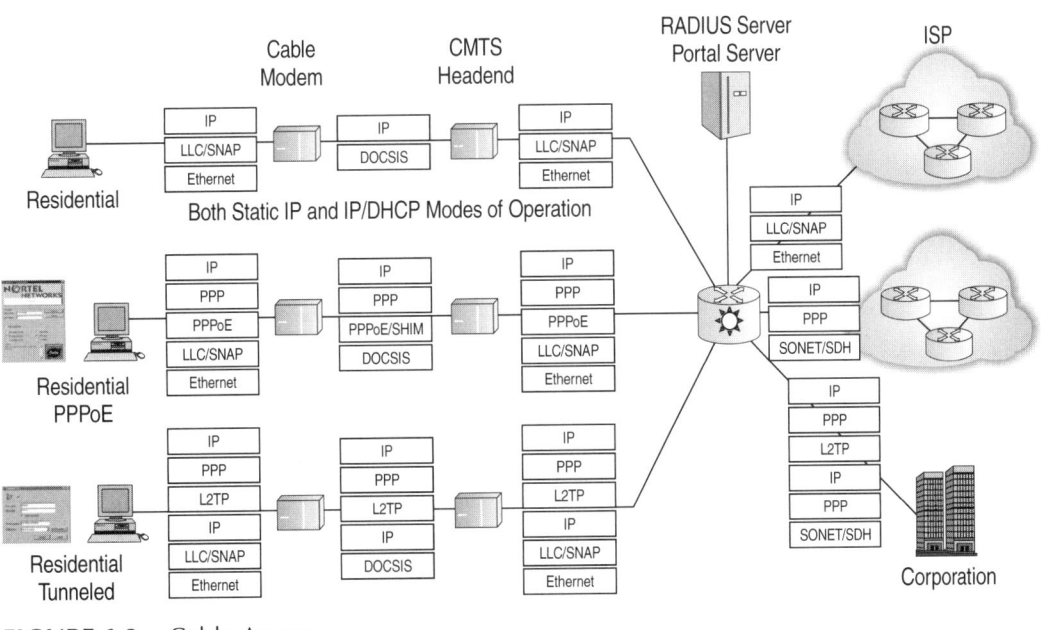

FIGURE 6.3 Cable Access

the initiative in bundling voice services with their cable modem offerings, providing the customer with one-stop shopping for video, voice, and data. The DSL providers are at a disadvantage in this regard in that they cannot offer the video, and in most cases they are incapable of bundling long-distance voice (with the exception of wireless). However, over time, the typical DSL or cable operator is expected to be capable of offering the full palette of services, including voice (local and long-distance, VoIP or PSTN), video, roaming net access (for those traveling away from their DSL or cable access), and even wireless.

Residential cable revenues in the United States are expected to grow from $850 million in 2000 (reflecting greater initial penetration than DSL) to $2.5 billion in 2003; at that point, DSL and cable will strike a closer balance (IDC, 1999a). In Europe, projected growth is steeper, with the market growing from $323 million in 2000 to over $2.5 billion in 2003 (IDC, 2000a). European cable penetration is expected to be greater than that of DSL over the next three years.

Cable modem penetration is expected to be even greater than that of DSL, with more than 3.2 million subscribers expected by the end of 2000 and 15.2 million by the end of 2004. This is a 30 percent consumer penetration rate, based on the 84 percent of cable subscribers connected to a cable-modem-capable plant. As with DSL, the global market size is expected to double this, though it too could be much greater.

The demographic split between DSL and cable subscribers is apparent when looking at service deployment. This split is a reason analysts traditionally report DSL revenue separately for businesses and consumers while lumping cable revenues into one statistic. Cable has the greatest appeal among residential subscribers, especially when bundled with telephony services. However, even with the relative QoS capabilities of DOCSIS 1.1, the cable modem specification, it is not considered a viable service for businesses looking for T1 and fractional T1 replacement. In contrast, DSL is quickly becoming the technology of choice for leased line and Frame Relay replacement. In fact, you can categorize DSL services into two types. The first offers low-cost Internet access based on a session protocol (e.g., PPPoE, described in chapter 2) and is priced to compete with cable modem services. Delivered via ADSL, this service is targeted at the residential subscriber. The second is targeted at the business customer and is offered via a bridged or routed connection via SDSL, HDSL, SHDSL, and sometimes ADSL.

Wireless Access and Market Opportunity

Fixed wireless bears a resemblance to cable since many subscribers share a single-access connection. The wireless base station connects to the IPSS via T1/E1 or channelized DS3. Individual subscribers arrive as RFC-2427 bridged or routed traffic or, alternatively, via L2TP or PPTP. In the case of bridging or routing, the IPSS must demultiplex the subscribers based on their source IP addressing (see Figure 6.4).

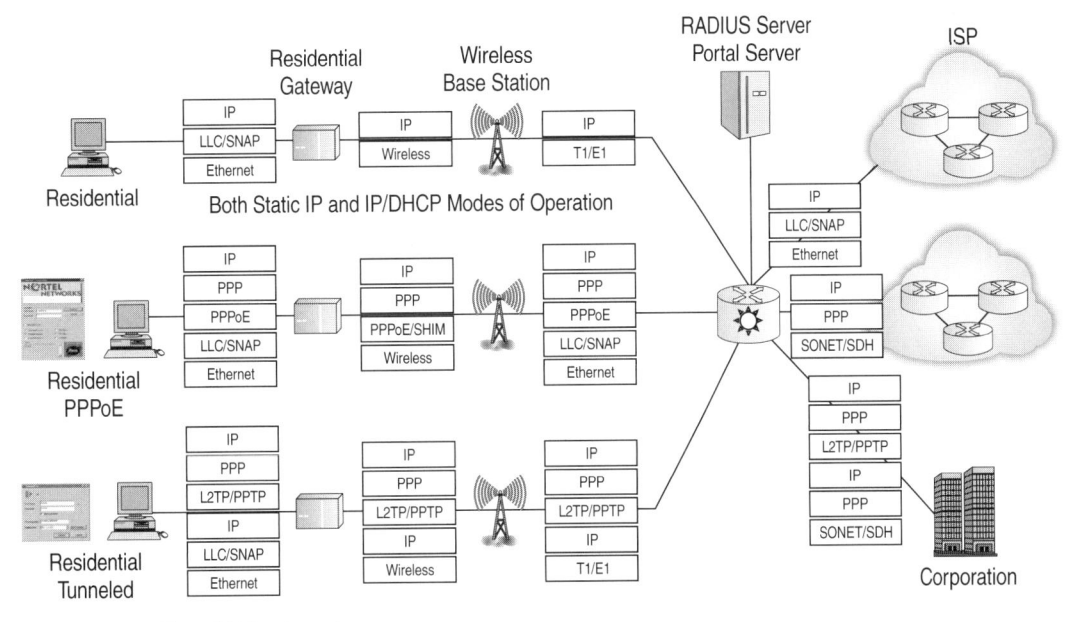

FIGURE 6.4 Fixed Wireless Access

During 2000, the first residential fixed-wireless services became available, at $34.95 for 1 Mbps of throughput. Although the system supports voice, voice service is priced separately, at $25.95 (AT&T, 2000). Residential wireless revenues in the United States are expected to increase from $539 million in 2000 to $2.2 billion in 2003. This figure, however, is questionable since both AT&T and Sprint backed away from their residential wireless deployments toward the end of 2001. During the same timeframe, business revenues will increase at a greater rate, from $827 million to $5.2 billion, reflecting growth in the metro areas (IDC, 1999c). In the case of one provider, business wireless fees ranged from $500 per month for 1 Mbps service with 10 Mbps burst capability to $2,500 per month for 5 Mbps service. Equipment was included, and installation was $750 (NextWeb, 2000). Note that this service, though more expensive than most DSL offerings, is still below that of legacy access and offers higher bandwidths. European revenues will grow from $23 million (reflecting a very early market) to $1.3 billion in the same timeframe (IDC, 2000a).

Legacy Access

Legacy access is supported with the IPSS accepting T1/E1 or channelized DS3/E3 connections from subscribers and acting as a replacement for a traditional Frame Relay edge switch. Subscriber encapsulations include Frame Relay (Brown and Malis 1998), bridged and routed, high-level data link control (HDLC), and PPP.

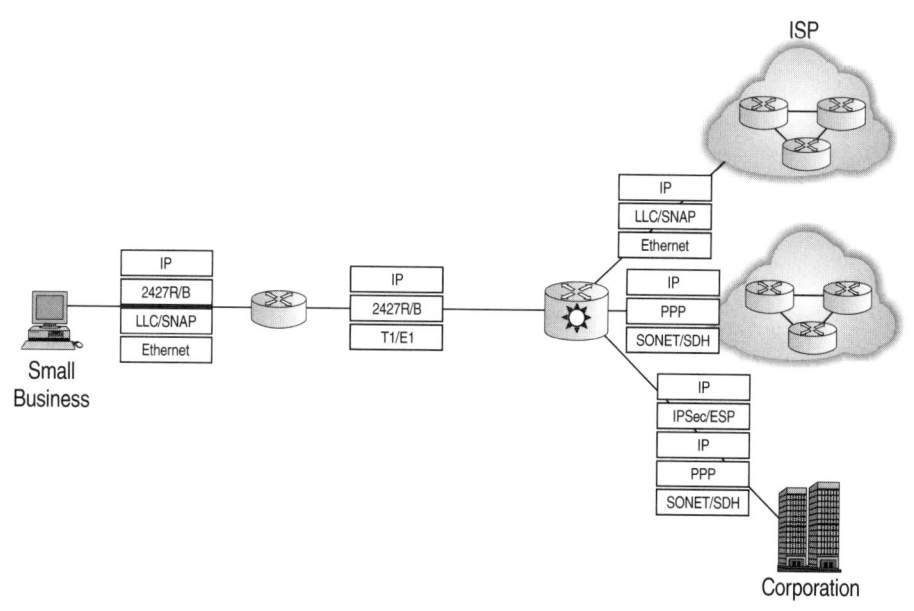

FIGURE 6.5 Frame Relay Access

Another use of the IPSS in this environment is to act in adjunct with an existing Frame Relay switch. The service provider continues to terminate the existing Frame Relay access connections on the switch (which may be a very large number of 64 Kbps and higher connections). Instead of forwarding these subscriber data link connection identifiers (DLCIs) into the existing Frame or ATM backbone, the service provider re-homes the connections onto the IPSS for additional IP layer processing (see Figure 6.5), either via Frame or ATM interfaces.

Satellite Access

Extending the reach of broadband services still further, satellite systems are also experiencing strong growth, with more than 3 million subscribers projected in the United States alone by 2004. The one problem with deployments before the end of 2000 was the lack of a high-speed return channel, with most systems limited to telco return where the link back to the provider was via a dial-up modem connection (a problem that plagued early cable modem systems as well). This severely limits the applicability to businesses or telecommuters and precludes any two-way broadband interaction. A good sign is the entry of multiple providers into the two-way satellite space, including StarBand, via the DISH Network; Earthlink, taking advantage of the Hughes DirecPC service; and MSN, also using StarBand's service. Also in this space is Gilat Satellite Networks, which focuses on the business space. These systems offer downstream bandwidth to 500 Kbps and upstream to 150 Kbps. Although this is not great compared with DSL and cable, in many rural areas it is the only option available. At the end of 2000, monthly service pricing started at about $59.95, plus installation which could run $400 or more (Current Analysis, 2000).

One advantage of satellite is that providers can bundle satellite TV and Internet services. This could significantly increase the potential subscriber base by targeting consumers who are unlikely to purchase a standalone PC with a Web-enabled set-top box. For providers looking at this segment as their major opportunity, the most telling number is the expected 50 percent or more satellite dish penetration among those not served by cable, primarily in rural areas. ISPs' offering services to these subscribers could also localize content accordingly based on these demographics. Analysts predict satellite Internet revenues approaching $7.4 billion yearly by 2003 (IDC, 2000b), with growth to $15 billion by 2008 (FCC, 2000). By mid-decade, other broadband satellite systems should also be operational, though the mass market may not adopt these technologies because of expected costs and concerns over latency due to the types of satellites deployed.

Comparison of DSL, Cable, and Fixed Wireless

Figure 6.6 summarizes the revenue opportunities across DSL, cable, and fixed wireless, the three areas usually tracked when considering mass-market broadband deployment. Table 6.2 lists expected buildout for these three technologies across the United States and Europe.

MDU/MTU Market Segment

Parallel to the growth of DSL, cable, and wireless is broadband deployment within the MDU/MTU and hospitality spaces. Although technologies such as cable may service this market segment, it is worth a separate discussion because of its size and importance. Based on numbers in IDC, the market opportunity for apartments is $20 billion per year, for businesses $59 billion (of which $14 billion is data, which

TABLE 6.2 DSL, Cable, and Fixed Wireless Deployment

	DSL		Cable		Fixed Wireless	
	USA	*Europe*	*USA*	*Europe*	*USA*	*Europe*
1999	500,000	25,000	1.4 million	367,000	none	none
2000	2 million	657,000	3.2 million	978,000	200,000	41,000
2001	4 million	2.7 million	6 million	2.4 million	500,000	386,000
2002	6 million	7.2 million	8 million	5.2 million	1.2 million	1.2 million
2003	9 million	14.7 million	12 million	9.6 million	3 million	2.8 million

Source: Estimates based on numbers in FCC, 2000, and IDC, 2000b.

FIGURE 6.6 Broadband Revenues

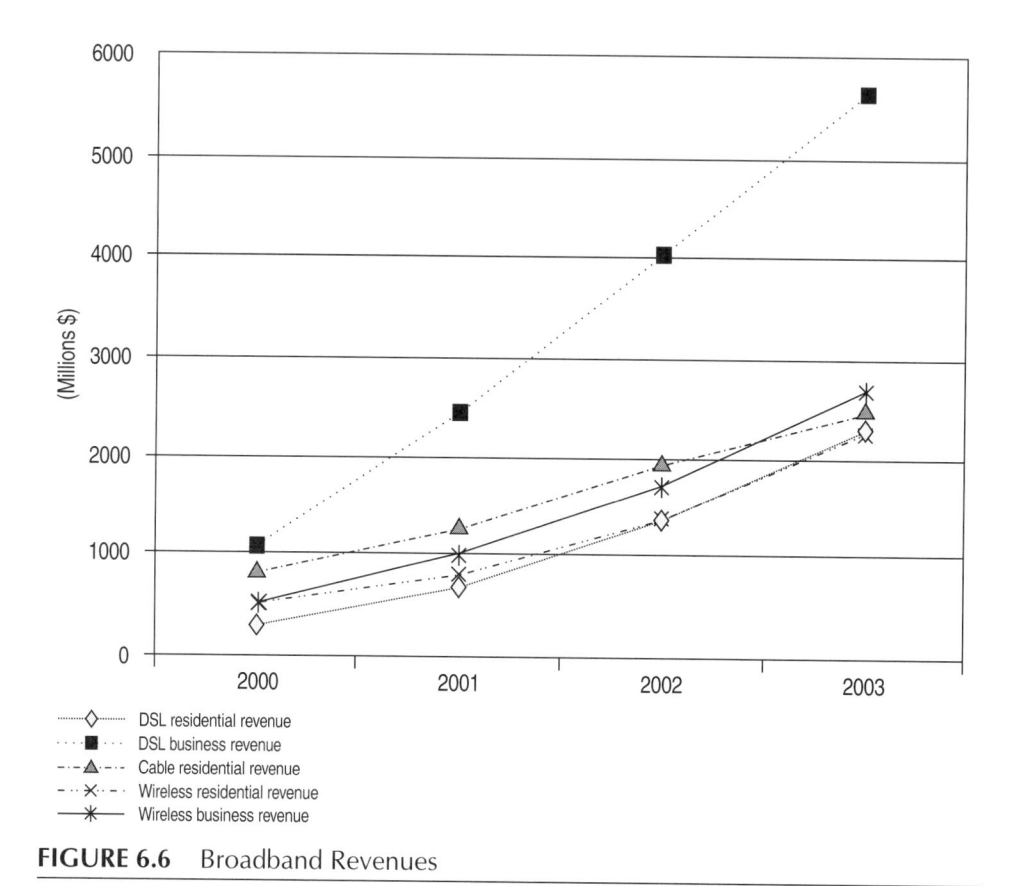

will grow to $40 billion by 2002 [Dun & Bradstreet]), and for hotels $1.5 billion. This opportunity will involve more than 21 million apartment units (National Multi-Housing Council), 750,000 multitenant commercial buildings (Building Office Management Association), and 3.6 million hotel rooms (*Hotel* magazine). Direct fiber connectivity to this space is expected to grow from 2.4 million subscribers in 2002 to 5.3 million in 2003. With landlords using broadband access as an attractor, this is a major growth area for both service providers (i.e., ISPs serving the hospitality industry) and infrastructure vendors. Deployment of the IPSS in this space is possibly more important than in some of the other market segments, because of the preponderance of small businesses, the requirement for mobility and security, and the demand for content services.

Dial Access Aggregation

The IPSS also plays a role in dial aggregation. In a dial wholesale environment, the IPSS may perform PPP and tunnel termination into ISP contexts or L2TP tunnel

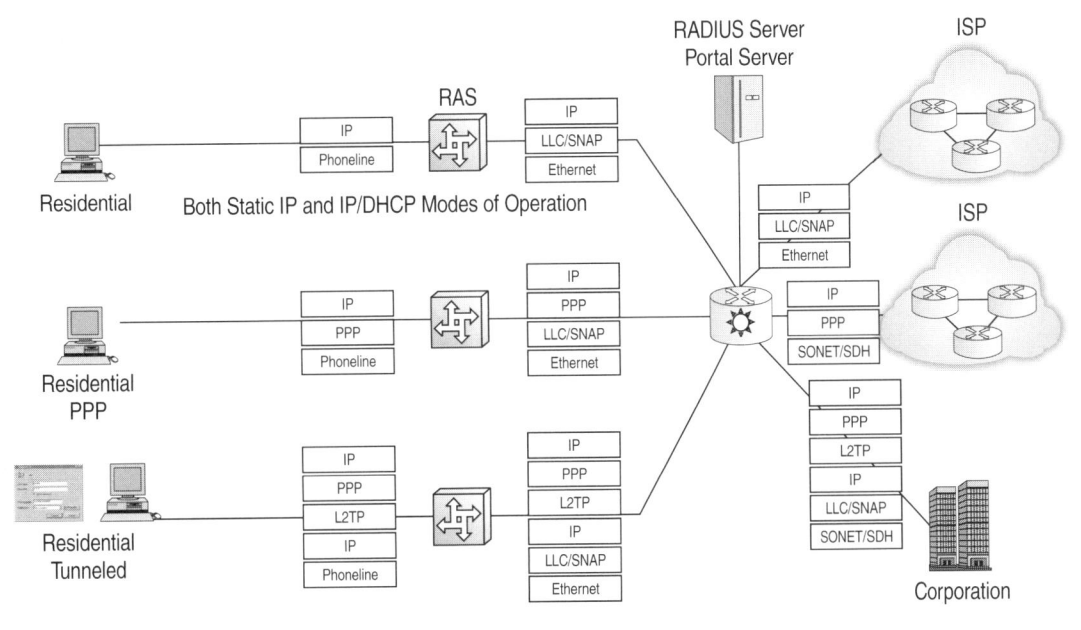

FIGURE 6.7 Dial Access

switching (see Figure 6.7). As part of tunnel termination, most of the functions described in the following sections are available to dial subscribers. Although the IPSS is not a requirement per se in dial, many providers want to aggregate both broadband and dial subscribers on a single service platform. The advantages are clear: The provider has a single place to define a subscriber service policy.

Mobile Wireless Access

One of the most recent applications of the IPSS is in support of 2.5G and 3G mobile wireless deployments. The IPSS is the first IP services node toward the network core from the subscriber perspective, and it provides access-side tunnel termination and mapping of the subscriber traffic into the provider's IP backbone. Access-side encapsulations are dependent on the type of wireless technology deployed. In the case of GSM GPRS, an evolution of TDMA and GSM, the IPSS acts as the gateway GPRS serving node (GGSN). This GGSN connects to the SGSN, and then to the base station controller (BSC). IP traffic between the SGSN and the GGSN is encapsulated via the GPRS Tunneling Protocol (GTP). Future UMTS deployments will follow this same architecture. Within CDMA 1xRTT and 3xRTT, the IPSS acts as a packet data serving node (PDSN), connecting to the BSC, which then connects to the actual radio system (see Figure 6.8). Note that traditional voice traffic does not enter the IPSS under either solution. In the case of both GPRS and CDMA 1xRTT, the BSC forwards this traffic to the voice network.

FIGURE 6.8 Mobile Wireless Access

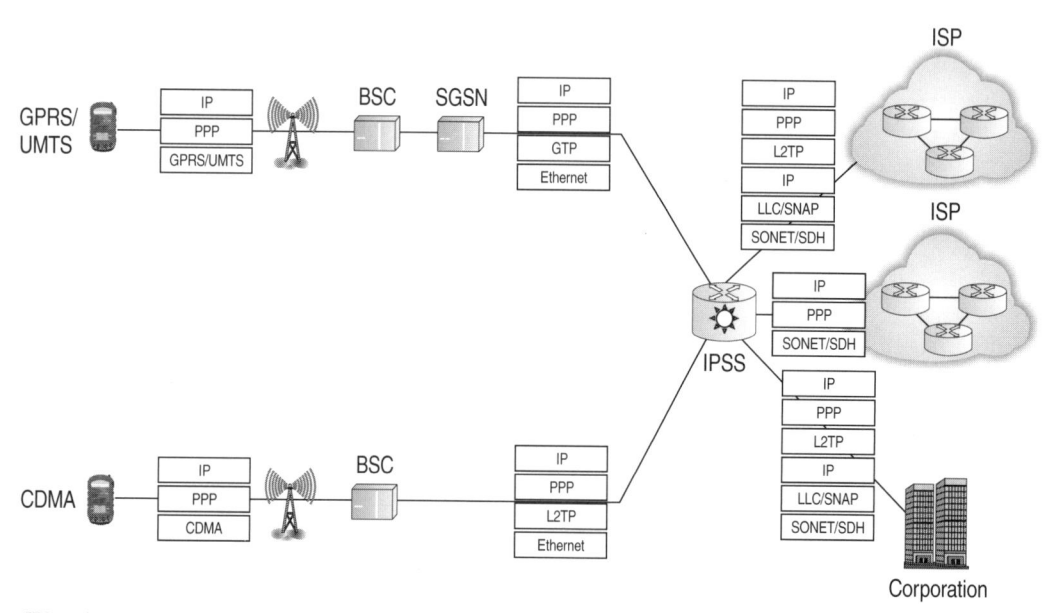

Note: IPSec also is an option between IPSS and ISP or corporation. IPSec or L2TP encapsulations may also originate at a subscriber's mobile terminal.

Although IP mobility was defined several years ago in RFC 2002, it has not seen much use to date. Reasons include the low penetration of mobile wireless PCs and other means of connecting remote users to the corporate intranet such as IPSec tunneling. However, this is expected to change with the deployment of GPRS, CDMA 1xRTT, and UMTS, technologies that will result in a large mobile IP population expecting seamless connectivity between the office and the road, the original intent of IP mobility.

A discussion of IP mobility introduces a number of new terms. A *foreign agent* (FA) is a router on a mobile node's visited network that provides routing services to the mobile node while it is registered on the visited network. This agent de-tunnels and delivers IP packets to the mobile node, packets that were originally tunneled by the node's *home agent* (HA). The HA is a router on the node's home network that tunnels the packets for the node while traveling and, just as important, maintains the current location of the traveling node. Finally, *mobileIP* is a term to describe the UDP-based signaling messages exchanged between the mobile node and the HA, relayed via the FA. When deployed, IP mobility operates as depicted in Figure 6.9.

HAs and FAs periodically broadcast agent advertisements. These are received by all nodes on a given link and include whether the device is an HA or FA. If the device is an FA, the advertisements include the "care-of" address for use by the mobile node. Mobile nodes examine these advertisements and determine whether

1. Home agents and foreign agents periodically broadcast agent advertisements, which are received by all nodes on the link.

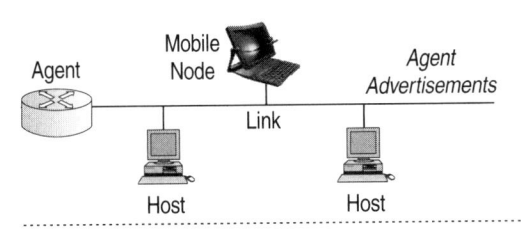

2. Mobile nodes examine agent advertisements and determine whether they are connected to their home or to a foreign link.

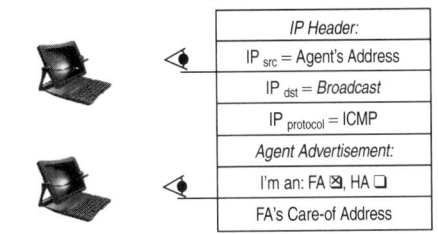

IP Header:
IP $_{src}$ = Agent's Address
IP $_{dst}$ = Broadcast
IP $_{protocol}$ = ICMP
Agent Advertisement:
I'm an: FA ☒, HA ☐
FA's Care-of Address

3. Mobile nodes connected to a foreign link obtain a care-of address from agent advertisement.

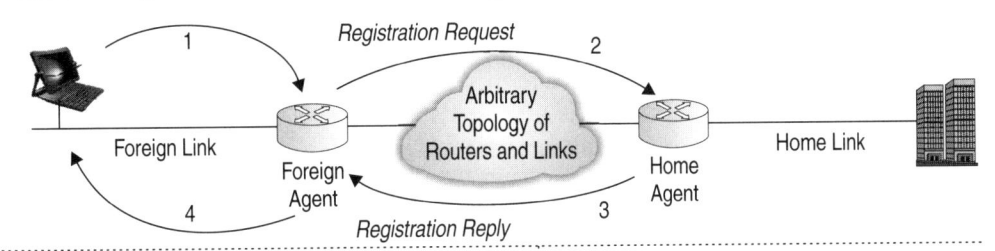

4. Mobile node registers its care-of address with its home agent.

5a. Home agent or other router advertises reachability to mobile node's home address . . .

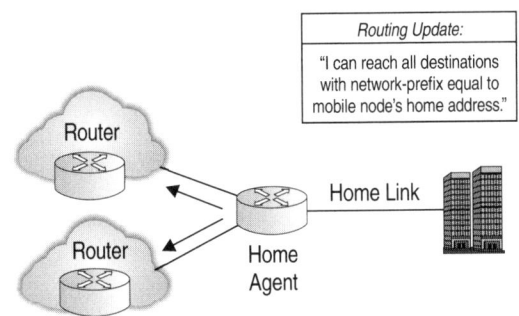

Routing Update:
"I can reach all destinations with network-prefix equal to mobile node's home address."

5b. . . . thus attracting packets destined to the mobile node's home address.

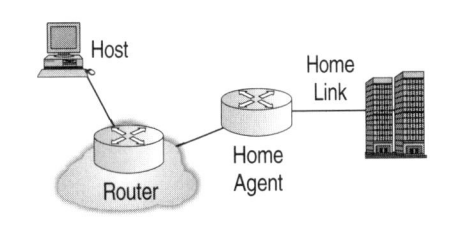

5c. Home agent intercepts packets destined for the mobile node's home address and tunnels them to the mobile node's care-of address.

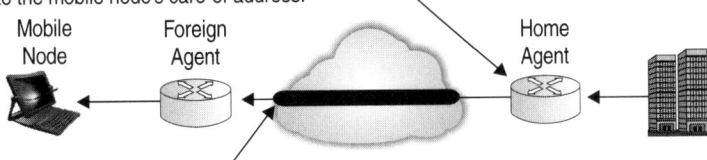

6. Foreign agent removes original packet from the tunnel and delivers the original packet to the mobile node over the foreign link.

FIGURE 6.9 IP Mobility Sequence of Events

they are connected to their home or a foreign link and, if connected to an FA, obtain the care-of address. The mobile node then registers itself with the FA, which forwards the request to the HA. The HA replies and advertises reachability for the mobile node. The HA then encapsulates the packets destined for the mobile node and tunnels them to the node's care-of address. The FA de-encapsulates the packet and forwards it to the node.

An interesting evolution in IP mobility is the role of IPv6. Providers are increasingly using the extensive addressing capabilities of IPv6 for wireless technologies, especially for 3G wireless systems. It seems that IPv6 has found a champion in the wireless space.

Traffic Management

Traffic management plays an increasingly important role in access for consumers and telecommuters, groups that expect a reasonable level of support for corporate access or media downloads. Effective support for traffic management permits a provider not only to meet these demands but also to set different rates for these services, resulting in greater revenue opportunities. Effective traffic management must result in a quantifiable outcome—the subscriber must have evidence in terms of throughput and application performance that the provider's offering is in fact equal to the subscriber's expectations. For example, it does no good to offer a 768 Kbps DSL service (and charge accordingly) when in fact the measurable throughput is on the order of 400 Kbps, even at idle hours. (Unfortunately, this is very much a reality for current DSL services.)

Effective traffic management must also include an awareness of what applications require what types of treatment. For example, some applications such as video distribution are tolerant of some data loss, while others are intolerant of any loss. In the same way, one-way video distribution is accepting of latency, but two-way interactions such as conferencing and gaming require tighter bounds on delay across the network.

The IPSS plays a key role in implementing traffic management at the network edge. This section covers important traffic management concepts: bandwidth allocation, capability to support and manage oversubscription, and provision of additional QoS guarantees. Because of their importance, the methods used to manage traffic are also covered as well as the role of MPLS in traffic management. This section concludes by looking at using traffic management to offer QoS and dynamic QoS.

The Role of the IPSS

Before looking at the ways in which traffic management is actually deployed, we first need to understand how the IPSS, as introduced in chapter 5, operates and where it plays a role in enabling application QoS support. Traffic management exists at multiple layers—in transmission systems, within Frame Relay and ATM, and at the IP layer. Most IPSSs, because of their location at the edge of an access network that often includes ATM, combine elements of traffic management on multiple layers. The question then is where to place the importance. Although an IPSS aggregating DSL subscribers services a larger number of ATM permanent virtual circuits (PVCs) than a traditional ATM switch, each with its own QoS, these PVCs are static and do not communicate the dynamic nature of the subscriber's traffic. The "intent" of the subscriber is discernible only from its IP flows.

Emphasis within the IPSS should therefore be placed on Layer 3 traffic management, as opposed to trying to somehow manage and bill for multiple PVCs at different QoSs from a single subscriber. Note that this arrangement is separate from a subscriber with data and voice PVCs, with the voice PVCs not terminating on the IPSS. Since the ATM network is used only for access, any true end-to-end QoS support must occur at the IP layer in any case. One requirement then is to construct the IPSS in such a way that it is as nonblocking as possible at the ATM layer, removing this from any QoS considerations. Proper fabric, virtual circuit (VC) capacity, and buffer engineering accomplish this. Given that the bottleneck in any IPSS is at the IP layer, because of the amount of processing required, this should not present a problem.

The goal of any IPSS is therefore to support and interact with other IP devices to offer consistent edge-to-edge Layer 3 QoS. The IPSS will include the various functions described in the following paragraphs to make this a reality.

Bandwidth

Basic services are most commonly specified with respect to the amount of bandwidth they provide. Higher bandwidth results in more expensive service. Two special cases apply to bandwidth: asymmetrical bandwidth and medium-induced variations in per-call available bandwidth, even before oversubscription and congestion are considered.

Asymmetrical bandwidth, when properly engineered and used for appropriate applications, can improve the cost-effectiveness of service delivered to the subscriber. Web browsing, video on demand, and related applications are inherently asymmetrical in their bandwidth requirements. The subscriber initiates content requests that are relatively small but receives large amounts of data in response.

Technologies such as ADSL split the available bandwidth to give the most resources in the direction they are needed. SOHO ADSL gives far more bandwidth from the provider to the subscriber than in the reverse direction, which is much cheaper than requiring the maximum application bandwidth requirement in both directions. In contrast, business-class DSL services such as SDSL and SHDSL emphasize symmetric bandwidth, more closely emulating traditional T1 connections. This provides better support for applications, such as interactive voice or video, that are inherently symmetrical and need to be provisioned with symmetrical bandwidth.

Services such as analog dial and data transmission over cellular radio may deliver different bandwidth depending on the quality of the medium committed for each call. A 56 Kbps modem, under ideal conditions, is actually limited to 53 Kbps. In practice, certain local loop equipment may limit it to 28 Kbps or less.

Oversubscription

In most deployed services, the bandwidth goal is an ideal. Factors that moderate the bandwidth expectations include the probability of connection in connection-oriented services, and competition for shared resources in always-on services.

Dial access services, for example, generally can deliver full modem bandwidth once a user is connected. The challenge with dial, ISDN, and cellular telephony is becoming connected. It is reasonable to assume that not all users will connect simultaneously, and it is therefore reasonable to provide fewer access ports than there are users. This assumption becomes complex, however, when there are multiple access points. It might be reasonable, for example, to assume that providing access for 10 percent or 25 percent of the user population at any one time is adequate for a consumer-grade service.

Coupled with the ability of the network elements to support effective traffic management, and therefore application QoS, is the extent to which the operator actually takes advantage of this functionality. For example, the provider may choose to offer only a best-effort residential ADSL service. This will require very little up-front

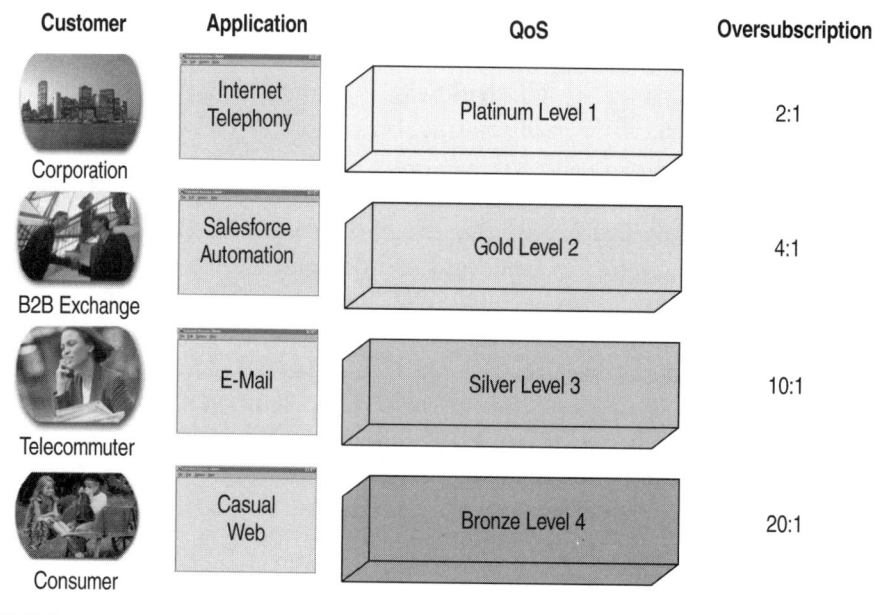

Customer	Application	QoS	Oversubscription
Corporation	Internet Telephony	Platinum Level 1	2:1
B2B Exchange	Salesforce Automation	Gold Level 2	4:1
Telecommuter	E-Mail	Silver Level 3	10:1
Consumer	Casual Web	Bronze Level 4	20:1

FIGURE 6.10 Oversubscription

engineering since the goal is to minimize cost per subscriber. However, the provider must still engineer for a certain oversubscription between the DSLAMs and the IPSS and/or between the IPSSs and the peering routers. In this case, a ratio of 20 to 1 is not unreasonable. In contrast, a provider may offer a high-end SDSL service at only 4 to 1 oversubscription (see Figure 6.10). The monthly fee an operator may charge for these two very different services will directly influence the incoming revenue.

The challenge then is for the provider to combine the traffic management functions just described into a set of services, marketed to the subscriber base and priced appropriately. The provider must demonstrate to the subscriber that different levels of service result in visible improvements in application performance, as opposed to attempting to explain to the subscriber the advantages of a specific IETF RFC. Typically, a provider will combine application prioritization, policing, and shaping into a single traffic management service.

For example, consider a CLEC offering a premium SDSL service to small businesses. In order to compete with the $39.95 ADSL services offered by the ILECs, the CLEC will want to demonstrate to its subscribers that its SDSL service offers superior QoS across the network. This, of course, requires support within the IPSS and also requires careful network engineering across the metropolitan ATM network between the DSLAM and the IPSS. Currently, most DSLAMs offer minimal QoS support. The provider must therefore be careful to provision the trunk PVCs in such a way that the premium subscribers always have access to their contracted bandwidth. Newer DSLAMs offer more possibilities by permitting the provider to prioritize subscribers at the ATM layer. More challenging is the CPE, an often-neglected component of end-to-end QoS. Although the IPSS protects traffic destined for the subscriber (e.g., shaping ASP-hosted applications over bulk HTTP traffic), data originating at the subscriber may be prioritized only at the CPE. If the subscriber is attempting to run real-time services such as VoIP, the CPE should queue the VoIP traffic accordingly. This is especially critical if the upstream connection is heavily loaded. Most providers and subscribers are just gaining experience with these issues.

Additional QoS Guarantees

Some services, such as voice over IP and video distribution, are concerned with more service parameters than just raw bandwidth. Both total latency across the network and variable latency (i.e., jitter) have strong impacts on service quality.

Interestingly, multimedia services tend to be more tolerant of errors than latency. Since human senses will interpolate errors in sound or vision, these services can drop occasional errored packets without seriously degrading the perceived service quality.

Delay, however, has a major impact on service quality. Providers of VoIP service must engineer their systems to avoid oversubscription and other bursty congestion mechanisms that cause variable delay.

A controversial QoS issue involves latency induced by "packet training," where, for example, a short VoIP packet queues behind a long FTP packet. No simple queuing mechanism solves this problem, since once the long packet occupies the transmitter, it may not be preempted. The conventional wisdom for solving the packet-training problem has been ATM's use of short cells, so no high-priority traffic is delayed by more than one cell of the same priority. Frame Relay fragmentation follows this model as well.

Advocates of optical Ethernet in the local loop, operating at 1 or 10 Gbps, claim that with a sufficiently fast transmission medium, packet-training delays become insignificant. With local loops of these speeds, the challenge is having a sufficiently fast PoP router to steer high-priority traffic onto paths engineered for its QoS requirements.

Traffic Management Concepts

The subject of traffic management is complex in that it involves many issues such as the capabilities (or lack thereof) of the underlying physical technologies, the way in which a provider designs the network, any peering relationships with other providers, and an awareness of the impact of different levels of oversubscription on revenue. The technologies behind effective traffic management include the following:

- Classification
- Policing
- Queuing at Layer 2 (i.e., ATM) and Layer 3 (IP)
- Congestion control and shaping

Classification is the task of identifying traffic coming into the network and setting its priority based on a number of factors, including the application, the policies of the service provider, and the services requested by the subscriber. Congestion control acts as a throughput regulator and is used to avoid network node congestion. This operates in conjunction with congestion avoidance mechanisms such as random early detection (RED) or weighted RED (WRED). The traffic may also pass through a shaping function, smoothing the peaks for more efficient data transfer across the network or to the subscriber.

Policing looks at the traffic coming into the network at each priority, compares it to the contract and current network load, and drops, forwards, or resets the priority as required. *Queuing* is then used to play out packets onto the network based on their priority or volume. It helps maintain QoS across the backbone. *Priority queuing* assigns priority to packets based on their protocol, interface, or address, while *customer queuing* assigns a specific account of queue space to each class of packets. They are then transmitted on a round-robin basis based on a weighted priority. *Weighted fair queuing* gives priority to low-volume traffic, with high-volume traffic sharing the remaining bandwidth proportionally.

Classification

An internetworking device must first be capable of identifying the subscriber traffic and then applying the various traffic management rules described in this section accordingly. At its simplest, this identification may apply to all traffic across a physical port or all traffic originating from a given IP subnet. More sophisticated classification relies on identifying the application's UDP/TCP ports. Having identified the traffic, the device may then mark, shape, or discard the traffic accordingly.

The most common method of marking subscriber traffic is based on DiffServ, which is standardized within the IETF and applies network resources on aggregated flows for a network-wide set of traffic classes. The DiffServ architecture describes a number of per-hop behaviors (PHBs), which defines the externally observable packet-forwarding treatment applied at an internetworking device. This description allows the construction of predictable services, while multiple services may be supported by a single PHB used in concert with a range of traffic conditioners.

A PHB group (PHBG) is a set of one or more PHBs that can only be meaningfully implemented simultaneously because of a common constraint applying to all PHBs in the set, such as a queue service discipline or queue management policy. Assured forwarding (AF) is an example of a PHBG, and although it offers better support for application QoS requirements than best-effort forwarding, it does not make any absolute guarantees. Under AF, the internetworking device may assign traffic to one of four queues (e.g., class-based queuing [CBQ]) according to some network-wide policies. In most cases, AF4 designates the highest priority and AF1 the lowest. At the same time the traffic is assigned an AF class, it is also assigned a drop precedence (DP) from 1 to 3. This designates the likelihood of the traffic being discarded in times of network congestion and is used by the policing function. In general, one would set DP3 for applications that are rather accepting of packet loss.

As an example, a given business subscriber may use Internet telephony (H.323), may deploy salesforce automation and office applications (e-mail), and may have employees access the Web (HTTP). In this case, the provider sets the following (see also Figure 6.11):

- Telephony to high priority with AF = 4 and DP = 2 (nontolerant to high latency, but may accept packet loss)
- Salesforce automation to medium priority with AF = 3
- E-mail to a low priority by setting AF = 2
- HTTP to lowest priority by setting AF = 1

Although the focus here is on provider marking, nothing precludes the subscriber from marking the traffic within the CPE. Therefore, an important capability at the network edge permits the service provider to re-mark the traffic if required.

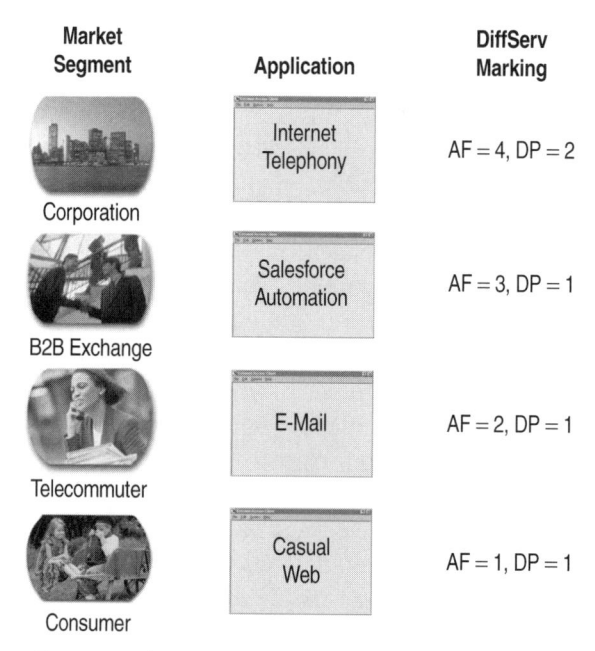

Market Segment	Application	DiffServ Marking
Corporation	Internet Telephony	AF = 4, DP = 2
B2B Exchange	Salesforce Automation	AF = 3, DP = 1
Telecommuter	E-Mail	AF = 2, DP = 1
Consumer	Casual Web	AF = 1, DP = 1

FIGURE 6.11 DiffServ Implementation

A second PHBG is expedited forwarding (EF) (Jacobson, 1999). EF seeks to offer a bounded loss, delay, and jitter, and assured bandwidth service. Such a service will appear to the endpoints as a point-to-point connection, a "virtual leased line." EF requires strict queue and bandwidth management across the network. Currently, few devices implement EF. At the opposite end of the spectrum is discard eligible (DE), the default class that offers only best-effort service.

The DiffServ architecture defines a set of "codepoints" used to specify the ways in which a networking device must interpret the DiffServ codepoint (DSCP) bits within the IP packet header in support of a PHBG. RFC 2597 (Heinanen et al., 1999) defines the various assured forwarding/drop precedence (AF/DP) combinations for the assured forwarding and expedited forwarding PHBGs.

Another Internet QoS protocol is RSVP (Resource Reservation Protocol) (Braden, 1997), standardized within the IETF's Integrated Services (IntServ) architecture. Although this protocol is capable of delivering stronger application QoS guarantees than DiffServ, it is implemented in fewer provider networks than originally intended because of difficulties in deployment. This is due to the fact that, although RSVP works in theory, it becomes exceedingly difficult to implement in current-generation routers over a wide area network IP infrastructure because each device is required to maintain session state per flow on a per-hop basis. The IETF work has assumed that signaling packets traverse a data path and set per-flow state in every router/switch along the way, an approach that is now understood to be untenable because of the large amount of state that must be kept at every node on the path and the need to classify every packet on a per-flow basis at every node on this path. Hence scalability becomes a major concern as the number of RSVP flows increase and the resources required on each intermediate device increase along with it. RSVP is, however, implemented as the label switched path (LSP) setup protocol for MPLS.

Compared to IntServ, DiffServ-based architecture is inherently much more scalable because of its simplicity. Intermediate devices in a DiffServ-based network do not require maintenance of session state but simply treat traffic according to pre-determined rules based on the DSCP. Hence in the DiffServ model, the load-of-traffic classification is distributed to the edge of the network. The core elements simply treat packets based on the DSCP value and are able to achieve end-to-end QoS in large-scale, distributed IP networks without sacrificing performance.

Policing

Application marking is only the first step in deploying an end-to-end architecture capable of supporting application QoS. Having marked the traffic, the provider must then ensure that the subscriber conforms to its SLA. This is the role of a policing function, matching the actual bandwidth from the subscriber at the different AF classes against a contract (i.e., the subscriber's committed information rate [CIR] and excess information rate [EIR]). There are two elements to a policing function—metering the traffic against parameters set by network management, and then discarding, remarking, or logging based on these parameters. A typical policer compares the subscriber bandwidth against average and peak bandwidths and burst sizes. Based on this comparison, the traffic enters a discard-marking function that may reset the DSCP with a net effect of altering the packet's likelihood for discard or preferential handling within the network. Note that the policing function assumes that the traffic has first passed through a classification function, either in the same network-based device or at the CPE.

As an example, under one scheme, known as the *two-rate, three-color marker* (Heinanen and Guerin, 1999), TCP packets arriving from the subscriber are compared against a contract consisting of a CIR, a peak rate (PIR), a committed burst size (CBS), and peak burst size (PBS). Depending on the packet's conformance with the traffic contract, the policer may drop the packet, reset its drop precedence, or reset its IP precedence.

Here, traffic arriving faster than the subscriber's CIR (measured in packets per second) but within the CBS (measured in bytes) is marked "green." Other packets exceeding the CIR, but below the PIR and PBS, are marked "yellow," while those exceeding the PBS are marked "red." These packets all enter the queue and are sent across the trunk in accordance with the CIR of the contract. If packets are delayed in the queue, TCP's backoff (which reduces throughput) may be activated because of the increase in latency, with a net effect of decreasing the data rate. If the queue

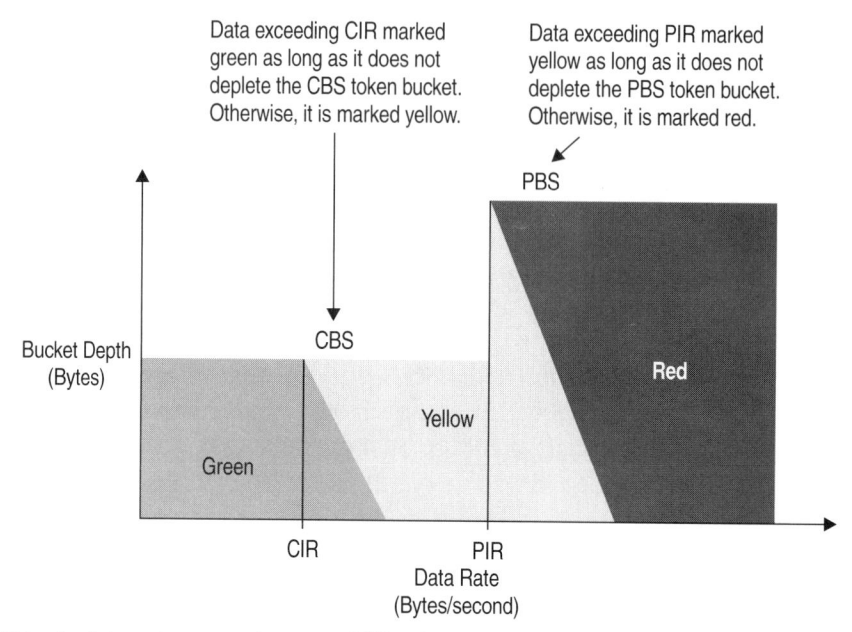

FIGURE 6.12 Policing: Two-Rate, Three-Color Marker

Note: Token buckets are incremented at a rate of CIR or PIR until they reach CBS and PBS, respectively.

depth grows too great, the system will begin by discarding the "red" packets. If this does not reduce the queue to acceptable levels, it will then discard the "yellow" packets. These color labels are coded within the DSCP field of the packet. In the case of the AF PHB, this usually involves setting its drop precedence. Figure 6.12 depicts this policy, whereby the different classes of traffic as defined in Figure 6.11 are individually acted on by the policy. Another scheme, known as the *single-rate three-color marker*, operates only on the committed rate and not on the peak rate (see Figure 6.13).

Queuing

Any successful traffic management implementation requires effective queuing support within the device. Depending on the type of policy implemented, the following techniques may be appropriate:

- *Single-queue mechanisms,* such as first-in, first-out (FIFO). The first packets entering the device are forwarded first. Although simple to implement, FIFO does not provide effective QoS support since high-priority packets may be delayed behind those requiring only best-effort service.

- *Single-queue discard strategies,* such as WRED. WRED helps reduce congestion across the backbone by discarding TCP traffic in such a way that retransmission is minimized. This is useful only if a significant percentage of the traffic continues to be TCP-based.

Traffic Management

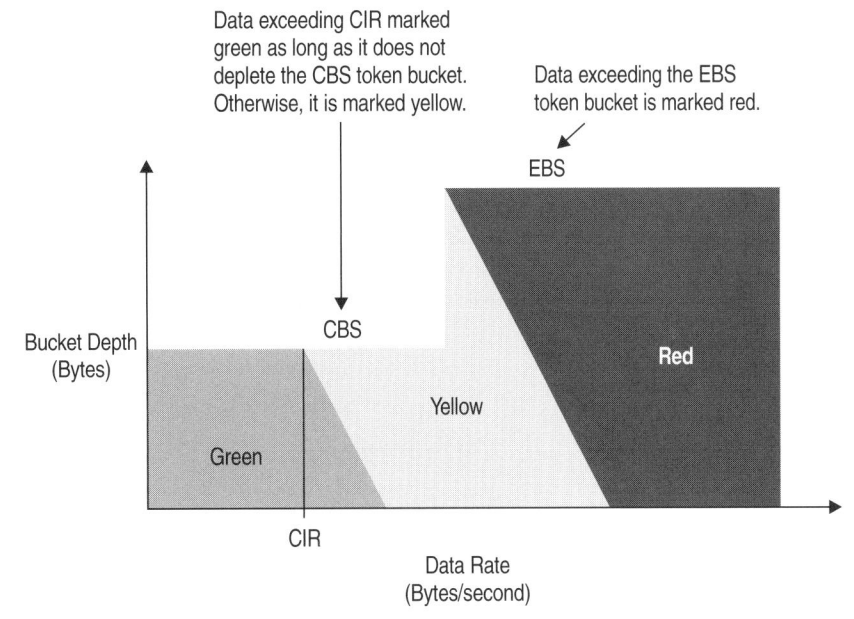

[Figure content: chart showing Bucket Depth (Bytes) vs Data Rate (Bytes/second), with Green, Yellow, and Red regions separated by CIR and EBS thresholds, and CBS level marked.]

Annotations on figure:
- Data exceeding CIR marked green as long as it does not deplete the CBS token bucket. Otherwise, it is marked yellow.
- Data exceeding the EBS token bucket is marked red.

Note: Both token buckets are incremented at a rate of CIR until they reach CBS and EBS, respectively.

FIGURE 6.13 Policing: Single-Rate, Three-Color Marker

- *Multiple-queue scheduling disciplines,* such as the following:
  - *Strict priority scheduling,* which serves the high-priority queue if there are packets waiting. Note that this technique may lead to starvation of lower-priority queues.
  - *Fair queuing,* which services all queues within a traffic class. This ensures that all queues receive equal treatment.
  - *Weighted fair queuing* (WFQ), where a given queue is serviced based on a weight proportional to allocated bandwidth. This helps with proper allocation of bandwidth among different applications and users.
  - *Class-based queuing* (CBQ), which maintains different queues for each traffic class.
  - *Hierarchical class-based queuing,* where classes have subclasses. Here, a given subclass may share bandwidth with another subclass, where both belong to the same higher-level class.

The IPSS then forwards the subscriber data into the core network. End-to-end QoS assumes that the core routers support DiffServ. Alternatively, if the core is ATM, the QoS looks into the DSCP field and maps packets into different ATM VCs—for example, AF4 into constant bit rate (CBR). Where the traffic transits multiple providers' networks, they will need to (or at least attempt to) implement bilateral agreements to preserve these mappings.

Shaping

Following the traffic flow from the network to the subscriber, we see that traffic accepted by the IPSS from the core network will first enter a policer that performs the same functions as the ingress policer. It then passes through a shaper, capable of assigning an absolute or percentage bandwidth to a given application or flow before forwarding it across the subscriber's local loop. The shaper operates on rate weights, global rate limits, and per-flow or per-policy rate limits. The rate weight determines what percentage of the available bandwidth a given traffic type can use during times of congestion, in effect giving precedence to specific traffic flows.

Figure 6.14 depicts a policy specific to RealAudio and SNMP. Rule 1 limits the total amount of RealAudio traffic between the subscriber and a group of servers (also known as a "server farm") to 1,024 Kbps and each session to 256 Kbps. Rule 2 then limits the SNMP traffic from a network management host to the subscriber

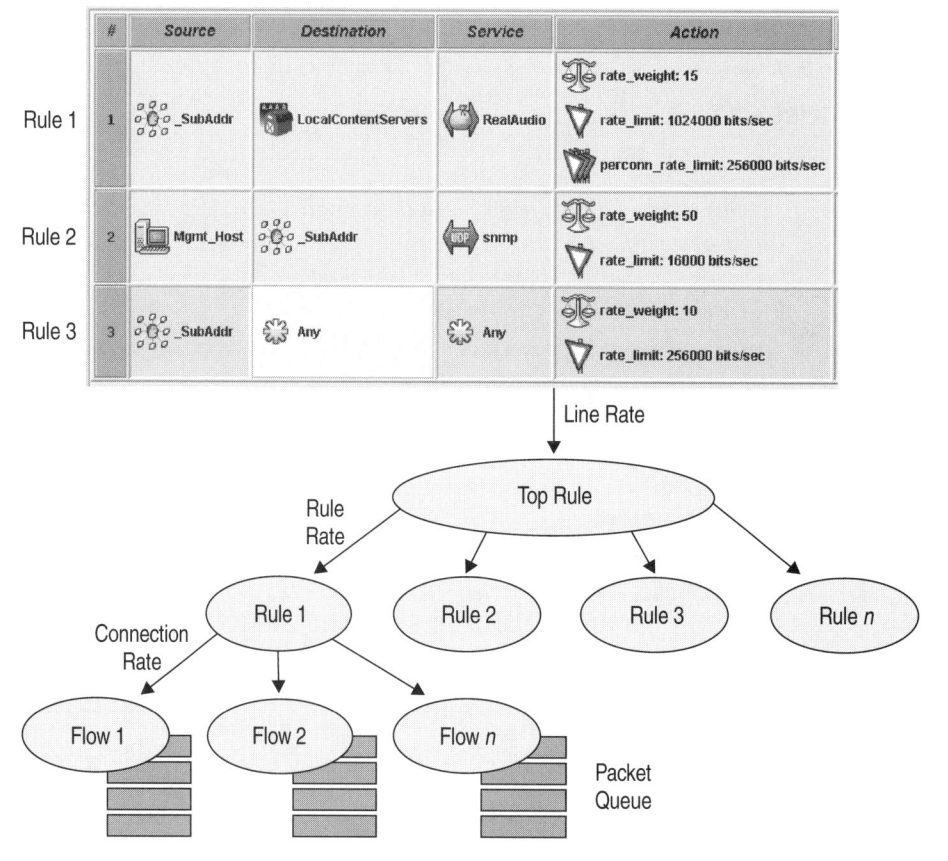

#	Source	Destination	Service	Action
Rule 1	1	_SubAddr	LocalContentServers	RealAudio	rate_weight: 15 rate_limit: 1024000 bits/sec perconn_rate_limit: 256000 bits/sec
Rule 2	2	Mgmt_Host	_SubAddr	snmp	rate_weight: 50 rate_limit: 16000 bits/sec
Rule 3	3	_SubAddr	Any	Any	rate_weight: 10 rate_limit: 256000 bits/sec

FIGURE 6.14 Shaping

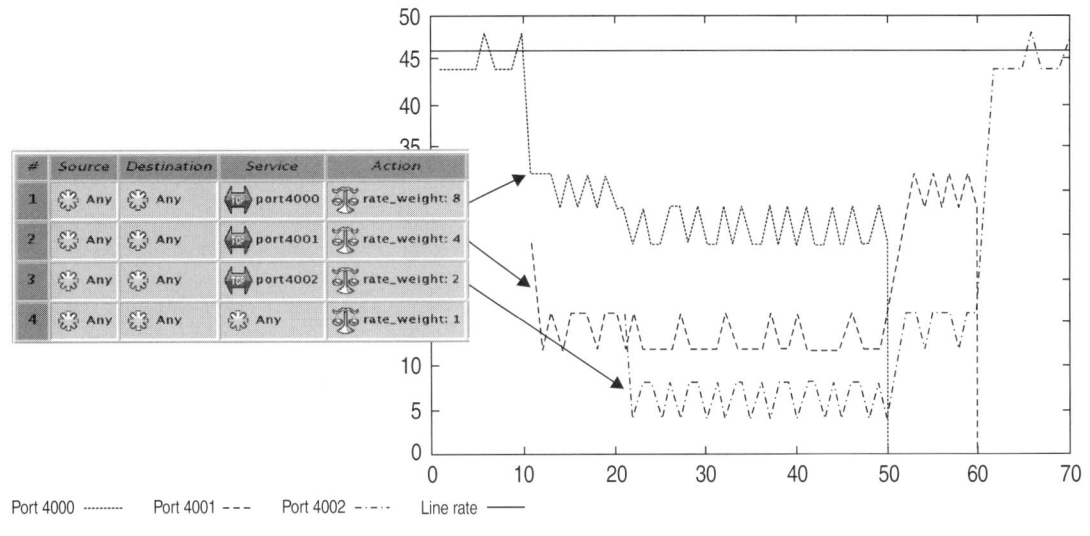

FIGURE 6.15 Shaping Policy Verification

to 16 Kbps. Rule 3 then applies to all other types of traffic, limiting them to 256 Kbps. In times of congestion, the rate weights specify that the SNMP traffic will have five times the priority (50/10) over ordinary subscriber traffic, and 50/15 priority over RealAudio. In any case, the sum total of the SNMP traffic is limited to 16 Kbps as described in Rule 2.

The bottom part of Figure 6.14 shows a hierarchical view of the rule implementation. Beginning with the overall line rate, we implement a rule for different traffic types. Within a given rule there are multiple connections, each limited by the connection rate. A single connection, or IP flow, is assigned to the necessary queue within the system.

Figure 6.15 demonstrates operation of a shaping policy. Rules for three arbitrary TCP ports—4000, 4001, and 4002—are set, each weighted at half the previous port. The graph on the right of Figure 6.15 depicts actual throughput as traffic is applied to each port in turn.

MPLS

Not to be forgotten is the role that MPLS is expected to play in traffic management. Unlike the QoS available via Frame Relay or ATM virtual circuits, MPLS permits the provider to deploy meaningful QoS across a pure IP backbone. It is therefore usable over any link-layer technology, including ATM and Frame Relay, as well as PPP, Ethernet, and even optical wavelengths. MPLS accomplishes this through the use of constraint-based paths that use CR-LDP or RSVP signaling to tell the network the QoS expectations based on demand at the edge. Metrics supported include delay and throughput.

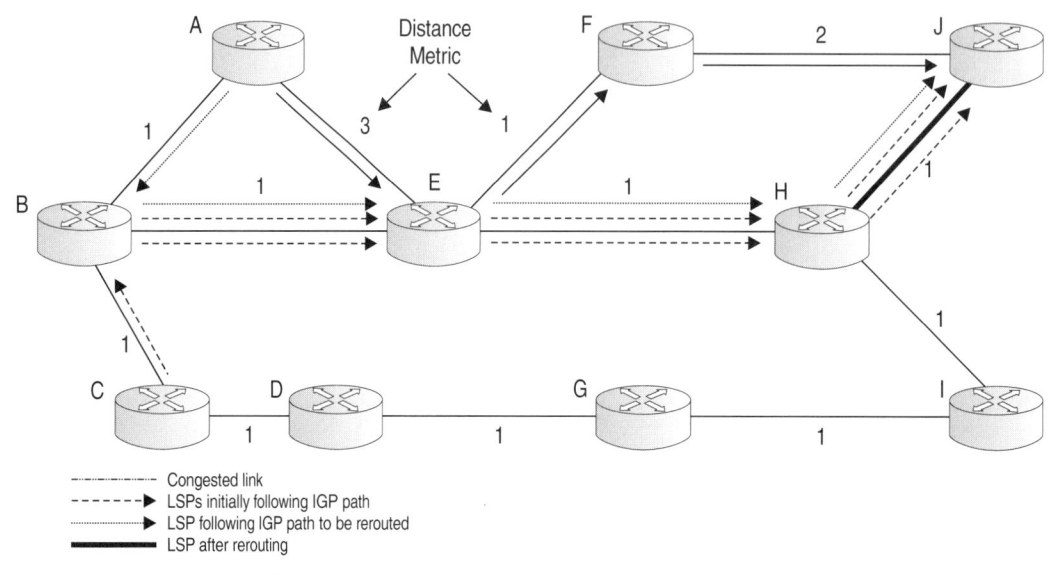

FIGURE 6.16 MPLS Traffic Engineering

Traditionally, packets will cross a router backbone based on a path determined by the interior routing protocol that the ISP is using. Depending on the metrics—that is, Border Gateway Protocol (BGP) or Open Shortest Path First (OSPF)—this may result in some links being overcongested, while others are lightly loaded. What MPLS permits the network designer to do is to selectively shift traffic between a source and destination from the congested path to an alternate. The most common protocol for accomplishing this is RSVP or LDP, used to signal a new LSP along the selected path. Traffic from the identified source to the destination will now follow this path. Figure 6.16 depicts a typical network core before and after this traffic engineering (Juniper, 1999). Packets, and therefore LSPs, that normally follow one path because of the interior routing protocol are redirected to the alternate path with this engineering. Some vendors support extensions to routing that permit automatic path selection, rather than requiring manual planning. MPLS-based traffic engineering is a key component of backbone QoS support, required for the end-to-end traffic management capability described in chapter 7. Also worth mentioning are efforts that are finally reaching fruition to integrate QoS into standard routing protocols such as OSPF and IS-IS.

Deploying QoS

An important point about traffic management is that it is an end-to-end function, unlike the security or IP-VPN services described later that may in fact not extend across the network. For example, a subscriber's router or integrated access device (IAD) may perform the initial DiffServ marking and queuing of the data. This is critical if both real-time and bulk IP or ATM traffic are to be properly supported in the upstream direction across the loop. In a DSL environment, the DSLAM also plays a critical role, in that it must be capable of maintaining QoS between different ATM virtual circuits. As an example, subscribers may generate ATM AAL5 PVCs for data and AAL2 for voice at a higher priority. The DSLAM must give preference to the AAL2 virtual circuits within the device and across the upstream trunk.

Contrast this QoS offering over different ATM virtual circuits with an all-IP environment, in which all subscriber traffic is carried over AAL5 PVCs. In the all-IP environment, the DSLAM must be capable of designating those subscribers with real-time applications as high priority. Necessary elements include the following:

- Large linecard buffers
- A nonblocking switching matrix
- CBR, VBR-rt, VBR-nrt, and possibly available bit rate (ABR)
- Congestion control mechanisms, including weighted fair queuing, connection admission control (CAC), user parameter control (UPC), per-VC policing, cell loss priority (CLP), tail packet discard (TPD), and early packet discard (EPD)

Many first-generation DSLAMs did not offer these capabilities, in effect relegating all subscribers to best-effort status.

Traffic now enters the IPSS, the focal point for many of the traffic management services, and then passes into the core network. This core may consist of ATM switches or routers. If consisting of the former, the architecture is much like that within the metropolitan area, with different QoSs mapped to different ATM VCs (if required). In the past, some ATM switches presented additional problems for IP traffic because of buffer sizing, but the current generation of deployed switches has mostly eliminated these problems. Router cores present additional challenges because of their varying support for QoS. This is a function of their buffering schemes, interface designs, and contention across the backplane or switch matrix. In 2001, a new class of QoS-optimized core routers with per-flow queuing arrived on the market. These are beginning to see deployment and should further assist in end-to-end application QoS support. Note that both ATM and router backbones support MPLS in support of QoS. As is obvious, every internetworking device must support some form of QoS if any end-to-end guarantees are to be meaningful.

The best way to look at the end-to-end requirements is through two examples focusing on DSL, the first dealing with retail services and the second with wholesale.

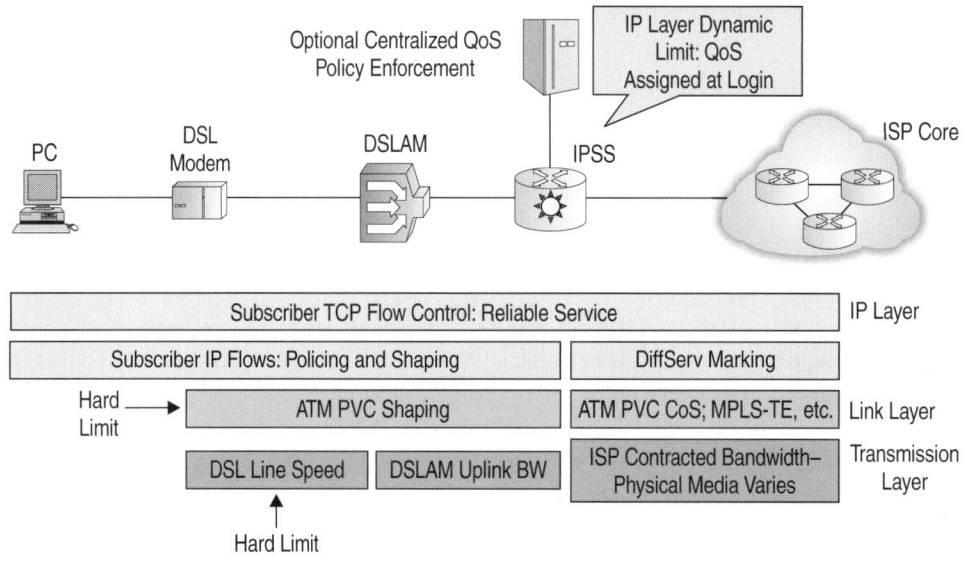

FIGURE 6.17 End-to-End QoS Requirements: Retail

DSL Retail QoS

Here (see Figure 6.17), the subscriber's PC connects to an ADSL modem and then to a DSLAM that connects to an IPSS and into an IP core. At the transmission layer, the DSL line speed, as well as the uplink bandwidth from the DSLAM to the IPSS, is set. Between the IPSS and the IP backbone, the ISP has purchased a given amount of bandwidth over any one of a number of technologies (ATM, SONET, FE/GE). Between the DSL modem and the IPSS, ATM layer shaping takes effect on a per-PVC basis using ATM classes of service (CoS) such as UBR+ and variable bit rate (VBR). Between the IPSS and the ISP's backbone, shaping may also be on a PVC-basis or may rely on MPLS traffic engineering. Finally, traffic management at the IP layer relies on shaping and policing the subscriber's IP flows between the PC and the IPSS. Between the IPSS and the backbone, DiffServ marking takes effect. The highest layer of traffic management takes place at the TCP layer, providing flow control in support of reliable transport.

DSL Wholesale QoS

A wholesale deployment consists of the subscriber's PC, modem, DSLAM, and IPSS, as in the retail scenario (see Figure 6.18). The first IPSS acts as an L2TP LAC, connecting across a backbone to another IPSS acting as an LNS. This then connects to the destination ISP's router. Traffic management at the transmission and ATM layers is the same as with retail services, with ATM CoS marking now extend-

FIGURE 6.18 End-to-End QoS Requirements: Wholesale

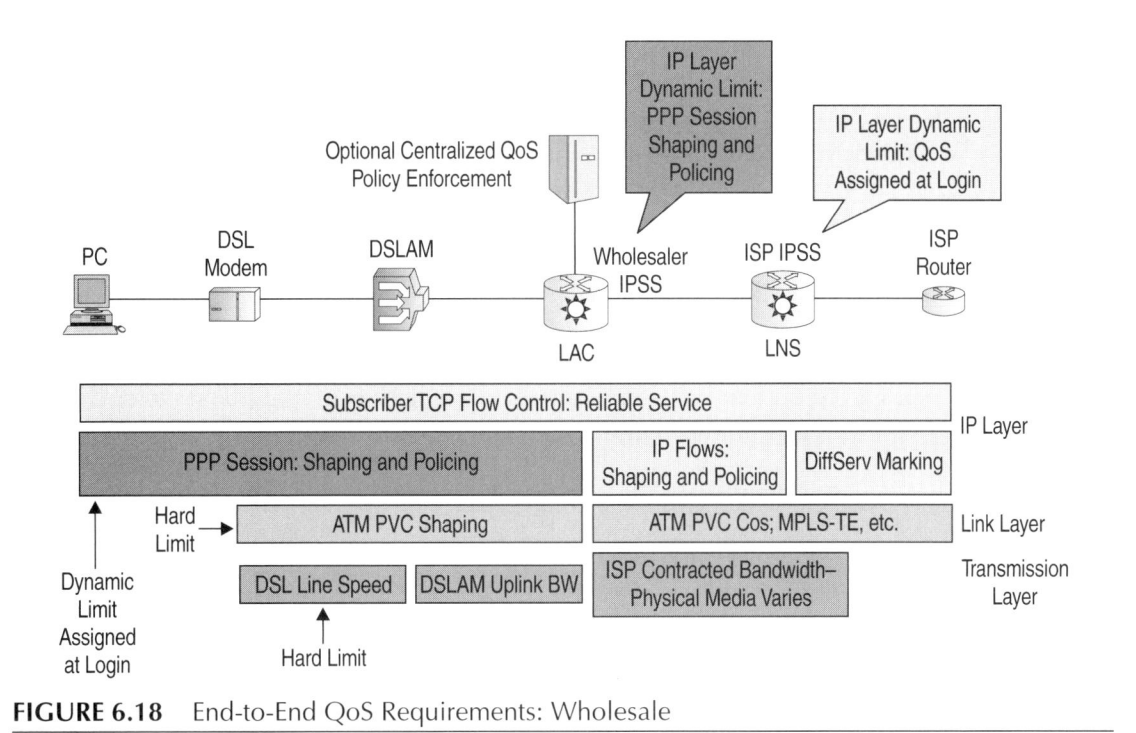

ing to the destination ISP's router. Across the access wholesalers' backbone, the individual IP flows are policed and shaped, with DiffServ marking in effect between the IPSS and the ISP's router. As in the retail scenario, end-to-end traffic management takes place at the TCP layer.

In order for the IPSS to play an effective role in traffic management, it must implement the various functions described earlier—classification, policing, shaping, queuing, and MPLS-based techniques, if appropriate. These all exist at Layer 3. Although the focus is not on ATM-layer QoS, the IPSS's I/O must still provide this support. As an example, a time wheel scheduler may be used for CBR and UBR+, playing out the traffic onto the link at either the peak cell rate (PCR), in the case of CBR, or the minimum cell rate (MCR), in the case of UBR+. The actual rates would be programmable via the provisioning system, and could correspond to the subscriber access or trunk rates. VBR support is provided the same way, shaping at an SCR and bursting to a PCR at a set maximum burst size.

Cable QoS

Traffic management across a cable infrastructure is very different from DSL, at least between the cable headend and the CPE. This is due to the shared nature of cable modem service, where hundreds of subscribers share a single downstream channel (usually supporting 27 or 39 Mbps). This sometimes results in the QoS complaints often heard during peak traffic times. The cable headend delivers an FE trunk to the IPSS, at which point Layer 3 processing takes place. Although early prestandard and DOCSIS 1.0 installations did not support QoS, the more recent DOCSIS 1.1 standard provides a way in which cable modems may request bandwidth from the network. One service enabled by this capability is Internet telephony. Note that from a 30,000-foot view, cable is not all that much different from DSL. Whereas cable is oversubscribed across the local loop, DSL is oversubscribed upstream from the DSLAM. In both cases, the network operator may engineer the service for as little or as much QoS in both the upstream and downstream direction as desired. Note that some cable technologies integrate non-IP voice on a different channel from the data traffic, as described in chapter 4.

Wireless QoS

Wireless technologies introduce an entirely new set of QoS concerns because of the inherent bandwidth limitations of the medium. Within a fixed wireless deployment, network design will include the amount of bandwidth available per subscriber within a given service area as well as the types of applications offered (i.e., voice and data). Depending on the type of wireless system, streaming media may present additional problems. For example, within a wireless sector, the base station may permit only a certain percentage of the users access at any given time, but once subscribers have access, if they transmit or receive data within a certain timeout, the system will not release them. With streaming media, the subscriber holds the connection by never timing out, effectively locking out others. This is a concern that wireless providers must address. Once a solution is in hand, traffic management concerns at the IP layer are no different from those within DSL or cable deployments. Even more complex is traffic management across mobile wireless. Here, the types of applications supported and their bandwidth requirements are central to the service definition.

Dynamic QoS

One area of intense interest, and a feature of the IPSS, is the ability to control QoS on the fly via a provisioning system. For example, a subscriber may enter the network via DSL and authenticate using RADIUS. The subscriber now has a basic connection into the network. However, if the provider offers premium services such as video, the subscriber could request these services via a portal (described in chapter 5), and his or her QoS will then be dynamically changed on the IPSS to correspond with the QoS requirements of the media. The portal also interfaces with any back-office systems involved with billing.

Wholesaling

Although many would consider wholesaling to be related to the physical infrastructure, it is actually a service offered by one provider on behalf of others (and ultimately the subscriber) and is independent in most cases of the underlying physical access technology. *Wholesaling* permits an access operator (i.e., ILEC, CLEC, PTT) to share infrastructure costs among multiple ISPs and corporations. As an example, a CLEC may deploy DSLAMs within central offices across a geographic region and offer this DSL access service to various ISPs and corporate clients. The ISPs and corporate clients benefit in that they no longer must deploy a dedicated access infrastructure. The deployment of this infrastructure is in fact not even an option for DSL or cable, since the ISP has no access to the central offices or cable headends. This outsourcing of access is therefore a win-win scenario for both parties. The ISP no longer needs to invest in modem pools or remote maintenance and may focus on marketing and services. In addition, it permits the ISP to extend the reach of its service by contracting with multiple DSL access wholesalers. The cost of wholesaling is comparable to direct modem ownership, as shown in the example in Table 6.3 taken from the dial space.

Even within a single technology, multiple wholesaling models exist. Initial DSL deployments relied on ATM PVCs spanning from the subscriber through the DSLAM and across the CLEC's access infrastructure (usually consisting of ATM switching) to a device at the corporate or ISP gateway site capable of terminating large numbers of ATM PVCs and subscriber sessions (see Figure 6.19). This is the

TABLE 6.3 Modem Ownership versus Wholesaling Costs

ISP Purchases and Maintains Modems.	$/subscriber/month	*ISP Leases Modems from Wholesaler.*	$/subscriber/month
Access equipment expense	1.25	Modem lease	5.50
Remote facilities expense	0.40	Subscriber management	0.25
Primary rate interface (PRI) access costs	2.80	Frame Relay trunk to wholesale PoP	0.40
RAS operations and remote staff	2.50	Subscriber management operations	0.60
Total	6.95	Total	6.75

Source: Weiner, 2000.

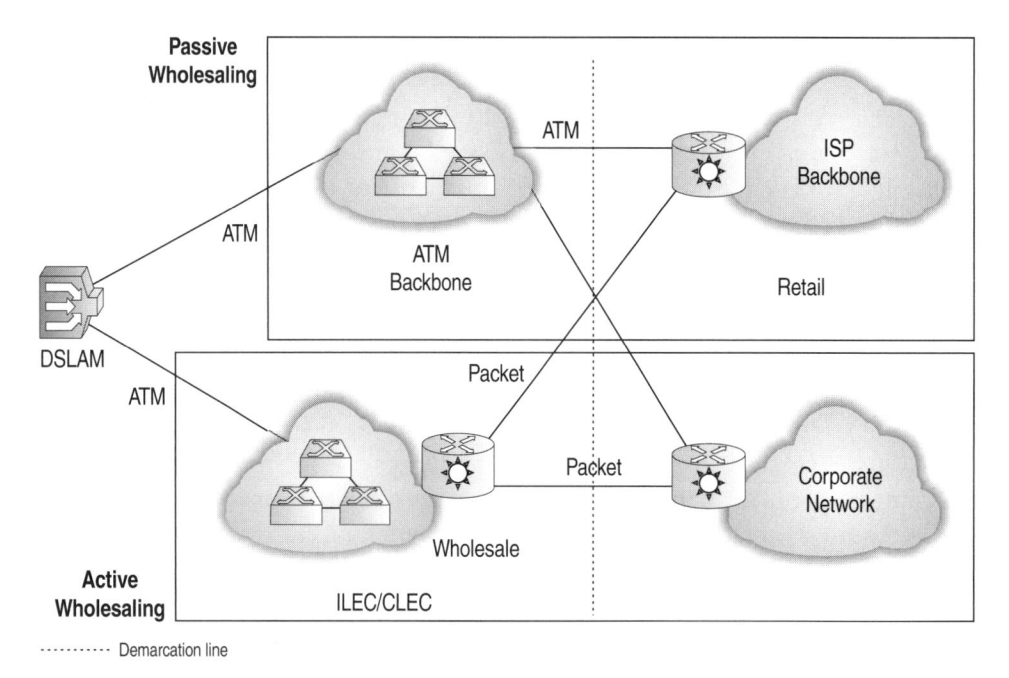

FIGURE 6.19 Active versus Passive Wholesaling

initial deployment scenario for the B-RAS or SMS and still comprises the majority of DSL deployments. Although this allowed for market entry, the wholesale provider was placed at a disadvantage for a number of reasons. These reasons, however, were transparent to the subscriber since the network was only called on to provide basic transport services. As more providers entered a given metro area, they were subject to increasing price commoditization, and since their model was predicated on basic connectivity, they could offer no real service differentiation. For example, the local DSL access provider was all but invisible after service installation (at least until the monthly bill arrived in the mail). DSL access providers were therefore looking for a different architecture, one in which they would play a more direct role in the subscriber's service path. We refer to this new model as *active wholesaling*, in comparison to older *passive*, or *transparent*, wholesaling deployments.

Active Wholesaling

With the availability of more scalable IPSS platforms, active wholesaling became a reality. Via the IPSS, an access provider is now able to terminate a very large number of subscriber PVCs, mapping them into ISP or corporate contexts or into secure tunnels. They may therefore play a more active role in content mediation by peering with content providers and ASPs and, in some cases, may function as ISPs in their own right. Effective wholesaling requires a number of capabilities within the IPSS:

- *Routing contexts (or virtual routers),* where the single platform maintains separate forwarding tables and runs separate instances of routing protocols for each ISP or corporation. This is effectively the same as having multiple routers in the wholesaler environment, but instead they are virtually hosted on a single platform.
- *Tunnel scalability,* permitting the access operator to terminate thousands of subscriber-side tunnels or originate a large number of tunnels across the backbone. Tunnel scalability protocols include IPSec, L2TP, L2F, and PPTP.
- *Management and resource partitioning,* permitting a given ISP to manage its own subscriber policies and reachability.
- *Integration with existing AAA systems,* such as RADIUS. This also involves CORBA APIs and interaction with LDAP, as well as the ability to alter subscriber configurations on demand.
- *Integration with content selection systems,* permitting the wholesale operator to peer directly with content providers.

Advantages of this active wholesaling to the ILEC include the following:

- Greater subscriber visibility by branding and portal services.
- The ability to offer additional content services.
- The ability to redirect VoIP traffic (where permitted).
- Optimization of the ATM switching infrastructure (i.e., PVCs across the backbone).

Advantages to the ISP include the following:

- Easier access to emerging markets because of lower cost of entry and ease of deployment
- Access to high-touch services via the wholesaler
- Choice of access technologies (no longer limited to ATM PVCs)
- Lower up-front capital costs

An even more sophisticated form of wholesaling relies on specialty providers offering services to both access wholesalers (the incumbents) and retail ISPs. The initial service is an IP-VPN, where the specialty provider offers this capability to multiple access providers or ISPs within a metro area. This provider has the expertise to deploy and manage the service. This service permits an incumbent to offer a more sophisticated service than would normally be possible. Depending on the business model of the incumbent, a combination of ILECs; CLECs; interexchange carriers (IXCs), such as Sprint and AT&T; ISPs; and application service providers (ASPs), such as Corio, offering specialized application services may deploy these platforms.

Although the focus in the previous paragraphs is on DSL wholesaling, the evolving cable and wireless wholesale offerings look much the same. Within cable, the headend connects to the IPSS, and with fixed wireless, the connection is between the radio base station and the IPSS. Dial wholesale is a bit different. Here, the RAS maps subscribers into multiple L2TP or PPTP tunnels, which traverse the Internet backbone and terminate at tunnel termination devices located at the ISP or corporate edge (see Figure 6.20). Alternatively, these tunnels terminate at an IPSS within the domain of the wholesaler. The IPSS then maps the subscriber traffic into multiple ISP contexts. Yet another model is where the wholesaler offers a *vanity ISP* service. Vanity ISPs provide subscriber services such as e-mail, Web hosting, and billing, but do not own any physical infrastructure. In this case, the wholesale operator assigns subscribers IP addresses native to its address space.

Although the architectures just described may seem complex, they are just an entry point to even more sophisticated wholesaling models, all with the goals of even greater scalability and reduced operational expenses.

Now consider a national or global wholesale operator with literally hundreds of PoPs and with peering relationships with hundreds of ISPs and corporations. In

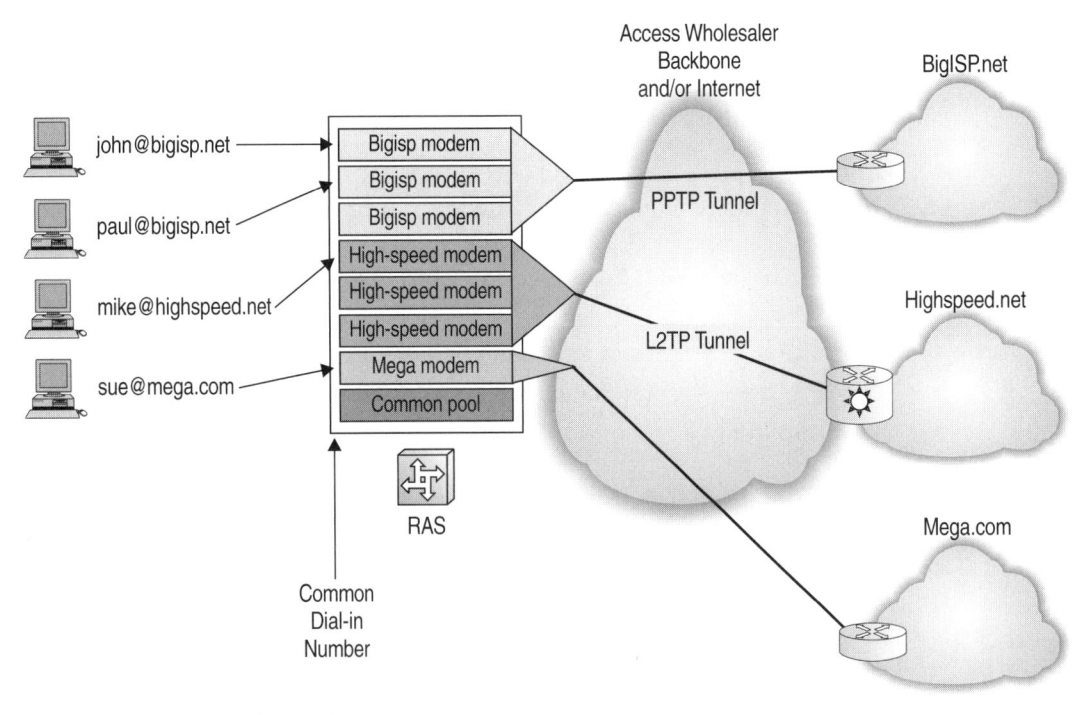

FIGURE 6.20   Dial Wholesaling

the architecture just described, hundreds of PPTP and L2TP tunnels may originate from each PoP, requiring even the smallest of client ISPs to install a device capable of supporting this tunnel scalability. The situation is actually worse in that a single PoP may be composed of a large number of loosely coupled RAS platforms, each generating individual tunnels. Thus, wholesalers and ISPs require a more scalable wholesale architecture. This is the role of the IPSS, aggregating traffic from multiple RASs within one or more PoPs in a given metropolitan area and then performing tunnel aggregation (see Figure 6.21). This "tunnel switching" was first deployed in 2000.

Some providers choose not to use a tunneling protocol to offer wholesaling. Instead, they use a RADIUS proxy that delegates authentication and authorization to the wholesaler. Although this eliminates the need for the ISP to have a router capable of performing tunnel termination, it necessitates that all ISPs share the same address pool from the wholesaler. In this scenario, the ISP "donates" its address pool to the wholesaler, who then serves these IP addresses as part of its global address pool. UUnet is an example of such a wholesaler in the dial space, while this address-assignment method is just now seeing deployment within DSL.

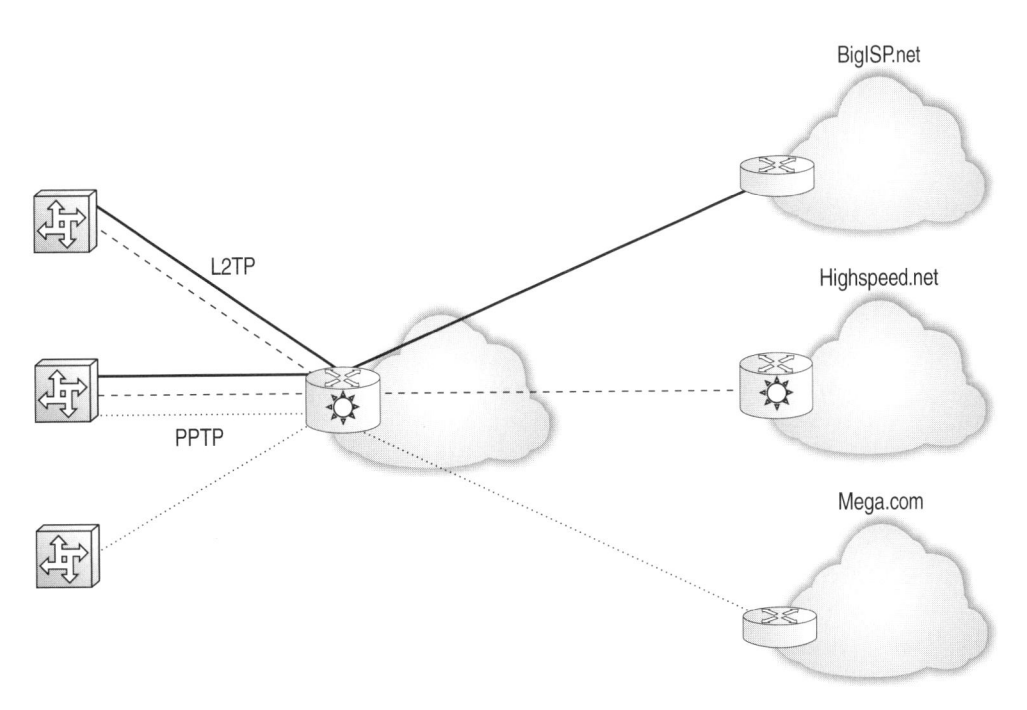

FIGURE 6.21 L2TP Tunnel Switching

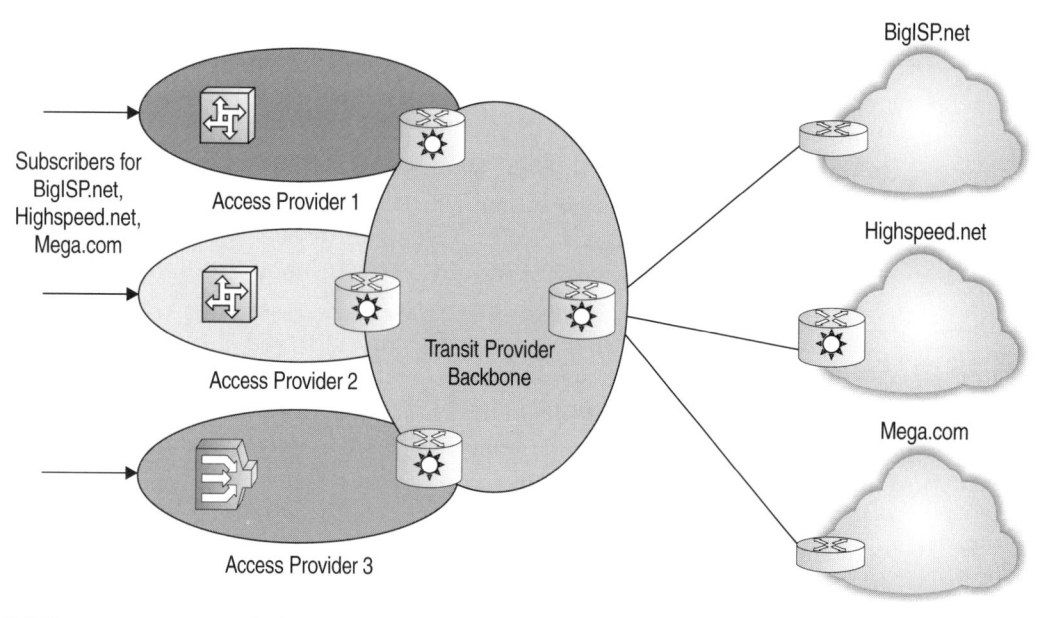

FIGURE 6.22 Transit Wholesaling

Transit Wholesaling

Another form of wholesale deployment is *transit wholesaling*. A CLEC deploying DSLAMs within a metropolitan area, and wishing to offer wholesale access service to ISPs in some other geographic area, will no longer need to extend its backbone connectivity to this second region. The added value for the ISP, of course, is that it may now offer service via some of the more regional CLECs as opposed to only the national providers. Here, the CLEC peers with a national (or international) transit provider, forwarding its PVCs to IPSSs within the destination ISP's backbone, which then terminates the sessions on an IPSS. A more scalable model is where the transit provider deploys the IPSS, terminating the CLEC's PVCs and forwarding traffic to the ISP via routed contexts or L2TP tunnels (see Figure 6.22).

Wholesaling Financial Comparisons

Now let's compare the financials for the two forms of wholesaling—passive and active. Under the passive model, ILEC charges the ISP a fixed amount for the DSL access connection (from the subscriber to the provider's ATM node), nominally based on bandwidth. The ILEC then charges an additional fee for transit across its backbone and a final fee for the PVC between the ATM node closest to the ISP and the

Wholesaling

ISP itself (based on bandwidth and distance). In some cases, two or three of these separate costs will be bundled into a single charge. Note the following example:

- The ILEC charges the ISP $10 per month for 256 Kbps DSL access and another $10 per month for PVC termination at the ISP's PoP (see Figure 6.23).
- For 2,000 subscribers, this is a $40,000 per month transfer fee from the ISP to the ILEC.
- For tariff justification, the ILEC may make the claim that the $10 per month for each "half-circuit" is based equally on the cost of infrastructure and provisioning (amortized across a given time period).

The ILEC evolves its business and service models by deploying an IPSS and aggregating the ISP's PVCs onto a single larger PVC. This is the active wholesaling described earlier. The ILEC still charges the ISP the $20,000 per month for the DSL access PVCs, but the ISP must now pay the ILEC only $200 per PVC (for example, based on a higher per-PVC bandwidth for the aggregate of the subscribers) for a smaller number of PVCs between the ILEC and its PoP. The ILEC may make the claim that the $200 is due to greater infrastructure cost, whereas the provisioning cost of the single PVC is no greater than that of each of the lower-bandwidth PVCs described in the previous paragraph. An ISP requiring 10 PVCs from the ILEC's IPSSs will therefore pay the ILEC $2,000.

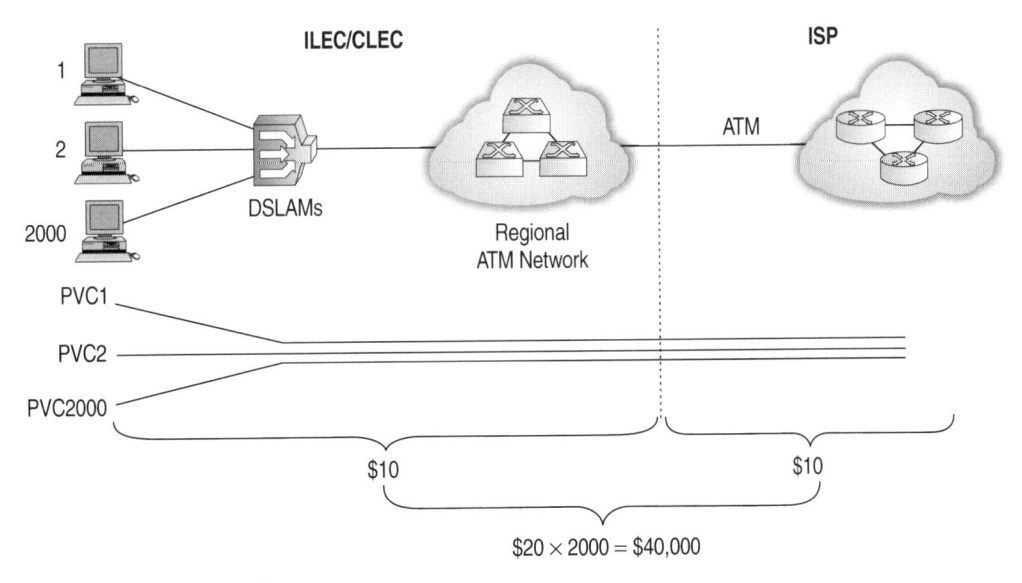

FIGURE 6.23 End-to-End PVCs

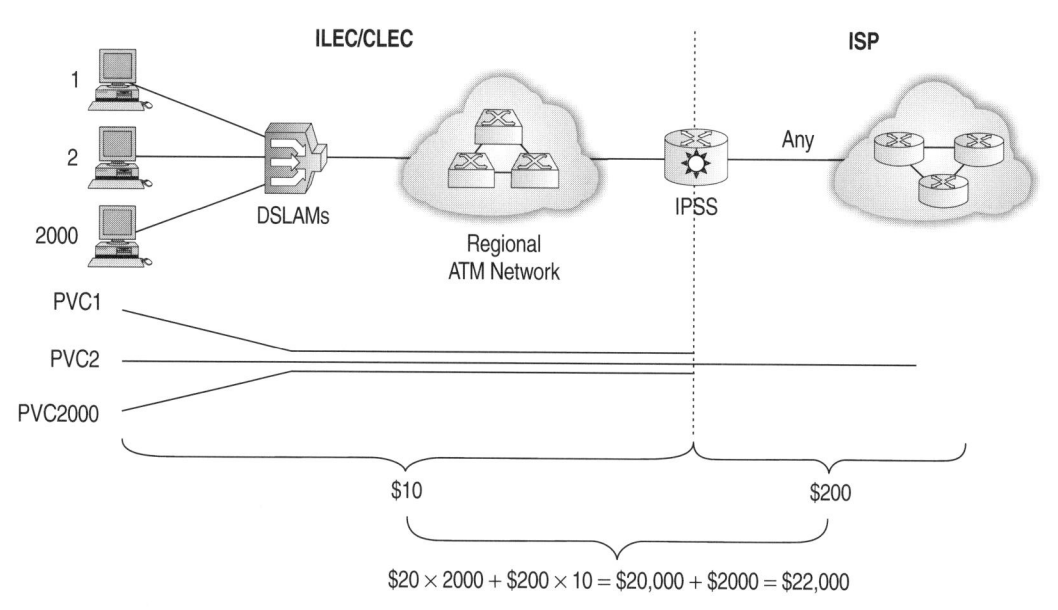

FIGURE 6.24 Wholesaler Deploys IPSS

The following is an analysis of how the ILEC recovers the cost of the IPSS and shows some cost advantages over the direct termination cost of $40,000:

- The ILEC's cost for the PVCs is $22,000 (see Figure 6.24).
- The ILEC sets a monthly transfer fee of $30,000 for the ISP.
- The difference between the ILEC's PVC cost and the ISP transfer fee ($8,000/month) is needed by the ILEC in order to recover the IPSS deployment cost.

The advantages of wholesaling to the ISP are the additional cost savings in that the ISP no longer must purchase a B-RAS/IPSS nor upgrade an existing router to serve larger numbers of ATM PVCs. This up-front cost could easily run from $10,000 in the case of an additional ATM interface on an existing core router to $50,000 or more for a dedicated subscriber management platform. If the ILEC is providing aggregation, then the ISP may still have to upgrade its router, but not to the same extent. In addition, since subscriber PVCs all terminate at the ILEC's IPSS, the ISP is not limited to ATM. FE/GE (within an exchange point), POS, and Frame are all possible access interfaces.

Examining the IPSS cost yields the following analysis: The ILEC will serve 16,000 subscribers from a single platform, which costs $250,000 (taking into account hardware and software, including provisioning software). Assume straight-line depreciation and $100,000 total for support and maintenance over the time period. This results in $70,000 per year (over 5 years), or $8,750 per year for the

2,000 subscribers served by the ISP. Now add in an initial per-subscriber provisioning charge of $5 (very conservative). The ILEC need only recover $18,750 in the first year to break even (and $8,750 plus an increment for new subscribers in years 2 through 5). In this example, the ILEC recovers $96,000 ($8,000 × 12 months) during the first year and every year thereafter. It has the additional benefits outlined earlier of subscriber visibility, new content services, and so forth.

The IPSS deployment therefore results in significant cost advantages to the ILEC. The ILEC needs only to convince the ISP that partnering with it as an active wholesaler is more beneficial in terms of cost savings and access to value-added services. Note that this analysis did not take into account absolute bandwidth per subscriber or distance. These values could be entered with similar results. Also note that the financials do not change based on the type of ISP connectivity. For example, a typical IPSS supports ISP routed contexts, L2TP tunneling, and/or generic router encapsulation (GRE). In all three cases, the ISP still requires an ATM PVC or a tunnel over FE/GE between the IPSS and its router or LNS.

Subscriber Experience in the Wholesale Environment

A typical subscriber experience within a wholesale deployment is as follows: Assuming that the provider deploys the PPP model, the subscriber logs in to the DSL service with a user ID of the form *dave@borg.net*. The DSL IPSS takes this incoming request and forwards the authentication string to a RADIUS server that maintains identity as to domains and tunnels. Based on this information, the IPSS maps the subscriber into the appropriate L2TP tunnel. This tunnel terminates on *borg.net*'s router. Authentication continues at *borg.net*, with the subscriber authentication string now passed to *borg.net*'s RADIUS server. Alternatively, *borg.net* could trust the wholesaler with operating the RADIUS server. If the wholesaler deploys contexts, the flow of events is a bit different. Here, the subscriber PPP session terminates at the IPSS, with traffic forwarded directly into the ISP's backbone.

As part of the provisioning process, the network assigns each subscriber an IP address via the Dynamic Host Configuration Protocol (DHCP). In an Ethernet environment, the PC client generates the request, and a router forwards it to the DHCP server (see Figure 6.25). The server responds, and the router forwards the response across the proper interface based on the "giaddr" field, which is the IP address of the router's Ethernet interface. Although multiple PCs on the segment receive the response, only the PC that generated the original request will take note. For dial, the RAS maintains state for each DHCP request, ensuring that the request is forwarded to the proper modem. However, this process breaks down in large DSL deployments, where the IPSS is not expected to maintain state for every DHCP request. DHCP Option 82 solves this problem by adding a new field to the request that contains the VPI/VCI pair (in the case of DSL) of the originating subscriber. The DHCP server responds, and the IPSS forwards this to the proper subscriber. Without Option 82, the IPSS would need to maintain the mapping for

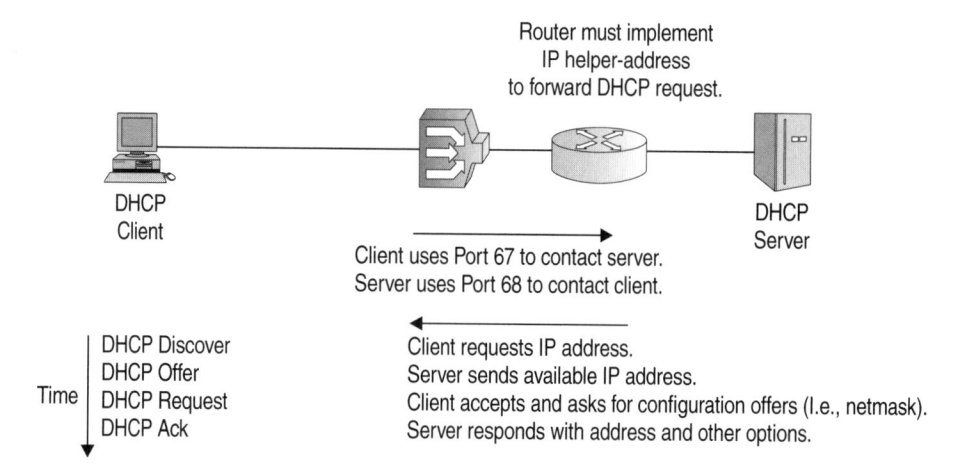

FIGURE 6.25 DHCP Flow of Events

Diagram shows DHCP Client connected through a switch and router to a DHCP Server. Labels indicate: "Router must implement IP helper-address to forward DHCP request." "Client uses Port 67 to contact server. Server uses Port 68 to contact client."

Time sequence:
- DHCP Discover — Client requests IP address.
- DHCP Offer — Server sends available IP address.
- DHCP Request — Client accepts and asks for configuration offers (I.e., netmask).
- DHCP Ack — Server responds with address and other options.

every subscriber, since the giaddr field is not usable (because many subscribers share a logical interface). Related to DHCP's Option 82 is the NAS port identifier, used within RADIUS. It functions in much the same way as Option 82, but is used as part of the RADIUS authentication process.

Probably the ultimate extension of wholesaling in the dial space, and a model that we may extend to broadband, is global roaming via the Internet, which allows a corporation to extend telecommuter access globally across many Internet access providers (IAPs). For example, with the iPass service, a subscriber connects via a special client to a roaming-enabled access point operated by one of a number of IAPs. This access point encrypts the connection request and forwards it to the iPass transaction center. Here it is decrypted, with the subscriber's domain name used to determine the destination enterprise. The transaction center encrypts the request once again and forwards it to the iPass-enabled server at the enterprise. Acceptance is forwarded via the transaction center to the local PoP, and the connection is established. If the enterprise requires a VPN client, this may be integrated with the roaming client.

The interesting part of this type of architecture is the fee settlement system. A transaction server tracks the logon location, time, and duration, forwarding this data to the enterprise, which then settles with iPass. iPass then settles with the local access provider, freeing the enterprise from having to deal directly with potentially hundreds of IAPs. The Open Settlement Protocol (OSP) standardizes much of this procedure.

Loyalty and Lock-in

Although much of the focus among service providers seems to be on the initial network buildout, subscriber acquisition, and basic service deployment, one of the real challenges is in retaining subscribers in the face of competition since many subscribers have little provider loyalty.

Basic services are a commodity. The main way of keeping customers from changing services is to sign them up for long-term contracts with premature termination clauses. Even with such contracts, some customers will leave out of sheer frustration when basic service is not well delivered. Less quantifiable than customers leaving is the impact of a provider developing a bad reputation for supplying basic services, with an impact on the provider's competitiveness in obtaining new customers.

Therefore, providers that are quick to introduce innovative services and personalization will prevail since they will have more perceived value to the customer. This personalization includes application and messaging hosting, broadband portals, service bundling, and sophisticated subscriber customization of service offerings via customer network management (CNM). Over a longer timeframe, providers offering these types of value-added services maintain or grow revenue, while revenue for those offering basic connectivity steadily decreases. This is despite the fact that the initial cost of service deployment is greater for these more sophisticated service offerings.

Minimizing Subscriber Churn

As providers layer these different services, the potential for subscriber lock-in increases. This is critical as new providers enter a given market and offer basic connectivity or even some of the more sophisticated services at a discount to the established players with a goal of growing market share. If a provider is able to avoid *subscriber churn* (subscribers leaving one provider for another) in the face of this competition, the return on investment (ROI) per subscriber increases since new subscriber acquisition cost is minimized. Providers may even offer bundles beyond Internet services. For example, they may combine wireless and traditional long-distance service, or cable providers may bundle a basic cable service with both telephony and Internet connectivity. These approaches all help maintain subscriber loyalty.

Basic connectivity does nothing to reduce subscriber churn based on performance or pricing pressures, nor does it build brand identity. In fact, positioning oneself as a purveyor of basic transport services may have the exact opposite effect. In the view of a major service provider, dark fiber services with network termination under the enterprise's responsibility may seem appealing to the enterprise from a financial perspective at first glance. However, after the first fiber outage, any advantage is all but eliminated because of the costs of network downtime to the enterprise, which may approach millions of dollars in certain sectors (e.g., the financial industry). An often-quoted statistic is that an increase of 5 percent in subscriber retention results in an increase of up to 255 percent on the bottom line.

Customer Support

An important but sometimes neglected aspect of retaining customer loyalty is support. Each and every customer must feel that he or she is important to the provider, even if he or she is on a discount plan or generates little revenue. What is sometimes forgotten is that a little customer may grow into a larger customer or that the IT staff at one enterprise may end up in the future at another. History travels with the decision makers and does not remain only at one enterprise. Once a provider has lost the business, it is very unlikely to get it back. We've witnessed many horror stories in the small-medium enterprise (SME) broadband access space, and there are all too many Web sites dedicated to comparing worst experiences in dealing with providers. The customer-facing staff, during the complete life cycle of the service, from the initial order, through the installation, and then into ongoing support and problem resolution, must be knowledgeable, courteous, and understanding of the impact of network problems on the customer's livelihood. It will be a long time before any of us in northern California forget the disasters caused by NorthPoint and a number of the DSL ISPs during the end of 2000 and into 2001. Let that be a lesson.

Conclusion

This chapter details basic access service deployment and revenue opportunities. As part of this service discussion, we introduce traffic management because of the role it plays at the congested network edge. We then look at how many providers actually deploy these services via wholesale models. The chapter also looks at often neglected aspects of offering a successful service—subscriber loyalty and support. The next chapter builds on these basic connectivity services by detailing the more advanced services at the core of many service provider IPSS deployments.

Chapter 7
Deploying Higher-Layer Services

This chapter addresses deployment of sophisticated service offerings such as IP-VPNs, content management, and voice. This discussion parallels the technology descriptions in chapters 3 and 4. These technology offerings are quite important to the provider, since the basic services described in chapter 6 do nothing to avoid commoditization, which erodes carrier margins; one subscriber management service is in most cases no different from another, and the objective of the basic services described in chapter 6 is to provide a solid foundation on which the provider can deploy these services.

One challenge with more sophisticated offerings is that they often rely on close cooperation between access providers and either enterprises or content providers or both. For example, virtual private networks (VPNs) are commonly used to connect telecommuters and small offices to enterprise sites, to link small enterprise sites, or to build extranets of various cooperating enterprises. No single user or site buys a VPN service, but rather multiple sites or multiple partners are involved.

This chapter details these more advanced service offerings by looking at security and IP-VPNs and then detailing content distribution and management, voice, and services bundling.

Firewalls and IP-VPNs

Corporate IT staffs are involved in many hours of discussions about firewall and IP-VPN deployment—what and where to deploy, what to block from the outside world, how to protect against the next attack if in a high-visibility environment, and the best way to provide remote access to corporate resources. Security hardware, software, and services are major expenses for enterprises, and providers have taken notice. The IPSS offers providers a platform on which providers can deploy network-based firewall and IP-VPN services. However, any network-based offering must meet the requirements of the customer, and in most cases customers will immediately compare the provider's offering against comparable standalone devices. The provider must therefore be careful to properly position the service, looking out for the most appropriate customers and their price sensitivities, and must understand that a complete service offering will consist of both network-based and CLE- or CPE-based solutions.

Firewalls

Firewalls are critical in protecting a large or small enterprise or even a residential customer from unwanted intrusion or denial-of-service (DoS) attacks. Although firewalling was considered almost a black art a few years ago, it has moved into the mainstream with the growth of the Internet and an awareness of the threats that a large Internet population poses. At the same time, corporations have opened up their intranets to Internet connectivity; gone are the days when corporate networks were walled off from the world or when only small, select groups of researchers in Fortune 500 corporations had Internet connectivity.

We've also seen a proliferation in the types and capabilities of firewall devices, from the simplest PC-based solutions or residential boxes to sophisticated enterprise platforms. This has caused a great deal of confusion about what is required in a firewall, who ensures that it actually works, and how to configure and deploy the device. The following sections address these considerations, including the capabilities required in a given type of firewall, how to verify that a vendor's claims are real, and where best to deploy the firewall within the network.

Firewall Capabilities

What should the subscriber or provider expect as baseline functionality in a firewall? A typical standalone device will include WAN, LAN, and LAN-side demilitarized zone (DMZ) interfaces and will be capable of supporting anywhere from T1/E1 to OC3/STM1 rates, depending on the customer's requirements and budget. If the customer requires redundancy, the provider deploys two separate devices, connected to redundant routers pointing toward the WAN. A dedicated firewall

---

♦ **DMZ**

DMZ is a term used to refer to a set of servers that sit on a special network accessible only from the outside world (the Internet) or from specific intranet servers. No traffic passes through the DMZ from the Internet to the company's internal network. Examples of DMZ servers include e-commerce and e-mail.

protects the site or enterprise from hacker attacks or from unauthorized users trying to access information.

Firewall devices also usually support complex rules and logging and may include a scripting language for the identification of new application types based on TCP/UDP ports. This is useful if the enterprise wants to run a new application. For example, many corporations develop proprietary expense-vouchering systems that allow access via a WAN connection. To support these proprietary applications and enable users to access them remotely, a new rule would need to be added to the firewall that would identify the TCP/UDP port over which this application operates. Although this functionality allows greater versatility, it is typically used by a small percentage of the subscriber base. Check Point's INSPECT engine is one example of this capability. Other functions common within enterprise firewalls include e-mail SPAM filtering, virus scanning, Java and ActiveX filtering, URL filtering, and intrusion detection.

The capabilities described in the preceding paragraphs are the baseline by which other (nonstandalone) firewalls are judged. Alternatives to standalone devices include PC- and server-based solutions (described later), routers with firewall capabilities, and network-based solutions using an IPSS.

IPSS-based firewalls offer most of the functionality found in standalone devices, but in the past they did not include some of the more sophisticated functions such as scripting languages, higher-layer application filtering (e.g., on URLs), and intrusion detection. However, most small businesses—the primary targets of the IPSS—do not utilize these capabilities. For customers that do require these additional services, many IPSSs are being enhanced to include this functionality or to operate with other specialty platforms that offer services such as content filtering and intrusion detection. In addition, as would be expected, standalone firewalls run a single instance of the firewall software and are therefore designed for a single enterprise. This contrasts with the IPSS firewall, which is capable of supporting hundreds or even thousands of customers, each with their own rules.

Where to Deploy Firewalls

The next question is where to deploy the firewall. Options include the network edge (via the IPSS and managed by the provider), as CLE (managed by the provider), as CPE (managed by the subscriber), and on the desktop. The customer's skill set, the criticality of the service, the availability of the service, and its cost will also play a part in this decision. One concern is whether a provider-based service is based at the provider's PoP or whether it is based on managed CLE. There is no correct answer, other than to say that a sizable proportion of the residential and small business subscribers will wish to outsource their security needs given an effective offering by the provider. This is similar to what occurred with network-based voicemail. End users purchased the first answering machines. When an answering machine service was offered as part of the telephone service, many customers started using that. Network-based offerings and CPE offerings offer a similar paradigm. IP-VPNs, described later in this chapter in the section "IP-VPNs," are a bit trickier in that a given VPN may contain both subscriber-based and network-based components.

Desktop-based solutions require installation on every PC; this is a questionable alternative for large businesses because of the requirement to update the software periodically. An interesting point, especially for residential PC-based firewall users, is that in order for the provider to update the software, it must have some access to the PC. This in itself may open vulnerabilities if the automated update process is in some way compromised.

CPE- and CLE-based solutions present their own set of problems. With CPE, the subscriber is responsible for device installation, configuration, and upgrade. Although this is a viable alternative for larger enterprises, smaller businesses do not have the in-house expertise for this task. CLE-based approaches relieve the subscriber from this task, placing the burden on the service provider to install and maintain the device. A subscriber contracts with the provider for a managed firewall service, and shortly thereafter, a firewall device arrives at the subscriber's front door (along with an installer in most cases). Between periodic truck rolls (where the provider must send a truck to the subscriber, costing money) and maintenance calls, a provider must usually price the service in the $1,000 per month range to achieve an adequate return on investment.

Another problem with many subscriber-based solutions is that they are often mission-specific. That is, they offer firewalling, traffic management, or IP-VPNs, but do not combine these various functions into a single solution. A customer requiring multiple services may be forced to deploy two or more platforms, each optimized for a single function. In contrast, a provider offering a network-based solution is able to upgrade features on demand. This, of course, has operational advantages for the provider as well as cost and ease-of-use advantages for customers in that they are not maintaining one or more separate boxes.

A third problem is that CLE, CPE, and desktop solutions do not stop unwanted traffic before it hits the local loop, thus tying up a scarce resource (the last and often congested mile) with traffic destined for discard.

The IPSS offers a new approach to the difficulty of providing firewall capabilities to large numbers of subscribers, by offering this capability to thousands of subscribers, thereby lowering the monthly fee substantially. In addition, the provider no longer must deploy a dedicated CLE device at the subscriber, resulting in savings on the initial installation. The trade-off is that a dedicated device may offer additional features for a subset of the subscribers. However, for the majority, the security offering of the IPSS is more than adequate. In the end, a provider may offer both solutions, marketing and pricing accordingly based on business requirements. Table 7.1 summarizes the four types of firewalls—personal, SME, enterprise, and network-based.

TABLE 7.1 Firewall Types and Features

Personal	SME	Enterprise	Network-Based
Is software-based. Is located at each subscriber PC. Includes only basic functions. Requires user configuration. If provider managed, requires provider support—software downloads, PC settings, updates. Is inexpensive.	Includes antivirus and content filtering, in most cases, as adjunct devices. Is similar in configuration to personal firewalls. Is priced per user—approximately $50. Includes dedicated hardware appliances.	Is a router or dedicated appliance integrating the necessary firewalling hardware and/or software. Includes antivirus, filtering, logging. Some include VPNs at $40–$80/user.	Configuration and upgrade are centralized. Is part of outsourced security solution. Introduces new cost profile for SME firewalling.

The important concept to note is that the real differentiator between firewall solutions is the cost and complexity of network-based deployment versus the simplicity and low expense of traditional enterprise solutions. One would expect more sophisticated customization available in a standalone device to cost up to 1,000 times more than a network-based solution. The total market size for this class of product is maybe 100,000 enterprise locations globally. In contrast, the potential market size for network-based firewalls is potentially 100 times greater than that.

One area to consider with network-based security solutions is how they deal with vulnerabilities across the local loop. True, a determined attacker may be capable of intercepting the subscriber's traffic between the PoP and the subscriber's location, but this vulnerability exists even with leased lines and Frame Relay (and also with telephony traffic, for that matter). If the subscriber is really concerned, both firewalling and encryption at the CLE are requirements. For this reason, as noted earlier, network-based solutions are not applicable for 100 percent of the subscriber population.

One evolving requirement in security deployments that is applicable to both CLE- and network-based deployment is *split-horizon management*, discussed in chapter 5. In split-horizon management, both the provider and the subscriber have management interfaces into the CLE device. For example, the subscriber may be permitted to alter firewalling policies and adjust logging, while the provider is responsible for connectivity into the network.

For verification of firewall rules on the IPSS, a number of programs are available, such as *nmap* for port-scanning networks. To test a firewall, traffic may first be sent through the IPSS with no firewall rules applied. The network administrator

> ◆ **ICSA Labs Certification**
>
> TruSecure's ICSA Labs (www.icsalabs.com) is an organization that provides certification for a given vendor's security capabilities. Product areas include antivirus software, network firewalls, IPSec products, and cryptography products. Certification is a way to ensure that a vendor's claims regarding security capabilities are in fact true and that the product is deployable and configurable. This last area is especially important in that a given firewall may have excellent filtering capabilities but may be too difficult to configure properly. An acceptance criterion is the firewall's default behavior—when first activated, it must immediately enter blocking mode. The purchaser then at his or her leisure may allow additional traffic types. The most recent firewall criteria list is 3.0a, which covers topics such as allowing or denying different types of traffic from the public or private side of the firewall, identifying and logging events so that the administrator may take appropriate action, administration of the firewall itself, and resilience of the firewall to common attacks.

sets policies to block the relevant ports, the traffic flow is halted, and the network management system logs the attempted security violation. For PCs, other programs such as *portscan* or *nessus* are available. The ICSA test suites also describe firewall verification procedures.

IP-VPNs

A VPN is the emulation of a private network over a shared infrastructure. While the idea of using a public IP network for private communications is not new, it is only recently that the appropriate mechanisms, standards, and technologies have come together to meet the customer requirements for quality of service (QoS), reliability, security, and cost-effectiveness. IP-VPNs are becoming the building blocks of next-generation enterprise WANs and provide the greatest potential source of future revenue for service providers. IP-VPNs offer corporations the ability to cost-effectively extend the corporate network to remote sites, telecommuters, and mobile workers. They also reduce communications costs among their existing corporate sites and with business partners. Once deployed, these services provide the infrastructure necessary to support additional IP-based services, such as hosted applications and voice services, with little incremental network cost.

Network-based IP-VPNs are the next evolution of CPE-based and Frame Relay-based VPNs. They enable enterprises to outsource a portion or all of their network to a service provider. Let's examine how and why CPE-based VPNs evolved to network-based VPNs.

Firewalls and IP-VPNs

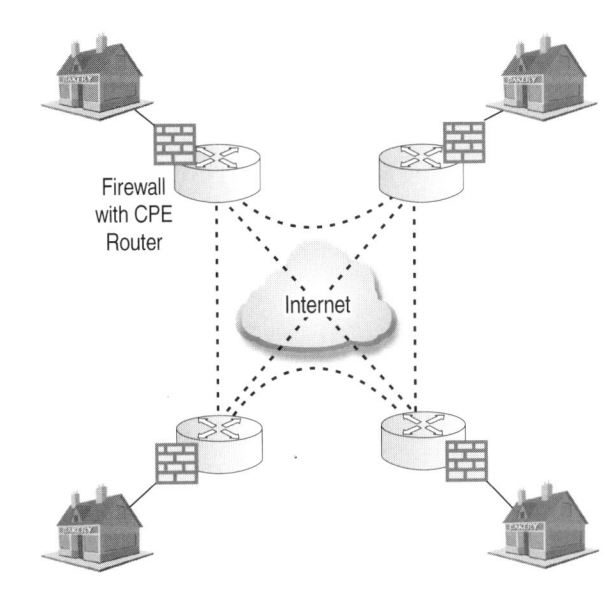

FIGURE 7.1 CPE-Based IP-VPNs

One type of CPE-based VPN evolved for smaller businesses that could not afford to use Frame Relay PVCs as dedicated links. This market used the Internet as its backbone in contrast to large businesses, which used dedicated carrier links, described next. In this VPN, a CPE router along with a firewall was used to create secure tunnels to the other sites. This topology is shown in Figure 7.1. The tunnels used IPSec to ensure that the data was encrypted and secure from the Internet traffic. Anyone in the enterprise could join this VPN as long as they had access to the Internet. In this scenario, Internet traffic would be directed immediately to the Internet and would not be backhauled to a headquarters location, saving on bandwidth. VPN traffic would be tunneled. The benefits of this type of IP-VPN were its simplicity and reduced cost. The drawbacks were a lack of guaranteed QoS.

The other type of CPE-based VPN relied on Frame Relay and leased lines to connect large corporate sites, as shown in Figure 7.2. In fact, this type of VPN is still the most common for Fortune 500 corporations. The enterprise obtains a dedicated Frame Relay link from the carrier for CPE routers at each branch location. Branch sites are aggregated to distribution, or hub, sites, also connected to the Frame Relay backbone. These hub sites interconnect via leased lines if the corporation requires the bandwidth, though both Frame Relay and ATM are widely deployed as well. Under this architecture, for each new site, a new link is required. Where hub sites are not deployed, each branch location would require individual PVCs to any other branch with which it needed to communicate.

Drawbacks of this architecture are the requirement to adapt the Frame Relay connections as topologies and bandwidth requirements change and the technical

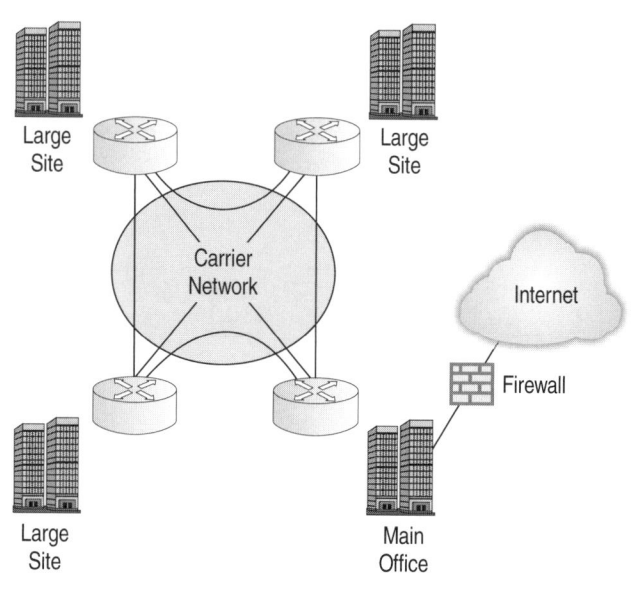

FIGURE 7.2 Frame Relay or Leased-Line IP-VPN

staff required to manage the CPE routers, hub sites, and circuits. An even larger problem is the requirement to backhaul all Internet traffic to one central site (or a few sites) where it will pass through a corporate firewall. With the growth of any-to-any Internet traffic patterns, this is not the most efficient solution.

Both of these types of CPE-based VPNs evolved into network-based VPNs, as shown in Figure 7.3. A new model emerged for small businesses; with this model, businesses were no longer required to have a router along with a firewall to provide connectivity. Instead, their access could be a simpler access device. The intelligence is migrated to the network. The network-based VPN would generate the secure tunnels, either over the Internet or, alternatively, over an opaque network if additional QoS guarantees and service level agreements were required.

An *opaque network* is so called because to the end customer it is irrelevant whether it is an IP, MPLS, or ATM network. The network provides the connectivity and the SLAs. Any traffic destined for the site would go through a network-based firewall. Any traffic coming from a site would go through the firewall and, depending on whether the traffic was destined for the Internet or for the VPN, would be forwarded appropriately. If it were for the VPN, the traffic would use a tunneling mechanism, such as IPSec tunnels, to reach its destination.

For Frame Relay–based networks the evolution to network-based VPNs aimed to simplify what was required at the end customer site and to move the complexity into the network. Now, instead of requiring a large router capable of terminating multiple PVCs as well as being responsible for their configuration and the cre-

Firewalls and IP-VPNs 227

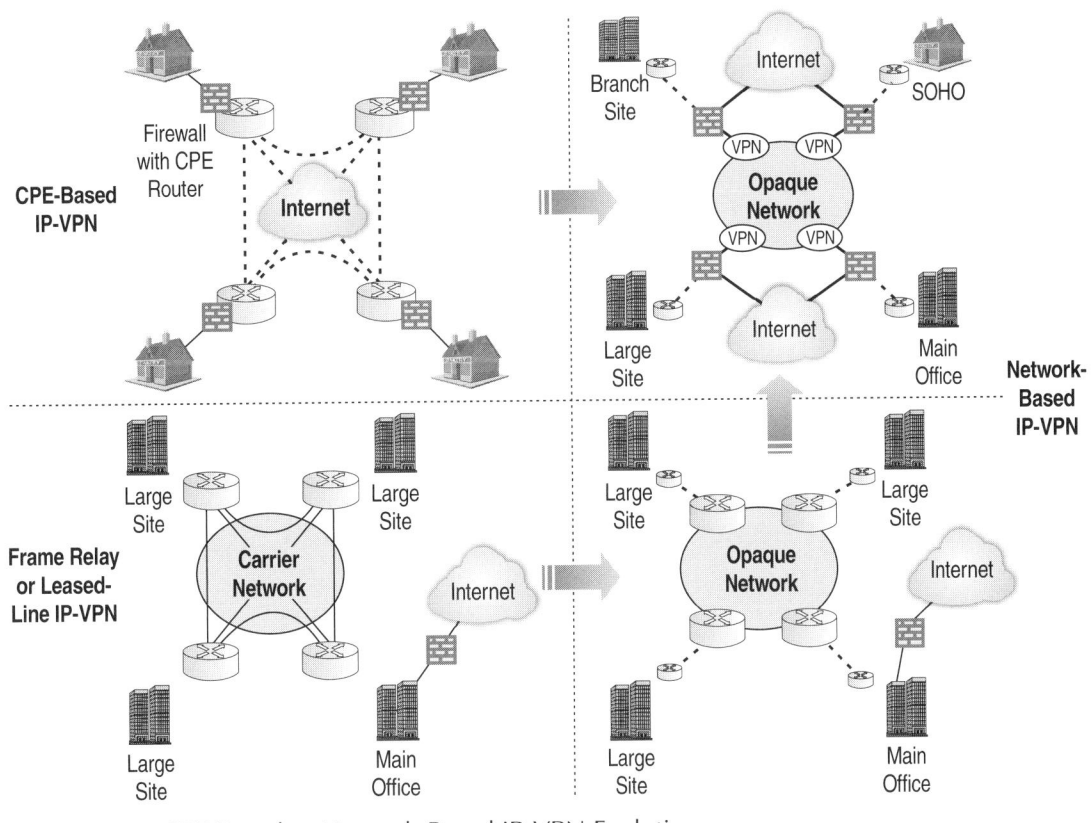

FIGURE 7.3 CPE-Based to Network-Based IP-VPN Evolution

ation of a mesh between the various sites, the corporation need only have one PVC that serves as its connection to the VPN. This migration is shown as the evolution of the lower-left quadrant to the lower-right quadrant in Figure 7.3. The service offered by the service provider makes the network opaque. The enterprise no longer has to worry about the underlying connectivity. The service provider delivers the QoS and the required connectivity.

In this version, the Internet traffic is still backhauled to the headquarters site and then goes through the enterprise firewall before reaching the Internet. This version is a very natural migration from Frame Relay–based services to a network-based IP-VPN. A further evolution is the migration from the lower-right to the upper-right quadrant of Figure 7.3, where the capability to offer network-based firewalls enables the service provider to direct the Internet traffic to the Internet without backhauling to the headquarters site. This results in significant bandwidth savings as well as in removing traffic that doesn't belong on the service provider network as soon as possible.

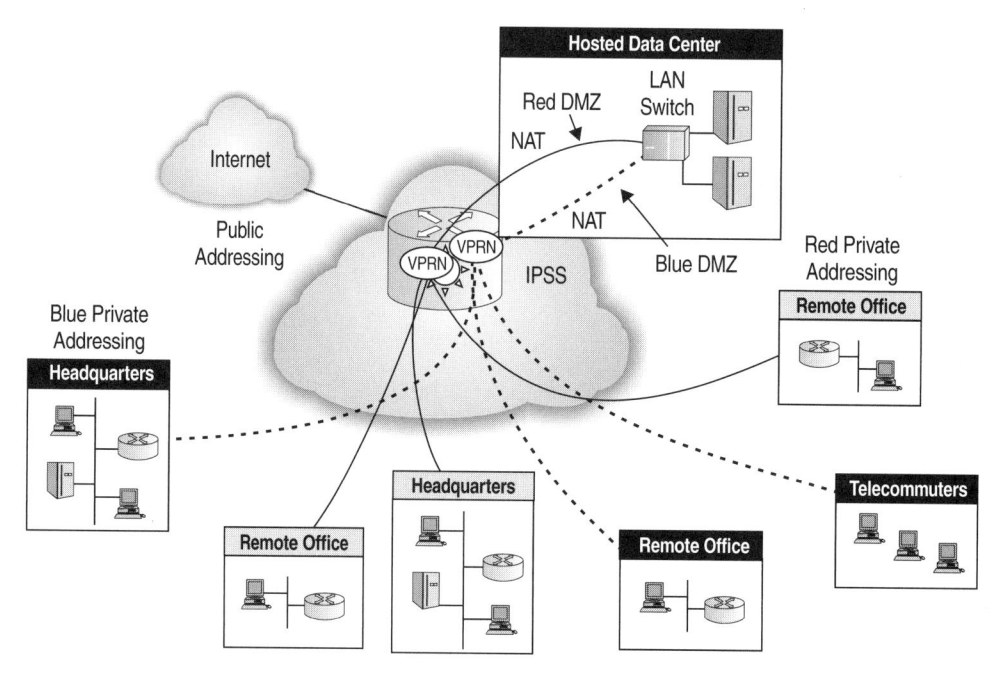

FIGURE 7.4 Network-Based IP-VPNs

Once the enterprise and small business have migrated to a network-based VPN, additional services may be offered, such as the creation of DMZ sites for servers, content server hosting, and connectivity to application service providers (ASPs) that may host the corporate applications. Such a topology is shown in Figure 7.4. In this topology, two VPNs exist: a red one (solid lines) and a blue one (dashed lines). The data center hosts servers that contain data for the red VPN and other servers that contain data for blue VPN. The IPSS uses its virtual private routed network (VPRN) technology in conjunction with firewalls to keep the servers logically separate even though they are housed in the same location. The IPSS also uses network address translation (NAT) to enable the corporate private address sites to be translated to public address sites so that they can access the Internet.

IP-VPN Device Characteristics

Given the evolution of the IP-VPN described in the preceding section, what types of platforms enable these capabilities? Dedicated IP-VPN platforms in their most basic form are used to securely connect two or more branch offices across a provider's backbone and many times include the firewalling functionality described in the previous section. CLE IP-VPN platforms became popular because of the lower cost of deployment when contrasted with Frame Relay–based VPNs. These devices typically use the Internet as their backbone and create secure tunnels over the Internet to connect the branch sites together.

In a carrier network, the IPSS needs to segregate traffic from different enterprises before forwarding it across the backbone. Techniques for this segregation, described in chapter 3, include virtual routers and multiple routers.

To secure the tunnel across the Internet, the IP Security protocol (IPSec) (also detailed in chapter 3) is used for authenticating and encrypting the data as it travels between two sites. Encryption of the data will be based on either software or hardware, depending on the throughput required. If this level of security is not required (i.e., all traffic traverses a single carrier's network deemed to be secure), MPLS or other techniques such as GRE or IP in IP are usually sufficient to separate traffic belonging to multiple enterprises.

Additional capabilities of dedicated IP-VPN platforms include traffic logging, NAT, DiffServ marking for application QoS support, and the ability to bypass non-VPN traffic, permitting customers to use these devices as the single point of entry into the WAN since performance is not impacted by VPN traffic. Representative vendors in the IP-VPN at the beginning of 2001 included VPNet Technologies, Check Point, TimeStep, RedCreek, Radguard, Nortel, Lucent, Cisco, and Microsoft.

One complexity with standalone IP-VPN devices is multivendor interoperability. Given the current state of IPSec's Internet key exchange (IKE) and limited multivendor testing, interoperability is problematic. One reason for this is that

♦ 3DES or Not 3DES

Over the past few years, there has been a great deal of discussion regarding encryption algorithm vulnerabilities. Originally, the Data Encryption Standard (DES), offering a 56-bit key length, was considered sufficient. However, with the advent of massively parallel processing, DES encryption keys based on the 2^{56} key space have been attacked and compromised with brute force, something unforeseen when the key length was selected over 20 years ago. Note that the actual algorithm is still secure. For this reason, most deployments are now based on 3DES (referred to as "triple-DES") with a 112-bit key space (2^{112}). One would expect that with this key length, the encryption key would be secure for some time. (The whole issue will be moot in a few years, however, with the deployment of the Advanced Encryption Standard [AES].)

DES is not the only algorithm in use. Other algorithms have been deployed in a more limited manner, but do not enjoy the almost universal support among the internetworking hardware community that DES has garnered.

Two good sourcebooks on encryption are *Internet Cryptography* by Richard Smith and *Applied Cryptography: Protocols, Algorithms, and Source Code in C* by Bruce Schneier.

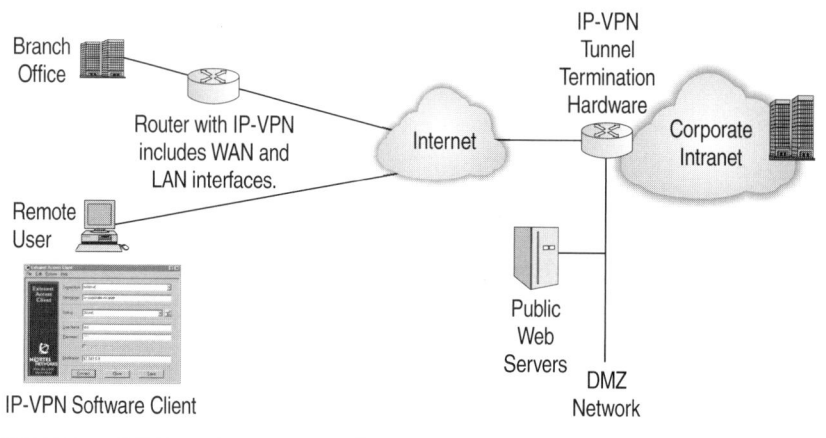

FIGURE 7.5 CLE-Based IP-VPN Architecture

although many vendors create standard-compliant IPSec, they often add many vendor-proprietary extensions that make multivendor interoperability very difficult.

A separate application for standalone IP-VPN hardware focuses on client-to-HQ connectivity, providing telecommuters with secure access to the corporate intranet. Here, CLE-based IP-VPN platforms support anywhere from tens to thousands of telecommuters based on the scalability required (see Figure 7.5).

As noted earlier, nothing precludes deployment of a router with many of these firewall or IP-VPN capabilities. Where the level of sophistication of dedicated platforms is not required, a router may suffice. In the DSL space, many DSL routers now come equipped with integrated IP-VPN and filtering capabilities, offering a subset of the functions available from standalone platforms. Note that at DSL rates in the 256 Kbps to 6 Mbps range, hardware encryption acceleration is not as much of a requirement, removing the necessity for dedicated hardware. One advantage of integrating IP-VPN capability within the router is that it may eliminate the need for PC IPSec client software. This permits multiple users within a site (e.g., branch office) to share the IPSec tunnel to the central location.

IP-VPN Desktop and Server Software

At the opposite end of the spectrum from network-based solutions is software running on the subscriber's PC or server. Where centralized management is not a requirement, or where a managed service is not available, these standalone programs have appeal. In fact, among DSL and cable subscribers, personal firewall utilities enjoy great popularity. The most sophisticated of these programs offer blocking of user-selectable incoming traffic types, include alerting and logging of suspicious activity (see Figure 7.6), and even provide traces back to the origin of

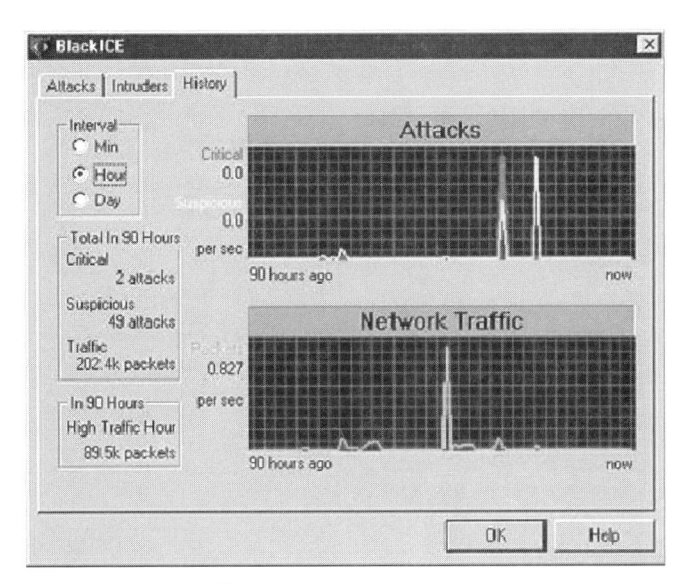

FIGURE 7.6 Personal Firewall Logging *Source:* Internet Security Systems.

an attack. One program representative of this class of applications, BlackICE Defender by Network ICE, permits the subscriber to set security levels such as "trusting," "cautious," "nervous," and "paranoid" with increasing levels of protection and logging. Although these subscriber-managed functions have their place within a network, they do not normally form part of a managed service and therefore are not described in any additional detail here.

Server-based, site-to-site IP-VPN gateways also exist, most notably by Microsoft and Novell. Although these include many of the functions of the hardware-based solutions described previously, they are limited in overall performance because of the lack of hardware acceleration. Note that this site-to-site application is different from client-to-HQ deployments, where a software-based solution for the client is quite acceptable. As with the PC applications described previously, these server-based solutions are not expected to see deployment as part of a managed service.

IP-VPN Implementation

Within an IP-VPN implementation, combinations of PC clients, CPE/CLE, and network-based devices will implement IPSec, L2TP, PPTP, MPLS, and virtual routing, depending on the business model of the service provider. Note that the remainder of this section assumes that the corporation has outsourced provisioning of the entire IP-VPN requirement to the provider, including any CLE devices as well as any PC client software. These components enable the following set of IP-VPN services, which are diagrammed in Figure 7.7.

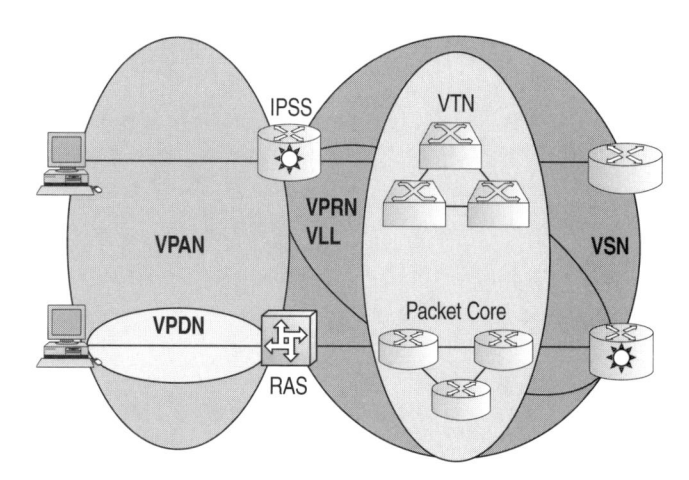

FIGURE 7.7 IP-VPN Services

- *Virtual transport networks* (VTNs) offer scalable intersite connectivity across a wide area. Protocols for VTNs include virtual and multiple routers at the edge, generic routing encapsulation (GRE), IP in IP, MPLS, and policy routing for interconnectivity, all in conjunction with the various traffic management techniques. An effective VTN, of course, must tightly integrate within the provisioning of other end-to-end IP-VPN services and will usually extend across platforms from multiple vendors.
- *Virtual service networks* (VSNs) offer "high-touch" VPN services to subscribers and are a superset of VTNs. These VSNs include traffic management, firewalling, and both Internet and extranet connectivity. Techniques for VSNs include IPSec as well as IP layer tunneling protocols such as the Layer Two Tunneling Protocol (L2TP), the Point-to-Point Tunneling Protocol (PPTP), and the Layer 2 Forwarding Protocol (L2F). VSNs at the network edge may feed into VTNs within the network core.
- *Virtual private access networks* (VPANs), sometimes referred to as "remote access VPNs," enable secure client connectivity into a corporate intranet. PC IPSec, L2TP, or PPTP clients establish secure tunnels across dial, DSL, cable, and so forth, to an IP-VPN termination device located at the provider's edge (the IPSS) or to a device dedicated to a given corporation (CLE/CPE).
- *Virtual private dial networks* (VPDNs) apply to traditional dial access and are a subset of VPANs.
- *Virtual private routed networks* (VPRNs) are constructs that tunnel across a network backbone and are a form of VSN. For security purposes, IPSec is often used as the tunneling technology. VPRNs offer secure intranet and extranet

connectivity between a corporation's offices, customers, and suppliers and usually rely on an IP services node at the provider's network edge.

Virtual leased lines (VLLs) are Layer 2, point-to-point constructs that connect across a network backbone, supporting all types of Layer 3 traffic (i.e., not limited to IP as is the case with VPRNs). They are the IPSec analogy of a traditional leased line and are also a form of VSN.

For example, an organization consisting of a small number of branch sites and telecommuters may outsource intranet connectivity to an IP-VPN provider, replacing an existing leased-line or Frame Relay infrastructure. Requirements on the provider's backbone are modest in this example. This VSN also includes remote access via PC-based IPSec clients (a VPAN). Branch offices connect via SDSL to IPSSs at the provider's edge for IPSec tunnel origination (see Figure 7.8). The central site is also connected to the same VPRN, either via a dedicated CLE device managed by the provider or by a connection to an IPSS.

Note that much of this IP-VPN terminology is currently under refinement within the IETF's Provider Provisioned Virtual Private Network working group. This group is chartered with defining the various types of provider-based IP-VPNs, combining both CLE- and PoP-based solutions. It is addressing both Layer 2 technologies, such as Frame Relay and ATM (as well as mapping these two technologies at the edge into IP), and Layer 3 solutions, such as MPLS and virtual routers. To base any solution in reality, the group is relying on service provider input for security, addressing, QoS, SLA, and management requirements.

With an understanding of the different types of tunneling and IP-VPN alternatives, we are now in a better position to contrast the various forms of client-side tunneling, comparing the techniques in ease of use, security, and application support. Table 7.2 provides this comparison.

Which IP-VPN protocol you select, as discussed in chapter 3, relates to what type of VPN you have. Issues include whether the IP-VPN is used for remote access, for interworking with extranet partners, for branch office connectivity within a small or large corporation, or for mobile access, potentially the most complex VPN architecture of all. The size of the corporation will also have a major impact on the type of IP-VPN deployed.

A complete IP-VPN offering will incorporate all the services described up to this point in the book. Permanent or transient subscribers will connect to the service via any one of the access technologies described. If the IP-VPN replaces the corporation's existing backbone, traffic management capability in support of application prioritization is a must. This includes both prioritization versus other IP-VPNs and prioritization within the IP-VPN. Security services are also a given, with firewalling a requirement when connecting the IP-VPN to the Internet or to extranet partners.

TABLE 7.2 Client Tunneling Alternatives

	PPTP/PPP	L2TP/PPP	L2TP/IPSec	IPSec
User authentication	Yes	Yes	Yes	In progress
Machine authentication	Yes, if gateway-to-gateway	Yes	Yes	Yes
NAT-capable	Yes	Yes	No	No
Multiprotocol	Yes	Yes	Yes	In progress
Dynamic IP address assignment	Yes	Yes	Yes	In progress
Encryption	Yes	Yes	Yes	Yes
Public key encryption (PKE)	Yes	Yes	Yes	Yes
Packet authenticity	No	No	Yes	Yes
Multicast	Yes	Yes	Yes	Yes

TABLE 7.3 IP-VPN Alternatives

	IP in IP	GRE	L2TP	IPSec	MPLS-VPN
Multiplexing	No	Varies	Yes	Yes	Yes
Signaling	No	No	Yes	Yes	Yes
Data security	No	No	Varies	Yes	Varies
Multiprotocol	No	Yes	Yes	Yes	Yes
Sequencing	No	No	Yes	No	Yes
Low overhead	Yes	Yes	Varies	Varies	Yes

Table 7.3 outlines the different options for IP-VPN deployment across a provider's backbone in terms of various implementation issues. *Multiplexing* is the capability of a single tunnel to transport multiple user sessions between a source and a destination. This helps to minimize overhead and state along the path. *Signaling* permits automatic tunnel establishment, reducing the need for manual configuration. Most of the techniques rely on the existing Layer 3 routing protocol for the exchange of reachability information. *Data security* protects the data from prying eyes and implies support for encryption, or in the case of L2TP, MPLS, and VRs, the capability to add encryption via a separate protocol. *Multiprotocol* is just that—the capability of the tunneling technique to support Layer 3 protocols other than IP. With the exception of IP in IP, all techniques support this. *Sequencing* prevents mis-ordering of subscriber traffic, but is not that great of an issue since, with IP, higher-order protocols (TCP) are responsible for this task. Finally, the amount of overhead is dependent on the encapsulation technique. Both L2TP and IPSec rely on larger headers than the other techniques.

Firewalls and IP-VPNs 235

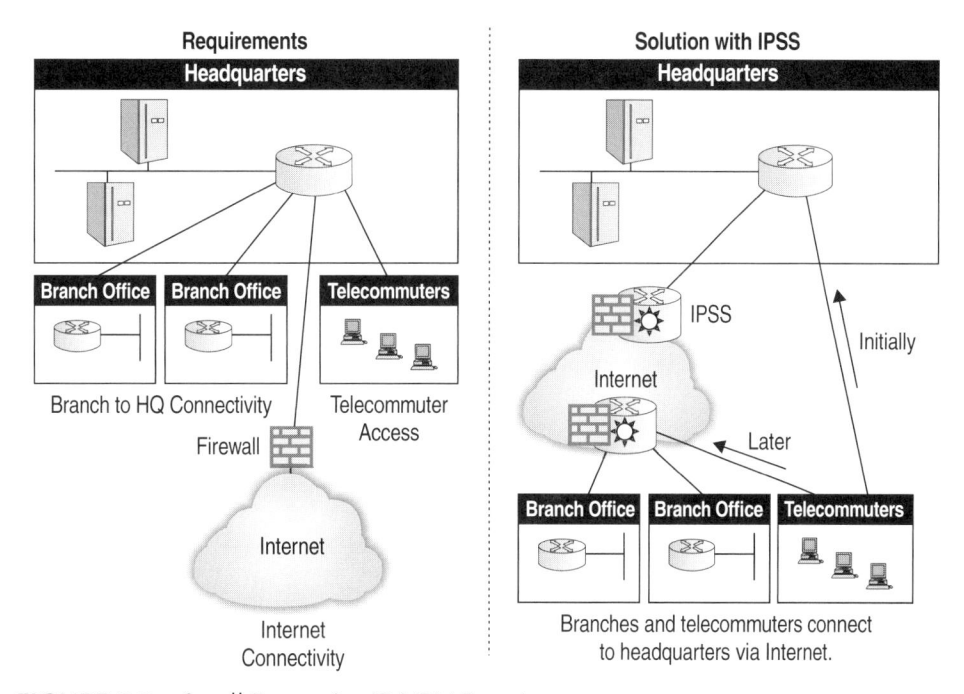

FIGURE 7.8 Small Enterprise IP-VPN Requirements

Which IP-VPN architecture is selected will depend on the type of enterprise being served. There are major differences in deployment between small and large enterprises.

Small Enterprise Deployment As an example, a small enterprise requires branch office and telecommuter connectivity to the headquarters site. The headquarters then has a single firewalled connection into the Internet. Branches connect via DSL, T1/E1, or fractional T1/E1 services, while telecommuters usually connect via dial, DSL, or cable directly into the headquarters site (see Figure 7.8).

With an IPSS, branches can connect directly to the Internet for outgoing traffic, accepting incoming traffic only from within the corporation's IP-VPN. The connection to the Internet from the headquarters site is also via the IPSS. Figure 7.9 depicts the rules for a branch office connecting to this network, as follows:

- Rule 1 permits only traffic from the corporate IP-VPN into the site.
- Rule 2 accepts any "harmless" traffic such as Ping.
- Rule 3 permits users in the branch office to initiate sessions into the Internet (avoiding the need to go through the headquarters site for all outgoing traffic).
- Rule 4 logs any incoming "malicious" traffic.
- Rule 5 drops any other traffic from the Internet to the branch office.

#	Source	Destination	Service	Action	Log	Remark
1	_VpnAddr	_VpnAddr	Any	accept_via_vpn		
2	Any	Any	Useful_ICMP	accept		
3	_SubAddr	Any	Any	accept		
4	Any	Any	ident	reject		
5	Any	Any	Any	drop	brief	

FIGURE 7.9 Small Enterprise IP-VPN Policy for a Branch

#	Source	Destination	Service	Action	Log	Remark
1	_VpnAddr	_VpnAddr	Any	accept_via_vpn		
2	Any	WebServer	http, https, ftp	accept		
3	Any	MailServer	smtp	accept		
4	Any	DNSServer	domain-udp	accept		
5	Any	Any	Useful_ICMP	accept		
6	_SubAddr	Any	Any	accept		
7	Any	Any	ident	reject		
8	Any	Any	Any	drop	brief	

FIGURE 7.10 Small Enterprise IP-VPN Policy for the Headquarters Site

The headquarters site is the only location that accepts incoming traffic from the Internet, diverting most of it to the DMZ LAN. Figure 7.10 depicts the rules for this location, as follows:

- Rule 1 permits incoming traffic from the corporate IP-VPN (the branch offices).
- Rule 2 accepts incoming traffic (http, https, ftp) from the Internet to the corporate Web server located on the DMZ LAN.
- Rule 3 does the same for mail (smtp).
- Rule 4 permits DNS queries.
- Rule 5 accepts any "harmless" traffic such as Ping.

- Rule 6 permits users at the headquarters site to initiate sessions into the Internet.
- Rule 7 logs any incoming "malicious" traffic.
- Rule 8 drops any other traffic from the Internet to the branch office.

As part of its service definition, the service provider must determine whether a branch office may connect directly to the Internet or must always tunnel through the provider's backbone to the corporate gateway site (see Figure 7.11). If this connection is permitted, this *split tunneling,* as it is known in IPSec terminology, in effect places the branch in an IP-VPN to the corporate intranet as well as on the Internet. An advantage of this architecture is that Internet access is now distributed, reducing the burden on the central site in regard to Internet bandwidth. The IPSS permits this distributed firewalling from the branch offices. Key exchange in this environment is relatively simple, in that it exists only across the provider's backbone, and the IP-VPN service is usually based on a single vendor's product. If this is not the case, interoperability testing is a requirement, though IP-VPN management and configuration will usually be a larger issue than the actual IPSec internetworking.

Note that split tunneling does introduce some security concerns since a user with simultaneous connections to both the corporate intranet and the Internet could conceivably route between the two. The network administrator in this case must maintain close control over the software running on the telecommuter's PC or the configuration of the branch office router (if one exists).

Building on this scenario, the enterprise now has the requirement to connect mobile workers across the Internet (see Figure 7.8). The solution here is a PC-based IPSec client, with the tunnel terminating on the IPSS (see Figure 7.12). Note that this implies that all telecommuters have access to the IPSS, by virtue of either

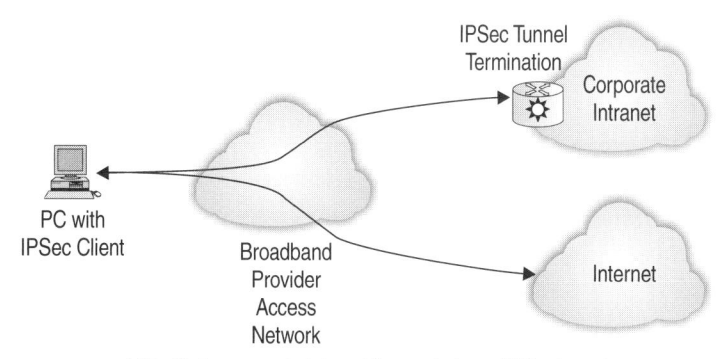

FIGURE 7.11 Split Tunneling

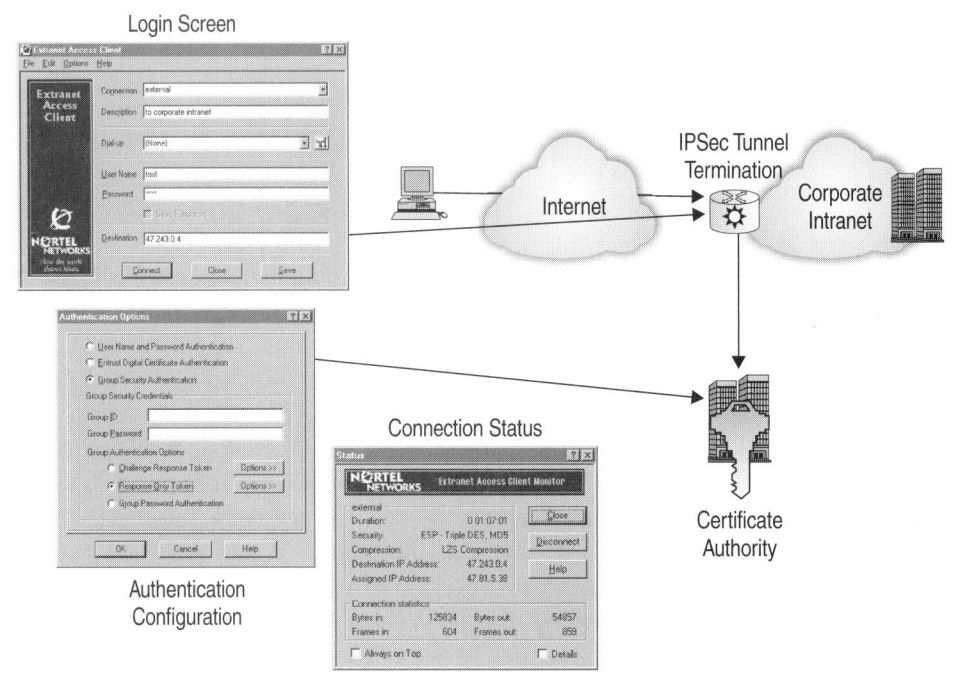

FIGURE 7.12 IP-VPN Client   *Source:* Nortel Networks.

being "on-net" (native to the provider's network) or having reachability via a wholesale operator. If this is not the case, the enterprise could operate a separate IP-VPN gateway, described later. Note that the IPSS brings to the table some of the same advantages to the telecommuter as it brings to the branch office, most notably distributed firewalling, NAT, and, therefore, Internet access. The use of IPSec clients also permits the corporation to dispense with a dedicated RAS infrastructure (and its operational costs).

Large Enterprise Deployment   A large corporation transitioning to a managed IP-VPN service requires a more complex architecture (see Figure 7.13). Consider a pre-VPN implementation, relying on leased lines or Frame Relay for branch connectivity. Instead of connecting to each other via Frame Relay data link connection identifiers (DLCIs), these branches now connect to distribution sites, which are then interconnected via a full mesh. This is a classic hierarchical router network overlaid on a Frame Relay backbone for branch access. As with the previous example, the enterprise requires telecommuter access and Internet connectivity and has one or more central sites with high bandwidth requirements. Branch office, telecommuter, and Internet connectivity falls into the realm of a VSN, as

Firewalls and IP-VPNs 239

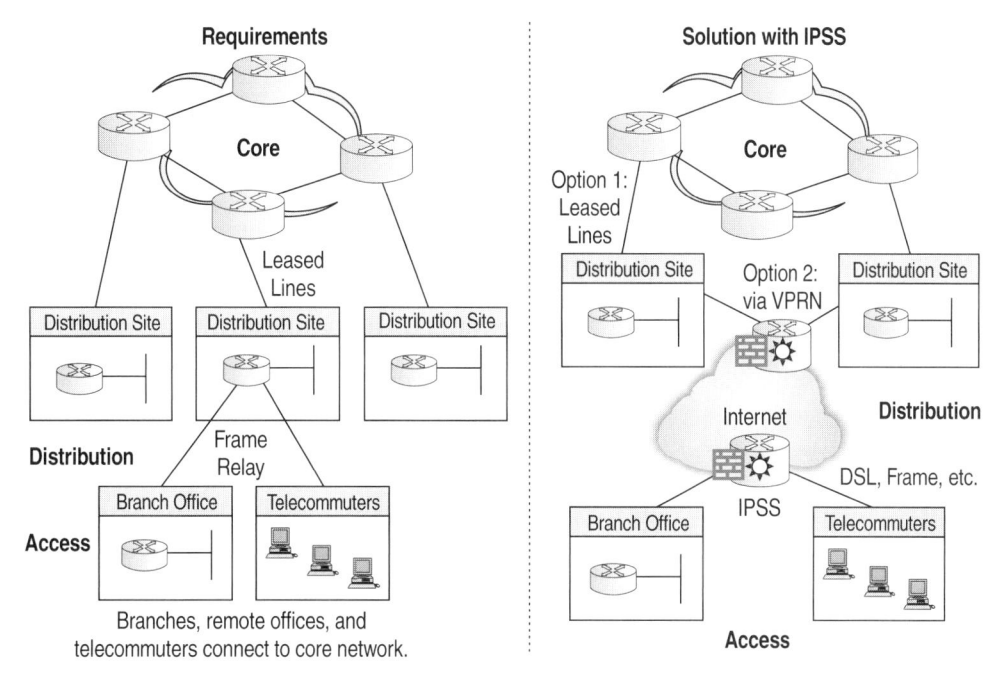

FIGURE 7.13 Large Enterprise IP-VPN Requirements

described earlier. In contrast, connectivity across the backbone calls for a VTN. Although IPSec could be used to construct both the VSN and VTN components, some providers prefer the use of vendor-specific virtual router implementations or MPLS-VPNs for the VTN component.

With an IPSS, branch offices connect via DSL or Frame Relay and map into edge VPRNs on the IPSS platform. These VPRNs rely on IPSec or MPLS-VPNs for site-to-site connectivity. The distribution sites also connect to this VPRN and are interconnected via leased lines (Option 1) or across the same VPRN (Option 2), depending on the bandwidth required and the scalability of the IPSS platform.

Note that the IPSS still does not solve the connectivity requirements of larger enterprises, which require a degree of routing isolation and manageability that an IPSec or even an MPLS-VPN solution cannot offer. Larger enterprises continue to require dedicated links or connectivity via more traditional means such as Frame Relay or ATM.

Recently, platforms have become available that permit carriers to offer dedicated router resources to these enterprises within a single platform. The enterprise would have the same degree of autonomy, scalability (including QoS support), and security as if it had its own dedicated router. In contrast to VPNs, backbone connectivity based on this architecture may be termed *real private networks,* or RPNs.

Extending the IP-VPN "Off-Net" Note that some sites beyond the service area of an IPSS-equipped provider (referred to as "off-net") may choose to deploy CLE-based firewalls. Figure 7.14 depicts a CLE-based IP-VPN policy. This device, the Check Point Firewall 1, also supports firewalling. Each rule is defined by source, destination, service type (application), action, and logging. Let's look at the configuration rule by rule:

- Rule 1 prohibits all access to the device itself, preventing attacks against the firewall. In addition, any attack against the firewall immediately results in an alert to the network administrator.
- Rule 2 invokes IPSec for sites within the IP-VPN.
- Rule 3 creates a remote access VPN, encrypting all traffic from the field destined for the corporate network.
- This is extended by Rule 4, which defines an extranet (with partners) and also encrypts the traffic.
- Rules 5 through 10 define the firewall policies.
- Rules 5 and 6 permit traffic to and from the mail server.
- Rule 7 permits pop-3 access to the mail server for mail retrieval.
- Rule 8 permits access to the Web and ftp servers.
- Rule 9 prohibits all access from the DMZ network to the internal network. This prohibits hackers from potentially using hosts on the DMZ net as jumping-off points for attacking the internal network.
- Rule 10 permits any traffic from the internal network to the Internet.

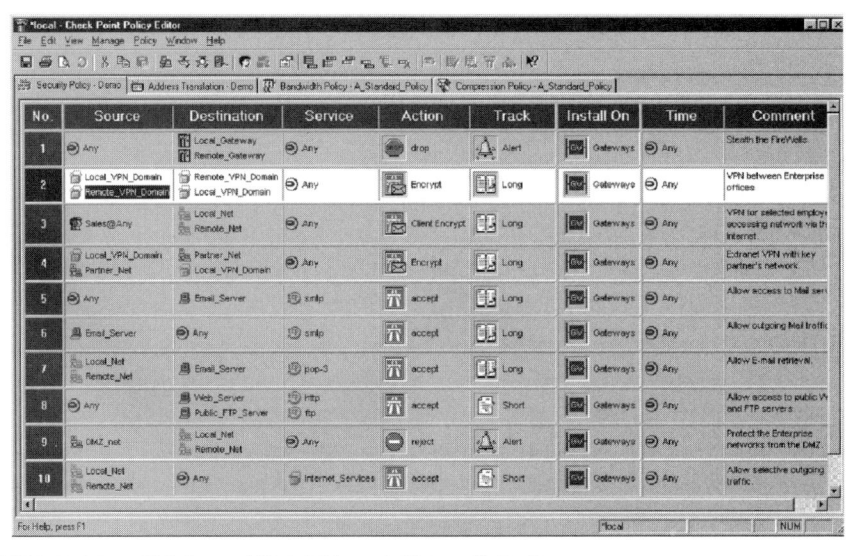

FIGURE 7.14 CLE-Based IP-VPN and Firewall Policy

Source: Copyright © 2001 Check Point Software Techologies Ltd. Used with permission.

The combination of these rules results in a policy applicable for an enterprise with remote users, extranet partners, branch offices across the Internet, and servers on a DMZ network.

Interoperability in this environment is probably more of a concern than with simpler IP-VPN deployments, since a single corporation's VPN may extend across multiple service providers. Within a managed service, one cannot guarantee that different providers will use the same CLE or even the same protocol to enable the VPN. The option here would be for the enterprise's primary provider to provision a CLE box at a site connected to the second provider but managed by the first. Interoperability is also an issue at the VSN-VTN boundary, where one vendor's IPSS may map into a second vendor's ATM switch or core router.

Another option is to connect some of the branches (over dedicated Frame Relay or ATM connections) directly into the core, bypassing the IPSS. These branches would then map directly into an MPLS-VPN, which could then connect to the IPSS. The IPSS could act as the go-between from the MPLS to the IPSec domain (see Figure 7.15). This may be a viable option if the provider has a large installed base of Frame or ATM switching and wishes to quickly deploy IP-VPN services. The provider therefore has a great deal of flexibility in how to connect a given site, based on the choice of access technology, the bandwidth requirement of the site, and whether the provider has deployed an IPSS. As with the first example, this application does not require a PKI either for the backbone or for telecommuters since IP-VPN membership is confined to trusted sites belonging to the enterprise.

A more complex application is secure supplier/distributor connectivity, where a large enterprise establishes linkages to other companies in its supply or distribution chain. The major focus is on interoperability and key exchange, as enterprises deploying IPSec devices from multiple vendors will connect to different service providers (unless the network is established as a closed service and confined to a single provider). Unlike the previous examples, this application

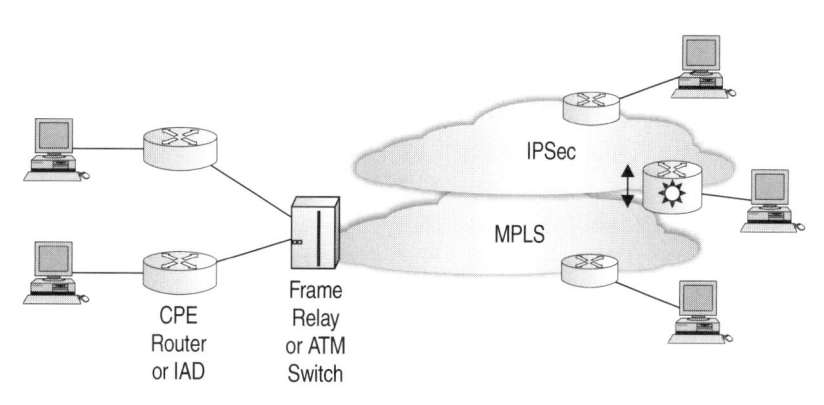

FIGURE 7.15 IP-VPN Internetworking

requires implementation of a PKI with one or more CAs since multiple enterprises must be capable of establishing IPSec tunnels between one another. One of the earliest examples of a multi-enterprise IPSec service was the ANX, which connected companies within the auto industry.

Advantages of IPSec to the provider include the ability to offer IP-VPN services to a subscriber base that may have been reluctant to use a managed service because of costs. In offering additional value to the subscriber, the provider also differentiates its offering from pure transport services. The subscriber also benefits by no longer having to manage its WAN connectivity, maintain complex CPE, or make guesses as to QoS or SLAs. In addition, the cost of using a managed IP-VPN service will be less than that for equivalent connectivity via leased lines or Frame Relay. The only potential pitfalls include reach of the provider's service, which can be addressed via remote placement of CLE, and the potential dependency on a single provider, which possibly can be addressed by provisioning backup links (no different than the backup requirements within Frame Relay). A potential drawback to encrypting at the IPSS instead of the CPE or CLE is that the local loop is unencrypted, making tapping a bit easier. This is no different than leased line or Frame Relay tapping. Since most security attacks come from the Internet, as opposed to physical tapping, encrypting at the network edge when required is an acceptable alternative given the advantages it provides.

Wireless VPNs

Although a great deal of emphasis has been placed on IP-VPN support for fixed subscribers, such as telecommuters accessing their corporate networks from home or from hotel rooms, a totally new type of VPN is in the early stages of deployment. This is the mobile VPN, which serves subscribers connected to 2.5G and 3G wireless networks who desire the same access to their corporate network or ISP as if they were connected via a landline.

The goal of the network operator is to provide mobile subscribers with connectivity to their home ISP or corporation across GPRS, UMTS, or CDMA 2000. Because of the nature of wireless connectivity—it offers limited bandwidth (in comparison to fixed broadband access)—as well as limited processing power and battery life on the handset, the proper VPN architecture with a goal to minimize overhead is critical.

GPRS and UMTS Architecture   As discussed earlier, there are two types of tunneling—voluntary and compulsory. Voluntary tunneling relies on end-to-end tunnels between the subscriber and his or her destination and, in most cases, is based on IPSec. Within a wireless deployment, this is not necessarily the most efficient use of resources since IPSec may use up to 30 percent of the wireless bandwidth. In contrast, compulsory tunnels are established within the provider's network, usually between the provider's edge PoP and the destination. They always remain active and are shared by multiple subscribers. However, the use of compulsory tunneling does assume that the provider's access network, in this case the wireless segment, is secure. This is accomplished through the use of encryption across the wireless link. The compulsory tunnels may be based on a number of techniques, including IPSec, L2TP, or MPLS.

As a review, within a GPRS or UMTS deployment, the SGSN and the GGSN perform two distinct functions. The former is responsible for mobility management, authentication, and packet data routing. Mobile devices attach to the SGSN via the base station, which also provides location tracking. The SGSN is also responsible for sending queries to the home location register (HLR) to obtain profile data for GPRS/UMTS subscribers. As part of this role, it detects new devices, processes registrations, and keeps track of subscriber locations. The GGSN, in contrast, terminates the GPRS Tunneling Protocol (GTP) originated by the SGSN and forwards the subscriber's session in tunnels to the home ISP or corporation. Other functions of the GGSN include routing, address management, firewalling, and AAA.

The challenge, then, is in connecting the subscriber from the GGSN to the ISP or enterprise network. Here, the GPRS specification offers two solutions. The first, *transparent mode,* permits the GPRS/UMTS operator to offer connectivity to the subscriber's IP network without any access authentication. The only authentication in this case is that between the mobile device and the SGSN via the HLR or the visitor location register (VLR). Under transparent mode, the GPRS/UMTS operator issues public IP addresses to GPRS/UMTS users. In effect, the subscriber becomes a part of the GPRS/UMTS operator's IP network. Note that this service could support an end-to-end voluntary IPSec tunnel once connectivity is established, as described earlier, though this may not be the ideal use of wireless resources.

Nontransparent mode may form a basis for network-based VPN services. Here, the subscriber is allocated an IP address from the ISP or enterprise. The GGSN plays an active role in RADIUS authentication by issuing the request at Packet Data Protocol (PDP) context activation. It is responsible for the creation of IPSec or L2TP tunnels, or the establishment of MPLS-VPNs, to the ISP or enterprise network.

If the GGSN does not support PPP, the operator will probably rely on IPSec for tunneling between the GGSN and the subscriber's home network. This is known as an "IP mode" PDP context. If mapping into IPSec, the GGSN must associate the subscriber's IP address with the specific IPSec tunnel. One problem in offering an IPSec-based solution is that the only user authentication is via the wireless segment via the HLR. If a phone has been hacked, an impostor could gain access to the enterprise network. For this reason, PPP-based solutions are preferred, though this assumes that the GGSN is capable of handling RADIUS.

Under an MPLS solution, PPP/IP traffic is encapsulated into an LSP by the GGSN acting as a label edge router (LER) and is then terminated at a label switch router (LSR) at the ISP or enterprise. The other option is for the GGSN to support L2TP. Here, mobile subscribers attach to the GPRS network and then initiate PPP sessions.

The GGSN therefore performs GTP to L2TP tunnel switching. This is probably the most secure mechanism, since the subscriber authenticates via the corporate or ISP AAA server and is then assigned an IP address from either of these two address spaces. The subscriber specifies the destination network through the use of access point names (APNs), identifiers managed by the wireless operator.

CDMA 2000 Architecture The mobile IP-VPN architecture within CDMA 2000 deployments is a bit different from that of GPRS/GGSN. Instead of the GTP, CDMA networks rely on mobile IP (MIP) tunneling between the subscriber and the wireless base station. MIP, described in chapter 6, permits subscribers to maintain their original IP address when traveling between regions. Subscribers connecting to their "home" IP network when not traveling are assigned IP addresses under the direction of a home agent (HA). When the subscriber leaves the home network, it registers with a foreign agent (FA). The FA assigns the subscriber an address native to the network to which the subscriber has attached (the foreign network) and relays this care-of address to the HA. One challenge is how the subscriber maintains the same IP address when crossing geographic boundaries. The packet-carrying function (PCF) and the packet data support node (PDSN) implement the mobile IP protocol stack. The wireless media terminate at the PCF, while the PDSN acts as the FA. As the subscriber moves, it will connect to multiple PCFs. However, each of these PCFs must be anchored to the same PDSN if the subscriber is to maintain its same IP address.

IP-VPN Market Opportunity

For enterprise customers, IP-VPNs are major drivers. Over a third of enterprises already have IP-VPNs, connecting either branch offices or telecommuters. With the growth of broadband access, this connectivity becomes even more valuable. Important components of these IP-VPN services include NAT, firewalling, SLAs, customer network management (CNM), and authentication. These different services are described in chapter 3. Content streaming and caching are also important. Centralized file backup and prioritized Web services are additional services. The first offers offsite file recovery and has been around in one form or another for a while. Web prioritization offers better response times to customers.

Security services include managed firewalls with intrusion detection (often in conjunction with IP-VPNs), as well as content and virus filtering. Unlike the residential space, where some of the additional services may be required just to head off customer defection, the opportunity for additional revenue in the enterprise space is great. For the SME, a provider may offer a firewall or IP-VPN service at set fees of anywhere from $50 to $250 or more per month (described as part of the financial models in chapter 8).

Another way to price some services is on an individual basis (also known as *price per seat*). In this model, anywhere from $2 to $5 per month is possible for firewalling, with automatic file backup pushing $10 per month. Given the potential value of automatic file backup, the higher pricing is not surprising.

An often-voiced concern is whether the various firewalling and IP-VPN requirements may be better met by a CPE- or CLE-based solution. Given client- or router-based firewalls and low-cost VPN hardware, this may be a consideration from the financial standpoint. However, the real criteria are the business model of the provider and the expectations of the subscriber. Network-based services may be appropriate where the subscriber wishes no role in deploying or managing these services. This contrasts to the costs associated with in-house solutions based on CPE that involve the following:

- Security personnel salaries, to include 24×7 availability
- Ongoing training and dedicated expertise in the latest intrusions/vulnerabilities, viruses, content-filtering categories and technology, and the latest security technologies (Note that some companies provide central updating in some but not all of these areas.)
- Installation expenses
- Downtime incurred during installation and provisioning

The IPSS allows the provider to deploy a single platform and, just as important, to allocate scarce staff among thousands of subscribers. For the first time, the small enterprise need not pay the $1,000 or more per month for firewall software and hardware, the installation fees of $500 to $5,000, and the initial security audit and configuration costs, sometimes running as high as $25,000. The availability of network-based security solutions will cause this segment of the security services market to grow from $512 million in 1998 to over $2.24 billion by 2003 (IDC, 1998). This network-based service may be offered as part of a larger security consulting solution—a market expected to reach $14.8 billion by 2003.

Today we can look back and see that the Fortune 500 have been in the forefront of advanced service deployment. They have contracted for leased lines, Frame Relay, and ATM services, and have used these technologies as a basis for their various security, QoS, and IP-VPN architectures. The enterprises have had both the funding and the expertise to deploy these services on a regional or even global basis and, in the case of some, such as AT&T GNS (the former IBM GNS) and FT/Equant, have even evolved into service providers in their own right. These primarily CPE-based services have met the needs of their customers for the last two decades, but have not been available at an acceptable cost for the evolving Internet business community, sometimes referred to as the Fortune (or unfortunate) 5,000,000. One cannot expect a small business paying $200 per month for an SDSL service to support a $1,500 per month managed firewall service.

However, the cost of advanced deployment service is just one aspect. Most businesses connecting to the Internet permanently for the first time do not have the expertise to either understand or deploy (in the case of CPE) the service. The IPSS enables a new class of network-based services, where the provider may offer the business a set of managed services appropriate to their business model. The cost barrier is overcome by being able to virtualize these services over a large number of subscribers, thereby minimizing the per-subscriber cost. For example, a provider could offer a managed firewall service to a small business at $50 per month or less, compared to the $1,500 just quoted, and still be profitable.

In 2000, 73 percent of local and regional ISPs, 80 percent of CLECs, and 88 percent of national providers and ILECs planned to offer IP-VPN services. Of these, 75 percent planned CPE-based and 63 percent planned network-based services. The growth in these services, from 44 percent the previous year, reflected the growing availability of network-edge IP service platforms. From the perspective of the subscriber, only 25 percent of small businesses made use of provider-based IP-VPNs in 2000. This is expected to grow to 50 percent by 2002. The uptake for medium and large enterprises was a bit stronger in 2000, at about 35 percent. The European numbers were much the same, with about 25 percent in 2000 and 50 percent in 2002. This growth in both CPE and network-based services is reflected in the revenue projections. Managed CPE-based service revenues will grow from $1.6 billion in 2000 to $7.4 billion in 2002 and then to $15.4 billion in 2004, while network-based services will grow at an even steeper rate, from $400 million in 2000 to $4.5 billion in 2002 and then to $10 billion in 2004 (see Figure 7.16) (Infonetics, 2000).

One reason for the growth in IP-VPNs is the cost advantage in comparison to leased-line or Frame Relay alternatives. This advantage becomes especially acute in a dynamic environment extending beyond a few sites, or where the customer wishes service beyond the geography served by a single provider. In addition, whereas past models relied on all Internet connectivity via a central site, many

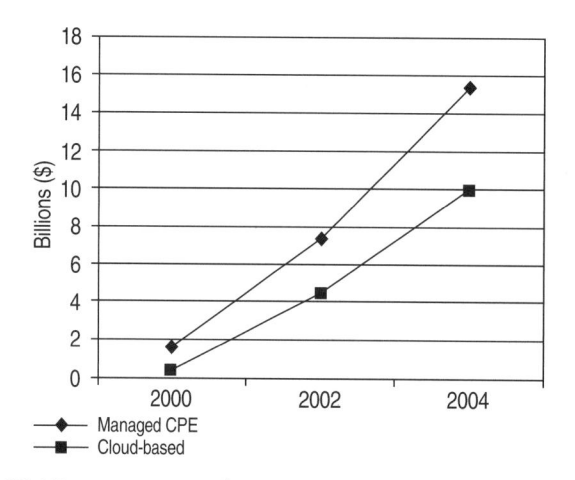

FIGURE 7.16 VPN Penetration and Revenue   *Source:* Infonetics

Firewalls and IP-VPNs 247

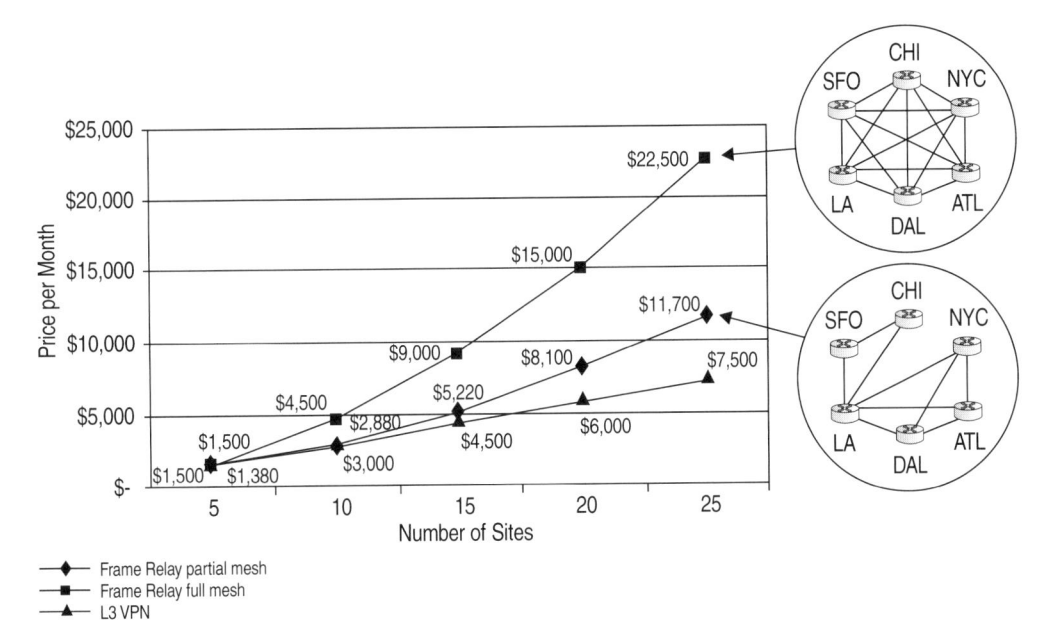

FIGURE 7.17 Example Frame Relay versus Layer 3 VPN Deployment *Source:* Nortel Networks

branches now require direct Internet connectivity. Figure 7.17 contrasts a Frame Relay with an IP-VPN deployment based on the number of sites and monthly pricing. Monthly Frame Relay pricing is mostly a factor of the number of Frame Relay PVCs required for full- or partial-mesh connectivity, as listed in Table 7.4. Other assumptions include $180 per port for basic Frame Relay connectivity and $60 per PVC (DLCI). IP-VPN pricing is $300 per port and includes provisioning of the in-cloud component and its associated SLAs.

TABLE 7.4 Frame Relay versus IP-VPN Connections

	Total Number of Connections (Frame Relay PVCs or IP-VPN Access Links)		
Sites	Partial Mesh	Full Mesh	IP-VPN
5	8	10	5
10	18	45	10
15	42	105	15
20	76	190	20
25	120	300	25

IP-VPN services therefore offer the greatest potential for revenue among the different service offerings from the perspective of provider deployment and subscriber acceptance. Analysts predict that the vast majority of service providers will offer a combination of in-cloud and CLE-based IP-VPN services during the coming years, offering their customers a choice of options.

Content Services Deployment

On par with IP-VPN services, in terms of potential revenue opportunity to the provider, is content distribution and management. Although a great deal of progress has been made in bringing to market the necessary infrastructure devices and protocols to enable these services, the real challenge is in deploying them in a way that will result in profitability to both the network provider and the content provider, and that will result in real value to the subscriber. Creating profitable financial relationships between these different entities is a major goal, and the IPSS plays a major role in bringing the access provider or ISP back into the content revenue flow. This section looks at content networking business requirements, the topologies and equipment required to meet these requirements, and the resultant market opportunity.

Business Relationships

One problem with the status quo is that many of the content management solutions deployed to date do not really address the need to create closer financial ties between subscribers and content providers. For example, an access provider may deploy caching, but it is usually with the goal of minimizing upstream bandwidth. Any reduction in subscriber latency to remote content is just a welcome by-product. Existing content distribution systems also do nothing to create closer ties with the subscriber, though they do provide the content provider with a better assurance that the content actually makes it to the network edge.

Consider a typical DSL subscriber, with a 384 Kbps connection across the access provider. Based on current revenue models, the subscriber's local ISP has no incentive to maintain this QoS across its backbone and into the transit provider and must therefore massively oversubscribe its service offering. The subscriber blames the access provider for poor service, and the access provider blames the content provider. It doesn't matter if this transit provider has terabits of bandwidth at its disposal, since the subscriber experiences suboptimal service. This is the reason many subscribers complain that access to distant content via their DSL connection is not better than that available via dial. The worldwide wait is not solely attributed to the last mile but to various bottlenecks throughout the network. There are also possible bottlenecks between the actual content providers and their backbone providers, though this has been mostly addressed by the hosting architectures described in chapter 4.

What really needs to happen is financial linkage between all parties in the broadband content distribution chain. This may happen in a number of ways. In one model, the subscriber communicates its desires directly to the content provider—that is, the entity that has either created the content or has distribution rights for the content. In the latter case, the distributor, who will probably have partnerships with a large number of content originators, is responsible for the transfer payments. The content provider then distributes the material via any ISPs and access providers, paying for this transit as required. In this case, the access provider or ISP plays no active role in acting as a portal to the content and is therefore potentially marginalized. Any rights management issues are also handled directly between the subscriber and the content provider.

A more evolved business model brings the network providers back into the loop. In this scenario, the access provider or ISP acts as a portal, or broker to the content, having established partnerships with multiple content providers. Subscribers request content via the portal and are billed by the network provider. This precludes the subscriber from having to deal directly with multiple content providers. The provider in turn pays the content provider, is responsible for ensuring the quality and security of the content across its infrastructure, and takes a cut of the action. These models apply whether the content provider is a traditional media company, an ASP, a gaming network, or a wide-area storage provider.

The portal is enabled via the IPSS. Subscribers arrive at the IPSS via any one of a number of access technologies, are authenticated if required, and are then presented with a generic or customized portal listing the available services and content providers. They select the content via this portal. Given a proper level of sophistication in the provisioning system, the subscriber's access characteristics, such as bandwidth, may be dynamically altered via this portal.

In a survey conducted by the Strategis Group (Stratagis, 1998), the availability of new content directly influenced the amount subscribers were willing to pay on a monthly basis. As an example, at $60 per month, a total of 700,000 subscribers would be "definitely interested" in a basic service and 3.3 million would be "interested" (see Figure 7.18). This is a marked decrease from the 6.2 million subscribers definitely interested in a service at $25 per month, showing the resistance to higher rates even for higher-speed connectivity.

According to the survey, the availability of enhanced content would shift most of these "interested" subscribers. From the perspective of the service provider, if the provider could offer the basic service at $19.95 per month, an additional $10 of revenue is possible via value-added applications and content, an additional $2 from advertising subsidization, and an additional $5 from service tier upgrades. This almost doubles the potential per-subscriber revenue.

One often-raised concern in any content architecture is privacy—how much the network and content providers learn about the buying habits of the subscriber. Note that this is not a new problem; the corner video store gathers much

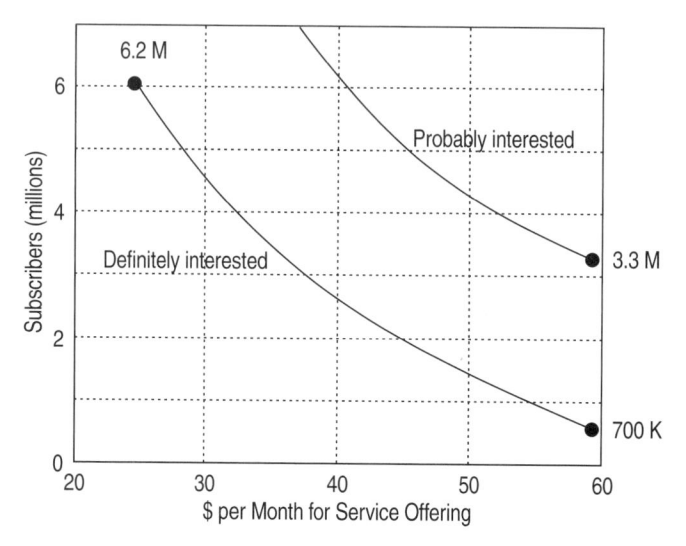

FIGURE 7.18 Service Penetration and Up-Sell   *Source:* Strategis Group

of the same information. In addition, the current cookie-based Web architecture (detailed in chapter 4) leaves little to the imagination of the Web site operator, as any and all types of information are often embedded in the cookie. Based on experiences thus far, the average online individual is willing to make the trade-off between privacy and convenience, and the Internet is just the latest means of information gathering.

Topologies for Content-Enabled Networks

Given the need to recognize revenue from content management, what network topologies will the provider deploy to enable this goal? An end-to-end topology (see Figure 7.19) of a content-enabled network includes the access link, the IPSS, content routing, content switches, and caches.

Figure 7.20 offers a closer look at the content delivery network itself and consists of the following components working in coordination:

- The *content cache* is responsible for caching and serving static objects and on-demand streaming media. It also includes a pipelined cache, splits live media, and ensures content freshness.
- The *overlay network* helps with streaming content pre-provisioning and prioritization of content delivery.
- The *personalization platform* is responsible for content injection (e.g., ads), content steering (e.g., personal home pages and walled gardens), and content filtering and customization.

Content Services Deployment

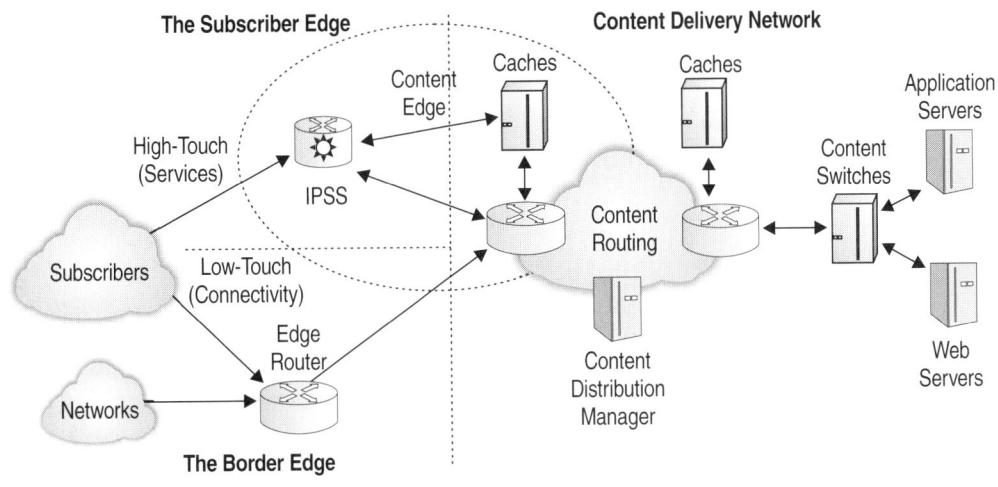

FIGURE 7.19 End-to-End Content Network

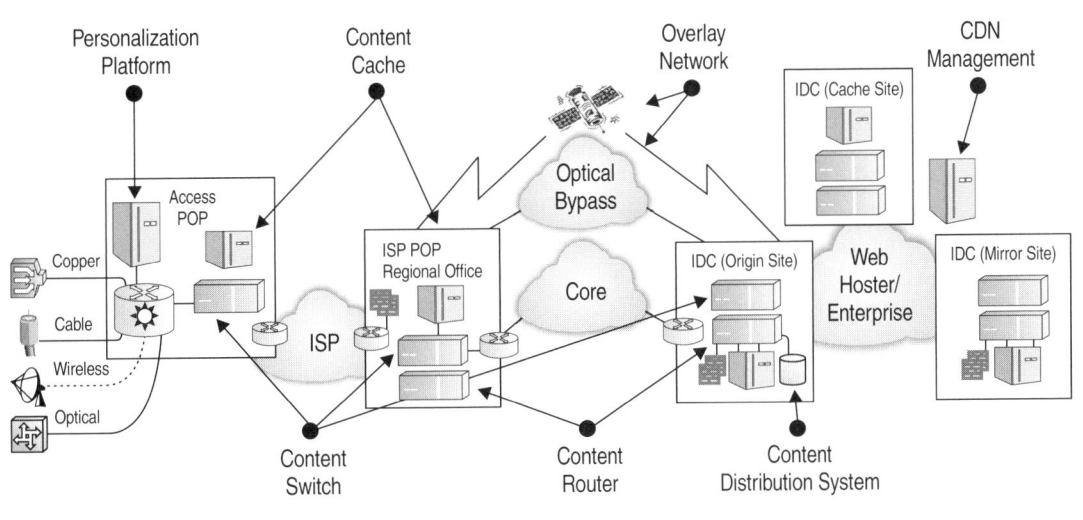

FIGURE 7.20 A Closer Look at the CDN

- The *content switch* is responsible for L2-7 policy redirection, cache load balancing, firewall load balancing, server load balancing, server offloads and acceleration, and server-side bandwidth management.
- The *content router* routes requests to content sites based on content availability, Internet load and reliability, server load and availability, and user proximity.
- The *content distribution system* helps with content pre-positioning and updates, as well as logging and accounting of the content.

* *CDN management* is responsible for the provisioning, monitoring, and troubleshooting of the end-to-end network.

In any content network, end-to-end QoS is a major concern. Various techniques, as described in chapter 6, are applicable at different points in the network (see Figure 7.21):

A link between the subscriber's PC (or other Internet-capable platform, such as a settop box) and a point in the network providing access-link termination. For DSL, this is normally the DSLAM in the central office. For cable, this is the headend. For wireless, it is the base station. QoS across this path will rely on technology-specific or IP layer techniques. For example, in the case of DSL, ATM traffic management will come into play.

A link between this termination device and the PoP. This PoP contains the IPSS along with any content-switching and caching systems. In most cases, traffic will pass over an ATM, Frame Relay, or router-based aggregation network between the central office or headend and the PoP. QoS across this path will rely on ATM, Frame Relay, or IP layer techniques.

A link between the content switch and the optical backbone. Here, content flows have been identified, and QoS is managed at layers 4 through 7 (in addition to the link and IP layers). Identification of flows at this point in the net-

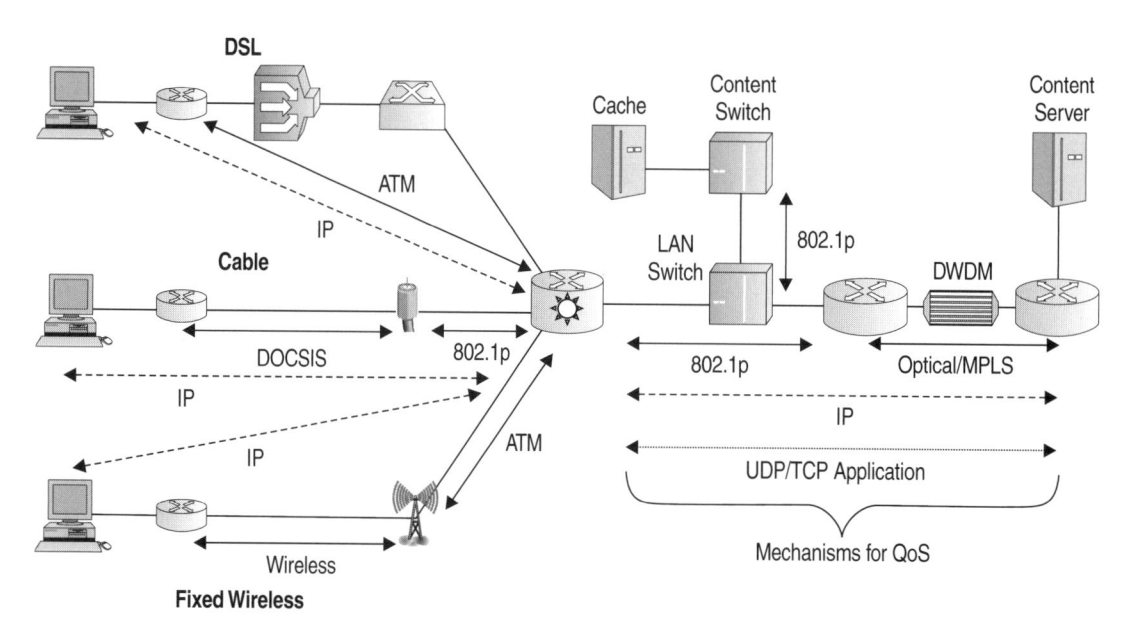

FIGURE 7.21 End-to-End Content Delivery QoS Requirements

work may be based on the IP source address, the destination address, the TCP or UDP port, the URL, a file type, a cookie, or even the Layer 7 application.

The link across the optical backbone that relies on optical QoS (such as that offered by evolving multiprotocol-over-lambda switching techniques). One promising technique is the deployment of a router-based overlay network for different content providers, permitting them to maintain better control over their content between their servers and the network edge. This overlay could be operated by the content provider or, alternatively, operated by a facilities-based carrier on the content provider's behalf using a new class of internetworking platform permitting router wholesaling.

A set of financial agreements, accounting mechanisms, and funds transfer mechanisms that make the whole thing commercially viable (as described earlier).

The Result

The net result of an end-to-end content architecture is to make available a set of potentially profitable services to both the network operator and the content provider. These services include content positioning, customization of content and delivery, and the ability to offer premium content and charge accordingly. For content positioning, providers may offer an enterprise customer of an ISP the ability to pre-fetch content during off-peak hours. Alternatively, the provider may pre-position content at strategic locations within the network in anticipation of high use. This is a lead-in to Web site overflow protection, capable of detecting which content needs replication on demand.

Content customization includes filtering, mediation, and customized content insertion. For example, a provider may offer a filtering service to an enterprise, to protect it from liability caused by inappropriate employee conduct (e.g., downloads of explicit material) or to increase productivity. This concept was introduced in the section on security in chapter 3, but is reinforced here because of its role within the content architecture. Schools benefit by shielding students from undesirable content, and in some areas, government regulations require this capability. Note that this filtering has an added advantage of freeing bandwidth, in that inappropriate or unproductive content never makes it across the local loop. One well-known filtering program is Symantec's I-Gear, which offers periodic updates and includes customizable databases.

Content mediation, or adaptation, permits the provider to compress content as appropriate for different access technologies (see Figure 7.22). This requires the deployment of special servers capable of identifying the access technology of the subscriber, its QoS capabilities, and what part of the content is critical and what is not. As an example, a subscriber may have subscribed to a set of news services through a content selection portal. At home, over a DSL or cable connection, this content may be displayed at a certain QoS. However, when wireless technology is

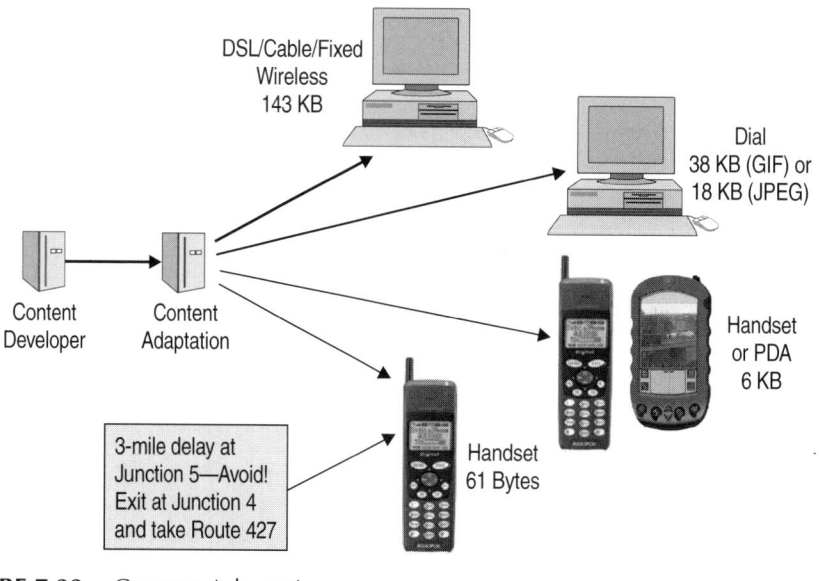

FIGURE 7.22 Content Adaptation

used (in an auto or on foot), the bandwidth of the content must be adjusted accordingly.

Another service is content insertion. For example, advertisements may be inserted on a regional basis into centrally generated content. This is no different than the architecture in place for traditional broadcast media.

An evolved content network permits the deployment of premium services, which allow targeting of a subset of the subscriber base for a higher-quality Internet experience. The protocols and architectures described earlier help enable this. Via the services and financial relationships already described, the provider may now selectively target subsets of its total subscriber base with premium, monetizable content.

Ultimately, an evolved content architecture results in the following:

- Higher QoS, by bypassing congestion and reducing latency through use of QoS-enabled backbones and caching
- Improved traffic management, by providing statistics on content and subscribers
- Tailored content, by allowing customization and binding to subscribers
- Improved network scalability and bandwidth savings
- New content services, resulting in increased revenue opportunities for wholesalers, ISPs, and content providers

Service providers benefiting from a "content-enabled" infrastructure include the following:

- Content delivery service providers (CDSPs), such as Akamai (described in chapter 4)
- Application service providers, such as Qwest and XO
- Hosted service providers (HSPs), such as Digex and Exodus
- Access service providers, including Covad (a CLEC) and Verizon (an ILEC)

The Content Distribution Market Opportunity

The content networking market segment is still in its early growth phase (especially as it relates to the Internet), but is expected to be an area of major growth in the coming years as higher-speed connectivity becomes available. The combined service revenue from Web hosting will grow from $4.3 billion in 2001 to over $19.7 billion in 2004 (Forrester, 2000). Content delivery and distribution revenues alone will grow from under $1 billion in 2001 to $6 billion in 2004. This market consists of streaming media (audio and video), HTTP graphics and text, and more advanced services such as the delivery of secure digital content, conferencing traffic, and software. (This revenue from Web hosting should not be confused with the service revenues to conferencing or software providers, which are much greater.) The top revenue generators within this segment include portals, business-to-business (B2B) transactions, business-to-consumer (B2C) transactions, and news and sports (IRG, 2000).

Although the ISPs and broadband access providers derive minimal direct revenue from content carriage at present, this is expected to change as they establish more effective peering relationships with the content providers. We may envision payment mechanisms where the service provider pays the content provider and then charges the subscriber, or other schemes where the subscriber has a direct relationship with the content providers. Existing broadband portals (e.g., MSN) are examples of another option, where content providers pay the service provider for presence on the portal home page. Here, subscribers do not pay for the individual content—they pay the service provider.

For higher bandwidth service, such as that needed for movies-on-demand, the service provider will still act as a portal from the content provider, but the service provider will charge the subscriber for the specific content. By movies-on-demand, we don't mean the digitization of existing movies that you can get from the video store. Instead, we mean the capability to request and view the last 10 episodes of "Friends" or "The Sopranos" or the baseball game you may have missed or forgot to tape. The service provider will receive a portion of this charge. Note that the reverse scheme could apply, with the subscriber being billed by the service provider and the service provider then paying the content provider. It is still too early to estimate revenue opportunities for this service, but if only a few percentage points of the total video rental market and existing broadcast market shift to broadband access over the coming years, it could be immense.

Separate from direct service revenues, but by no means insignificant, are indirect revenues derived from advertising. Although the viability of "click-through" and banner advertising by the dotcoms has come into serious question, this is still a market expected to grow to over $11 billion by 2003 (Jupiter, 1999b) given proper targeting. It will remain a major source of profitability for the retail ISPs and portal sites as more of the "click-and-mortar" operations accept online advertising. In 2000, the going price for a typical banner ad targeting an unspecified audience was $33 per thousand impressions (also known as $33 CPM). Providers would receive 55¢ for every click-through and $3.45 for every click-through resulting in a registration. When partnering with commerce sites, the provider usually received a 9 percent commission on sales. Using one of the larger ISPs, Netzero, as an example, its rate was $20 CPM for untargeted ads and $40 CPM for those targeted at a certain segment of the subscriber base. Where the ad was targeted at a specific URL typed by the subscriber, the rate went up to $65. Average click-through rates were 1 to 2 percent (Merrill Lynch, 1999). In the future, advertisers are expected to be able to further refine their target audiences. One method will be to embed more messaging in streaming content where there is more of a captive audience.

It may also be useful to look at network services growth from the perspective of e-commerce. Any network infrastructure buildout must offer the necessary QoS, security, and content management for this class of services. This market currently enjoys a 60 percent annual growth rate, which will result in B2C transactions approaching $358 billion and B2B transactions approaching $2.1 trillion annually by 2005 (from a combined market of $250 billion in 2000) (Ovum, 2000c). The segment therefore offers a massive opportunity to service providers and to equipment vendors supplying the hardware, provisioning, and services infrastructure.

Finally, another way to look at the opportunity is in terms of the complete broadband value chain—the underlying technology, clients, infrastructure, and content and applications. Cahners IN-Stat predicts this market to be worth over $450 billion by 2004, growing from $90 billion in 2000. The $450 billion consists of $329 billion in services and content, $61 billion in infrastructure spending, $49 billion for clients and associated equipment, and $24 billion for basic technology, such as chipsets (Cahners, 2000). This content revenue component will be a major driver for network buildout over the coming years. This opportunity is immense for the content originators, as well as for the access providers, ISPs, and content networkers peering with these entities.

Voice Services Deployment

Some of the most sophisticated services yet deployed at the network edge are those combining voice (in one of its many forms) with the data traffic. It is quickly becoming clear to the ILECs and especially to the remaining data CLECs that a combined voice and data bundle is required for profitability. Depending on the type of service provider, the architecture and protocols used may differ, but the ultimate goal is the same—to have the subscriber use the provider for both data and voice services.

In the case of the ILEC, the gateway is placed within the local CO or at an aggregation point within the metropolitan area. CLECs will select the latter option, since they will usually have a single point of entry into the PSTN within a given metropolitan area. Some CLECs, with origins in the voice world, may already have a wide-area voice infrastructure in place. In this case, they may choose to forward the voice traffic across their backbone, sending it to the ILEC serving the recipient. An ISP offering voice services may situate the gateway at its local PoP or, in some cases, may find it more efficient to backhaul the VoIP traffic to the destination city. The other question is the choice of technologies—when to deploy an ATM-based solution and when an IP-centric solution might prove better. Table 7.5 lists the differences between these two approaches.

So how is the provider's voice network expected to evolve? Some vendors are now proposing an evolution of the PSTN from traditional local and transit voice switches to a new architecture based on call servers, media gateways, voice servers, and an ATM or packet backbone. A typical deployment may consist of the following components (see also Figure 7.23):

- *Backbone and user access gateways,* offering POTS, DSL, ISDN, DS1/E1, DS3/E3, and OC3/STM1. One role of this gateway is to interface existing circuit-switched trunking with an ATM or packet backbone.
- *Call servers,* providing standard and value-added telephony features. A call server closely interfaces with an audio server providing the necessary voice announcements, conferencing, and speech recognition functions.
- *Signaling network interfaces,* providing internetworking (connection) to the SS7 environment for intelligent networking services. These include toll-free and number-portability services.

TABLE 7.5 VoATM and VoIP Comparison

Voice over ATM (VoATM)	Voice over IP (VoIP)
POTS quality and services	Some POTS features (more in future)
Existing CPE in most cases	New CPE in most cases
Multiple phone lines	Voice and data integration
Fax and modem support	Internet focus
Small business focus	VPNs

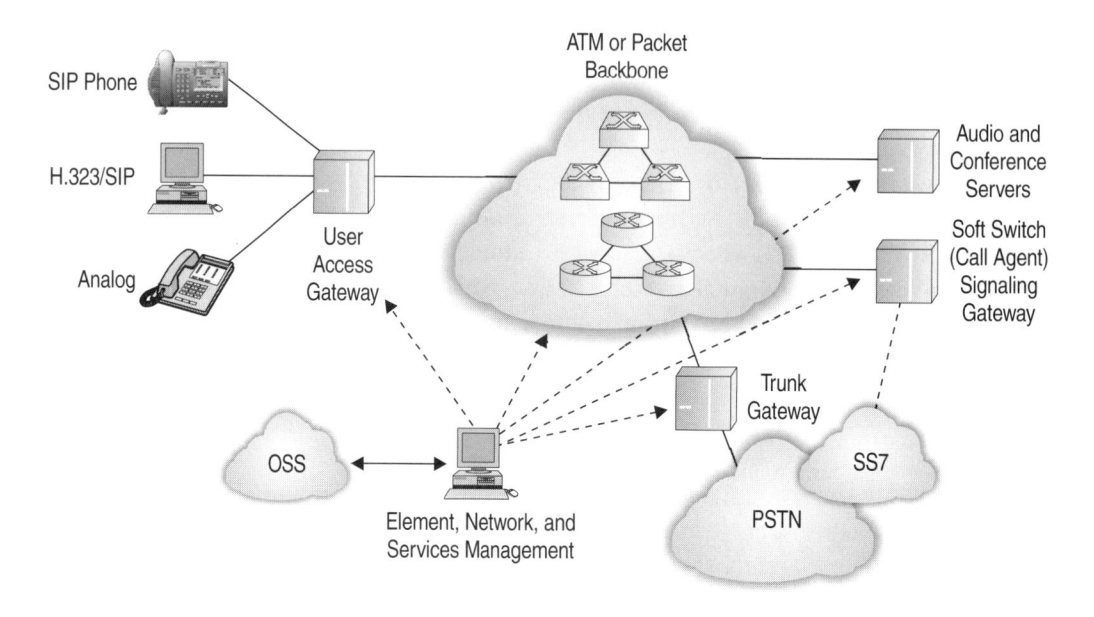

FIGURE 7.23 Voice Network Evolution

- *Core switching,* providing the QoS-enabled backbone for the voice services.
- *Element, network, and services management,* tying these various components together and into the provider's existing OSS.

The goal of this next-generation voice architecture is to provide subscribers with the same set of services currently available via the existing PSTN. The service provider benefits through greatly reduced operational and upgrade costs, as well as by being able to standardize on a single multiservice backbone for both voice and data (ATM, Frame, leased line, and some IP) services.

Service Bundling

Service bundling is the art of combining the various security, traffic management, content, and IP-VPN services described in the previous sections of this chapter into an offering tailored to the subscriber. For example, a residential DSL subscriber may request a combination of a security service and a certain application QoS from the network provider, while a small business may have more complex IP-VPN requirements in addition to basic security and traffic management. The marketing and sales organization within the service provider will combine these service bundles into offerings, with monthly fees based on the included services, whether the competition has a comparable offering, whether the subscriber is willing to commit to the bundle for a period of time, and possibly whether the subscriber has contracted for additional services from the provider (e.g., a DSL subscriber signing up for an ILEC's long-distance service). Given a sophisticated service-provisioning system, the provider may create these bundles easily and apply them to a given subscriber upon service activation. Even more sophisticated is an environment where the subscriber self-provisions the bundle and can change the level of service on demand.

Residential

In the residential space, where cost sensitivities are paramount, the provider has little leeway in charging a premium for added functionality. For example, DSL providers may offer a selection of downstream and upstream bandwidths, each at a different price point, but will find that most subscribers will sign up for the most basic service. When the subscriber is paying $39.95 a month for a combination of the DSL access and the ISP, any additional services must be at a little or no additional cost. Examples may include content filtering at $2 per month, or a basic network-based firewalling service at $2 per month or even offered for free if the provider wishes to differentiate the service offering. Given effective marketing and a way to demonstrate the benefits, the provider could also make a case for prioritization of Internet telephony traffic and charge accordingly. The subscriber may be willing to pay up to $5 per month more if the provider could maintain end-to-end QoS for the voice call. However, in the low-end residential space, there is resistance to any service offering beyond $50 per month (though this could change as premium streaming content becomes a larger part of the service offering). One way to stay within this limit is by grouping sets of features into pricing bundles, much as voice providers do today. A residential bundle could consist of basic security policies (firewalling, antispoofing), QoS enforcement, and a portal.

Telecommuter

Sponsored telecommuters, for which the corporation pays for Internet connectivity, are more willing to partake of premium services. Here, the subscriber may sign up for additional bandwidth, more sophisticated security policies, and possibly an IP-VPN service. The best example of this is where the subscriber's job depends on the network connection. The corporation may be willing to pay for a service offering, such as guaranteed QoS, if it improves productivity. In the case of a distributed call center application, this may make or break the service. The subscriber may also map into an IP-VPN for corporate intranet access. This IP-VPN service may be a major revenue generator for the provider. Figure 7.24 depicts this combination of traffic management and security services.

Small Business

A small business will have more sophisticated requirements in security, QoS, and IP-VPN services than telecommuters. For example, it may operate servers on the

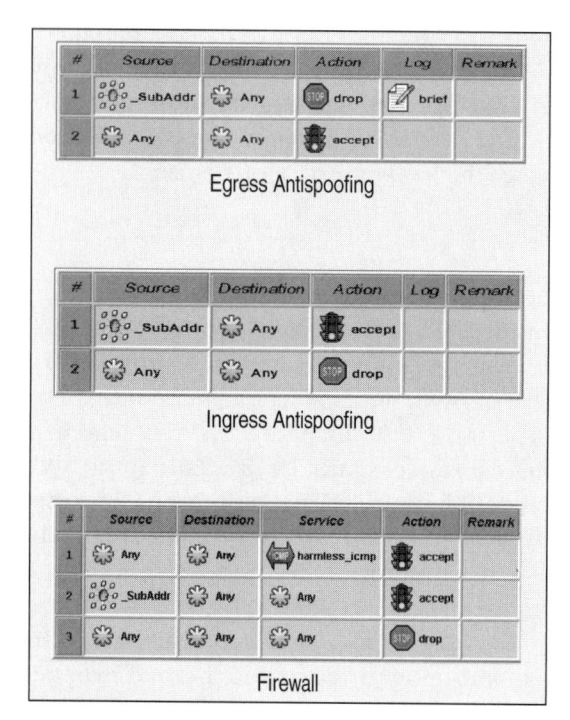

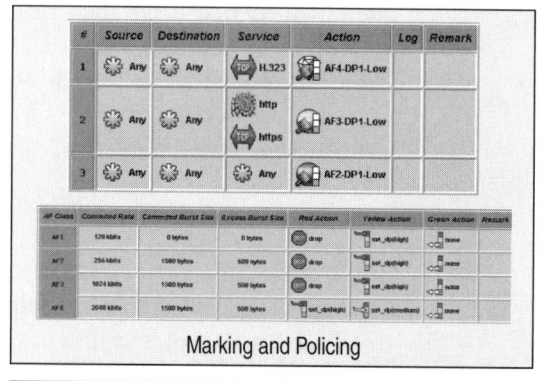

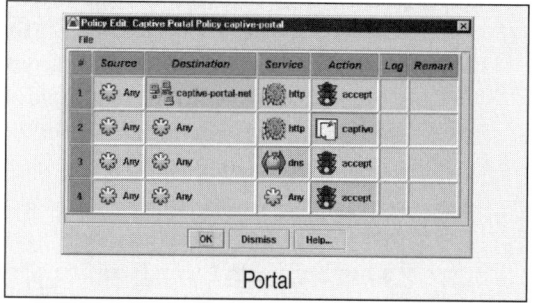

FIGURE 7.24 Telecommuter Bundle

premises. Any firewall policy must therefore support access to these servers from the Internet. Where the SME operates from more than one location, its branches will connect across the backbone, and the network must provide adequate QoS and security for any mission-critical applications. In many cases, the customer will demand an SLA for this service and may also require the capability to change service parameters on the fly. Figure 7.25 depicts a typical SME service bundle. Note that it may also apply to branch offices of a larger enterprise.

Multiservice Bundling

Although the previous discussions focus on bundling of IP services, bundling also occurs at a higher level. For example, a service provider will seek to offer a residential subscriber, telecommuter, or small business a bundle of voice (including wireless), data, and, in some cases, video services. As discussed in chapter 6, this service bundling helps to minimize subscriber churn and generates a balanced revenue flow for the service provider.

Conclusion

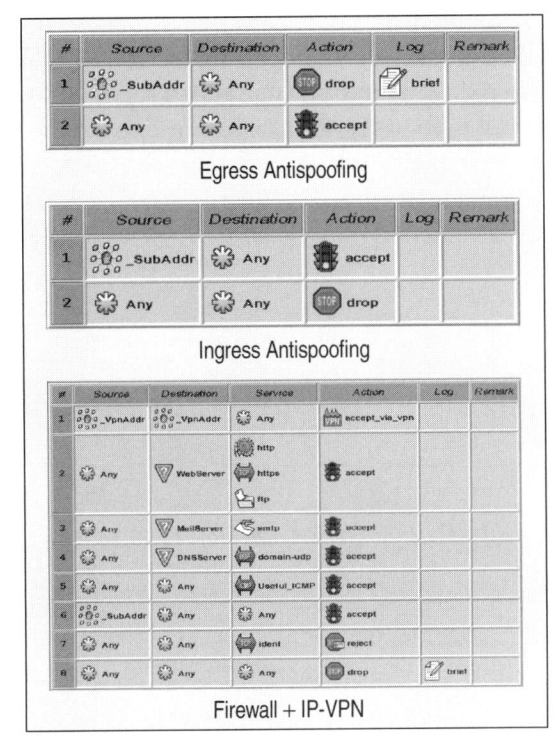

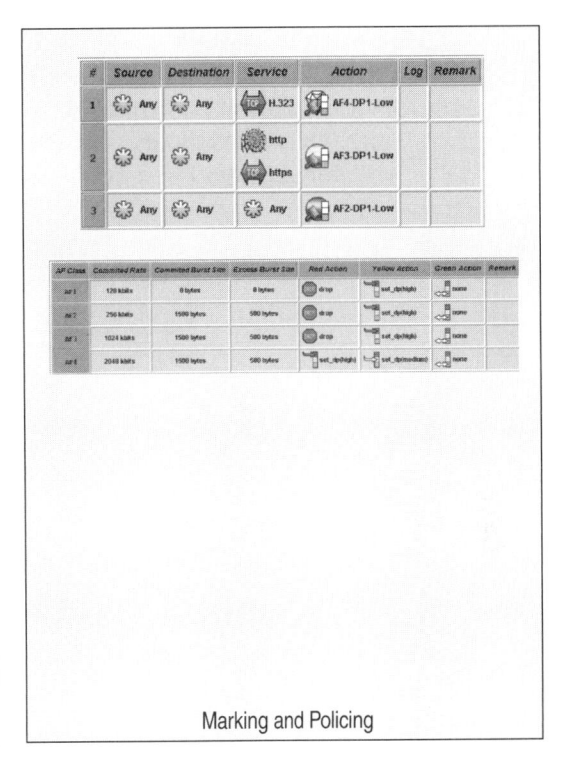

FIGURE 7.25 SME Bundle

Conclusion

This chapter details higher-layer security and media services, building on the basic services described in chapter 6, as well as the technologies and platforms introduced in the earlier chapters. By this time, you should have a good understanding of the capabilities of an IPSS, as well as its deployment possibilities. The concluding chapter of this book, chapter 8, looks at a number of actual IPSS deployments in the DSL, cable, wireless, and content management spaces.

It is probably fitting to close with a statistic on the sheer magnitude of the services opportunity. Analysts predict total network services spending will grow from $1 trillion in 2000 (yes, trillion) to over $3 trillion a decade later. Part of this is due to business and consumer spending habits. In the consumer space, percentage of income spent on telecommunications services is three to four times that of a decade ago and is expected to double once again by the middle of the decade because of the proliferation of additional communications services (e.g., wireless Internet). During this interval, residential revenues will grow to 15 percent of the total, while SMEs will generate 50 percent. This SME market is critical, in that many of the higher-margin, network-based services deployed via the IPSS are initially targeted at this segment—it is the path of entry for value-added services. The other element is the explosive growth of mobile services, expected to be responsible for almost 50 percent of the total revenue by mid-decade (Nortel, 2000).

Chapter 8
Deployment Examples

Building on the descriptions of the technologies, topologies, and services throughout this book, this chapter details real-life examples for the following deployments:

- Residential PPPoE DSL service
- DSL wholesaling and portals
- Cable open access
- Fixed wireless wholesaling
- 3G mobile wireless services
- IP-VPNs and firewalls
- Broadcast video distribution
- Internet data center

For each of these examples, this chapter describes the business model of the service provider and what it is trying to accomplish, the service offering (including equipment, topologies, and service costs), and how the service adds to the competitiveness of the provider. In essence, this is a guide to high-value service deployments, which use the technologies and hardware described in chapters 2 through 5, and the services described in chapters 6 and 7. This chapter comes full circle back to chapter 1, which describes the financial models behind some of these services.

Residential PPPoE DSL Service

PPPoE, introduced in chapter 6, is the most widely deployed encapsulation for subscriber access to DSL, a broadband access technology introduced in chapter 2. This example details the deployment of PPPoE within an ISP.

Background

When DSL was first introduced, provisioning and scaling of the access infrastructure to support end-to-end service were recognized problems. Early deployments of DSL were usually provisioned with ATM virtual circuits (VCs) that extended from the subscriber modem, all the way across the access provider's network, and into an ISP PoP. The rapid rise in popularity of residential DSL services placed a severe strain on existing networks, which were not designed for very large-scale deployments of DSL transported over ATM. Fortunately, a solution to the scaling problem in the access network emerged in the form of the Layer 2 Tunneling Protocol (L2TP), which allowed for massive aggregation of ATM virtual circuits in the access network and a tunnel handoff of PPP sessions to upstream ISPs.

L2TP addressed scaling problems in the access network, but other problems remained. Speeding up deployments would require simplifying the residential provisioning process. It also became clear that many consumers had a desire to connect more than one PC in their homes to the broadband network. Protocols and encapsulations available at the time required either the use of a router, which greatly complicated provisioning, or the use of bridging across the access network, which caused undesirable security and scaling problems. The only alternative for authenticated access was PPP over ATM (PPPoA), which required complicated configuration at the consumer end and restricted network access to a single PC unless the provider provisioned multiple PVCs for the subscriber and installed an ADSL modem functioning as an ATM switch. A more fundamental disadvantage with PPPoA was that it required installation of a new interface card within the PC, either an ATM card connecting to an external DSL modem or an integrated DSL modem card. For the service provider, this was a real problem, since it would result in a service call every time there was a problem with the subscriber's PC. Given the cost of service calls, this quickly eliminated any profit on the service.

Again, the industry responded with a solution, a new protocol called PPP over Ethernet (PPPoE). PPPoE has all the inherent benefits of PPP—dynamic authentication, dynamic addressing (which enables dynamic service selection), personalized network configuration, and embedded accounting mechanisms, all driven from a centralized subscriber database. It greatly simplifies the provisioning process because it works over Ethernet and thus eliminates ATM VC configuration and the requirement for an expensive ATM network interface card (NIC). PPPoE also includes an important extension to PPP that enables a service provider to forward its subscribers to a customized Web page for service advertisement after they are authenticated on the network. Finally, since almost all PCs are now equipped with Ethernet, PPPoE avoids the requirement to introduce a new interface card, minimizing the possible support costs described in the previous paragraph.

Services Description

A very large ISP, Marslink, was predisposed to a PPP-based solution for residential broadband deployments since it had a substantial investment in infrastructure to support existing dial subscribers and the technical staff was familiar with PPP and RADIUS. The ISP considereed PPPoA, but it wanted to make certain that it could easily accommodate residences with multiple PCs. In fact, Marslink saw an opportunity to offer additional broadband access accounts to such homes for a modest incremental fee. For this reason Marslink was attracted to PPPoE. After learning more about the protocol, the company realized it could use the service advertisement function to implement highly automated Web-based registration for subscriber services. Another of Marslink's goals was to permit subscribers to connect to the network in a transmission-neutral manner, abstracting the customer from the transmission network. The provider would also be freed from having to individually provision subscribers, permitting the activation of thousands as opposed to dozens of subscribers in a given time period. This is much like the existing dial model, which relies on central RADIUS servers.

Marslink relies on the local ILECs for the DSL access service (see Figure 8.1). For the initial deployment, these included SBC and Verizon. The residential subscribers connect to the ADSL service via modems supplied by these providers (so

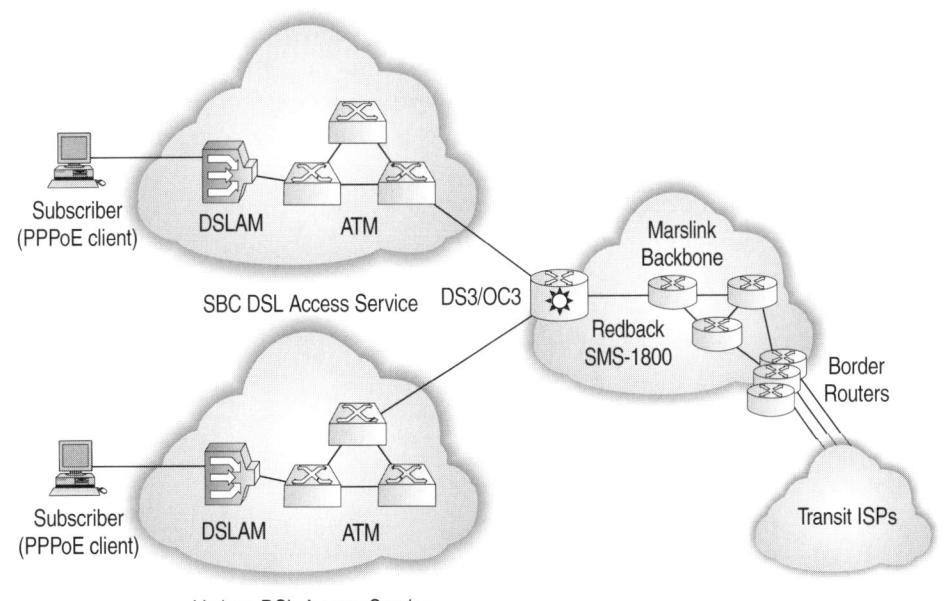

FIGURE 8.1 Marslink PPPoE DSL Access Architecture

as to be compatible with their DSLAMs). ATM trunks connect these DSL access services with Redback subscriber management systems (SMSs) located within Marslink's PoPs. These SMSs then connect to the existing routers within Marslink's backbone. For connectivity to other ISPs, and thus the Internet as a whole, subscriber traffic passes through Marslink's border routers and onto a transit provider such as Worldcom/UUNet or AT&T.

Marslink came up with a solution that included the following:

- PPPoE client software
- A Web portal that serves subscriber registration pages
- An SMS that is highly optimized for PPP-based service provisioning
- A billing system that includes an embedded RADIUS server

Figure 8.2 depicts the end-to-end encapsulations used between the subscriber and the ISP's backbone.

The system was designed to allow subscribers to initialize services on Marslink's network with a guest login consisting of a published *username@domain* and password. The guest login allows access only to a privately addressed network that hosts a registration server with no connectivity to the Internet or any other network.

After the subscriber is authenticated on the guest network, Marslink uses the service advertisement feature of PPPoE to forward a URL to the PPPoE client software. The client launches the default browser on the client desktop and points the browser at the URL. The subscriber gets a Web page containing a registration form. After filling out the form (which includes name, address, credit card, and so forth) and selecting a new username and password, the subscriber logs out. The registration server uses the subscriber information to create a billing record. The username and password selected by the subscriber are also checked against the

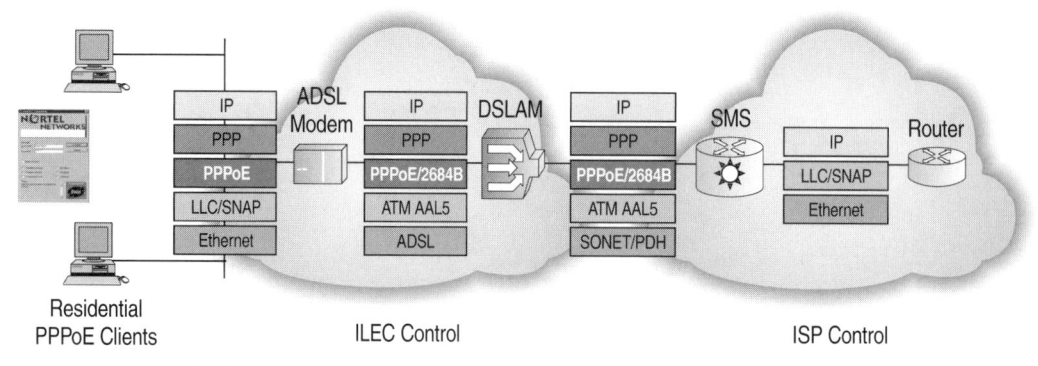

FIGURE 8.2 Marslink PPPoE Encapsulations

Residential PPPoE DSL Service

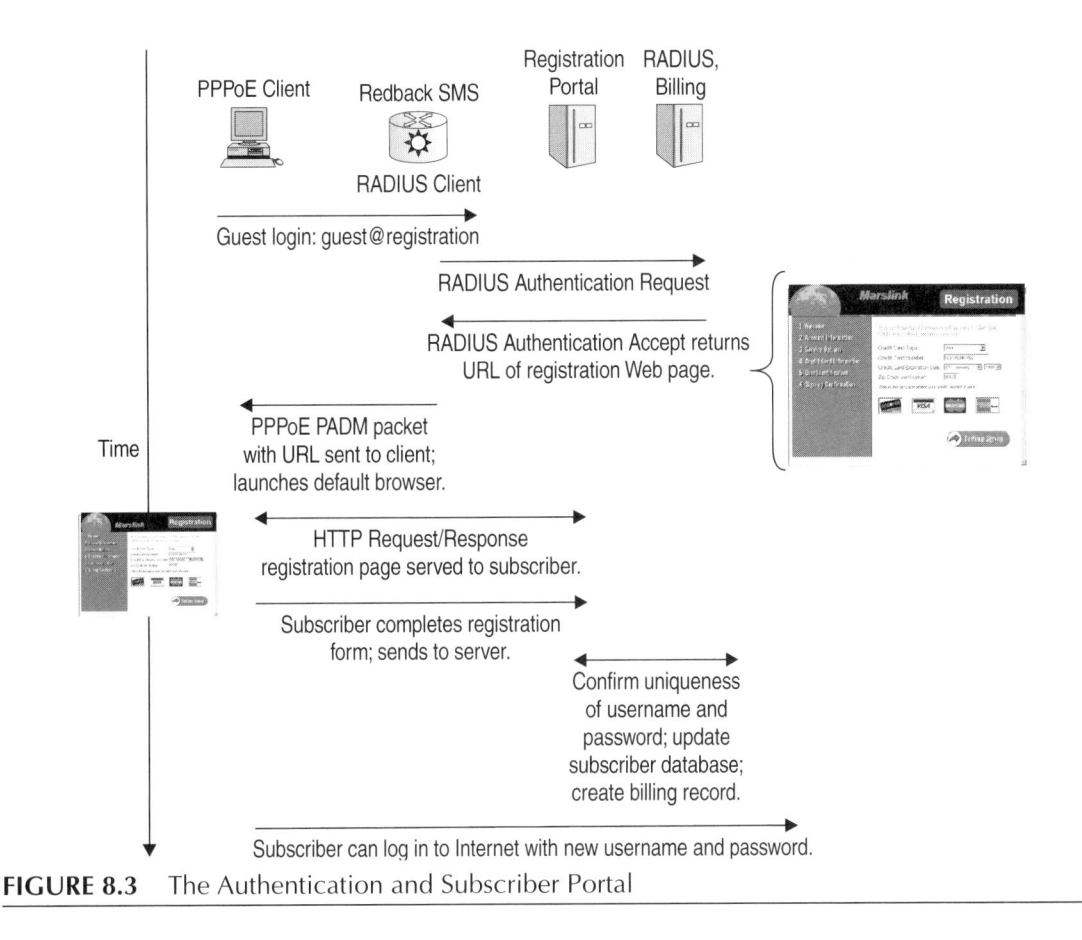

FIGURE 8.3 The Authentication and Subscriber Portal

subscriber database to ensure uniqueness. The subscriber can now log in to the ISPs Internet backbone. The process is diagrammed in Figure 8.3.

The same system was adapted to support broader service advertisement and service selection capabilities. The ISP has placed a service portal in its network that it uses to host customized welcome pages for subscribers. After a subscriber is authenticated at login, he or she is presented with a branded page, as shown in Figure 8.4. The page is customized for each subscriber and displays services that subscribers can access. It can also be used to order additional services or for service upgrades. For example, a subscriber could order a basic firewall service online and have the firewall automatically deployed. When the subscriber selects a new service or service upgrade, the service portal collects the information from the subscriber and uses it to populate the subscriber database as well as modify his or her billing record. As with the initial registration process described earlier, when the subscriber logs in to the network, he or she can immediately enjoy the new service. The entire process is diagrammed in Figure 8.4.

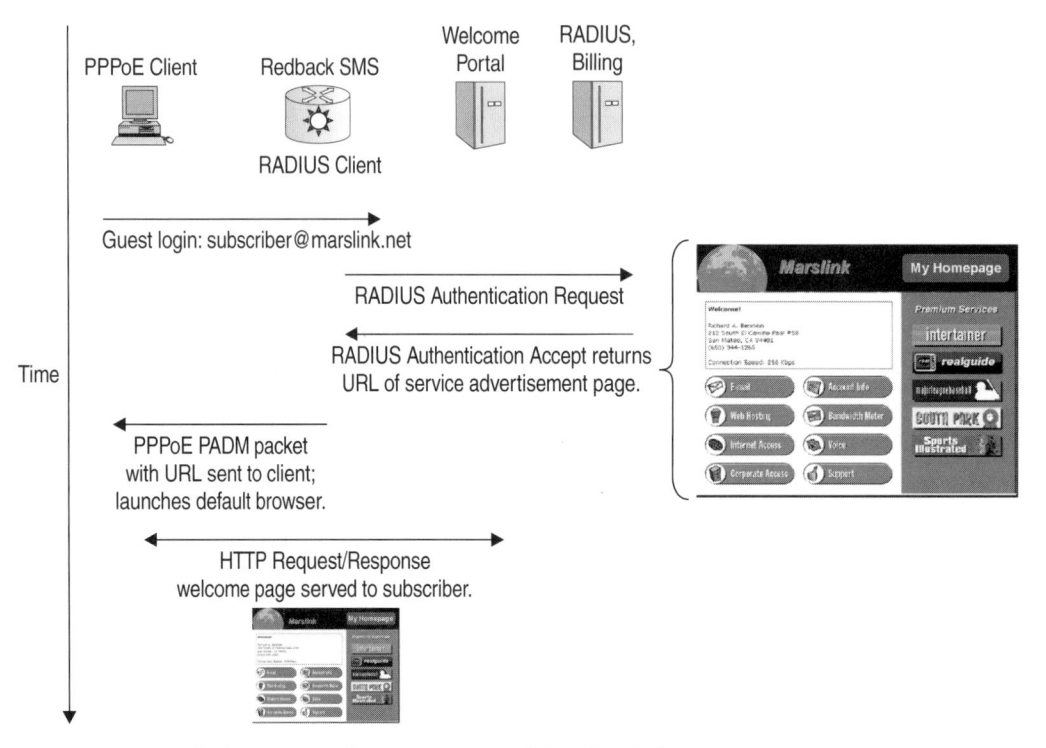

FIGURE 8.4 Branded Service Advertisement and Service Selection

Advantages

Marslink recognizes that it has a very flexible infrastructure that can easily be adapted for a variety of purposes. It has already begun to investigate how to extend the service portal model to enable access to digital content that is hosted on a high-speed network. The necessary mechanisms to secure the network are already in place, and the ISP is investigating how to deploy caching to ensure that subscribers have a quality experience as they browse bandwidth-intensive content.

The Financial Model

The financial model described in this section is based on hypothetical expenses, revenues, and profit. In this model, the assumptions and results are typical of the service in question; they do not reflect Marslink's actual financials.

Spreadsheet 8.1 lists the assumptions that underlie Marslink's DSL service offering:

- Lines 2 through 9 list the different SLAs—the service parameters, the ratio of oversubscription to trunk bandwidth, the expected subscriber penetration,

Residential PPPoE DSL Service

SPREADSHEET 8.1 DSL ISP Assumptions

1	ISP-Only		
2	SLA1 - 1.5 Mbps / 128 Kbps residential (60:1)	Percentage	40%
3	SLA2 - 1.5 Mbps / 384 Kbps telecommuter (30:1)	Percentage	25%
4	SLA3 - 768 Kbps / 768 Kbps business (10:1)	Percentage	25%
5	SLA4 - 1.5 Mbps / 1.5 Mbps business (10:1)	Percentage	10%
6	SLA1	Quarterly	$60
7	SLA2	Quarterly	$120
8	SLA3	Quarterly	$225
9	SLA3	Quarterly	$400
10	Growth Rate	Quarterly	20%
11	Aggregation Per Metro	One-time	$100,000
12	Routing Per Metro	One-time	$50,000
13	Operational	One-time	$100
14	Operational - per subscriber	% of revenue	3.5%
15	SG&A	% of revenue	2.5%
16	Bandwidth - Metro	Quarterly per Mbps	$500
17	Bandwidth - Peering	Quarterly per Mbps	$1,500
18	Installation	One-time	$50
19	**Trunk Bandwidth**		
20	SLA1	Mbps	0.025
21	SLA2	Mbps	0.05
22	SLA3	Mbps	0.0768
23	SLA4	Mbps	0.15

Note: All spreadsheets are available at www.daveginsburg.com/users/gins/ipss.htm.

and the quarterly fee. The subscriber fees listed only apply to the ISP portion—the subscriber pays an additional fee to the ILEC. Of note is the oversubscription ratio since Internet transit fees are one of the largest expenses. The ISP must set this ratio and the DSL fee to cover this expense.

- Line 10 lists the growth rate, a conservative number, at least for the first year of deployment. This growth rate applies to all SLAs.
- Line 11 lists the price for the subscriber management system in each of the metropolitan areas.
- Line 12 lists the incremental router fee in each of the metropolitan areas. This reflects the price of either a new router to support the additional DSL traffic or additional capacity on an existing core router.
- Line 13 reflects the one-time operational expense of provisioning the subscriber, while Line 14 reflects the ongoing cost of maintaining the customer. Line 15 includes the general overhead of maintaining this subscriber.

- Line 16 is the cost the ISP incurs for metropolitan bandwidth (connecting to the access provider's network), while Line 17 is the transit fee to the ISP for backbone Internet connectivity. This last fee is a major element of the ISP's expenses and is managed by the oversubscription ratios in Lines 2 through 5.
- Line 18 reflects the revenue from the initial installation fee. Note that in many instances this may be waived.
- Lines 20 through 23 detail the actual trunk bandwidth per class of customer, taking into account oversubscription. For example, customers with SLA2, a telecommuter service offering 1.5 Mbps downstream and 384 Kbps upstream, are actually allocated a trunk bandwidth of 50 Kbps on average. This is due to statistical multiplexing.

Figure 8.5 depicts the major growth assumptions of the model—metropolitan areas served, total number of central offices, and total number of subscribers. By Q6, the service is totally deployed and is available in ten metropolitan areas and 200 central offices (COs).

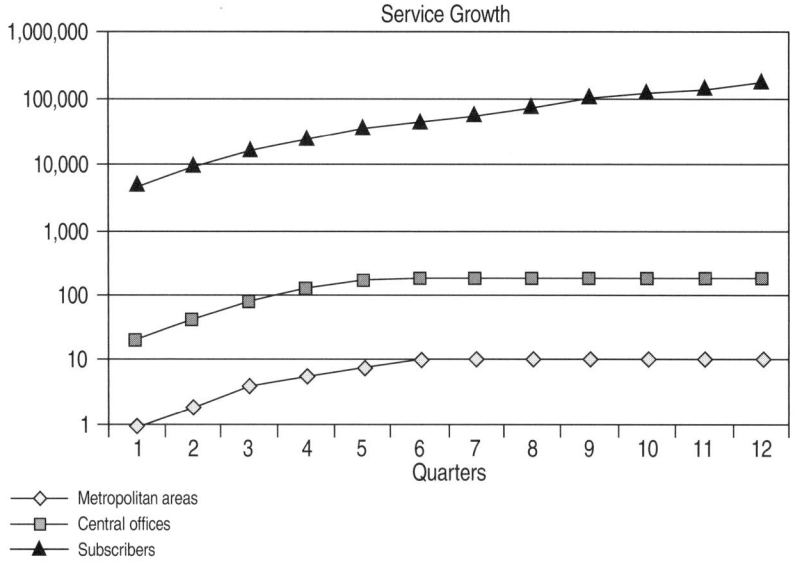

FIGURE 8.5 Service Assumptions

SPREADSHEET 8.2 DSL ISP Revenue Breakdown (Basic Service)

		Q1	Q12
1	Metros	1	10
2	COs	20	200
3	Subs per CO	250	990
4	Total Subs	5000	197,903
5	New Subs	5000	37,150
6	Subs SLA 1	2,000	79,161
7	Revenue SLA 1	$120,000	$4,749,660
8	Subs SLA 2	1,250	49,476
9	Revenue SLA 2	$150,000	$5,937,075
10	Subs SLA 3	1,250	49,476
11	Revenue SLA 3	$281,250	$11,132,016
12	Subs SLA 4	500	19,790
13	Revenue SLA 4	$200,000	$7,916,100
14	Installation	$250,000	$1,857,521
15	**Total Revenue**	**$1,001,250**	**$31,592,373**
16	**Capital Expenses**		
17	Aggregation	$100,000	
18	Routing	$50,000	
19	**Total Capital Expenses**	$150,000	
20	**Total Invested Capital**	$150,000	$1,500,000
21	**One-Time Operational Expenses**		
22	Operational	$500,000	$3,715,042
23	**Recurring Operational Expenses**		
24	Operational-Recurring	$60,075	$1,895,542
25	Bandwidth - Metro	$141,750	$5,610,536
26	Bandwidth - Peering	$425,250	$16,831,609
27	Equipment Leasing	$15,210	$152,100
28	**Total Expenses**	**$1,142,285**	**$28,204,829**
29	**Service Revenue**	$1,001,250	$31,592,373
30	**Cost of Sales**	$1,142,285	$28,204,829
31	**Cost of Sales as % of Revenue**	1.14	0.89
32	**EBIT**	($141,035)	$3,387,544
33	**EBIT as % of Revenue**	-14%	11%

EBIT = Earnings before interest and taxes

Spreadsheet 8.2 details the first and last quarters of the actual revenue in the hypothetical model. Important observations include the following:

- The revenue generated by service installation continues to play an important role in the model, and if the ISP waives this in most cases, it must recover the revenue in some other way.

- By far the greatest element of the model is bandwidth. If the ISP is in a position to procure cheap bandwidth from the DSL access provider, and if it has low-cost transit (or even peering) into an Internet transit provider, the model will be improved.
- Leasing charges are a small percentage of the overall model. Here, the lease rate is set to approximately 14 percent.
- Given these assumptions, the service is not especially profitable to the ISP. In fact, this is pretty much the case for the majority of pure DSL plays—they suffer from low margins.

The ISP then decides to offer additional IP services beyond basic connectivity (see Spreadsheet 8.3). These services include business firewalls, content brokering, as well as business and telecommuter VPNs. Spreadsheet 8.3 lists both the quarterly service fees (in addition to the basic DSL service) and the expected penetration. These services result in additional hardware requirements—the installation of an IPSS (Line 8), as well as additional ongoing expenses.

SPREADSHEET 8.3 DSL ISP Assumptions with Services

1	Additional Services		
2	Business Firewalls	Quarterly	$75.00
3	Business FW Penetration	Percentage	25%
4	Business VPN	Quarterly	$300.00
5	Business VPN Penetration	Percentage	25%
6	Telecommuter VPN	Quarterly	$30.00
7	Telecommuter VPN Penetration	Percentage	25%
8	Hardware and Provisioning	One-time	$150,000.00
9	Ongoing Operational Business Customer	Quarterly	$75.00
10	Ongoing Operational Telcommuter	Quarterly	$10.00
11	Content	Quarterly	$30.00
12	Content Penetration	Percentage	25%

The interesting part about these new service offerings is their impact on the gross margin, as depicted on Line 17 of Spreadsheet 8.4. The gross margin increases from 11 percent to 24 percent, making this service viable.

Finally, Figure 8.6 contrasts the revenue possibilities of basic service depicted in Spreadsheet 8.2 with those of the premium service described in Spreadsheet 8.4.

SPREADSHEET 8.4 DSL ISP Revenue Breakdown (Premium Service)

	Services:	Q1	Q12
1	Original Revenue	$1,001,250	$31,592,373
2	Business Services	$164,063	$6,493,676
3	Telecommuter Services	$9,375	$371,067
4	Content	$15,000	$593,708
5	**Adjusted Revenue**	**$1,189,688**	**$39,050,824**
6	Original Cost of Sales	$1,142,285	$28,204,829
7	Business Operational	$32,813	$1,298,735
8	Telecommuter Operational	$3,125	$123,689
9	Additional Hardware	$50,000	$0
10	Total Additional Hardware	$50,000	$500,000
11	Equipment Leasing	$5,070	$50,700
12	**Adjusted Cost of Sales**	**$1,183,293**	**$29,677,953**
13	**Service Revenue**	$1,189,688	$39,050,824
14	**Cost of Sales**	$1,183,293	$29,677,953
15	**Cost of Sales as % of Revenue**	0.99	0.76
16	**EBIT**	**$6,395**	**$9,372,871**
17	**EBIT as % of Revenue**	1%	24%

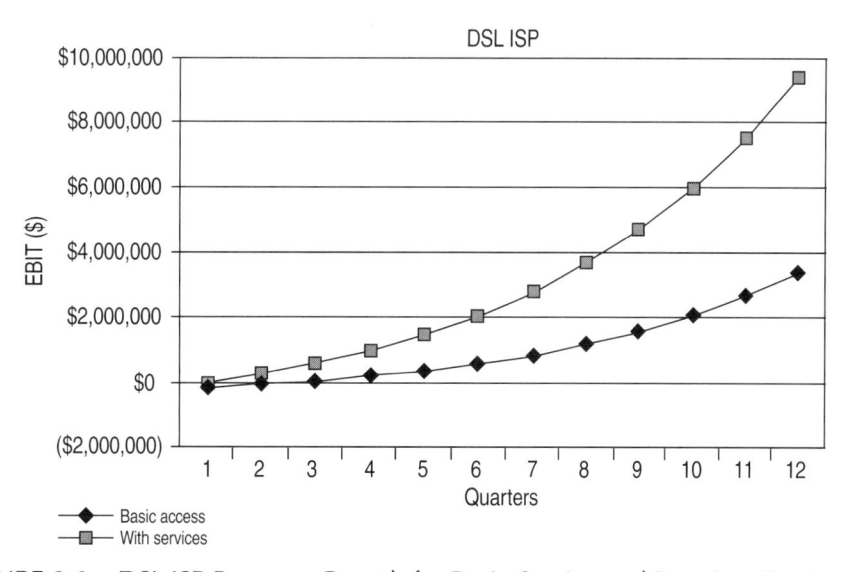

FIGURE 8.6 DSL ISP Revenue Growth for Basic Service and Premium Service

DSL Wholesaling and Portals

DSL wholesaling, as introduced in chapter 3, permits DSL access providers to resell their access infrastructure to multiple ISPs and enterprises. Although the first wholesale deployments relied on dedicated PVCs between the subscriber and the ISP, this is now changing. More sophisticated and optimized service models are being deployed.

Background

BellSouth is an ILEC that offers DSL access throughout the southeastern United States. Traditionally, the company has deployed DSLAMs within its COs. It then runs ATM PVCs across its regional ATM network to different ISPs and enterprises. Although this is an effective tactical market entry approach, BellSouth wants to implement a more scalable wholesale model. The new model no longer relies on backhauling individual PVCs for each and every subscriber (and sometimes multiple PVCs per subscriber), a situation that places strain on the capacities of BellSouth's installed ATM switches as well as posing provisioning difficulties. The new model implements L2TP tunneling across BellSouth's backbone, mapping subscriber PVCs into tunnels at aggregation PoPs via an IPSS and then terminating these tunnels at IPSSs serving the destination ISPs or enterprises. Although the L2TP tunnels traverse the ATM backbone, far fewer PVCs are required to support this new service model than previously required. In addition, there is no longer any need for end-to-end PVC provisioning, as the ATM virtual circuit now terminates in the aggregation PoP. The tunneled architecture also provides an avenue to additional revenue possibilities.

Services Description

Before IPSSs were deployed, the BellSouth DSL access service consisted of the following:

- Alcatel DSLAMs (and smaller remote DSLAMs known as Mini-RAMs) connected to a Lucent GX-550 ATM regional network.
- ISPs connected to this ATM backbone via DS3 or OC3 ATM (see Figure 8.7). This was a bridged service (RFC-2684), requiring no subscriber support for PPP or PPPoE.

After deployment of the tunneling architecture, the subscriber is equipped with a DSL CPE or PC client capable of supporting PPPoA or PPPoE. The subscriber's ATM PVC, containing one or more user sessions via PPPoE or PPPoA encapsulation, terminates at the ingress IPSS, known as the *ingress broadband gateway* (IBG). The IBG in this case is a Nortel/Shasta 5000 broadband service node (BSN).

DSL Wholesaling and Portals 275

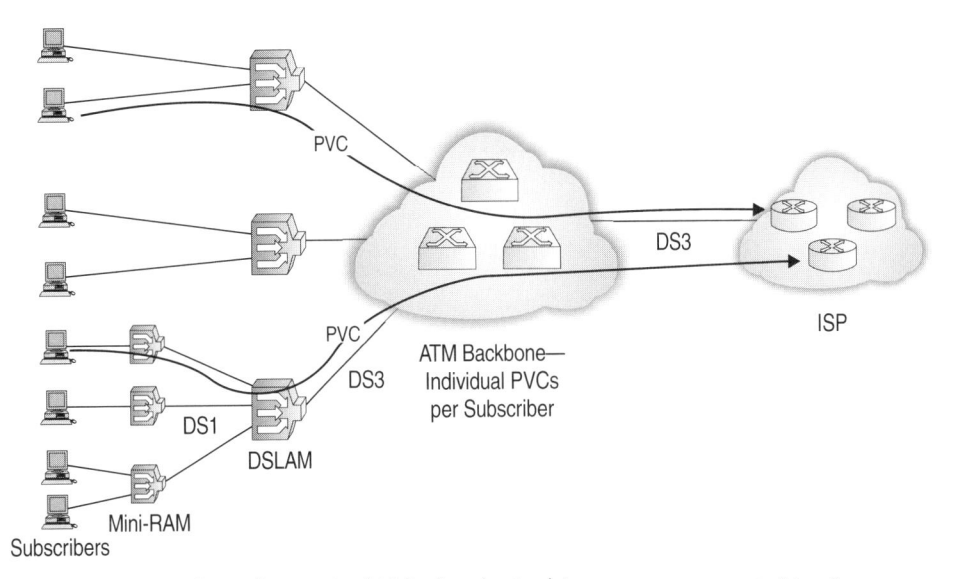

FIGURE 8.7 BellSouth Original Wholesale Architecture *Source:* BellSouth.

The BSN is a subscriber management and IP services platform offering many of the services described in chapters 6 and 7.

The IBG aggregates the sessions into an L2TP tunnel for transport across the regional ATM network to a second IPSS, known as an *egress broadband gateway* (EBG). Here, the L2TP tunnels arriving from multiple IBGs are further aggregated into another L2TP tunnel for transport to the network service provider (NSP), which is the ISP. A single EBG services multiple NSPs, with the destination NSP determined by the domain name entered by the subscriber during the authentication phase. Although subscribers enter authentication information in the form *user@domain.net*, the IBGs map subscribers into the L2TP tunnels based only on the domain name. Also, multiple domains belonging to the same ISP may share the same L2TP tunnel from the EBG to the NSP. Figures 8.8 and 8.9 depict this architecture.

Following the physical topology, DSLAMs connect to the backbone ATM switches via DS3 or OC3 ATM interfaces. These switches then trunk to the IBGs via one or more ATM OC3 interfaces depending on traffic requirements. Note that a single DSLAM's subscribers may be serviced by one or more IBGs. Each IBG will handle up to 6,000 subscribers per physical interface and on the order of 16,000 per system. IBGs and EBGs usually connect to the ATM backbone via OC12. NSPs then connect to the EBGs via ATM OC12, OC3, or DS3. Since the EBG does not support direct DS1 connectivity, NSPs requiring this interface will connect via an ATM switch located in the same CO as the EBG.

The service architecture defines two types of L2TP tunnels, originating at an L2TP access concentrator (LAC) and terminating at an L2TP network server (LNS).

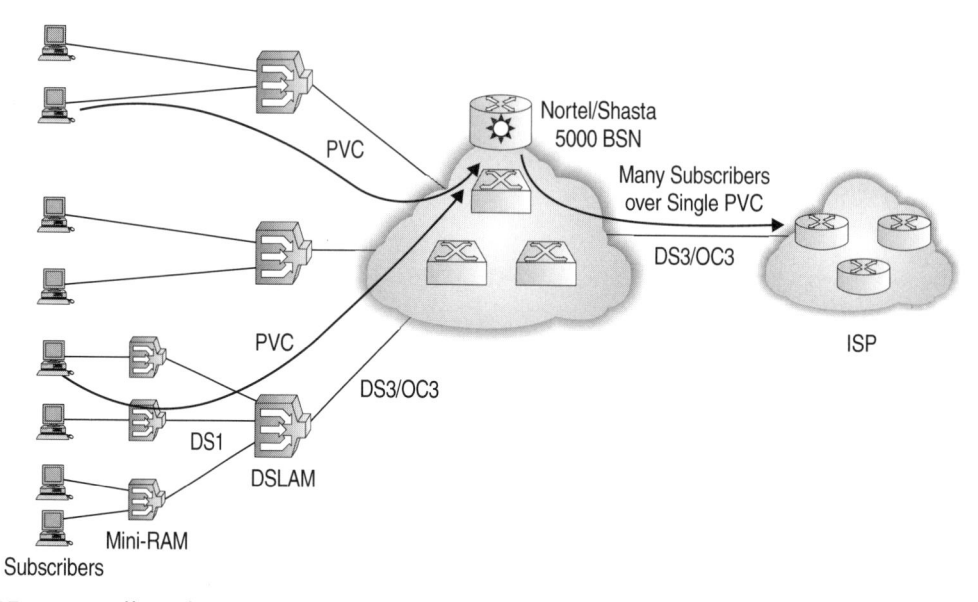

FIGURE 8.8 BellSouth New Wholesale Architecture *Source:* BellSouth.

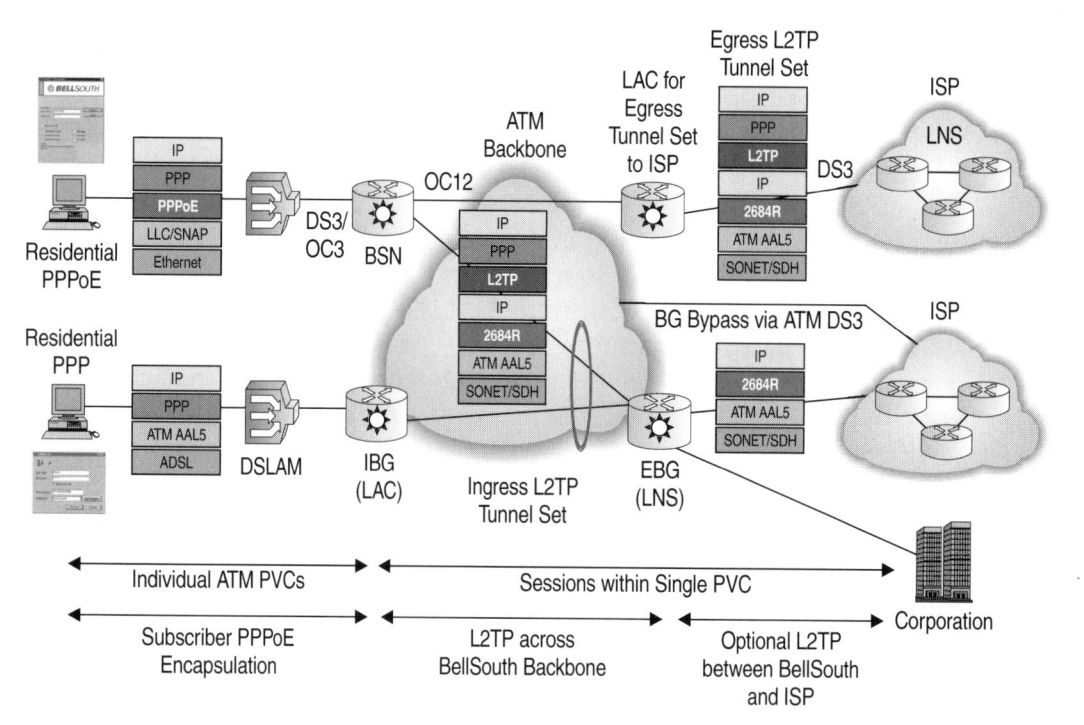

FIGURE 8.9 BellSouth Wholesale Encapsulations *Source:* BellSouth.

The first set of tunnels transport the PPP sessions for a particular NSP between the IBGs and the EBGs, while the second set aggregate the PPP sessions belonging to a single NSP for transport between the EBG and the NSP's L2TP-capable router. Note that multiple L2TP tunnels may share a single ATM PVC. Figure 8.9 depicts L2TP carried over UDP/IP and then over ATM, with IP addresses assigned to the endpoints of the tunnel. There is an alternative, where L2TP may be carried directly over ATM. However, although this configuration reduces the encapsulation overhead, it is incapable of supporting multiplexing of tunnels. It is expected that this option may be deployed in the future.

The basic service supported by the tunneling architecture is *subscriber aggregation*—the mapping of a single subscriber to a single destination NSP. As noted earlier, subscriber data is encapsulated in either PPPoE or PPPoA (assuming an ADSL NIC). This of course requires appropriate client PPPoE software, either supplied by the NSP or integrated within an ADSL modem with native PPPoE support. When a PC PPPoE client is deployed, any existing ADSL bridge may be used. Devices initially supported by BellSouth include the Alcatel 1000, the Alcatel Speedtouch Home, Alcatel Manta, and the Siemens Efficient 4060. PCI modems supporting PPPoA include the 3Com Homeconnect, the Siemens Efficient 3060, and the IteX Apollo 2. DSL routers in use include the Cayman, the Cisco 827, the Alcatel Speedtouch Pro, and the WebRamp. Chapter 6 describes both the PPPoA and PPPoE encapsulations in use. At the IBG, any PPPoE headers are stripped off, and the domain name, as specified during session establishment by the subscriber, is used for L2TP tunnel mapping.

The management system ensures that no port on the ATM switch or the IBG exceeds session limitations. It also ensures resources tracking for the L2TP tunnels created on demand across the backbone. During the provisioning process, the network management system (NMS) associates a given subscriber with an IBG ATM PVC (VPI/VCI, port), the NSP, the protocol, and the domain name. If the subscriber is permitted to access multiple destinations, then additional allowable domains must be entered, along with the total number of permitted simultaneous sessions.

Subscriber configuration and tunnel provisioning are under the control of the Nortel/Shasta Service Creation System (SCS). This is a client/server-based system that is responsible for IPSS element and network management. Each Nortel/Shasta 5000 BSN connects to the SCS server via an in- or out-of-band management connection. The system identifies faults via SNMP traps and may forward these to an external NMS (e.g., HP OpenView). The server requires a Sun Enterprise 250 or larger, while the client is any Pentium-based system running Windows or Sun Solaris. Each IPSS queries the server database for subscriber information upon session establishment. This architecture therefore requires a robust management system and network.

Between the EBG and the NSP's router, parameters of the L2TP connections include the IP addresses, any Layer 3 routing required, the domain name(s) associated with the tunnel set, and the total number of sessions permitted. Note that this connection may traverse any Internet link—it is not limited to any physical encapsulation.

For a multiple-destination service, the IBG must be capable of accepting a list of allowable domain names on a per-subscriber basis. If the service supports multiple simultaneous sessions, the IBG needs to limit the number of allowable PPPoE sessions for an individual subscriber. Note that PPPoA supports only a single session because of its lack of a session multiplexing layer.

Taking a broader view of wholesale DSL services in general, we see that pricing differs by provider but, as a general guideline, an ILEC will traditionally charge the ISP on the order of $25 to $35 per month for a basic consumer service. The ISP must then go ahead and add its expenses into the mix, and will end up charging the subscriber $39.95 per month or more for the DSL service. This pricing model does present a problem to dial ISPs, which derive an acceptable margin from their subscribers. For this reason, initial ISP successes in the DSL space are by those ISPs attached to the ILECs and by those ISPs specializing in broadband access and which therefore have no dial service to cannibalize. The ILEC is in a prime position as part of this wholesale offering, in that it may now create direct partnerships with content providers and may offer premium bandwidth services based on market demand. To encourage ISPs to partake of their tunneling service as opposed to the earlier direct PVC model, an ILEC may offer discounts on the transfer charge. For example, the ILEC may charge $30 per subscriber if the ISP demands an end-to-end PVC, precluding the ILEC offering a broadband service selection portal. However, if the ISP agrees to the tunneled service, the ILEC, realizing that the subscriber now has access to other ISPs and content providers, may reduce this to $25 per subscriber.

Challenges in deploying this tunneled architecture included deployment and training of the management team, the additional ATM links required between the IPSSs, integration within the existing provisioning systems, documentation for NSPs (L2TP, CPL, service order entry), and tariff compliance (NECA 4).

Although not an element of the initial service deployment, the use of tunneling permits the provider to take a more active role in the subscriber experience. As part of this, the provider may offer a broadband portal, initially offering the subscriber a choice of ISPs and content sources. After selecting these services, the subscriber will be presented with a customized home page displaying entries for the selected ISP, value-added content providers, and other information of interest. This portal in an always-on environment in effect becomes the broadband equivalent of the dial tone.

Advantages

Advantages of the tunneled service include a reduction of ILEC and NSP infrastructure costs. This is due to a current limitation in the number of ATM PVCs supported on a given ATM switch interface (2,000 per DS3) compared to the number of subscribers supported via a single L2TP tunnel (4,000 or more). To better understand these efficiencies, first consider a typical dial service at a 12:1 oversubscription ratio. Based on historical data, average use per subscriber is between 4 percent and 6 percent of a 64 Kbps channel. The bandwidth averaged across the subscriber base is therefore 267 bps. Extending this to DSL, and taking into account the growth of multimedia traffic, the average bandwidth per DSL subscriber is still only a bit over 1 Kbps at the service inception. In a given service area, 4,000 subscribers therefore equate to about 4 Mbps on average, or about 20 Mbps at peak (5 percent at 1.5 Mbps and 95 percent at 640 Kbps) use. These theoretical numbers have been backed up by empirical evidence in live networks (Redback, 2000).

Given a 1:10 concurrent usage pattern, out of a population of 8,000 subscribers, only 800 will be active at once, generating approximately 3.2 Kbps on average during peak times. In a non-IPSS model, each of these 8,000 subscribers would require an individual PVC. Since most ATM switches are limited to 8,000 PVCs across an OC3 or 2,000 across a DS3, the OC3 trunk would be very lightly utilized at only 2.5 Mbps. Obviously, this is an inefficient approach and would require many more trunks between BellSouth and the ISP than are required based on bandwidth requirements. Terminating the ATM PVCs within the BellSouth backbone and mapping the subscribers into L2TP tunnels serving many subscribers across a single PVC is therefore the only way to cost-effectively scale the service.

This solution also provides additional opportunity for ILEC revenue, including providing access to multiple NSPs from a single DSL connection, the support for multiple sessions per host, and the opportunity for additional value-added services such as firewalling, mapping into IP-VPNs, and partnering with content providers. These are all services being investigated. From the perspective of the NSP, this solution permits access to corporate LANs, bypassing the NSP's facilities, though the NSP may still offer the service. This therefore allows the ILEC to implement multisession charging.

The Financial Model

A financial model covering the ILEC's expenses, revenues, and basic assumptions concerning service deployment backs up the service just described. Spreadsheet 8.5 lists the assumptions underlying the service offering:

- The first section covers general assumptions. Line 2 is the one-time service installation revenue. As with the ISP model, the ILEC may waive this fee through special promotions. Line 3 is the quarterly service fee for the basic consumer (PPPoE) service, equating to $40 per month, while Line 4 is the expected quarterly growth rate.
- Next are the capital expenses. Line 6 is the one-time operational cost for establishing the service, while Line 7 is the additional cost per metropolitan area. In the same way, Line 8 is the one-time cost to establish the OSS, while Line 9 is the incremental cost per metro. The regional switching expense

SPREADSHEET 8.5 DSL ILEC Wholesaler Assumptions

1	**General Assumptions**		
2	Service Installation	One-time	$250.00
3	DSL service	Quarterly	$120.00
4	Growth Rate	Quarterly	20%
5	**Capital Expenses**		
6	Operations - overall	One-time	$250,000.00
7	Operations - per metro area	One-time	$25,000.00
8	OSS - overall	One-time	$300,000.00
9	OSS - per metro area	One-time	$25,000.00
10	Regional Switching - per metro	One-time	$150,000.00
11	**Central Office Expenses**		
12	Colocation fee	One-time	$35,000.00
13	Backbone into network	One-time	$2,500.00
14	DSLAM hardware	One-time	$13,000.00
15	**Operational Expenses**		
16	Customer Acquisition	One-time	$120.00
17	Unbundled Loop	One-time	$125.00
18	Provisioning - Data	One-time	$110.00
19	**Recurring Expenses**		
20	Loop	Quarterly	$60.00
21	Colocation - per CO	Quarterly	$4,200.00
22	Bandwidth - Backbone per DSLAM	Quarterly	$2,850.00
23	Bandwidth - Per Mbps to Internet	Quarterly	$1,500.00
24	Operations	% of revenue	3.50%
25	Customer service	Quarterly	$18.00
26	SG&A	% of revenue	2.50%
27	Lease Factor	Quarterly	0.1014
28	Subscriber Peering Bandwidth	Mbps	0.025

listed in Line 10 is the cost to deploy the ATM switch for DSLAM aggregation as well as the cost of the IPSS.

- The next section outlines one-time CO expenses. These include establishing the trunk link into the metro network (Line 13) and the cost of the DSLAM (Line 14). The collocation fee (Line 12) applies to the CLEC model detailed later in this section.

- One-time operational expenses include the cost of customer acquisition (Line 16) and the cost of provisioning (Line 18). Line 17, the unbundled loop charge, also applies to the CLEC model.

- The next section lists the recurring expenses. Line 20, the recurring loop charge, and Line 21, the collocation fee, only apply to the CLEC model. Line 22 is the cost to the DSL access provider of the bandwidth per DSLAM, while Line 23, the cost of transit bandwidth into the Internet backbone, is based on the total subscriber bandwidth. This is listed in Line 28 as an average of

DSL Wholesaling and Portals

25 Kbps per subscriber, reasonable for a residential-grade service. Depending on the business model of the ILEC and how it accounts for bandwidth, Lines 22 and 23 may vary greatly. Line 24 is the ongoing operational expense, a percentage of revenue, while Line 26 is the same for SG&A. The customer service cost listed in Line 25 is constant per subscriber. Line 27 is a derived lease factor equating to a loan rate of 14 percent.

Based on these assumptions, we can now calculate the service revenue model. Spreadsheet 8.6 details this for the first and twelfth quarters of the service.

SPREADSHEET 8.6 DSL ILEC Revenue Breakdown

	Q1	Q12
Metros	1	10
COs	20	200
Subscribers per CO	250	990
Total Subscribers	5000	197,903
New Subscribers	5000	37,150
Revenue		
Service	$600,000	$23,748,301
Installation	$1,250,000	$9,287,605
Total Revenue	$1,850,000	$33,035,906
Capital Expenses		
Operations+OSS	$650,000	
Operations+OSS metro	$200,000	
Regional SW - CO	$150,000	
BB+DSLAM	$310,000	
Total Capital Expenses	$1,310,000	$0
Total Invested Capital	$1,310,000	$6,485,000
One-Time Operational Expenses		
Customer Acquisition	$600,000	$4,458,050
Provisioning	$550,000	$4,086,546
Recurring Operational Expenses		
Bandwidth - Backbone from DSLAMs	$57,000	$1,140,000
Bandwidth - Peering into Internet	$187,500	$7,421,344
Operations + SG&A	$111,000	$1,982,154
Customer Service	$90,000	$3,562,245
Leasing Fee	$132,834	$657,579
Total Cost of Sales	$1,728,334	$23,307,919
Service Revenue	$1,850,000	$33,035,906
Cost of Sales	$1,728,334	$23,307,919
Cost of Sales as % of Revenue	0.93	0.71
EBIT	$121,666	$9,727,987
EBIT as % of Revenue	7%	29%

Subscriber growth is the same as the ISP model, depicted in Figure 8.5. Revenues in fact are close to that of the ISP, although expenses are lower because of a reduction in the bandwidth transit fees. Note that capital expenses that occur during Quarters 2 through 11 are hidden in Spreadsheet 8.6. The model results in a service with a margin acceptable to the ILEC—29 percent—by the third year of service.

For comparison, Spreadsheet 8.7 details the same model as in Spreadsheet 8.6, but for a DSL CLEC. The main difference between the models is that the CLEC must pay loop and collocation fees. This has a major impact on the model, since

SPREADSHEET 8.7 DSL CLEC Revenue Breakdown

	Q1	Q12
Metros	1	10
COs	20	200
Subscribers per CO	250	990
Total Subscribers	5000	197,903
New Subscribers	5000	37,150
Revenue		
Service	$600,000	$23,748,301
Installation	$1,250,000	$9,287,605
Total Revenue	**$1,850,000**	**$33,035,906**
Capital Expenses		
Operations+OSS	$650,000	
Operations+OSS metro	$200,000	
Regional SW - CO	$150,000	
Colocation+BB+DSLAM	$1,010,000	
Total Capital Expenses	$2,010,000	$0
Total Invested Capital	$2,010,000	$13,485,000
One-Time Operational Expenses		
Customer Acquisition	$600,000	$4,458,050
Loop	$625,000	$4,643,802
Provisioning	$550,000	$4,086,546
Recurring Operational Expenses		
Loop	$300,000	$11,874,151
Colocation	$84,000	$840,000
Bandwidth - Backbone from DSLAMs	$57,000	$1,140,000
Bandwidth - Peering into Internet	$187,500	$7,421,344
Operations and SG&A	$111,000	$1,982,154
Customer Service	$90,000	$3,562,245
Leasing Fee	$203,814	$1,367,379
Total Cost of Sales	**$2,808,314**	**$41,375,672**
Service Revenue	$1,850,000	$33,035,906
Cost of Sales	$2,808,314	$41,375,672
Cost of Sales as % of Revenue	1.52	1.25
EBIT	($958,314)	($8,339,766)
EBIT as % of Revenue	-52%	-25%

Cable Open Access

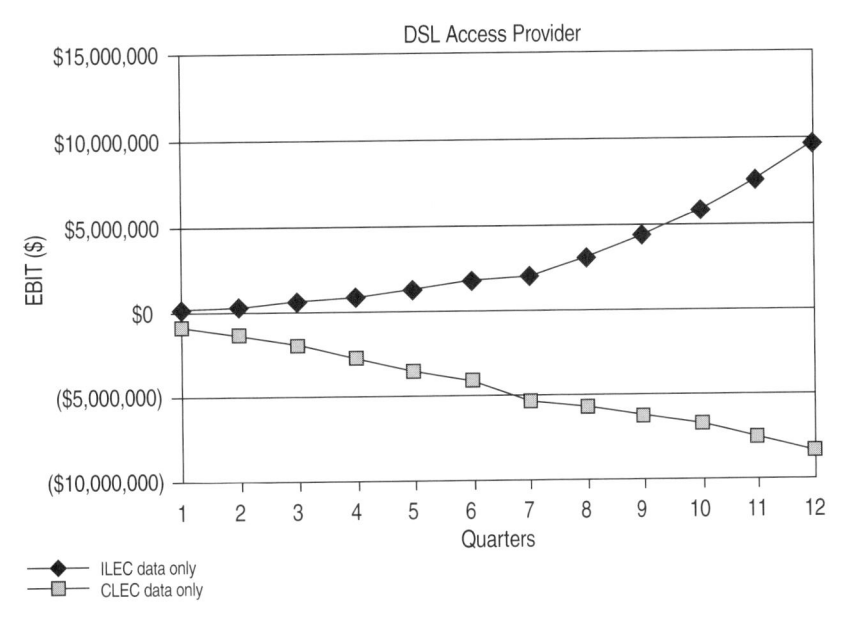

FIGURE 8.10 DSL Access Revenue

the DSL fee of $40 per month is no longer sufficient to cover operational expenses. Figure 8.10 graphically depicts the diverging revenue curves between the ILEC and the CLEC. The additional costs all but preclude the ability of the CLEC to offer a basic residential service, thus the focus on business services. However, even with increased revenues, the margins are still quite thin. Adjusting the fee to $100 per month and the average backbone bandwidth to 75 Kbps still results only in a 15 percent margin at Q12. Note that a business case distributed by Copper Mountain (Copper Mountain, 2000) presents a good voice-focused DSL business model, from which some of the fields presented here are derived.

Cable Open Access

Cable modem service, a technology introduced in chapter 2, is currently the most popular form of broadband connectivity, at least for residential subscribers. An evolving trend is to permit the cable modem subscriber to have access to multiple ISPs, a capability referred to as *open access*. In this section, we describe an early open access service.

Background

Canbras TVA is a leading cable provider in Brazil and is the result of an association between Canbras Communications Corporation of Canada and TVA, a subsidiary of the group Abril. It offers cable TV services and has recently rolled out a cable modem service for faster access to the Internet. Its (headend) sites are in São José dos Campos, Guarulhos, São Vicente, Guarujá, Mogi das Cruzes, and Santo André. Its cable TV system consists of multiple receivers installed in Brazilian cities and various satellite systems, as well as the necessary fiber and coaxial infrastructure. Canbras is dedicated to providing the best entertainment and information to its viewers as well as the best Internet connectivity. Its cable modem service is called Canbras Acesso and competes with dial-up modems as well as DSL access to the Internet.

Services Description

Canbras's initial focus is on providing a methodology to offer high-speed Internet access, competing with the existing dial infrastructure. Its competitive offering is based on the fact that dial service in Brazil is metered, so it has developed a business model that results in savings if a user is dialed in to the Internet for more than two and a half hours per day. The result is that, if the user is a cable modem subscriber, significant savings are realized; plus there is an additional incentive that the phone line remains free to be used for voice conversations. Additionally, Canbras's service enables faster downloads of data, effective participation in videoconferences, and faster downloads of music clips.

Although the hardware deployed by Canbras TVA meets DOCSIS 1.1 standards (described in chapter 2), the firmware meets DOCSIS 1.0 standards. This deployment ensures that the cable modem can be updated remotely by software. Thus, the cable modem needs to be DOCSIS 1.0–compliant and on the list of homologated cable modems by Canbras TVA or, alternatively, one of the cable modems sold by Canbras TVA.

Figure 8.11 depicts Canbras's initial rollout. In this scenario, a DOCSIS-compliant cable modem is connected via the hybrid fiber-coax (HFC) access network to a cable modem termination system (CMTS). Canbras TVA has selected Nortel Networks/Arris to supply the CMTS headend. The product used by Canbras TVA is the CMTS 1000. From the CMTS, the subscribers are connected to a Nortel Networks/Shasta 5000 BSN. From here, the subscribers leave the Canbras TVA network and are switched to different ISPs, which operate the routers that provide the Internet connectivity needed to comply with open access. The initial phase does not take full advantage of the services value of the IPSS, limiting Canbras TVA to offering a connectivity service. The next phase of the deployment will include open access to other valuable services.

The second phase is required to support an open access environment with additional security and services. This permits subscribers to select any ISP serving

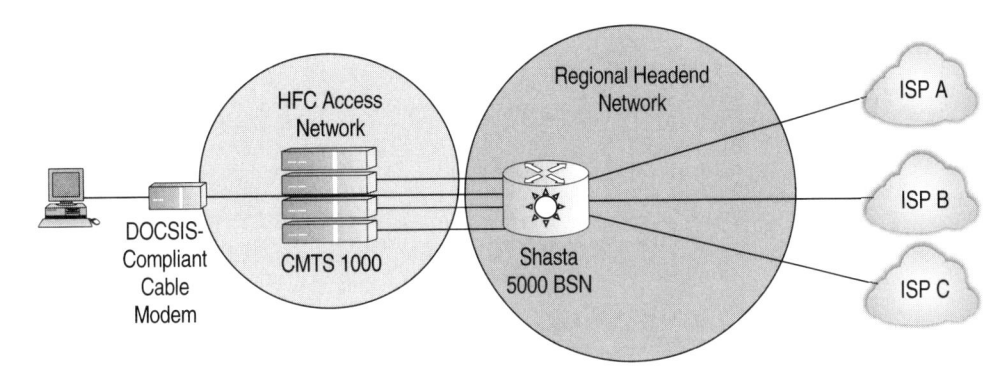

FIGURE 8.11 Canbras Cable Modem Deployment

their area and not just the two affiliated with Canbras TVA—@Jato (www.ajato.com.br) and CanbrasNet (www.canbrasnet.com.br).

In cable deployments, there is a growing awareness of the lack of security within an "always-on" architecture. Lack of security in cable deployments received heavy press coverage because of hacker attacks and the initial capability of subscribers on the same subnet to view other computers. Although some protection has been implemented via DOCSIS, the cable operators have not had the means at their disposal to truly protect their subscribers and their networks. Thus, although DOCSIS provides security from the cable modem to the CMTS, it does not protect the end user from hackers coming from the Internet. Although dial and DSL deployments do not offer any additional security, cable seems to have suffered the brunt of the negative publicity surrounding security.

Canbras TVA wanted to offer customers additional services, such as QoS management, IP-VPNs, and network-based firewalls, to protect its "always-on" subscribers. As a result, the second phase of its rollout incorporates the services capabilities of the IPSS. This scenario includes PPPoE subscribers belonging to multiple ISPs arriving from the CMTS to the Shasta 5000 BSN. In order to support this, the Shasta 5000 BSN has a feature called PPPoE Aggregator, which provides the flexibility of having multiple subscribers behind one access connection. Each subscriber can have his or her own set of services that could include membership in a VPN. There could also be static or preconfigured subscribers with their own IP addresses, or subscribers with multiple IP address ranges with a list of services. These statically addressed subscribers could also have local subnets reachable via the Internet. With PPPoE tunneling, the operator may automatically create subscribers based on a template with a set of services upon detection of a new login

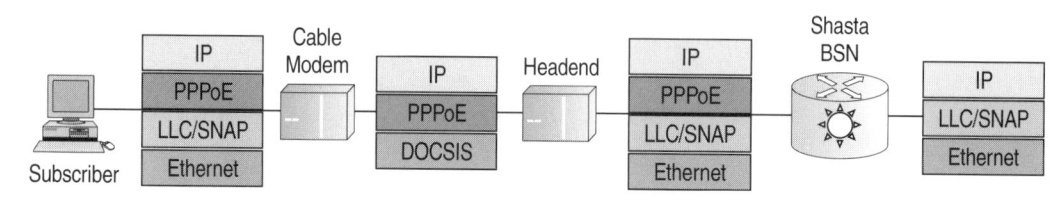

FIGURE 8.12 Cable Modem Encapsulations

name. Figure 8.12 depicts the encapsulations used within this architecture between the subscriber's PC, the cable modem, and the CMTS headend.

With the addition of the Shasta 5000 BSN, Canbras TVA can protect subscribers against hackers. Additionally, it secures the network from users who violate its acceptable use policies (AUPs). For example, if a subscriber has not signed up as a Web hoster, then the firewall rules can ensure that packets are blocked from reaching the unauthorized server. In the future, Canbras TVA will implement the Personal Portal to present a home page to the subscriber that is used for self-configuration, provider selection, and content selection. The Shasta 5000 BSN will then route or tunnel subscribers into an ISP backbone or enterprise network via FE or ATM.

To get started with the service, the initial equipment cost (year 2000 figures) is R$599 ($300 U.S.) without a service contract or R$299 with a service contract for 18 months. There are two service offers: 64 K service for R$29.95 a month and 256 K service of R$49.95 a month. In addition, there is a one-time initial configuration fee of R$150 for residential users or, alternatively, R$99 per subscriber in a building as long as there are at least five subscribers to the service at that location.

Business subscribers can participate in IP-VPNs for site-to-site connectivity. This service is provided to branch offices interconnecting via cable modem to their headquarters site. In this scenario, the Shasta 5000 BSN sets up IPSec tunnels to interconnect members of a VPN. The specific VPN supported for this topology is the virtual private routed network, in which the Shasta 5000 BSN creates the VPN topology from information stored in the service creation system. Canbras TVA can easily provision cable modem subscribers to become members of a VPN. Additionally, because of the firewall capabilities in the Shasta 5000 BSN, the same coaxial connection serves to connect the subscriber to both the Internet and Canbras's VPN. Offering these value-added services in addition to Internet connectivity enables Canbras TVA to receive additional revenues.

Advantages

Canbras TVA is still at an early stage of developing its data topology, but it is preparing for the future by putting in place an intelligent subscriber edge device.

Although Canbras is very familiar with Internet connectivity via cable modems, the requirement to offer open access is forcing it to enable dynamic ISP selection. The intelligent subscriber edge device makes it easier for Canbras to offer open access. Also, the self-provisioning capabilities of the intelligent edge device result in significant savings to the operator. Since the subscriber can self-provision, Canbras TVA can save on operating costs. Additionally, as its data service grows, Canbras can offer services beyond IP-VPNs and firewalls. These additional offerings will help Canbras TVA to remain profitable while providing its subscribers with new and desired services.

The Financial Model

The financial model for the Canbras cable modem service is much like that of the Marslink DSL service described earlier in the chapter. First, we will outline the various assumptions and then detail the revenues. Spreadsheet 8.8 depicts subscriber growth for the cable service, which is identical to the growth projected for DSL.

SPREADSHEET 8.8   Cable Modem Service Assumptions

1	**Cable Assumptions:**		
2	Residential Service	Quarterly	$90.00
3	SOHO Service	Quarterly	$150.00
4	Growth Rate	Quarterly	20%
5	Operational	One-time	$50.00
6	Operational - ongoing - residential	Quarterly	$10.00
7	Operational - ongoing - telecommuter	Quarterly	$20.00
8	G&A - % of revenue	Quarterly	2.50%
9	Telecommuter - firewall and IP-VPN	Quarterly	$60.00
10	Telecommuter - firewall and IP-VPN	Penetration	50.00%
11	Content	Quarterly	$30.00
12	Content	Penetration	25.00%
13	Operational - ongoing - telecommuter services	Quarterly	$10.00
14	CMTS Initial Cost (4000 subs)	One-time	$60,000
15	Aggregation and Routing / Metro area	One-time	$100,000
16	CMTS Upgrade for 2000 subscribers		$10,000
17	Equipment Lease Factor		0.1014
18	**Trunk Bandwidth**		
19	Residential	Mbps	0.025
20	Telecommuter	Mbps	0.05
21	Peering Bandwidth	Quarterly/Mbps	$ 1,500

This permits a like-to-like comparison. However, this model involves some assumptions that are different from those in the Marslink model:

- The basic residential service fee is $90 per quarter, equating to $30 per month. Average trunking bandwidth for this service is 25 Kbps (Line 19). A premium SOHO (telecommuter) service with additional bandwidth is offered at $150 per quarter, or $50 per month. Average trunking bandwidth for the SOHO service is 50 Kbps (Line 20). In both cases, the cable provider must pay $1,500 per Mbps per quarter for transit into the Internet backbone (Line 21).
- Operational expenses, listed in Lines 5, 6, and 7, are on a per-subscriber basis. The G&A listed in Line 8 is still a percentage of the total revenue.
- Beyond the basic service, the provider offers a telecommuter firewall and IP-VPN service at an additional $60 per quarter (Line 9). Canbras expects this service to be adopted by 50 percent of the telecommuters (where the telecommuters compose less than 20 percent of the total cable modem population). Line 13 lists the additional ongoing operational expense for this service. Canbras also expects 25 percent of the total subscriber base to sign up for value-added content services at a cost of $30 per quarter (Line 11).
- Line 14 lists the initial CMTS cost. The systems deployed support 4,000 subscribers each, with an upgrade required (Line 16) for each increment of 2,000 subscribers. The other major expense is for subscriber aggregation and routing, at $100K per metro area (Line 15).
- The equipment lease factor (Line 17) is set for 14 percent, which is identical to the other models in this chapter.

Given these assumptions, the basic service generates the following return (see Spreadsheet 8.9): Residential subscribers grow from 5,000 in Q1 to almost 200,000 in Q12, while SOHO (telecommuters) grow from 1,000 to almost 40,000 during the same timeframe. For recurring expenses, backbone bandwidth is the greatest cost, as would be expected. The model generates a margin of 34 percent after three years of service. This may seem acceptable, but the provider could do better.

Spreadsheet 8.10 depicts the addition of IP-VPNs and advanced content to the basic service offering. These two services generate additional revenue (Lines 2 and 3) exceeding their cost of implementation. Leasing fees grow (Line 9) because of the additional hardware required (Line 8). The bottom line is an increase in the gross margin (Line 15).

SPREADSHEET 8.9 Cable Modem Service Revenue Breakdown

		Q1	Q12
1	**Number Of Homes Passed**	2,500,000	2,500,000
2	New Residential Subscribers	5,000	37,150
3	Total Residential Subscribers	5,000	197,903
4	Residential Penetration	0.20%	7.92%
5	New SOHO Clients	1,000	7,430
6	Total SOHO Clients	1,000	39,581
7	**Total Revenue**	$600,000	$23,748,301
8	**Capital Expenses**		
9	Aggregation and Routing	$1,600,000	$200,000
10	**Total Invested Capital**	$1,600,000	$2,700,000
11	**One-Time Operational Expenses**	$300,000	$2,229,025
12	**Recurring Operational Expenses**		
13	Subscriber Maintenance	$70,000	$2,770,635
14	Bandwidth - Peering	$262,500	$10,389,882
15	Equipment Leasing	$162,240	$273,780
16	**Total Expenses**	$794,740	$15,663,322
17	Service Revenue	$600,000	$23,748,301
18	Cost of Sales	$794,740	$15,663,322
19	Cost of Sales as % of Revenue	1.32	0.66
20	EBIT	($194,740)	$8,084,979
21	EBIT as % of Revenue	-32%	34%

Figure 8.13 contrasts the cable modem and DSL revenue curves. Note that the cable modem service is generally less expensive to deploy than the DSL service. It generates higher margins and, although not as optimal a solution for businesses as DSL, may still generate acceptable revenue and margin from the residential and SOHO customers. The cable modem service will leave the majority of the business traffic to the DSL operators.

Figure 8.14 contrasts the gross margins for the different services—DSL wholesale (ILEC), DSL ISP, and cable modem. Although not a true apples-to-apples comparison, it does provide some insight into the decision making that occurs when service providers select which services to offer.

SPREADSHEET 8.10 Cable Modem Value-Added Services Revenue Breakdown

	Services:	Q1	Q12
1	Original Revenue	$600,000	$23,748,301
2	Telecommuter Services	$30,000	$1,187,415
3	Content	$37,500	$1,484,269
4	**Adjusted Revenue**	**$667,500**	**$26,419,985**
5	Original Cost of Sales	$794,740	$15,663,322
6	Telecommuter Operational	$5,000	$197,903
7	Additional Hardware	$50,000	$0
8	Total Additional Hardware	$50,000	$500,000
9	Equipment Leasing	$5,070	$50,700
10	**Adjusted Cost of Sales**	**$804,810**	**$15,911,925**
11	**Service Revenue**	$667,500	$26,419,985
12	**Cost of Sales**	$804,810	$15,911,925
13	Cost of Sales as % of Revenue	1.21	0.60
14	**EBIT**	($137,310)	$10,508,061
15	**EBIT as % of Revenue**	-21%	40%

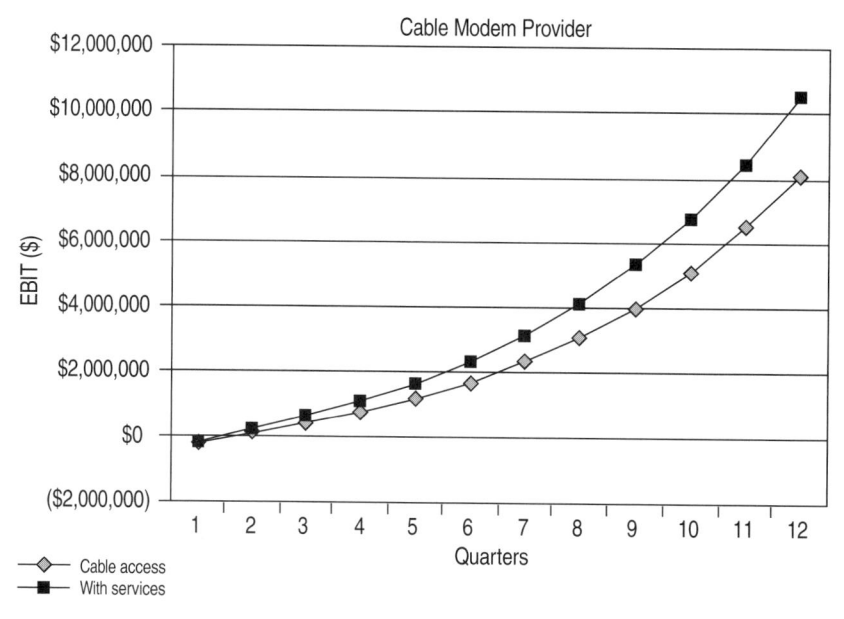

FIGURE 8.13 Cable Modem Service Revenue Comparisons

Fixed Wireless Wholesaling

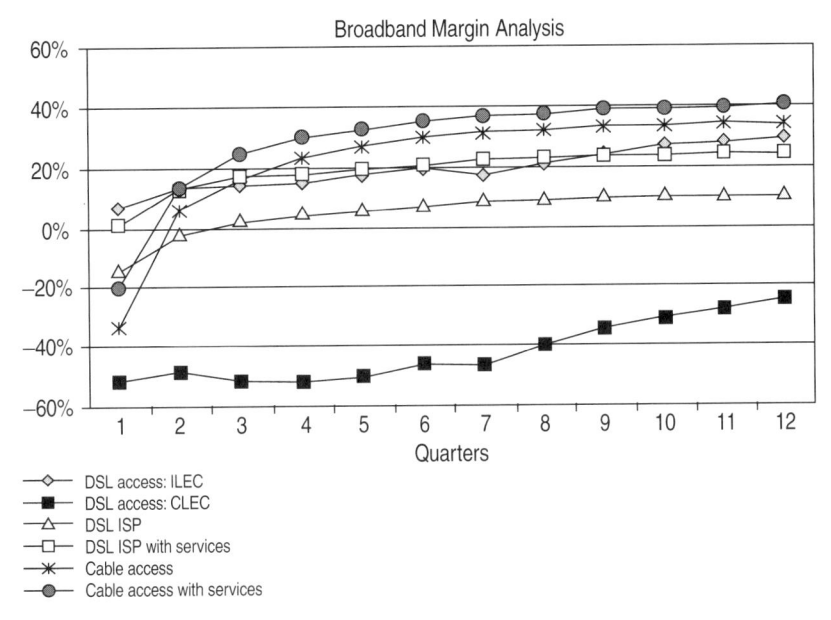

FIGURE 8.14 Services Margin Analysis

Fixed Wireless Wholesaling

Although DSL and cable access receive the lion's share of publicity (partially because of the visibility of the ILECs, the CLECs, and the MSOs), broadband fixed wireless could be considered the "dark horse" because of its appeal in some regions. Chapter 2 introduced this emerging technology, and here we document an actual deployment.

Background

Los Gatos Wireless (LGW), a major wireless operator in North America, wishes to more effectively compete against DSL and cable operators in offering high-speed data services. Since it is not the incumbent carrier, and therefore does not control the local loop, it has two alternatives. The first is to build out a DSL infrastructure along the lines of Covad's or Rhythms', leasing both collocation and copper from the ILEC. Although this is a possibility, there is a second alternative. LGW may leverage its existing cellular infrastructure and customer contacts, adding technology that will permit it to offer residential (and some business) high-speed data and voice services. Now able to offer data, fixed voice, and cellular services, LGW is better able to avoid subscriber churn and better able to protect itself against the ILECs offering cellular in addition to DSL and fixed voice.

Fixed wireless service for residential subscribers is a fairly recent development, which relies on technology specific to a given vendor for deployment (i.e., there is no interoperability as of yet). Chapter 6 outlines the projected market size for this technology over the next few years.

Services Description

LGW deploys a fixed wireless system that leverages the existing cellular towers and data infrastructure in more than 50 major metropolitan areas. Subscribers have access to high-speed data services as well as telephony.

The system architecture, depicted in Figure 8.15, consists of a vendor-proprietary wireless link operating at 1.9 Ghz in the PCS band between the remote unit attached to the residence and the base station. Within the residence, multiple PCs (a maximum of five) connect over a home phone networking alliance (HPNA) LAN to the remote unit. HPNA is a low-cost, in-home network that relies on installed phone lines. Multiple devices access the network through a variation of the Ethernet MAC. The wireless base stations are located on the existing cellular towers, and each tower serves on the order of 150 households within a one-mile radius. Between 50 and 250 radio towers will serve a given metropolitan area, with a total of 200 to 1,000 T1 trunks. A given radio tower initially offered 1 Mbps of bidirectional capacity shared among 150 households. This has since evolved to 4 Mbps with 4xT1 of uplink capacity. This bandwidth,

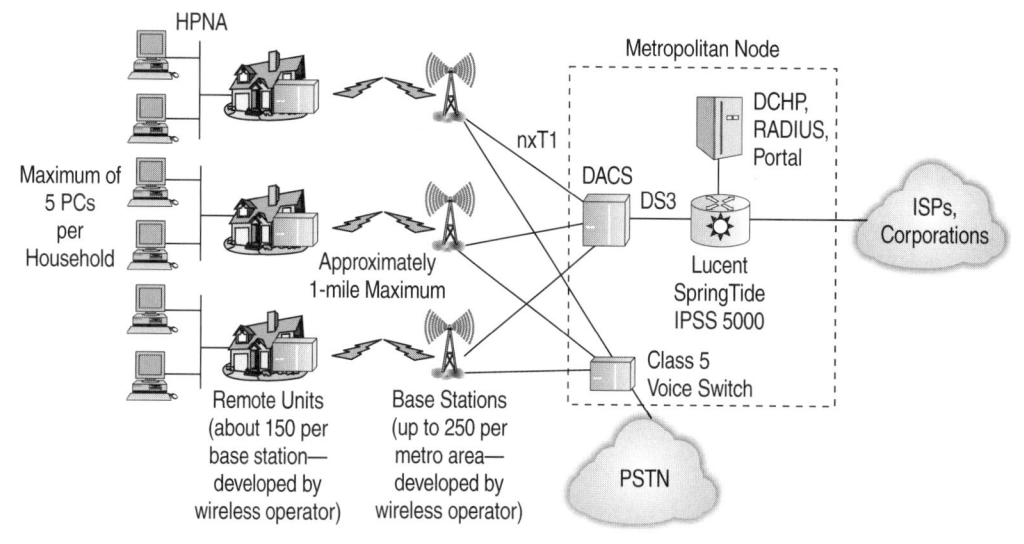

FIGURE 8.15 LGW Fixed Wireless System Architecture

taking into account the number of residences and the trunk capacity, is roughly equivalent to other basic residential cable and DSL deployments.

Multiple T1s extend from each base station to a metropolitan node containing a digital access cross connect (DACS) and a Lucent/SpringTide 5000 IPSS, as well as additional routers, DHCP servers, and mail servers. The DACS converts the individual T1s to channelized DS3 links for connectivity to the IPSS. One optimization between the base station and the IPSS is the use of multilink PPP (MLPPP). This extension to PPP permits the provider to better distribute subscriber traffic among the T1 uplinks by avoiding the need to map individual subscribers to individual links. Other T1s extend to the existing Class 5 switches. Connectivity to the Internet from the IPSS is over any supported interface, including ATM, PPP over SONET, and GE. The IPSS also connects through the network to DHCP and authentication servers.

Let's look more closely at encapsulations and the authentication process. The wireless provider equips the subscribers with a provider-branded L2TP client. This client is used to select ISP and enterprise destinations across the network, but may also be used to gain access to a management network that is used for service enhancements and troubleshooting. After activating the client and logging in to the service, the subscriber has access to the management network and is presented with a menu of destinations (or may enter additional destinations at will). The subscriber now selects a destination (e.g., *big.net*) and enters a user ID and password.

At the IPSS, subscriber traffic is mapped into a given tunnel based on an FQDN selection, the combination of the destination and the user ID and password. These tunnels terminate at a selected ISP or enterprise. Initially, the wireless operator deployed PPTP for tunneling since it was available on the first-generation tunnel termination equipment (the Nortel Contivity) and was also supported on Microsoft Windows at the time. Later, in selecting the production hardware, the operator required a platform supporting both PPTP and L2TP. L2TP was selected for wide-scale deployment because of better resiliency as well as wider support by routing hardware.

Why go through the complexity of using a tunneling protocol at all, when native IP could possibly meet the needs of the service? The problem with this approach is that there is no clean way of assigning subscribers addresses native to the different ISPs—the wireless provider would have to act as an intermediary for all DHCP requests, control that some ISPs and enterprises will not release. In addition, support of multiple PCs in the household with multiple destinations is problematic. An alternate native approach using NAT at the provider–Internet boundary was not seriously considered because of the effects of NAT on different protocols and applications (described in chapter 3). Yet another option is PPPoE, a lightweight protocol offering many of the same address assignment capabilities as L2TP without the tunneling overhead. In this case, PPPoE was not considered an option because of the system modifications required.

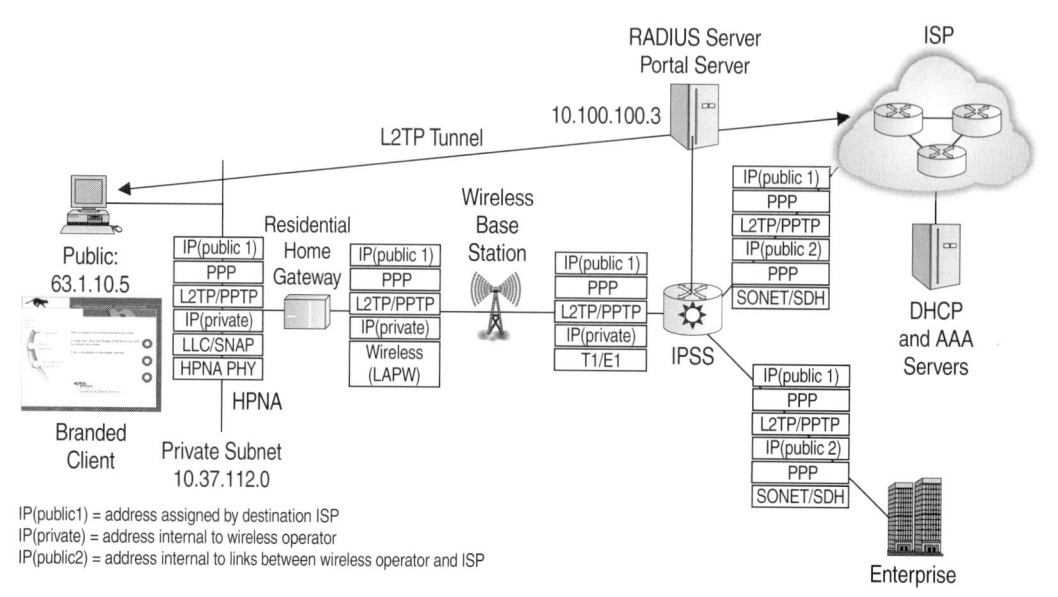

FIGURE 8.16 LGW Fixed Wireless Encapsulations and Addressing

Within the network, as shown in Figure 8.16, each household is assigned a separate subnet belonging to a private address space invisible to the outside world. The subnet mask is set so a given subscriber may operate up to five PCs. The operator's DHCP server, IPSS, and other servers internal to the service offering are all within this private address space.

Within the home, the remote unit acts as a DHCP relay and substitutes its IP address in all DHCP responses so as to be considered the default gateway for the home. It also performs filtering, ensuring that only IP addresses assigned to the given household are forwarded across the link. It also filters out any destination addresses not native to the wireless operator's network, precluding home-to-home transmissions. Finally, it helps minimize any extraneous wireless traffic by filtering out any broadcast or unknown unicast traffic.

Advantages

The fixed wireless service provides advantages to both the subscribers and the service provider. For the subscribers, it permits a bundled high-speed data and voice service in areas where DSL and cable may not be available. Monthly pricing is comparable to these alternatives. From the perspective of LGW, it permits a service offering in those geographies where the provider may not have incumbent status or any DSL or cable ownership. This allows a wider palette of service offerings, encouraging subscriber loyalty. In the future, broadband fixed wireless will offer residential subscribers a viable alternative to DSL and cable services.

3G Mobile Wireless Services

By the end of the decade, over 1 billion individuals will connect to the Internet, with over 750 million via mobile wireless. With the advent of next-generation wireless deployments, more sophisticated subscriber services, including access to rich media, become a reality.

Background

3GNet is one of the leading mobile Internet providers in Europe. More than 7 million customers use its wireless voice services, and more than 750,000 customers subscribe to its Internet service. 3GNet was the first provider to launch a mobile ISP service and offered commercial Wireless Application Protocol (WAP) service in the year 2000. Based on the success and demand for mobile Internet service, the company is currently building out its general packet radio services (GPRS) network to offer mobile data services that are faster than existing GSM services offering transmission rates of 9.6 Kbps.

In anticipation of the tremendous bandwidth demand for content, 3GNet bid and won a universal mobile telephone system (UMTS) license for its primary service area, with expected commercial deployment in 2003. UMTS is one of the technologies that support IMT-2000 and is commonly known as 3G (for third generation). The idea behind 3G is to unify the disparate radio and data standards in today's second-generation wireless networks. Instead of different network types being adopted in the Americas, Europe, and Japan, the plan is for a single network standard to be agreed on and implemented. Figure 8.17 shows the allocation of worldwide IMT-2000–standard frequency allocation bands. Note that on a region-by-region basis there is some conflict in spectrum allocation in that some existing

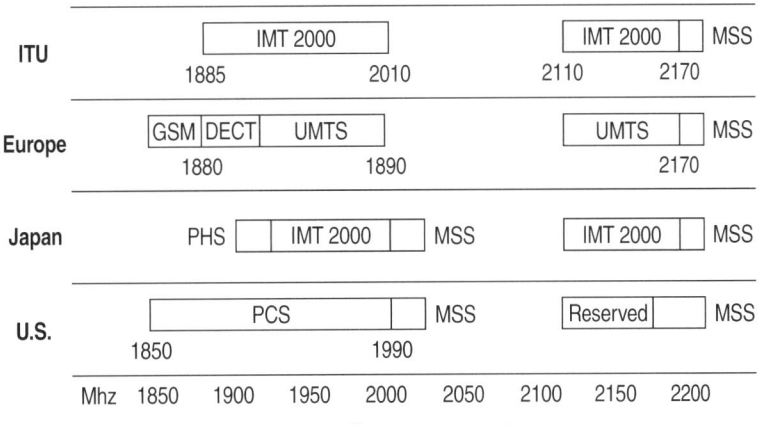

FIGURE 8.17 IMT-2000 Frequency Allocation Bands

services (e.g., DECT or personal handy-phone system [PHS]) overlap with what is considered the IMT-2000 spectrum.

The company awarded Nortel Networks a contract to be the principal supplier of the end-to-end UMTS network infrastructure, including both radio and core elements. Since both GPRS and UMTS services will be offered simultaneously, the UMTS network will overlay the GPRS network but will require a brand-new backbone and base station subsystem.

Services Description

3GNet's Internet Mobility service is currently evolving from GSM to GPRS. The GPRS network consists of a Motorola network solution with an Internet infrastructure supplied by Cisco Systems. Its GPRS network is shown in Figure 8.18.

GPRS will support the increased demand for mobile Internet services. It allows the mobile user to access Internet services three to five times faster than first-generation GSM technology. Additionally, with GPRS, the mobile user is always online, and there is no requirement to log on to the network. As well, GPRS provides greater bandwidth to enable better access to images, video, and multimedia applications on the mobile phone.

One of 3GNet's current services is Internet Mobility. It uses a combination of the cellular service, a WAP phone, and the Internet (ISP). WAP, an international standard, allows mobile phones to send and receive information from the Internet. WAP technology is designed to display Web information as text and pictures on the mobile phone, enabling online services while moving around. The ISP was the first Web site to bring WAP-enabled data to mobile phones.

The WAP phones supported by the Internet Mobility service include the Motorola T2288, which allows subscribers to talk on the handset; send and receive e-mails and text messages; and access up-to-the-minute information on just about

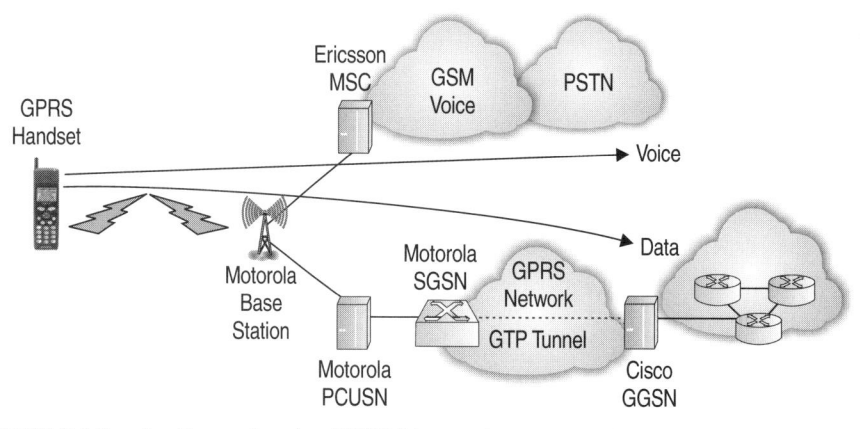

FIGURE 8.18 An Example of a GPRS Network

TABLE 8.1 Service Tariffs

Tariff Name	Pay-as-You-Go Plan
Phone and connection	€39.99
Inclusive call value	€5
Local call charges	€0.35 peak; €0.10 off-peak
Calls to 3GNet phones	€0.10 peak; €5 weekend
Internet calls via Genie	€0.10
VM message retrieval	€0.10
Calls to other networks	€0.50 peak; €0.25 off-peak
Top-up vouchers	€5, 10, or 15
Text message	€0.10

anything, such as sports, news wire stories, stock information, and lottery winning numbers. Additionally, the Motorola T2288 services offer capabilities that allow one to avoid delays on the roads by receiving an early warning of congestion on major roads up to 150 miles ahead and 5 miles on either side. Other services allow a subscriber to locate hotels, restaurants, gas stations, ATM machines, and other necessities via the mobile handset based on the subscriber's current location. These services are offered on a pay-as-you-go plan—the user prepurchases connection time via the phone. Table 8.1 shows some of the tariffs in effect in 2001.

The Financial Model

In developing the business plan that results in the tariffs described in Table 8.1, the typical wireless operator looks first at the total expected market share, taking into account competition and other technologies. This total available subscriber base is then qualified against the market segments—business, mobile workers, residential, and casual subscribers. Depending on the subscriber type, voice and data uptake will have different penetration. The net result of this calculation is what the probable revenue for the service will be. Using the United Kingdom as an example, by 2010 more than 10 million UMTS subscribers are expected, divided almost evenly among four operators. The business and mobile worker segments will form the majority of the subscriber base in the early years of the service (2003 and beyond), while casual use will grow in the later years. Voice is the primary use of the network, while additional services include voice mail and SMS. Data is segmented into four bands—64, 144, 384, and 2,048 Kbps. One possibility to encourage the uptake of data is to offer aggressive pricing on the lower-bit-rate services.

When you take into account a typical service mix, the total monthly bill could be on the order of €50 per month for residential subscribers, €100 per month for mobile workers, and €150 or more per month for regular business users. To determine the ultimate profitability of the service, these revenues are then balanced against the initial network license cost, the capital expense for the service deployment, ongoing operational expenses including transmission, and SG&A (which includes any handset subsidies and promotions). The cost of the initial license cannot be understated, running in the billions of dollars in some European countries. The cost of the build-out is also a major element, running over €1 billion during the 10-year network license. Based on the expected subscriber penetration and revenue per subscriber, the provider expects the service both to be profitable and to generate a positive cash flow during the license period.

The technical advances of 3G applications will enable radically different services beyond GPRS. They will provide additional capacity that will enable faster and more efficient transmission of bandwidth-intensive applications such as graphics and video content. In addition to conventional voice, fax, and data services, 3G also enables fast transmission and high-resolution video and multimedia services on the move, such as for mobile office services, videoconferencing, entertainment, shopping, and banking.

3GNet has announced plans for a UMTS offering (3G wireless) by 2003. One can envision that the first phase of a migration path from a GPRS network to a UMTS-enabled network would occur as shown in Figure 8.19.

Although it is too early at this point to identify which wireless data services 3GNet will offer as part of its UMTS rollout, there are some obvious possibilities. Early adopters of wireless data are expected to be business users who have the need to stay in touch when they are away from their office desks. As intranets become the means for communication within a corporation, the need to access them securely from anywhere and at anytime is growing. With the increased data capabilities of UMTS, road warriors are more apt to use wireless data to connect to corporate databases instead of wireline dial-up modems (see chapter 7 description on wireless VPNs). Another application involves the use of the short message service currently offered by many GSM operators. With this service, subscribers can receive the latest information on sports scores, stock quotes, and so forth. With UMTS, these currently text-based services will be offered with increased graphical richness that enhances the user experience.

Other applications involve telemetry or remotely monitored devices such as meters or vending machines, as well as e-business. The subscriber identity module (SIM) is unique to each phone and can be used as an identifier in conjunction with a personal identification code to approve e-transactions. Thus the GPRS and UMTS technologies help solve many of the user security problems associated with Internet commerce. Additionally, being able to access online applications to compare prices and products while shopping will change consumer purchasing habits, since comparing a product while in a store with the same product available via an Internet store will enable the consumer to have greater bargaining power. This will be easy

3G Mobile Wireless Services

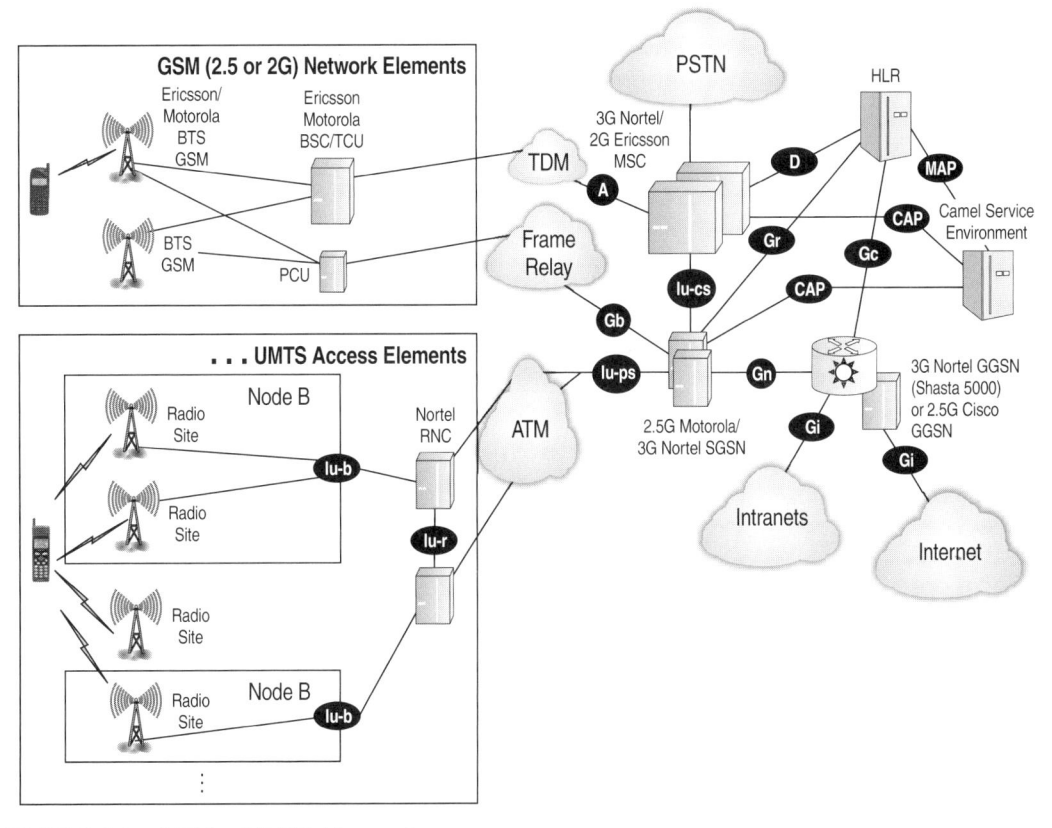

FIGURE 8.19 3GNet UMTS Network

through the enhanced graphics that are achieved with a UMTS network. Also, location-based services will likely be offered. By understanding where the subscriber is, information can be customized by location and sent to each individual subscriber. Other possible services that 3GNet may offer include customized vertical applications for medical or emergency services. Figure 8.20 shows some of these potential services.

In addition to the enabling capabilities of UMTS technology are the value-added capabilities of the GGSN in the network. In wireless networks, with the introduction of packet data in addition to voice, two domains exist. The circuit network services the *voice domain,* and the packet network services the *data domain.* With next-generation "always-on" mobile devices, packet sessions from a mobile terminal all terminate at a GGSN before accessing the Internet or intranet, and all incoming sessions from the Internet pass through the GGSN.

FIGURE 8.20 Potential 3G Services

The GGSN is at the packet edge in mobile networks and is a key area for subscriber services, including content, VPNs, and firewalls. In the 3GNet solution, the Nortel Networks/Shasta 5000 BSN is used as the GGSN. Some of the services enabled with the Shasta 5000 BSN are IP-VPNs and a firewall offered on a per-subscriber basis for the "always-on" UMTS user. With the Shasta 5000 BSN, templates are used to add subscribers to the network core quickly and easily. The templates can define the users by market segment, such as corporate users, SOHO, remote office/branch office (ROBO), commuters, and residential users. For example, a small business may take advantage of a silver pack (see Figure 8.21) offering access, IP-VPNs, sophisticated traffic management, and firewalling, while a SOHO pack may offer only firewalling and IP-VPNs. A breakdown of these types of profiles is shown in Figure 8.21. One requirement is that the GGSN must effectively interoperate with 3G subscriber provisioning. This requires interoperability with some of the 3G control protocols as well as support for a large number of tunnels via the GPRS Tunneling Protocol (GTP).

Although a great degree of skill is required to design the templates and understand 3GNet's market segments, once the marketing and network operations staff have defined these templates, subscribers can potentially sign up for services by themselves using a self-service portal. With self-provisioning, operational costs are reduced and faster and customized access to the network is made available for subscribers. A sample exchange involving subscriber self-provisioning is shown in Figure 8.22. Here, the network directs a new subscriber (who has been provided with basic network access) to a provisioning portal where he or she may sign up for the type of service required and any additional capabilities, such as IP-VPNs. Once provisioned, the subscriber's traffic bypasses this portal unless the subscriber wishes

FIGURE 8.21 Service Profiles

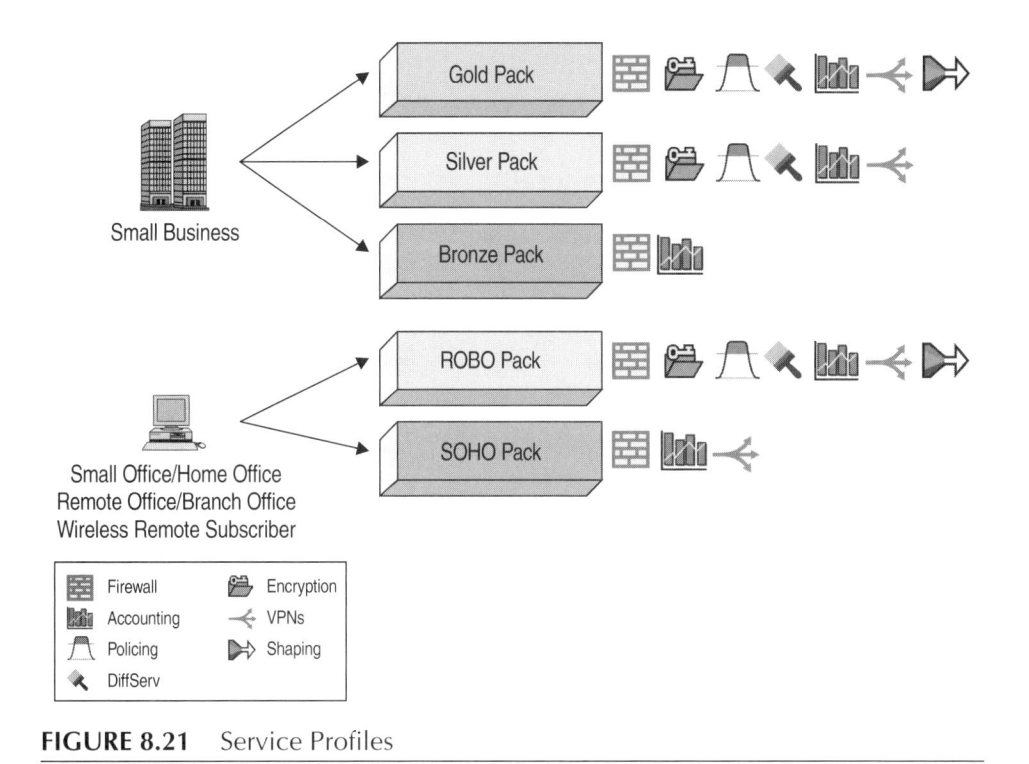

to change his or her service profile. Note that this provisioning paradigm is no different from what is becoming commonplace for Internet dial and DSL.

Further in the future, an end-to-end packet architecture for both voice and data will eventually replace the separate circuit-switched voice and packet data architectures deployed within GSM and GPRS. The UMTS architecture shown in Figure 8.23 will be fairly typical in the years 2003 onward.

Within this architecture, 3GNet can extend its services to offer ISP wholesale services. In this scenario, the Shasta 5000 will act as a bridge between the GGSN and the different ISPs, which will use the mobile operator as another access network to their service portfolios. The Shasta 5000 will use the subscriber information to steer the traffic to the preferred ISP. Even when end users are roaming on other mobile networks, GPRS and UMTS standards will ensure that they are forwarded to their home GGSN and hence the correct Shasta 5000 (as described in chapter 7). Figure 8.24 shows a typical wholesale scenario where subscribers will have access to different ISPs and ASPs. Once again, this is no different from what exists within DSL and cable.

Advantages

3GNet's plans for rolling out GPRS and UMTS will allow it to participate in the many future applications that will unfold with the evolution of wireless data.

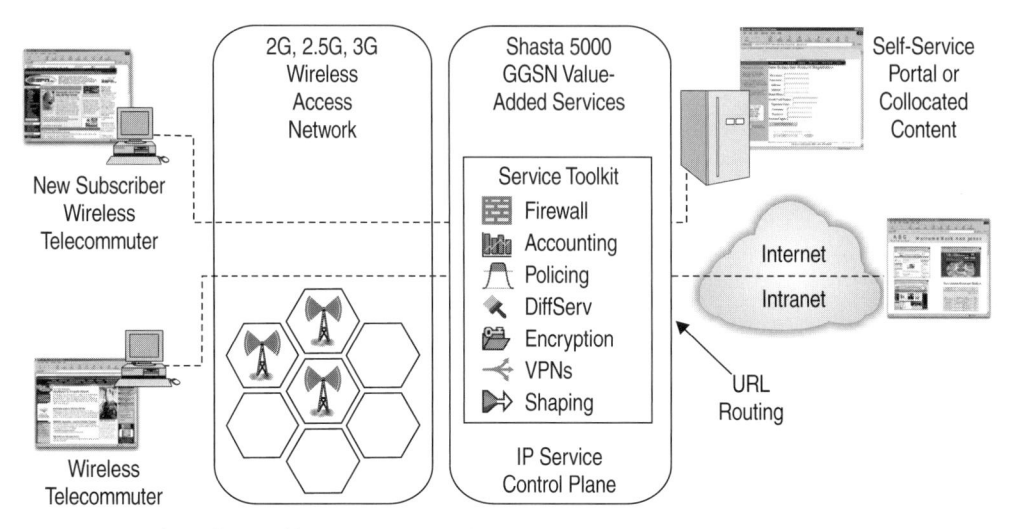

FIGURE 8.22 Subscriber Self-Provisioning

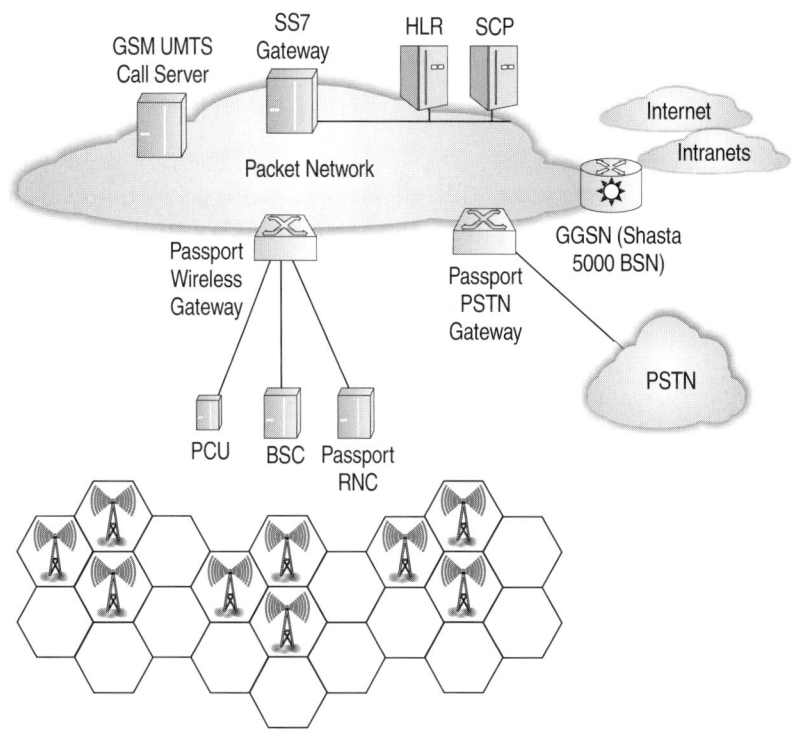

FIGURE 8.23 Future UMTS Network Architecture

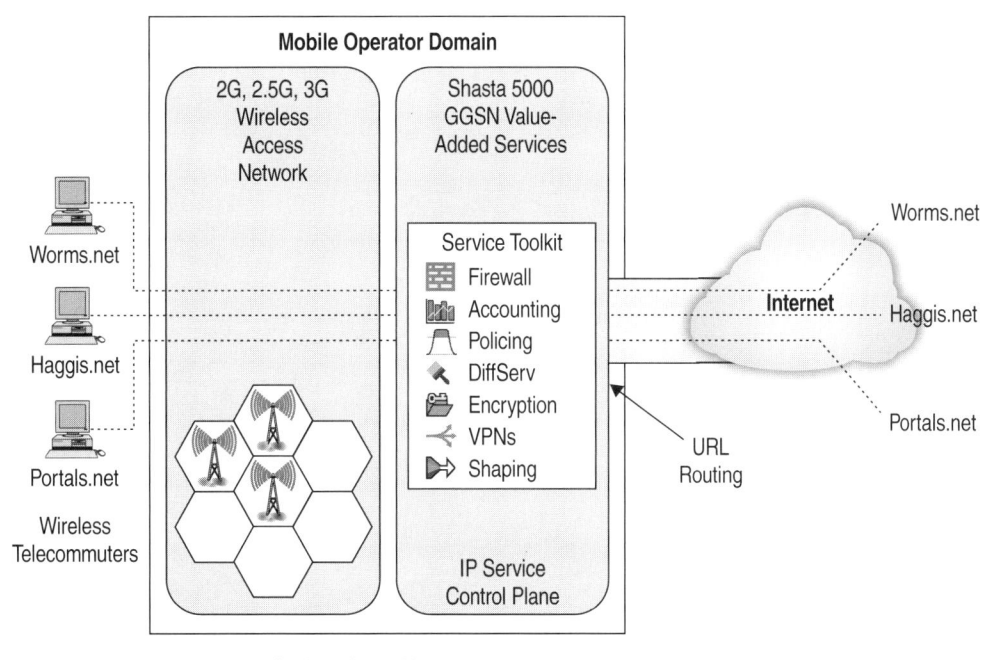

FIGURE 8.24 3GNet ISP Wholesale Offerings

However, by introducing service-enabling platforms, such as the Shasta 5000 BSN as the GGSN, 3GNet now can offer many IP services, such as VPNs and firewalls, and can obtain service revenues immediately rather than depending solely on the future wireless data applications. With an understanding of the subscriber and application of the subscriber profile, wireless data applications can be customized to the users' needs and can be priced according to what they are willing to pay.

IP-VPNs and Firewalls

Moving up the value chain from basic DSL, cable, and wireless access, service providers are seeking to offer more sophisticated in-the-cloud services. These advanced services, detailed in chapter 7, include IP-VPNs and firewalls. Toward the end of 2000 and into 2001, providers first rolled out these sevices based on IPSSs.

Background

SAVVIS Communications is a global internetworking services provider that supports Internet and managed IP e-business solutions in 43 countries. It focuses on providing services to financial institutions and corporate customers that demand superior QoS for real-time transactions. Via SAVVIS's ATM/IP backbone, customers

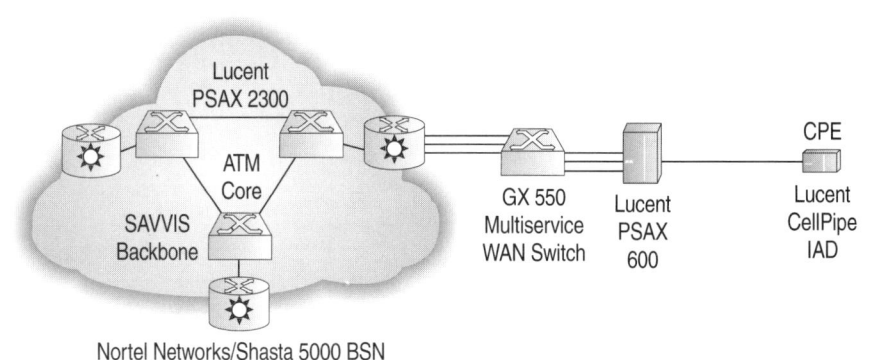

FIGURE 8.25 SAVVIS Network Architecture

can choose end-to-end QoS levels for each discrete application as well as bundled pricing on a per-site basis. SAVVIS offers Internet access from DSL up to OC-3, as well as security solutions, IP-VPNs, and managed IP solutions. The SAVVIS network consists of Lucent ATM switches and Cisco and Nortel routers (see Figure 8.25).

SAVVIS has built out a private network that offers customers the reliability and services that can be guaranteed only via a controlled environment, as opposed to potentially congested public Internet exchange points. It offers both CPE-based and network-based IP-VPNs. The Financial Xchange™ IP-VPN network consists of a combination of ATM switches and Nortel BSNs. The BSNs are located at the edge of their network and focus on transforming Frame Relay VPNs into reliable IP-VPNs that traverse SAVVIS's ATM infrastructure to maintain reliable bandwidth for its customers and its customers' applications. Corporate customers can connect their branch offices to headquarters sites easily and can additionally provide Internet access off the same connection. Customers now need only one connection or PVC from the service provider to each site to hook all the branch sites together. In addition, Internet access is offered off the same PVC. The IP-VPN architecture built on a private network, as opposed to the public Internet, is the key differentiator in enabling SAVVIS to offer guaranteed SLAs.

Services Description

SAVVIS is focusing on offering a new level of service with its managed IP network, which leverages its ATM backbone and the virtual router capabilities of the Shasta 5000 BSN. SAVVIS brings the network core to the customer's premises by deploying an integrated access device (IAD) that provides ATM class of service (CoS) and ATM QoS from the customer's premises to the backbone switching equipment. SAVVIS also has an extensive integrated provisioning system, referred to as the network creation system (NCS), which joins the hardware infrastructure configura-

IP-VPNs and Firewalls

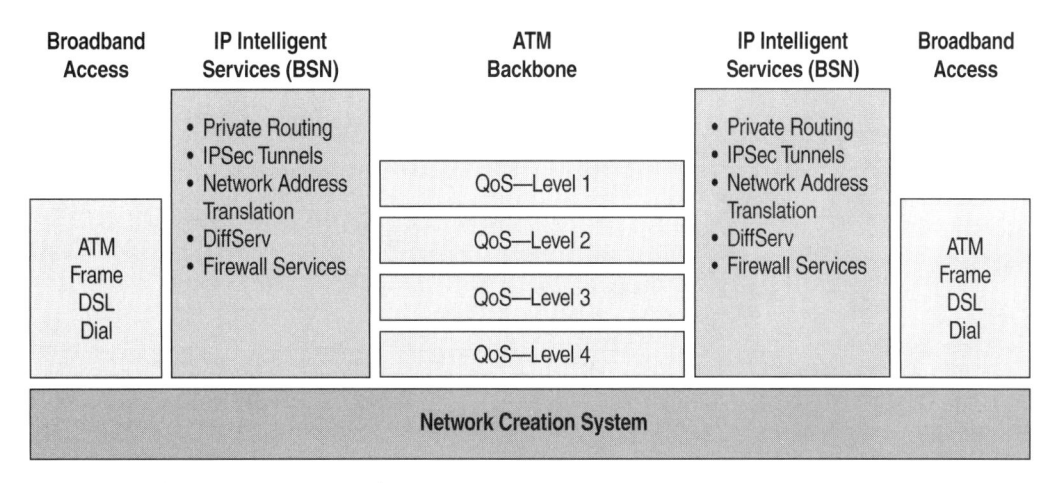

Broadband Access	IP Intelligent Services (BSN)	ATM Backbone	IP Intelligent Services (BSN)	Broadband Access
ATM Frame DSL Dial	• Private Routing • IPSec Tunnels • Network Address Translation • DiffServ • Firewall Services	QoS—Level 1 QoS—Level 2 QoS—Level 3 QoS—Level 4	• Private Routing • IPSec Tunnels • Network Address Translation • DiffServ • Firewall Services	ATM Frame DSL Dial
		Network Creation System		

FIGURE 8.26 SAVVIS Service Architecture

tion with the operation support systems (OSSs). Using the NCS, SAVVIS customers can self-provision many of the features and services that SAVVIS is offering.

The core network and IPSS are "access independent," allowing customers to choose the access method that best meets their requirements. SAVVIS can define and enforce Layer 3 application-aware private networking features, including QoS, auditing, policing, shaping, firewalls, antispoofing, and differentiated services (DiffServ). Figure 8.26 shows the SAVVIS service network architecture.

Customer traffic enters the network with an ATM QoS applied at the Lucent IAD on the customer's premises. At the IPSS (see Figure 8.27), the data first passes through an ingress antispoofing policy that discards any traffic (based on its source address) from the customer with an IP address different from the known address or addresses on the IPSS port assigned to the customer. Antispoofing prevents masquerade attacks from hackers. The traffic then passes into the traffic management elements. The first traffic management function marks different types of traffic via DiffServ markings. These DiffServ markings map to certain Layer 2 QoS on the SAVVIS network. Once the DiffServ marking is set, routers within the network core will use this information to queue and/or discard the traffic in a set priority.

The policing function then presents traffic to the network core so as to conform to the customer's requested rate defined at Layer 2. The traffic then enters a VPN-steering function. This directs the data either to a VPN community or to SAVVIS's Internet. It is in the VPN-steering function that the firewall policies are applied. The IPSS has a robust stateful inspection firewall that applies rules based on source and/or destination, service type (HTTP, HTTPS, SMTP, and so forth), and action (drop, reject, accept). Finally, based on the earlier DiffServ marking, SAVVIS assigns each assured forwarding (AF) class to a different PVC within the trunk

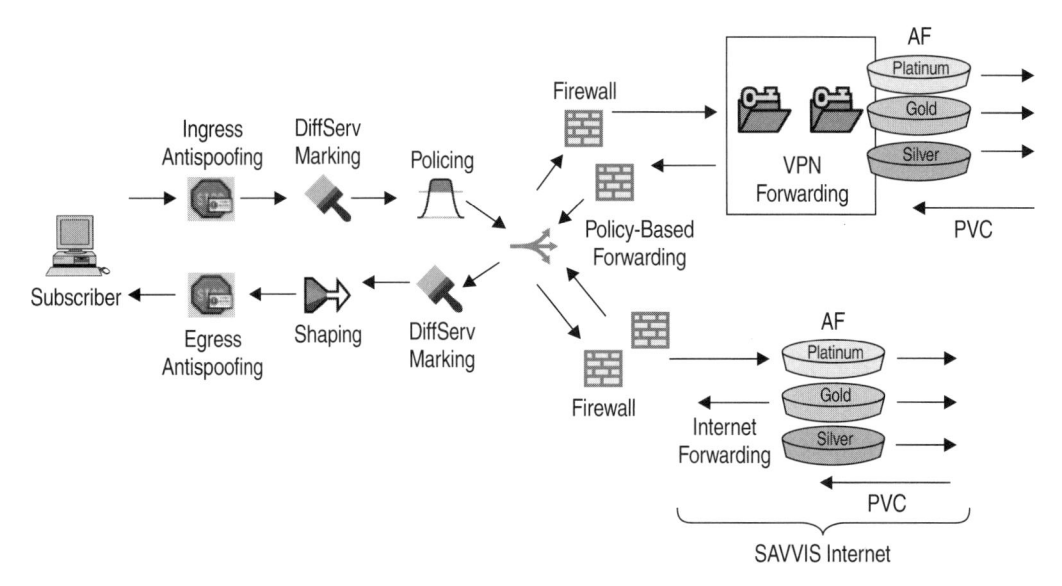

FIGURE 8.27 SAVVIS Service Application

group or assigns application-aware QoS values within an AF class. This separates the different traffic types across the backbone and provides QoS enforcement in support of SLAs.

In the opposite direction, traffic entering the IPSS from the network core may or may not have been subject to DiffServ marking, based on the customer's requirements or the origin of the packet (such as off-net Internet). In any case, the traffic passes through the filter rules of the firewall. By placing the firewall in the network, traffic sent to the customer's premises has already been filtered—eliminating the need for the customer to deploy costly premises-based firewalls at every location. The in-network firewall also reduces the amount of wasted bandwidth, which may have been taken up by data that would be restricted/dropped at the customer's premises. The data then enters the traffic-shaping function, also responsible for protecting bandwidth of the customer's access link so that mission-critical applications may receive higher prioritization over delay-tolerant applications. Here, weight and bandwidth limits are assigned based on source, destination, and traffic type.

Finally, the data passes through an egress antispoofing policy that discards any traffic with a source address equal to the customer's own network, which implies that an external entity is attempting to masquerade as the customer.

With its IP-VPN offerings, SAVVIS aims to define various communities of interest networks (COINs), with each COIN segmented into controllable levels of quality. The first COIN is focused on business Internet customers. The deployment scenario is shown in Figure 8.28. This environment provides traditional Internet

IP-VPNs and Firewalls

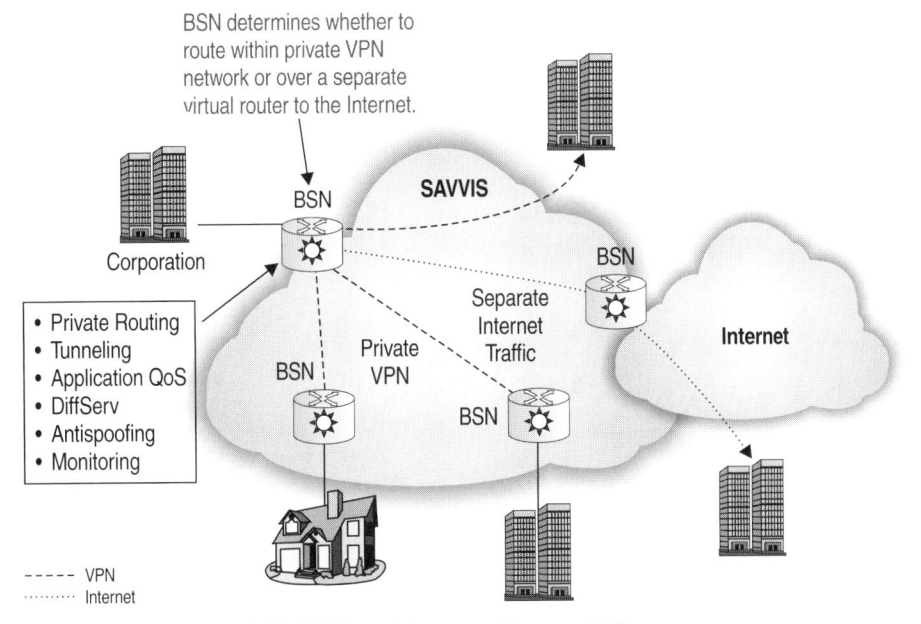

FIGURE 8.28 SAVVIS IP-VPN and Internet Connectivity

access and allows for defined IP addresses to be segmented off to their own VPN environment. Users who are part of the customer's defined VPN list are protected from Internet users at large. SAVVIS also offers firewall functionality when the user leaves the VPN community to provide added security. Other features that may be set include private routing (the VPN locations), tunneling (e.g., IPSec connections to off-net locations), application QoS (policing and shaping), DiffServ, antispoofing, and monitoring (IP accounting of certain events).

The second COIN, shown in Figure 8.29, is what SAVVIS refers to as a shared "IP Xchange" environment where multiple application/service providers in the same vertical market want to reach multiple clients/recipients in the same, or similar, vertical market. Since this is an "extranet" of multiple providers and multiple recipients, it is critical to provide many of the same features as in the VPN-plus-Internet environment described earlier. In this environment, network address translation (NAT) is also added because of the use of private IP addresses for the private data networks. SAVVIS provides either legal IP addresses for the networks or NAT on the addresses the customers currently may be using.

The third community of interest is a *private IP Xchange* environment, where a single application/service provider within a specific vertical market wants to reach multiple clients in the same, or similar, vertical market. The key difference between IP Xchange and private IP Xchange is the application provider's requirement to

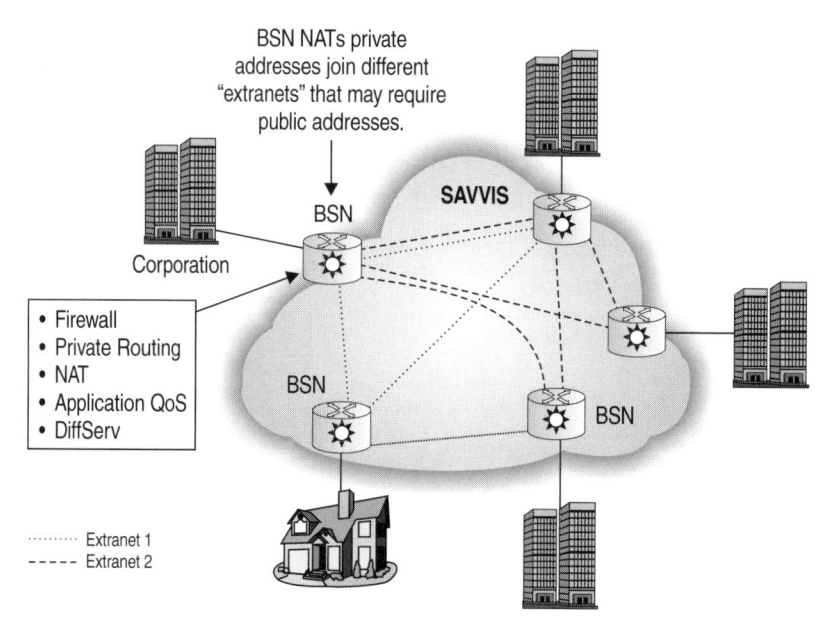

FIGURE 8.29 SAVVIS IP Xchange

have the exclusive use of the network service level (e.g., a dedicated PVC) for its application(s). Also, with private Xchange, the service provider may choose from any of the four ATM levels of services (see Table 8.2). In the IP Xchange, SAVVIS has predefined the quality level and the IPSS rules. Private Xchange provides a more flexible environment for services providers. Since this is also an "extranet" of multiple recipients, SAVVIS provides many of the features in VPN plus Internet.

The other IP-VPN service is a private network, shown in Figure 8.30, traditionally described as an intranet. SAVVIS enhances this by enabling the buildout of a VPN within the intranet. Most intranets require very expensive, fully meshed, point-to-point networks to be deployed. SAVVIS offers a fully meshed intranet, in which the individual sites need only connect to the VPN community. The value-added feature of the service is the security that previously required customers to deploy expensive VPN and firewall devices at each location.

Subscriber configuration and VPN provisioning are under the control of the Nortel/Shasta Service Creation System (SCS) discussed earlier. VPN provisioning is simplified using the SCS-as-VPN membership, and tunnels are automatically created since the SCS has a network map.

A service policy that may be applied to a VPN-plus-Internet user is shown in Figure 8.31. This policy allows the customer to reach an Internet site. Additionally, it allows access from the Internet to a mail server, a Web server (using HTTP and HTTPs), a DNS server, and a customer-defined server. This policy allows reachability of all VPN members.

IP-VPNs and Firewalls

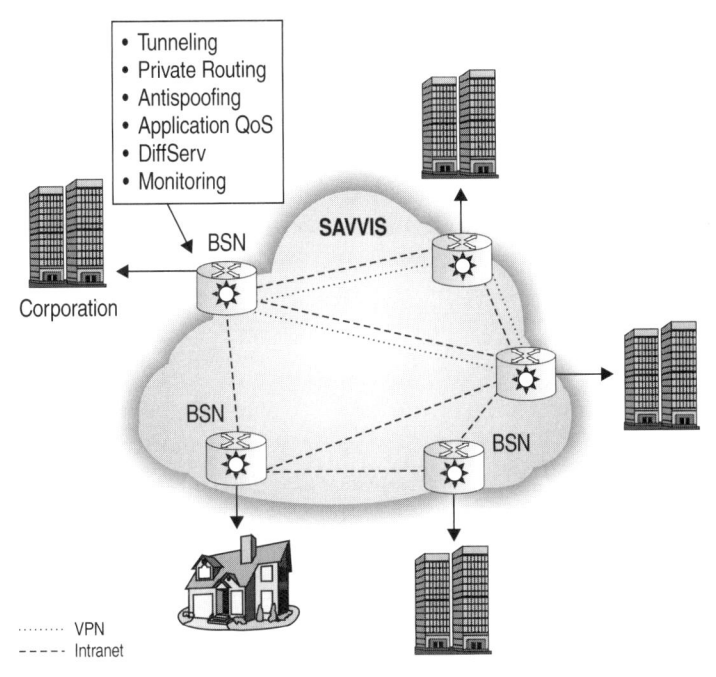

FIGURE 8.30 SAVVIS Private Network Offering

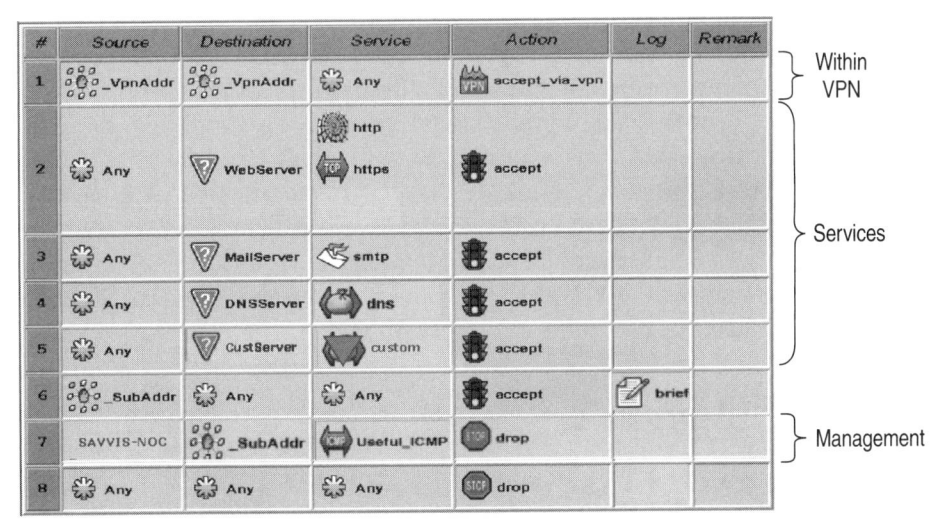

FIGURE 8.31 SAVVIS IP-VPN Host Policy

Source: Information and screenshots in Figures 8.25 through 8.31 used with permission.

TABLE 8.2 SAVVIS SLAs

ATM Service Level	DiffServ Default Setting	Application	Availability	Latency	Packet Loss
1 (VBR-nrt-1)	AF4 DP1	Real-time market data	100%	50 ms	< 0.1%
2 (VBR-nrt-2)	AF3 DP1	Real-time video or voice	100%	60 ms	< 0.25%
3 (VBR-nrt-3)	AF2 DP1	File transfer, transaction processing	100%	70 ms	< 0.5%
4 (UBR)	AF1 DP1	E-mail, Internet access	100%	75 ms	< 1%

Traffic that is on the VPN traverses PVCs based on the QoS purchased. Internet traffic is segmented off and traverses another set of PVCs. This enables SAVVIS to offer the extensive SLAs. Table 8.2 lists some of the available SLAs for the SAVVIS network.

Advantages

The advantage of the IP-VPN service that SAVVIS offers is the simplification of traditional Frame Relay service while adhering to the service guarantees that subscribers are accustomed to with Frame Relay. This is mainly due to the ATM backbone of SAVVIS and the segregation of VPN traffic onto PVCs separate from Internet traffic. Using an IPSS enables SAVVIS to further differentiate its various IP-VPN offerings and allows it to simplify customer connectivity to either a VPN or the Internet via the embedded firewall software in the IPSS. Enterprise customers benefit by having a single connection to carry their traffic to the Internet or to other VPN members. Additionally, with the Nortel Networks/Shasta 5000 BSN, VPN provisioning and membership are greatly simplified, as the IPSS automatically creates the tunnels to other IPSSs as long as there are VPN members provisioned. This eliminates tedious site-to-site provisioning or manual IPSec tunnel setup. Additionally, SAVVIS can create different pricing levels based on the types of services administered via the VPN. By enabling additional services to the enterprise customer, SAVVIS is able to maintain a continuous revenue stream from customers wanting to outsource their networks.

Broadcast Video Distribution

Service providers are looking for additional ways to leverage their broadband service infrastructure beyond the advanced services described earlier in the book. This is especially true for the incumbent operators offering DSL, who wish to compete with the cable providers by offering a complete range of data and entertainment services. The use of the DSL infrastructure for video is by no means a new idea. In fact, video distribution was the original intent of DSL technology when it was first proposed almost ten years ago. The technology now exists, both at the subscriber site and within the network infrastructure, to make this a viable business proposition. However, the bandwidth and QoS requirements, as well as the provisioning infrastructure required for subscriber channel selection, do introduce challenges.

Background

Aliant Telecom is the incumbent telephony provider in the Canadian Maritime Provinces. The company was formed in 1999 by combining NB Tel (New Brunswick), MT&T (Nova Scotia), NewTel (Newfoundland), and Island Telecom (Prince Edward Island). It currently offers a DSL high-speed data service and wishes to better compete with the cable providers by offering broadcast video services across the same DSL access. Its strategy is to offer a bundle of three services—high-speed data, PC-based video (PC-TV), and broadcast-quality video delivered via a settop box (IP-TV) to the TV and DSL modem and then to the PC. Its partner for video services is iMagic, a company also based in New Brunswick. Early on, Aliant recognized the synergy that could be gained by combining high-speed Internet access with broadcast and unicast video services. For example, one could access the local weather map and then immediately segue to the actual broadcast for additional information (see Figure 8.32). Although many refer to this capability as interactive TV, it is actually much more than that; this service provides a complete linkage between the Internet and the broadcast world via a single DSL access to the home.

Content sources include commercial specialty networks, local affiliates, national broadcasters, stock footage, and free Web content. Support systems include caching, content management, merchant relationships, reporting, targeting, billing, and the consumer database. These all form the backend requirements for the actual subscriber applications—the TV interface, the personalized portal, and any commerce and communications components.

FIGURE 8.32 Aliant Video and Web Convergence

Services Description

Subscribers receive both high-speed Internet access, marketed as Vibe, and broadcast video, called VibeVision, via a single ADSL connection. Depending on the service mix, the subscriber must reside within a certain distance of the CO because of the bandwidth versus distance limitations of DSL. For example, the complete service requires about 6 Mbps of bandwidth—4 Mbps for MPEG2 (for ITV), 1.5 Mbps for MPEG1 (for TV on the PC), and some additional bandwidth for the high-speed Internet access. In contrast, an MPEG1-plus-data service requires under 2 Mbps because of different encoding, greatly expanding the possible subscriber base. Given the deployment of DLC-based DSLAMs in the future, Aliant could therefore greatly expand the footprint of the MPEG2 service. This upgrade is being planned. (As an aside, SBC's Project Pronto in the United States is a fiber buildout of the DLCs and remote deployment of DSLAMs. This project is expected to provide over 50 percent of homes in the Pronto-equipped service area with 6-Mbps-capable service. Thus, high-speed DSL in the future will not be a niche market.)

The Aliant network, shown in Figure 8.33, currently consists of the following:

- Alcatel 350 DSLAMs and Pace CPE connected to a regional ATM network based on the Alcatel 36170.
- A control center in Saint John, where satellite systems feed the incoming video signals into a bank of more than 100 PixStream VDS 5000 MPEG2 encoders. A smaller percentage (on the order of 15 channels) is also fed into MPEG1 encoders. The encoders deliver their output, MPEG2 within IP, into a Cisco 7500. The router then forwards them across individual ATM PVCs to the Alcatel (Newbridge) DSLAMs.
- These DSLAMs perform ATM point-to-multipoint (pt-to-mpt) replication—in effect, Layer 2 multicasting.
- When a given subscriber wants to receive a particular video signal, his or her settop box signals its intent to join the associated IP Multicast (IPmc) group. This is accomplished via an Internet Group Management Protocol (IGMP) join request to the DSLAM, which then grafts the subscriber onto the appropriate pt-mpt virtual circuit connection (VCC) serving the multicast group. Thus the settop box directly controls the ATM provisioning within the DSLAM.

This is an effective scalable architecture, with the video transported over ATM and the service managed through IP capability. This architecture is currently deployed with 55,000 homes passed by the service and 2,100 customers.

Although this is an effective first-generation architecture, since the video stream is IP-based, handling all replication at the IP layer using IP multicasting is more efficient and scalable. Another architecture supporting this IP-based replication is currently under evaluation (see Figure 8.34) and is based on Shasta 5000

Broadcast Video Distribution 313

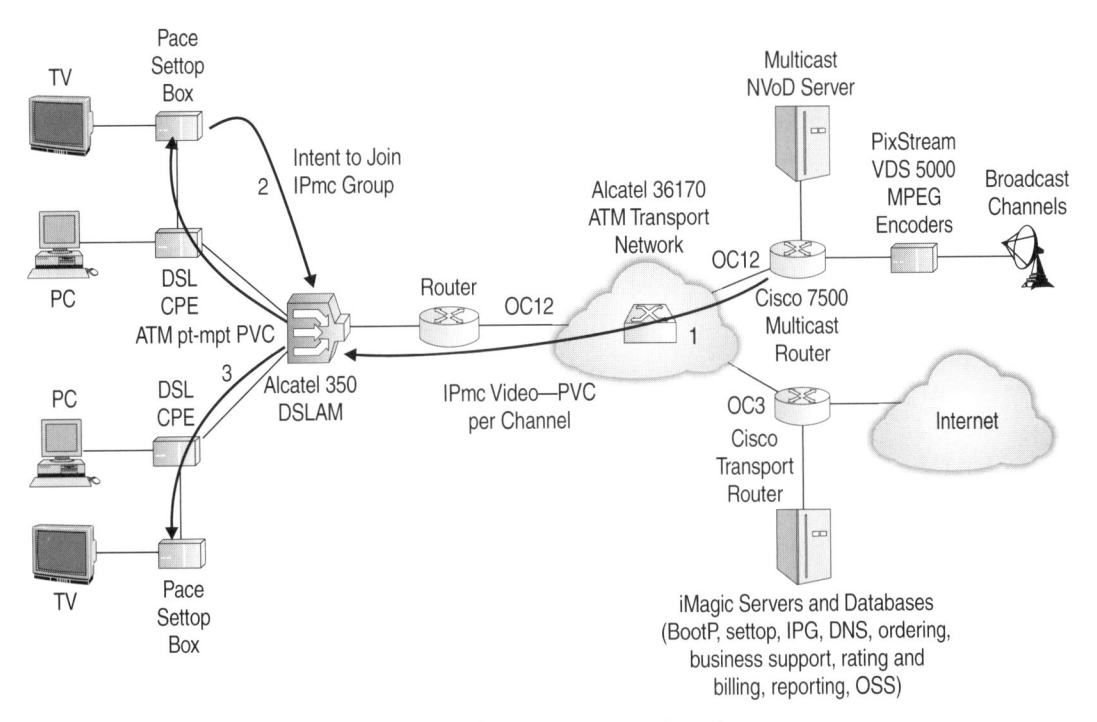

FIGURE 8.33 Aliant Video over DSL Architecture: ATM-Centric

BSNs providing the IPmc replication. At each CO, Aliant locates an IPSS with one or more DSLAMs, depending on subscriber density.

The key to the VibeVision service offering is a video distribution architecture developed by iMagic. This infrastructure enables Aliant, through software, to deliver IP-based broadcast content and, when combined with other sources of IP content including Web, telephony, and streaming media, creates a compelling convergent experience for the customer. As introduced earlier, the network consists of codecs, routers, DSLAMs, and settop boxes. This section describes this architecture in additional detail.

The centerpiece of the subscriber experience, for the iMagic software, is an electronic program guide (see Figure 8.35) that lists programs and permits the user to create customized program groups. In the future, the system will support network-based VCR functionality, much like TiVo, but not requiring a dedicated appliance. A business support system includes customer provisioning, channel packaging, headend content management, and status reporting. The iMagic system also provides the necessary interfaces to a provider's rating and billing systems, reporting systems, and OSSs.

Via the program guide, the subscriber decides what channel to view. Selecting a given channel causes the settop box to add the subscriber to the IPmc group

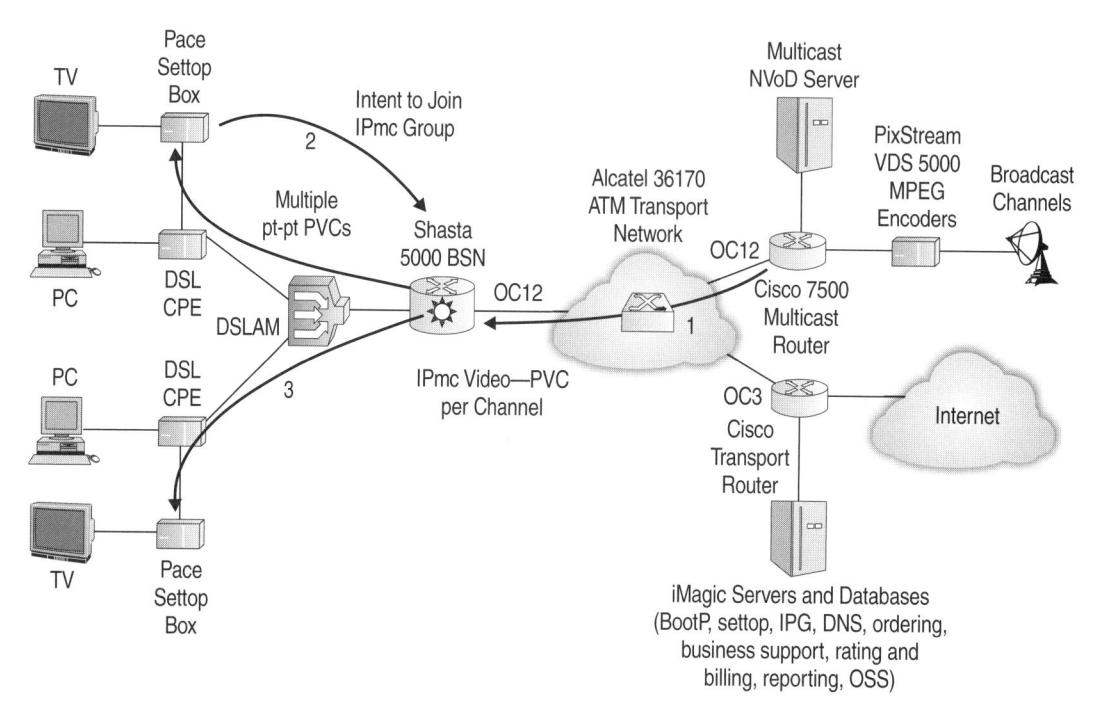

FIGURE 8.34 Aliant Video over DSL Architecture: IP-Centric

FIGURE 8.35 Aliant iMagic Program Guide

serving the specific channel. The request arrives at the IPSS, which performs the actual addition. This video traffic now traverses the subscriber's PVC from the IPSS through the DSLAM and to the settop box. Note that all channels are delivered in parallel with the IPSS—the only dynamic selection is the decision as to which subscribers will receive a given channel.

Service tariffs are designed to encourage up-sell, in terms of both additional channel packages and additional voice services. The basic VibeVision channel package without high-speed Internet access is $19.95 per month and includes a palette of the most-watched channels (see Figure 8.36).

Broadcast Video Distribution 315

FIGURE 8.36 Aliant Basic Programming

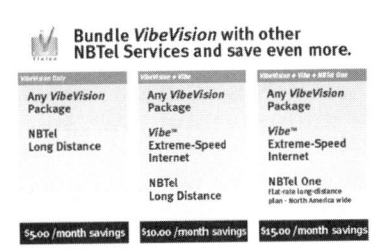

FIGURE 8.37 Service Bundles

Separate from this is the Vibe high-speed Internet offering at $39.95 per month (plus $101 for installation). If a subscriber uses both services, the total is about $50 per month, resulting in a $10 per month discount (see Figure 8.37).

Additional discounts take effect if the subscriber also signs up for long-distance service. The VibeVision service includes various bundles of channel packages and movies, ranging anywhere from the $39.95 just mentioned to $59.95 for eight program bundles and all movies. Aliant has stated that the majority of the subscribers do sign up for these additional packages. This bundling has the added advantage of providing the subscriber with a single bill. Although some would state that "sticker shock" results from video, Internet, and voice services all appearing on a single statement, experience proves that the convenience to the subscriber outweighs this possible problem.

Another element of the service offering is a broadband portal, which provides access to the different content sources (see Figure 8.38). This is different from the iMagic front end for video programming. One differentiator is its use of XML for content description, as opposed to the more common use of HTML or DHTML. XML encodes characteristics of the object, in effect adding intelligence to the displayed data. For example, customers will view content optimized for the TV or PC. The portal also recognizes different settop vintages and will optimize the consumer experience accordingly. The portal also adjusts for appliance context, such as navigation, fonts, and media types presented.

When service providers consider offering a video service, one common concern is how pricing for equivalent bandwidth relates to traditional data services. For example, the MPEG2 broadcast described earlier requires 4 Mbps on average. However, the total monthly price to the subscriber starts at $19.95 per month. This is clearly a different pricing model from what would exist for 3.5 Mbps of

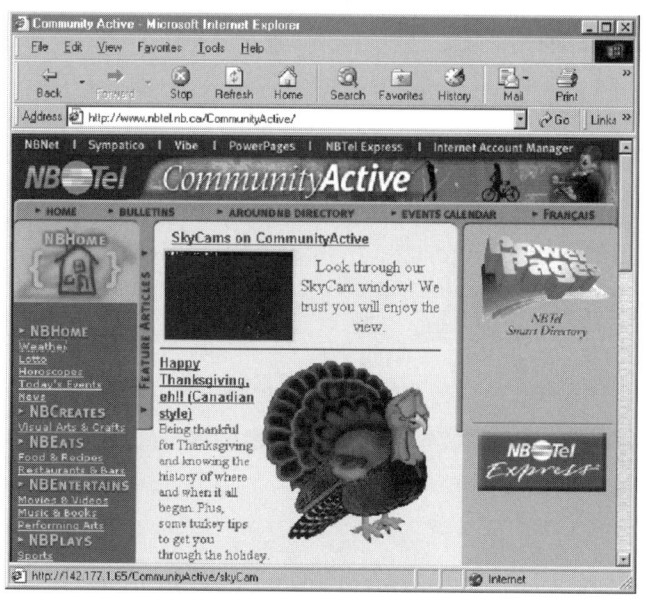

FIGURE 8.38 Aliant Portal

Source: Figures 8.32 through 8.38 used with permission of Aliant.

data. The service provider must understand that video and data are two totally separate services, each subject to its own price sensitivities. This awareness is critical since a video service will also require additional bandwidth delivered to the DSLAM in the CO. If the provider uses data pricing as a metric, the potential revenue from the DS3, OC3, or even OC12 dedicated to the video service is not justified. However, if considered strictly as a video service, and compared to the opportunity cost of not competing with the cable provider, then the video bandwidth is clearly justified.

Note that the Aliant offering is only one solution to solving the video over DSL problem. Other more ATM-centric solutions exist, whereby a settop box may signal a unicast SVC to the content server. Depending on the bandwidth requirements of this video SVC and whether additional services are required, the video stream may bypass the IPSS and terminate directly on an ATM-connected media server. However, this architecture limits the provider to an ATM-centric approach, and although the vast majority of DSLAMs are ATM-connected at present, this may not be the case in the future. In addition, other technologies, such as Ethernet extension, do not rely on ATM as a transport. Any video solution deployed should be compatible with all planned physical access technologies if the provider hopes to reach the greatest potential subscriber base.

Advantages

This combined DSL video and high-speed data service permits Aliant Telecom to better utilize its investment in a DSL infrastructure and play a greater role in subscriber services beyond providing basic connectivity. It also allows Aliant to better compete against the local cable operator, which is also offering high-speed Internet access in addition to broadcast video. Although the service is based on a more complex architecture than basic Internet services, subscribers find the service quite appealing in terms of usability and cost.

Internet Data Center

Earlier, we addressed Internet security and the threats facing Web sites from DoS attacks. This is a very real concern for data center operators, and they are actively looking for ways to provide security against such attacks while not sacrificing performance. Any firewall solution must also retain compatibility with installed server load-balancing solutions, as these are critical in maintaining Web site performance. Content providers are concerned not only about protecting the content servers but also about the content distribution mechanisms to various caches located in multiple remote locations. This example describes one solution and may form the basis of a service differentiating a given provider from its competition.

Background

Solstice, an Internet data center (IDC) operator, offers a service protecting its Web site clients from external attacks. It accomplishes this by deploying firewalling capability in conjunction with existing server load balancers (SLBs), or *Web switches,* as they are more commonly called (see Figure 8.39). Web switches distribute incoming client (Internet) traffic among multiple servers belonging to a single customer. This helps optimize server performance while improving response time for the Internet user. For larger customers, these switches may distribute traffic across a large number of servers.

The firewalls deployed in addition to the Web switches have the capability of filtering other types of traffic (other than malicious). For example, the Web site operator could permit traffic only from certain users or even restrict access to users within a given IP-VPN. The Web switch offloads the traffic-filtering responsibility from the firewall to a DMZ LAN. The switch can perform this task with greater efficiency, since it is designed for higher-layer filtering (but not port-following inspection, the firewall's forte). When deploying Web switches in conjunction with firewalls, we introduce the concept of "dirty" and "clean" networks. The dirty network is on the Internet side of the firewall, while the clean network is on the server side. Note that in a basic configuration, the operator could deploy

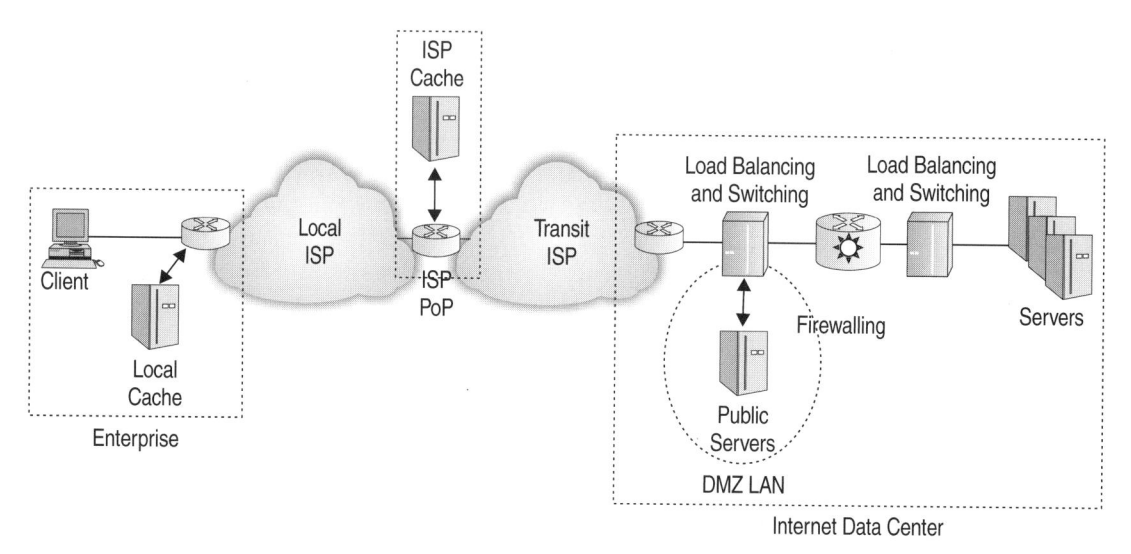

FIGURE 8.39 Content Distribution

a single Web switch and firewall, while deploying two of these switches in parallel results in increased reliability.

Beyond providing a scalable firewall solution to the content origin servers, Solstice is also concerned with ensuring that the original content being placed on the various cache servers traverses securely over the Internet. Traditionally, content providers have a backdoor to populating the origin servers, but distributing and pre-positioning the original content at various caches and mirror sites in the Internet pose a security risk of some malicious hacker altering the content at these sites. Therefore, IDC operators also offer a secure method of content distribution to the various other caches and mirror sites.

Services Description

Solstice deploys a number of devices to meet this service requirement, each of which performs a specific role. Client requests arriving at the data center first pass through dual Juniper M160 routers. The Juniper routers peer the IDC with the Internet via BGP and direct the incoming traffic to two Nortel Passport 8600s operating in parallel. This is accomplished via load balancing within OSPF. The Passports provide intra-IDC routing and also redundancy via the Virtual Router Redundancy Protocol (VRRP) (RFC 2338). VRRP normally implements this redundancy by configuring two or more VRRP routers (those routers participating in VRRP) into a virtual router. Via a selection protocol, one of the VRRP routers is designated as the master and forwards all incoming traffic. If the master fails, one of the backups takes over.

Subscriber traffic enters two Nortel Alteon 184 Web switches. The role of these switches is to balance the incoming traffic across the IP-VPNs on the Shasta 5000 BSN by mapping the traffic into 802.1Q-tags associated with IP addresses used for virtual LANs to identify subscribers. The way the Shasta is architected, it is more efficient for the firewall function to process the traffic in this way, as opposed to having all of the traffic arrive on a single IP address. This permits the Shasta to scale to 1 Gbps or more of firewall processing. Traffic leaving the Shasta on the clean side of the network now enters a second set of Alteon 184s. These switches perform two roles. The first is to map traffic leaving the servers in the direction of the Internet to the 802.1 Q-tags, while the second is to load-balance traffic arriving at the servers. In this direction, traffic now enters paired Passport 8100s performing Layer 2 switching and providing physical fan-out to the actual servers.

The Alteon switches build on VRRP by permitting the designation of dual masters, permitting the Passports to balance the incoming and outgoing traffic across both switches (as opposed to the normal mode of VRRP operation, where one switch would be designated as a standby). The Web switches monitor their ports to the Shastas and are connected via a failover link. Under normal operation, subscriber traffic is load-balanced to the two Shastas across this failover link through the use of Q-tagging. However, if the physical connection to the Shasta fails on either of the Web servers, signifying a device failure, all traffic will pass over the failover link to the Web switch connected to the remaining operational Shasta. This procedure is repeated on the server side of the Shasta. Figure 8.40 depicts this topology, along with the IP addresses in use. Although this implementation requires a diversity of platforms, the net result is a very scalable and redundant solution providing both server balancing and high-speed firewalling. The initial deployment cost, well under $1 million at list pricing, is minimal compared to the multimillion-dollar potential financial damage caused by DoS attacks or site hacking.

Distributing content securely to other mirror sites and caches is done via IP-VPNs that establish IPSec tunnels between the origin server location and the various data centers' servers and caches (see Figure 8.41). This ensures that the origin data center is authenticated and, more important, that the data has not been tampered with as it traverses the dirty network. In this topology, in addition to providing a firewall service for users accessing the origin servers, the Shasta 5000 BSN utilizes its VPRN capability to create an IP-VPN between the origin server location and the various hosting data centers. A different VPRN can be set up for different content being hosted by the IDC, so although websearch.com and webbooks.com may both be hosted by the same data center and need to be distributed to the same set of caches, a different VPRN may be used for each content provider.

The Shasta 5000 BSNs establish the IPSec tunnels from the IDC main hosting location to the other Shasta 5000 BSNs at other data centers. Nortel's Service Creation System maintains the network map of the VPN topology that identifies the location of the various IPSSs. When content providers want to update mirror

FIGURE 8.40 Data Center Firewalling

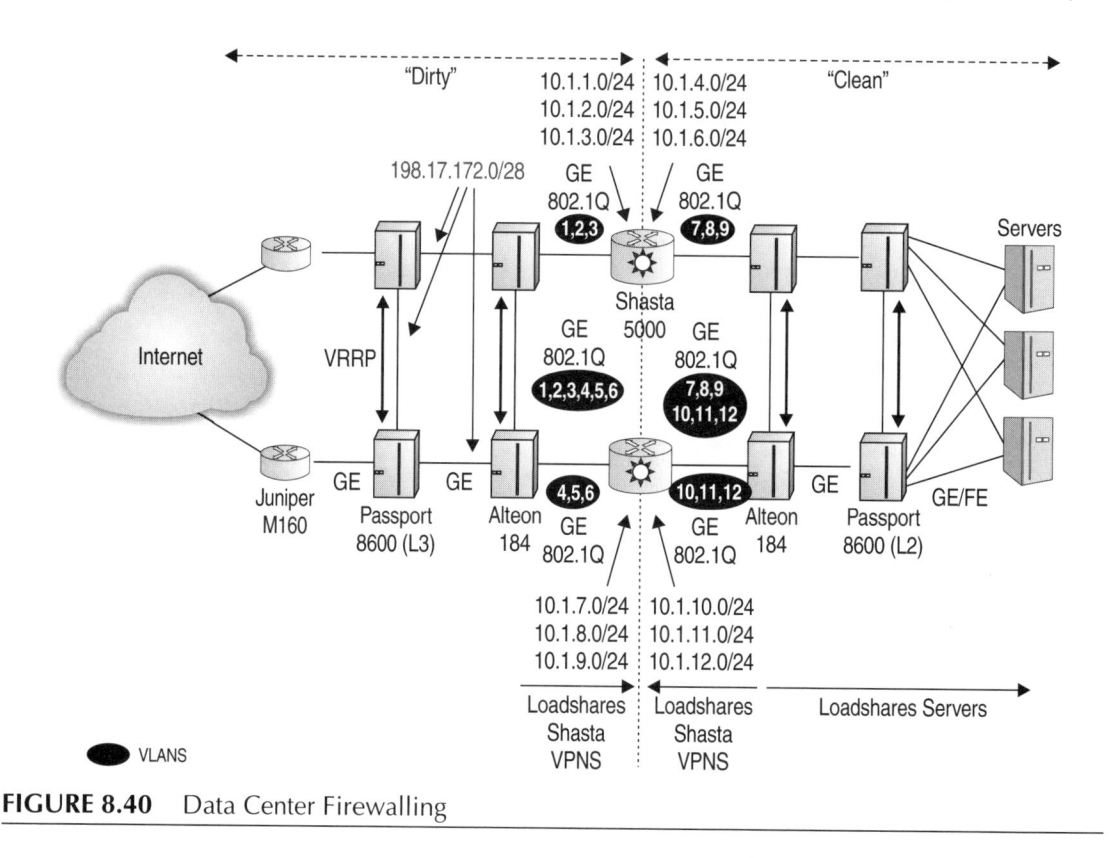

servers or pre-position content on caches, the information passes through the Alteon 184 switch, where the different content providers can be load-balanced via different Q-tags as opposed to arriving as a single IP address. The data, after arriving at the Shasta 5000 BSN, is encapsulated, encrypted, and sent through an IPSec tunnel. The Shasta 5000 BSN enables the operator to specify DES or 3DES encryption as well as a no-encryption option if the data is to traverse a private network. After arriving at the destination site as part of a VPRN, the Shasta at the remote location decrypts the data and enables the caches and mirror servers to be populated. This method ensures that only members of the IP-VPN can adjust the content at the remote data centers, providing a secure method for content distribution.

Advantages

The combined Web site load-balancing and firewall service offers advantages to the Internet subscriber, to Solstice, and to the Web site content owner. For the subscriber, access to Web content is accelerated since incoming requests are now distributed among multiple servers in parallel. This is especially important with Inter-

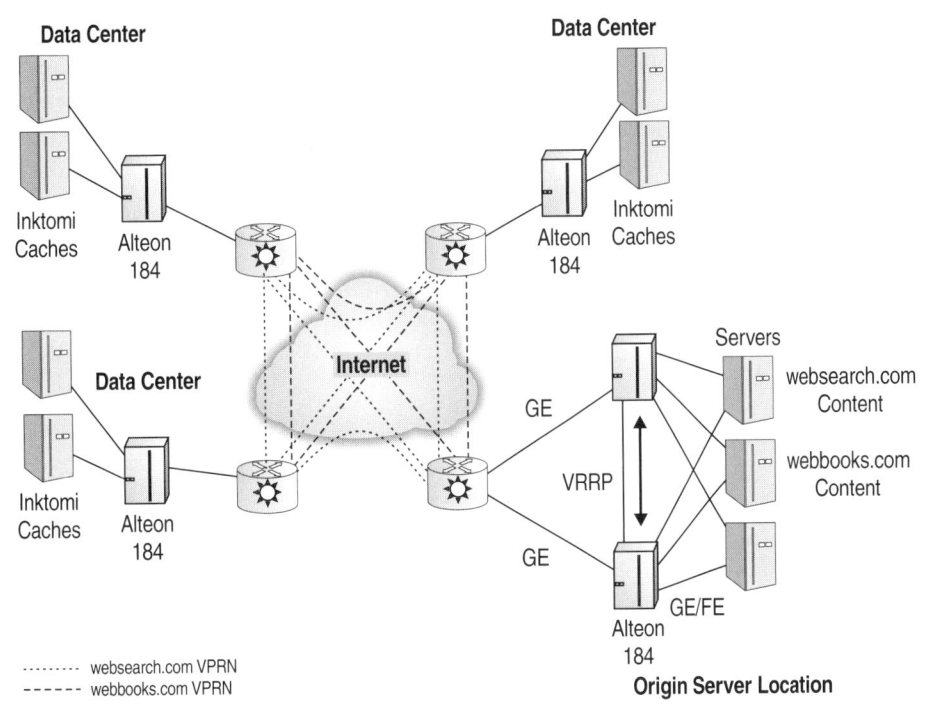

FIGURE 8.41 Secure Content Distribution

net commerce or multimedia. The deployment of a firewall also helps prevent hacker attacks, with a resulting improvement in Web site availability. Next, the data center operator benefits by being able to offer a differentiated service to the Web site content owner. In addition, by being able to prevent denial-of-service attacks, the hosting operator may be less vulnerable to legal action. By ensuring that content is securely distributed to other servers and sites, the hosting operator eliminates the possible embarrassment of some hacker tampering with content at cache sites. Finally, Web site owners benefit by being able to offer better-quality service in terms of response time and availability to the subscriber.

Conclusion

This chapter details the different services available at the network edge, beginning with basic connectivity and then introducing more complex offerings such as IP-VPNs and content distribution. It is important to note that, although some services are mapped to specific access technologies such as DSL or cable, in most cases the actual service is access technology neutral. What is important is an appreciation of the wide mix of revenue-generating services now available at the edge both to the service provider and to the customer or subscriber. It is up to the service provider to take advantage of the various hardware, software, and provisioning technologies necessary to offer these services, and it is up to the subscriber to seek out a provider offering the mix of services best suited to his or her requirements. A part of the subscriber's decision will be based on how well the provider markets the services and its success in customer retention. These are the challenges, and those providers able to effectively execute these tasks will prosper.

Appendix
Resources

This appendix includes a list of standards and recommendations relevant to broadband services deployment; a list of well-known applications, service providers and vendors active in broadband deployment; and the most relevant industry associations.

Standards and Recommendations

The tables in this section list the standards and recommendations relevant to broadband services deployment. These include those from the Internet Engineering Task Force (www.ietf.org); the DSL Forum (www.dslforum.org); the ATM Forum (www.atmforum.org); CableLabs (www.cablelabs.com); as well as those pertaining to fixed wireless and mobile wireless; and, finally, the ITU (www.itu.ch).

TABLE A.1 IETF

Standard Number	Standard Title
RFC-894	Standard for the Transmission of IP Datagrams over Ethernet Networks
RFC-1332	The PPP Internet Protocol Control Protocol (IPCP)
RFC-1631	The IP Network Address Translator (NAT)
RFC-1662	PPP in HDLC-Like Framing
RFC-1723	RIP Version 2—Carrying Additional Information
RFC-1771	Border Gateway Protocol 4 (BGP-4)
RFC-1901	Community-Based SNMPv2
RFC-1918	Address Allocation for Private Internets
RFC-1973	PPP in Frame Relay
RFC-2138	Remote Authentication Dial-In User Service (RADIUS)
RFC-2225	Classical IP and ARP over ATM Update (obsoletes RFCs 1577 and 1626)
RFC-2251	Lightweight Directory Access Protocol (v3)
RFC-2272	Message Processing and Dispatching for SNMPv3
RFC-2273	SNMPv3 Applications
RFC-2328	OSPF Version 2
RFC-2331	UNI Signaling 4.0 Update (obsoletes RFC-1755)
RFC-2363	PPP over FUNI
RFC-2364	PPP over AAL5
RFC-2401	Security Architecture for the Internet Protocol
RFC-2402	IP Authentication Header
RFC-2406	IP Encapsulating Security Payload (ESP)
RFC-2408	Internet Security Association and Key Management Protocol (ISAKMP)
RFC-2409	Internet Key Exchange (IKE)
RFC-2427	Multiprotocol Interconnect over Frame Relay (obsoletes RFC-1490)
RFC-2516	Method for Transmitting PPP over Ethernet (PPPoE)
RFC-2547	BGP/MPLS VPNs
RFC-2597	Assured Forwarding PHB Group
RFC-2598	Expedited Forwarding PHB Group
RFC-2615	PPP over SONET/SDH
RFC-2661	Layer 2 Tunneling Protocol (L2TP)
RFC-2684	Multiprotocol Encapsulation over ATM Adaptation Layer 5 (obsoletes RFC-1483)
RFC-2764	A Framework for IP-Based Virtual Private Networks
RFC-3031	Multiprotocol Label Switching Architecture

TABLE A.2 DSL Forum

Standard Number	Standard Title
TR-001	ADSL Forum System Reference Model
TR-002	ATM over ADSL Recommendations
TR-003	Framing and Encapsulation Standards for ADSL
TR-004	Network Migration
TR-005	ADSL Network Element Management
TR-006	SNMP-Based ADSL Line MIB
TR-007	Interfaces and System Configurations for ADSL: Customer Premises
TR-008	Default VPI/VCI Addresses for FUNI Mode Transport: Packet Mode
TR-009	Channelization for DMT and CAP ADSL Line Codes: Packet Mode
TR-010	Requirements and Reference Models for ADSL Access Networks: The "SNAG" Document
TR-011	An End-to-End Packet Mode Architecture with Tunneling and Service Selection
TR-012	Broadband Service Architecture for Access to Legacy Data Networks over ADSL Issue 1
TR-013	Interfaces and System Configurations for ADSL: Central Office
TR-014	DMT Line Code Specific MIB
TR-015	CAP Line Code Specific MIB
TR-016	CMIP Specification for ADSL Network Element Management
TR-017	ATM over ADSL Recommendation (TR-002 Issue 2)
TR-018	References and Requirements for CPE Architectures for Data Access
TR-019	ADSL Recommendation Number 1—Splitter Mode Operation (PR-001)
TR-020	ADSL Recommendation Number 2—Splitterless Operation (PR-002)
TR-021	ADSL Recommendation Number 3—ATM Compliance (PR-003)
TR-022	The Operation of ADSL-Based Networks
TR-023	Overview of ADSL Testing
TR-025	Core Network Architecture for Access to Legacy Data Network over ADSL
TR-026	T1.413 Issue 2, ATM-Based ADSL ICS
TR-027	SNMP-Based ADSL Line MIB
TR-028	CMIP Specification for ADSL Network Element Management
TR-029	ADSL Dynamic Interoperability Testing
TR-030	ADSL EMS-to-NMS Functional Requirements
TR-031	ADSL ANSI T1.413-1998 Conformance Testing
TR-032	CPE Architecture Recommendations for Access to Legacy Data Networks
TR-033	ITU-T G.992.2 (G.lite) ICS
TR-034	Proposal for an Alternative OAM Communications Channel across the U Interface
TR-035	Protocol-Independent Object Model for ADSL EMS-NMS Interface
TR-036	Requirements for Voice over DSL
TR-037	Auto-Configuration for the Connection between the DSL Broadband Network Termination (B-NT) and the Network using ATM
TR-038	DSL Service Flow-Thru Management Overview
TR-039	Addendum to TR-036 Annex A: Requirements for Voice over DSL
TR-040	Aspects of VDSL Evolution
TR-041	CORBA Specification for ADSL EMS-NMS Interface
TR-042	ATM Transport over ADSL Recommendation (update 017)
TR-043	Protocols at the User Interface for Accessing Data Networks Using ATM/DSL

TABLE A.3 ATM Forum

Standard Number	Standard Title
AF-UNI-0010.002	ATM User-Network Interface Specification 3.1
AF-SIG-0061.000	UNI Signaling 4.0
AF-ILMI-0065.000	Integrated Local Management Interface (ILMI) v4.0
AF-TM-0056.000	Traffic Management 4.0
AF-RBB-0099.000	Residential Broadband Architectural Framework
AF-VTOA-0083.001	Voice and Telephony over ATM to the Desktop
AF-VTOA-0089.000	ATM Trunking Using AAL1 for Narrow Band Services v1.0
AF-SEC-0100.002	ATM Security Specification v1.1

TABLE A.4 CableLabs (Cable Modems)

Standard Number	Standard Title
DOCSIS 1.0	Data over Cable System Interface Specification (now known as CableLabs Certified Cable Modem)
DOCSIS 1.1	(Adds QoS in support of IP telephony)
PacketCable 1.0	Real-Time Multimedia Services
J.112	ITU Recommendation for Data over Cable (Annex B is DOCSIS-specific)
Euro-DOCSIS	(Adaptation of DOCSIS to European 7/8 Mhz channel spacing versus 6 Mhz in North America)
EuroModem (DVB/DAVIC)	(Developed by the European Cable Communications System—cell-based)

TABLE A.5 Fixed Wireless

Standard Number	Standard Title
MMDS (in progress)	Multichannel Multipoint Distribution System (Multiple vendor proprietary solutions exist)
LMDS (in progress)	Local Multipoint Distribution System (Multiple vendor proprietary solutions exist)
802.16.1 (in progress)	Broadband Access Air Interface for 10 to 66 GHz (http://standards.ieee.org/wireless)
802.16.3 (in progress)	Broadband Access Air Interface for 2 to 11 GHz

Resources

TABLE A.6 Mobile Wireless

Standard Number	Standard Title
ETSI GSM Series 1–12	Global System for Mobile Communications (GSM)
TIA IS-136	Time Division Multiple Access (TDMA)
TIA IS-95	Code Division Multiple Access (CDMA)
ETSI GSM 03.3	High-Speed Circuit-Switched Data (HSCSD)
TIA/EIA IS-2000/cdma2000	(3G evolution path for CDMA)
ETSI GSM 02.60/03.60	General Packet Radio Service (GPRS) (evolution phase to 3G for GSM)
GPRS-EDGE	GPRS—Enhanced Data for GSM Environment (additional evolution)
W-CDMA	(3G evolution path for GSM)
ITU-T IMT-2000	Universal Mobile Telephone System (UMTS) (integrates multiple 3G standards)
Bluetooth 1.0/IEEE 802.15	Short-Range Wireless Interface (www.bluetooth.com)
HomeRF	In-Home Wireless Interface (www.homerf.org)
802.11b (and other)	Wireless LANs (www.wirelessethernet.com)

TABLE A.7 ITU

Standard Number	Standard Title
G.991.1	High Bit Rate Digital Subscriber Line (HDSL) Transmission System on Metallic Local Lines
G.991.2	Single-Pair High-Speed Digital Subscriber Line (SHDSL) Transceivers
G.992.1	Asymmetrical Digital Subscriber Line (ADSL) Transceivers
G.992.2	Splitterless Asymmetric Digital Subscriber Line (ADSL) Transceivers
G.993.1	Very-High-Speed Digital Subscriber Line (VDSL)—in Progress
G.994.1	Handshake Procedures for Digital Subscriber Line (DSL) Transceivers
G.995.1	Overview of Digital Subscriber Line (DSL) Recommendations
G.996.1	Test Procedures for Digital Subscriber Line (DSL) Transceivers
G.997.1	Physical Layer Management for Digital Subscriber Line (DSL) Transceivers

Table A.8 lists examples of the types of applications that a state-aware firewall must follow. Some applications, such as Apple's QuickTime (port 458) and Lotus Notes (port 1352), have well-known port numbers (as defined at http://www.iana.org/assignments/portnumbers). Others are totally dynamic or private.

TABLE A.8 Well-Known Applications

Category	Application
Representative Multimedia Applications	Apple: QuickTime; Eloquent: Presenter!; Emotion: Creative-Partners; IDT: Net2Phone; Liquid Audio: Liquid Music; Macromedia: Flash; Microsoft: Conferencing, Media Player, Windows Media Services, NetShow; Netscape: Conference, CoolTalk, NetMeeting; Real: Encoder, Audio, Guide, JukeBox, Player, Video; Vivo: VivoActive; White Pine: CU-SeeMe
Representative Database Applications	Sybase: Jconnect for JDBC, Open Client, SQL Server; Lotus: Notes; Microsoft: SQL Server; Oracle: SQL*Net
Representative Audio Applications	Lycos: Sonique; Conduits: packetplayer; Nullsoft: WinAmp; Xaudio: MP3 Player
Representative Chat Applications	Yahoo Messenger, AOL Instant Messaging, MSN Messaging

Representative List of Service Providers

Tables A.9 through A.13 list the major carriers and service providers in the broadband sector. The tables include the DSL access providers, cable operators, and wireless providers. In the DSL space, a given provider's Web site will usually include links to the ISPs with which the provider partners.

TABLE A.9 U.S. and Canadian DSL Access Providers

Service Provider	Web Site
United States	
Covad Communications	www.covad.com
BellSouth	www.bellsouth.com
Qwest/US West	www.qwest.com
SBC	www.sbc.com
Verizon (former GTE and Bell Atlantic)	www.verizon.net
Canada	
Aliant	www.aliant.ca
Bell Canada	www.bce.ca
MTS	www.mts.mb.ca
SaskTel	www.sasktel.com
Telus (BC Tel)	www.telus.com

TABLE A.10 Overseas DSL Access Providers

Provider	Region Served	Web Site
Europe		
FirstMark Communications	Pan-European	www.firstmark.net
VersaPoint	Pan-European	www.versapoint.com
Telekom Austria	Austria	www.telekom.at
Belgacom	Belgium	www.belgacom.be
TeleDanmark	Denmark	www.teledanmark.dk
CyberCity	Denmark	www.cybercity.dk
World Online	Denmark	www.worldonline.nl
Sonera	Finland	www.sonera.fi
Elisa Communications	Finland	www.elisa.fi
France Telecom	France	www.francetelecom.fr
Deutsche Telecom	Germany	www.telekom.de
Mannesmann Arcor	Germany	www.arcor.net
KKF.net	Germany	www.kkf.net
Eircom	Ireland	www.eircom.com
Telecom Italia	Italy	www.telecomitalia.it
KPN	Netherlands	www.kpn.com
Telenor	Norway	www.telenor.com
Telefonica	Spain	www.telefonica.com
Telia	Sweden	www.telia.com
BT	United Kingdom	www.bt.com
Asia		
Primus	Australia	www.primustel.com
Telstra	Australia	www.telstra.com
Cable and Wireless Optus	Australia	www.optus.net.au
Pacific Internet	Australia	www.pacific.net.sg
Pacific Century CyberWorks	Hong Kong	www.cyberworks.com
China Telecom	China	www.chinatelecom.com.cn
Chunghwa Telecom	Taiwan	www.cht.com.tw
Korea Telecom	Korea	www.koreatelecom.com
Dishnet DSL	India	www.ddsl.net
Telekom Malaysia	Malaysia	www.telekom.com.my
SingTel Magix	Singapore	www.magix.com.sg
Latin America		
TelMex	Mexico	www.telmex.com.mx
Telesp	Brazil	www.telesp.com.br
Vesper	Brazil	www.vesper.com.br
Entel	Chile	www.entel.cl
Cantv	Venezuela	www.cantv.com.ve

TABLE A.11 U.S. and Canadian Cable Access Providers

Provider	Web Site
AOL/Time-Warner	www.timewarner.com
AT&T (TCI)/@Home	www.athome.att.com
Cablevision Systems	www.cablevision.com
Charter Communications	www.chartercom.com
Comcast Online (@Home)	www.comcast.com
Cox Communications	www.cox.com
MediaOne (now AT&T)	www.broadband.att.com
RCN	www.rcn.com
Rogers	www.rogers.com
Shaw Communications	www.shaw.ca
Videotron	www.videotron.com

TABLE A.12 Overseas Cable Access Providers

Provider	Region Served	Web Site
Europe		
Callahan Associates International	Pan-European	www.callahanassoc.com
Liberty Media Group	Pan-European	www.libertymedia.com
NTL	Pan-European	www.ntl.com
United Pan-Europe Communications	Pan-European	www.upccorp.com
UPC Telekabel (chello)	Austria	www.telekabel.at
Brutele	Belgium	www.brutele.be
Telenet	Belgium	www.telenet.be
UPC Belgium	Belgium	www.upcbelgium.be
TeleDanmark	Denmark	www.teledanmark.dk
Sonera	Finland	www.sonera.fi
UPC France	France	www.upcfrance.com
France Telecom Cable	France	www.francetelecom.com
Noos (former Lyonnaise Cable)	France	www.noos.com
Est Videocommunication	France	www.evc.net
Primacom	Germany	www.primacom.de
CMI	Ireland	www.cablenet.ie
Cablelink	Ireland	www.cablelink.ie
Irish Multichannel	Ireland	www.irish-multichannel.ie
Casema	Netherlands	www.casema.net
CasTel/Palet	Netherlands	www.castel.nl

Provider	Region Served	Web Site
UPC	Netherlands	www.upc.nl
Telenor Avidi	Norway	www.telenor.com
UPC	Norway	www.upc.no
Cabovisao	Portugal	www.cabovisao.pt
TV Cabo	Portugal	www.tvcabo.pt
Menta	Spain	www.menta.net
Cableuropa	Spain	www.ono.es
Supercable	Spain	www.supercable.es
B2 Bredband AB	Sweden	www.bredband.com
Cablecom	Switzerland	www.cablecom.ch
NTL	United Kingdom	www.ntl.com
Asia		
Telstra	Australia	www.telstra.com
Cable and Wireless Optus	Australia	www.optus.net.au
China Broadband Corporation	China	www.chinabroadband.com
Thrunet	Korea	www.thrunet.com
Hanaro Telecom	Korea	www.hanaro.net
Korea Telecom	Korea	www.koreatelecom.com
GiGaMedia	Taiwan	www.giga.net.tw
Hathway Cable	India	www.hathway.com
Hinduja IN2Cable	India	www.hindujagroup.com
Destiny Cable	Philippines	www.mydestiny.net
Singapore Cable Vision	Singapore	www.scv.com.sg
Latin America		
Multicanal	Argentina	www.multicanal.com.ar
TCI/Fibertel	Argentina	www.fibertel.com.ar
Canbras	Brazil	www.canbras.com.br
Globo Cabo	Brazil	www.globocabo.com.br
TVA	Brazil	www.tva.com.br
Metropolis Intercom	Chile	www.tvcable.cl
TV Cable Ecuador	Ecuador	www.tvcable.com.ec
Cablevision	Mexico	www.cablevision.com.mx
Megacable	Mexico	www.megacable.com.mx
SuperCable	Venezuela	www.supercable.com
Intercable	Venezuela	www.intercable.com.ve

TABLE A.13 Fixed Wireless and Satellite Access (Residential/SOHO)

Service Provider	Web Site
Fixed Wireless	
AT&T	www.iatt.net
Sprint	www.sprintbroadband.com
Satellite	
Hughes/EchoStar DirecPC	www.direcpc.com
Europe Online Networks	www.europeonline.com

Most existing CDMA/TDMA/GSM mobile wireless access providers offer 2.5 and 3G services at the end of 2001 and beginning of 2002 timeframe.

Representative List of Vendors

Table A.14 lists those equipment vendors active in the broadband hardware, services, and provisioning marketplaces.

TABLE A.14 Broadband Hardware, Services, and Provisioning Vendors

Vendor	Service Area	Web Site
2Wire	DSL	www.2wire.com
Adaptive Broadband	DSL	www.adaptivebroadband.com
Akamai	Content networking	www.akamai.com
Alcatel	Multiple	www.alcatel.com
Alidian	Optical metro	www.alidian.com
Allegro Networks	Edge	www.allegronetworks.com
Accelerated Networks	Edge	www.acceleratednetworks.com
AccessLAN	Edge	www.accesslan.com
Avici	Core	www.avici.com
Axient	Content	www.axient.com
BroadJump	Clients	www.broadjump.com
Caspian	Core router	www.caspiannetworks.com
Celox	Edge	www.celoxnetworks.com
Ceyba	Core DWDM	www.ceyba.com
Check Point	Security	www.checkpoint.com
Ciena	Core DWDM	www.ciena.com
Cisco Systems	Multiple	www.cisco.com
CopperCom	Voice over DSL	www.coppercom.com
Copper Mountain	DSL	www.coppermountain.com
Corvis	Core DWDM	www.corvis.com

Vendor	Service Area	Web Site
Crescent Networks	Edge	www.crescentnetworks.com
CoSine	IP services	www.cosinecom.com
Efficient Networks (Siemens)	NICs	www.efficient.com
Eicon Technology	DSL	www.eicon.com
Ellacoya	Optical metro	www.ellacoya.com
epicRealm	Content	www.epicrealm.com
Ericsson	Multiple	www.ericsson.com
Force10	Ethernet metro	www.force10networks.com
Gotham Networks	Edge	www.gothamnetworks.com
iBeam	Content	www.ibeam.com
Jetstream Communications	Voice over DSL	www.jetstream.com
Juniper	Core/edge	www.junipernetworks.com
Lucent (with SpringTide)	Multiple	www.lucent.com
Marconi	Multiple	www.marconi.com
Merlot Communications	DSL	www.merlot.com
Mirror Image	Content	www.mirror-image.com
Motorola	Cable	www.motorola.com
Network ICE	Security	www.networkice.com
Nightfire	Management	www.nightfire.com
Nokia (and Amber, plus Ramp Networks)	Multiple	www.nokia.com
Nortel Networks	Multiple	www.nortelnetworks.com
Optimight	Core router/DWDM	www.optimight.com
ONI	Optical metro	www.oni.com
Orckit	DSL	www.orckit.com
PairGain	DSL	www.pairgain.com
Paradyne	DSL	www.paradyne.com
Portal	Management	www.portal.com
Pluris	Core	www.pluris.com
Procket	Core	www.procket.com
Quarry	Edge	www.quarrytech.com
Redback	Edge/optical	www.redback.com
RiverDelta (Motorola)	Cable	www.riverdelta.com
Riverstone	Cable	www.riverstonenet.com
Sonus	Voice	www.sonusnet.com
Speedera	Content	www.speedera.com
Syndesis	Management	www.syndesis.com
Sycamore	Optical metro	www.sycamorenet.com
Tellium	Core DWDM	www.tellium.com

continued

TABLE A.14 Broadband Hardware, Services, and Provisioning Vendors *continued*

Vendor	Service Area	Web Site
Tenor	Core	www.tenornetworks.com
Timetra	Ethernet metro	www.timetra.com
TollBridge Technologies	Voice over DSL	www.tollbridgetech.com
Tollgrade	Loop qualification	www.tollgrade.com
Turnstone	Loop management	www.turnstone.com
Unisphere Networks	Edge	www.unispherenetworks.com
Village Networks	Core router/DWDM	www.villagenetworks.com
Westell	DSL	www.westell.com
Worldwide Packets	Ethernet metro	www.worldwidepacket.com
Xtera	Core DWDM	www.xtera.com

Industry Forums and Associations

Table A.15 lists a subset of the major industry forums and associations active in broadband. They span from more technology-focused groups, such as the DSL Forum, to groups that focus more on business implications, such as the Broadband Content Delivery (BCD) Forum.

TABLE A.15 Industry Forums and Associations

Forum or Association	Web Site
ATM Forum	www.atmforum.org
Broadband Content Delivery (BCD) Forum	www.bcdforum.org
Content Bridge	www.contentbridge.org
DSL Forum	www.dslforum.org
IETF	www.ietf.org
ITU	www.itu.ch
North American Network Operators Group (NANOG)	www.nanog.org
Optical Internetworking Forum (OIF)	www.oiforum.com

Glossary

3G (third generation)—Term for the third generation of cellular technology. Based on CDMA-Wideband, it combines both voice and high-speed data switching across a packet network.

AAA (authentication, authorization, and accounting)—The process of identifying a user accessing network resources and then billing for the usage if required. The IETF has focused on the most widely deployed use of authentication, Remote Authentication Dial-in User Service (RADIUS) (Rigney, 1997b), and its expansion, called Diameter (a "radius" pun and not an acronym) (Calhoun, 2000).

AAL2 (ATM Adaptation Layer 2)—ATM adaptation layer optimized for transport of real-time data. Used for VoDSL.

AAL5 (ATM Adaptation Layer 5)—ATM adaptation layer optimized for data. Used for most traffic between DSL modems and DSLAMs.

ADSL (asymmetric digital subscriber line)—Technology offering asymmetric and symmetric bandwidth of up to 8 Mbps downstream over one copper pair and supporting POTS splitters. Encoding based on DMT standardized by ANSI and the ITU-T.

ANSI (American National Standards Institute)—U.S. telecommunications standards-setting body. European equivalent is ETSI.

BSN (broadband service node)—IP services platform offering subscriber management and high-touch IP services. Also known as a broadband remote access server (B-RAS), a subscriber management system (SMS), or an IPSS.

CDMA (code division multiple access)—Cellular technology that uses digital codes rather than different frequencies to differentiate subscribers. Sprint PCS is an example of a CDMA network.

CLE (customer located equipment)—Networking equipment located at the subscriber site and managed by the service provider.

CLEC (competitive local exchange carrier)—Service provider category created to offer value-added voice and data services in competition with the ILEC. Formalized as part of the 1996 Telecommunications Act in the United States.

COPS (Common Open Policy Service)—A simple query and response TCP-based protocol that can be used to exchange policy information between a policy decision point (PDP) and its clients, policy enforcement points (PEPs) (Durham, 2000). (See also PDP and PEP.)

CORBA (Common Object Request Broker Architecture)—Messaging API for interconnections of different vendor management systems.

CPE (customer premises equipment)—Networking hardware located at the subscriber's site.

DEN (directory-enabled networks)—DEN's goals are to enable the deployment and use of policy by starting with common service and user concepts, specifying their mapping/storage in an LDAP-based repository, and using these concepts in vendor- and device-independent policy rules.

DES (Data Encryption Standard)—Encryption standard based on 56-byte key length. Used widely in commerce and no longer considered secure. 3DES uses an effective 112-byte key.

DHCP (Dynamic Host Configuration Protocol)—A protocol that is used to automatically assign IP addresses to computers.

DOCSIS (Data over Cable System Interface Specification)—Standard for transmission of data over cable networks by cable modems. Now know as CableLabs Cable Modem.

DS (differentiated services)—The IP header field, called the *DS-field*. In IPv4, it defines the layout of the ToS (Type of Service) octet; in IPv6, it is the Traffic Class octet (Nichols, 1998), in support of QoS policies. DS requires a policy to define the correspondence between codepoints in the packet's DS-field and individual per-hop behaviors (to achieve a specified per-domain behavior).

DS3 (Digital Signal 3)—Payload and framing structure for the North American 45 Mbps transmission system.

DSL (digital subscriber line)—Refers to any of the DSL technologies, including ADSL, HDSL, IDSL, SDSL, SHDSL, and VDSL.

DSLAM (digital subscriber line access multiplexer)—A chassis containing DSL modems, which aggregates them onto an ATM, Frame, or packet uplink.

ESP (Encapsulating Security Payload)—IPSec encapsulation method that supports encryption.

ETSI (European Telecommunications Standardization Institute)—European standards organization. The United States equivalent is ANSI.

GE (gigabit Ethernet)—A 1000 Mbps Ethernet standard that builds on the 100 Mbps Fast Ethernet standard. Used within campuses, across metro areas, and as intra-PoP links.

GGSN (gateway GPRS support node)—Within GPRS, provides the point of interconnection with external networks and tunnels traffic to the SGSN.

GPRS (General Packet Radio Service)—Standard for carrying packetized data over an existing 2G (e.g., GSM) wireless network.

GSM (Global System for Mobile Communications)—A digital cellular telephony standard.

HDSL (high-speed digital subscriber line)—Symmetric technology supporting bandwidths to T1/E1 over one or two pairs. It does not support POTS splitters. Deployment overlaps somewhat with SDSL, and it is expected to be replaced with SHDSL.

HFC (hybrid fiber-coax)—Architecture within cable TV distribution in which fiber is run to a neighborhood distribution point, where the signal is then converted to coaxial cable. Required for effective cable modem deployments.

Glossary

IAD (integrated access device)—CPE/CLE device combining data and voice. Commonly refers to a device with an ATM uplink.

ILEC (incumbent local exchange carrier)—The original telephony provider within a geographic area; the RBOC.

IPmc (IP Multicast)—Set of IETF protocols permitting efficient replication of data within an IP network. Protocols include Protocol Independent Multicast (PIM), Internet Group Management Protocol (IGMP), Multicast Source Discovery Protocol (MSDP), and Multicast-BGP (MBGP).

IPSec (IP Security)—Set of IETF protocols defining security framework, including authentication, encryption, and key management.

IPSS (IP services switch)—A system that is capable of IP services processing. Includes broadband service nodes, broadband remote access servers, and some subscriber management systems. Supports subscriber management, firewalling, and IP-VPNs.

IPv6 (IP version 6)—Next-generation IP protocol offering greater address ranges and better provisions for autoconfiguration, security, and QoS.

IP-VPN (IP virtual private network)—Refers to an IP-based VPN across a public Internet. Supplements earlier Frame and ATM-based VPNs.

ISP (Internet service provider)—A provider that offers basic Internet connectivity. Recent regulations state that an ISP may not own the facilities it uses.

IXC (interexchange carrier)—A U.S. service provider that offers long-distance telephony services.

L2TP (Layer 2 Tunneling Protocol)—Means of encapsulating multiple subscriber sessions (e.g., PPP) across arbitrary backbone links. A tunnel exists between a LAC and an LNS.

LAC (L2TP access concentrator)—Internetworking device providing L2TP tunnel creation.

LCP (Layer Control Protocol)—Used for negotiation of PPP configuration between two peers.

LDAP (Lightweight Directory Access Protocol)—Method of storing subscriber profiles in central X.500-based directories. Part of DEN.

LMDS (local multipoint distribution system)—Wireless system offering megabit data rates to subscribers across a small radius within a metropolitan area.

LNS (L2TP network server)—Internetworking device providing L2TP tunnel termination.

MD5 (Message Digest 5)— One-way hash function for IPSec that generates digest of input message. Ensures that the input message has not been tampered with.

MMDS (metropolitan multipoint distribution system)—Wireless system offering megabit data rates to subscribers across a metropolitan area.

MPLS (multiprotocol label switching)—Integrates a label swapping and switching framework with network layer routing (RFC-3031). The basic idea involves assigning short, fixed-length labels to packets at the ingress to an MPLS cloud. Throughout the interior of the MPLS domain, the labels attached to packets are used to make forwarding decisions (usually without recourse to the original packet headers). Based on earlier Cisco Tag Switching proposal.

NAP (network access provider)—A provider that offers telephony services in the United States.

NSP (network service provider)—An entity that offers value-added services and connectivity within a telecommunications network. ISPs, ILECs, and CLECs are examples of NSPs.

NTE (network termination equipment)—The devices that terminate each end of the transmission line.

OC3 (Optical Carrier 3)—Defines the 155 Mbps transmission rate within the North American SONET hierarchy. (See STM-1.)

PCLEC (packet CLEC)—A competitive provider that offers only advanced data services.

PDP (policy decision point)—A logical entity in the network that makes policy decisions for itself or for other network elements that request such decisions (Yavatkar, 2000). Sometimes referred to as a *policy server*.

PDSN (packet data serving node)—Performs routing and external data connectivity within CDMA 1xRTT network.

PEP (policy enforcement point)—A logical entity that enforces policy decisions (Yavatkar, 2000).

PIM (Protocol Independent Multicast)—Scalable IP multicast protocol, permitting distribution of a single source's data to multiple recipients.

Policy—A set of rules influencing the subscriber's service, either determined by the network operator or contracted by the subscriber. Policies are created and enforced in the network by PDPs and PEPs.

PoP (Point of Presence)—Location where a carrier or ISP deploys its internetworking equipment.

POS (PPP over SONET)—Method of encapsulating IP traffic across a SONET/SDH backbone. Relies on PPP.

PPP (Point-to-Point Protocol)—Method of encapsulating IP packets across point-to-point links. Most Internet access uses PPP encapsulation.

PPPoE (PPP over Ethernet)—Encapsulation of PPP within Ethernet frames (RFC-2516). Used for DSL access between the PC and the IPSS.

PSTN (public switched telephone network)—Global telephony network.

PTT (post, telephone, and telegraph)—Used in Europe and elsewhere to refer to the former state-owned telephone companies.

QoS (quality of service)—At a high level, QoS refers to the ability to deliver network services according to the parameters specified in a service level agreement. "Quality" is characterized by service availability, delay, jitter, throughput, and packet loss ratio. At a network resource level, "quality of service" refers to a set of capabilities that allow a service provider to prioritize traffic, control bandwidth, and control network latency. There are two different approaches to QoS on IP networks: integrated services (Braden, 1994) and differentiated services (Blake, 1998).

RADIUS (Remote Authentication Dial-In User Services)—Protocol used by ISPs for subscriber authorization and accounting. It has all but replaced the earlier TACACS+ protocol.

Glossary

RBOC (Regional Bell Operating Company)—Regional carriers resulting from the AT&T divesture. Also known as ILECs. Only BellSouth, SBC (including Ameritech and Pacific Telesis), Verizon (including Bell Atlantic, Nynex, and GTE), and Qwest (including US West) remain.

RSVP (Resource Reservation Protocol)—A setup protocol designed for an integrated services Internet to reserve network resources for a path (Braden, 1997). Also, a signaling mechanism for managing application traffic's QoS in a differentiated services network.

SA (security association)—A relationship that is set up by two peers within an IPSec environment.

SDH (Synchronous Digital Hierarchy)—An international optical hierarchy offering different multiplexing rates and including resilience. North American equivalent is SONET.

SDSL (symmetric digital subscriber line)—Offers symmetric service over two or four copper wires and may support POTS. Most SDSL uses 2B1Q (two-binary, one-quaternary physical layer) encoding.

Service—From the perspective of the subscriber, a service is a fee-based network offering, such as hosting, IP-VPN, and firewall. The IETF is developing a more rigorous definition as to how a provider may actually define and offer services. RFC-2216 defines a *service* as the functions to be performed, the information required to perform these functions, and the way network elements interact to enable the service. Service application across a network is made possible by policy definition and enforcement.

SGSN (serving GPRS support node)—Within GPRS, performs mobility management, implements authentication procedures, performs traffic management, and routes packet data.

SHDSL (single-pair HDSL)—Recent form of HDSL based on new encapsulation permitting operation over a single pair. Should replace HDSL, SDSL, and HDSL2 over time. Systems may negotiate ATM, Frame, or packet encapsulation and can support multiple data rates due to spectral compatibility of HDSL2.

SLA (service level agreement)—The documented result of a negotiation between a customer/consumer and a provider of a service. Specifies the levels of availability, serviceability, performance, operation, and other attributes of the service.

SMS (subscriber management system)—Provides circuit and session aggregation and services for broadband subscribers. (See IPSS and BSN.)

SONET (Synchronous Optical Network)—North American optical hierarchy offering different multiplexing rates and including resilience. International equivalent is SDH.

STM-1 (Synchronous Transport Module 1)—Basic transport rate and framing of 155 Mbps within the SDH hierarchy. Other well-known rates include STM-4 at 622 Mbps and STM-16 at 2.4 Gbps.

TDMA (time division multiple access)—Cellular technology using timeslots to separate customers. AT&T Wireless is an example of a TDMA network.

UMTS (universal mobile telecom system)—Next-generation global standard for mobile wireless based on wideband-CDMA. Also known as 3G.

VDSL (very-high-speed digital subscriber line)—Asymmetric or symmetric technology based on a variation of CAP/QAM or DMT encoding. Delivering up to 52 Mbps over shorter distances (4,500 ft. maximum) than ADSL. Proposed for high-quality video distribution.

VLL (virtual leased line)—Emulation of a point-to-point connection across a public IP backbone. Layer 3 protocol independent.

VoD (video on demand)—Refers to a service allowing subscribers to request video content at any time. ADSL offers the bandwidth required for VoD. A variation of VoD is Near-VoD (or stagger casting) where content is streamed at set intervals (such as a popular movie every 15 minutes). More recently, VoD has relied on IPmc optimization.

VoIP (voice over IP)—Generic term referring to IP-based voice.

VPRN (virtual private routed network)—Separate instance of an IP-VPN across a public Internet.

VSN (virtual services network)—IP-VPN providing advanced subscriber-aware services such as firewalling.

VTN (virtual transport network)—IP-VPN providing basic transport. (See MPLS.)

Bibliography

Akamai, 2000. Service description at http://www.akamai.com/html/en/tc/core_tech.html.

Arango et al., 1999. M. Arango, A. Dugan, I. Elliott, C. Huitema, and S. Pickett. "RFC-2705: Media Gateway Control Protocol (MGCP), Version 1.0." October 1999.

Ashwood-Smith, 2000. P. Ashwood-Smith et al. "Generalized MPLS Signaling—CR-LDP Extensions." Internet draft, draft-ietf-mpls-generalized-cr-ldp-04.txt. July 2001.

Ashwood-Smith, 2001. P. Ashwood-Smith. "Generalized MPLS—Signaling Functional Description." Internet draft, draft-ietf-mpls-generalized-signaling-05.txt. July 2001.

AT&T, 2000. AT&T announcement of fixed wireless Internet services at http://www.att.com/press/item/0,1354,2706,00.html. 22 March 2000.

Blake, 1998. S. Blake, D. Black, M. Carlson, E. Davies, Z. Wang, and W. Weiss. "RFC-2475—An Architecture for Differentiated Service." December 1998.

Braden, 1994. R. Braden, D. Clark, and S. Shenker. "RFC-1633—Integrated Services in the Internet Architecture: An Overview." June 1994.

Braden, 1997. R. Braden, L. Zhang, S. Berson, S. Herzog, and S. Jamin. "RFC-2205: Resource Reservation Protocol (RSVP)." September 1997.

Brown and Malis, 1998. C. Brown and A. Malis. "RFC-2427: Multiprotocol Interconnect over Frame Relay." September 1998.

CableLabs, 1999. "DOCSIS 1.0 and 1.1." http://www.cablemodem.com/specifications.html.

Cahners, 2000. "Entering the Broadband Era." Cahners IN-Stat Group. May 2000.

Calhoun, 2000. P. Calhoun, G. Zorn, P. Pan, and H. Akhtar. "DIAMETER Framework Document." Internet draft, draft-letf-aaa-diameter-framework-01.txt. March 2001.

Callon, 2000. R. Callon, A. Viswanathan, and E. Rosen. RFC-3031: "Multiprotocol Label Switching Architecture." January 2001.

Cieslak, 2000. M. Cieslak, G. Tiwana, and R. Wilson. "Web Cache Coordination Protocol." Internet draft, draft-wilson-wrec-wccp-v2-01.txt. April 2001.

Note: The various protocol and standards documents referenced here are available at the respective Web sites (e.g., ww.ietf.org; www.ieee.org; www.itu.ch). Analyst documents and reports are available on a subscription basis from the respective firms (e.g., IDC, Gartner, Infonetics).

CIMI, 1998. CIMI Corporation. "IP-VPNs and MPLS: Twin Keys to 21st Century Public IP Success." 1998.

CIMI, 2001. CIMI Corporation. "Netwatcher." 2001.

Cook, 2001. "Scaling the Internet via Exchange Points." *Cook Report.* January 2001.

Copper Mountain, 2000. "DSL Architecture and Business Case." Copper Mountain. http://www.coppermountain.com/library/whitepapers/pdf/80030wp.pdf. September 1999.

Covad, 2000. "Covad Communications Acquires Bluestar Communications." Covad. http://www.covad.com/companyinfo/pressreleases/pr_2000/061600_press.shtml. 16 June 2000.

Current Analysis, 2000. "Two-Way Satellite Broadband: No Panacea for the Broadband Blues." *Current Analysis.* 18 December 2000.

Durham, 2000. D. Durham, J. Boyle, R. Cohen, S. Herzog, R. Rajan, and A. Sastry. "RFC-2748: The COPS (Common Open Policy Service) Protocol." January 2000.

EETimes, 2001. "Analysts Remain Rosy about DSL." *EETimes.* 12 April 2001.

Egevang, 1994. K. Egevang and P. Francis. "RFC-1631: The IP Network Address Translator (NAT)." May 1994.

Exchange Point, 2000. http://www.ep.net/naps_na.html.

FCC, 2000. "Deployment of Advanced Telecommunications Capability: Second Report." http://www.fcc.gov/Bureaus/Common_Carrier/Orders/2000/fcc00290.pdf. August 2000.

Forrester, 2000. "Hosting's Moving on Up." Forrester Research. May 2000.

GAO, 2001. "Characteristics and Choices of Internet Users." U.S. General Accounting Office. February 2001.

Gilder, 2000. "The Post-Diluvian Paradigm." *Gilder Technology Report.* February 2000.

Ginsburg, 2000. "1 Mbps Forwarding Takes 1 MIPS." Empirical formula derived from processor (in MIPS) vs. bandwidth (in Mbps) performance of major core router designs including the Cisco 7500, Cisco 12000 (GSR), Cisco 10000, and Juniper M40.

Greene et al., 2000. N. Greene, M. Ramalho, and B. Rosen. "RFC-2805: Media Gateway Control Protocol Architecture and Requirements." April 2000.

Gross et al., 1998. G. Gross et al. "RFC-2364: PPP over AAL5." July 1998.

H.323, 2000. "Packet-Based Multimedia Communications Systems." ITU Recommendation H-323. November 2000.

Hamzeh, 1999. K. Hamzeh et al. "RFC-2637: Point-to-Point Tunneling Protocol." July 1999.

Harkins, 1998. D. Harkins and D. Carrel. "RFC-2409: The Internet Key Exchange (IKE)." November 1998.

Heinanen et al., 1999. J. Heinanen, F. Baker, W. Weiss, and J. Wroclawski. "RFC-2597: Assured Forwarding PHB Group." June 1999.

Heinanen and Guerin, 1999a. J. Heinanen and R. Guerin. "RFC-2698: A Two Rate Three Color Marker." September 1999.

Bibliography

Herzog, 2000. S. Herzog. "RFC-2750: RSVP Extensions for Policy Control." January 2000.

HomePNA, 2000. "HPNA 2.0 Specification." Home Phoneline Networking Alliance. www.homepna.org. December 1999.

IDC, 1998. "US Managed Security Services: Market Overview and Forecast, 1997-2002." June 1999.

IDC, 1999a. "The Cable Man Cometh: United States Residential Data Cable Service Market Assessment Forecast, 1998-2003." November 1999.

IDC, 1999b. "Preparing for Liftoff: US Residential DSL Market Assessment and Forecast 1998-2003." October 1999.

IDC, 1999c. "United States Broadband Fixed Wireless Market Assessment and Forecast, 1998-2003." December 1999.

IDC, 2000a. "DSL, Cable, and FWA: European Broadband Access Services Forecast and Analysis, 1999-2004." April 2000.

IDC, 2000b. "The Need for Speed: Residential High-Speed Data Services Market Assessment, 1999-2003." May 2000.

IEEE, 1998. "IEEE 802.1Q—IEEE Standard for Local and Metropolitan Area Networks: Virtual Bridge Local Area Networks." IEEE. 1998.

IEEE, 1999. "Information Technology—Telecommunications and Information Exchange between Systems—Local and Metropolitan Area Networks—Specific Requirements—Part 11: Wireless LAN Medium Access Control (MAC) and Physical Layer (PHY) Specifications." IEEE. 1999.

IEEE, 1999a. "Supplement to Information Technology—Telecommunications and Information Exchange between Systems—Local and Metropolitan Area Networks—Specific Requirements—Part 11: Wireless LAN Medium Access Control (MAC) and Physical Layer (PHY) Specifications: High Speed Physical Layer (PHY) in the 5 GHz Band." IEEE. 1999.

IEEE, 1999b. "Supplement to Information Technology—Telecommunications and Information Exchange between Systems—Local and Metropolitan Area Networks—Specific Requirements—Part 11: Wireless LAN Medium Access Control (MAC) and Physical Layer (PHY) Specifications: Higher Speed Physical Layer (PHY) Extension in the 2.4 GHz band." IEEE. 1999.

Infonetics, 2000. "User Plans for VPN Products and Services in the US." Infonetics Research. 2000.

Infonetics, 2001. "Service Provider Core and Edge Hardware: Quarterly Worldwide Market Share and Forecasts for 4Q00." *Infonetics Research.* February 2001.

IRG, 2000. "The 2000 Content Delivery and Distribution Report." Internet Research Group. February 2000.

ITU, 1999a. "G.994.1 (G.hs) Handshake Procedures for Digital Subscriber Line (DSL) Transceivers." June 1999.

ITU, 1999b. "G.992.2 (G.Lite): Splitterless Asymmetric Digital Subscriber Line (ADSL) Transceivers." July 1999.

ITU, 2000. "G.991.2 (G.shdsl): Single-Pair HDSL." April 2000.

Jacobson, 1999. V. Jacobson, K. Nichols, and K. Poduri. "RFC-2598: An Expedited Forwarding PHB." June 1999.

Juniper, 1999a. "Deploying MPLS Traffic Engineering." Juniper Networks application note. http://www.juniper.net/techcenter/app_note/350000.html. October 2000.

Jupiter, 1999b. "Online Advertising through 2003." Jupiter Research. July 1999.

Jupiter, 2000. "US Online Demographics: Fundamentals and Forecasts, Spring 2000." Jupiter Research. July 2000.

Kent, 1998a. S. Kent and R. Atkinson. "RFC-2402: IP Authentication Header." November 1998.

Kent, 1998b. S. Kent and R. Atkinson. "RFC-2406: IP Encapsulating Security Payload." November 1998.

Kent, 1998c. S. Kent and R. Atkinson. "RFC-2401: Security Architecture for the Internet Protocol." November 1998.

Keynote Systems. http://ww.keynote.com.

Malis, 2001. A. Malis et al. "SONET/SDH Circuit Emulation Service over MPLS (CEM) Encapsulation." Internet draft, draft-malis-sonet-ces-mpls-05.txt. July 2001.

Mamakos, 1999. L. Mamakos et al. "RFC-2516: Method for Transmitting PPP over Ethernet (PPPoE)." February 1999.

Martini, 2001a. L. Martini et al. "Encapsulation Methods for Transport of Layer 2 Frames over MPLS." Internet draft, draft-martini-l2circuit-encap-mpls-03.txt. July 2001.

Martini, 2001b. L. Martini et al. "Transport of Layer 2 Frames over MPLS." Internet draft, draft-martini-l2circuit-trans-mpls-07.txt. July 2001.

Maughan, 1998. D. Maughan, D.M. Schertler, M. Schneider, and J. Turner. "RFC-2408: Internet Security Association and Key Management Protocol (ISAKMP)." November 1998.

Merrill Lynch, 1999. "Internet@Latam: The Current State and Prospects of the Internet in Latin America." Merrill Lynch. 19 August 1999.

NextWeb, 2000. http://www.nextweb.cc/datasheets.html/BusinessInternetaccess.pdf.

Nichols, 1998. K. Nichols, S. Blake, F. Baker, and D. Black. "RFC-2474: Definition of the Differentiated Services Field (DS Field) in the IPv4 and IPv6 Headers." December 1998.

Nortel, 2000. "The Shifting Services Cash Flow." Nortel Networks. May 2000.

NYT, 2000. "High Technology Stew." *New York Times,* 28 December 2000: 1C.

Ovum, 2000. "Global Telecoms and IP Markets." Ovum Forecasts. 2000.

Ovum, 2000a. "Access@Ovum." Ovum Forecasts. 2000.

Ovum, 2000b. "The Business Case of Next Generation IP Networks." Ovum Forecasts. August 2000.

Perkins, 1996. C. Perkins. "RFC-2002: IP Mobility Support." October 1996.

PointTopic, 2000. "DSL Worldwide Directory." PointTopic LTD. 2000.

Redback, 2000. "Subscriber Aggregation for Broadband Networks." Redback Networks internal document. 2000.

Bibliography

Redpoint, 2000. "Investments in Networking: Dawn or Dusk." Presentation by Redpoint Ventures at the Next-Generation Networks Conference. November 2000.

Rigney, 1997a. C. Rigney. "RFC-2139: RADIUS Accounting." April 1997.

Rigney et al., 1997b. C. Rigney et al. "RFC-2138: Remote Authentication Dial In User Service (RADIUS)." April 1997.

Rosen, 2000. E. Rosen et al. "BGP/MPLS VPNs." Internet draft, draft-ietf-ppvpn-rfc2547bis-00. July 2001.

Shasta, 2000. Description of Shasta (Nortel IP Services) products at http://www.nortelnetworks.com/ipservices.

Simpson, 1994. W. Simpson, ed. "RFC-1661: The Point-to-Point Protocol (PPP)." July 1994.

Simpson, 1996. W. Simpson. "RFC-1994: PPP Challenge Handshake Authentication Protocol." April 1996.

Simpson, 1997. W. Simpson. "RFC-2153: PPP Vendor Extensions." May 1997.

Solomon and Glass, 1998. J. Solomon and S. Glass. "RFC-2290: Mobile IPv4 Configuration Option for PPP IPCP." February 1998.

SpringTide, 2000. Description of SpringTide (Lucent) products at http://www.lucent.com.

Strategis, 1998. "High Speed Internet." Strategis Group. December 1998.

Telechoice, 2000. "Moving Broadband to the Next Level." Telechoice. July 2000.

Townsley, 1999. W. Townsley. "RFC-2661: Layer Two Tunneling Protocol L2TP." August 1999.

UMTS, 1997. "Evolution of Land Mobile Systems towards IMT-2000." August 1997. (Provides cross-references to other ITU-R "M" series recommendations.)

Wahl et al., 1997. M. Wahl, T. Howes, and S. Kille. "RFC-2251: Lightweight Directory Access Protocol (v3)." December 1997.

Weiner, 2000. M. Weiner. "Dial Off-Load—A Win-Win for ISPs and LECs." *Boardwatch*. June 2000.

Westerinen et al., 2000. "Policy Terminology." Internet draft, draft-ietf-policy-terminology-01.txt. November 2000.

Wired, 2001. F. Rose. "Telechasm" *Wired*. May 2001.

Yavatkar, 2000. R. Yavatkar, D. Pendarakis, and R. Guerin. "RFC-2753: A Framework for Policy-Based Admission Control." January 2000.

Yankee, 2000. "US Residential Broadband Forecast." The Yankee Group. 2000.

Zona, 1999a. "Estimated $4.35 Billion in Ecommerce Sales at Risk Each Year: Zona Research Report Reveals Consequences of Unacceptable Download Times." Zona Research. http://www.zonaresearch.com/info/press/99-jun30.htm. June 1999.

Zona, 1999b. "The Need For Speed." Zona Research. June 1999.

Index

AAA (authentication, authorization, and accounting), 63
AAA servers, 154–157
AAA system integration, wholesaling and capabilities within IPSS, 209
AAL2. *See* ATM Adaptation Layer 2
AAL5. *See* ATM Adaptation Layer 5
Abatis, 174
ABR (available bit rate), 203
Abril group, and Canbras TVA, 284
Abstract objects, *68,* 70
Acceptable use policies, 285
Access control, 51
Access control list, 64
Access devices, at subscriber site, 33–34
Access encapsulations
  across cable, 181
  choice of, 174
Access network, 34–60
  cable access networks, 41–47
  dial-up RAS, 59–60
  DSL access technologies, 35–40
  fixed wireless access technologies, 47–49
  metropolitan Ethernet access technologies, 55–58
  mobile wireless access technologies, 49–55
  traditional dedicated access technologies, 58–59
Access operators, and wholesaling, 207
Access point names, 244
Access protocol, and provider differentiation, 179
Access providers
  and element provisioning, 151
  and last mile problem, 7
  and modem wholesaling, 8
  service, 255
  for video distribution, 117
Access-Request command, 155
Access-Response command, 155
Access technologies, *33, 34*
Access wholesalers, 17, 140
Accounting, 79, 151
Accounting functions, with network subsystem, 52
Accounting Start command, 155
Accounting Stop command, 155
ACL. *See* Access control list
Active agent architecture, *164*
Active wholesaling, 210–211
  advantages with, 209
  passive wholesaling *versus,* 208
Addresses/Addressing
  IPSS and management of, 140
  with Los Gatos Wireless, 293, *294*
  resolution, 66
ADSL. *See* Asymmetric DSL
Advanced Encryption Standard (AES), 80, 229
Advanced services, FCC definition of, 178
Advanced Services Order of 1998, 9
Advertisements/Advertising
  agent, 188
  click-through, 256
  CSPs and revenue from, 17
  rates, 256
  service revenues from, 256
AF. *See* Assured forwarding
Aggressive Mode, with IKE, 88, 89
AH. *See* Authentication header
Akamai, 113, 255
  architecture, 110, *111*
  network, 101
Alcatel, 41, 133, 174
  1000, 277
  36170, 312
  DSLAMs, 274, 312
  Onestream Broadband Access Server, 145

Note: Italicized page locators refer to figures and/or tables.

Alcatel *continued*
   Speedtouch Home, 277
   Speedtouch Pro router, 277
Alcatel Manta, 277
Aliant Telecom, 311
   advantages with, 317
   Aliant basic programming, *315*
   Aliant portal, *316*
   Aliant video over DSL architecture, *312, 314*
   service bundles, *315*
   services description, 312-316
   video and Web convergence, *311*
Alteon Web Systems (Nortel), 105
"Always-on" architecture, security issues with, 285
Amazon, 319
Amber Networks, 133, 145
American National Standards Institute (ANSI), 38
Amplifiers, 39
Analog copper transmission systems, 6
Analog services, 2, 3
Antispoofing, 62, *71*, 74, 172, 305, 307
Antivirus software, 224
ANX, 242
AOL Time-Warner, 97, 98
APNs. *See* Access point names
Application prioritization, 193
Application proxy firewalls, 63, 64-65, 66
Applications, services, technologies, and, *171*
Application service providers, 16, 29, 117, 209, 255
   and CSPs, 16-17
   as IPSS deployment option, 140
Application Specific Integrated Circuits, 134
APS. *See* Automatic protection switching
Architecture
   active agent, *164*
   active wholesaling, 210
   BellSouth new wholesale, *276*
   BellSouth original, *275*
   broadcast video distribution, *118*
   CDMA 2000, 244
   central headend with secondary hub, *46*
   CLE-based IP-VPN, *230*
   content distribution, 98
   COPS, *154*
   dial access, *59*
   DiffServ, 196, 197
   future UMTS, *302*
   Global System for Mobile Communications, *51*
   GPRS and UMTS, 242-244
   GSM, 51
   high-level Internet, 14-15
   H.323 voice, *120*
   IntServ, 196
   IP-centric, 124
   IPSS, 134-136
   Los Gatos Wireless system, *292*
   Marslink PPPoE DSL access, *265*
   OSS, *163*
   SAVVIS, *304, 305*
   single headend, *45*
   wireless system, *49*
ARPANET, Internet Procotol suite in, 4
ArrowPoint (Cisco), 105
AS (autonomous system), 14
Asia/Pacific Rim
   DSL buildout plans in, 176
   DSL revenue growth in, 180
ASICs. *See* Application Specific Integrated Circuits
ASPs. *See* Application service providers
Assured access, 133, 174
Assured forwarding, 195, 305
Asymmetric attacks, 72
Asymmetric DSL, 35, 36, 182
   and bandwidth, 191
   interoperability problems: CAP *versus* DMT, 38
   G.Lite/DSL-Lite and, 37
Asynchronous transfer mode (ATM), 3, 34, 91
   deployments, 141
   DSLAMs based on, 40
   and MPLS, 201
   networks, 1
   PPP over, 176
   radios connected to, 48
   switches, 141
   traffic management within, 190
   and virtual circuits, 264
   and virtual routers, 93
ATM Adaptation Layer 2, 120
ATM Adaptation Layer 5, PVCs, 120
ATM aggregation platform, management of, 149
ATM-based voice service, 120, *121,* 122
ATM Forum, 323, *326*
ATM networks, and rural schools, 19
ATM voice IAD, and PSTN gateway, *121*
Attack prevention, 70-74
AT&T, 6, 7, 12, 13, 15, 47, 176, 209, 245, 266
AUC. *See* Authentication center
AUPs. *See* Acceptable use policies
Authentication, 8, 61, 79, 151, 215, 243
   and IP-VPNs, 244
   and key management, 81
   Los Gatos Wireless, 293
   via Web interfaces, 158
   and wholesaling, 211
Authentication center, 52
Authentication header, 88
Authorization, 79, 211
Automatic protection switching, 136

Index

Backbone
    and bandwidth improvements, 2
    and Internet dial wholesaling, 85
    tunneling across, 62, 83
Backhaul, and exchange points, 16
Bandwidth, 169
    for ADSL, 37
    and broadcast video distribution, 311
    and cache deployment, 103
    and circuit switching, 1
    commoditization, 18
    and content management, 99
    and DDoS attacks, 73
    and filtering, 253
    higher services, 255
    and latency, 3
    and oversubscription, 192
    and packet switching, 2
    and policing, 197
    pricing, 29
    with satellite systems, 184
    and second mile problem, 8
    and service charges, 178
    and shaping, 200
    and technology access choices, 34
    with third-generation wireless access, 54
    and traffic management, 190, 191
    unbundling, 11
    with VDSL, 39
    and video distribution, 118
    and voice protocols, 119
    and WDM, 58
    with wireless connectivity, 242
    and wireless QoS, 206
Bang Networks, 111
Banner advertising, 256
Base station system, 50, 51, 187
Base transceiver station, 51
Basic services, 169, 172
    deployment of, 169-218
    loyalty and lockin, 216-218
    service basics, 170-173
    subscriber aggregation and basic access, 173-190
    traffic management, 190-206
    wholesaling, 207-216
BCD Forum, 336
Bell Atlantic/GTE, 176
Bellcore. *See* Telcordia
BellSouth, 7, 176, 274, 279
    advantages with tunneled service, 278-279
    architecture, 275, *276*
    financial model, 279-283
    services description, 274-275, 277-278
    wholesale encapsulations, *276*

Bell System, 6
BGP. *See* Border Gateway Protocol
BGP4, 91, 92
BigIP (F5 Network), 105
BigIron (Foundry), 105
Bilateral file sharing, 38
Billing, 149. *See also* Prices/Pricing
    and management systems/vendors, *160,* 161
    of subscriber services, 146
    systems, 99
    with vanity ISPs, 210
Biometric systems, 81
BlackICE Defender, 231
BLES. *See* Broadband loop emulation service
Blocking, 78, 230
BOOTP, 65
Border edge, 99
Border Gateway Protocol, 202
Border Gateway Protocol, version 4 (BGP-4), 14
Branch offices. *See also* Telecommuters
    connectivity to, 233
    and IP-VPNs, 244
    and small enterprise deployment, 235
Brand identity, 217
B-RAS. *See* Broadband remote access servers
Brazil, Canbras TVA in, 283-284
Bridged headends, 181
Bridged pricing model, 174
Broadband access, 10-11
Broadband buildout, 176, *177*
Broadband content distribution chain, financial linkage between parties in, 249
Broadband content management and distribution, 97
Broadband fixed wireless, deployment example for, 291-294
Broadband hardware vendors, *333-335*
Broadband loop emulation service, 122
Broadband portals, with wholesale DSL services, 278
Broadband remote access servers, 132, 133, 134, 144, 174
Broadband revenues, *185*
Broadband satellite systems, 185
Broadband service node, 25, 274-275
Broadband services, 2
    help desk requests for, 148
    and second mile problem, 8
Broadband subscriber aggregation, 172
Broadcast video distribution, 97, 118, 180, 263, 310-317
BroadJump, 162, 163
BSC. *See* Base station controller
BSN. *See* Broadband service node
BSS. *See* Base station system
BTS. *See* Base transceiver station

Buffering, 142
Buffer sizing, 203
Building Office Management Association, 186
Buildout, 27
   broadband, 176
   of data centers, 12
   DSL, 35
   fixed wireless, 47
   global broadband, *177*
   ILEC, 19
   infrastructure costs and, 18
   revenue growth, 256
   3GNet, 298
Bulk policies, 152
Bulk provisioning, 150
Bundled services, 170, 172, 177, 184, 217, 311
Burstiness, 3
Business, revenue growth in, 180, 183
BusinessFirewall, 70
Business-grade services, residential-grade services *versus,* 21
Business management, within ITU's TNM, 147
Business relationships, and content services deployment, 248–250
Business subscribers, SLAs for, 179
Business-to-business, revenue from, 255, 256
Business-to-consumer, revenue from, 255, 256

CA. *See* Certificate Authority
Cable, 17, 31, 34, 60
   buildout of, 27
   comparison of DSL, fixed wireless and, 185, *186*
   and fiber, 44–45, 47
   high-speed connectivity via, 8
   provisioning, *152*
   quality of service, 205–206
   and subscriber self-provisioning, 158
   subscription costs, 22
   technology, 10
   topology, *43*
   voice traffic, 126, *127*
   wholesaling, 210
Cable access, 180–182
Cable access providers, *331–332*
Cable access technologies, 41–47
   evolving role of fiber in cable systems, 44–45, 47
   headend, 42, 44, *46*
Cable and Wireless, 15
Cable headends, *43*, 205, 206
CableLabs, 42, 323, *326*
Cable modems, 32, 33, 41, 42
   deployment of, *46*, 151
   encapsulations, *286*
   headends, 42, 44
   penetration of, 182
   service, 19, 205, 283, *287*
   termination system, 41, 42, 145, 151, 284
Cable open access, 263, 283–290
   advantages with, 286–287
   cable modem service revenue, *289, 290*
   financial model, 287
CAC. *See* Connection admission control
CacheFlow, 102
Cache misses, 100
Caches/Caching, 4, 30, 97
   characteristics of, 101–103
   content, 100–103
   and IP-VPNS, 244
   and load balancing, 251
   personal information, 127, 128
   proxy, 100–101
   servers, 100
Cageless deployments, 10
Cahners IN-Stat, 256
CALA. *See* Central and Latin America
CALEA. *See* Communications Assistance for Law Enforcement
Call acceptance, 66
Call agents, 120
Call control, 52
Caller ID, 18, 122
Call forwarding, 52, 122
Calling station IDs, 157
Call servers, 257
Call waiting, 122
CAMEL, 52
Canadian Maritime Provinces, Aliant Telecom in, 311
Canbras Acesso, 284, 287–288
Canbras Communications Corporation (Canada), 283
CanbrasNet, 284
Canbras TVA, 283–284
   advantages with, 286–287
   cable modem services, *285, 287, 289, 290*
   financial model for service, 287–291
   services description, 284–286
Carrier amplitude and phase (CAP), 38
Carriers, 1
   evolution of: divestiture and consequences, 6–13
   and TDMA, 50
Carrier technological problems, 7, 8
Category 5 unshielded twisted pair, 32
Cayman router, 277
CBQ. *See* Class-based queuing
CBR (constant bit rate), 199
CBS (committed burst size), 197
CCC. *See* Circuit Cross Connect
CDMA. *See* Code division multiple access
CDMA 1xRTT, 187, 188
CDMA 3xRTT, 187
CDMA 2000, 55, 244

Index

CDN. *See* Content distribution network
CDPs. *See* Content distribution providers
CDSPs. *See* Content delivery service providers
Cell loss priority, 203
Cell phones, 25, 34
Cellular, evolution of, 52–53
Cellular masts, 48
Cellular provisioning systems, 133
Cellular radio, 191
Cellular telephones, 192
Celox, 133, 145, 174
Central and Latin America, DSL revenue in, 180
Centralized file backup, and IP-VPNs, 244
Centralized management goals, 153
Central office, 35, 37, 39, 118
Centrex for business, 21, 122
CE routers, 91, 92
Certificate Authority, 81, 82, 88, 242
Certificates, 63, 82–83, 88
Certification, ICSA, 224
Challenge Handshake Authentication Protocol (CHAP), 79, 84
Channelized DS3 and E3, 182, 183
Channels, 50
Chargen services, 73
Check Point, 229
Check Point Firewall 1, 240
Check Point SecuRemote, 175
Checksums, and authentication headers, 88
ChOC12 Frame, 135
Ciphering algorithms, 89
Circuit Cross Connect, 91
Circuit emulation service, over MPLS, 91
Circuit-level firewall, 64
Circuit-oriented DSLAMs, 40
Circuit-switched services, 1
Cisco Systems, 57, 84, 102, 174, 229, 296
    ArrowPoint, 105
    DPT, 135
    routers for SAVVIS network, 304
    Sightpath acquired by, 113
    routers, 132, 143, 144, 145, 277
    VPN 5000 Concentrator, 145
    Web Cache Coordination Protocol, 103
Class-based queuing, 199
Classes of service, 204
Class 5 office, 7
Class 5 voice switch, 122
Classification, 194, 205
CLE. *See* Customer localized equipment
Clean networks, 317, 319
CLE-based IP-VPN and firewall policy, *230, 240*
CLEC. *See* Competitive local exchange carrier
CLE/CPE. *See* Customer localized equipment/customer premises equipment

CLE devices, monitoring/altering configuration of, 164–165
CLI. *See* Command line interface
"Click-and-mortar," *26,* 256
"Click-through" advertising, 256
Client registration, 163
Client software, IPSS, service provisioning and, 146, 162–164
Client-to-HQ connectivity, 230
Client tunneling alternatives, *234*
Client updates, 163
CLP. *See* Cell loss priority
CMDA 2000, 242
CMTS. *See* Cable modem termination system
CNM. *See* Customer network management
CO. *See* Central office
Coaxial cable, 3, 7, 45, 126
Codecs, 119
Code division multiple access, 49, 50
COINs. *See* Communities of interest networks
Collocation agreements, 9
Collocation fees, with wholesale DSL services, 280
"Colors," 56, 57, 58
Command line interface, 150
Committed information rate, 179, 197
Common element redundancy, and IPSS, 136
Common Object Request Broker Architecture (CORBA), 149, 157
Common Open Policy Service, 146, 153, *154*
Communications Assistance for Law Enforcement Act, 125
Communities of interest networks, 306, 307
Competitive LECs, 8, 11, 35
    and ADSL, 38
    economic viability of, 12–13
    and incumbent local exchange carriers, 9–10
    and provisioning, 148
    and rural areas, 19
Compulsory tunneling, 84, *85,* 242, 243
Condominiums, metropolitan fiber extension to, 55
Conferencing, and traffic management, 190, 255
Congestion, 191, 218. *See also* Traffic management
    and content routing, 107
    control, 194
    reducing, 198
    and shaping, 200, 201
Connection admission control, 203
Connectivity costs, 21, 22–25
Content, 99
    adaptation, *254*
    condensation, 102
    customization, 253
    distribution, *113, 318, 321*
    insertion, 254
    positioning, 253

Content *continued*
   routing, 99, 107-108
   streaming, 244
Content architecture, evolved, 254
Content caches/caching, 97, 99, 100-103, 105, 250
Content delivery service providers, 255
Content distribution and management, 99, 108-117, 248
   digital rights management, 116
   evolution of content distribution, 109-112, *110*
   hosted applications, 117
   streaming content, 112-116
Content distribution architecture, elements, 98
Content distribution market opportunity, 255-256
Content distribution network (system), 99, 251, 252
Content distribution providers, 6, 17
Content edge, 99
Content-enabled networks, topologies for, 250-253
Content filtering/blocking, 24, 61, 62, 77-78, 244, 253, 259
Content management, 61, 95, 98-117
Content mediation, 132, 208
Content mediation/adaptation, 253-254
Content networking, evolution of, 30
Content PoP, *100*
Content providers, 7, 31, 98, 248-249
Content router, 251
Content selection system integration, 209
Content servers, 29
Content service providers, 6, 16-17
Content services, edge and intelligent placement of, 28
Content services deployment, 248-256
   closer look at CDN, *251*
   end-to-end content network, *251, 252*
   net result of end-to-end architecture, 253-255
   service penetration and upsell, *250*
Content switching/switches, 30, 97, 99, 103, 104, 110, 137, 145, 251
Content Tunnel, 114, 115
Contracts, 217
Control messages, and L2TP, 84
Convergence, 1, 2, 5-6, 97
Cookies, 104-105, 106, 253
CopperCom, 123
Copper loop-based technologies, 36, 151
Copper Mountain, 283
Copper pairs, 3, 7, 149
   reuse of, 57
   sharing, 11
   and voice, 119, 125
COPS. *See* Common Open Policy Service
COPS-PR, 153, 154
Copy protection of content, 99
Core network, in mobile network, 50
Core router, IPSS *versus*, 133, 134

Core switching, 257
Corio, 209
CoS. *See* Classes of service
CoSine Communications, 133, 137, 145, 174
Costs. *See also* Billing; Prices/Pricing
   financial wholesaling comparisons, 212-215
   for residential service bundling, 259
Covad, 8, 11, 29, 176, 178, 179, 255, 291
CPE. *See* Customer premises equipment
CPE-based service revenues, 246
CPE-based VPNs, 224-226, *225, 227*
Crescent Networks, 133
CRLDP signaling, and MPLS, 201
Cryptography, 87, 224
CSPs. *See* Content service providers
CT. *See* Content Tunnel
Customer care, 149, *160,* 161
Customer-facing providers, 30
Customer localized equipment, 17, 18, 20, 29, 35, 221, 222
   services, 170
   and transit wholesaling, 212
   and voice distribution, 119
   and voice services, 256, 257
Customer localized equipment/customer premises equipment, 27
Customer network management, *165,* 217
   IPSS, service provisioning and, 146, 164-165
   and IP-VPNs, 244
Customer premises equipment, 4, 20, 35
   and firewall deployment, 221, 222
   and oversubscription, 193
   transition from leased lines to managed, 5
Customer requirements for advanced services, 25
Customers, 1. *See also* Subscribers
   effective provisioning for, 147-149
   loyalty and lockin, 216-217
   queuing, 194
   retaining, 322
   segments, *21*
   support, 218
Customization, 217
Customized applications for mobile enhanced logic. *See* CAMEL
Customized dictionary, 77
Customized services, with IPSS provisioning, 146

DACS. *See* Digital access cross connect
Dark fiber, 58, 217
Data, 5, 6, 12
Data center operator, 317, 318, 321
Data domain, 299
Data encoding, with HDSL, 39
Data Encryption Standard, 80, 87, 229
Data-forwarding path, 146

Data link connection identifiers, 184, 238
Data LEC, 161
Data messages, and L2TP, 84
Data Over Cable System Interface Specification, 42, 151, 182, 284
"Data pump," 111
Data-replication architecture, 110
Data security, 234
Data services, 2-6, 13
DE. *See* Discard eligible
Dedicated access technologies, 58-59
Dedicated resources, 3
Default forwarding, 15
Default-free zone, 15
Delays, 193, 196, 201
Demilitarized zone interfaces, 220
Demographics, DSL, cable subscribers and, 182
Denial of service, 317
Denial-of-service attacks, 62, 71, 72, 172, 220, 321
Dense wavelength division multiplexing, 30, 56
Deployment examples, 263-322
    broadcast video distribution, 263, 310-317
    cable open access, 263, 283-290
    DSL wholesaling and portals, 263, 274-283
    fixed wireless wholesaling, 263, 291-294
    Internet data center, 263, 317-321
    IP-VPNs and firewalls, 263, 303-310
    residential PPPoE service, 263-273
    3G mobile wireless services, 263, 295-303
Deregulation, 2
DES. *See* Data Encryption Standard
DFZ. *See* Default-free zone
DHCP. *See* Dynamic Host Configuration Protocol
DHCP Option 82, 215
Dial access, 59, 186, *187,* 192
Dial-up remote access servers, 59-60
Dial-up users, and security by obscurity, 62
Dial wholesaling, 60, 156-157, *210,* 211
Diffie-Hellman key exchange, 87
DiffServ, 172, 195, 197, 199
    codepoint, 196
    implementation, *196*
    markings, 205, 229, 305, 306
Digex, 255
Digital access cross connect, 293
Digital certificates, 87
Digital Island, 111
Digital loop carrier, 39, 41, 176
Digital networking, 3
Digital rights management, 116
Digital signatures, 63, 82
Digital subscriber line, 8, 10, 17, 31, 34, 60, 155-156
    access, 33, *175*
    and bandwidth, 191
    and broadcast video distribution, 180
    buildout of, 27
    cable modem service *versus,* 41
    comparison of cable, fixed wireless, and, 185, *186*
    costs of, 22
    IP-based voice technology support with, 124
    management domains, *148*
    marketing opportunities and access to, 173-180
    modems, 32, 38
    providers, and incumbent LECs, 10-11
    provisioning tasks, *150,* 151
    rates, 181
    retail quality of service, 204
    routers, 230
    and rural areas, 19
    and subscriber self-provisioning, 158
    taxonomy, *37*
    topology, *36*
    urban area access to, 19
    and video distribution, 117
    and voice services, 257
    wholesale quality of service, 204-205
    wholesaling, 207-209
Digital subscriber line access multiplexer, 8, 11, 17, 36, 40-41, 173
    and ATM-based voice services, 120
    with BellSouth, 274
    circuit-oriented, 40
    and DSL wholesaling, 275
    and element provisioning, 149, 150
    IP-DSLAMs, 40-41
    and IPSS deployment, 137, 138
    headends, 145
    and oversubscription, 193
    and QoS, 203
    and transit wholesaling, 212
    and video distribution, 118, 180
Digital subscriber line integrated access device, 35
Digital subscriber line technologies, 35-39, 40-41
Digital subscriber line wholesaling and portals, 263, 274-283
Digital technologies, 3
Digital TV, 177
Digital Video Broadcasting, 42
Directory replication, with LDAP, 157
Dirty networks, 317, 319
Disaster recovery, 128
Discard eligible, 196
Discrete multitone, 38
Dish Network, 184
Distributed denial of service, 71
Distributed DoS attacks, 72, 74
Divestiture, evolution of carriers and consequences of, 6-13
DLC. *See* Digital loop carrier
DLCIs. *See* Data link connection identifiers

DLEC. *See* Data local exchange carrier
DMT. *See* Discrete multitone
DMZ interfaces. *See* Demilitarized zone interfaces
DMZ1 and DMZ2, 228
DNS. *See* Domain name service
DOCSIS. *See* Data Over Cable System Interface Specification
Domain name service, 170
Domain Naming System, 17
Domain of interpretation (DOI), 88
DoS. *See* Denial of service
Downstream, 37
Downstream data, 45, 47
Downtime, 217
DPT (Cisco), 135
DRM. *See* Digital rights management
Drop precedence (DP), 195
DSCP. *See* DiffServ codepoint
DS1/E1, and voice services, 257
DS3/E3, 135, 257
DSL. *See* Digital subscriber line
DSL access providers, 149, *329, 330*
DSLAM. *See* Digital subscriber line access multiplexer
DSL Forum, 323, *325,* 336
DSL-Lite, 38
Dumb terminals, 4
Dun & Bradstreet, 186
DVB. *See* Digital Video Broadcasting
DVDs, piracy of, 116
DWDM. *See* Dense wavelength division multiplexing
Dynamic Host Configuration Protocol, 71, 149, 215, *216*
Dynamic Packet Transport (Cisco), 57
Dynamic quality of service, 190, 206
Dynamic updates, *112*

EAP. *See* Extensible Authentication Protocol
Early packet discard, 203
Earthlink, 184
Eavesdropping, 88
EBG (egress broadband gateway), 275
EBS. *See* Excess burst size
Echo services, 73
e-commerce, 169
　and cookies, 106
　and DMZ, 220
　and firewalls, 68
　and network services growth, 256
EDGE, *53,* 54
Edge aggregation routers, 144-145
Edge caching, 100, 101, 103, 113
Edge routers, 93, 136
　IPSS *versus,* 133, 134, 142-143
Edge services, 1, 28-30
Education services, spending on, *26*

EF. *See* Expedited forwarding
Efficiencies
　optimizing data network, 3
　with wholesale DSL services, 279
Efficient 4060, 277
Egress antispoofing and filtering, 71
802.1Q tagging, 57
EIR. *See* Equipment identity register
Electronic picket fences, 73
Element management/provisioning, 146, 149-152
　within ITU's TMN, 147
　and management systems/vendors, *160*
　and voice services, 258
Ellacoya, 133, 174
e-mail, 16, 17, 129
　and DMZ, 220
　with vanity ISPs, 210
Embedded operations channel (EOC), 122
Emerging technologies, hype cycle of, *146*
Encapsulating security payload, 76, 88
Encapsulations, Los Gatos Wireless, 293, *294*
Encryption, 61, 63, 79-80, 84, 87, 93, 133, 229, 230, 243
End office, 7
End-to-end architecture, net result of, 253-255
End-to-end content delivery, QoS requirements, *252*
End-to-end content network, 250, *251*
End-to-end management service, 173
End-to-end PVCs, *213*
End-to-end QoS, 199, 252
End-to-end requirements, 203, 204, *205*
End-to-end service implementations, 170
Enhanced Data Rates for Global Evolution. *See* EDGE
Enhanced services, 159, 169
Enterprise firewalls, 222, *223*
Enterprise markets, and SOHO market, 21
Enterprise resource planning (ERP), 128
Entertainment, 129
Entertainment-quality video distribution, 117
Entrust, 82
E1, 20, 39, 58, 257
EPD. *See* Early packet discard
Equal access, through MSOs, 13
Equinix, 15
Equipment identity register, 52
Error correction, 4
ESCON, 58
ESP. *See* Encapsulating security payload
Ethernet, 33, 35, 39, 45, 58, 91
　bridging, 181
　extension, 55-56, 316
　installations, 32
　MAC, 292
　MPLS, 201
　switching, 33

Index

E3, 257
Europe
    DSL, cable, and fixed wireless buildout across, 185
    DSL buildout plans in, 176
    DSL revenue growth in, 180
    IP-VPN revenue growth in, 246
    residential cable and wireless revenues, 182, 183
    3GNet in, 295
    voice services in, 126
Excess burst size, 197
Excess information rate, 197
Exchange points, 15–16
Excite@home, 255
Exodus Communications, 15, 255
Expedited forwarding, 196
Extensible Authentication Protocol, 84
External management systems, 159–162

FA. *See* Foreign agent
Fair queuing, 199
Fast Ethernet (FE), 40, 42, 56, 57, 59, 135
Fast packet services, 3
Fault management, *160*
FCC (Federal Communications Commission), 9
FDDI. *See* Fiber distributed data interface
FDMA. *See* Frequency division multiple access
Federal Communications Commission, 9
Federal Information Processing Standard, 80
Fees, 34, 58. *See also* Billing; Costs; Prices/Pricing
F5 Networks, BigIP, 105
Fiber, evolving role of, in cable systems, 44–45, 47
Fiber Channel, 58
Fiber distributed data interface, 57
FIFO. *See* First-in, first-out
File backup, automatic, 245
File recovery, 244
File transfer, 16
File Transfer Protocol, 66, 69
Filtering, 77, 78
    with Los Gatos Wireless, 294
    services, 253
Financial agreements, 253. *See also* Service level agreements
Financial information, 129
Financial wholesaling comparisons, 212–215
Financial Xchange IP-VPN network, 304
FineGround, 102
FIPS. *See* Federal Information Processing Standard
Firewall certification standards bodies, 78
Firewall criteria list 3.0a, 224
Firewall logging, personal, *231*
Firewall policy, 63, *70*
Firewalls/Firewalling, 27, 34, 61, 63–68, 70, 74, 125, 129, 142, 220–224, 233, 240, 321. *See also* VPNs and firewalls

application proxy, 64–65
applications followed by, *328*
and caches, 102
capabilities of, 220–221
comparison of, 65
and customer network management, 164
deployment of, 221–224
distributed, 237
H.323, 67
and Internet data centers, 317, 318, *320*
and IPSS, 132
and IP-VPNs, 244
load balancing, 251
and L2TP, 86–87
packet-filtering, 64
policy definition for, 68, 70
and protocols, 65–68
with residential service bundling, 259
stateful, 64, 172
types and features, 63, 222, 223
voice traffic, 124
Firewall software development, 67
First-generation (1G) cellular deployments, 52
First-in, first-out, 198
Fixed wireless, 60, 182, 323, *326*
    comparison of cable, DSL, and, 185, *186*
    deployment, *48,* 151
    and voice distribution, 126
Fixed wireless access, 47–49, *183*
Fixed wireless service providers, *333*
Fixed wireless wholesaling, 263, 291–294
    advantages with, 294
    background to, 291–292
    service description, 292–294
"Flooding" of network, 72
Flood protection, 74
Floor space, and CLECs, 10
Flow-through provisioning, *160, 162*
Foreign agent, 188, 190, 244
Fortune 5 million, 20, 245
Forward caching, 100
Foundry, BigIron, 105
4G wireless, 55
FQDNs. *See* Fully-qualified domain names
Fractional T1, 182
FRAD. *See* Frame Relay access device
Frame Relay, 3, 20, 34, 35, 54, 58, 91, 137, 141, 238, 242, 245
    access, 183, *184*
    and CPE-based VPNs, 225
    DSLAMs based on, 40
    fragmentation, 194
    IP-VPN connections *versus,* 247
    IP-VPN cost advantages over, 246
    Layer 3 VPN deployment *versus,* 247

Frame Relay *continued*
 and MPLS, 201
 networks, and rural schools, 19
 OC3/STM1, 135
 radios connected to, 48
 and services, 170
 T1/E1, 135
 traffic management within, 190
 and virtual routers, 93
Frame Relay access device, 34
Frame Relay edge switch, 34
Frame Relay IP-VPNs, *226*
France, DSL-capable lines in, 176
Frequency division multiple access, 50
FTP. *See* File transfer protocol
Full-content filtering, 107
Full-mesh connectivity, 247
Fully-qualified domain names, 155
Funds transfer mechanisms, 253

Gambling, online, 129
Games/Gaming, 25, 69
 consoles, 32
 spending on, 25, *26*
 and traffic management, 190
Gartner Group, 146
Gateway GPRS serving node, 187
Gateway GPRS support node, 50, 54, 127, 152, 243
Gauntlet software (Network Associates), 137
GE. *See* Gigabit Ethernet
General Bandwidth, 124
Generalized MPLS, 91
General Packet Radio Service, 49, 53, 54, 188
 architecture, 242–244
 network, example of, *296*
 and 3GNet, 295
Generic router encapsulation, 89, 90, 215, 229, 232
Geographical mobility, 299
Geographic issues, and large users, 19
GeoPoint (Quova), 112
Germany, DSL-capable lines in, 176
GGSN. *See* Gateway GPRS support node
G.hs handshake protocol, 39
Gigabit Ethernet, 42, 56, 59, 135, 144
Gilat Satellite Networks, 184
G.lite, 38
Global broadband buildout, *177*
Global load balancers, 103
Global roaming, via Internet, 216
Global System for Mobile Communications, 49, 50, 51, 298, 299
Gotham Networks, 133, 145
GPRS. *See* General Packet Radio Service
GPRS Tunneling Protocol (GTP), 187, 243, 300
GRE. *See* Generic router encapsulation

GRE tunneling, *90*
GR-303, 122–123
GSM. *See* Global System for Mobile Communications
GSM GPRS, and mobile wireless access, 187
GTE, 82

HA. *See* Home agent
Hacker attacks, 285, 221, 321
Hackers/Hacking, 61, 318, 319
 and IP address spaces, 62
 SMURF attacks by, 72
 spoofing by, 70
Half-bridging, 175
Hardware, and provisioning, 149
Hash algorithms, 89
HDLC. *See* High-level data link control
HDSL. *See* High-speed DSL
HDSL2, 36, 39
HDTV (high-definition television), 7
Headend cable, beyond, *43*
Headends, 42, 44
 within cable, 180
 central, with secondary hub architecture, *46*
 and element provisioning, 151
Headquarter sites, and small enterprises, 236–237
Help desk requests, 148
HFC. *See* Hybrid fiber-coax
Hierarchical class-based queuing, 199
High-density subscriber aggregation, 27
High-end business services, pricing for, 179
Higher-layer technologies, 97–129
 content management, 98–117
 video distribution, 117–118
 virtual hosting services, 127–129
 voice distribution, 119–127
Higher-level services deployment, 219–262
 content services deployment, 248–256
 firewalls and IP-VPNs, 219–248
 service bundling, 258–260
 voice services deployment, 256–258
High-level data link control, 183
High-speed access, *20*
High-Speed Circuit-Switched Data, 52, *53*
High-speed DSL, 36, 38
High-touch packet-processing modules, 135
High-touch services, 131, 232
High-value service deployments, 263
Hit rates, of caches, 100, 101
HMAC + MD5 and HMAC+SHA-1, 87
Home agent, 188, 244
Home gateway, 32
Home location register (HLR), 52, 243
Home networking, *32*
Home Phone Networking Alliance (HomePNA), 32, 48, 292

Home security, 32
Home workers, bandwidth needed by, 178
Hong Kong, DSL-capable lines in, 176
Hosted applications, 117
Hosted service providers, 255
Hosted Web servers, with virtual hosting services, 127
Hosting facilities, and network peering, 16
Hot software upgrade, 123
Hot swap, 123
HP OpenView, 277
HSCSD. *See* High-Speed Circuit-Switched Data
HSPs. *See* Hosted service providers
H.323, 64, 65, 66, 67, *120*
HTTP, and firewalls, 66
H.245 exchange, and firewalls, 67
Hughes DirecPC service, 184
Hybrid fiber-coax, *44*, 151, 284

IAD. *See* Integrated access device
IANA. *See* Internet Assigned Numbers Authority
IAPs. *See* Internet access providers
IBG. *See* Ingress broadband gateway
iBlast, 114
IBM GNS. *See* AT&T GNS
ICMP, and firewalls, 65
ICSA. *See* International Computer Security Association
IDC. *See* Internet data center
IDSL. *See* ISDN DSL
IETF. *See* Internet Engineering Task Force
IETF Policy Framework Working Group, service defined by, 170
I-Gear (Symantec), 253
IGMP. *See* Internet Group Management Protocol
IGs. *See* Interface groups
IKE. *See* Internet Key Exchange
ILECs. *See* Incumbent local exchange carriers
iMagic, 311, 313, 315
Incumbent local exchange carriers, 2, 6, 7, 8, 34, 35
　and ADSL, 38
　and competitive LECs, 9–10
　and DSL providers, 10–11
　financial wholesaling comparisons and, 213–215
　for flow-through provisioning, 161
　and voice distribution, 119
　and voice services, 256, 257
Independent operating companies, 6, 11–12
Independent voice service providers, 7
Industry forums and associations, *336*
Infonetics, 58
Information services, 25, *26,* 129
Ingress antispoofing, 71, 74
Ingress broadband gateway, 274, 275, 278
Ingress filtering, 71
Initial loop qualification, 149
Inktomi, 102

Innovative servicing, 217
Installed capacity, ratio of lines in service *versus,* 145
Integrated access device, 34, 35, 120, 203, 304
Integrated services digital network, 1, 3, 37, 58, 192
　DSL, 37, 39
　encoding, 39
　and H.323 protocol, 66
　RASs, 17
　and voice services, 257
Integrated Services (IntServ), 196
Intelligent edge caching, 101
Intelligent network (IN), 52
Interactive TV, 117
Interexchange carriers, 6, 29
　and IOCs, 11–12
　and wholesaling, 209
Interface groups, 122
Interface management, 142
International Computer Security Association, 78, 224
International Mobile Telecommunications 2000 (IMT 2000), 53, 55, *295*
Internet, 2, 4, 25, 80, 97, 99
　accelerators, 24
　architecture, high-level, 13–14
　dial provisioning, 158
　dial wholesaling, 85
Internet access
　dial-up, 59–60
　and digital rights management, 116
　exchange points in, 15–16
　global roaming via, 216
　and regulation, 30
　over TADs, 22
　providers, 216
　telephony, *125*
　video distribution over, 117
Internet Assigned Numbers Authority, 68, 69
Internet data center, 263, 317–320
　advantages with, 320–321
　background to, 317–318
　IPSS uses for within, 140
　services description, 318–320
Internet Engineering Task Force, 59, 90, 91, 323
　Integrated Services, 196
　Provider Provisioned VPN working group, 233
　standards, *324*
Internet Freedom and Broadband Deployment Act, 10
Internet Group Management Protocol, 312
Internet Key Exchange, 88, 229
Internet Mobility (3GNet), 296
Internet Protocol, 4, 65
Internet radio, 129
Internet Security Association and Key Management Protocol, 88

Internet service providers, 1, 7, 29, 140, 255
   active wholesaling and, 209
   creation of, 9
   and element provisioning, 151
   evolution of, and Internet architecture, 13-17
   and modem wholesaling, 8
   and packet-switched services, 2
   services, 170
   and subscriber evolution, 18
   and wholesaling, 207, 214
Internet telephony, 42, 66, 206
Intranets, 81
   IP-VPN access to, 129
   and universal mobile telecom system, 298
Intrusion, 62, 244
IOCs. *See* Independent operating companies
IP. *See* Internet Protocol
IP addresses
   assigning, 175
   and firewall policy definition, 70
   and hackers, 62
   and masquerade attacks, 71
   and NAT, 74
iPass, 216
IP-based voice services, 123-126
IP-DSLAMs, 40-41
IP in IP, 89, 90, 229, 232
IPmc. *See* IP Multicast
IP mobility, 188, *189*
"IP mode" PDP context, 243
IP Multicast, 40, 113, 312
IP-network-based services, spending on, *26*
IP Security (IPSec), 76, 77, 81, 87-89, 149, 181, 231, 243
   advantages with, 242
   products, 224
   session establishment, *89*
   tunneling, 187
IP Security Protocol, 76, 229
IP service routers, 145
IP services
   categories of, 169
   role of, at network edge, 25, 27-28
IP services switch (IPSS), 22, 60, 129, 131-133, *132*, 174
   architecture for, 134-136
   and cable headends, 42, 44, 180
   and content revenue flow, 248
   and content switches, 105
   deployment, 137-140
   in dial aggregation, 186
   and dynamic QoS, 206
   edge and core routers *versus*, 133, 134
   edge routers *versus*, 142-143
   elements within, 136
   and firewall deployment, 222
   forwarding performance, *135*
   interaction with RADIUS, *155*
   and IP-based voice services, 124
   and large enterprise deployment, 239
   and legacy access, 183
   in MDU/MTU market segment, 186
   and mobile wireless access, 187
   network engineering with, 140-142
   packet flow through, 136-137
   provisioning, 146-147
   radios connected to, 48
   role of, 190-191
   and services location, 172
   and small enterprise deployment, 235, 237, 238
   and subscriber self-provisioning, 158
   and traffic management, 203
   and traffic segregation, 229
   and tunnel switching, 211
   vendor revenue opportunity, 143-146
   wholesaler deployment of, *214*
   and wholesaling, 208-209, 210, 212
   wholesaling and capabilities within,
   and wireless access, 182
IP services switch I/O, and DSL wholesale QoS, 205
IP services switch I/O modules, components, 135
IP services switch provisioning, 146-167
   and client software, 162-164
   COPS, 153-154
   customer network management, 164-165
   dial wholesaling and RADIUS, 156-157
   external management systems, 159-162
   LDAP, 157
   need for, 147-149, 152-153
   RADIUS, 154-156
   SLAs, 165-167
IP-TV, 311
IPv6 (IP version 6), and IP mobility, 190
IP-virtual private network (IP-VPN), 27, 76, 105, 142, 224-248, 321
   alternatives, *234*
   blades, 143
   clients, 238
   and DCN, 99
   and CNM, 164
   desktop and server software, 230-231
   device characteristics, 228-230
   extending "off-net," 240-242
   and firewall deployment, 222
   Frame Relay or leased-line, *226*
   and hosted applications, 117
   implementation of, 231-238
   interworking, *241*
   and IPSS, 132
   large enterprise deployment, 238-239

market opportunity for, 244-248
network-based, 228
service level agreements, 166
services, 91, 232
small enterprise deployment, 235-238
and wholesaling, 209
IP VPNs and firewalls, 303-310
advantages with, 310
background to, 303-304
services description, 304-308, 310
IP Xchange, 307
ISAKMP. *See* Internet Security Association and Key Management Protocol
ISDN. *See* Integrated services digital network
IS-IS, 202
Island Telecom (Prince Edward Island), 311
ISPs. *See* Internet service providers
IteX Apollo 2, 277
ITU, 38, 323
standards, 327
Telecommunications Management Network, 147
IXCs. *See* Interexchange carriers

Japan, 295
@Jato, 284
Jetstream, 123
Jitter, 193, 196
Juniper, 91
Juniper M160 routers, 318
JUNOS software, 91

Kerberos, 88
Keyed hash algorithms, 87
Keys, 82
exchange of, 241
management of, 63, 80-82, 88
Kingsbury Commitment (1913), 6
Korea, DSL-capable lines in, 176

Label edge router, 243
Label switched path, 197
Label switch router, 243
LAC. *See* L2TP access concentrator
LANs. *See* Local area networks
Laptops, 32, 34
Large enterprises, 238-239
requirements, 19-20
Last-meter, business, SOHO, and residential LANs, 31-33
Last-mile problem, 7, 129
Latency, 3, 39, 110, 193, 198
Layer 1/Layer 2 technologies, 91
Layer 2 Forwarding Protocol, 84, 87, 232
Layer 2 Tunneling Protocol, 83, 84-87, 169, 232, 243, 244, 264
advantages with, 86, 87

and IP addressing, 175
and Los Gatos Wireless, 293
and wireless access, 182
Layer 3 protocols, 234
Layer 3 traffic management, 191
Layer 3 VPN deployment, Frame Relay *versus*, 247
LDAP. *See* Lightweight Directory Access Protocol
LDAPv3, 157
Leased-line IP-VPN, 226
Leased lines, 5, 245, 246
LECs. *See* Local exchange carriers
Legacy access, 183
Legacy systems, 29
Legacy technologies, 35
LER. *See* Label edge router
Level 3 Communications, 12, 29
LGW. *See* Los Gatos Wireless
Lightweight Directory Access Protocol, 82, 146, 153, 157, 158
Linux, 163
LNS. *See* L2TP Network server
Load balancing, 251, 318, 319, 320
Local area networks, 31, 33
Local exchange carriers, 6
Local load balancers, 103
Local loops, vulnerabilities across, 223
Local mobility, 299
Local multipoint distribution system (LMDS), 47, 48
Local Number Portability, 125
Location
for services, 172-173
tracking, 243
Lockin, 169, 171, 216-218
Logging and protection, 231
Loop extenders, 39
Loop unbundling, 12
Los Gatos Wireless, 291-292
advantages with, 294
service description, 292-294
Losses, and traffic management, 190
Lotus Notes, 68, 328
Loyalty, 169, 216-218
LSP. *See* Label switched path
LSR. *See* Label switch router
L2F. *See* Layer 2 Forwarding Protocol
L2-7 policy redirection, 251
L2TP. *See* Layer 2 Tunneling Protocol
L2TP Access Concentrator, 85, 156, 275
L2TP Network Server, 85, 156, 275
L2TP tunnels/tunneling, 155, 211, 275
Lucent, 133, 174, 229
ATM switches for SAVVIS network, 304
DSL Terminator 100, 145

Lucent *continued*
   5ESS, 122
   SpringTide, 137, 145, 293

MAC. *See* Media access control
Mac operating system, 163
MAE. *See* Metropolitan Area Exchange
Main distribution frame, 10, 35
Mainframe-based networks, 3
Main Mode, with IKE, 88, 89
Malicious attacks, 73, 79
Malicious traffic, 235, 237
MAN. *See* Metropolitan area network
Managed services, 35
Management/resource partitioning, 209
Management systems and vendors, *160,* 161
Man-in-the-middle attacks, 81
Market opportunities
   cable access and, 180–182
   content distribution, 255–256
   DSL and, 173–180
   IP-VPN, 244–248
   magnitude of, 261–262
   and pricing, 176
   wireless and, 182–185
Marslink, 268
   advantages with, 268
   DSL service, 287
   financial model, 268–273
   PPPoE DSL access architecture, *265*
   PPPoE encapsulations, *266*
Mass-market IP services, 4–5
Master computers, 73, 74
MCUs. *See* Multipoint control units
MDF. *See* Main distribution frame
MDU/MTU. *See* Multidwelling unit/multitenant unit
Mean time between failures, 167
Media access control, 57
Media Gateway Control Protocol, 120
Media servers, 32
Megaco, 120, 125
Messaging, 25, 129
Messaging bus, 161
Messaging services, spending on, 25, 26
Metropolitan Area Exchange, 15
Metropolitan area network, 57, 180
Metropolitan carriers, and multiservice operators, 12
Metropolitan Ethernet, 31, 35, 60
   access technologies, 55–58
   and video distribution, 117, 118
Metropolitan exchange points, 16
Metropolitan fiber extension, *56*
Metropolitan statistical areas, 11
MGCP. *See* Media Gateway Control Protocol
Microsoft, 69, 83, 229, 231, 293

Microwave transmission systems, 3
Mini-RAMs, 274
Mirroring, 109, 110
Mirror servers, 319, 320
MLPPP. *See* Multilink PPP
Mobile IP (MIP), 188, 244
Mobile networks, components within, 50–51
Mobile nodes, 188
Mobile services, explosive growth of, 262
Mobile station, 50
Mobile switching center, 51, 52
Mobile terminal, 50
Mobile VPNs, 242
Mobile wireless, 35, 60, 323, *327*
   access, 34, 187, *188,* 190
   and element provisioning, 152
   traffic management across, 206
   voice over, 127
Mobile wireless access technologies, 49–55
   cellular evolution, 52–54
   EDGE, 54
   GPRS, 54
   3G wireless access and UMTS, 54–55
Mobile wireless deployment components, 51–52
   base station system, 51
   network subsystem, 51, 52
   operation and support system, 51, 52
Mobility management, 243
Modem ownership, wholesaling costs *versus,* 207
Modems, 3
   cable, 41, 42
   and dial access, 59
   wholesaling, development of, 16
Monitoring services, 25, 26, 129
Motorola, 133, 296–297
Movies-on-demand, 255
MPEG1, 115, 117
MPEG2, 115, 117, 312
MPLS. *See* Multiprotocol label switching
MP3, 115, 206
MSAs. *See* Metropolitan statistical areas
MSC. *See* Mobile switching center
MS-CHAP (v2), 84
MSN, 184
MSOs. *See* Multiservice operators
MSO wholesaler, and access encapsulation, 181
MTBFs. *See* Mean time between failures
MT&T (Nova Scotia), 311
Multicasting, 99, 118
Multichannel multipoint distribution system, 47, 48
Multidwelling units/multitenant units, 11, 41, 55, 186
Multi-homing strategy, 15
Multilink PPP, 293
Multimedia services, and errors, 193
Multiple queue scheduling disciplines, 199

Index

Multiple-service bundles, 23
Multiplexing, 234, 270
Multipoint conferencing, 66, 119
Multipoint control units, 119
Multiprotocol, 234
Multiprotocol label switching, 30, 90–93, 201–202, 231, 232, 233, 239, 241, 243
Multi-routers, *94,* 95
Multiservice bundling, 260
Multiservice operators, 12, 34
Multivendor interoperability, 229
Music on demand, 129
Music services, spending on, 25, *26*

Napster.com, 116
NAS. *See* Network access server
NAT. *See* Network address translation
National Multi-Housing Council, 186
NB Tel (New Brunswick), 311
nessus, 224
Network access server, 16, 59
Network address translation, 61, 62, 74, 75, 76–77, 87, 229, 244, 307
Network Address Translation/Protocol Address Translation (NAT/PAT), 34
Network and host attacks, 75
Network Associates, 137
Network-based caching, 129
Network-based devices, 77
Network-based firewalls, 222, 223
Network-based IP-VPNs, 224, 228
  CPE-based VPNs evolution into, 224–226, *227*
Network-based services, 170
  revenue growth with, 246
  transition from leased lines to managed CPE to, 5
Network-based voicemail, 18
Network caching, 113
Network convergence, 5–6
Network creation system (NCS), 304
Network edge, ISPs, 113, 131, 321
  evolution of, 2
  and firewall deployment, 221
  rich services at, 95
  role of IP services at, 25, 27–28
  traffic management at, 190
Network engineering, with IPSS, 140–142
Network ICE, 231
Networking, 3, *32*
Network interface card, 264
Network management, 277
  within ITU's TMN, 147
  and voice services, 258
Network provisioning, 149
Networks, "flooding" of, 72
Network service provider, 275

Network side caching, 100, 102
Network subsystem, in wireless network, 51, 52
Netzero, 256
News, *128,* 255
NewTel (Newfoundland), 311
NIC. *See* Network interface card
Niche providers, and wholesaling, 209
nmap, 223
Nokia, 133
Nontransparent mode, 243
Nortel, 57, 174, 229
  Alteon 184 Web switches, 319, 320
  Alteon Web Systems, 105
  Contivity, 293
  DMS-100 or 500, 122
  IMAS DSLAMs, 312
  Passport 8600s, 318
  routers, for SAVVIS network, 304
  Service Creation System, 277, 308, 319
Nortel/Shasta 5000 BSN, 136, 145, 274, 284, 285, 286, 310
Northpoint, 20, 29, 218
Novell, 113, 231
NSP. *See* Network service provider
NTS, 162
Nynex, 7

OC3, 98, 118, 257
Office buildings, metropolitan fiber extension to, 55
Offline households, income-based categories of, *24*
Offload servers, 77
"Off-net," 172, 240–242
Online advertising, 256
Online backup, with virtual hosting services, 127
Online expenses, household, *26*
Online gambling, 129
"On-net," 172
Opaque networks, 226–227
Open access, 9, 13, 42, 87, 283
Open Settlement Protocol (OSP), 216
Open Shortest Path First (OSPF), 91, 202
Operational support system, 159
Operation and support system (OSS), 51, 52, 305
OPTera Packet Edge (Nortel), 57
Optical carriers (OCs), 135, 136. *See also* OC3
Optical backbones, 27, 252
Optical cross-connect architectures, 91
Optical Ethernet, 194
Optical fiber systems, 7
Optical transmission systems, 3
Optical wavelengths, and MPLS, 201
OSS architecture, *163*
Outages, 217
  and SLAs, 166, 167
Outsourcing of access, 207

Overbuild, 145
Overlay network, 250
Oversubscription, 172, 175, 178, 190, 191, *192*, 206, 269, 270

PacBell, 178, 179
Pace CPE, 312
Packet-based (air) interface, 54
Packet carrying function, 244
Packet control unit support node, 54
Packet Data Protocol, 243
Packet data routing, 243
Packet data serving node, 50, 127, 152, 187
Packet data support node, 244
Packet encapsulation, 88
Packet-filtering firewalls, 63, 64, 66
Packet flow, through IPSS, 136–137
Packet switching, 2, 3
"Packet training," 193–194
Parallel processing, 229
Parsing, and content filtering, 77, 78
Partial-mesh connectivity, 247
Partner interaction models, 161
Passenger protocol, 90
Passive wholesaling, active wholesaling *versus*, 208
Passport 8100s, 319
Password Authentication Protocol (PAP), 79
Passwords, 81
PAT. *See* Port address translation
Path-protection switching, 122
Payroll, 117
PBX market, 21
PC client, 162, 163
PC-equipped households, high-speed access for, 176
PCF. *See* Packet carrying function
PCTs, 115–116
PC-TV, 311
PCUSN. *See* Packet control unit support node
PDP. *See* Policy decision point
PDSN. *See* Packet data serving node
PDUs. *See* Protocol data units
Peak cell rate (PCR), 205
Peak rate, 197
Peering, 13, 14, 15, 17, 30, 98, 255, 272
PEPs. *See* Policy enforcement points
Per-call available bandwidth, 191
Per-flow queuing, 203
Performance reporting, 160
Per-hop behaviors (PHBs), 195
Peripheral ports, footprint for, 32
Permanent virtual circuits, 35, 40, 191
PE routers, 91, 92
Personal caching, 24–25
Personal computers (PCs), 4, 32
Personal content tunnels, *114*

Personal digital assistants (PDAs), 25, 34
Personal firewalls, 222, *223*, *231*
Personal information caches, 127, 128
Personalization, 217, 250
Personal Portal, 286
Per-subscriber state, maintaining, 134
PHB group, 195
PIMs. *See* Partner interaction models
Ping, 235, 236
Piracy, and DRM, 116
PKI. *See* Public key infrastructure
Plain old telephone service (POTS), 35, 257
PNA. *See* Home Phone Networking Alliance
Point-of-presence (PoP), 4, 29, 31
    IPSS connectivity within, 137, *138*
    link between termination device and, 252
    and services location, 172
Point-to-multipoint (pt-to-mpt) replication, 312
PointTopic, 176
Point-to-point protocol (PPP), 16, 40, 42, 157
    and ATM, 176
    and MPLS, 201
Point-to-point technologies, tunneling, 83
Point-to-Point Tunneling Protocol (PPTP), 84, 87, 182, 231, 232
Policing, 172, 193, 194, 200, 205
    single-rate, three-color marker, *199*
    two-rate, three-color marker, *198*
Policy decision and enforcement points, 153, 154
Policy provisioning, 174
Polling technologies, 111
Port address translation, 76
Portals. *See also* Digital subscriber line wholesaling and portals
    Aliant, *316*
    with residential service bundling, 259
    revenue generation from, 255
    and subscriber self-provisioning, 158
Portal services, 27
Port remapping, 76
portscan, 224
Port-scanning networks, 223
Post, telephone, telegraph (PTT) monopolies, 2
POTS splitters, and ADSL, 38
PPP over ATM (PPPoA), 264
PPP over Ethernet (PPPoE), 143, 176, 181
    Aggregator, 285
    and IP addressing, 175
    L2TP *versus*, 86
Pre-shared keys, 81, 88
Prices/Pricing, 174, 178-179
    and buildout, 177
    of cable, 181
    with Canbras TVA services, 286, 287, 288
    financial wholesaling comparisons, 212–215

and IP-VPNs, 244–245, 247
and market opportunity, 176
modem ownership *versus* wholesaling costs, *207*
and oversubscription, 192–193
and satellite systems, 184
and service selection, 173
subscriber evolution, 18–19
3GNet, 297
VibeVision channel package, 314–315
wholesale DSL services, 278
of wireless, 183
Printers, 32
Priority queuing, 194
Privacy, 106, 249–250
Private IP address, 76
Private IP Xchange, 307
Private keys, 81
Profitability, 18, 29
Project Pronto (SBC), 312
Promotions, 179
Proprietary applications, and firewall capabilities, 221
Protection and logging, 231
Protection switching, 123
Protocol conversion, 51
Protocol data units, 54
Provider quandary, and subscriber evolution, 18–25
Providers, 14, 178–179
Provisioning
  bulk, 150
  effective, 147–149
  element, 149–152
  portals, 158
  services, 152–153
  subscriber, 158–159
  vendors, *333–335*
Proxy caches, 100–101
Public IP address, 76
Public keys, 87
  encryption of, 81
  infrastructure, 81, 82
Public switched telephone network (PSTN), 2
  and H.323 protocol, 66
  and regulation, 30
Push technologies, 111
PVCs, end-to-end, *213*

Q.931 messages, 67
Q-tags, 320
Quality of service (QoS), 3, 4, 17, 20, 40, 66, 115, 169, 202–206
  additional guarantees, 193–194
  and broadcast video distribution, 311
  cable, 205–206
  and CDN, 99

and convergence, 6
DSL, 204–205
dynamic, 190, 206
and IP-VPNs, 224
and residential service bundling, 259
and SLAs, 165
support, 27
and traffic management, 190, 193–194
and tunnel grooming, 83
wireless, 206
Quarry, 133, 145, 174
Queuing, 194, 198–199, 205
Quick Mode, with IKE, 88, 89
QuickTime (Apple), 328
Quova, GeoPoint, 112
Qwest, 12, 176, 255

Radguard, 229
Radio
  cellular, 191
  and fixed wireless access, 48
  Internet, 129
Radio access network, 50, 53
Radio base stations, 50
Radio frequency, 34
Radio network, in mobile network, 50
Radio spectrum, and wireless access methods, 50
RADIUS. *See* Remote Authentication Dial-in User Services
RAN. *See* Radio access network
Random early detection (RED), 194
RAS. *See* Remote access server
Rates. *See* Billing; Prices/Pricing
Rating database, 77
RealAudio, 200, 201
Real private networks, 239
Recurring loop charges, 280
RED. *See* Random early detection
Redback, 132, 133, 143, 145, 174, 266
RedCreek, 229
Reference libraries, 129
Regional Bell Operating Companies (RBOCs), 7
Regulation
  and economic viability of CLECs, 12–13
  evolution of, 8–13
  ILECs and CLECs, 8–10
  ILECs and DSL providers, 10–11
  IOCs and IXCs, 11–12
  MSOs and metropolitan carriers, 12
  and network evolution, 30
  of telephone companies, 6
Regulators, and subscribers, 5
Reliability, and SLAs, 165
Remote access server, 16, 59, 60
Remote access VPNs, 232

Remote Authentication Dial-in User Services, 59, 79, 149, 151, 154-157, 175, 211, 216, 243
   attributes, 157
   dial wholesaling and, 156-157
   IPSS interaction with, *155*
Remote office/branch office, 300
Remote units, 151
Repeaters, 39
Request-to-content router, 107
Residential cable revenues, 182
Residential Ethernet extension, 57
Residential markets, 18, 19, 27
Residential PPPoE DSL service, 263-273
   advantages with, 268
   assumptions, *270*
   authentication and subscriber portal, *267*
   branded service, *268*
   DSL ISP assumptions, *269, 272*
   DSL ISP revenue breakdown and growth, *271, 273*
   financial model, 268-273
   Marslink PPPoE, *265, 266*
Residential services, 179, 259, 261-262
   business services *versus*, 21
Residential users, 22-25
Resource Reservation Protocol, 153, 196, 197, 201
Response times, 20
Retention, subscriber, 217
Retransmission, 4
Return on investment (ROI), 217
Reverse proxy caches, 101
RF. *See* Radio frequency
RFC-2684 bridging, 174, 176
RF splitters, 45
Rhythms, 29, 291
Rich content, 28, 178
Rich media, 295
Rich services, 95
Rijndael encryption formula, 80
"Ripped" DVDs, 116
RIPv2, 91
RiverDelta, 133
Rivest-Shamir-Adelman (RSA) public-key algorithm, 80, 81, 83
Roaming-enabled access point, 216
Roaming software structures, 16
ROBO. *See* Remote office/branch office
Rogue programs, 73
Routed headends, 181
Routers, 19
   content, 107-108, 251
   DSL, 230
   and edge caching, 101
   and element provisioning, 150
   function of, 141
   and MPLS, 91
   multi-, *94, 95*
   packet-filtering, 64
   QoS-optimized core, 203
   for SOHO users, 34
   virtual, 93, *94,* 95
RouterWare, 162
Routing contexts, 209
RPNs. *See* Real private networks
RSVP. *See* Resource Reservation Protocol
Rural access, to broadband connectivity, 19
RUs. *See* Remote units

SA. *See* Security association
Sales tracking, 117
SAR. *See* Segmentation and reassembly
Satellite access service providers, *333*
Satellite dish penetration, 185
Satellite Internet revenues, 185
Satellite system growth, 184
SAVVIS Communications, 303, 304-310
   advantages with IP-VPN service, 310
   background, 303-304
   IP-VPN and the Internet, 307, *309*
   IP Xchange, *308*
   network architecture, *304*
   private network offering, *309*
   service application and architecture, *305, 306*
   service level agreements, *310*
SBC, 7, 176, 265
Scalability, 197
   with active wholesaling, 210
   IPSS, 141
   and streaming content, 112
   wholesale, 156
Schneier, Bruce, 229
Schools, high-speed access to, 19
SCS. *See* Service Creation System
SDH. *See* Synchronous Digital Hierarchy
SDSL. *See* Symmetric DSL
Second-generation (2G) cellular deployments, 52-53
Second mile problem, 8
Secret keys, 87
Secure digital content delivery, 255
Secure networking, 6
Secure socket layer, 79
Secure supplier/distributor connectivity, 241
Security, 27, 50, 57, 62-83, 95, 129, 133, 233, 317, 318. *See also* Firewalls/Firewalling
   and "always-on" architecture, 285
   attack prevention, 70-74
   AAA, 78-79
   and basic services, 172
   certificates and digital signatures, 82-83
   and CDN, 99
   content filtering, 77-78

data, 234
encryption, 79-80
expenses, 219
firewalls, 63-68, 70
home, 32
with IPSS, 140
and IP-VPNs, 244
key management, 80-82
NAT, 74-77
and provisioning, 149
and SLAs, 165, 166
and split tunneling, 237
through obscurity?, 62-63
user focus on, 61
with virtual hosting services, 128, 129
Security association, 87
Security by obscurity, 62
Segmentation and reassembly, 137
Self-installation, 179
Sequencing, 234
Server load balancers/balancing, 97, 103, 251, 317
Servers, 27
Server-side caching, 101, 103
Service activation, 158, 160
Service assurance, and management systems/vendors, 161
Service basics, 172-173
Service bundles/bundling, 217, 258-261
  Aliant, *315, 316*
  multiservice, 260
  residential and small business, 259-260
  SME, *261*
  telecommuter, 259, *260*
Service creation platforms, in mobile network, 51
Service Creation System (Nortel/Shasta), 277, 308, 319
Service level agreements, 58, 62
  for business subscribers, 179
  IPSS, service provisioning and, 146, 165-167
  IP-VPN, *166,* 244
  and policing, 197
  SAVVIS, *310*
  service parameters and, 166
Service management, within ITU's TMN, 147
Service monitoring, and systems/vendors, 160
Service providers, 13, *14,* 30, 31, 329-333
  and "content-enabled" infrastructure, 254-255
  fixed wireless and satellite access, *333*
  requirements, 28
Service quality, 193-194
Service(s), 170, *171*
Service selection portals, 97
Services management, and voice services, 258
Services processing redundancy, and IPSS, 136
Services provisioning, 131, 146, 152-153

Services vendors, *333-335*
Serving central office, 7
Serving GPRS support node, 54, 243
Session Initiation Protocol (SIP), 119, 125
SGSN. *See* Serving GPRS support node
Shaper, 200
Shaping, 172, 193, 194, *200,* 201, 205
Shaping policy verification, *201*
Shared-cage deployments, 10
Shared IP Xchange, 307
Shasta 5000 BSN, 303, 319, 320
Shasta Networks, 133
SHDSL. *See* Symmetric HDSL
Short cells, 194
Short Message Service, 53, 298
Siemens EWSD, 122
Sightpath, 113
Signaling, 51, 234
Signaling network interfaces, 257
Signaling System 7, 120
SIM. *See* Subscriber identity module
Single headend architecture, *45*
Single-queue mechanisms and discard strategies, 198
Single-rate, three-color marker, 198, *199*
SITA/Equant, 245
Site hacking, 319
"Skills gap," 4
SLA systems/vendors, 160
SLAs. *See* Service level agreements
Slave computers, 73, 74
SLBs. *See* Server load balancers
Small businesses, 133, 259-260
Small enterprise, *235, 236*
Small-medium enterprises (SMEs), 27, 218, *261*
  and firewalls, 222, *223*
  growth in, 262
  requirements for, 20-21
Small office/home office (SOHO), 21, 117
  and Canbras TVA, 287
  LAN options in, 31, *32,* 34
  requirements for users and economics of, 21-22
Smart cards, 81
Smart content parsing, 78
Smith, Richard, 229
SMS. *See* Short Message Service
SMSs. *See* Subscriber management systems
SMURF attacks, 71, 72
SNMP, 65, 149, 157, 200
  and COPS, 153, 154
  and element provisioning, 149, 150
Soft switches, 120, 124
Software and games, 25
Software applications, spending on, 25, *26*
SOHO ADSL, and bandwidth, 191

Solstice, 317-320
  advantages with, 320-321
  content distribution, *318*, *321*
  data center firewalling, *320*
SONET. *See* Synchronous optical network
Split horizon capabilities, 164
Split-horizon management, 35, 223
Splitters, 35, 38
Split tunneling, *237*
Spoofing, 70
Sports, revenue generation from, 255
SpringTide, 133, 174
Sprint, 8, 47, 209
SSL. *See* Secure socket layer
StarBand, 184
State maintenance, 106-107
Stateful firewalls, 63, 64, *66*, 172
Statistical multiplexing, 270
Storage, 32
Strategis Group, 249
Streaming content, 112-116
Streaming media, 24, 206, 255
Strict priority scheduling, 199
Sub-loop unbundling, 9
Subscriber aggregation/basic Internet access, 169, 173-190, 277
  cable access and market opportunity, 180-182
  comparison of DSL, cable, and fixed wireless, 185-186
  dial access aggregation, 186
  DSL access and market opportunity, 173-180
  mobile wireless access, 187-188, 190
  wireless access and market opportunity, 182-185
Subscriber and service provider requirements, *28*
Subscriber churn, minimizing, 169, 217, 260, 291
Subscriber edge, 99, 143-144
Subscriber evolution, and provider quandary, 18-25
Subscriber identity module, 298
Subscriber management platforms, edge routers in place of, 143
Subscriber management routers, 144, 145
Subscriber management systems, 25, 174, 266
Subscribers
  address hiding for, 61
  building base of, 177
  closer financial ties between content providers and, 248-249
  and ISPs, 16
  loyalty and lockin, 216-217
  management of, 133, 173
  and regulators, 5
  requirements for, *28*
  and second-mile problem, 8
  security wanted by, 61
  and wholesale environment, 215-216
Subscriber segregation, 62, 93-95
  multi-routers, *94*, 95
  virtual routers, 93, *94*, 95
Subscriber self-provisioning, 153, 158, *159*, 300, *302*
Subscriber site, access devices at, 33-34
Subscriber tracking, 102, 104, 106
Subtending, 40
Sun Enterprise 250, 277
Sun Solaris, 277
Switched VCs, 40, 203
Switching fabric, 59, 107
Switch throughput, *107*
Symantec, 253
Symmetric DSL, 36
  and bandwidth, 191
  and high-speed DSL, 38
Symmetric HDSL, 37, 39, 191
Synchronous CDMA, 42
Synchronous Digital Hierarchy, 42
Synchronous optical network, 91
Synchronous optical network/synchronous digital hierarchy (SONET/SDH), 40, 42
Syndesis, 161
SYN flood attacks, 72

Tail packet discard (TPD), 203
Taiwan, DSL-capable lines in, 176
Tapping, 242
TCP
  and firewalls, 65
  splicing, 104, *105*
  SYN flood protection, 74
TCP/UDP ports, and IANA, 69
TDD CDMA. *See* Time division duplex CDMA
TDM. *See* Time division multiplexing
TDMA. *See* Time division multiple access
TDM-based IAD, and PSTN gateway, *126*
Technologies, applications, services, and, *171*
Telcordia, 122, 161
Telecommunications Act of 1996, 8, 12
Telecommunications Management Network (TMN), 147
Telecommunications services spending, 261-262
Telecommuters/Telecommuting, 24, 31, 84, 117, 119, 129, 242
  bandwidth needed by, 178
  bundling, 259, *260*
  and client-to-HQ connectivity, 230
  and enterprise markets, 21, 22
  global, 216
  high-speed access for, 176
  and IPSS platforms, 133
  and IP-VPNs, 244

pricing for, 178, 179
and small enterprise deployment, 235
and traffic management, 190
Telephone access device (TAD), 22
Telephone industry, evolution of, 1, 6–7
Telephony, 117, 129
and classification, 195
Internet, *125*
TeleSpeed, 178
TeleSurfer, 178
10GE, 135
"10 networks," 76
Terabit routing, 27
Terminal, in mobile network, 50
Terminal Access Controller Access Control Server (TACACS+), 151, 154
Thawte, 82
Third-generation (3G)
cellular systems, 53
mobile wireless networks, 127
universal mobile telecom systems, 49, 50
wireless access, 54
wireless deployments, 133
Third-party ISPs, 179
3DES, 87
3G mobile wireless services, 295–303
advantages with, 301, 303
background, 295–296
financial model, 297–301
services description, 296–297
3GNet, 295
advantages with, 301–303
background, 295–296
financial model for, 297–301
future UMTS network architecture, 302
GPRS network, *296*
Internet Mobility service, 296
ISP wholesale offerings, *303*
potential 3G services, *300*
service profiles, *301*
services description, 296–297
service tariffs, *297*
subscriber self-provisioning with, 300, *302*
UMTS network, 298, *299*
3G wireless, 54–55, 190
Three-way calling, 122
Throughput, 201
Tier-1 connectivity, 16
Tier-1 providers, 14, 15
Tier-2 providers, 15
Time division duplex CDMA, 55
Time division multiple access, 49, 50, 53
Time division multiplexing, 35
Timeslot management channel (TMC), 122

Timeslots, 50
TimeStep, 229
Time-Warner, 97
Time window, of SLAs, 165–166
T1, 3, 20, 35, 58, 143, 182
and HDSL, 39
IP-based voice technology support for, 124
TiVo, 313
Token cards, 84
Tokens, 79
TollBridge, 124
Total latency, 193
Traffic concentration, 51
Traffic filtering, 27
Traffic logging, with IP-VPN platforms, 229
Traffic management, 169, 172, 173, 190–206, 218
additional QoS guarantees, 193–194
and bandwidth, 191
with IPSS, 140
oversubscription, 192–193
role of IPSS, 190–191
Traffic management concepts, 194–201
classification, 194, 195–197
policing, 194, 197–198
queuing, 198–199
shaping, 200–201
Transit providers, 14
Transit relationship, 14
Transit wholesaling, 212, *212*
Transparent mode, 243
Transparent wholesaling, 208
Transport mode, 88, 89
Transport protocol, 90
Triple DES (3DES), 80, 229
Tripwire, 74
Tunneling, 42, 62, 95, 97, 129, 133
client alternatives, *234*
GRE, *90*
mobile IP, 244
modes of, 84, *85*
split, 237, *237*
with wholesale DSL services, 278
Tunneling technologies, 83–93
GRE, IP in IP, and UTI, 84, 89–90
IPSec, 84, 87–89
L2TP, 84–87
MPLS, 84, 90–93
PPTP, 83, 87
Tunnel mode, 88, 89
Tunnels
grooming services for, 83
optimization of, *86*
and personal content, *114*

Tunnels *continued*
   scalability of, 209
   termination of, 50
Tunnel switching, 156
   L2TP, *211*
Two-rate, three-color marker, 197, *198*

UBR+, 204
UDP
   and firewalls, 65
   message types carried over, 84
Unbundled Network Element, 9
Unisphere, 133, 144-145
United Kingdom, UMTS subscribers in, 297
United States
   broadband access in, 8
   DSL, cable, and fixed wireless buildout across, 185
   DSL customers in, 176
   residential cable revenues in, 182
   residential DSL revenue growth in, 180
   residential wireless revenue growth in, 183
Universal access concentrators (UACs), 25
Universal content locator (UCL), 115
Universal mobile telecom system (UMTS), 49, 53, 188
   architecture, 242-244
   with 3GNet, 298, *299*
   and 3G wireless access, 54
   and 01 deployments, 187
Universal mobile telephone system, 295
Universal serial bus (USB), 32, 33, 35, 45
Universal service, 6
Universal Tunnel Interface (UTI), 90
Updates, dynamic, *112*
Uplinks, 33-34
Upstream, 37
Upstream data, 45, 47
Uptime guarantees, and SLAs, 165
URLs, 77, 78, 108
U.S. Supreme Court, regulatory decisions by, 9
User names, and RADIUS, 157
User parameter control (UPC), 203
Users, 1. *See also* Customers; Subscribers
US West, 176
UTP, 32
UUnet (Worldcom), 15, 266

Vail, Theodore, 6
Value-added services, 22, 27, 32, 95, 129, 131, 217, 262
   with network subsystem, 52
   with UMTS, 299
Vanity ISPs, 17, 210
Variable bit rate (VBR), 204
Variable latency, 193
VC. *See* Virtual circuit
VCC. *See* Virtual Circuit Connection

VCI. *See* Virtual circuit identifier
Vendors
   broadband hardware, services, and provisioning, *333-335*
   IDs, 157
   revenue opportunities for, IPSS, 143, *144,* 145-146
Vendor-specific attributes (VSAs), 157
Verio, 15
VeriSign, 82
Verizon, 8, 176, 255, 265
Very high-speed digital subscriber line (VDSL), 37, 39
V5.2 interface, 122
Vibe, 312
VibeVision, 312, 313, 314
Video, 95
   and convergence, 5, 6
   through MSOs, 13
Video conferencing, 64, 66, 69, 119, 129
Video distribution, 97, 117-118, 129, 180, 193
   and IP-DSLAMs, 40, 41
   and state maintenance, 106
   and traffic management, 190
Video on demand (VoD), 7, 129
Video services, spending on, 25, *26*
Virgin, 98
Virtual circuit, 191, 264
Virtual circuit connection, 312
Virtual circuit identifier, 157
Virtual hosting services, 98, 127-129
Virtual ISPs, 16, 17, 140
Virtualized routing, 30
Virtual leased lines, 196, 233
Virtual LANs, 57
Virtual path identifier (VPI), 157
Virtual private access networks (VPANs), 232
Virtual private dial networks (VPDNs), 232
Virtual private networks (VPNs), 4, 219
   Frame Relay or leased-line, *226*
   penetration and revenue, *246*
   wireless, 242
Virtual private routed networks (VPRNs), 228, 232-233
Virtual Router Redundancy Protocol (VRRP), 136, 318, 319
Virtual routers, 93, *94,* 95, 174, 209, 231, 233
Virtual services network (VSN), 232, 238
Virtual transport network (VTN), 232, 238
Virtual truck, 163
Virus filtering, 244
Virus scanning, 78
Visitor location register (VLR), 52, 243
Vitria BusinessWare, 161
VLANs. *See* Virtual LANs
VLLs. *See* Virtual leased lines
VoATM, VoIP compared with, *257*

Index 369

Voice, 95
  and convergence, 5, 6
  domain, 299
  gateways, 119
  integration, 98
  and latency, 3
  support at subscriber edge, 119
Voice distribution, 119–127
  ATM-based voice services, 120–122
  IP-based voice services, 123–126
  other voice services, 126–127
  voice protocols, 119–120
Voice-mail services, 52
Voice network, and mobile wireless, 187
Voice over cable and wireless, 126, *127*
Voice over DSL (VoDSL), 39, 40, 120
Voice over IP (VoIP), 21, 29, 119, 193
  across fixed wireless, 126
  VoATM compared with, *257*
Voice over multiservice broadband networks (VoMBN), 124
Voice protocols, 119–120, *121*
Voice services
  ATM-based, 120, *121, 122*
  bundling of, 182
  deployment, 256–258
  through MSOs, 13
VoIP gateway, and element provisioning, 151
VoIP IAD, and PSTN gateway-traditional class 5 and MGCP, *123*
Volera, 102, 113
Voluntary tunneling, 84, *85*, 242
VPI/VCI cell header, 90
VPNet Technologies, 229
VPN-IPv4, 92
VRs. *See* Virtual routers

WAN. *See* Wide area network
WAP. *See* Wireless Application Protocol
WAP technology, 296
Wavelength division multiplexing (WDM), 56
WCDMA. *See* Wideband CDMA
Web, 16
Web accelerators, 101, 102
Web Cache Coordination Protocol (WCCP), provisions by, 103
Web caches, 29, 100, 101
Web convergence, Aliant video and, *311*
Web hosting, 128
  service revenue from, 255
  with vanity ISPs, 210

Web interfaces, authentication via, 158
WebRamp router, 277
Web redirectors, 105
Web services, and IP-VPNs, 244
Web site overflow protection, 253
Web switches, 317, 318, 319
WebTV, 22
Weighted fair queuing (WFQ), 194, 199
Weighted RED, 194, 198
Wholesaling, 169, 207–215
  active, 210–211
  costs, modem ownership *versus, 207*
  financial wholesaling comparisons, 212–215
  subscriber experiences and, 215–216
  transit, 212
Wide area network, 29
Wideband CDMA, 53
Wi-Fi solution, 32
Williams Communications, 12
Windows, 163, 277
Windows 2000, 84, 86
Windows ME, L2TP within, 86
Wind River, 162
Wireless, 31, 35
  buildout of, 27
  high-speed connectivity via, 8
  IP-based voice technology support for, 124
  and subscriber self-provisioning, 158
  voice over, *127*
  wholesaling, 210
Wireless access
  major methods of, 50
  and market opportunity, 182–185
  protocol, 50
  providers, 17
Wireless access technologies, 47–48, 49–55
Wireless Application Protocol, 295
Wireless modems, 34
Wireless operators, and element provisioning, 151, *152*
Wireless QoS, 206
Wireless systems, 7, *49*
Wireless technology evolution, 53
Wireless VPNs, 242
WorldCom, 12, 15, 176
WRED. *See* Weighted RED

XO, 255
X.25 technology, 3, 4

Yahoo, 319
Yankee, 176

Register Your Book

at www.aw.com/cseng/register

You may be eligible to receive:
- Advance notice of forthcoming editions of the book
- Related book recommendations
- Chapter excerpts and supplements of forthcoming titles
- Information about special contests and promotions throughout the year
- Notices and reminders about author appearances, tradeshows, and online chats with special guests

Contact us

If you are interested in writing a book or reviewing manuscripts prior to publication, please write to us at:

Editorial Department
Addison-Wesley Professional
75 Arlington Street, Suite 300
Boston, MA 02116 USA
Email: AWPro@aw.com

Visit us on the Web: http://www.aw.com/cseng